D0752928

DEMOCRATIC DEVELOPMENT AND POLITICAL TERRORISM

Democratic Development

EDITED BY WILLIAM CROTTY

Other volumes in the Northeastern Series on Democratization and Political Development
The Politics of Terror: The U.S. Response to 9/11, edited by William Crotty (2003)

Political

& Terrorism

THE GLOBAL PERSPECTIVE

NORTHEASTERN UNIVERSITY PRESS · BOSTON

Northeastern University Press

Copyright © 2005 by William Crotty

All rights reserved. Except for the quotation of short passages for the purposes of criticism and review, no part of this book may be reproduced in any form or by any means, electronic or mechanical, including photocopying, recording, or any information storage and retrieval system now known or to be invented, without written permission of the publisher.

Library of Congress Cataloging-in-Publication Data

    Democratic development and political terrorism : the global perspective /
    edited by William Crotty.
        p.   cm.
    Includes bibliographical references and index.
    ISBN 1-55553-625-5 (cloth : alk. paper)
        1. Democratization. 2. Terrorism. 3. Political violence. 4. War on Terrorism, 2001- —Political aspects. 5. Terrorism–Government policy–United States. I. Crotty, William J.
    JC423.D46 2005
    303.6'25–dc22   2004009740

Project management by Book Production Resources, Tampa, Florida. Composed in Bodoni Book by Van-garde Imagery, Inc, Clearwater, Florida. Printed and bound by Sheridan Books, Ann Arbor, Michigan. The paper is House Natural, an acid-free stock.

MANUFACTURED IN THE UNITED STATES OF AMERICA
08   07   06   05   5   4   3   2   1

Contents

Preface

The terrorist acts of September 11, 2001, created a new political world, one less secure than before and one in which terrorism forced itself onto the international stage. Almost three thousand people died in one day, the result of terrorist attacks on American civilians. The attacks would have worldwide consequences and would be the beginning of a new era of global concern about terrorist networks.

The images transmitted by television of the horrors of the planes crashing into the World Trade Center and their resultant collapse, the loss of life, and the heroic firefighters and other emergency workers who responded to the crisis (many sacrificing their lives in the process) were all seared into the collective memory of Americans. The attacks in New York, the targeting of the Pentagon, and the crashing of a fourth plane into the fields of Pennsylvania (after passengers had charged the hijackers) that was apparently headed for an additional target in Washington (the Capitol? the White House?) brought home to Americans and to the free world the reach, consequences, and determination of modern-day terrorist movements.

How could such a thing happen? Why? What would motivate people to commit such acts? What could be done about it? Was there more to come? Answers were not quick in coming. The immediate call was for revenge—targeting and eliminating to the extent possible those responsible for the attacks. Retribution was the order of the day.

But retribution proved not to be easy and raised more questions than anyone was to anticipate. Two wars, both brief, were to follow, as was a new sense of urgency and determination in dealing with terrorist threats internationally.

The war in Afghanistan, the base for the terrorist operations of September 11, led to the fall of the Taliban government that supported Osama bin Laden and al

Qaeda. Leaders (although not bin Laden) and followers of al Qaeda were killed or captured, severely disrupting the group's operations. This war was succeeded by a military invasion of Iraq, a brief war, the replacement of Iraq's authoritarian/totalitarian government, and later the capture of Saddam Hussein. The postwar occupation of Iraq has proven to be longer than anticipated and has been costly, both in terms of casualties (more American lives have been lost in the occupation than during the war itself) and financing. Occupation has also caused rifts in America's alliances with its European allies and with the United Nations. Among other things, the Iraqi operation in particular raised issues as to the ability of Western countries, and most specifically the United States in this case, to institutionalize democratic government in a society with no such traditions that is historically used to authoritarian rule.

What September 11, 2001, and the train bombings in Madrid of March 11, 2004, did do is raise terrorism to the level of prime international concern. Questions arose as to how best to contain terrorist activities and how to successfully democratize societies in the Middle East and elsewhere. The very conceptions of democratic operations are foreign to most. Is military force the best option? Are there other alternatives? Is there a relationship between authoritarian repression and terrorist activities? If so, how best can these be approached in the ever-broadening effort to establish a stable, peaceful world, one built on a respect for the rights of the individual?

The chapters in this book deal with these and related issues. The problems of advancing democratic development while dealing with terrorism produce tensions that, at times, appear unsolvable in any reasoned or moderated manner. The root causes of terrorism, the regional and international impact of terrorists, the transitions under way and the problems associated with these, and the disruptions caused by political violence of the most extreme kind, as well as the way in which the West, including the United States, has chosen to confront the problems are treated in the pages to follow. Terrorism is a large subject with even greater implications for democratic development within a cooperative and mutually tolerant international community.

Acknowledgments

I wish to thank Bob Gormley, editor-in-chief, Northeastern University Press, for his help in all phases of this project. I wish to also thank Ann Twombly, production director, and Jill C. Bahcall, associate press director, both of Northeastern University Press, and the others who contributed to the publishing of this book—Fred Thompson, director of Book Production Resources, and associates Yvonne Ramsey, copyeditor, Polly Linthicum, proofreader, and Darlene Swanson, typesetter. Amy Richey and Ben Lampe, research associates at the Center for the Study of Democracy at Northeastern University, contributed significantly to the development of this volume. Janet-Louise Joseph, administrator, Department of Political Science, was a consistent source of support. Guy B. Peters and James M. Scott provided quite helpful and inclusive reviews, which I appreciate. Most of all, I wish to thank Mary Hauch Crotty, who works in the area of crisis management and health and emergency delivery services and who has a fundamental appreciation for the issues involved.

DEMOCRATIC DEVELOPMENT AND POLITICAL TERRORISM

PART ONE

Introducing the Problem

CHALLENGES OF DEMOCRATIZATION

WILLIAM CROTTY

1 Democratization and Political Terrorism

INTRODUCTION

Political terrorism is the international community's biggest contemporary threat to a stable world order. The signal event in bringing global terrorism to the world's attention has to be the September 11, 2001, attacks on the World Trade Center and the Pentagon. Approximately three thousand people died in a horror broadcast throughout the world. On March 11, 2004, approximately two and one-half years later, the terrorist bombings of commuter trains in Madrid killed approximately two hundred people and injured another fifteen hundred. This was the greatest loss of life on the European continent since the end of World War II (other than the ethnic cleansing and genocide in Bosnia and Kosovo). The Spanish authorities blamed the bombings on Basque terrorists, a continuing problem for the country. Al Qaeda, the terrorist organization that planned and executed the September 11 attacks, claimed responsibility. Political terrorism, if not fully appreciated before, had become a worldwide threat.

SEPTEMBER 11 AND THE DAWN OF A NEW AGE OF INTERNATIONAL TERRORISM

The attacks on the World Trade Center and the Pentagon on September 11 set off a chain of reactions, the ultimate consequences of which will be a new world order, one in which governments are more security-conscious, more guarded in regard to international movements (this in an era of the globalization of trade, finance, communications, and political institutionalization), more sensitive to the threat of terrorist activity, and, although this is less clear, more dependent on military force and procedures to implement security and retaliatory measures. The world has changed.

The terrorist attacks of September 11 in the United States were followed by horrific scenes of fires, mutilations, and death, as well as the heroic efforts of, in particular, the New York City Fire and Police Departments and emergency workers. The scenes of destruction, death, and heroism were captured by television and transmitted nationally and internationally. All would share in one way or another the shock, confusion, and, for Americans and many others, anger that were to follow.

The U.S. government followed the period of grief with military retaliations against al Qaeda, the sponsor of the attacks, and Afghanistan's Taliban government, which housed and supported al Qaeda. Later, American troops would invade and occupy Iraq in an effort to uncover weapons of mass destruction (WMD), punish the country for its support of al Qaeda (despite the lack of evidence of any such link), introduce democracy to an autocratic/totalitarian regime, and depose the Iraqi leader, Saddam Hussein. The war ended quickly. The occupation that followed has proven to be troublesome, with more American casualties than during the war itself.

For Americans, this all represented a new and less secure world. For many others, it was a forceful reminder of the power of terrorist actions and the necessity of dealing with these on an international scale.

The Bush administration would implement its war on terrorism, complete with a restructuring of the American government (via the creation of the Department of Homeland Security) in a manner the administration felt would best meet the threat and the addition of restrictions on the legal, privacy, and political rights of both U.S. citizens and those "detained" in combat or as terrorists or alleged supporters of terrorist networks. The Bush administration would also initiate the military actions that led to the wars in Afghanistan and Iraq.

COUNTING THE COSTS

The new world order was less secure, more militarized, and less stable than before. Political terrorism would be seen as a global threat. How best to deal with it? What factors provide for (or explain) terrorist acts? What countries are most susceptible to terrorist movements and why? What differences can be found in the various regions of the world and what explains those differences? And, compared to other areas, what explains the sources of terrorism in the Middle East? How receptive are countries in the region to democratization, the creation of inclusive and effective political institutions of representation, the nurturing of an independent and vital civil culture, and the development of a democratic ethos that would pervade a country's society and provide a direction for its political (and social) actions and its relationships with the rest of the global order?

These are some of the issues and questions that the chapters in this book deal with. There are no clear-cut or relatively simple answers. The problem of terrorism, its sources, and the means to combat it are not easily resolved. Efforts to democratize authoritarian countries most likely will be long and hard. The movement will require patience and understanding of the depths of the problems to be encountered, a perspective that this volume attempts to convey.

DEFINING WHAT IS DEMOCRATIC

There is no single, universally accepted definition of democracy or, for that matter, model of what a democracy should be. The emphases vary in accordance with the history of a country, its culture and the strength of its civic society, and the conditions under which democratic institutions were introduced (economic or military crises, outside or international intervention, mass revolt or the threat of it). One consequence is that countries that use the term "democratic" to describe their governing systems can range from Western European nations (and the United States) to China and the former Soviet Union to autocracies in the Middle East, Africa, and Latin America. At the same time, many would argue that democracy is the one game in town. As Phillipe Schmitter writes, "'Democracy,' in some form or another, may well be the only legitimate and stable form of government in the contemporary world" (Schmitter 1996, 77).

Democracy has no ideological rivals. The criteria for being considered "democratic" are universally invoked (if not always put into practice) to justify regimes or their actions. Democracy sets the standards, and terms of debate, as to how nations are to be viewed and dominates the contemporary political landscape.

Democratic systems can be minimalist democracies in which the citizenry mainly has the right to vote but enjoys few other political freedoms; democracies that incorporate such freedoms (press, association, religion, assembly, speech) within their conceptions of a democratic culture, the approach favored in this book; or democracies that would expand conceptions of democracy to full participation in all civic institutions and/or the equitable distribution of resources (social policies, economic prosperity) to all segments of the population.

For those who choose to emphasize a liberal democracy associated with the freedoms indicated and the direct accountability of the political leadership to the citizenry, the argument would be that while perhaps not ideal, it has been implemented in a number of nations and, most importantly, it works. Moving beyond such standards may be fanciful, putting pressure on the state and its institutions through a series of guarantees that it cannot readily meet in the real world.

Given this range of democratic types, the paradigm put forth by Robert A. Dahl in his conception of "polyarchy" (democracy) to measure democratization within a society provides an attractive basis for comparative judgments as to performance and functioning that can be quite useful. Dahl stipulates the conditions critical to the institutional forms and qualities that initialize a democratic state:

> The government must be responsive to its citizenry with all considered equal. The citizens . . . have "unimpaired opportunities" "to formulate their preferences," make their preferences known to other citizens and the government through collective (political parties, civic and professional associations, the media); and their preferences will be "weighed equally in the conduct of government" and distribution of resources. (Dahl 1971, 2)

The institutions needed to achieve such objectives include:
1. Freedom to form and join organizations
2. Freedom of expression
3. Right to vote
4. Eligibility for public office
5. Right of political leaders to compete for support . . .
6. Alternative sources of information
7. Free and fair elections
8. Institutions for making government policies depend on votes and other expressions of preference (Dahl 1971, 3)

In this same context, Arend Lijphardt endorses Dahl's now familiar polyarchical approach: "It is not a system of government that fully embodies all democratic ideals, but one that approximates them to a reasonable degree" (Lijphardt 1977, 4). There is a utilitarian advantage to such an approach in assessing democracy in states that provide criteria for comparison and judgment. Participation, inclusiveness, and representation are key elements of any form of democratic governance.

WHAT IS TERRORISM?

Terrorism can be defined as extralegal acts of violence directed against civilian (primarily), official, or military targets in an effort to induce fear and disorder into a society in advancing ideological, religious, ethnic, or other agenda. Its toll and its impact can be significant. Yet terrorism is the act of minorities, excluded from the normal political avenues of representation, repressed in one manner or another, and determined to advance their cause or fight their enemies in the one way they believe effective (see also Odgen pp. 228–31 in this volume). Terrorism on any large scale can be an indication of the failures of a country's efforts or will to be inclusive or representative of all segments of its society and thus, in turn, a negative gauge of a state's degree of democratization.

As Jessica Stern indicates, there are literally hundreds of definitions of terrorism. One reason for this is the difficulty of distinguishing terrorism from normal dissent or factious groups in a society (that can be labeled "terrorist" by a regime) or traditional criminal activity or, alternatively, any type of antistate expression. As Stern points out, some definitions focus on the groups (or terrorist states) involved, others on their motivations, and still others on the techniques and targeting objectives they use. Terrorism has

> two characteristics [that] are critical for distinguishing terrorism from other forms of violence. First, terrorism is aimed at noncombatants. This is what makes it different from fighting in war. Second, terrorists use violence for a dramatic purpose: usually to instill fear in the targeted population. This deliberate evocation of dread is what sets terrorism apart from simple murder or assault. (Stern 1999, 200)

Stern contends that terrorism in the contemporary era has reached its most extreme form due to the relatively easy availability of nuclear weaponry and other WMD.

Terrorists, whatever their political objectives, have a need for ultimate control over the thinking and actions of those in their group. They rationalize violence as a legitimate means to achieve much larger ends, provide an ideology and belief system that rewards those who advance the group's ends through terrorist acts, and have the discipline, expertise, and technology to successfully operationalize their plans. Terrorism is not an ad hoc, spur-of-the-moment series of acts borne of repression, zealotry, frustration, and anger (although these can be motivating forces).

Quite the opposite is the case. Terrorist acts are paramilitary operations, carefully planned and normally not concerned with the amount of damage inflicted or the lives lost (among terrorist agents or in civilian populations). Included in the terrorist arsenal, and one reason terrorism is difficult to deal with effectively, are a range of options, some favored by one group, others by another. These include car bombs, plane bombings, airplane hijackings, assassinations, ambushes, biochemical attacks, hostage-taking, kidnappings for ransom, drug trafficking, revenge killings, sabotage, and threats to disrupt societies or frighten opponents (Combs 2000). The one factor terrorists have in common is the willingness to carry these actions out whatever the cost.

A word of caution is relevant in all of this. Groups can be labeled "terrorists" at the will of governments, but not all "terrorist groups" are terrorist. Such labeling is a convenient way of stigmatizing what under other conditions would be a gitimate opposition to a regime, its leadership, or its policies.

DEMOCRATIZATION AND POLITICAL TERR

The definition of terrorism depends on political power. Governments can increase their power when they label opponents as "terrorists." Citizens seem willing to accept more abuses of governmental power when a counterterrorist campaign is in progress. "Terrorists" do not enjoy the same humanitarian privileges as "people." In the public mind, illegal arrest and sometimes even torture and murder are acceptable methods for dealing with terrorists. Labeling can have deadly results. (White 2003, 6)

This is a caution worth keeping in mind. There can be state-sponsored terrorism as well as group-driven terrorist networks. Discretion in applying the label "terrorist" and a close examination of the dynamics of the processes in play within a state or a group are necessities. Terrorism is the most extreme form of political violence. In today's world, it can be extremely dangerous and is dealt with harshly. At the same time, terrorism should be approached as a political act, even if carried out at a different level of threat to a society and with a higher degree of consequence than, for example, nonviolent political dissent or "normal" criminal activity.

Terrorism is deadly. No one argues against this. Unfortunately, it can be unusually effective in promoting a group's aims, calling attention to alleged deprivations, psychologically frightening a population, and, not to be dismissed, mobilizing mass citizenries and government forces against perpetrators.

Terrorism is not new. It has its root causes, is persistent, and is present in some form or another in all regions of the world. This book looks at the terrorist threat within the context of the international community, weighing the efforts to develop democratic institutions of representation against the terrorism that is bred in the societies most resistant to such objectives. Terrorism, in itself, is another kind of war, one that will be with us for a long time to come. It is the major contemporary issue of our times.

LINKAGES: DEMOCRATIZATION AND TERRORISM

Democracy and terrorism represent the extremes of the political continuum. Democracy, that is, a fully functioning liberal democracy—one that includes political rights; accountability of elected officials; inclusive electorate, competitive, and policy-relevant political parties; an independent legal system, and normal individual freedoms—effectively offers the norms, values, motivations (the expansion of political support), and institutions that help effuse terrorist developments. This is not to say that democracies do not suffer from terrorism. However, they do so at a much lower level and by clearly distinguishable groups of actors: the lone terrorist (such as Ted Kaczynski, Eric Robert Rudolph, or the individuals charged with assassinating U.S. presidents from Lincoln on) or a small number of terrorists acting on their own (as with Timothy McVeigh and Terry Nichols in the bombing of the Oklahoma City federal building in which 168 people were killed) are two examples. Political assassinations by disturbed individuals is another (Crotty 1970). Regional secessionists (the Basques in Spain) or out-of-the-mainstream groups (for example, religious fanatics, radical communitarians, right-wing militia, the Ku Klux Klan historically, antinativists or antireligious organizations) can author limited, and largely isolated, terrorist acts. Democracies can also serve as targets for terrorist attacks, as the September 11 attacks in New York City and Washington, D.C., and the later train bombings in Madrid demonstrated.

The point is that inclusive, representative democratic systems offer outlets to identify and address social and economic inequalities effectively enough to make terrorism as a political act moot and, when engaged in, largely ineffective. Terrorism, at least internal terrorism, is viewed as principally a criminal act. In a fully democratic society, terrorism is neither encouraged nor viewed as a logical course of action to achieve a group's ends.

This is also not to say that in the process of democratization, much of which this book is concerned with, terrorism won't offer a threat to a state's evaluation that can vary from a nuisance level up to an indirect derailing of the emerging democratic process. The unfortunate fact is that during the variety of stages of democratic development, terrorism can be very effective in achieving its ends. It can also be effective in preventing countries from beginning the long, extraordinarily difficult, and sensitive task of turning from an authoritarian/totalitarian past to an increasingly democratic future. In fact, terrorism may have the most impact at this stage in that the normal, or traditional, reaction to terrorist acts is the use of military force and a further repression of the groups seen as sponsoring the terrorism in question.

Force does not lead to toleration, inclusive representation, fair electoral systems, and the freedoms associated with liberal democracies. If anything, it gives the elites in power an excuse not to begin or, depending on the stage of development, to engage in further experiments in democratization. The terrorist group, outside of the success of its acts, targets itself for the wrath of the society as well as those in power and, consequently, the necessity of putting security above political freedoms. This strategy works. In effect, the terrorists manage to keep a political system from which they are excluded continuing in operation. Calls for social order and an end to politically inspired violence, while reasonable enough in their own right, reaffirm the rule of force and build support for an authoritarian and repressive government. In one sense, it validates the right of democratic leaders both to rule and to engage in their repressive acts. It is the antithesis of democratization. Even if successful in undermining a regime, which can happen sporadically, a new government built on the seizure of power through violence serves only to reiterate the old ways, albeit with a new set of actors and new priorities. Terrorist takeovers of countries do not normally signal the introduction of a greater sense of social justice or a more open and responsive political system—in fact, quite the opposite. And despite a handful of exceptions (South Africa being a prime example, and, to a lesser extent, El Salvador, Argentina, Nicaragua, Chile, and some of the former Soviet republics, most of which evolved from elite bargaining), the ultimate outcome is more of the same. The outcome may be a little worse in that large-scale repressive acts usually follow political uprisings, and thus any roadways to more democratic societies become something of a lost cause.

Terrorism flourishes in autocratic, authoritarian, and totalitarian societies. Such societies provide the economic, religious, ethnic, or regional bases for extremism to develop and terrorism to take root. This would indicate that democratization processes, whatever the initial costs, are (in the long run) the best means to eventually alleviate terrorist behavior.

There are policy concerns in such developments, ones clearly unwelcome to those elites (economic, political, social, military, religious) holding power. A sharing of society's resources through an open and responsive political system should help overcome the conditions that sustain terrorist groups. The equation is not immediately direct or obvious; generations of abuse, repression, ignorance, or blind fundamentalism does not give way readily or quickly to tolerance, equality, acceptance, and a respect for human rights.

Wealthy countries in past generations (or centuries in some cases) have established themselves as colonial powers, extracted resources, and used subject countries as geopolitical strategic pawns in world-power conflicts. In contemporary times, these world powers, in a globalized economy strategic approach, have disposed of consumer goods in the same once-subject nations and thus provided convenient targets for impoverished and antidemocratic terrorist groups. It is not difficult to understand why some Muslim nations saw Osama bin Laden as a "Robin Hood" or, less enthusiastically, supported Saddam Hussein in the days in which he presented himself as a pan-Arab leader.

Little from the past experiences of world powers has been of lasting help to the subjugated countries involved; the foundations alleged to be introductory steps to the establishment of fully democratic societies have disappeared (or been adapted to authoritarian ends) almost as quickly as the colonial masters withdrew peacefully or were forced out. That such Western nations, and the United States as the world's richest and most powerful superpower, should serve as obvious—and even popular in some countries—targets for retribution for real or alleged wrongs by terrorist groups should not prove overly surprising. Even easier to comprehend is the resentment Muslim societies feel when what they see as a secular, godless, consumer- and sex-driven, alien civilization intrudes, replacing their traditional ways of life. The anger and frustration of the powerless under such conditions has to be great. The people of these cultures can little understand the forces they are competing against, much less survive and prosper in a world economy they essentially reject.

The most available and justifiable targets, from the terrorist's perspective, may well be the Western nations they have so long fought. If you add Israel to the equation along with the unqualified support by the United States for Israeli actions against the Palestinians and other neighbors, which if conducted by Arab nations would be (justifiably) condemned as terrorist acts (from which Israel also suffers), it is not difficult to appreciate why Western nations, and the United States in particular, serve as symbols of all that the Muslim societies resent.

The problems posed by terrorist groups and networks are not easily addressed. The conditions that provide the basis for grievances that result in random attacks on civilians are complex. They are also basic. To say that terrorism will not exist in a vibrant, liberal democratic culture is too strong an expectation. Clearly, terrorism does ingrain itself in repressive, authoritarian regimes. To the extent that these regimes can be politically liberalized and to the degree that effective and open political institutions and norms can be cultivated (the pace and forms of which will clearly vary in different societies), the greater, in effect, the fundamental effort to alleviate political terrorism and the conditions that condone (from the terrorist's point of view) the use of political violence.

INTRODUCING THE CHAPTERS

The chapters in this volume raise issues basic to the understanding of contemporary terrorism, its corrosive effects on political institutions, and the social and economic factors most closely associated with the repressive regimes that foster and support terrorist networks.

In the remainder of the introductory section, Amílcar Antonio Barreto presents a rational actor model in an effort to gain perspective on those who participate in terrorist acts and the reasons for these acts. John S. Jackson III and Chris Barr examine the American reaction to September 11, the issues raised, and the governmental actions taken. Irene Gendzier assesses presidential decision-making, the institutional use of agencies, and the balance of power among these in planning and executing the war on terrorism. Karla J. Cunningham studies the role of women in terrorism and political violence, a little-understood and particularly underdeveloped area of study. One consequence she presents is the underutilization of women in the structuring of postviolent states.

The Middle East

The Middle East is, in the contemporary period, the focus of much of the concern over terrorism. The societies are not modernized; political rule is authoritarian; the people are poor; educational systems can be primitive, allowing few opportunities to a country's citizenry to advance themselves; distaste for the West and its ideas and concepts of consumerism and spirituality (or lack thereof) is strong; democratic values of tolerance and individual protections have yet to take root; and Islam in its various shades of interpretation can be employed, directly or indirectly, to legitimize autocratic states and to offer a rationale (martyrdom) for political violence. This is a volatile mix, brought into sharp relief by the war on terrorism and the U.S. invasion of Iraq.

Rein Taagepera assesses democratic and authoritarian systems in Muslim countries and the reasons for those developments. Democratic societies do not normally foster state-sponsored international terror; authoritarian countries by the very nature of their exclusionary rule often provide a basis for terrorism, internally repressing their own people and providing a culture of fear in which terrorist networks can successfully recruit. James W. Roberts asserts that there are inherent tensions within Islam and between the West and Islamic nations. Roberts critiques the stresses within Islam and Islamic nations that create problems for any democratization effort, a sensitive issue, as he acknowledges, for all sides. Irm Haleem discusses developments in one of the key areas. Pakistan and its neighbors are crucial to efforts toward identifying and controlling terrorist activities. Pakistan has experienced Islamic government and is a majority-Muslim state. Haleem believes the real cause of extremism is best explained by social conditions, especially poverty. A number of factors combine to produce terrorist movements, but poverty and the absence of an inherited democratic tradition rank high on the list. These are emphases shared by most of the selections in this section and in this book. Abdullah Al-Faqih examines Yemen, prominent in both hosting terrorist groups and witnessing terrorist attacks, and the contradictions he sees in promoting a democratic movement while attempting to suppress terrorism itself. Mehran Kamrava assesses the interplay between radical Islam (and the political violence associated with it) and Islam's more liberal strains. The concern is with fundamentalist Islam, its emergence on a national and international scale, and its relationship to authoritarianism.

Asia and Southeast Asia

What kinds of nations do not suffer from international terrorism of any magnitude? What are the conditions that make for little to no terrorist activities of significance? How do these measures relate to criteria of democratic performance? These are issues addressed by examining China and selected East Asian countries. Suzanne Ogden's finely tuned analysis of China reviews the political violence that has occurred there but emphasizes that the nation's security policies, culture, and politics do not encourage dissent. Any type of violence, political or otherwise, is dealt with severely. Situations peculiar to the assertion of internal national and ethnic identities fall short of the terrorist challenges faced by other countries. Lawrence C. Reardon presents an overview of conditions in Southeast Asia, the variety of circumstances and cultures encountered, and the forms of political violence and terrorism present and how these have been dealt with. Dan G. Cox looks at Indonesia and the secessionist movement in East Timor (and elsewhere). In the case of East Timor, the movement was successful. Years of arbitrary or exclusionary policies by a state can lead to the mass movement of political violence faced by Indonesia and other countries. Yet the effort to keep a state from fragmenting, a priority for governments in these situations, combined with pressures to open and democratize the political system can create enormous tensions within any society, as they have in Indonesia and other countries in Southeast Asia.

Africa

Africa presents a variety of perspectives on the relationship between democratization and terrorism. The continent's experience has not always been positive—quite the opposite in the majority of cases. A number of incidents of violence, and regimes that propagated them, rank among the worst in contemporary history: for example, the genocide in Rwanda; the ever-continuing "liberation" fights in the Congo, Liberia, and Angola; and the transitions from relatively moderate and broadly functioning democracies to quasi-autocratic systems in Kenya, Mozambique, and elsewhere. The one success story, after centuries of apartheid, is South Africa.

Capturing the panoramic series of events that constitute the African story is well beyond the scope of this volume. Instead, we chose to focus on selected transitions and what can be learned from them. John Harbeson provides an introductory overview to the continent, its struggles, and its never-ending concerns. There are examples, few in number, that have combined an established institutional structure with efforts at electoral democracy. In particular, we have assessed the situations in Algeria, a country that undertook a relatively systematic and sophisticated experiment in democratization. Once under way, threats implicit in any democratization effort surfaced. This led to the potential (and likely) victory of a fundamentalist Islamic movement that in turn led to state repression. No one example can cover the full range of situations found on a continent as large as Africa. What a case study can do is help us to understand the processes under way and the risks, and potential rewards, involved.

Yahia Zoubir emphasizes the complexity of the situation involved in Algeria and the forces that gave rise to a radical Islam that undercut what had been achieved in terms of democratic pluralism. Mohammed Hafez focuses on the civil war that arose between the state and the fundamentalists and on the consequences this had for a nation attempting, and to an extent initially succeeding, the difficult task of turning a highly authoritarian regime into a representative political system. The case is a rare one for the region, which gives it added importance. Unfortunately, the lessons to be learned are unclear. The introduction of democracy can incite violence and encourage exclusions from a nation's policymaking. It is, for all African nations (and others), a difficult path. A healthy respect for human rights should represent an antidote to terrorism. In itself, it is a "good" and one promoted by the United Nations and the international community. The adoption of human rights treaties, as Iris Mwanza shows, does not always guarantee that human rights will be operationalized or respected in practice. She examines conditions in Ghana, Uganda, and Zambia (and elsewhere) in assessing the differences evident in symbolic acceptance and application of human rights imperatives.

Western Europe and Eastern Europe

Lada Parizkova assesses the reaction of the European Union (EU) to the terrorist threat as well as the different manner in which it has been handled in such countries as Germany, France, the United Kingdom, and Italy. There is both a common policy established through the EU and approaches followed by a given nation. The assessment is inclusive. One thing is clear—while the EU and Western European countries and their allies generally favor more humanitarian measures that attack (modestly it would seem) the roots of terrorist activities, the United States has focused more on the use of military force to attack terrorist bases and punish terrorist states. However, the EU and the United States both share the same concern: No one has yet to come up with plans acceptable to all countries or acknowledged as effective in preventing international terrorism. Parizkova develops a broad picture of the actions being taken in Europe. The conclusion would indicate that the real battle has just begun.

David E. Schmitt focuses on the Northern Ireland peace process and the continuing, extraordinarily difficult, long-term effort to end terrorism, provide an ecumenical basis for human rights, and resolve a conflict that has gone on for most of the twentieth century. The peace initiatives involve the United States, the United Kingdom, and the Republic of Ireland. It has been a taxing process, one filled with violence and one that is difficult to bring to any agreeable conclusion. The effects of September 11 have impacted all parties in the efforts to bring peace, tolerance, and nonviolence to a place that has known little of such conditions in the past. Lenard Cohen and Richard Farkas examine Serbia and Kosovo in relation to the extraordinary political violence and ethnic cleansing these areas have experienced and how such extreme conditions impact any efforts to democratize the countries involved and basically realign their treatment of human beings in general, their opponents in particular, with any criteria of democratic tolerance and accountability consistent with the EU.

Latin and Central America

Howard J. Wiarda and Susan L. Macek make the point that Latin American countries have long histories of violent behavior, some state-sponsored (Chile, Argentina, and Brazil, during the "dirty war" period), and have yet attempted to systematically develop democratic institutions and allow for political freedoms. The record has been uneven. The authors survey contemporary terrorist movements and the efforts to meet these in what are transitional attempts to fully democratize countries. Unfortunately, these events come at a time when the attention of the U.S. government has largely turned elsewhere.

Steven L. Taylor makes the point that the number of victims of political violence on a daily basis in Colombia reaches staggering proportions. It is a country that lives under the threat of unchecked violence, an unpredictable military, and a weak and personalized government. It is a poor country with immense drug cartel problems. Taylor contends that drug trafficking and the efforts to crack down on it (with assistance from the United States) has become the "new communism." The efforts to curtail the cultivation and transmission of cocaine and other drugs come at a high price in terms of the civil liberties abdicated to achieve what is believed to be a greater good. The violence and terror relied on by drug traffickers creates enormous difficulties for establishing any type of stable and orderly political society.

Jack Spence examines terrorism in Central America, especially during the 1970s and 1980s, when the area was considered a battlefront in the war against communism. It is not a pretty picture. State-sponsored or group-based assassinations, indiscriminate killings, and torture by military and paramilitary states and, to a lesser extent, guerrilla forces were common. Spence examines the efforts to come to terms with the past in Nicaragua, El Salvador, and, least successfully, Guatemala.

Each of the studies in the volume contribute to the understanding of political terrorism, in its many guises, and how it relates to efforts to democratize societies. The problems are complex and the solutions elusive, but the ultimate goals are eminently worthy of pursuit.

2 Toward a Theoretical Explanation of Political Extremism

Dividing discussions of individual participation in democratic politics and political extremism into two fundamentally different spheres of social reality may seem reasonable to the average observer. Democratic politics is often regarded as an example of reasonable if not rational politics, while political extremism is typically deemed an example of politics at its most irrational. Images of citizens lining up on election day are rarely juxtaposed with images of martyrs charging into battle on behalf of their venerated cause. Dichotomies are easily drawn between the politics of the expected and the unforeseen, the politics of tranquility and strife. Even in terms of frequency, elections are cast in the role of ordinary, perhaps even common, politics. But with acts of political violence, the unanticipated is usually the name of the game. Still, these very distinct forms of political action share common problems related to the cost-benefit calculus of any individual participant. Why should individuals participate in politics, whether in an electoral or combative alternative? Why do citizens in democratic societies, or militants in an extremist organization, bother to engage in politics rather than simply freeload off the efforts of others? What incentives are necessary to entice or encourage the sedentary to become active? These questions are not sensitive to temporal, cultural, or geographic boundaries. Interestingly, this debate impacts the rationality behind individual political participation regardless of its type.

Policymakers and scholars interested in the motivating factors behind terrorism and extremism need to move beyond the limited assumptions associated with traditional analyses that all too frequently presume that individuals are engaged in a constant struggle to accrue the greatest number of material goods. Certainly, individuals do strive for pecuniary gain. Still, such a framework may be better apt to describe the employee who changes one workplace for a higher paying substitute or even the astute politician altering their party's platform in a bid to appeal to the electorate's sway. Conjectures that all people seek to improve their material lot fail to explain the sacrifices made while engaging in other activities, particularly politics.

Although some governments mandate electoral participation, most voters, at least in liberal democratic regimes, are not remunerated for the time spent registering to vote or standing in line to cast their ballots. As motivating variables, material rewards and patronage are ill equipped to deal with the terrorist who may risk personal injury, if not martyrdom, for planting a bomb or driving a vehicle loaded with explosives into a police station. Interestingly, the same point may apply to the dutiful soldiers, particularly nonconscripts, who sacrifice their lives on behalf of the state and the existing order. Studies of political participation—in its electoral and extremist varieties—need to look to some of the fundamental assumptions underlying the works of many sociologists and cultural anthropologists. When analyzing individual behavior, we must recognize that under some circumstances individuals act like the typical *Homo economicus*; at other times, they comport themselves like the classic *Homo sociologicus*. They are not separate people per se but rather different dimensions of who we all are. What separates these realms is the degree to which we identify with particular groups and the personal satisfaction we derive from acknowledging that identity through performance, whether subtle or vicious.

A TRANSNATIONAL CASE IN POINT

Students of American politics often forget that the federal system comprised of fifty states and the District of Columbia has authority over millions of citizens living in various territories. Overseas territories are usually overlooked because of their distance from continental North America and also, perhaps, because of the lack of ethnic and racial characteristics that have historically linked most of the American states to one another. By far the most populous of the distant territories is the Commonwealth of Puerto Rico in the northeastern Caribbean. Its four million inhabitants are U.S. citizens constitutionally prohibited from directly participating in presidential or congressional elections. The only exceptions to that rule are that Puerto Ricans can elect a territorial nonvoting delegate to the U.S. House of Representatives and that the mainland Democratic and Republican parties can choose territorial residents as delegates to the national party conventions.

For more than a century, Puerto Ricans have lived under American rule, and the character of that relationship lies at the heart of insular politics—whether to remain a semiautonomous U.S. Commonwealth, join the federal union as a state, or separate and become an independent country. Without question, a clear majority of Puerto Ricans favor strong ties with the United States, either through statehood or the status quo. "Material prosperity, coupled with repression and intimidation, have blunted the demand for independence" (Weisskoff 1985, 121). At the same time, and perhaps paradoxically, Puerto Ricans are fervent cultural nationalists (Trías Monge 1997, 11). Rather than yield to the federal government's policy of "Americanization" (1899–1949) or forced linguistic and cultural assimilation, Puerto Ricans defiantly became more nationalist—both in terms of the more moderate and popular variant of autonomism and its more obdurate variant, separatism (Barreto 1998). This soft, less aggressive variant of cultural nationalism is widespread within elite and nonelite strata of society, both on the island and within Puerto Rican communities on the U.S. mainland (Morris 1995, 151–52; Rivera 1996, 500). Political elites on the island have on occasion flaunted this nationalism in an attempt to play on Washington's anxieties about its cultural and political periphery (Barreto 2001).

For a century and a half, a revolutionary fragment of that separatist movement endured despite varying degrees of persecution under a multitude of administrations in Madrid and Washington. In the late nineteenth century, Puerto Rican activists in New York City organized activities on behalf of the island's independence movement (Vega 1984, 48–54). They organized the Puerto Rican section of the Cuban Revolutionary Club—a group committed to eradicating Spain's remaining Caribbean territories, Cuba and Puerto Rico. Inspired by the 1868 *Grito de Lares* (Lares Uprising) against the Spanish Crown, the Puerto Rican activists promised to continue the struggle until the American flag was lowered in this Antillean island for the last time.

This activism did not wane in the advent of U.S. rule or with the federal government's decision to grant Puerto Ricans American citizenship in 1917. On the contrary, backing for greater degrees of home rule increased sharply during the Great Depression. Some supporters of Puerto Rican independence, even on the U.S. mainland, actively campaigned on behalf of Pedro Albizu Campos, the uncompromising Harvard-educated revolutionary who led the *Partido Nacionalista* (Nationalist Party) in the second quarter of the twentieth century (Vega 1984, 186–97). According to Lolita Lebrón, the New York City-based Puerto Rican nationalist who led the March 1, 1954, machine gun attack on the U.S. House of Representatives, the image of Albizu Campos served as an inspiration for her and her comrades (Ribes Tovar 1974, 111–14). A generation later, militant separatists lent their support to the Marxist Puerto Rican Socialist Party in various U.S. mainland cities (Velázquez 1998). While this party staged no insurgencies against the American federal government, it certainly applauded those individuals who defended the cause of independence regardless of strategy.

Perhaps the most familiar revolutionary organizations of the 1970s and 1980s were the Macheteros (Machete Wielders) and the Fuerzas Armadas de Liberación Nacional (Armed Forces of National Liberation [FALN]), both active on the U.S. mainland (Fernandez 1987). President Clinton's decision to grant conditional clemency to a dozen individuals connected to the Macheteros and FALN was applauded by Puerto Ricans and condemned by many in the United States as a capitulation to terrorists (Barreto 2002, 53–57). Sympathy for this cause—even its most militant strains—endures in many inner-city communities and is even seen by some as a gauge of Puerto Rican cultural authenticity (Ramos-Zayas 2003).

Today, the vast majority of Puerto Rican separatists—themselves a minority of the Puerto Rican electorate—are committed to self-determination via the ballot box. Only a tiny splinter pledges itself to secession from the United States by armed resistance or any other extralegal means. The existence of fringe armed organizations advocating independence is far from novel, even in well-established Western democracies. In Canada, the nationalist Parti Québécois won the momentous 1976 Quebec provincial elections despite the kidnappings and bombings carried out by the Front de Libération du Québec (Front for the Liberation of Quebec) in the 1960s and 1970s. Likewise, in Basque provinces, the armed activities of Euskadi Ta Askatasuna (Basque Homeland and Liberty) has not altered the fact that most Basque nationalists express their desire for separation from Spain by voting for the Partido Nacionalista Vasco (Basque Nationalist Party [PNV]), as the party is known in Spanish, or Euzko Alderdi Jeltzalea (EAJ), as the party is known in the Basque language. A plethora of other examples abound. Thus, the existence of extremist separatists within Puerto Rico's independence movement is far from unique.

One fascinating aspect of the Puerto Rican case, particularly its most militant manifestation, is that standard rationality assumptions in the social sciences—particularly in economics and mainstream political science—propose that extremist groups within diasporic communities should not even exist. Though one may vehemently disagree with the aims, and certainly the tactics, of extremist organizations, one can at least understand a particular reasoning behind the generic individual political extremist. Imagine if the terrorist's cause succeeded; the organization's leadership would be situated in a prime position to distribute rewards to its hard-core adherents. Of course, by definition such privileges are limited. What benefits would be left over for noncombatants or overseas lieutenants outside their jurisdiction?

Let us elaborate on the aforementioned point using the current example. One could imagine the insurgent fragment of the independence movement attempting to end U.S. rule in Puerto Rico. This is what happened when Pedro Albizu Campos led the Gesta de Jayuya (Jayuya Uprising) against Governor Luis Muñoz Marín on October 30, 1950. This declaration of independence was followed a couple of days later by an attack on Blair House in Washington, D.C., the temporary residence of President Harry Truman. Both of the Puerto Rican nationalists who attempted to storm the president's residence were from New York (Vivas Maldonado 1974, 304). Assume for a moment that Albizu Campos had succeeded. One could envision, supposing a purely rational calculus, a nationalist leader promising supporters valued positions in the forthcoming sovereign administration. Quite likely, an Albizu Campos administration would distribute the most valued positions to the highest-ranking members of his party and movement. Below them the ordinary militants would probably expect midrange positions in the impending sovereign government. One would be hard-pressed to imagine any of these prized positions apportioned to anyone else. Certainly we are looking at a high-stakes gamble on the part of prospective warriors in this endeavor. Indeed, the collapse of Albizu Campos's Gesta de Jayuya summoned more than a decade of varying degrees of repression by the federal and commonwealth governments against all independence sympathizers, even those who deplored violence (Bosque Pérez and Colón Morera 1997).

From the early 1950s, let us fast-forward to the present. Presumably, there remain individuals who sympathize with the Macheteros and the FALN in Puerto Rican enclaves such as New York City, Hartford, and Chicago. To gauge with any precision a community's support for extremists is, of course, very difficult. Nonetheless, since members of this ethnic community have promoted the island's independence since the nineteenth century, such support is not an unreasonable conjecture. Let us imagine they resumed their armed activities and somehow pushed Washington to a new cost-benefit calculation—one where the federal government opts to withdraw from Puerto Rico. The insurgents win in this scenario. Despite the victory, a question remains. Why did their companions in arms on the U.S. mainland bother to participate in the first place?

These individuals and their unarmed well-wishers live in the United States. Currently, out of more than seven million Puerto Ricans, approximately 40 percent live in the United States. A successful revolutionary regime in San Juan would be in no condition to encourage the mass migration even of its most ardent supporters several hundred kilometers away on the U.S. mainland. How a revolutionary government could reward its activists in another country is difficult to imagine. Such a regime would have to take care of its soldiers on the island before it could contemplate providing assistance, let alone patronage, to a transnational regiment. Metaphorically speaking, these insurrectionists would be working for the "promised land" knowing full well that they would likely not personally benefit from the journey. Barring the availability to generate and distribute selective incentives—incentives confined strictly to participants—a collective enterprise such as a terrorist movement would fail (Olson 1971, 51).

THE FREE-RIDER PARADOX

The conceptual problem highlighted above was stressed in Olson's renowned *Logic of Collective Action.* Movement leaders may be in a position to offer their key activists selective incentives for participation. Elites distribute the limited number of these selective incentives only to those who actively participate. In the context of social movements and revolutionary organizations, the incentives offered are dependent on future success. Still, the potential benefit—such as a post in the new government—can be rather enticing.

Selective incentives differ substantially in frequency and kind from their collective counterparts. Collective benefits are nonexcludable to group members regardless of level of participation. People travel on roads paid by public funds regardless of the size of their individual tax returns or whether they paid any taxes at all. Citizenship is certainly a nonexcludable good as is the franchise, under most circumstances. Even in restrictive cases—for example, lack of Israeli citizenship for Palestinians in the Occupied Territories or denial of South African citizenship for the country's nonwhite majority under Apartheid—the citizenship conferred by the regime to in-group members is not dependent on an individual's partisan ideology or adherence to the state's limitations on citizenship rights to particular groups. Individuals living in a postrevolutionary regime may benefit, for example, from the adoption of their vernacular as the government's official language regardless of how much time and energy they invested in the struggle. Again, what incentives a postrevolutionary Puerto Rican government could tender to its supporters living under another's jurisdiction is exceedingly difficult to imagine.

Barring the availability of selective incentives, individuals are tempted to "free ride" (Olson 1971). We can imagine a political extremist deciding on whether or not to actively participate. Even if we assume victory, a movement embracing hundreds of thousands or even millions will not be in a position to selectively reward all its militants. Indeed, many frontline activists know they will not live to enjoy the fruits of their labor. An ordinary person can expect to receive only a series of collective incentives. However, our pondering extremist will receive these rewards regardless of participation since these are public goods and, by definition, are nonexcludable. Our representative extremist will be tempted to let others perform the hard work, imperil their lives, or risk incarceration. Of course, if everyone thought that way, most social and revolutionary movements would fail. Government may solve this problem by way of employing enforcers (Hechter 1987). Laitin (1999) suggests that enforcement helps to explain how terrorists maintain in-group obedience. Still, few governments and even fewer extremist organizations could afford to hire sufficient regulators to monitor everyone based on the principle of disseminating selective incentives.

Since the publication of Olson's work, many social scientists have attempted to tackle the presumed irrationality of large-scale collective endeavors that include voting, ethnic mobilization, and political extremism. Collective action has been described as the most difficult and important problem to solve in the social sciences (Elster 1985). For the political extremist, particularly the martyr, there is no room left for possible material payoffs. Indeed, here we have the ultimate illogicality of people making the supreme tangible sacrifice—their very existence. Given their paucity, the selective tangible benefits distributed by elites to a limited number of activists are simply insufficient to explain mass movements or the behavior of individuals who forego their very lives (Popkin 1979). The current framework, as it stands, is inappropriate for explaining extremist political action given that militants are likely to risk, if not forfeit, their lives. This has led some scholars to question the rational actor framework in part (Green and Shapiro 1994) or in whole (Geertz 1973; Malešević 2002) as an analytical dead end. Some have even suggested that involuntary thought processes drive many actions. Boudon posited that "people unknowingly adhere to false ideas because they are impelled by *unconscious* forces outside their control which make them slaves either to their own interests (if they belong to the ruling class) or to the interests of the ruling class (if they belong to the underclass)" (1989, 41, emphasis in original).

A salient conceptual hurdle lies with the manner in which the rational actor model entered the social sciences—via economics (Von Neumman and Morgenstern 1953). Naturally, this discipline was eager to develop Bentham's (1988) assumptions that individuals seek to maximize their material benefits. Such postulations reconfirmed the underlying principles of capitalism. Even classic Marxist scholarship is founded on the logic of materially driven motivation. The bourgeoisie is expected to advance its selfish interests that are irreconcilably at variance with the material interests of the peasantry and the proletariat. Many economists ignore Bentham's contention that some individuals forego tangible gains in order to satisfy their lust to fulfill a social payoff. Certainly, this is not the case with all economists. Veblen (1973, 29) argued that more than a century ago notions of dignity and honor emerged as a consequence of the development of classes.

Can material selective incentives alone explain collective action or its subvariant extremist action? Disagreeing with some of the scholars previously cited, others emphatically answer that question in the negative. One group of analysts insists that the key to understanding collective action is found in group identity and solidarity (Dawes, Van de Kragt, and Orbell 1990, 99). Pride in and an individual's identification with a collectivity lie at the root of collective action (Breton 1964; Coleman 1995; Lichbach 1994). They recognize, as did Aristotle (1987, 22), that "man is naturally a social being." Social incentives are particularly effective in small stable groups (Taylor 1988, 84). Yet, such incentives may also apply well to large groups as long as the enforcement of these norms is implemented at the grass roots. Chong's analysis of the American Civil Rights movement insists that the possible long-term material benefits associated with the movement were not enough to foment collective action without additional social and psychological incentives (1991, 9, 196). Civil rights activism was aided by the fact that it operated as a vast coalition of likeminded groups and churches, each with the ability to encourage individual-level participation in a mass movement. Chong's analysis shares important parallels with Laitin (1999, 60), who insists that preexisting social networks and their codes of honor are key to understanding collective action (Chong 1991, 34–35).

IDENTITIES AND ACTION

Political extremists often have low regard for their personal security. After all, these individuals voluntarily put themselves in exceedingly vulnerable positions or even sacrifice their lives, as is the case with the exemplary suicide bomber. A focus on material payoffs will help us little to understand the motivating factors behind such irregular politics. Studies of political extremism will have to take into account dimensions of human motivation other than love of profit. Other emotions—such as love of community, hatred for the out-group, or resentment toward real or perceived injustices—will be key to understanding collective action in general and politics in the extreme in particular. Self-sacrifice exists in society because of feelings of solidarity (Durkheim 1973, 83), and the longing to connect to a group fulfills vital psychological needs (Kecmanovic 1996).

This comment in no way denies the existence of the material egoists. It does recognize our nonmaterial side. Material maximizers are frequently portrayed as truly rational beings, while those seeking emotional payoffs are often painted as unstable and irrational. Interestingly, research in the biological sciences is enlightening social scientists that preconceived notions about separateness between the rational and emotional realms of the mind are founded on false premises—the two processes are in fact rather integrated (Damasio 1995, 70). Group solidarity or emotional attachments to groups are not dichotomous; rather, they flow along a continuum, with the pure material maximizer on one end and the pure social maximizer on the other. In between these two endpoints lay a host of mixed or hybrid loyalties. Like Tsebelis's (1990) notion of a nested game, we sometimes favor one arena over the other.

After all, we all belong simultaneously to familial, linguistic, ethnic, religious, civic, political, and other groups or organizations. Yet, we rarely feel the same level of attachment to all of them. Some of us feel a greater attachment and sense of responsibility to one or a few. We would not be surprised to hear that someone jeopardized his or her life for child, confessional community, or ethnic group. However, many of us would be astonished to hear the same devotion exerted for a social club or neighborhood association. "Utility maximization should not only take into account the utility of what *we have* (and the activities we carry out) but also the utility we get from what (we think) *we are*" (Pagano 1995, 190, emphasis in original).

Who we are, or who we believe ourselves to be, is strongly influenced by our socialization. Naturally, the most important ideological beliefs are acquired during childhood (Hogan 2001, 74). As Coles (1986, 24) indicates in his study of political socialization in children, acquiring political beliefs is not limited to older children aware of government branches, map boundaries, and the differences between objective cultural traits used to separate particular groups. Coles describes a Catholic adolescent exhibiting a clear understanding of the subservient station of his group vis-à-vis Ulster Protestants. His status as an outsider, or a lower-ranking member of that society, was evident by the "dirty Fenian" label attached to him and his friends. Their response was to describe their rivals as "Prods" or the "Brits" (83). Prejudicial comments depend on stereotypes and a very selective knowledge of the rival group (Cullingford 2000, 9, 102). Or, as Hogan (2001, 71) put it, identification is founded on a sense of "shared subjectivity." Such notions about the "other" may be exaggerated, nonrepresentative of the unbiased present or past, or even completely fabricated (Roosens 1989, 161). A profound understanding of the theological schism separating the two communities was unnecessary. Let us return to the boy in Coles's study. The child's identification as a Catholic came from two primary sources: his family and peers who told him he was one of *us*, and the rival society that let him know he was *not* one of them.

Memories of atrocities, defeats, and humiliations help construct future victims. Subjective interpretations of the past are important to understanding political extremism.

Pastness is a mode by which persons are persuaded to act in the present in ways they might not otherwise act. Pastness is a tool persons use against each other.

Pastness is a central element in the socialization of individuals, in the maintenance of group solidarity, in the establishment of or challenge to social legitimation. Pastness therefore is pre-eminently a moral phenomenon, therefore a political phenomenon, always a contemporary phenomenon. That is of course why it is so inconstant. (Wallerstein 1991, 78)

Objective histories and studies circumvent the aim of stereotypes. Subjective readings of the past open the possibility of creating victims. "Being a victim confers upon us a kind of moral authority—a sense that we *deserve* to be treated specially" (Searle-White 2001, 92, emphasis in original). The child in Coles's study would grow up to become a victim like everyone else in his community. His people had little hope, so he had little incentive to excel in school and plan for the future. This child, at aged ten, was already a junior-grade veteran of the struggle. At the age of seven this child was delivering messages from one place to another "in the service of the resistance" (Coles 1986, 84).

What are the emotional sentiments that nourish the quest for vengeance and encourage political extremism? Petersen's (2002) study of ethnic violence in Eastern Europe looked into the roles of ethnic fear, hatred, rage, and resentment. Of these, he found that resentment explained more incidences of ethnic violence than the rest. Resentment, naturally, is ineffectual unless the person in question already has a strong identification with a particular community—whether that identity is chosen or imposed. Resentment is a comparative venture energized by a livid sense of injustice at the group's social, political, and economic status vis-à-vis its counterparts. Such feelings do not create prime opportunities for political violence, but they provide the groundwork that takes advantage of such occasions. Violent actions, when undertaken, do not create identities but rather safeguard them. "Brutality, ethnic cleansing, and so forth are not part of our ethnic identification. They are merely a means to the protection of that identification" (Hardin 1995, 9).

A sense of group belonging fuels a longing to defend one's honor in cases of perceived crass injustice. Norms of honor link individuals to their respective society. As Hobbes (1962, 81) noted, "Desire to praise, disposeth to laudable actions, such as please them whose judgment they value. . . . Desire of fame after death does the same." Justice and respect demand that the individual incarnate the collective's values and in so doing reinforce the group's identity.

Honour, therefore, provides a nexus between the ideals of a society and their reproduction in the individual through his aspiration to personify them. As such, it implies not merely an habitual preference for a given mode of conduct, but the entitlement to a certain treatment in return. The right to pride is the right to status (in the popular as well as the anthropological sense of the word), and status is established through the recognition of a certain social identity. (Pitt-Rivers 1996, 22)

Satisfying a violated sense of honor, the decisive cure for resentment, is a selective social incentive. Acquiring or fulfilling a sense of honor is valued only to the degree that one identifies with a particular group. Identification with a group is a powerful forecaster of negative attitudes as well as conflictual behavior toward out-groups (Kelly and Kelly 1994, 77). Such identification will naturally vary from person to person (Breton and Dalmazzone 2002, 46). It is selective in the sense that the only way to generate a positive social selective incentive is to participate. Through action, individuals "perform" their identities (Guss 2000). Actions that promote pride and diminish a sense of shame fuel self-esteem and may trigger some of the most determined and extreme forms of collective action (Breton and Dalmazzone 2002; Elster 1999).

Indeed, as Blumer (1969, 71) put it, "Without action, any structure of relations between people is meaningless." Active believers generate a positive payoff every time they express their beliefs (Chong 2000; Chwe 2001; Schuessler 2000). As La Rochefoucauld (1959, 64) noted in his 213th maxim, "Love of fame, fear of disgrace, schemes for advancement, desire to make life comfortable and pleasant, and the urge to humiliate others are often at the root of the valour men hold in such high esteem." The reverse also holds true. Inaction in the context of a strong identification with a group generates a negative social selective payoff, such as ostracism. Negative social sanctions shape behavior, not beliefs (Breton and Dalmazzone 2002, 53). As with its positive counterpart, shame works only to the degree that one identifies with a particular group.

Political extremists committing acts of violence voluntarily submit themselves to the court of public opinion. Naturally, their concerns lay with their particular community; no concern is given for the opinion of the outsider. "Public opinion forms therefore a tribunal before which the claims to honour are brought, 'the court of reputation' as it has been called, and against the judgements there is no redress" (Pitt-Rivers 1966, 27). The community has the means to confer praise and honor to its champions. Warriors may be showered with praise. "Status-enhancement is most likely to occur when the donor's generosity can be prominently memorialized" (Posner 2000, 61). The ultimate commendation—not surprisingly—goes to the martyr. On the other hand, the public also doles out the maximum discommendation. Nonconformers may be attacked by way of gossip and public ridicule (Lancaster 1988; Scott 1985). These weapons have no meaning unless and until they are internalized as legitimate expressions, even if negative, of one's identity.

What may not be clear at this juncture is why ordinary community members would bother to judge—positively or negatively—community norms and values. This too could be described as another free-rider paradox or "second order" free-rider paradox. The solution here is that regardless of the outcome in the court of public opinion, the judges always win. Members of the public at large pronouncing someone honorable, or not, generate for themselves positive social rewards. After all, every pronouncement for or against a fellow community member is a de facto reconfirmation that those sitting in judgment are worthy to adjudicate. At the grass roots, communities make sure that villains are condemned and heroes are extolled.

CONCLUSION

The microlevel of society is where we find the true battleground of political extremism. States may send in battalion after battalion in a quest to maintain order and suppress political violence. Indeed, many states actually instigate political violence. Negative sanctions are rarely sufficient to restrain terrorism. Future material rewards do not explain why individuals sacrifice their goods or lives for an array of causes. Policymakers interested in diminishing extremist politics will need to look to the social side of individuals rather than the egotistical materialist. Our identities, though they vary with intensity, shape our actions.

Individuals may seek to surround themselves with select material goods, but that does not alter the fact that people are also social beings forging robust emotional ties with a host of groups ranging in size from the nuclear family to the nation. Assuming the progression of strong social ties—a frequent occurrence in confessional, national, and ethnic identities—we should expect to find increases in various forms of collective action. Where there are strong identities, shifts in social hierarchies—whether perceived or real—may generate resentment. This emotion, coupled with an individual's sense of obligation to community, may be responsible for fomenting politics in the extreme. Of course, a comprehension of the origins of political violence does not guarantee a solution. After all, in the short run, privileged groups in society may be unwilling to surrender their social or economic advantages. Protracted conflicts may, however, change that cost-benefit assessment on the part of privileged groups.

REFERENCES

Aristotle. 1987. The *Nicomachean Ethics*, trans. J. E. Welldon. Amherst, N.Y.: Prometheus.
Barreto, Amílcar A. 1998. *Language, Elites, and the State: Nationalism in Puerto Rico and Quebec*. Westport, Conn.: Praeger.

————. 2001. *The Politics of Language in Puerto Rico*. Gainesville: University Press of Florida.

————. 2002. *Vieques, the Navy, and Puerto Rican Politics*. Gainesville: University Press of Florida.

Bentham, Jeremy. 1988 [1781]. *The Principles of Morals and Legislation*. Amherst, N.Y.: Prometheus Books.

Blumer, Herbert. 1969. *Symbolic Interactionism: Perspective and Method*. Berkeley: University of California Press.

Bosque Pérez, Ramón, and José J. Colón Morera. 1997. *Las Carpetas: Persecusión política y derechos civiles en Puerto Rico*. Río Piedras, Puerto Rico: Centro para la Investigación y Promoción de los Derechos Civiles.

Boudon, Raymond. 1989. *The Analysis of Ideology*, trans. Malcolm Slater. Chicago: University of Chicago Press.

Breton, Albert. 1964. "The Economics of Nationalism." *Journal of Political Economy* 72(4): 376–86.

Breton, Albert, and Silvana Dalmazzone. 2002. "Information Control, Loss of Autonomy, and the Emergence of Political Extremism." In *Political Extremism and Rationality*, ed. Albert Breton, Gianluggi Galeotti, Pierre Salmon, and Ronald Wintrobe, 44–66. Cambridge: Cambridge University Press.

Chong, Dennis. 1991. *Collective Action and the Civil Rights Movement*. Chicago: University of Chicago Press.

————. 2000. *Rational Lives: Norms and Values in Politics and Society*. Chicago: University of Chicago Press.

Chwe, Michael S. 2001. *Rational Ritual: Culture, Coordination, and Common Knowledge*. Princeton, N.J.: Princeton University Press.

Coleman, James S. 1995. "Rights, Rationality, and Nationality." In *Nationalism and Rationality*, ed. Albert Breton, Gianluggi Galeotti, Pierre Salmon, and Ronald Wintrobe, 1–13. Cambridge: Cambridge University Press.

Coles, Robert. 1986. *The Political Life of Children*. Boston: Atlantic Monthly Press.

Cullingford, Cedric. 2000. *Prejudice: From Individual Identity to Nationalism in Young People*. London: Kogan Page.

Damasio, Antonio R. 1995. *Descartes' Error: Emotion, Reason, and the Human Brain*. New York: Avon Books.

Dawes, Robyn M., Alphons J. C. Van de Kragt, and John M. Orbell. 1990. "Cooperation for the Benefit of Us—Not Me, or My Conscience." In *Beyond Self-Interest*, ed. Jane J. Mansbridge, 97–110. Chicago: University of Chicago Press.

Durkheim, Emile. 1973. *On Morality and Society*, ed. Robert N. Bellah. Chicago: University of Chicago Press.

Elster, Jon. 1985. "Rationality, Morality, and Collective Action." *Ethics* 96(1): 136–55.

————. 1999. *Alchemies of the Mind: Rationality and the Emotions*. Cambridge: Cambridge University Press.

Fernandez, Ronald. 1987. *Los Macheteros: The Wells Fargo Robbery and the Violent Struggle for Puerto Rican Independence*. New York: Prentice Hall.

Geertz, Clifford. 1973. *The Interpretation of Cultures*. New York: Basic Books.

Glazer, Amihai. 1993. "Political Equilibrium under Group Identification." In *Information, Participation, and Choice: An Economic Theory of Democracy in Perspective*, ed. Bernard Grofman, 81–92. Ann Arbor: University of Michigan Press.

Green, Donald P., and Ian Shapiro. 1994. *Pathologies of Rational Choice Theory: A Critique of Applications in Political Science*. New Haven, Conn.: Yale University Press.

Guss, David M. 2000. *The Festive State: Race, Ethnicity, and Nationalism as Cultural Performance*. Berkeley: University of California Press.

Hardin, Russell. 1995. *One for All: The Logic of Group Conflict*. Princeton, N.J.: Princeton University Press.

Hechter, Michael. 1987. *Principles of Group Solidarity*. Berkeley: University of California Press.

Hobbes, Thomas. 1962 [1651]. *Leviathan. Or the Matter, Forme, and Power of a Commonwealth Ecclesiasticall and Civil*, ed. Michael Oakshott. New York: Collier Books.

Hogan, Patrick C. 2001. *The Culture of Conformism: Understanding Social Consent*. Durham, N.C.: Duke University Press.

Kecmanovic, Dusan. 1996. *The Mass Psychology of Ethnonationalism*. New York: Plenum Press.

Kelly, Caroline, and John Kelly. 1994. "Who Gets Involved in Collective Action?: Social Psychological Determinants of Individual Participation in Trade Unions." *Human Relations* 47(1): 63–88.

Laitin, David D. 1999. "National Revivals and Violence." In *Critical Comparisons in Politics and Culture*, ed. John R. Bowen and Roger Petersen, 21–60. Cambridge: Cambridge University Press.

Lancaster, Roger N. 1988. *Thanks to God and the Revolution: Popular Religion and Class Consciousness in the New Nicaragua*. New York: Columbia University Press.

La Rochefoucauld, François. 1959 [1665]. *Maxims*, trans. Leonard Tancock. London: Penguin Books.

Lichbach, Mark I. 1994. "What Makes Rational Peasants Revolutionary? Dilemmas, Paradox, and Irony in Peasant Collective Action." *World Politics* 46(3): 383–418.

Malešević, Siniša. 2002. "Rational Choice Theory and the Sociology of Ethnic Relations: A Critique." *Ethnic and Racial Studies* 25(2): 193–212.

Morris, Nancy. 1995. *Puerto Rico: Culture, Politics, and Identity*. Westport, Conn.: Praeger.

Olson, Mancur. 1971 [1965]. *The Logic of Collective Action*. Cambridge: Harvard University Press.

Pagano, Ugo. 1995. "Can Economics Explain Nationalism?" In *Nationalism and Rationality*, ed. Albert Breton, Gianluggi Galeotti, Pierre Salmon, and Ronald Wintrobe, 173–203. Cambridge: Cambridge University Press.

Petersen, Roger D. 2002. *Understanding Ethnic Violence: Fear, Hatred, and Resentment in Twentieth-Century Eastern Europe*. Cambridge: Cambridge University Press.

Pitt-Rivers, Julian. 1966. "Honour and Social Status." In *Honour and Shame: The Values of Mediterranean Society*, ed. John G. Peristiany, 17–77. Chicago: University of Chicago Press.

Popkin, Samuel L. 1979. *The Rational Peasant: The Political Economy of Rural Society in Vietnam*. Berkeley: University of California Press.

Posner, Eric A. 2000. *Law and Social Norms*. Cambridge: Harvard University Press.

Ramos-Zayas, Ana Y. 2003. *National Performances: The Politics of Class, Race, and Space in Puerto Rican Chicago*. Chicago: University of Chicago Press.

Ribes Tovar, Federico. 1974. *Lolita Lebrón, la prisionera*. New York: Plus Ultra.

Rivera, Angel I. 1996. *Puerto Rico: Ficción y mitología en sus alternativas de status*. San Juan, Puerto Rico: Ediciones Nueva Aurora.

Roosens, Eugeen E. 1989. *Creating Ethnicity: The Process of Ethnogenesis*. Newbury Park, Calif.: Sage.

Schuessler, Alexander A. 2000. *A Logic of Expressive Choice*. Princeton, N.J.: Princeton University Press.

Searle-White, Joshua. 2001. *The Psychology of Nationalism*. New York: Palgrave.

Scott, James C. 1985. *Weapons of the Weak: Everyday Forms of Peasant Resistance*. New Haven, Conn.: Yale University Press.

Taylor, Michael. 1988. "Rationality and Revolutionary Collective Action." In *Rationality and Revolution*, ed. Michael Taylor, 63–97. Cambridge: Cambridge University Press.

Trías Monge, José. 1997. *Puerto Rico: The Trials of the Oldest Colony in the World*. New Haven: Yale University Press.

Tsebelis, George. 1990. *Nested Games: Rational Choice in Comparative Politics*. Berkeley: University of California Press.

Veblen, Thorstein. 1973 [1899]. *The Theory of the Leisure Class*. Boston: Houghton Mifflin.

Vega, Bernardo. 1984. *Memoirs of Bernardo Vega: A Contribution to the History of the Puerto Rican Community in New York*, ed. César A. Iglesias, trans. Juan Flores. New York: Monthly Review Press.

Velázquez, José E. 1998. "Coming Full Circle: The Puerto Rican Socialist Party, U.S. Branch." In *The Puerto Rican Movement: Voices from the Diaspora*, ed. Andrés Torres and José E. Velázquez, 48–68. Philadelphia: Temple University Press.

Vivas Maldonado, José L. 1974. *Historia de Puerto Rico*. New York: Las Américas Publishing.

Von Neumann, John, and Oskar Morgenstern. 1953 [1944]. *Theory of Games and Economic Behavior*. 3d ed. Princeton, N.J.: Princeton University Press.

Wallerstein, Immanuel. 1991. "The Construction of Peoplehood: Racism, Nationalism, Ethnicity." In Etienne Balibar and Immanuel Wallerstein, *Race, Nation, Class: Ambiguous Identities*, trans. Chris Turner, 71–85. London: Verso.

Weisskoff, Richard. 1985. *Factories and Food Stamps: The Puerto Rican Model of Development*. Baltimore: Johns Hopkins University Press.

3 The View from America

PRESIDENTIAL POLICY, ELECTIONS, AND THE CONGRESS

INTRODUCTION

The terrorist attacks of September 11, 2001, on the United States were a national trauma that will be permanently seared into our collective memories. The attacks and their aftermath have already become a prominent influence on our political culture, and the images they engendered have become one of the most widely recognized components of the popular culture. The picture of firemen raising the flag at ground zero, the ubiquitous use of the acronyms "FDNY" and "NYPD," the graphic pictures of the fireballs in the twin towers, even the evocation of the shorthand "9/11" became almost instantly the iconic symbols of these tragic events. Almost twenty-eight hundred people lost their lives in the twin towers in New York alone, according to the final official account. Including the losses at the Pentagon and at the plane crash site in Pennsylvania, more than three thousand were killed in the span of just a few minutes. Commentators quickly compared the occasion to the Japanese attack on Pearl Harbor, which began the American entry into World War II. Others noted that more Americans were killed in these attacks than on any single day since the battle of Antietam in the American Civil War. September 11 was a day that, like Pearl Harbor, would live in infamy as a tragic legacy that has changed American politics and the American political system in some very important ways.

THE POLITICAL PARAMETERS OF THE WAR ON TERRORISM

Now that some time has passed and we have gained the advantage of hindsight, we can draw some conclusions regarding the impact on American politics and government of the September 11 attacks and the ensuing war on terrorism. To assess the political consequences of the attacks that drove the institutional changes that have taken place, we must first review briefly the political situation at the beginning of the twenty-first century, particularly the 2000 presidential election. The fact that the nation was very closely divided politically hardly needs embellishing (Ceaser and Busch 2001; Simon 2001; Schier 2003). The 2000 presidential election was the first since 1888 where one candidate won the popular vote and another candidate won the electoral vote. Gore won the popular vote by approximately 537,000 votes, while Bush won the electoral vote by a narrow margin (271 to 266). Of course, the Bush victory was only settled thirty-six days after the vote when the Supreme Court of the United States in a narrowly drawn decision dictated that the Florida recount, which had been ordered by the Supreme Court of the State of Florida, not proceed, and Bush was certified as the winner in Florida and thus the winner in the electoral college (*Bush v. Gore* 2000).[1] While the 2000 race was not absolutely the closest in popular or electoral votes, it certainly ranks as one of the closest, and it was certainly one that was more prolonged in the aftermath of the election than almost any other. The bitterness of this dispute left some observers speculating as to what it would mean for the legitimacy of a George W. Bush presidency and whether he could govern in the sense of getting his policy proposals through Congress.

Further underscoring how narrowly divided the nation was politically is the fact that the original count in the U.S. Senate after the 2000 election put the partisan division at an exact tie of fifty Republicans and fifty Democrats. This meant that Vice President Dick Cheney had to cast the tie-breaker vote for the chamber to get organized, and presumably he would have cast many other tie-breaker votes if that situation had continued. Then in May of 2001, Senator James Jeffords of Vermont announced that he was switching from the Republican Party to become an Independent and that he would not vote with the Republicans in organizational and leadership matters. This meant that former Republican majority leader Trent Lott of Mississippi would become the minority leader, and former Democrat minority leader Tom Daschle would become the majority leader. The Democrats took over control of the U.S. Senate by one vote, while the U.S. House of Representatives remained in Republican control by a very narrow majority. Thus, the nation was about as closely divided in terms of party control of the government as it could possibly be.

This narrow margin in both houses of Congress, and divided government between the executive and legislative branches, meant that partisanship would continue to be very important in the policymaking process and that a certain amount of give-and-take and compromise between Democrats and Republicans would be necessary to pass any ambitious policy initiatives. September 11, 2001, certainly altered that equation in fundamental respects, especially after the 2002 midterm elections were over.

There is absolutely no question about the fact that the events of September 11 and its aftermath materially strengthened George W. Bush as president and strengthened the Republican Party politically. Just before September 11, President Bush's job approval ratings stood at 51 percent. This was good, but not particularly outstanding, for a first-term president. He was getting credit for honesty and an appealing personality; however, there were still persistent doubts about whether he was up to the job and especially whether his economic policies were working. He was not particularly more popular than other first-term presidents at that stage of their presidency. After September 11, however, President Bush's job approval ratings soared to 90 percent and stayed extremely high for well over a year (see table 3.1). They only declined to below 50 percent in the spring of 2004 as the occupation of Iraq dragged on and the costs mounted.

The terrorist attacks and the war on terrorism changed everything for President Bush. A presidency that had been ill defined and not particularly focused became a wartime presidency with a tremendous amount of support from the mass public and political elites alike. The immediate aftermath of the attacks did not begin well for President Bush, who was in Florida with a group of school children when he was first notified of the attacks. Bush appeared stunned in the initial moments and hours after the attacks, and he meandered around the country, flying first from Florida to Barksdale Air Force Base in central Louisiana, and then to Offitt Air Force Base in Omaha, Nebraska, issuing statements from each stop (Jamieson and Waldman 2003). Even the White House later admitted that those were not the president's finest hours. When he returned to the White House later in the evening on September 11, he seemed to find his voice and to begin a resolute plan of action. His performance at the Washington National Cathedral two days later, when, in effect, the whole nation drew together for a national funeral for the victims of terror, drew very positive reviews from both friends and former foes. The president, as had been demonstrated by Bill

TABLE 3.1 **George W. Bush approval rating**

Period	Date	Approval
Preelection	July 8–11, 2004	47%
Postwar	July 25–27, 2003	58%
Highest	Sept. 21–22, 2001	90%
Pre-9/11	Sept. 7–10, 2001	51%
Lowest	May 7–9, 2004	46%

SOURCE: Jones (2003, 2004).

Clinton in the wake of the Oklahoma City bombings in 1994, had become the "mourner-in-chief," and it was a role that Bush played well in the aftermath of the tragedy that had overtaken the whole nation.

Just as important as the symbolic role, the president also aggressively assumed the role of commander in chief and started planning for a military response. Attention fixed almost immediately on Afghanistan, the home of the Taliban and the source of at least some of the training and support for the terrorists. The fact that fifteen of the nineteen hijackers and Osama bin Laden, leader of al Qaeda, were all Saudi Arabians was noted; however, the nation of Saudi Arabia itself was not held responsible for harboring or providing material support for the terrorists. The Taliban government of Afghanistan was a harsh regime of fundamentalist Islamic zealots who had repressed its own people, particularly women, and had committed a number of other acts, particularly the destruction of the giant Buddha statues—all of which had certainly alienated the regime in Western public opinion. More importantly, Afghanistan had also been the home of terrorist training camps, and the Taliban had given safe haven to Osama bin Laden for a number of years. So, when President Bush identified the Taliban government of Afghanistan as the initial enemy and the supporters of the terrorists who had attacked the World Trade Center, there was relatively little debate about the matter in the United States, and apart from some of the Arab world, relatively little resistance in international quarters. The United States built up its forces in that area and then invaded Afghanistan with the avowed purpose of wiping out the Taliban government and bringing Osama bin Laden and his supporters to face judgment for the planning of the terror attacks. Of course, the first objective was achieved, but the second has remained elusive. U.S. forces swept into Afghanistan and within a matter of weeks effectively destroyed the Taliban as a fighting force, and the government of Afghanistan was turned over to a group much more friendly to the United States. Casualties, while always painful and tragic, were limited enough, with approximately seventy-four U.S. troops killed, that the American public was never outraged about the human costs (Reardon 2003). The human costs among the indigenous population of Afghanistan was noted and decried in some peace activist circles in the United States; however, overall those losses of Afghan lives and property were largely written off as the inevitable "collateral damage" that goes along with any military operation of this magnitude. In spite of much hard and dangerous searching on the part of the American military, the leader of al Qaeda, Osama bin Laden, escaped capture in Afghanistan and continued to plague American plans there and in the entire Middle Eastern region. After the immediate fighting ended, a relatively small contingent of American troops, approximately eleven thousand, were left in Afghanistan to continue to provide security for the new government and to look for Osama bin Laden. They continued to suffer sporadic attacks and to lose lives and sustain wounds as they were subjected to hostile forces who waged something of a war of attrition against the American and allied forces. Mostly, however, the scene shifted rather rapidly to Iraq.

Even before the war in Afghanistan ended, many in Washington began to focus on Saddam Hussein and the potential for regime change in Iraq. Ever since 1991, when U.S. forces had first entered Iraq after expelling Iraqi forces from Kuwait, which Iraq had invaded the previous year, there had been a strong body of opinion in Washington that insisted Saddam Hussein and his regime had to be displaced. He was deemed a bloody dictator who had not only invaded Kuwait but who had also fostered a horrific war with Iran that lasted most of the 1980s with tens of thousands killed on both sides. The fact that the first Bush administration had pulled back before going all the way to Baghdad had always rankled many people in Washington, and the most prominent of the war hawks were people who became influential in the second Bush administration. Vice President Dick Cheney, Secretary of Defense Donald Rumsfeld, Assistant Secretary of Defense Paul Wolfewitz, and a variety of other "defense intellectuals" had long advocated the elimination of Saddam Hussein and his Baathist Party regime by any means possible and by American military force if necessary. They were joined in this campaign by a chorus of conservative media pundits who became a persistent voice for the elimination of Hussein. So, when the war on terrorism was declared, and the immediate objective in Afghanistan was accomplished, the time seemed ripe for the next target to become Iraq. President Bush had prepared the way rhetorically in his State of the Union address in January of 2002 when he denounced Iraq, along with Iran and North Korea, as part of "the axis of evil." After that speech, a steady drumbeat of criticism of Iraq and Hussein came from Washington. Clearly elite-level support existed for an invasion of Iraq, and public opinion was being prepared.

An inconvenient fact, but a fact nevertheless, was that there was very little, if any, evidence that the regime in Iraq had anything at all to do with directly encouraging or subsidizing the September 11 attacks (Kemper 2003; Bovard 2003; McConnell 2003). None of the nineteen hijackers was Iraqi, and nothing directly linked them to Hussein. The war on terrorism became the catch-all reason for opposing Iraq, and it was then linked to the charge that Iraq had weapons of mass destruction. Hussein was known to have such weapons in the early 1990s, and he had been under U.N. sanctions for having those weapons and for refusing to allow U.N. inspectors to verify that they had been destroyed. President Bush increasingly depicted Hussein as a clear and present danger to the security of the United

States, the Middle East, and the world. In addition, Hussein's internal record of brutality against any perceived threat from his own people had led to many reports of atrocities committed domestically in Iraq in the 1980s and 1990s. Vilifying Saddam Hussein was not difficult to do, particularly among the American public who had seen him as an outlaw at least since 1990.

Of course, as we now know, much of the rest of the world was unconvinced of the case for war with Iraq. President Bush at first reluctantly and under immense pressure from domestic critics, some within his own party, agreed to take the case to the United Nations. He pressed for a vote allowing military force, if necessary, to reenter Iraq and to verify whether there were weapons of mass destruction. The president was opposed rather forcefully in this policy by several traditional allies, including France and Germany; however, he was joined by, most notably, Prime Minister Tony Blair of Great Britain as well as by Italy, Poland, and several other smaller countries. This was the rather limited coalition the Bush administration was ultimately able to assemble, and while it was decidedly less than the coalition that the first Bush administration had assembled against Iraq in 1990–91, it did provide the president some cover in the U.S. Congress and the rationale for considerable support from the American people. In general, a majority of the public wanted U.N. support if possible but also wanted action and would support whatever the president deemed to be necessary to fight those who had brought terror to our shores (Kull 2003).

THE RALLY EFFECT

The best way to describe what happened in American public opinion after September 11 is to adopt the rally-round-the-flag concept that was first expounded systematically by the political scientist John E. Mueller (Mueller 1973). Mueller analyzed public opinion longitudinally in the World War II, Korean War, and Vietnam War eras. He noted that the first tendency of the American people, when faced with external threat, and certainly when attacked militarily, was to rally round the flag. We want to support our government; we want to believe that our president and our elected officials know what they are doing and that they know how to respond to external challenge. We are generally a patriotic people, and comparative poll data have consistently shown that Americans are consistently proud of the nation and of our political institutions. Mueller noted the phenomenon in the following terms:

> It is somewhat surprising that the wars in Korea and Vietnam generated about the same amount of support at the beginning. . . . The comparability of war sup-

port at this point suggests that the principal motivating element in the public response to the Korean decision was similar to that in Vietnam—a desire to support the country's leadership in time of trouble, the rally-round-the-flag phenomenon. (Mueller 1973, 58)

Mueller went on to note that this phenomenon particularly strengthens the hand of the president. Most Americans know that our constitution places the president at the apex of the military pyramid, as the civilian commander in chief of all the armed forces. He is solely responsible for deploying our troops overseas and for directing military responses to any military challenge. Of course, declaring war is not the constitutional role of the president. That duty is given to the Congress of the United States; however, Congress has not exercised this duty officially since December 8, 1941. Congress never did declare war in Korea, Vietnam, Kuwait, Iraq, Panama, Grenada, Somalia, Kosovo, Bosnia, or a wide variety of other places where American troops have fought and died in the last fifty years. The president has arrogated to himself, with the active and tacit approval of Congress, the right to make war. The U.S. Congress is complicit in all of these shooting wars by giving approval to various needs to fund the war, by passing various surrogate resolutions that are taken by the president to be support for what he is doing, and by other official legislative acts of support such as the draft or the all-volunteer military. (For example, in August of 1964 Congress essentially gave Lyndon Johnson carte blanche to do whatever he deemed appropriate to respond to two purported attacks by the North Vietnamese on American destroyers in the Gulf of Tonkin. This resolution became Johnson's general congressional cover for the war in Vietnam.) However, Congress has completely abrogated its constitutional duty to actually declare war. Congress likes for the president to take the leadership role, and all recent presidents have been happy to accommodate.

As Mueller noted, and as other scholars such as Richard Neustadt (1990) had emphasized earlier, war has been a particularly effective instrument of presidential power. Americans want to believe in someone in times of crisis, and the president, the authoritative voice of the nation, becomes the most likely source of reassurance. Early political socialization research showed that the president symbolizes and epitomizes the aspirations of the collective whole of the people in unique ways that cannot be approximated by any other official (Easton and Hess 1961; Easton and Dennis 1965; Jaros 1967). Mueller, after noting that war naturally creates uncertainty and fear, put the proposition in the following words:

To deal with this uncertainty and indecision, many in the population grope for cues on which to base their opinion. The perceived issue position of various opinion leaders is very often taken as an important guide. While many public figures and institutions influence public opinion in this way, the most important by far is the president. Thus there exists, particularly in the area of foreign affairs, an important group of citizens—they can be called "followers"—who are inclined to rally to the support of the president no matter what he does. (Mueller 1973, 69)

As other scholars have emphasized, there is also a crucial role played by political elites, both public officials and members of the media, in the Washington community. They often provide the opinion leadership that is a crucial part of the president's policymaking preparation (Neustadt 1990; Rosenau 1968, 1984). Thus, the policymaking process in foreign and defense affairs is driven by the president with his close advisors at the center, the attentive media and opinion leaders who provide close support, and public opinion rallied to support the president and the nation, who are often initially identified as being pretty much the same. This is the record of what happened during the first years of our military engagement in both Korea and Vietnam. Of course, we also remember that both Vietnam and Korea became very unpopular wars in their later stages and liabilities for the presidents and administrations who initially engaged them. Korea was a part of the undoing of the Truman presidency and figured significantly in Eisenhower's victory in 1952. Vietnam led directly to Lyndon Johnson's decision not to seek reelection and indirectly hurt Richard Nixon's credibility and ability to get other things done (although Watergate was the precipitating factor in his resignation). But these negative effects beset the presidents involved long after the initial rally phenomenon boosted their job approval ratings. Negative impacts on the presidencies happened after casualties began to mount, when many Americans were torn apart by the terrible costs of Korea and Vietnam—loved ones were lost or returned to the United States with serious wounds, or many were held for years in POW camps. Even the leaders of the war, such as former secretary of defense Robert McNamara, later acknowledged the toll taken on the nation by their decisions on Vietnam (McNamara 1995).

The Korean War lasted 1,126 days and resulted in 36,913 total U.S. deaths. The Vietnam War lasted 3,921 days and resulted in 58,177 total U.S. deaths (Reardon 2003). In those conflicts, we tended to count the duration of public support in terms of years. Now we count in days and speculate before the war begins about the role of public opinion and loss of support. The loss of support for the president and the war in Vietnam also took place when there was an elite-level opinion that developed against the war, articulated by prominent officeholders such as Senator J. William Fulbright and the Senate Foreign Relations Committee, and after office-seekers arose to challenge the president, particularly in his own party as in the case of Senator Eugene McCarthy and Senator Robert Kennedy in the 1968 Democratic Party primaries. The public did finally lose confidence in their leaders over Vietnam, especially, but only after the "credibility gap" had been created by Lyndon Johnson and exacerbated by Richard Nixon in explaining and defending the war. The negative toll on public support for the president and for the war built up, but only gradually and long after the war had inflicted great personal losses on many American families. Also notable is that the Korea and Vietnam conflicts, like World War II, were wars fought with the draft in effect. Most of the deaths were among the enlisted men and women, many of whom were draftees. In short, these were wars that extracted a terrible cost on the civilian population. Not surprisingly, near the end of the Vietnam War the Nixon administration led the way in the creation of the all-volunteer military, which we now have. Avoiding military service is a lot easier than it used to be, and many Americans in elite-level positions in the government and in the mass media no longer have the experience of military service. Most middle-class American families can shield themselves from the ravages of war in twenty-first-century America if they choose to do so. Table 3.2 provides a summary of the duration, military involvement, battle deaths, and total deaths for all American wars since the Civil War.

The prescription for a popular war, based on the recent experiences in places as diverse as Iraq, Kuwait, Kosovo, Bosnia, Somalia, Panama, and Grenada, is to have a short and relatively low-casualty war that ends in victory within one or two weeks, a month at the most. If the war is to be protracted, say for more than a year, it should be in an obscure place such as Kosovo or Bosnia, with seemingly little relevance to American interests and where the battlefield casualties are kept low and the press and the public fairly quickly lose interest (Halberstam 2001; Clark 2001). It should also be fought with the dedicated and highly trained professionals who make up the American military today. The United States clearly has the best-trained, the best-equipped, and the most capable standing military in the world today and perhaps that has ever been assembled. The military budget, at $367 billion, is greater than that of the next twenty highest nations combined. Our military is certainly capable of handling any adversary in the world in any kind of conventional warfare. Such warfare where we are the dominant force can demonstrably be sustained by public opinion at least for a considerable length of time. Just how long that sustaining public opinion will exist is open to question, and we have not until recently tested the outer limits of the public's patience. If the United States enters military conflict, it should not appear to extract much of a price on middle-class American life. If it can be paid for without a tax increase, this will also help to ensure its popularity at home, if not abroad. This is largely the record of the wars fought by American

TABLE 3.2 Summary of duration, military involvement, battle deaths, and total deaths for all American wars since the Civil War

U.S. Casualties in Major Wars

	Civil War* 1861–65	WW I 1917–18	WW II 1941–45	Korean War 1950–53	Vietnam War 1964–75	Persian Gulf War 1991
Duration in Days	1,440	584	1,365	1,126	3,921	84
Total Military/ Deployed	3,263,363	4,734,991	16,112,566	1,789,000	33,403,000	665,476
Battle Deaths	214,938	53,402	291,557	33,651	47,378	148
Total Deaths	526,832	116,516	405,399	36,913	58,177	383

Conflicts in the Last Twenty Years

	Grenada 1983	Panama 1989–90	Somalia 1992–93	Kosovo 1999	Afghanistan 2001–
Duration in Days	51	14	153	77	540 (ongoing)
Deployed U.S. Troops	5,000	27,000	26,000	7,000	9,000†
U.S. Battle Deaths	18	23	29	0	21
Total U.S. Deaths	19	43	43	2	74

SOURCE: Reardon (2003).

*Civil War includes Union and Confederate Armies.

†At the point when President Bush declared an end to major combat on May 1, 2003, 59 Americans had been killed in action. By July 20, 2004, this figure had risen to 896 killed.

forces since the end of Vietnam. It is presidential war at its finest, and it is widely supported, with careful preparation of the case presented by the president as commander in chief. Such wars can be sustained in American public opinion and warmly embraced by a wide spectrum of elite level opinion.

This certainly seems to capture what happened in the cases of the first and second wars in Iraq as well as conflicts in Grenada, Kosovo, Bosnia, Somalia, and Afghanistan in recent cases of presidential deployment of American military forces to foreign trouble spots. Wars of brief duration can quickly boost presidential popularity because of the rally-round-the-flag effect. Leading the United States in popular victories in Afghanistan and Iraq at least initially was a great boost to President Bush's job approval ratings and to his 2004 reelection chances. Less clear, however, is how much that popularity could be sustained in the face of continued loss of life in both places. In particular, the continued occupation of Iraq and the attempts to build a successful civilian and secular government there presented a long-term challenge to the Bush administration. As the casualties mounted in Iraq, support for the occupation there and for President Bush's original decision to go to war in Iraq declined. The United States became deeply divided over Iraq as it had been earlier over Vietnam, although the reaction set in more quickly on Iraq. By the time of the transfer of authority on June 28, 2004, 51 percent of those polled said that the war was not worth the cost, while 46 percent said it was (Saad 2004). Equally unclear is how long the United States can sustain public support for the unprecedented war on terrorism that the president has declared. This is war without any of the normal identification of who the enemy is in the sense of what nation state to blame and oppose, where the enemy can be engaged, and how our conventional forces can be employed against unconventional tactics such as suicide bombers and planes used as instruments of terror. Fighting a war on terrorism is uncharted territory.

Secretary of State Colin Powell was one of the architects of the first war with Iraq in 1990–91. He was also an advocate for not continuing to pursue Saddam Hussein and his army all the way into Baghdad for a final and decisive battle. Powell had occasion over the next decade to explain and defend that decision. His writings and public comments on the subject of the employment of American military power became avidly sought after and became codified into what was often called the "Powell Doctrine." In short, this doctrine maintained that the United States should not commit military force to a battle unless there were clear and definable military goals to be reached and only if the political elites and the American public were reasonably united behind the military objectives. Then the military was to be employed with overwhelming force to virtually outclass and overwhelm the enemy very rapidly. Just as importantly, there should be an end game, that is, a plan for withdrawal from the battlefield and the country involved in the American military action. While most of those conditions were realized in Afghanistan and some were realized in the second war with Iraq, an end game with a realistic timetable and plan for withdrawal from Afghanistan is difficult to see, and this is even more true for Iraq. Ironically, Powell himself helped implement an invasion plan for Iraq that seemingly ensured the end to the Powell strategic doctrine that he had been so closely associated with in the past.

THE ROLE OF THE MEDIA

The role of the mass media has become pervasive in American government and politics. The media are so important that a former newsman, Douglas Cater, as far back as 1959 termed them "the Fourth Branch of Government" (Cater 1959). Candidates cannot run for office successfully without a carefully planned media strategy. They must elicit an enormous amount of free media coverage, and they must buy even more paid advertising in order to successfully pursue higher office, particularly the presidency. The mass media, particularly television, have become the interpreters and the gatekeepers for the presidential campaigns in ways that rival the role formerly played by the political parties and in ways that make the media among the most important influences on what the public knows about the candidates and issues involved in any single election.

The mass media are also extremely important to public officials who want to use the media to get their messages out to the American people. The officials want people to see them in action and to learn about their policies and plans. The president is first among those officials who can use the media to great advantage in getting his message out to average citizens throughout the nation. In fact, the president is in a good position to dominate the media in ways that cannot be duplicated by other public officials. The president and what he did or said that day is the major story on many nightly newscasts. One of the leading scholars in this field, Doris Graber, cites data indicating that in one twelve-month period in 1990–1991, the three major networks ran news stories on the presidency 30 percent of the time (Graber 1993, 289). This significantly exceeded the percentage of coverage of the Congress and far exceeded coverage for the Supreme Court. In the competition for news attention, the president has little competition from other elected officials.

As anyone who has studied American history over the past three or four decades understands, the news coverage of the government and the president has often been adversarial and downright negative. The American media value their role as watchdogs, and they often concentrate on looking for wrongdoing and scandal in high places. The First Amendment guarantees their freedom to serve the watchdog function, and the media value and honor that commitment. In the wake of Vietnam and Watergate in the 1960s and 1970s, the relationship between journalists and the White House became particularly adversarial and contentious. Both Lyndon Johnson and Richard Nixon railed against their perceived enemies among the working press who covered them, and they sought to control and manipulate their news coverage at every turn. As their troubles mounted, both presidents became increasingly secretive and increasingly inaccessible to those in the media they perceived to be "enemies." The press, in turn, coined the term "credibility gap" and became increasingly skeptical of the official party line coming out of the White House, whether it was about progress in the war in Vietnam or the role of the president in commissioning or covering up the deeds of those who broke into the Watergate complex during the election of 1972. From that point onward, there has been significant strain in the relations between the president and those assigned to cover him from the television networks and the major newspapers. Some scholars have gone so far as to suggest that this adversarial situation has become so extreme that it threatens the fabric of trust that must exist for a successful representative democracy to function (Patterson 1994; Fallows 1995). In short, they have raised thoughtful questions regarding the possibility that the press became too adversarial and cynical in the last quarter of the twentieth century.

Any scholar or observer raised on a steady diet of negative stories regarding public officials and scandal in the White House, the Congress, or other corridors of power will have to take some time to adjust to the possibility that this typical description of the adversarial relationship between the media and the government has been altered, if not changed permanently, by the events of September 11 and its aftermath. The media reacted to September 11 in some ways quite typical and in other ways that are quite atypical and surprising. First, typically, the mass media, especially television, and later the print media, immediately sprang into action to try to bring the story to the American people. They were themselves largely headquartered in downtown New York, and their Washington bureaus were located close to the Pentagon. For some of the television people, getting live shots of the second plane hitting the twin towers or the burning debris of one section of the Pentagon was a matter of taking a short walk and aiming their cameras (Schieffer 2003). The four or five major television networks went on the air live soon after the first plane hit the first tower and did not cease their continuous coverage for at least forty-eight hours, and in some cases, of course, the cable news networks are on the air continuously and did not cease their coverage of the terrorist threats for months and years. In times of crisis, such as a terrorist attack, an assassination, a war somewhere, or a natural disaster, the American people want to know first what is happening, and then they want some interpretation of what it all means. Is this event an awful aberration, an isolated incident, or part of a larger plot by a foreign power and a potential strike against the government and the nation? Those were the kinds of worried questions people raised in 1963 when John F. Kennedy was killed, and the great mass of Americans turned to the media to find answers as to what was going on and what it all meant. The pattern of continuous and largely thoughtful coverage established in 1963 was repeated again in the immediate aftermath of the terrorist attacks of September 11. Indeed, some of the news people who had been young reporters covering the Kennedy story, such as Dan Rather, Bob Schieffer, Tom Brokaw, and Daniel Schorr, occupied the anchor desks and other crucial positions on September 11, 2001. They had some idea of what to do because they had been through so many other periods of national crisis in the preceding three or four decades. The people turned to the news organizations for basic information, for directions from their government, and for reassurance from their leaders. Generally, this is what they got from the media in the first few days after the September 11 tragedy.

Interestingly enough, those who might have expected a skeptical, questioning, even cynical performance from the mass media would have been surprised by the outpouring of patriotism and communalism they encountered on television, in the newspapers and the news magazines, and on the radio. The media people apparently felt that it was their duty to be good citizens and to help rally the nation to some common causes. The first responders, that is, the firefighters, the police, and the emergency personnel who crowded into lower Manhattan and up into the twin towers, became instant and highly recognizable heroes. Many of them lost their lives in unselfish sacrifice trying to help others escape the burning towers. The firefighters raising the flag in an Iwo Jima-type salute in the middle of the World Trade Center rubble became the emblematic picture of the destruction and the hope that the city and the nation would prevail in spite of the very real losses (Jamieson and Waldman 2003). There could have been instant recriminations and rampant scapegoat-seeking as people sought someone to blame for this unparalleled disaster; however, there was relatively little of this, at least in the mainstream media. The Internet undoubtedly abounded with conspiracies and recriminations especially in some of the more fringe group corners; however, the mass media, especially television, mostly rallied round the flag. They stressed community, country, and the national interest and told heartwarming stories about how usually cynical and abrasive New Yorkers and other victims were coping with adversity and pulling together to help each other out and be better citizens and kinder human beings.

In some fundamental respects, this very positive, very communitarian reaction by the mass media should not be surprising given the circumstances created by September 11. Indeed, well before the September 11 attacks, in the era of Watergate and Vietnam, one major communications scholar wrote the following prescient words:

In American political culture the normal feuds of politics are suspended when the nation is in danger. . . . When life and property are endangered, when sudden death and terror reign, when well-known leaders are assassinated, or when the nation goes to war, normal media coverage practices are suspended. During crises, the media tend to abandon their adversarial role. They become teammates of officialdom in attempts to restore public order, safety, and tranquility. (Graber 1993, 166–67)

This quote from Graber captures quite cogently the role the American media played in the aftermath of September 11. In a real respect, they continued to play the supportive, nonadversarial, patriotic role more than two years after the events of September 11. In fact, the war in Iraq, with its embedded reporters, allowed the media to go to war in an immediate and personal sense that few of this generation of reporters had experienced, and they, in turn, were quite grateful for the security and protection that the American military and their equipment provided to them during the second war in Iraq.

Two of the most accomplished commentators on the role of the American media in the aftermath of September 11, Kathleen Hall Jamieson and Paul Waldman, discussed the "death of irony" among the media in the wake of the terrorist attacks. "Journalists may express cynicism toward the individuals who seek and hold power, but they are reverent toward the institutions of power. . . . Reporters were now participating with the government in a common enterprise: unifying the citizenry, reasserting the strength of democracy and America itself, and memorializing the victims. Journalists turned from cynics to eulogists in the immediate days and weeks following September 11, 2001" (Jamieson and Waldman 2003, 136–39).

In a further interesting observation, Jamieson and Waldman analyzed the rally-round-the-flag patriotism so evident among the mainstream American media with regard to the war in Iraq. They noted that most media people of today, like most young people and like most elite-level occupation holders, are not military veterans. They have little or no experience with the military, and they are personally easily impressed with those who are protecting our country and risking life and limb on the battlefields. These media people are largely products of the all-volunteer military era, and except for the most senior of them, they mostly missed Vietnam. Thus, when they got the opportunity to see the battlefield and to be protected by the American soldiers and marines in the second war with Iraq, they were impressed, as anyone might have been. In the wake of their attempt to gather information and impressions to report back to the American people, they were naturally going to give most of the story from the American perspective. This, in turn, helped to create the conditions back home for the American people to rally round the flag in support of the Iraq war effort, which they largely did. While there were critics remaining at home who had not favored the war in the first place, there were not a lot of cynics among the journalists in the foxholes and humvees in the Iraqi desert. Only later, after President Bush had effectively declared victory, when the occupation dragged on without identification of the location of weapons of mass destruction or any evidence of direct support from Saddam Hussein for the September 11 terrorists, and with doubts cast about the accuracy of the president's claims regarding Iraq's attempts to purchase nuclear materials in Niger did a note of the old skepticism and cynicism begin to creep back into the news reports. This

skepticism was fueled by various high-level former Bush administration officials who claimed that Iraq was the chief Bush administration target well before
September 11. Even then, though, the critique was very subdued and carefully
couched in phrases that were not likely to arouse much antagonism back in the
United States.

All of these events, after the first twenty-four hours of the September 11 attacks, worked to the net advantage of George W. Bush and his presidency. The
most common theme among the media commentators was that Bush had been
"transformed" by September 11. The once halting syntax was often absent, and
even when it returned, reporters were eager to overlook it while seeking the
larger meaning of his words. The president performed his symbolic functions
well, appearing genuine and honest in his approach to the victims of the terrorist acts. He launched two military campaigns with alacrity, and he displayed
a steely determination not to be deterred from his mission to punish those he
held responsible for the attacks. He faced down his critics, both domestic and
foreign, and exercised his authority, especially the authority of commander in
chief, with a single-minded devotion to taking what he defined as the necessary steps to root out the evil that had beset the United States. There are lots
of problems with letting one person so totally dominate the foreign and defense
agenda and so easily determine the best course of action in declaring a war on
terrorism, and then directing it toward two nation states as well as a wide variety
of shadowy groups and individuals around the world who may want to do harm to
the United States. Since George W. Bush also headed a very unified Republican
Party, and since the party controlled all three branches of the government in the
aftermath of the 2002 congressional elections, he was able to provide unified
leadership that had not been seen in the foreign policy realm since Franklin
Roosevelt during the apex of his power in World War II. While one can certainly
object to the direction in which Bush chose to lead the nation, and many critics
especially among the Democrats did, there was no doubt that he was exercising
leadership. For a long period, public opinion polls showed a surprising resilience to the very positive job approval ratings Bush was enjoying, especially on
foreign and defense issues. Bush's overall job approval ratings compared to his
two immediate predecessors are provided in table 3.3. It was only after the occupation of Iraq dragged on and American losses mounted that the president's
job approval ratings began to decline.

The president's success and popularity also worked to the advantage of the
Republican Party in the aftermath of September 11. The Republicans ordinarily
enjoy a positive margin over the Democrats on the national security and robust
defense dimensions, and this margin increased in the wake of the September 11

TABLE 3.3 **Job approval ratings of George W. Bush and two previous predecessors**

George W. Bush's Job Approval Ratings

Period	Date	Approval
Preelection	July 8–11, 2004	47%
Postwar	July 25–27, 2003	58%
Highest	Sept. 21–22, 2001	90%
Pre-9/11	Sept. 7–10, 2001	51%
Lowest	May 7–9, 2004	46%

Bill Clinton's Job Approval Ratings

Period	Date	Approval
Left Office	Jan. 2000	52%
Highest	Jan. 1999	71%
Lowest	June 1993	37%

George H. W. Bush's Job Approval Ratings

Period	Date	Approval
Left Office	Jan. 1993	36%
Highest	Feb. 1991	89%
Lowest	June 1992	35%

SOURCE: Jones (2003, 2004).

attacks and the wars in Iraq and Afghanistan. The polls continued to provide the president with the kind of mass popular support that he needed to get his military objectives in Iraq addressed, especially during the immediate shooting war, and he continued to use those levers of power to get Congress, under control of his own party, to approve pretty much whatever he wanted in the security field. The September 11 attacks led originally to the proposal of the Department of Homeland Security, the largest reorganization of the U.S. government since the creation of the Department of Defense in 1948. Initially, some of the Democrats in Congress resisted some details of this reorganization, especially at the behest of the public employee unions who wanted some guarantees of job security and protection of grievance rights. When the Democrats in the Senate stopped the reorganization bill from passing before the 2002 congressional elections, Bush took to the campaign trail saying that he needed a Republican-controlled Senate to do what was necessary to fight the war on terrorism.

Included in the president's plan of action against terrorism was passage of the Homeland Security Act in the form the White House wanted it. President Bush appealed for the voters to send him Republican members of Congress who would support the war against terrorism, particularly by supporting him on Iraq and on the Homeland Security Act. It was an appeal that resonated well with many voters. In a narrow group of very closely contested races, most notably the race for the Senate seat in Georgia and the races in Missouri and Minnesota, Mr. Bush's intervention appeared to spell the difference. He also got credit for campaigning vigorously in the most competitive House districts, and he weighed in on several gubernatorial races as well. In effect, President Bush, his White House political director Karl Rove, and the Republican Party leadership on Capitol Hill nationalized the congressional elections of 2002. When it was all over, the president prevailed and the Republicans controlled both houses of Congress, although the victory in the Senate was very close with a final 51:49:1 count. In the House, the Republicans continued the majority they had established in 1994 and even widened their majority by a few additional votes. More importantly, Mr. Bush was widely credited with making the difference. The Democrats were vanquished and reeling in disarray and recriminations. The House Democratic leader immediately resigned his post to run for president in 2004. The Senate Democratic leader, Tom Daschle, was barely able to help colleague Tom Johnson survive in their native South Dakota. Daschle stayed on as the Senate Democratic leader, but he was reduced from majority to minority leader. Whatever doubts had existed because of President Bush's narrow and contested victory in 2000 seemed to immediately evaporate after the votes were counted in 2002. The president was clearly in command, and a workable majority of those who bothered to vote seemed to endorse his presidency with some warmth. Those who were opposed had a very difficult time finding a voice, and they appeared to be divided and leaderless. The Democrats had nine announced candidates for president in 2004, who disagreed prominently among themselves about the president's Iraq policies. They were most often described by the media as being in "disarray" and "demoralized."

ENHANCING THE EXECUTIVE BRANCH

One of the important generalizations about the impact of war and external threats is that institutionally they enhance the size and scope of the national executive branch vis-à-vis both state and local government and the other branches of the national government (Schilling, Hammond, and Snyder 1963; Kettl 2003). We expect the national government to preserve and protect the hard external shell of the nation, to protect the borders and the territorial integrity of the nation state. All other functions take second place to that fundamental mission of the national government, and presidents generally appreciate the ramifications of that axiom. We need essentially executive agencies of defense, public safety, public health, and border control to protect us in times of peril. If state and local governments have to be pressed into duty, or ignored, in such causes, then doing so is quite acceptable in public opinion. The national government leads the way, and those "governments closest to the people" are relegated to support roles in the challenge of meeting national security threats.

The Homeland Security Act of 2002 illustrates the potential for national government and executive branch growth during times of security threat. This act brought about the largest reorganization of the national government since the organization of the Department of Defense in 1947. It assembled 169,000 employees from 22 preexisting governmental agencies, and parts of dozens of others, into a single super agency headed by a cabinet-level secretary. It also vastly expanded the scope of the authority of some of these agencies. The first year's budget was projected to be $37 billion. The reorganization was accomplished with a minimum of national debate, and it was certainly accomplished with much less study and debate than the act creating the Department of Defense, which is comparable in size and scope. From initial introduction to final passage and signing the act into law on November 25, 2002, hard on the heels of the midterm elections, took just over a year. Such debate as did take place was used as grist for the campaign mills of those supporters who championed the power of the national government and the need to do whatever the president deemed necessary in order to meet the external threat of terrorism in the beginning of the twenty-first century. Those members of Congress who stood in the way, even temporarily, were threatened during their campaigns in 2002 with loss of their office, and as former Senator Max Cleland of Georgia and former Senator Jean Carnahan of Missouri discovered, they were vulnerable to charges of being "soft on security" (Jackson and Barr 2003). So, the Homeland Security Act provides a vivid case study of the marked intersection of security policy, institutional change, and domestic politics.

There was also the impact of extending the size and scope of the federal government vis-à-vis individual civil liberties. This impact came from a combination of the Homeland Security Act, the Domestic Security Enhancement Act (or the Patriot Act), and various actions taken by the U.S. attorney general and the intelligence agencies of the federal government. In the wake of the terrorist attacks of September 11, President Bush, acting usually through the office of Attorney General John Ashcroft, issued a number of decrees extending the power of the government in investigating citizens and noncitizens and in some cases holding them without trial, without benefit of attorney, without an opportunity to face their accused, and without their families being told where they were being held. This expansion of the power of the federal government and the attendant loss of civil rights for the accused evoked a loud outcry of opposition from civil libertarian groups. Even some conservative commentators worried aloud about this loss of civil liberties. Nevertheless, it was justified by the president and the attorney general as the actions that must be taken by a prudent government under attack from an unknown enemy. In so doing, President George W. Bush was acting in the tradition of several pervious wartime presidents, and he had much precedent on his side. Presidents, and their agents, have taken actions and issued decrees against known and suspected enemies of the United States with relative impunity from court action and with minimum dissent from the U.S. Congress (Mileur and Storey 2003). The courts and Congress have tended to ratify and legitimize those actions immediately when they were challenged, and they have almost exclusively followed the president's lead and endorsed virtually any vigorous action taken by the president (*Hirabyashi v. U.S.* 1943; *Korematsu v. U.S.* 1944).[2] It is only later, if at all, that any court has acted to repudiate executive actions taken in the name of national security, and by then the hostilities have been long settled and damage to the rights of the accused endured for many years. President Lincoln, for example, suspended the right of habeas corpus during the Civil War (*Ex Parte McCardle* 1869),[3] and he approved the use of a military tribunal rather than a civil court to try a Southern sympathizer (*Ex Parte Milligan* 1866).[4] The Supreme Court upheld both actions. President Franklin Roosevelt ordered the removal of Japanese citizens from their homes along the West Coast at the beginning of World War II. The Japanese-Americans were interred by the thousands in refugee camps or prison camps during the war, and their property was often confiscated with little or no compensation. It was only much later that Congress took action to offer an apology and restitution to the Japanese survivors who were by then quite elderly. President Roosevelt's administration also presided over the capture and quick execution of three German saboteurs on the East Coast, who were determined to be "enemy combatants" and executed within one month. The courts upheld this action in the Quirin case (*Ex Parte Quirin* 1942).[5] In *Johnson v. Eisentrager* (1950) the Court held that aliens in military custody outside U.S. sovereignty do not have access to the American judicial system.[6] These cases then became the official governmental rationale for the holding of the prisoners in a number of cases without benefit of counsel, or even the right to trial, during the Bush administration's war on terrorism. The lower courts generally upheld this action and accepted the Quirin and Eisentrager cases as precedent. The American people accept aggressive executive action in such cases, and they do not worry a great deal about the civil liberties of those accused. The polls constantly affirm that we will support executive action and will not condone inaction in times of perceived external threats. It was something of a surprise, then, in 2004 when the U.S. Supreme Court ruled that prisoners in custody at Guantanamo Bay, Cuba, had to be given access to federal courts (*Rasul v. Bush* 2004; *Al Odah v. U.S.* 2004).[7]

Clearly, the president and the executive branch benefited initially from the rally-round-the-flag syndrome in the wake of September 11 and from the renewed sense of patriotism that was fanned by the American victories in the wars in Afghanistan and Iraq. The presidency is, after all, what most people think of as the embodiment of the nation in a single office and in one person. There is simply no rival for the dominance of the American presidency in the everyday political discourse. Most Americans want to be patriotic, and one manifestation of being patriotic, as many see it, is to "support the president." Another manifestation frequently asserted during the war in Iraq was to "support the troops." Since President Bush sent the troops to Iraq, the tendency was frequently to equate support for the troops with support for the president. Many conservatives and Republicans encouraged this equation and this tendency to elide the two together. The Democrats and the critics of the war were easily placed on the defensive, and they had a very difficult time explaining how they could be very supportive of the troops in the field and wish them safe passage while at the same time expressing great skepticism about the policies and rationale that put them there in the first place. These finely tuned gradients of philosophy and points for public debate are not easily reduced to bumper stickers. "Support Our Troops," "God Bless America," and "These Colors Don't Run" displayed alongside large stick-on American flags abounded on cars and trucks throughout the nation. The American people truly rallied round the flag with the flag symbol being prominently displayed in big and small versions on the sides of urban buildings and in rural yards across the nation. It was about as material a manifestation of that scholarly concept as one could find.

Only the aftermath of the war in Iraq, with its seeming anarchy and continuing death and wounding of American troops, gave some pause and began to eat away at some of the easy assumptions about how well the United States could guarantee the peace and establish a functioning government and economic system in the middle of a nation that did not entirely seem to welcome our presence and that remained deeply divided by ethnic and religious strife. The long-term record of our involvement in Vietnam and Korea provided a cautionary note. The long-term effect could still hurt President Bush during a second term or hamper his attempts to influence whoever his successor will be. A long-term occupation, a stalemate in the search for a successful government, and economic chaos could still start a steady erosion of the public's patience and approval of what the United States had accomplished by the war in Iraq. For the short term, for the preparation for the 2004 elections, it was all a win for the president and for his supporters in the Republican Party and for American conservatives in general. The liberals and the loyal opposition among the Democrats have found no effective strategy for opposing the war and the president's national security policies without appearing to be soft on security issues.

CONCLUSION

Ultimately, the story of the congressional elections in 2002 and the preparations for the presidential election of 2004 illustrate some fundamental points about the American political system early in the first decade of the twenty-first century. First, the president can utilize his power as commander in chief and his powers of political persuasion to dominate the debate about national security. When the 1973 War Powers Act was passed in the wake of the Vietnam War, there was much talk about Congress reasserting its powers in war-making and in the conduct of national security policy. It has not happened. President George H. W. Bush barely acknowledged the role of Congress in making war policy in the first Persian Gulf War, and Congress was glad to leave it up to him. Republicans challenged President Bill Clinton at every turn on domestic policy during his two terms. Since they controlled Congress after 1994, they were very effective in stopping or significantly modifying many Clinton initiatives, especially on the domestic front. The Republicans also criticized freely Clinton's foreign and defense policies; however, when it came to American military engagement in Kosovo and Bosnia, they preferred to let Clinton take the lead and the credit or blame (Halberstam 2001). George W. Bush has been even more assertive of presidential power and prerogative in the making of national security policy. His doctrine of preventive war overturns many generations of a bipartisan consensus in the making of American foreign and defense policy; however, Congress has not even debated, much less effectively challenged, this sharp departure. There has been no voice of dissent, as with Senator J. W. Fulbright in the Johnson era, to challenge the president, and the Democrats have been divided and ineffectual in raising a coherent challenge from the loyal opposition. The congressional hearings on September 11, the war in Afghanistan, or the lead-up to the war in Iraq have been carefully controlled by Republican majorities in both the House and the Senate. That control is crucial in containing the debate and defining the contours of the discourse.

Second, in the area of foreign and defense policymaking, with a unified Republican government, we have developed a twenty-first-century American version of the well-known Responsible Parties model (Pomper 2001; Green and Herrnson 2002). Bush campaigned vigorously for congressional Republicans, and he got his majority, however narrow it may be in the Senate. More importantly, he received popular credit for having achieved a "political mandate" out of the 2002 election, whatever the policy-based validity of that claim. Bush, in turn, received very high levels of deference from congressional Republicans especially since the 2002 elections. His sway over the core conservative constituency of the GOP gave him enormous political freedom to maneuver and leverage to achieve his goals. Bush even effectively, if indirectly, intervened in the ouster of one Senate majority leader, Trent Lott, and the selection of his successor, Bill Frist. In the midst of Lott's crisis, the president did nothing overt to save Senator Lott's job, and by letting it be known that he favored Frist as the new leader, Bush helped elect Frist with a minimum of internal party bickering. Bush's role in the selection of a Senate majority leader harkens back to the Lyndon Johnson era of presidential intervention into legislative prerogatives and is unprecedented since then.

For some time, scholars have been writing about the dominance of the president's role in "agenda-setting" for the national government (Graber 1993). Bush has pushed that role to its extreme form. Congress, especially the opposition party, simply has no one who can come close to competing with the president in the development and advocacy of policy, especially in the foreign and defense policymaking fields. This axiom was true in the last half of the twentieth century; however, it has been magnified by the September 11 disaster. George W. Bush has been steadily consolidating the power of the president to dominate policymaking in the area of national security, and he is using his access to the national media and the bully pulpit to dominate the political discourse in this area. His dominance also extends into the domestic policy field, although there it is not as complete as in foreign and defense policy. The Democrats, and a handful of moderate Republicans, have tried to make modest changes, at the margins, on some of the Bush legislation. For instance, three Republican moderates, Chaffee of Rhode Island and Snowe and Collins of Maine, were able to amend three of the most controversial provisions of the Homeland Security Act, but only after the basic legislation was passed in the form demanded by the White House. The Democrats had some marginal influence over the Iraq War Resolution by helping force a delay for UN action; however, they exercised only a delaying action at the most. It was clear early in the process that Bush was going to use the original resolution to do whatever he deemed best, acting under his power as commander in chief, as to the timing of the war with Iraq.

President George W. Bush is proving how thoroughly a determined president with a clear-cut, some would say myopic, worldview can dominate the national security policymaking field. With the addition of the war on terrorism, this whole national security field has expanded dramatically into the domestic theater of political conflict. With the constant raising and then lowering of the national security alert system, with a color-coded shorthand that most people do not understand, there is a constant element of foreboding in the popular and political culture reminiscent of the various nuclear war planning steps of the 1950s. The president, the director of Homeland Security, the attorney general, and the directors of the FBI and the CIA are familiar faces on the nightly news discussing the latest alert, possible source of terrorism, potential attacks on airliners or public buildings, or sighting of alleged terrorists. These are all executive branch leaders, and Congress is content to play a very timid and secondary role in the unfolding security drama. The leadership of the executive branch in the national security field was definitely demonstrable before 9/11; however, it has been enlarged and intensified since that tragic event. The results of the 2002 midterm elections simply gave political credence and a form of legitimacy to the claims of expanded presidential and executive branch power. The 2004 election results will probably reinforce these same trends. We now have evolved into an especially vigorous and assertive model of presidential government leading the expanding executive branch coupled with a hybrid of Responsible Parties government under a remarkably unified and disciplined Republican majority on the congressional side of the equation. Whether the nation and the world will ultimately like and approve this uniquely American hybrid that has evolved early in the twenty-first century is much more problematic and remains to be seen. The first test of that proposition only came in the aftermath of the war with Iraq and the challenge of nation building that followed. Like all wars, the war on terrorism has helped create and augment a very politically and institutionally powerful American chief executive.

NOTES

1. *Bush v. Gore* 121 S. Ct. (2000).
2. *Hirabyashi v. U.S.* 320 U.S. (1943); *Korematsu v. U.S.* 323 U.S. 214 (1944).
3. *Ex Parte McCardle* 74 U.S. 506 (1869).
4. *Ex Parte Milligan* 4 Wall 2 (1866).
5. *Ex Parte Quirin* 317 U.S. 1 (1942).
6. *Johnson v. Eisentrager*, 339 U.S. 763 (1950).
7. *Rasul v. Bush*, 3 F.3d 1134, 2004; *Al Odah v. U.S.*, 28 U.S.C. 131 (2004).

REFERENCES

Bovard, James. 2003. "By Accident or Design, Bush Hyped Case for War." *USA Today*, August 14, 2003, 13A.
Cater, Douglas. 1959. *The Fourth Branch of Government*. Boston: Houghton Mifflin.
Ceaser, James W., and Andrew E. Busch. 2001. *The Perfect Tie*. Lanham, Md.: Rowman and Littlefield Publishers, Inc.

Clark, Wesley K. 2001. *Waging Modern War: Bosnia, Kosovo and the Future of Combat*. New York: Public Affairs.

Easton, David, and Jack Dennis. 1965. "The Child's Image of Government." *Annals of the American Academy of Political and Social Science* 36 (September): 40–57.

Easton, David, and R. D. Hess. 1961. "The Child's Changing Image of the President." *Public Opinion Quarterly*, 24: 632–644.

Fallows, James. 1995. *Breaking the News*. New York: Pantheon Books.

Graber, Doris. 1993. *Mass Media and American Politics*. 4th ed. Washington, D.C.: CQ Press.

Green, John C., and Paul Herrnson, eds. 2002. *Responsible Partisanship? The Evolution of American Political Parties Since 1950*. Lawrence: University of Kansas Press.

Halberstam, David. 2001. *War in a Time of Peace*. New York: Scribner.

Jackson, John S., III, and Chris Barr. 2003. "The Congressional Reaction to Political Terror: Support, Restraint, and Fear." Paper delivered at the Midwest Political Science Association Meeting, Chicago, Illinois, April 3.

Jamieson, Kathleen Hall, and Paul Waldman. 2003. *The Press Effect*. New York: Oxford University Press.

Jaros, Dean. 1967. "Children's Orientations toward the President: Some Additional Theoretical Considerations and Data." *Journal of Politics* 29 (May): 368–387.

Jones, Jeffrey M. 2003. "Bush Approval Ratings Stabilize." The Gallup Organization. July 31.

———. 2004. "Bush's Latest Quarterly Rating His Worst." The Gallup Organization. July 27.

Kantor, Shira. 2002. "U.S. Image Waning Despite 9/11 Sympathies, Poll Finds." Report of Pew Global Attitudes Project results. *Chicago Tribune*, December 5.

Kemper, Bob. 2003. "Overstatement Seen in Bush's Case for War." *Chicago Tribune*, August 6, 2003, Sec. 1, p. 4.

Kettl, Donald F. 2003. *Deficit Politics: The Search for Balance in American Politics*. New York: Longman Press.

Kull, Steven. 2003. "New Poll Says Public Conflicted Whether UN Should Strengthen Inspections or Authorize Invasion." PIPA Knowledge Network. February 21, 1–2.

McConnell, Michael. 2003. "Administration's Argument Long on Drama, Short on Facts." *Chicago Tribune*, August 3, 2003, Sec. 2, p. 5.

McNamara, Robert S. 1995. *In Retrospect: The Tragedy and Lessons of Vietnam*. New York: Random House.

Mileur, Jerome, and Ron Storey. 2003. "America's Wartime Presidents: Politics, National Security, and Civil Liberties." Paper delivered at the Midwest Political Science Association Meeting, Chicago, Illinois, April 3.

Mueller, John E. 1973. *War Presidents and Public Opinion*. New York: John Wiley and Sons.

Neustadt, Richard E. 1990. *Presidential Power*. 3d ed. New York: Free Press.

Patterson, Thomas. 1994. *Out of Order*. New York: Vintage Books.

Pomper, Gerald M. 2001. "Party Responsibility and the Future of American Democracy." In *American Political Parties: Decline or Resurgence?*, ed. Jeffrey Cohen, Richard Fleisher, and Paul Kantor, 162–83. Washington, D.C.: CQ Press.

Reardon, Patrick. 2003. "As Bodies Pile Up, Support Can Slip." *Chicago Tribune*, March 30.

Rosenau, James N. 1968. *Attentive Public and Foreign Policy: A Theory of Growth and Some New Evidence*. Princeton, N.J.: Center of International Studies, Princeton University.

Rosenau, James N. 1984. *American Leadership in World Affairs: Vietnam and the Breakdown of Consensus*. Boston: Allen & Unwin.

Saad, Lydia. 2004. "Power Transfer in Iraq Doesn't Alter Perceptions of Iraq War." The Gallup Organization. July 19.

Schieffer, Bob. 2003. *This Just In*. New York: G. P. Putnam's Sons.

Schier, Steven E. 2003. *You Call This an Election? America's Peculiar Democracy*. Washington, D.C.: Georgetown University Press.

Schilling, Warner R., Paul Y. Hammond, and Glenn H. Snyder. 1963. *Strategy, Politics, and Defense Budgets*. New York: Columbia University Press.

Simon, Roger. 2001. *Divided We Stand: How Al Gore Beat George W. Bush and Lost the Presidency*. New York: Crown Publishers.

4 Who Rules the Middle East Agenda?

According to *The Washington Post*, "on Sept. 17, 2001, six days after the attacks on the World Trade Center and the Pentagon, President Bush signed a 2½-page document marked 'TOP SECRET' that outlined the plan for going to war in Afghanistan as part of a global campaign against terrorism. Almost as a footnote, the document also directed the Pentagon to begin planning military options for an invasion of Iraq, senior administration officials said." As a result, some in the administration began to probe the possible connection of the Iraqi regime with those presumed to be responsible for the attacks on the United States. The *Post* reported that on September 19 and 20 the "Defense Policy Board met at the Pentagon—with Rumsfeld in attendance—and animatedly discussed the importance of ousting Hussein" (Kessler 2003).

What of the nature and timing of the U.S. response? What of the credibility of the assumptions underlying the probe? And, above all, what was the purpose of the U.S.-led invasion and occupation of Iraq? Who shaped the Middle East agenda, of which Iraq became a centerpiece?

Some claimed that the decision to "hit" Iraq was made within hours of the September 11 attacks.[1] In the view of Bush apologists, the answer was self-evident: the catastrophic events of 9/11 transformed the United States, its president, and its foreign policies (Kaplan and Kristol 2003, 63). So argued Lawrence F. Kaplan and William Kristol in *The War Over Iraq*. "That day may not have changed the views of some of the president's diplomatic counselors. It may not even have changed the threat posed by Saddam Hussein. But it did change the president, and therefore the direction of his foreign policy" (71). From this perspective, the events of 9/11 shaped "an entirely new concept of national security—one that intercepted threats early, before they could damage American citizens" (Sanger and Wiesman 2003).

That "new concept" was not, in fact, new, nor was it relevant to the present case, given the absence of evidence that Iraq constituted an imminent threat.[2]

Others argued that the Bush administration chose the "narrow approach" in responding to the events of 9/11. According to Andrew Bacevich, the administration focused on Osama bin Laden, al Qaeda, and the Taliban, even as the U.S. president "in an unscripted moment referred to it as a 'crusade' against evildoers everywhere." Bacevich argued that 'Operation Enduring Freedom' was useful in that it freed the administration from the constraints of using force and from the related "obsession with avoiding casualties" (Bacevich 2002, 231). The references were to the Vietnam War. 'Operation Enduring Freedom,' then, provided "a compelling rationale for a sustained and *proactive* use of American power on a global scale justified as a necessary *protective* measure" (229). As the same author conceded, the administration's identification of the enemy in terms of "terror" permitted it to blunt public attention away "from evidence suggesting that it was America's quasi-imperial role that was provoking resistance—and would continue to do so" (231).

The disclosures of a former cabinet official cast a different light on 'Operation Enduring Freedom.' Former secretary of the treasury Paul O'Neill described a meeting of the National Security Council in February 2001 in which he observed that "from the start, we were building the case against Hussein and looking at how we could take him out and change Iraq into a new country. And, if we did that, it would solve everything. It was all about finding a way to do it. That was the tone of it. The President saying, 'Fine. Go find me a way to do this'" (Suskind 2004, 86). As O'Neill claimed, "the administration's consistent goal has been to eliminate any constraints on their exercise of raw power, whether by law, regulation, alliance or treaty" (Herbert 2004).

More than six months after the U.S.-led invasion was declared a victory, the "irrefutable proof" that the Iraqi regime possessed weapons of mass destruction had not been found. As *The New York Times* announced, "No Illicit Arms Found in Iraq, U.S. Inspector Tells Congress" (Risen and Miller 2003). Evidence of Iraqi collaboration with al Qaeda was also not substantiated. As a result, the administration shifted its justification for going to war. A succession of rationalizations was offered that ranged from Iraq's alleged possession of the stated weapons, to claims of programs designed to acquire such weapons, to claims with respect to those weapons' potential and or intended use, to the overriding objective of regime change minus such weapons, and finally to the goal of imposing democracy in Iraq and the Middle East.

Administration apologists continued to defend the decision to invade Iraq, claiming, as did Robert Kagan and William Kristol (2004) in *The Weekly Stan-*

dard, that "while his weapons were a key part of the case for removing Saddam, that case was always broader." That the U.S. public was not so informed was apparently of little consequence. The Kagan and Kristol reaffirmation of Bush administration policy appeared a month after the U.S.-appointed weapons inspector, David Kay, "concluded that Iraq had no stockpiles of chemical and biological weapons at the start of the war last year." As Richard W. Stevenson (2004), *The New York Times* reporter, added, "Dr. Kay's statements undermined one of the primary justifications set out by President Bush for the war with Iraq."

But such justification was challenged long before Dr. Kay's final assessments. The U.S. and British claims with respect to the imminent threat posed by Iraq were challenged prior to the U.S.-led invasion of Iraq (von Sponeck 2002).[3]

The underlying reasons for U.S. intervention—as opposed to the justifications of the U.S. invasion—were not addressed in Kay's remarks or in those of the administration (Stevenson and Sanger 2003). On the contrary, the Bush administration avoided public discussion of past or present U.S. interests in Iraq. Furthermore, until undeniable reverses in Iraq undermined administration claims, mainstream media coverage hewed closely to the administration's language and position, relying on 'embedded journalists,' avoiding too close a look at 'collateral damage,' and reiterating administrative charges against unidentified enemy insurgents attacking 'Operation Enduring Freedom.'

Under the circumstances, the past history of U.S.-Iraqi relations was omitted from public discussion. But the record was available, and it provided evidence of the pro-Iraqi policies pursued by the Reagan and first Bush administrations in the period following the Iranian Revolution of 1979. The second Bush administration made no mention of this phase of U.S.-Iraqi relations. When George W. Bush claimed that Washington had "acquired irrefutable proof" at the time of the first Gulf War "that Iraq's designs were not limited to the chemical weapons it had used against Iran and its own people, but also extended to the acquisition of nuclear weapons and biological agents," he made no mention of the role of the United States and other industrial states in providing matériel to produce such weapons and agents. On the contrary, the U.S. president insisted that "we must be prepared to stop rogue states and their terrorist clients before they are able to threaten or use weapons of mass destruction against the United States and our allies and friends."[4]

U.S. intervention in Iraq, according to this administration, was "the first step in a new strategy, one that promised, they said, to spread democracy in the Mideast, create a new beginning for the Israeli-Palestinian peace process, and to send what President Bush called 'a clear warning' to other regimes 'that support for terror will not be tolerated'" (Sanger and Weisman 2003). In practice,

U.S. intervention in Iraq sent "a clear warning" to some of America's close allies, making it clear that in exchange for their support they would be free to act as they chose. Israel and its policies toward Palestinians in the West Bank and Gaza constitute one such example, whose impact on the Palestinian population, as on the region in general, were matters of secondary interest in Washington.

What the second Bush administration chose not to recall concerning Iraq was instructive. It included the record of past U.S.-Iraqi relations, including the role of the first Bush administration in facilitating Iraq's acquisition of some of the very weapons that the second Bush administration identified as justifying invasion.

From 1990 through the mid-1990s, the U.S. House and Senate focused attention on the manner in which the first Bush administration facilitated the arming of Iraq as part of its "tilt" toward the very regime that the second Bush administration was determined to eliminate (Gendzier 2003, 2004). There was no fundamental contradiction in the objectives underlying these policies, which were designed to assure U.S. oil interests. And, indeed, many implicated in the promotion of the policies of the first Bush administration in Iraq were subsequently involved in the undoing of the same policies during the second Bush administration. Among those responsible, such as then Undersecretary for Policy Paul Wolfowitz, then Secretary of Defense Richard Cheney, and then Chairman of the Joint Chiefs of Staff Colin Powell, the long-term objectives remained the same.

To some in Congress, however, notably in the 1990s, the "tilt" toward Iraq pursued by the Reagan and first Bush administrations was deeply troubling.[5] Over the course of several years, as congressional hearings demonstrated, the first Bush administration obtained broad support to promote U.S. exports to Iraq, including the export of matériel that would eventually enhance Iraq's military infrastructure. This came to an end at about the time of Iraq's invasion of Kuwait, at which point Washington's assessment of the Saddam Hussein regime underwent a sharp turnabout. The sometime ally was now regarded as an enemy, but not because of the brutality of his regime, which was overlooked by Washington in the previous period. It was Iraq's invasion of Kuwait—an act that was viewed as a threat to U.S. oil interests in the Gulf—that became the justification for the change in U.S. policy.

The Defense Planning Guidance document of 1992, which appeared after the first U.S.-led Gulf War, was subsequently integrated into George W. Bush's National Security Doctrine. As in earlier such pronouncements, the National Security Doctrine left no doubt as to the importance of oil and energy resources in the construction of U.S. foreign policy or the role of U.S. allies in the region in implementing it. Described as designed to preserve "American global military supremacy and to thwart the emergence of a rival superpower in Europe, Asia or the former Soviet Union," the 1992 document affirmed the importance of preserving "US and Western access to the region's [Middle East] oil." Such an objective was considered paramount, as was the U.S. commitment to "foster regional stability, deter aggression against our friends and interests in the region, protect US nationals and property, and safeguard our access to international air and seaways and to the region's oil." Integral to the implementation of this project, according to its authors, was U.S. support for Israel that included the maintenance of its "qualitative edge," which was regarded as a contribution to "the stability of the entire region, as demonstrated once again during the Persian Gulf War" (Gellman 1992).

The above document was subsequently revised and reissued under the title "Rebuilding America's Defenses: Strategy, Forces and Resources for a New Century" by the Project for the New American Century (PNAC), established in 1997. PNAC's document reflected the strategic and political thinking of neoconservative publicists, writers, and future officials of the second Bush administration, some of whom had been key figures in the previous Bush administration such as William Kristol, Robert Kagan, and Paul Wolfowitz as well as Dov Zakheim, Abram Shulsky, and I. Lewis Libby. The PNAC posture was that "America should seek to preserve and extend its position of global leadership by maintaining the preeminence of US military forces."[6] Such a position implied maintaining nuclear superiority and "control [of] the new 'international commons' of space and cyberspace," to be assured through "a new military service—US Space Forces—with the mission of space control."[7] Those familiar with the Clinton administration's Space Command will recognize the similarities in objectives.

Closer to earth, PNAC defined the U.S. role in terms of securing and expanding "zones of democratic peace" that were designed "to deter the rise of a new great-power competitor; [to] defend key regions of Europe, East Asia and the Middle East; and to preserve American preeminence through the coming transformation of war made possible by new technologies."[8] Competitors and potential enemies included China, Iran, and North Korea.

Talk of democracy aside, the primary emphasis in such discussions was the move to guarantee the uncontested dissemination of U.S. military power in the Middle East after the first Gulf War. Moreover, the presence of U.S. military forces was not made contingent on the improvement in relations with states of the region, including Iran.

The above scenario, moreover, included an explicit endorsement of U.S. ties with Israel, whose military as well as political function was crucial to U.S. policy.

As the United States sought to maximize its military presence in the Gulf region as a whole following the first Gulf War, it collaborated with Britain in policies directed at Iraq, in particular. London joined Washington in patrolling the so-called no-fly zones over northern and southern Iraq in pursuing a sanctions policy, whose punishing effects on the Iraqi population became the basis for international condemnation, and in manipulating UN arms inspectors appointed by the Security Council to oversee the disarmament of the Saddam Hussein regime.

Critics of the Clinton administration who considered such policies inadequate demanded a change of regime in Baghdad. In January 1998, officials of past administrations, some of whom had been emissaries to the Taliban and indicted conspirators in the Iran-Contra affair, sent a letter to Speaker of the House Newt Gingrich calling for "regime change" in Iraq. Those who subsequently became part of the George W. Bush administration included Zalmay Khalilzad, Elliott Abrams, John R. Bolton, Richard Perle, Peter Rodman, Donald Rumsfeld, Paul Wolfowitz, R. James Woolsey, and Robert Zoellick.

In a May 1998 sequel sent to Newt Gingrich and Senate majority leader Trent Lott, the same above signatories argued against the "containment" of Saddam Hussein as endangering U.S. interests and those of its allies, claiming "that the only way to protect the United States and its allies from the threat of weapons of mass destruction was to put in place policies that would lead to the removal of Saddam and his regime from power." They urged Washington to "establish and maintain a strong US military presence in the region [Iraq] and be prepared to use that force to protect our vital interests in the Gulf—and, if necessary, to help remove Saddam from power." [9] Among justifications offered for this position was that the Iraqi leader threatened the so-called Middle East peace process, which some of the very signatories had in the past called on Israel to reject.

Writing of the 1990s, Andrew Bacevich described "the emergence of a new class of uniformed proconsuls presiding over vast quasi-imperial domains [that] was only one development among many making the 1990s arguably the most portentous and troubling period in the history of U.S. civil-military relations" (Bacevich 2002, 167). A decade later, the proconsuls drawn from the Republican administrations of Ronald Reagan and George H. W. Bush were key figures shaping the domestic and foreign policy agendas of the George W. Bush administration. Insofar as Iraq was concerned, regime change became the de facto U.S. policy. And as insiders as well as allied lobbyists made clear, they envisioned such change as part of a far broader reconstitution of what was referred to as the Near East, in the post–World War I period, when major Western powers partitioned the Ottoman Empire, rearranging borders and defining would-be nations to suit their interests.

The civilian/military triumvirate that shaped U.S. policies in Iraq and the Middle East in the aftermath of the collapse of the former USSR and in the aftermath of the first Gulf War included the vice president (Richard Cheney), secretary of defense (Donald Rumsfeld), and undersecretary of defense (Paul Wolfowitz). Collaborators in a realignment and concentration of power with vast domestic implications, they enhanced the role of the Pentagon in policymaking and relied on privatized bureaucracies offering custom-made intelligence whose role in the months leading up to the U.S.-led invasion of Iraq would prove of major importance. Key to the operations of such arrangements were subordinates selected for their political loyalty and ideological compatibility and such advisory institutions as the Defense Policy Board (DPB), whose sometime chair, Richard Perle, remained a staunch advocate—if not architect—of George W. Bush's Middle East policy. Finally, cooperating at a different level was the network of allied lobbyists and activists housed in conservative think tanks that provided a broad base of support and a ready audience for administration pronouncements.

In historical perspective, the Middle East agenda of the George W. Bush administration was built on the legacy of its predecessors. U.S. policy in Iraq, however, became a test case in this context, one designed to challenge existing international law on the basis of uncontested American hegemony. If the flaunting of international law assumed new proportions in the second Bush administration, the fundamental interests shaping U.S. policy in the Middle East were those rooted in an earlier era, one that originated in the period following the Second World War. Then and throughout the coming years that coincided with the first Lebanese civil war—in which the U.S. intervened—and the Iraqi revolution of 1958, the Eisenhower administration made clear its commitment to access of and control over Gulf oil. The importance of Saudi Arabia as well as the Gulf became a hallmark of U.S. Middle East policy, one in which the allied role of politically compatible regimes was an indispensable adjunct. The U.S.-Israeli relationship was eventually built into this framework, as Israel was recognized as critical to the maintenance of what U.S. documents referred to as the 'stability' of the region.

Under the second Bush administration, the aggressive pursuit of the Middle East agenda entailed no diminution of U.S. interests in Saudi or Gulf oil. By virtue of its occupation of Iraq and long-term commitment to maintaining U.S. military forces in the country, however, Washington positioned itself to dominate the oil-rich region while reordering its politics. Israel's supportive role in the process entailed no less an expansion of its own power, with tacit U.S. accord.

In the spring of 2001, with the second Bush administration in power, the Baker Institute for Public Policy prepared a report on energy policy that identified the importance of Iraqi reserves in the overall context of Middle East oil. The report contained the key elements of the administration's future policies in Iraq.

In the same period, as later disclosed, a secret Pentagon task force on Iraqi oil suggested a high level of interest not meant for public exposure (Gerth 2003). Efforts by the Government Accounting Office (GAO) and the public interest group Judicial Watch to determine the nature of such interests revealed that the 2001 president's Energy Task Force had mapped out information on "Iraq's oil fields, pipelines, refineries and terminals," along with the identities of foreign companies engaged in or considering negotiations with Baghdad.[10] It further revealed high-level consultations with "nonfederal energy stakeholders, principally petroleum, coal, nuclear, natural gas, and electricity industry representatives and lobbyists."[11] According to the same source, "representatives of many foreign oil concerns have been meeting with leaders of the Iraqi opposition to make their case for a future stake and to sound them out about their intentions" (Morgan and Ottaway 2002). The task force was reported to have consulted with domestic oil companies, a matter of some interest in terms of domestic political constituencies and political alignments.

Reflecting on the inside workings of the Bush administration, former Treasury Secretary Paul O'Neill emphasized the conformist ambiance in a political consortium averse to open debate, whether on Iraq or on matters of tax policy (Suskind 2004, chap. 2). O'Neill's views confirmed the realignment of power within the upper levels of the administration, notably the concentration of power in the hands of the vice president. Others observed that the staff of the office of the vice president had "eclipsed both the State Department and the National Security Council as the primary source of foreign policy initiatives—one not beholden to any bureaucratic constituency."[12]

Pentagon analysts arrived at the same conclusions, persuaded that policymaking in the Middle East rested in the hands of appointees of the vice president, such as David Wurmser, former head of Middle East studies at the conservative think tank, the American Enterprise Institute, who was reported to have "more direct influence on US policymaking in the Middle East than the entire staff of the State Department's Near East Affairs bureau" (Sieff 2002).

The emergence of privatized intelligence staffs was regarded by critical observers as undermining the conventional roles of the Departments of State and Intelligence. Air Force Lt. Col. Karen Kwiatkowski, a senior Pentagon Middle East specialist, argued that the Office of Special Plans (OSP) represented part of the "neoconservative capture of the policy-intelligence nexus in the run-up to the invasion of Iraq." Kwiatkowski further remarked on "seizure of the reins of U.S. Middle East policy" that resulted from the operations of the OSP and that included a greater reliance on conservative think tanks such as the Washington Institute for Near East Policy (WINEP) and the pro-Israeli lobbying group American Israel Public Affairs Committee (AIPAC) (Kwiatkowski 2004).

Those favorable to the above realignments interpreted the enhanced role of the military in policymaking as favorable. From this perspective, according to a *Wall Street Journal* report, officials bent on integrating the Defense Department in "the inter-agency process, where its proposals are thrashed out along with those from State, CIA, the National Security Council and others," represented a positive innovation (Kirkpatrick 2003). Such reports failed to consider the response within the military establishment itself that was far from uniform in its evaluation of the administration's policies (Hersh 2003).

At another level, external critics pointed to the administration's "intimate ties with corporate interests," including those representing defense and energy, referring to these as unprecedented (Sridhar 2003). The Center for Public Integrity calculated that of the Defense Policy Board's thirty members, "at least nine have ties to companies that have won more than $76 billion in defense contracts in 2001 and 2002. Four members are registered lobbyists, one of whom represents two of the three largest defense contractors." According to the same source, "the companies with ties to Defense Policy Board members include prominent firms like Boeing, TRW, Northrop Grumman, Lockheed Martin and Booz Allen Hamilton and smaller players like Symantec Corp., Technology Strategies and Alliance Corp., and Polycom, Inc." (Verlöy and Politi 2003).

Jack Sheehan, previously a member of the DPB, and the former general who was NATO's supreme allied commander Atlantic and commander in chief U.S. Atlantic Command until 1997, was senior vice president of Bechtel. As of the fall of 2002, Sheehan was "senior vice president and partner and responsible for the execution and strategy for the region that includes Europe, Africa, the Middle East and Southwest Asia" (Verlöy and Politi 2003). There were other major figures representing Bechtel on the DPB, including former Secretary of State George Schultz. Following the U.S.-led invasion and occupation of Iraq, Bechtel was awarded a contract worth some $680 million for "reconstruction work on airports, water, power, schools, roads and government buildings" (King and Kerr 2003). The sum was subsequently increased on repeated occasions, even as controversy surrounding the granting of such contracts intensified.

James Woolsey, former CIA director and a member of the DPB, was a key figure in the Paladin Capital Group, a venture-capital firm that was reported to be "soliciting investment for homeland security firms" (King and Kerr 2003).

Chris Williams, also a DPB member, was special assistant to Secretary of Defense Donald Rumsfeld on policy issues and worked as a lobbyist for Johnson and Associates, who, in turn, represented Lockheed Martin, Boeing, TRW, and Northrop Grumman.

Richard Perle, chair of the DPB until his resignation due to charges of conflict of interest, had been closely associated with "Global Crossing—a telecommunications firm that had sought his help in winning government approval for a deal with an Asian firm" (Tran 2003). He was also managing partner of Trireme Partners, LP, a company with an interest in issues of homeland security and defense; chair and CEO of Hollinger Digital, Inc.; and director of the Israeli newspaper *The Jerusalem Post,* among other positions.

Of the service contractors, Halliburton, of which Vice President Richard Cheney had been CEO, "emerged as the biggest single government contractor in Iraq," with Bechtel not far behind and DynCorp in next place. Halliburton, the oil and pipeline servicing and construction company with an international network of engineering affiliates, was reported to have obtained "over $443 million in defense related contracts to provide services ranging from logistical support to building enemy prisoner of war camps and refueling military tanks" (Donnelley and Hartung 2003). It received a contract estimated to be valued at $1 billion for its role in protecting Iraqi oil fields, according to the same source. Estimates of Halliburton's contracts at the time this essay was written were in the vicinity of $1.7 billion, with others anticipated in the future (Dobbs 2003).

In the months that followed, controversy surrounded the Halliburton subsidiary Kellogg Brown and Root (KBR). *The Wall Street Journal* reported that "the top Defense Department auditor asked the office [of the Pentagon inspector general] to investigate whether Halliburton subsidiary Kellogg Brown and Root overcharged for fuel deliveries by more than $61 million." Further, as journalist Neill King Jr. reported, the work being done in Iraq by KBR was reported to cost "nearly $6 billion, well over twice what has gone to all of the other 40 US contractors in Iraq, according to government records." According to *The Wall Street Journal* account, the U.S. Congressional General Accounting Office and the Pentagon were engaged in investigations of Iraqi reconstruction projects funded by U.S. companies (King 2004).

In comparison to the DPB, think tanks—some going back as far as the Reagan era—represented the organization of common interests in a nonformal setting that included former officials, lobbyists, and their respective staff members. The Center for Security Policy, the Heritage Institute, the Hudson Institute, and the American Enterprise Institute (AEI) supported the administration's Middle East policies, but these were by no means their dominant concerns. For WINEP, AIPAC, the Jewish Institute for National Security Affairs (JINSA), and the Institute for Advanced Strategic and Political Studies (IASPS), based in Washington and Jerusalem, the Middle East agenda as defined by Israeli policy was a matter of dominant concern (Beinin 2003a, 2003b).

In the spring of 2002, AIPAC held its annual conference, which "half the US Senate, ninety members of the House," and administration officials attended. Subsequently, "the US House of Representatives passed a resolution by 352 to 21, with 29 abstentions, that expressed unqualified support for Sharon's Israel" (Farsoun 2003). A similar outcome occurred in the Senate vote held on the same day. JINSA, whose vice chairman was the former director of AIPAC, focused on U.S.-Israeli military and intelligence relations while advertising Israeli military exports to third world countries, such as India. JINSA cited U.S. Marine Corps praise of "an Israeli-developed navigation pod used in the campaign against the Taliban and al Qaeda in Afghanistan," noting that the pod was made in the United States by Northrop Grumman with Rafael, an Israeli company (Cleven 2002). Similarly, JINSA tracked awards to major defense contractors, such as Boeing for a "$21 million contract to provide Israel with 1,000 Joint Direct Attack Munition (JDAM) MK-A4 guided vehicles." There were other notices, including upgrades to "Israel's Boeing-made Harpoon anti-ship missiles" and news of cooperation between Israeli and U.S. law enforcement agents. JINSA's director, Tom Neumann, endorsed the Pentagon's choice Iraqi exile, Ahmed Chalabi, explaining that he not only had ties with the Pentagon and the White House, "but he has built a strong following in the American Jewish community," as the *Jewish Bulletin News* reported in April 2003 (Davis 2003).

There are other examples of the political networking in which some of the above think tanks and activists played a significant role. They included the creation of a host of hybrid organizations defined as supporting American goals in the Middle East, whether of Lebanese, Iranian, Turkish, or Kurdish origin. The Middle East Forum issued a report of the Lebanon Study Group entitled "Ending Syria's Occupation of Lebanon: the US Role." Signatories included, among others, Richard Perle, Douglas Feith, Paula Dobriansky, and David Wurmser. The co-chairs of the Lebanon Study Group, Daniel Pipes and Ziad Abdelnour, were also members of the so-called Golden Circle of special members of the U.S. Committee for a Free Lebanon (USCFL), an advocacy group for Lebanon's right-wing exiles and former militia leaders. The Golden Circle identified those responsible for shaping U.S. policy toward Lebanon, a list that reproduced some of the signatories of the Pipes-Abdelnour circle as well as members of the Bush administration's support network, including Michael Ledeen of the American Enterprise Institute.

In the fall of 2002, an Israeli journalist writing in the mainstream Israeli daily, *Ha'aretz,* reported on an event that illustrated the interaction among the Pentagon, the Defense Policy Board, and an unnamed think tank. Their common purpose was consideration of a slide show whose policy implications involved U.S. intervention in the political redesign of the Middle East. According to journalist Akiva Eldar, a number of "Pentagon chiefs" were invited to view a special slide show organized by "researchers from a Washington think tank with particularly close relations with the Defense Department" (Eldar 2002).

The host responsible for inviting Pentagon officials was Richard Perle, then chair of the Defense Policy Board. According to an Israeli source familiar with the situation, Pentagon officials were shown slides of the "three goals in the war on terror and the democratization of the Middle East." The slides depicted Iraq as "a tactical goal," Saudi Arabia as "a strategic goal," and Egypt as "the greatest prize." In the remaining slide, "Palestine is Israel, Jordan is Palestine, and Iraq is the Hashemite Kingdom." Ehud Sprintzak, the Israeli military analyst who was the source of the above report, observes that civilian officials of the Pentagon viewed the Arab world as "a world of retards who only understand the language of force" (Fishman 2002). That observation did not appear in the *Ha'aretz* account. There, Akiva Eldar underscored the resemblance between the above scenario and the 1996 proposal written for the figure who was the leader of Israel's right-wing incumbent.

In 1996, according to Eldar, a group of consultants—including Richard Perle, Douglas Feith, and David Wurmser—had been invited to "help Israeli [right-wing leader] Benjamin Netanyahu in his first steps as prime minister. They could not have known that four years later the working paper they prepared, including plans for Israel to help restore the Hashemite throne in Iraq, would shed light on the current policies of the only superpower in the world" (Eldar 2002).

The 1996 report, "A Clean Break," was commissioned by the Washington and Jerusalem-based Institute for Advanced Strategic and Political Studies. It advocated an Israeli policy toward the Palestinians based on force, "the *right of hot pursuit* for self defense into all Palestinian areas and nurturing alternatives to Arafat's exclusive grip on Palestinian society," and demanded that "Only the unconditional acceptance by Arabs of our rights, *especially* in their territorial dimension, *'peace for peace,'* is a solid basis for the future." As the report further noted, "Israel's efforts to secure its streets may require hot pursuit into Palestinian-controlled areas, a justifiable practice with which Americans can sympathize." In addition, it endorsed a restoration of right-wing leaders in Lebanon, following Syria's removal and containment, as well as the restoration of monarchical figures to lead Iran and Syria. Similarly endorsed was "removing Saddam Hussein from power in Iraq—an important Israeli strategic objective in its own right—as a means of foiling Syria's regional ambitions."[13]

Four years later, Perle, Feith, and Wurmser were part of the George W. Bush administration, with Perle as chair of the Defense Policy Board. In 2004, Perle was no longer officially serving the administration as the U.S. president prepared his electoral campaign to extend his term in office. What was certain to remain unchanged in this period was the central role of the Middle East. Whether the agenda defined by those who shaped its course in the second Bush administration persisted unchanged as well remained to be determined.

NOTES

The original draft of this text was written in November 2003 and partially revised in March 2004. The abundant evidence of government policies and deception that have since been revealed confirm the principal arguments of this essay.

1. "Pilger Claims White House Knew Saddam was no Threat," *Sydney Morning Herald,* September 23, 2003.

2. As Daniel Webster wrote in the Caroline case, which provides the recognized legal basis for claims of preemption, the following conditions would have to be met: "It will be for that Government to show a necessity of self-defence, instant, overwhelming, leaving no choice of means, and no moment for deliberation," as cited in Shewmaker (1983, 67).

3. In March 2003, *Newsweek* reported that the director of the UN nuclear agency, Mohamed ElBaradei, had informed the Security Council in March 2003 that "there was no evidence of resumed nuclear activities . . . nor any indication of nuclear-related prohibited activities at any related sites" (Zakaria 2004). For a general review of the subject, see Cirincione, Mathews, Perkovich, and Orton (2004).

4. The full text of President Bush's "The National Security Strategy of the United States" is available online at Common Dreams News Center, www.commondreams.org/headlines02/0920-05.htm.

5. On this theme, see Chomsky (2003).

6. "Rebuilding America's Defenses: Strategy, Forces and Resources for the New Century," a report of the Project for the New American Century, Washington, D.C., September 2000, Statement of Principles, Section IV.

7. Ibid., v.

8. Ibid., 2–3.

9. Available at www.newamericancentury.org/iraqletter1998.htm.

10. "Cheney Energy Task Force Documents Feature Map of Iraqi Oilfields," Judicial Watch, July 17, 2003, www.judicialwatch.org/071703.b_PR.shtml. In a memo in its "National Briefing" column of Wednesday, September 17, 2003, *The New York Times* (p. A21) indicated that "the Bush administration told a federal appeals court that it would ask the Supreme Court to review a decision that requires Vice President Dick Cheney to give the Sierra Club documents from his task force on energy. Last week, the full United States Court of Appeals for the District of Columbia Circuit let stand a panel's decision that the government had no basis to ask the appeals court to block a lower court's ruling that called for disclosure of information. Mr. Cheney has invoked executive privilege in keeping the documents secret."

11. "Energy Task Force: Process Used to Develop the National Energy Policy," United States General Accounting Office, Report to Congressional Requesters, August 2003, www.gao.gov/cgi-bin/getrpt?GAO-03-894.

12. Petroleum Finance Company, "Saudi Arabia Country Report," Report written for a private corporation, September 2002, p. 15.

13. "A Clean Break: A New Strategy for Securing the Realm," The Institute for Advanced Strategic and Political Studies, Jerusalem, Washington, 1996, www.israeleconomy.org/strat1.htm.

REFERENCES

Bacevich, A. J. 2003. *American Empire*. Cambridge: Harvard University Press.

Beinin, Joel. 2003a. "Pro-Israel Hawks and the Second Gulf War." Middle East Report Online, April 6. www.merip.org/mero/mero040603.html.

———. 2003b. "US: The Pro-Sharon Thinktank." *Le Monde Diplomatique*, July 2003.

Chomsky, Noam. 2003. *Hegemony or Survival*. New York: Metropolitan Books.

Cirincione, J., J. Mathews, G. Perkovich, and A. Orton. 2004. *WMD in Iraq: Evidence and Implications*. Washington, D.C.: Carnegie Endowment for International Peace.

Cleven, Kristen. 2002. "U.S.-Israel Strategic Relations in 2002: Counter-Terrorism, Missile Defense and High-Tech Research Remain Priorities." JINSA, November 21. www.jinsa.org/articles/articles.html/function/view/categoryid/658/documentid/1825/history/3,2360,658,1825.

Davis, Douglas. 2003. "New Iraq May Recognize Israel, Bring Financial Relief." *Jewish Bulletin News*, April 25. www.jewishsf.com/bk030425/i20a.shtml.

Dobbs, Michael. 2003. "Halliburton's Deals Greater than Thought." *Washington Post*, August 28, p. A1.

Donnelley, Ceara, and William D. Hartung. 2003. "New Numbers: The Price of Freedom in Iraq and Power in Washington." Arms Trade Resource Center, World Policy Institute, August. www.worldpolicy.org/projects/arms/updates/081203.html.

Eldar, Akiva. 2002. "Perles of Wisdom for the Feithful." *Ha'aretz*, November 2.

Farsoun, Samih. 2003. "Roots of the American Anti-Terrorism Crusade." *Holy Land Studies* 1(2) (2003): 154.

Fishman, Alex. 2002. "Iraq and Jordan Will Become One Hashemite State." *Yediot Ahronot*, September 6.

Gellman, Barton. 1992. "Keeping the US First: Pentagon Would Preclude a Rival Superpower." *Washington Post*, March 11, p. A1.

Gendzier, Irene. 2003. "Dying to Forget: The U.S. and Iraq's Weapons of Mass Destruction." *Logos Online*, March 14, reproduced on ZNet. www.zmag.org/content/showarticle.cfm?ItemID=3233.

———. 2004. "Reflections on the Start of the New Year," Znet, January 18. www.zmag.org/content/showarticle.cfm?ItemID=4832.

Gerth, Jeff. 2003. "Report Offered Bleak Outlook about Iraq Oil." *New York Times*, October 5, p. 1.

Herbert, Bob. 2004. "Masters of Deception." *New York Times*, January 16, p. A21.

Hersh, Seymour M. 2003. "Annals of National Security: Offense and Defense." *New Yorker*, April 7.

Kagan, Robert, and William Kristol. 2004. "The Right War for the Right Reasons," *Weekly Standard* 9(23) (February 23). www.weeklystandard.com/Content/Public/Articles/000/000/003/735tahyk.asp.

Kaplan, Lawrence F., and William Kristol. 2003. *The War Over Iraq*. San Francisco: Encounter Books.

Kessler, Glenn. 2003. "US Decision on Iraq Has Puzzling Past," *Washington Post*, January 12, p. A01.

King, Neil Jr. 2004. "Halliburton Tells Pentagon Workers Took Kickbacks to Award Projects in Iraq." *Wall Street Journal*, January 23, p. 1.

King, Neil Jr., and Simeon Kerr. 2003. "US to Boost Bechtel's Funding to Rebuild Iraqi Electricity Grid." *Wall Street Journal*, August 28, p. A1.

Kirkpatrick, Melanie. 2003. "Clear Ideas versus Foggy Bottom." *Wall Street Journal*, August 5, p. A8.

Kwiatkowski, Karen. 2004. "The New Pentagon Papers." March 10. www.archive.salon.com/opinion/feature/2004/03/10/osp/index_np.html.

Morgan, Dan, and David B. Ottaway. 2003. "In Iraqi War Scenario, Oil Is Key Issue." *Washington Post*, September 15, p. A01.

Risen, James, and Judith Miller. 2003. "No Illicit Arms Found in Iraq, U.S. Inspector Tells Congress." *New York Times*, October 3.

Sanger, David E., and Steven R. Wiesman. 2003. "Bush's Aides Envision New Influence in Region." *New York Times*, April 10, p. B11.

Shewmaker, Kenneth E., ed. 1983. *The Papers of Daniel Webster*, vol. 1, 1841–1843. Hanover, New Hampshire, and London: University Press of New England.

Sieff, Martin. 2003. "Global Politics Divvying Up the Spoils of Iraq: The Pentagon's Vision." *Globalist*, September 12.

Sridhar, V. 2003. "Bush and Co. Private Limited." *Frontline* 20(5) (March 1–14). www.hinduonnet.com/fline/fl2005/stories/20030314006302400.htm.

Stevenson, Richard W.. 2004. "Iraq Illicit Arms Gone Before War, Inspector States." *New York Times*, January 24, p. 1.

Stevenson, Richard W., and David E. Sanger. 2003. "Calling Iraq a Serious Threat, Bush Vows That He'll Disarm It, and Also Rebuild US Economy." *New York Times*. January 29, p. 1.

Suskind, Ron. 2004. *The Price of Loyalty*. New York: Simon and Schuster.

Tran, Mark. 2003. "Halliburton Misses $600 Million Iraq Contract." *Guardian*, March 31. www.guardian.co.uk/business/story/0,,926400,00.html.

Verlöy, André, and Daniel Politi. 2003. "Advisors of Influence: Nine Members of the Defense Policy Board Have Ties to Defense Contractors." Center for Public Integrity, September 2. www.publicintegrity.org/report.aspx?aid=91&sid=200.

von Sponeck, Hans C. 2002. "Iraq: Four Questions, Four Answers." UN Humanitarian Coordinator for Iraq (1998–2000) at the European Colloquium, Brussels, September 25. www.irak.be/ned/bivv/iraq4questions4answers.htm.

Zakaria, Fareed. 2004. "We Had Good Intel—The U.N.'s," *Newsweek*, February 9. www.msnbc.msn.com/id/4122113.

KARLA J. CUNNINGHAM

5 Women, Political Violence, and Democratization

INTRODUCTION

Historically, women have engaged in a range of activities such as intelligence gathering, recruitment, hostage-taking, and suicide bombing within politically violent settings (revolutionary, guerrilla, "terrorist"[1]) in diverse geographical locales (e.g., Vietnam, Colombia, Palestine, the United States). The literature on this phenomenon is small and generally shares several common features that have important methodological and theoretical ramifications, especially for emergent democratic settings. First, the overall literature on political violence[2] suffers from a "small-N" problem in that few actors overall engage in political violence to precipitate political change. This problem is compounded by gender, as among politically violent actors more men than women have traditionally engaged in this behavior. While some scholars have not found the low-frequency argument to be a deterrent to studying politically violent women (Benson and Simon 1982; Broido 1977; Cooper 1979; Cunningham 2003; Decker 1990; Fangen 1997; Galvin 1983; Georges-Abeyie 1983; Neuburger and Valentini 1996; Powers 1971; Steel 1998; Weinberg and Eubank 1987), overwhelmingly the terrorism and political violence literatures assume that the object of their analysis will be male. The female is seen as an aberration from the norm and is studied, if at all, through the application of male-derived theories and assumptions regarding her behavior. Compounding this process are gendered assumptions of female behavior that have high cross-cultural durability and meaning.[3]

Women's utilization and embrace of political violence challenges cross-cultural gendered normative assumptions governing human behavior and subsequent socioeconomic-political structures and processes. Assumptions that women avoid violence because they are biologically, and thereby "naturally," peaceful have been largely disproved (Björkqvist and Niemelä 1992; Campbell 1995; Camp-

73

bell 1999). More convincing, although not fully explanatory, is the importance of society on socializing women (and men) with respect to aggression and violence. While most societies associate aggressiveness with masculinity,[4] contextual changes (namely war) have briefly altered social constraints on women's roles to encompass a range of politically active and violent behaviors, including combat. Similar to O'Donnell and Schmitter's (1986) contention that civil society temporarily surges into the public sphere to precipitate and propel political transition, so too have women been temporarily mobilized under extraordinary conditions only to find themselves returned to their private roles once the crisis is over.

The overall result is that the limited literature on politically violent women tends to restrict and reframe female motivations for engaging in political violence and the types of actions in which they engage. With respect to the former, politically violent women are overwhelmingly denied conscious reasons for their behavior. Their violence is attributed to one of three motives: they are either "dupes" of men, victims of men, or irrational if not insane actors. None of these motives implies conscious agency and, as a result, women's activities within politically violent organizations are assumed to be secondary, peripheral (and often sexually ancillary), and unimportant. Even in settings where women have engaged in combat activities (e.g., Sri Lanka, Palestine), their actions are dismissed by referring to one or more of the aforementioned motives. For example, Dhanu, the Sri Lankan woman who assassinated Prime Minister Rajiv Gandhi, was said to have committed the act as revenge for her rape at the hands of Indian forces. Her motive and action have subsequently been extended to much of the small literature on the Birds of Paradise, the female suicide bombing unit of the Black Tigers. In contrast, men do not need a motive for political violence per se; their willingness to fight corresponds to the political conflict itself.

The gendered dichotomous framing of female political violence has significant ramifications for postviolent contexts and particularly the political structures and processes that result. These outcomes overlap with, and reinforce, the framing in two ways. Since women engage in political violence for the "wrong" reasons and are thereby not politically conscious agents, their right to fully participate in creating postconflict structures is highly circumscribed. This process is reinforced by three factors: firstly, nascent political elites are usually loathe to isolate male actors whose support is crucial as power creation and consolidation occurs; secondly, women do not represent a unified political front, and divisions between "traditional" and "modern" women are particularly visible in the early postconflict phase; and thirdly, women's political goals such as liberation and equality were, at best, secondary to the larger politico-ideological motives of their respective organizations.

The second way framing is significant in postconflict settings is specifically centered on women's activities during the conflict period. Women involved in political violence up to and including combat are seen as rare from both historical and cross-cultural perspectives. In the rare instances when women are acknowledged in politically violent settings, their roles are viewed as peripheral and range from comfort services (e.g., nursing, camp maintenance, and even prostitution), to moderate active behavior (e.g., propaganda dissemination, intelligence gathering and infiltration, and infrastructure maintenance or repair), to overt active behavior (e.g., combat, shootings, hijackings, and suicide bombings).

Whether the activities women have engaged in are peripheral or whether the activities are peripheral because women engage in them remains unclear. Certainly, comfort services are traditionally viewed as almost exclusively female, and their separation from active behavior embodies their peripheralization. Active behaviors are normally associated with males; however, women do perform these activities, and where this occurs either the activity slowly becomes associated with women as personnel shifts occur or women's activity is seen as temporary and anomalous, not necessitating fundamental attitudinal changes in operational roles for male members. Cynthia Enloe's (1983) notion of "combat elasticity" and rollback explains why women were almost invariably relegated to support positions once Israel's security posture improved due to technology (155–59). Where women have been militarily engaged in the Israeli context, their commanders' decisions seemed to have more to do with emasculating the enemy through the use of a female opponent than with genuine promotion of female roles within the military (Halpern 1992). In both the United States and Britain, women were assigned specifically noncombat jobs "for the duration," meaning that "[de]mobilisation was built into the programmes to mobilise women in both the first and second world wars" (Enloe 1983, 158, emphasis in original).

CITIZENSHIP THROUGH POLITICAL VIOLENCE

Women's political violence is often visible within nationalist/resistance settings, as the rebellion tends to be all-encompassing for the society in question, altering a variety of social structures including those related to age and gender. With respect to the latter, women are permitted and even encouraged to broaden roles insofar as they remain within, and subsumed to, the nationalist/resistance framework that maintains gendered normative structures and assumptions (Chatterjee 1989; Kandiyoti 1991). Thus, women may be encouraged to produce more soldiers through higher birthrates (e.g., Vietnam, U.S. white separatists), protect young men by their presence and with their bodies (e.g., Palestine), engage in demonstrations and assist nationalist enterprises (e.g., Algeria, Palestine, Sri Lanka), and even act as warriors when personnel shortages or operational imperatives demand (e.g., Sri Lanka, Palestine, Colombia). In these settings, the primary goal for women and men is some form of liberation or independence.

Within most nationalist/resistance settings there is also a secondary goal of social change; however, this is conceptualized differently for men and women. While normally not explicitly stated, men generally want social change that maintains patriarchy while women want social change that will undermine patriarchy. Importantly, while women concur about the legitimacy of the primary nationalist goal, they differ regarding women's roles in achieving this goal and with respect to the secondary goal of social change. While men want to alter political structures to include different groups, these are understood to be largely different groups of men. Where women are part of this process, there is generally no recognition or effort to alter the fundamental sociopolitical structures that retain male advantages. As a result, full equality with respect to any measure (social, economic, political) is not pursued, is not a goal, and where women are courted by the state they are instrumentally co-opted to weaken key male opponents to the new statist structures, as demonstrated by Brand (1998), not to advance the rights and advantages of women as an end.

Gendered dichotomous framing of political action often ascribes political violence as masculinized, whereas nonviolent activities (e.g., grassroots organizations, nongovernmental organizations) are feminized. The efficacy of each approach is highly contextualized, but oftentimes when grassroots approaches are viewed as unsuccessful, militancy becomes a more attractive approach. This process has been visible in several recent settings. In the Palestinian setting, for example, the grassroots approach—or more specifically the lack of militancy in the first intifada—has been partly viewed as responsible for the loss of Palestinian rights since Oslo, leading to greater societal acceptance of the male/militancy path and the rejection of the female/grassroots path (Hasso 1998, 454) during the second intifada. The sense of grassroots failure in this setting, however, has two sides. On one side it has led to the embrace of militancy by both men and women in an effort to achieve the primary goal of Palestinian autonomy from Israel. More importantly for this analysis, however, is that on the other side women are increasingly associating political violence, particularly combat roles, with expanding citizenship claims and rights based either on their own or others' real or apparent failings to use nonmilitaristic tactics to achieve political change. Mirrored in other settings (e.g., Colombia, Peru, and Sri Lanka), women appear to have calculated that without greater militarism their ability to achieve broader rights and freedoms will resemble Vietnam, Algeria, and Palestine after the first intifada, and they are not willing to accept that outcome. However, this conclusion is not supported by historical or theoretical evidence.[5]

To date, neither militancy nor nonviolent political action has resulted in political equality for women. Less clear is how repeated female violence and mobilization will affect political structures over the long-term. Evidence from the United States with respect to the altering dynamics of the armed forces for African Americans, and even the citizenship demands from many former colonies in the developing world, suggest that multiple mobilizations—and disappointments—influence society to facilitate and propel future political demands. Whether this process can succeed in eradicating gendered normative assumptions remains unrealized to date, and earlier mobilizations of the type described have not eliminated structural racism and inequality, raising troubling implications. The cases of Algeria and Palestine highlight some of these themes.

ALGERIA'S DASHED EXPECTATIONS

During the 1950s' Algerian resistance against the French, women became actively mobilized into a politically violent setting based on their own initiative and organizational imperatives driven by personnel shortages and operational constraints. Jeffrey Decker (1990) argues that connected with the entrance of women into the revolution was a rise in violence and the association of the "technique of terrorism" with their participation. Women's operational success was gendered and played into the biases held by both sides of the conflict. Specifically, the veil became "both a dress and a mask," facilitating women's operational utility during the Revolution (180–81).

The phased mobilization of women into the Algerian resistance movement had three discernable junctures, corresponding to Frantz Fanon's (1965) stages of veiling (and unveiling) of women in Algeria. Before 1956, only men were involved in armed struggle, but French adaptation to resistance tactics prompted male leaders to hesitantly transform their strategy and include women in the "public struggle." Women's willingness to join with the resistance was a product of both nationalist fervor and a response to colonial attempts to dominate society. While the French offered to liberate Algerian women from Islam, women's anticolonial activities gave them new ways to challenge tradition from within (Roy and Korteweg 1999, 56). During this period, the veil was worn out of tradition and to resist French attempts to unveil Algeria (Fanon 1965, 63).

During the second phase of women's mobilization, three changes occurred: terrorist tactics were more readily employed, the conflict became more urbanized, and women were unveiled to exploit French biases. Fanon (1965) recognized the temporal, contextual, and exceptional features of this occurrence, stating that "the mutation occurred in connection with the Revolution and under special circumstances. The veil was abandoned in the course of revolutionary action. What had been used to block the psychological or political offensives of the occupier became a means, an instrument" (63). By 1957, the final phase occurred when veiling combined with militarism. "Resistance [was] generated through the manipulation, transformation, and reappropriation of the traditional Arab woman's veil into a 'technique of camouflage' for guerilla warfare" (Decker 1990, 193).

Algeria is a benchmark case because its lessons have been learned by women in other revolutionary and nationalist settings. While Fanon's (1965) second chapter envisions a fundamental transformation of Algerian families, largely precipitated by female roles in the resistance, postconflict structures did not fundamentally alter. At best, what occurred was "transformation of the Muslim notion of femininity, even if only momentarily during decolonization, [which] is central to theorizing the general range of *possibilities* for Algerian women's subjectivity and agency" (Decker 1990, 183, emphasis in original). In reality, little change took place because women's action was utilized and framed within existing gendered structures. Unveiling itself was viewed as a "mutation," as described by Fanon (1965, 63), and highly contextualized. Women's veils were transformed contemporaneously and externally without any alteration of the fundamental pillars of traditional society. Women mobilized within this framework for lack of other alternatives, exacerbating and reinforcing their position within, and implicit acceptance of, those very structures. Thus, corresponding to virtually all nationalist movements, while Algerian men and women generally shared the same political objective—in this case freedom from French colonial domination—women and men held differing secondary goals where women clearly wished for greater equality, albeit not in the Western feminist sense, while men viewed social change as asserting more authentic cultural forms (e.g., Islam) and maintaining male political primacy within the polity. The sociopolitical structures that were constructed after the revolution institutionalized men's secondary goal rather than women's and retained tiered citizenship in which women remained protected and dependent peripheral members of the polity.

The articulation of the latter's vision of social change is captured in *La Charte d'Alger*, the Algerian charter of 1964. There we observe similarities with the Bengali case highlighted by Partha Chatterjee (1989) in which modernity was made consistent with traditional culture, replacing Western patriarchy with a "new" traditional patriarchy designed to reform the Western degeneracy of women in a manner that balanced secular nationalist goals with traditional social forces (239–45). Similarly, in the Algerian case women's inferiority under colonialism was

blamed on poor interpretations of Islam to which women "naturally" reacted to become freer. However, that response occurred within existing structures and did not
fundamentally alter the status quo. "The war of liberation enabled the Algerian
woman to assert herself by carrying out responsibilities *side by side* with man and
taking part in the struggle. . . . In this sense the charter reveals its unwillingness
discursively to allow women's participation in the war to be the product of their
chosen activity. Women's historical action is legitimized by their proximity to men
. . . not by their agency" (Lazreg 1994, 62, emphasis in original).

Women's participation within the resistance was reinterpreted or reframed as
less authentic, allowing them to be politically peripheralized and their objectives, particularly with respect to social change, to be dismissed. Also, women's
participation was not viewed as individually chosen; rather, it was facilitated by
relationships with others or structural factors (such as poverty) that distanced
women from the violence they participated in, allowing society (and emergent
political leaders) to not only separate women from the citizenship rights inherent in combat roles, and to a lesser extent military service, but also placed
women's violence within a more palatable context.

PALESTINE: MILITANCY GROWS TO AVOID OTHERS' FATE

As early as the Balfour Declaration of 1917, educated women demonstrated and
opposed the limitations of Palestinian autonomy in their lands (Strum 1992, 28;
Kuttab 1993, 3). Between 1936 and 1939 women became more heavily involved
in both the military and civil aspects of resistance (Kuttab 1993, 3), although
women's activities were closely coordinated by the nationalist superstructure.
Women's roles expanded further by 1948 when they began to create and en-
large social structures to serve people during the war (e.g., social and medical
services) and when they joined the underground in Jordan. While "[t]hese developments created a new image of women's militancy though special cells were
created for women . . . gender segregation and the traditional division of labor,
where women's roles were sexually defined and limited to providing service support, were maintained" (Kuttab 1993, 4).

For Palestinian women (and women in many other settings), motherhood has
been synonymous not only with sustaining the family but also sustaining the
nation ("child") in the face of occupation. This phenomenon was furthered by
the locus of conflict that concentrated on the home and family, whereby "the
willingness to die has been more significant than the willingness to kill." This
endured that "the space of combat and violence was not defined as exclusively
male" in the Palestinian context, where "a willingness to sacrifice and an ability

to organize to fight . . . [meant that] women were not excluded on the grounds of unfitness" (Peteet 1997, 4). The very nature of the conflict (e.g., locus, goals) facilitated the inclusion of women first, and as most socially acceptable, as mothers but later as militants, corresponding to a wide array of cases including Ireland, Colombia, Sri Lanka, and Vietnam.

Despite early evidence of the range of women's political action, most observers date widening female roles to the Six-Day War, when women moved from being the "mothers" of the nation to more militant involvement, and the two intifadas have accelerated this process. Women's mobilization during the Six-Day War created female leaders and activists who subsequently formed women's committees that proved significant during the first intifada (Strum 1992). The earlier mobilization created the functional structures through which women were able to mobilize politically both during and after open conflict, and they also included "some of the first Palestinian women to politicize their individual female identities. In other words, they organized women as women, not as wives or mothers" (Hammami 1997, 165–66). However, Joost Hiltermann (1991) questions the overall importance of the committees for women's politicization, as the organizations achieved very few political outcomes. Rather, he argues that the true source of future women's power within the society would stem from their direct politicization in the streets (48–57), a theme embraced by younger women especially during the second intifada.

With the creation of groups such as the General Union of Palestinian Women (1969) and the spread of education, women had a public presence and ambition that coincided with secularist Palestinian leaders. For the latter, there was a growing awareness "that women constitute half the available manpower resource, one that a small, embattled nation cannot afford to waste. Women began to participate, publicly, in every crisis, from Wahdat camp in the 1970 Amman battles to the latest Israeli invasion in South Lebanon" (Antonius 1979, 28–30). While women were willing to participate, Arafat's conception of their public role did not correspond to societal norms, making full participation in the conflict difficult for women. Militant women became vanguards in the same way their feminist sisters were during the first intifada (Strum 1992, 273); in both instances, these public and nontraditional women were seen as being out of step with society and making life more difficult for other women.

Nevertheless, the early vanguard following the Six-Day War created a new image for women, as one activist woman noted, where there were now "two faces of woman: the strong mother, the home and the land, who encourages her son to fight, and the young woman, the beloved, who is herself a fighter and active in the struggle" (Antonius 1979, 31). A woman who fought during this period summed up her commitment: "I am a woman. . . . I feel the Palestine cause is mine and the work is mine. . . . Socially we haven't caught up with our political development—we're all walking on an advanced political leg and dragging a backward social leg behind, impeded and crippled" (30–39). These same sentiments would reemerge and magnify with the first and second intifadas.

The intifada is often viewed as the first real Palestinian mass mobilization—an organized resistance that has confronted Israel and an organized process that has shaken Palestinian society, particularly with respect to gender and generational issues (Kuttab 1993, 1). As a distinct stage in the national liberation struggle of the Palestinian people, the intifada "assumes that common interests unite all sectors and classes in society" (2), and since women are being affected they become part of the struggle. The all-encompassing features of the intifada have softened traditional societal cleavages and include gender, generation, class, and urban/rural populations, providing an opportunity for new forms of interaction and leadership. As in other national liberation settings, most notably Vietnam and Algeria, the war has become a people's war, and "[p]eople's war is a woman's war because women's participation is essential for success. The concept that every citizen must become a solider is a tested and tried tradition in revolutions and histories of self-defence against invaders. The front has been everywhere, a peaceful village or town one day may become a combat-zone the next so everyone is needed to contribute to the battle" (Kuttab 1993, 2).

During the first intifada, women's participation included three elements: martyrs, prisoners, and protesters (Kuttab 1993). Between December 1987 and December 1991, 11 percent of 903 martyrs were women; 1 out of 7 people hospitalized between December 1987 and November 1988 for shootings or beatings were women; and by July 1991, 3,000 women had been arrested and 18 were being held in administrative detention without charges (10). Based on numerous accounts of women's activities during the first intifada, a fourth category could be added; women also became men's protectors. As Strum (1992, 80) notes, "Women picked up the motto 'He's my son!' and extended their traditional function of protecting their families to protecting all men at demonstrations." She also quotes an unidentified scholar who commented that "it has become dangerous for men to participate in demonstrations or marches in the absence of women."

Women's mobilization during the first intifada went through two phases that built upon the structural developments that had occurred since 1967 but also was heavily influenced by complex social forces contending with escalating Israeli violence, heightened national expectations, and expanding female roles. Initially, women mobilized as either mothers or warriors, mirroring the events of the 1967 War but also involving more women in a wider array of roles. Women at this time mobilized for a number of reasons, including personnel shortages, public organizations such as neighborhood committees, and their support by the Palestinian leadership (Usher 1993, 38). However, after about a year the Hijab Campaign (Hammami 1997; Hammer 2000; Usher 1993) evolved as a complex reaction to secularist-Islamist competition over nationalism, women's mobilization by the secularist forces, and societal ambivalence over this expanding female public role. The result was that young "warrior" women, whose public but usually not violent activities challenged social norms of appropriate female behavior, if not emerging conflict-driven norms regarding manhood (Peteet 1994), were pushed out of the visible ("unveiled") public ("warrior") realm, and mothers expanded their symbolic and support roles. Thus, by the second stage of the first intifada, "only the 'mother' generation played a role in public while younger women were kept at home, the main argument . . . being for their safety" (Hammer 2000, 304).

Female activism did not lead to political power in the period of quasi-state-building that occurred in the wake of the 1993 Oslo Accord for several reasons. First, Islamists and the Palestinian Authority (PA) created a "matrix of domination" that limited women's roles (Jamal 2001) for many of the accomodationist and state consolidation reasons noted by Brand (1998). Being Palestinian and having Palestinian rights continued to mean having Palestinian male rights because they are conceptually masculinized (Massad 1995). Second, women's roles during the first intifada were generally fairly proscribed and limited, specifically with respect to violence. Finally, women's public mobilization outside of the mother framework lasted for only about a year.

Women's roles in the second intifada have continued to range along the mother-warrior continuum. However, evidence suggests that women have been more heavily attracted to a more activist "warrior" stance in this intifada than in earlier cases and that their roles were being expanded quite early during the uprising. These phenomena are largely responses to the deeper features of the second intifada, the scope of Israel's response, and a reaction to the first intifada. Beginning in late 2000 and then escalating throughout 2001, women were becoming more visible participants in a range of violent activities, including shootings and planting bombs, that presaged their role as suicide bombers. On January 28, 2002, Wafa Idris reportedly detonated a twenty-two-pound bomb in Jerusalem that killed her and an eighty-one-year-old Israeli man and injured more than one hundred others. While there remains skepticism about the incident because its method (not to mention its perpetrator) did not conform to "standard operating procedure," by February Israel declared that the incident was an intentional suicide bombing and the Fatah-linked Al-Aqsa Martyr's Brigade (Al Aqsa Brigades) claimed responsibility. Idris's attack was followed by three other female suicide bombings in as many months.[6] Consistent with observer scrutiny of female political violence, a great deal of attention was devoted to identifying the motive(s) of each woman, and less attention has been devoted to exploring the tactical significance of the actions.[7]

CONCLUSION

Women's mobilization in resistance and crisis settings has historically included a wide variety of roles, and as the struggle intensifies women are included in greater numbers through their own initiative, as a result of leaders' calculations, and through softening societal controls. However, the mobilization of women into politically violent settings is not traditionally precipitated by altered social structures. In nationalist settings, this has meant that nationalism for women is different than it is for men. Deniz Kandiyoti (1991) argues that for men nationalism is a rights expander but for women it is a rights limiter; while women are allowed to be linked to the nation, and indeed they are indelibly—if not bodily—part of the nation, they are not indelibly part of the polity. Women are "protected" citizens (429) through the extension of the social construction of "protected dependents" based on the tradition of male protection (*nafaqa*, or maintain) of women in exchange for female obedience (*ta'a*) (Hammami and Johnson 1999, 329). This "gender contract," not unlike Carol Pateman's (1988) sexual contract, is a formula that has been institutionalized in virtually every postnationalist setting.

Men generally view altered gender roles created by political crisis as temporary because the mobilization occurs within existing social parameters. Thus, women were demobilized in the United States and Britain after World War II, politically peripheralized in the wake of the Russian Revolution, and socially ostracized after the Vietnam War. In Palestine, economic necessity in rural areas has created the social structure upon which women's temporary mobilization into politically violent contexts is enabled, wherein "[w]omen frequently participated in 'men's work'; Palestinian men, like those everywhere else, normally played no role in the 'women's work' of childrearing, cooking, and housekeeping" (Strum 1992, 27).

Since the beginning of the Palestinian conflict, women have been twice-removed citizens. The two-tiered features of nationalism and citizenship were maintained following the first intifada, wherein women generally remained the (passive) symbols of Palestinian culture, specifically as mothers (Hammami and Johnson 1999, 321). The social construction of women's roles in society, and especially their identification with the private realm, must be reconciled with the need to mobilize women, albeit temporarily, into the public realm. Franz Fanon (1965) captured how Algerian women were mobilized in defense of the private and how their very location there is an act of nationalist resistance and action. However, by mobilizing as mothers in defense of the family, women invariably are unable to secure the greater sociopolitical rights they were fighting for (Chatterjee 1989; Kandiyoti 1991).

The political rights of the tiered system have been ascribed to the Islamic principle of complementarity, not equality; thus, women are to receive equivalent but not equal rights (Hammami and Johnson 1999, 315). Importantly, this tiered system is not culturally limited as it corresponds to political action as well. First-tiered citizenship is correlated with "active" behavior, most notably combat, and second-tiered citizenship is correlated with less active roles such as educating future citizens (Arnot 1997; Brindle and Arnot 1999; Burk 1995; Quicke 1992; Rose 2000). The implications of women's greater militarism during the second intifada remain unknown at this juncture, but earlier cases provide insight into the likely outcome.

While military service has theoretically been associated with citizenship claims for some minority groups, "[t]here are no historical precedents that show women transforming themselves from subjects into citizens through their exploits as soldiers" (Burk 1995, 510). Precedent from the U.S. experience is useful in examining this issue, as conceptualizations of citizenship at the country's founding trace back to Roman definitions wherein "the citizen was the man who is prepared to take up arms to defend the republic, and so, in reciprocal relations, had a right to claim a voice in the decision to resort to arms" (Kerber 1998, 26). Women in the United States were viewed as residents of the state, not members, in the same way as resident aliens and children. However, this would suggest that simply taking up arms would secure for women rights similar to those held by their male counterparts, which has not occurred because female citizenship is not merely linked to combat roles, suggesting further that neither are men's. To trace the idea further, note that Aristotle viewed women and slaves as inherently unable to exercise authority over others with the result that "[n]atural subjects can never be citizens" (Tétreault 2000, 75–76).

Women's exclusion from political rights through combat or other means in the United States was originally grounded in coverture, wherein married women were subsumed within and under the legal person of their husbands. Under coverture "a wife, like a slave, was civilly dead" (Pateman 1988, 119). The role of unmarried women is a bit more complex, mirroring similar discourses on "maiden warriors" and single militant women in other settings such as Sri Lanka, Colombia, Palestine, and Vietnam. Contradictions between marriage and warfare have been recognized by some scholars (Adams 1983, 1992) who cite patrifocal marital residency (wives leave their families to live with their husbands) as highly correlated with female exclusion from warfare, a finding consistent with coverture that continues to possess resonance to varying degrees in many societies today. More generally, women are assumed to owe their primary allegiance to their families, while the state comes in second (Kerber 1998, 237), raising the prospect of female loyalty during war. This has implications even for the broader conceptualizations of citizenship that provide equivalence between combat roles and allegiance (241). While citizenship has been located in the family in many Middle Eastern states (Joseph 2000, 24), and the same relational basis for citizenship is visible in many other societies (frequently relying on proof of paternity to establish citizenship obligations and rights), male status in this realm continues to imbue men with greater obligations and rights, both vis-à-vis the family and the state.

Women have participated in every American war, usually in support roles, and their participation has been viewed as particularly patriotic because it was voluntary. However, these two features—support roles and volunteerism versus conscription—are reflective of differential gendered obligations and resulting citizenship rights. Males overwhelmingly, and often exclusively, serve in combat roles because their maleness is synonymous with this aspect of citizenship. This is also true with conscription, as males possess the inherent obligation to take up arms corresponding both with their gender role as well as their civic role. When women fight, they do so voluntarily; they are not expected to fight and as such acquire none of the additional entitlements to accompany their service (Kerber 1998, 223), which is framed as corresponding with traditional female attributes of self-sacrifice and protection of the private (family) sphere. The very character of war that threatens the assumed private realm of women, and represents male failure to protect this dimension upon which their privilege is in part assumed to be based, represents an underlying paradox.

While combat roles have traditionally served as a rights expander in many social settings, the crucial determinant lies in the expectation of obligations to the state and thereby the subsequent expectations of rights resulting from the fulfillment of the obligation. Frequently, this conceptualization is gendered, as reflected in tiered citizenship wherein women are "protected citizens" and as such possess differing obligations to the state and rights vis-à-vis the state related to their status. Over time, many previously disenfranchised groups (e.g., landless, poor, racial or ethnic minorities) have secured political rights through military service, but overwhelmingly this was and remained a male enterprise. None of these groups were necessarily "protected" citizens; they were just excluded and unequal. The "protected" status of women in many societies is reflective of institutionalized gendered assumptions of female roles and behavior. Military combat in itself will likely be unable to undermine this "protected" status insofar as female mobilization remains framed within structures that retain, reinforce, and legitimate the assumption of female protection.

Nevertheless, women in a variety of settings and in this study most notably Palestine increasingly appear to associate militancy with future claims to citizenship, with respect to both Israel and their male counterparts. However, the young women who are willing to die for the cause, particularly as suicide bombers, with the thought that they or their sisters will receive fuller citizenship may very well be disappointed on several levels. Dead women cannot push for fuller rights, and those rights do not extend to the women they leave behind who did not "actively" serve. As one Mozambican female activist noted, ending colonialism was easier than getting rid of the social structures designed to maintain traditional female and male roles (Kuttab 1993). This same frustration is evident in the comments of a female committee member who admitted toward the end of the first intifada that "[u]nfortunately, women's role in the street has not been reflected in their social situation in general, as they are still under a great deal of social pressure; even women who are educated and economically independent or nationally and socially active still experience this pressure. Our journey is still a long one" (Strum 1992, 256).

Despite the fact that women have embraced and successfully fulfilled the action most closely associated with "maleness" (the warrior) that possesses cross-cultural meaning (Adams 1983; McCarthy 1994), they have not received the political advantages normally linked to the behavior and, in fact, have often suffered social ostracism. The political marginalization and social stigma associated with female militarism have been institutionalized in the postconflict and postcrisis structures that women were instrumental in securing. However, despite their optimism, political violence is not the panacea many young women seem to be hoping for, because it is not the method of political change that is ultimately significant, but rather the goal the action is directed toward. Until women are able and willing to address the social structures that perpetuate tiered citizenship, political violence will not secure their political ends.

NOTES

1. One widely utilized definition is Hoffman's (1998, 43), wherein terrorism is "the deliberate creation and exploitation of fear through violence or the threat of violence in the pursuit of political change."

2. The study of political violence will follow Ted Robert Gurr's (1970, 3–4) conceptualization, which

> refers to all collective attacks within a political community against the political regime, its actors—including competing political groups as well as incumbents—or its policies. The concept represents a set of events, a common prop-

erty of which is the actual or threatened use of violence, but the explanation is not limited to that property. The concept subsumes revolution, ordinarily defined as fundamental sociopolitical change accomplished through violence. It also includes guerilla wars, coups d'état, rebellions, and riots. Political violence is in turn subsumed under "force," the use or threat of violence by any party or institution to attain ends within or outside the political order. The definition is not based on a prejudgment that political violence is undesirable. Like the uses of violence qua force by the state, specific acts of political violence can be good, bad or neutral according to the viewpoint of the observer.

Notably absent from inclusion in Gurr's definition is terrorism, and he only briefly treats the topic later in this important study where he considers it a tactical use of violence oriented toward conversion and publicity (the "propaganda by deed") by using indirect and threatened violence (212–13). For the purposes of this analysis, "terrorism" will be subsumed within the political violence concept, except where its attributes utilizing Hoffman's (1998) definition are warranted. The rationale for subsuming terrorism within the political violence conceptual framework is to reduce some of the pejorative features of the term. Women's involvement with political violence for this analysis can include, but is not limited to, guerrilla and revolutionary movements, terrorist groups, rebellions, and rioting.

3. For example, with few exceptions women are seen as passive, private, and emotive; males are viewed as active, public, and rational. More importantly, the former traits are generally viewed rather negatively across cultures, the latter more positively. There is an enormous literature on this subject. Three illustrative readings are Eagly (1987), Goldberg (1993), and Kimmel (2000).

4. There are some notable exceptions, such as in Margarita, Venezuela (Cook 1992), and the aboriginal Australia (Burbank 1994).

5. Interestingly, both of these arguments also correspond to male political behavior. For example, in the Palestinian context, the failure of more grassroots and nonviolent political action in the first intifada has increased the perceived utility of violence during the second intifada.

6. Following Idris's apparent attack were three subsequent suicide bombings on behalf of Al-Aqsa Brigades in as many months by three young women, who put to rest many of the doubts surrounding Idris's action: on February 27, 2002, Darin Abu Aysheh detonated an explosive device at an Israeli checkpoint in the West Bank; on March 29, 2002, Ayat Akhras blew herself up at a grocery store in a Jerusalem neighborhood during a wave of Passover attacks; and on April 12, 2002, Andalib Takafka blew herself up in a crowded Jerusalem market, killing six and wounding more than fifty people. Abu Aysheh had approached Islamist groups to carry out the attack but was rejected and subsequently tasked by Al-Aqsa Brigades.

7. Idris's motives have been attributed to a variety of factors, including nationalist fervor, hopelessness and rage created by occupation, and the daily human casualties she witnessed as a medic with the Red Cross. Described as irreligious, her family's connection to Fatah (her brothers were members) were explored, and much was made of her status as a childless divorcée. Abu Aysheh's motives for the attack were linked to the death of a relative who

carried out a suicide mission in Tel Aviv the month before and her attending the funeral of one of the six Palestinian soldiers killed in Nablus, days before her own attack, where she dipped her handkerchief in his blood and vowed revenge. Akhras's attack possessed greater military and political significance, occurring within a wave of Passover attacks following Israeli attacks against Arafat's headquarters and helping prompt further widespread Israeli intervention in the West Bank during Spring 2002. However, her motive was also said to be personal, prompted by the death of a close male relative or neighbor, depending on the report. Takafka's attack was also strategically timed to undermine peace talks that were under way between U.S. Secretary of State Colin Powell and Israeli Prime Minister Ariel Sharon. Her motives have never been fully explained.

REFERENCES

Adams, David B. 1983. "Why There Are So Few Women Warriors." *Behavior Science Research* 18(3) (Fall): 196–212.

———. 1992. "Biology Does Not Make Men More Aggressive Than Women." In *Of Mice and Women*, ed. Kaj Björkqvist and Pirkko Niemelä, 17–25. San Diego: Academic Press.

Antonius, Soraya. 1979. "Fighting on Two Fronts: Conversations with Palestinian Women." *Journal of Palestine Studies* 5 (October): 26–45.

Arnot, Madeline. 1997. "'Gendered Citizenry:' New Feminist Perspectives in Education and Citizenship." *British Educational Research Journal* 23(3): 275–95.

Benson, Mike, Mariah Evans, and Rita Simon (1982). "Women as Political Terrorists." *Research in Law, Deviance and Social Control* 4: 121–30.

Björkqvist, Kaj, and Pirkko Niemelä, eds. 1992. *Of Mice and Women*. San Diego: Academic Press.

Brand, Laurie A. 1998. *Women, the State, and Political Liberation: Middle Eastern and North African Experiences*. New York: Columbia University Press.

Brindle, Patrick, and Madeleine Arnot. 1999. "'England Expects Every Man to Do His Duty': The Gendering of the Citizenship Textbook, 1940–1966." *Oxford Review of Education* 25(1/2) (March–June): 103–23.

Broido, Vera. 1977. *Apostles into Terrorists: Women and the Revolutionary Movement in the Russia of Alexander II*. New York: Viking Press.

Burbank, Victoria K. 1994. *Fighting Women: Anger and Aggression in Aboriginal Australia*. Berkeley: University of California Press.

Burk, James. 1995. "Citizenship Status and Military Service: The Quest for Inclusion by Minorities and Conscientious Objectors." *Armed Forces and Society* 21(4) (Summer): 503–29.

Campbell, Anne. 1995. "A Few Good Men: Evolutionary Psychology and Female Adolescent Aggression." *Ethology and Sociobiology* 16: 99–123.

———. 1999. "Staying Alive: Evolution, Culture, and Women's Intrasexual Aggression." *Behavioral and Brain Sciences* 22: 203–52.

Chatterjee, Partha. 1989. "The Nationalist Resolution of the Women's Question." In *Recasting Women: Essays in Colonial History*, ed. Kumkum Sangari and Sudesh Vaid, 233–53. New Delhi: Kali for Women.

Cook, H. B. Kimberley. 1992. "Matrifocality and Female Aggression in Margariteño Society." In *Of Mice and Women*, ed. Kaj Björkqvist and Pirkko Niemelä, 149–61. San Diego: Academic Press.

Cooper, H. H. A. 1979. "Woman as Terrorist." In *The Criminality of Deviant Women*, ed. Freda Adler and Rita Simon, 150–57. New York: Houghton Mifflin.

Cunningham, Karla J. 2003. "Cross-Regional Trends in Female Terrorism." *Studies in Conflict & Terrorism* 26(3) (May–June): 171–95.

Decker, Jeffrey Louis. 1990. "Terrorism (Un)Veiled: Frantz Fanon and the Women of Algiers." *Cultural Critique* 17 (Winter 1990–91): 177–95.

Eagly, A. H. 1987. *Sex Differences in Social Behavior: A Social-Role Interpretation*. Hillsdale, N.J.: Lawrence Erlbaum Associates.

Enloe, Cynthia. 1983. *Does Khaki Become You? The Militarisation of Women's Lives*. Boston: South End Press.

Fangen, Katrine. 1997. "Separate or Equal? The Emergence of an All-Female Group in Norway's Rightist Underground." *Terrorism and Political Violence* 9(3) (Autumn): 122–64.

Fanon, Franz. 1965. *Studies in a Dying Colonialism*, trans. Haakon Chevalier. New York: Grove Press.

Galvin, Deborah M. 1983. "The Female Terrorist: A Socio-Psychological Perspective." *Behavioral Sciences and the Law* 1(2): 19–32.

Georges-Abeyie, Daniel E. 1983. "Women as Terrorists." In *Perspectives on Terrorism*, ed. Lawrence Zelic Freedman and Yonah Alexander, 71–84. Wilmington, Del.: Scholarly Resources, Inc.

Goldberg, Steven. 1993. *Why Men Rule: A Theory of Male Dominance*. Chicago and La Salle, Ill.: Open Court.

Gurr, Ted Robert. 1970. *Why Men Rebel*. Princeton, N.J.: Princeton University Press.

Halpern, Micah D. 1992. "Middle East Women." *Pravda*. http://english.pravda.ru/hotspots/2002/05/16/28857.html.

Hammami, Rema. 1997. "Palestinian Motherhood on the West Bank and Gaza Strip." In *The Politics of Motherhood: Activist Voices from Left to Right*, ed. Alexis Jetter, Annelise Orleck, and Diana Taylor, 161–68. Hannover: University Press of New England.

Hammami, Rema, and Penny Johnson. 1999. "Equality with Difference: Gender and Citizenship in Traditional Palestine." *Social Politics* 6 (Fall): 314–43.

Hammer, Juliane. 2000. "Prayer, Hijab and the Intifada: The Influence of the Islamic Movement on Palestinian Women." *Islam and Christian-Muslim Relations* 11(3) (October): 299–320.

Hasso, Frances S. 1998. "The 'Women's Front': Nationalism, Feminism, and Modernity in Palestine." *Gender and Society* 12(4) (August): 441–65.

Hiltermann, Joost R. 1991. "The Women's Movement during the Uprising." *Journal of Palestine Studies* 20(3) (Spring): 48–57.

Hoffman, Bruce. 1998. *Inside Terrorism*. New York: Columbia University Press.

Jamal, Amal. 2001. "Engendering State-Building: The Women's Movement and Gender-Regime in Palestine." *Middle East Journal* 55(2) (Spring): 256–76.

Joseph, Suad. 2000. "Gendering Citizenship in the Middle East." In *Gender and Citizenship in the Middle East*, ed. Suad Joseph, 3–30. Syracuse, NY: Syracuse University Press.

Kandiyoti, Deniz. 1991. "Identity and Its Discontents: Women and the Nation." *Millennium: Journal of International Studies* 20(3): 429–43.

Kerber, Linda K. 1998. *No Constitutional Right to Be Ladies: Women and the Obligations of Citizenship*. New York: Hill and Wang.

Kimmel, Michael S. 2000. *The Gendered Society*. New York: Oxford University Press.

Kuttab, Eileen S. (1993). "Palestinian Women in the Intifada: Fighting on Two Fronts." *Arab Studies Quarterly* 15(2) (Spring): 69–85.

Lazreg, Marnia. 1994. *The Eloquence of Silence: Algerian Women in Question*. New York: Routledge.

Massad, Joseph. 1995. "Conceiving the Masculine: Gender and Palestinian Nationalism." *Middle East Journal* 49(3) (Summer): 467–83.

McCarthy, Barry. 1994. "Warrior Values: A Socio-Historical Survey." In *Male Violence*, ed. John Archer, 105–20. London, New York: Routledge.

Neuburger, Luisella De Cataldo, and Tiziana Valentini. 1996. *Women and Terrorism*, trans. Leo Michael Hughes. New York: St. Martin's Press.

O'Donnell, Guillermo A., and Philippe C. Schmitter. 1986. *Transitions from Authoritarian Rule: Tentative Conclusions about Uncertain Democracies*. Baltimore: Johns Hopkins University Press.

Pateman, Carole. 1988. *The Sexual Contract*. Cambridge, UK: Polity Press.

Peteet, Julie. 1997. "Icons and Militants: Mothering in the Danger Zone." *Signs* 23(1) (Autumn): 103–29.

Powers, Thomas. 1971. *Diana: The Making of a Terrorist*. Boston: Houghton-Mifflin Company.

Quicke, John. 1992. "Individualism and Citizenship: Some Problems and Possibilities." *International Studies in Sociology of Education* 2(2): 147–63.

Rose, Sonya O. 2000. "Women's Rights, Women's Obligations: Contradictions of Citizenship in World War II Britain." *European Review of History* 7(2) (Autumn): 277–89.

Roy, R., and A. C. Korteweg. 1999. "Women's Movements in the Third World: Identity, Mobilization, and Autonomy." *Annual Review of Sociology* 25: 47–51.

———. 1999. "Is Political Conflict a Setback or Springboard to Gender Equality? Reflections on Women's Struggles in Israel/Palestine and the North of Ireland." *Gender, Armed Conflict and Political Violence*. Washington, D.C.: The World Bank (June 10–11), 1–9. www.worldbank.org/gender/events/Sharoni.doc.

Steel, Jayne. 1998. "Vampira: Representations of the Irish Female Terrorist." *Irish Studies Review* 6(3) (December): 273–84.

Strum, Phillipa. 1992. *The Women Are Marching: The Second Sex and the Palestinian Revolution*. New York: Lawrence Hill Books.

Tétreault, Mary Ann. 2000. "Gender, Citizenship, and State in the Middle East." In *Citizenship and the State in the Middle East*, ed. Nils A. Butenschon, Uri Davis, and Manuel Hassassian, 70–87. Syracuse, NY: Syracuse University Press.

Usher, Graham. 1993. "Palestinian Women, the Intifada and the State of Independence: An Interview with Rita Giacaman." *Race & Class* 34(3) (January–March): 31–43.

Weinberg, Leonard, and William Lee Eubank. 1987. "Italian Women Terrorists." *Terrorism: An International Journal* 9(3): 241–62.

PART TWO

Middle East

6 Prospects for Democracy in Islamic Countries

Currently, no democratic country with an Islamic majority exists. In his *Patterns of Democracy*, Arend Lijphart (1999) deems thirty-six countries to be stable democracies during the past twenty years. Only five of them are geographically located in Asia or Africa (Botswana, India, Israel, Japan, Mauritius), and none has an Islamic majority (though India has a Muslim minority of some one hundred million).

When the Soviet empire crumbled, democracy took root the quickest in countries with a Catholic-Protestant background. It did so more hesitatingly in Orthodox countries and not at all in Islamic countries. Fond hopes lasted for a long time in the West that Kyrgystan would be an island of democracy in Central Asia, but by now even the greatest optimists must have given up such hope. In the Balkans, democracy is fragile in predominantly Muslim Albania, and in Bosnia and Kosovo it has survived only thanks to the bayonets of international peace-keeping forces. Further east, note that India has maintained democracy pretty steadily while Pakistan, with the same British colonial inheritance, has oscillated between short-lived attempts at democracy and longer periods of dictatorship. Separated from Pakistan, Bangladesh has followed a similar course. Since achieving independence, Indonesia did not make it to democracy for fifty years, and democracy there is not yet out of the woods.

Turkey has rehearsed for democracy for more than eighty years, but dress rehearsal is still to come. Iran has an elected parliament and president, but major decisions are made by nonelected clerics. Among the Arabic countries, the half-Christian Lebanon had hopes for democracy forty years ago, but it has moved backwards. South of the Sahara, we do not encounter anything close to stable democracy, be it in Muslim-majority or other countries, until we reach Botswana.

One may therefore ask with good reason whether a culture based on Islam is as unsuitable a ground for democracy as is the Sahara for agriculture. Before drawing such a conclusion, however, one should take a look at the broader history of democracy, brief as it is, focusing on Catholic countries in particular.

CATHOLICISM, DEMOCRACY, AND ISLAM

Seventy-five years ago, in 1928, democracy may have looked like a peculiarity of Protestant culture, finding little fertile ground in Catholic lands. The entire Protestant Europe was democratic, from Britain, the Netherlands, and Switzerland to Latvia, Estonia, and Finland, while among the Catholic countries this was the case only in Belgium, France, and Czechoslovakia. Democracy had recently crumbled in Catholic Italy, Portugal, Hungary, Poland, and Lithuania, and it was shaky in Austria and Spain. The Americas offered a similar contrast between the predominantly Protestant and democratic North America and proneness to dictatorship in Catholic Latin America.

Of course, the picture looked different seven years later, in 1935, when the predominantly Protestant Germany had given up on democracy and when Estonia and Latvia followed in the footsteps of Poland and Lithuania. But even so, the shrinking island of democracy remained overwhelmingly Protestant, ranging from the British dominions to the Nordic countries. In the 1930s, one could have presented a conference paper titled "Prospects for Democracy in Catholic Countries" and concluded that such chances were slim.

As of now, the picture has changed altogether. Democracy tends to look like a characteristic of the entire Protestant-Catholic cultural area, from the Mediterranean to South America. Of course, democracy also extends to Japan, India, Israel, and Greece—and there are gaps in South America. The point, however, is that prospects for democracy in Catholic countries has become a moot issue.

As communism crumbled in Central and Eastern Europe, the first free elections produced a clear pattern. Democrats won in traditionally Catholic-Protestant countries, while communists survived in Orthodox and Islamic countries. The difference became blurred later on, especially on Croatia's account. But economic reform indicators preserved the gradient, from Catholic-Protestant countries to the Orthodox ones and on to the Islamic. By one rating (Cameron 2000), Catholic-Protestant countries ranged from 29.5 points in Hungary down to 24.0 points in Croatia, while Islamic countries ranged from a mere 22.7 in Kyrgystan to a pitiful 11.4 in Turkmenia.

The Russian Federation came in at 20.3 points. Of course, market economy is not the same as democracy, but there is some connection. Regarding political and individual freedom in 1999 to 2000, Cameron (2000) gave 12 to 13 points to all post-communist Catholic-Protestant countries, except Croatia (7 points), while the score in Orthodox and Islamic countries ranged from 11 points in Romania to 1 point in the realm of the megalomaniac boss of Turkmenia. Russia rated 6 points. Democracy hardly has persisted anywhere for more than two centuries, if that much. Against the backdrop of humankind's fifty centuries of written history, future historians may well consider it mere chance that democracy first took root in Protestant countries. Instead of Protestantism, one might as well ascribe democracy to a Germanic influence, including formerly Celtic areas colonized by Anglo-Saxons or named after the Germanic Frankish tribes. A few centuries from now, who will care that democracy tended to take root in Catholic countries in the mid- to late twentieth century?

In that light, what are the chances that Orthodox countries and then Islamic ones could surmount the threshold the Catholic countries surmounted during my lifetime? Which Islamic countries might lead? Potential favorable factors might include the following:

1. Geographical closeness to Europe. It strengthens hope for Bosnia, Albania, and Turkey but also for Algeria, Tunisia, and Morocco, due to the persistent influence of the French language.

2. Use of Latin script, which reduces the psychological-cultural distance to Europe. This factor favors not only Bosnia, Albania, and Turkey but also Indonesia.

3. Low corruption, given that heavy corruption may make people wish for a strong hand at the helm. The Elite Integrity Index, which is the reverse of the Perceived Corruption Index and ranges from 0 to 10, places Malaysia, Tunisia, and Jordan highest among Islamic countries, with a middling 5 points (Sandholtz and Gray 2000; Sandholtz and Taagepera 2003). They are followed at a distance by Morocco (around 4 points) and Turkey and Egypt (around 3.5 points). All other predominantly Islamic countries are below 2.5 points. The aforementioned Albania has 2.4 and Indonesia 1.8, while figures for Algeria and Bosnia are lacking. Bangladesh (0.8 points) is perceived as the world's most corrupt country.

4. Current strength of democratic grass roots. Here I would place Iran ahead of countries such as Turkey and Indonesia where democracy seems an elite idea. They are followed by Morocco, Malaysia, Pakistan, Jordan, and maybe others where elections hover in between real and fake.

On the basis of these four considerations above, the following coarse rankings emerge in regard to the current stage of predemocracy (real or fake) in Islamic countries:

1. Turkey, Bosnia, and Albania;
2. Indonesia, Malaysia, Tunisia, and Jordan;
3. Iran and Morocco; and
4. the rest.

However, my final gut-feeling ranking is somewhat different.

ELEMENTS OF DEMOCRACY IN NON-ARAB ISLAMIC COUNTRIES

The label "Islamic" makes some of us think of Arab countries, given that Arabic is the language of the Koran. Although the present Arab vernaculars differ from classical Arabic as much as Spanish does from Latin, the Koran still gives the Arab countries a central place in the Islamic world. This Arab core has the strongest self-awareness and seems the least willing to accept Western ideas, democracy included. Yet, an overwhelming majority of Muslims live in Pakistan, India, Bangladesh, and Indonesia.

Location, Latin alphabet, and desire to participate in European well-being give hope to Bosnia and Albania (if it were not for corruption!). Turkey has desired to join Europe ever since Ataturk's reforms, but more at the elite level than the mass levels. Setbacks to democracy have been so numerous that even the carrots offered by the European Union may not change Turkey soon. Pakistan and Bangladesh lack even that carrot, and their attempts at democracy have repeatedly drowned in corruption. Indonesia's present attempt faces the same challenge. East of Iran, multicultural Malaysia looks the most promising, at least in terms of limited corruption. However, the Malaysian elites seem afraid that democracy might upset the ethnic-religious balance. And this was the consideration that delayed reforms in the Soviet Union until it was too late.

Paradoxically, I have high hopes for a country that, at least in the United States, is viewed as the worst example of Islamic extremism—Iran. True, supreme power is in the hands of unelected clerics, but underneath that superstructure genuine presidential and parliamentary elections take place. These institutions lack power, but electoral victory requires superiority over the clerics in local grassroots organizing. There are countries where democracy has been introduced by the elites (Turkey) or imposed through student demonstrations (Indonesia), while a civic society is missing. In contrast, the struggle with the clerics in Iran seems to represent tremendous grassroots schooling in democracy. If and when democracy wins in Iran, its society might be as well prepared for it as the Spanish society was at Franco's twilight.

ELEMENTS OF DEMOCRACY IN ARAB COUNTRIES

Let us not forget that not all "Arab countries" are purely Islamic. Christianity exists in Lebanon, Egypt (the Copts), and elsewhere. Nor are these countries entirely Arabic. A large portion of Moroccans and Algerians speak Berber at home, and the language landscape becomes quite varied in Sudan and beyond, despite the elite attempts to go Arab. This said, I resign myself to using the term "Arab countries" in its customary broad sense.

Most of these countries have held elections at least occasionally, but all too often these have been fake elections orchestrated by the government in favor of one party. Formal choice among several parties was available during the 1990s in Morocco, Algeria, Tunisia, Egypt, Lebanon, Palestine, Jordan, Kuwait, and Yemen. But genuine competition has been sadly limited. Marsha Posusney (2000) has characterized the conditions with two terms: *taddaxxul* (intervention) prior to elections and *tazwir* (falsification of results) thereafter. These tactics make it certain that the existing power-holders do not risk replacement. The legislative and judicial powers are firmly under control. Opposition parties find it difficult to achieve legal status, reach the media, and carry out campaigning. Voters are pressured to vote for the government party. Advances toward *ta'adudiyya*, a multiparty system, are conceivable but difficult.

Posusney (2000) has made the argument that inventing peculiar electoral rules is part of governmental games. A favorite rule is that winner takes all—in single-seat districts or even in multiseat districts, where all seats go to the largest party—and *taddaxxul* makes certain that the winner is the government party. If proportional representation rules are used, they are combined with a high countrywide votes threshold. In Egypt in 1984, the threshold was 8 percent—and all votes for parties failing to surpass it were transferred to the successful. As a result, the government party supposedly received 73 percent of the votes and most assuredly pocketed 87 percent of the seats. The rules of the game have varied in Egypt, but the government party's seat share never has fallen below 79 percent. Along with co-opted "independents," it rose as high as 94 percent in 1995.

When the king of Jordan deemed to have elections in 1989, after a hiatus of twenty-two years, the rules fired back. They turned out to favor the Muslim Brotherhood and other Islamics hostile to the king (and to democracy), giving them 42 percent of the seats on the basis of a much lower share of votes. So, for the next elections in 1993, the government made rules that favored tribal fractionalization, thus cutting the Islamist representation down to 25 percent.

In Palestine in 1996, Fatah received 30 percent of the votes but 58 percent of the seats. In southern Yemen in 1993, the socialists received 57 percent of the votes and 95 percent of the seats. In Tunisia in 1989, the ruling Democratic Constitutional Coalition won *all* the seats; in 1994 it was down to 88 percent, only because 12 percent were reserved for other parties. In 1999, this reserved share was even raised to 20 percent—generously, and without any risk to the government, thanks to *taddaxxul* and *tazwir*.

The Algerian presidential elections of 1999 started out well with seven candidates, including some who addressed the Kabyl Berber voters in their own language. The press looked free, and the general tone of the campaign was constructive. Then came *taddaxxul*, some sort of intervention that made six candidates give up. On the eve of the elections, the spokesperson for one of the candidates announced, in the name of six candidates: "We withdraw from the presidential elections and do not recognize their outcome" (Bouandel 2001). The sole remaining candidate, the army favorite Abdelaziz Bouteflika, raked in 73.8 percent of the votes. The remaining 26.2 percent of the votes were for the other candidates, despite their withdrawal. Officially, participation was 61 percent, but some journalists estimated it no higher than 30 percent.

Morocco has the longest record of multiparty elections—from 1963 on. Yet whenever the king's men risked losing, the king dissolved the assembly and changed the rules. In 1993, the two main opposition parties avoided competition and, together, won 45 percent of the directly elected seats. In 1997, they even surpassed the governmental bloc. By this time, however, an indirectly elected second chamber was in place, where the government enjoyed an advantage of 76 to 44 representatives. Nonetheless, Morocco may still offer the most hope among the Islamic Arabic countries. (I will bypass the fuzzy half-Christian Lebanon.) French influence remains strong in Morocco, which means contact with the democratic world. Corruption is relatively limited. The oldest opposition party, Istiqlal (Freedom), has survived ever since the times of French occupation. In contrast to neighboring Algeria, the risk seems low that antidemocratic fundamentalists could carry free and fair elections in Morocco.

Distorted electoral rules and practices present the opposition parties with a dilemma: Do they get more out of boycott or participation? They have tried both. If democracy is to come to the Arab world, Posusney (2000) feels that reforms are needed that go beyond formally allowing opposition parties to run. Respect for individual and group rights must become reality. The overriding power of the executive must be hemmed in. In monarchies, executive power must shift to elected bodies.

As of now, Arab rulers have not introduced multiparty elections so as to proceed toward such goals but rather to preempt them. Still, some of those limited elections may unintentionally lead toward democracy. By tying their legitimacy to electoral campaigns, the autocratic rulers give the democratic activists not only an opportunity to participate in elections but also to protest their limitations.

SHARI'A AND WORLD VALUES

When facing past attempts to explain social reality in the Soviet Union through Marxist holy scripts, I countered with a recommendation to try to explain Western society on the basis of the Bible. Such attempts are hopeless. Voluminous holy scripts always contain contradictory dictums that can be used to explain and justify anything, from slavery to freedom. Islam differs in that the Koran is complemented by shari'a, a detailed collection of behavioral and administrative norms. To base state administration solely on the Bible or the Koran, without additions that fill in essential blanks in the holy script, is not possible. However, in principle, basing state administration on the shari'a is possible. Such attempts have been made in the past and are likely to continue. This particularity has been pointed out to argue that democracy and Islam are contradictory, so that one cannot develop as long as the other prevails.

I can think of more creative developments. The Western world has been able to preserve a Christian format while no longer literally believing that the world was created in seven days. If so, then selective interpretations may occur in other cultures, too. I do not know how Muslims north of the polar circle, where the sun does not set for an entire month, carry out their Ramadan fast during which eating and drinking are forbidden before the sun sets. Never mind; they will find a solution. Justifying democracy in Islamic terms, once the need for it is felt, is far easier. Is there such a need?

Yes and no. One may well desire the fruits of democracy but not be willing to pay the price in terms of cultural change. The results of a World Values Survey (Inglehart and Long 2002) place the Islamic and African countries in a very special location. Answers to this large set of questions organize themselves, to a remarkable extent, along two axes: traditional versus secular-rational values, and survival concerns versus self-expression. Stable democracies tend to be high both on secular-rational values and self-expression. Latin America is traditional and moderately high on self-expression. Postcommunist countries (and South Korea) are secular-rational but stress survival over self-expression. Muslim and African countries are both traditional *and* survival-oriented—which places them in the opposite corner, compared to stable democracies. Partial exceptions are postcommunist Albania, Bosnia, and Azerbaijan that hover between traditional and secular-rational values. The least survival-oriented Islamic countries are Turkey, Indonesia, and Iran, but they too fall markedly short of even the most survival-oriented countries among Lijphart's (1999) thirty-six stable democracies—Colombia, Venezuela, and Portugal.

Self-expression values load heavily on gender equality and tolerance. Secular-rational values go light on belief in god, faith, obedience, and national pride. If such values look conducive to democracy, would the Islamic peoples be willing to shift in such a direction, or would they feel that possible material gains would not offset the loss of their very identity? Democracy requires not only an abstract will but certain skills in interpersonal transactions. Are the present values in Islamic countries conducive to such skills, where democracy is proclaimed? This may be the crux of Turkey's delayed democratization. The democratic shell has been around for eighty years now, but Turkish values have remained traditional and survival-oriented.

I started out with a question that could have been posed seventy-five years ago: Is democracy possible in Catholic countries? We now can answer "yes," but is it that democracy has been adjusted to Catholic values or that Catholics have adjusted their values to be more conducive to democracy? I suspect that West European Catholics seventy-five years ago were appreciably more traditional and survival-oriented than they are now—more like today's Poland or Brazil. Has their democracy been stable because their values shifted, or has practice of democracy caused their values to shift? It may be a two-way street.

In this light, I have to conclude that democracy is possible in Islamic lands, too. But what is possible is not always inevitable. The fruits of democracy in terms of well-being may well have an appeal in Islamic countries. But do they have the skills needed to implement democracy, and are they willing to shift their values in the direction conducive to such skills? Much will depend on a demonstration effect in one country. If I had to name three top candidates pre-9/11, these would be Bosnia, Morocco, and Iran.

While change is possible, it comes at a price. Some givens in the history of civilizations have considerable inertia.

REFERENCES

Bouandel, Y. 2001. "The Presidential Elections in Algeria, April 1999." *Electoral Studies* 20: 157–63.

Cameron, D. R. 2000. "Constitutions, Institutions and Elections: The Politics of Economic Reform in the Post-Communist World." Paper presented at the American Political Science Association annual meeting, Washington, D.C., August 31–September 3.

Inglehart, R., and K. Long. 2002. "Clash of Civilizations or Trauma of Modernization? Support for Democracy in Islamic Societies." Paper presented at the annual meeting of the Midwest Political Science Association, Chicago, 25–28 April.

Lijphart, A. 1999. *Patterns of Democracy*. New Haven and London: Yale University Press.

Posusney, M. P. 2000. "Multi-Party Elections in the Arab World: Institutional Engineering and Oppositional Strategies." Paper presented at the American Political Science Association annual meeting, Washington, D.C., August 31–September 3.

Sandholtz, W., and M. Gray. 2000. "International Norms and National Corruption." Manuscript, University of California, Irvine.

Sandholtz, W., and R. Taagepera. 2003. "Corruption, Culture, and Communism." Manuscript, University of California, Irvine.

7 Political Violence and Terrorism in Islamdom

In addressing the nation after the attacks of September 11, 2001, President George W. Bush said, "Islam is a religion of peace." Given the circumstances, this was probably a statesmanlike and humane thing to say. It would have been foolish to put the United States in a position of adversarial relationship with a great world religion, and it was both wise and humane for the president to head off the natural human impulse to view American Muslims with suspicion or hostility because of what their co-religionists had done in the name of their religion.

As an empirical description of contemporary Islamdom,[1] however, the president's statement is seriously deficient. The world of Islam today is not at peace. First, and most importantly, it is not at peace with itself. And because the ramifications of its coexistence with Western civilization are inextricably woven into the issues that drive its internal disputes, a peaceful relationship between Islamdom and the West is not the present condition, and will not be so for some time.

The terrorist acts that hit the United States in 1993, with the bombing of the World Trade Center, and more massively on September 11, 2001, were unique only in that the U.S. homeland had never before been subjected to this sort of attack from abroad. We and other industrial nations have had our own homegrown radicals who have sometimes resorted to violence in the hope of shaking the system and forcing it to respond to their actions. Clearly, terrorism is not simply a resort of the weak—that is, something that occurs only in weak polities. In modern times, Italy has had its Red Brigades, Germany its Baader-Meinhof group, and Japan its Red Army Fraction, and of course Britain has had the Irish Republican Army (IRA) in its various permutations. Except for the IRA and the Basque ETA, however, terrorist episodes in the stronger polities have not so far had any sort of base in the public opinion of their respective countries.[2] Thus, even when the event itself is spectacular—for instance, the kidnap and murder of the former Italian Prime Minister Aldo Moro—it remains an isolated event, a one-day wonder that proves to be no more than a temporary nuisance, utterly failing to trigger the follow-on effects hoped for by the perpetrators.

The terrorism emanating from those parts of the world where Islam is the predominant religion is quite another matter. It clearly does have a mass base in important sectors of public opinion there. The various actions have spanned a considerable period of time and have undeniably impacted the internal situations of the societies from which they spring. Likewise, they have had resonances across state borders—and even across oceans—that most of the terrorists of the strong polities could only dream of.

Obviously, at the present time, the threat of terrorist acts directed against the U.S. homeland and against U.S. interests and agents abroad emanates from Islamdom. But the United States is by no means the sole—or even the principal—target of this terrorism. Terrorism has occurred throughout the Muslim world, as evidenced by bombings in Indonesia in the fall of 2002. India too has had its experiences. Nevertheless, the terrorism that currently threatens the United States originates from within the world of Arab Islamdom.

Why a particular person commits a terrorist act is a matter of individual life experience and psychology, and this topic is beyond the scope of this essay. Our concern is with a group phenomenon, where the actor is an agent acting somehow at the behest or direction of the group. This definition eliminates the actions of the Oklahoma City bomber Timothy McVeigh and the Washington-area sniper John Allen Muhammed from the list of terrorist events, insofar as no evidence has yet surfaced that in either of these cases the act was directed by, or part of the planning of, any group or association with which the perpetrator had a relationship. While these two individuals may perhaps have been self-appointed identifiers with some cause or other, their cases seem to present a different problem from the highly organized collective action that produced the events of September 11, 2001.

Why do organized acts of terrorism and other kinds of political violence occur so frequently today in Arab societies as well as being projected outward? The cause is their self-perceived failure to solve the problem of modernization, to keep up with the rest of the world. This paper explores the deep resentment and sense of victimization this generates. We make four assumptions about the dynamics of the contemporary situation.

First, we cannot understand the contemporary Arab predicament without taking into account the deep cultural drivers at work in that world, of which the greatest is the religion of Islam.

Second, Islamdom, and especially the Arab part of it, is undergoing an intense and far-reaching inner crisis right now, and the tensions produced by this are responsible for the terrorist acts that emanate from the Arab world.

Third, these inner-Arab tensions (to a considerable extent also at work in the non-Arab part of Islamdom, which constitutes at least 80 percent of the whole) must be worked out by the Islamic peoples themselves—there is little that we can do directly to affect the outcome, even though our existence as an alternate model of a way of life is deeply intertwined with the Arab predicament.

Finally, between the worldviews and values of the societies that have grown out of Western Christendom and the values and worldviews of the Muslim world, there are almost certainly some ineradicable incommensurabilities. Even so, this does not commit us to the view that Muslims are exotic creatures, somehow outside of the purview of universal human experience. In fact, some of the feelings of discontent now raging within the Arab world are by no means unknown to contemporary Western societies. Some of the same pressures are to be found in our own political life.

ISLAM AS THE DOMINANT FORCE

Since at least 90 percent of the people in the Arab countries consider themselves to be Muslims, and since their public discourse is saturated with the rhetoric of Islam (to say nothing of the rhetoric of the militants and avowed terrorists or jihadis of that world), it might seem that giving pride of place to the religion and its derivative social phenomena, as against all the other possible drivers at work in Islamdom, is simply laboring the obvious.

Nevertheless, this is a disputed point in some circles. Not only that, but those Western scholars who hold the view expressed above are excoriated as, at best, taking an arrogant and patronizing attitude toward the Arab peoples and, at worst, being outright hostile to their interests. In either case, scholars' understanding of their subject is deemed sadly lacking.

The best known exponent of this view is Edward Said, who first expressed his ideas in his 1978 book *Orientalism* and argued his points thereafter in various other venues. His views have been highly influential and have been taken up by many others. Said was born to a Christian identity in a family with roots and relatives in what would now be called the Palestinian Arab community. Although he does not seem to have actually spent much time in that community, aside from visits to relatives who in fact lived there, he did, in his mature years, choose to become a passionate advocate of the Palestinian cause and a fierce opponent of the Zionist project. He resigned his position as a member of the

Palestinian National Council in protest against the Oslo Agreement, for the apparent reason that the Palestinian Liberation Organization (PLO) agreed therein to the principle of a two-state solution—meaning that the Jewish state was to be accepted as permanent.

Said is a scholar who comes from the Arab world—but that does not make him a scholar *of* that world anymore than being born in the United States and to the English language means that one necessarily has a deep understanding of American history, political culture, intellectual history, and so on. He was, in fact, a professor of English who spent most of his career at Columbia University, and he gave no indication in his writings that he had devoted the time and effort it would have taken to have established himself as a profound scholar of Islam, Arab culture, or Arab-Islamic intellectual history. The work that brought him fame, *Orientalism*, is not a piece of scholarship on the Middle East and its issues; rather, it is a harsh critique directed against many of the scholars who *are* specialists and have a deep knowledge of the area.

Deploying the methodology of "lit-crit" postmodernism, mobilizing ideas from Foucault and Gramsci with a bit of Franz Fanon thrown in, along with the sort of antibourgeois, anticapitalist sensibility that is fairly typical of the Western left intelligentsia, Said rages through the serious Western writing on Middle Eastern topics, from the nineteenth century to the present, and does not like much of what he finds. It is important to note that although his own expertise is that of a man of letters, he does not limit his attack to those Western writers who specialize in literature and language studies of the area. Intellectual historians and those who presume to present history-based interpretations of Arab culture and political experience in the last two centuries also come in for his ire. Indeed, they are his real targets. He seeks to discredit much, if not most, of the received serious Western writing on the area.

One result of the wide currency of his ideas—and the reason for this exposition of his views here—is that advancing an interpretation of the contemporary Arab predicament that finds Islam and the culture it has created to be a central determinant of contemporary events has become a very sensitive matter. Such interpretation brings a charge from Said and his many followers (who include many scholars in the social sciences) that one has committed the dreaded sins of "orientalism" or "essentialism."

Said's argument has of course been subjected to a vigorous rebuttal, and a sizable literature has come into being. This, however, is not our topic here. The reader who wishes to pursue it further is referred to *Orientalism: History, Theory and the Arts*, by the British scholar John M. Mackenzie (1995). In any case, one of the effects of Said's work is that it is necessary to be as clear as possible about the chain of thought when one essays to establish a link among the history and dynamics of the religion of Islam, its cultural surround, and the contemporary situation in Islamdom—as we do here. And whether one accepts Said's thesis or not, this is, after all, not an unreasonable demand.

ISLAM AND POLITICS

The Prophet Muhammad, whom Muslims believe was chosen by God to be the Messenger who would transmit God's revelation to the world, was Prophet. He was the leader of a religious community, the leader of a political community, and the director and leader of his community's military ventures—all these roles in one person. This has set the pattern ever since; Islamdom does not have the division of realms between the sacred and secular that Christianity developed naturally, as it evolved from obscure Jewish sect into the official religion of the Roman Empire. In the eyes of Islam, God's revelation, as embodied in the Koran and in the record of the divinely directed doings of the Messenger and his immediate associates, has given man all the guidance he needs to find the right path in all his endeavors. Whatever the activity of mind or hand—private, social, or public—the revelation, rightly understood, provides an answer; there is no area of human thought or activity that it does not encompass. A slogan commonly deployed by contemporary Islamists is "Islam is the Answer." This unity of all things is called *tawhid*.

Obviously, then, the conduct of political affairs can only be justly done under the prescriptions contained in the revelation. In the vocabulary of political science, the legitimation of the polity comes, and can only come, from God's directions to mankind.

How has this conception played out in the fourteen centuries or so of political experience in Islamdom? Is it really true that all politics has been conducted according to understood Islamic principles? In the instance where this has been demonstrably not the case, has this invariably led to resistance and rebellion? Not at all. Most, if not all, political conduct in the history of Islamdom is explainable in terms of the same secular determinants we would use to describe politics anywhere else. In practice, Muslim religious scholars (the ulema) have evolved a political theory according to which the evils of serious political discord are so great that it is advisable to suffer even the bad ruler who is not guided by Islamic precepts, so long as he does not overtly and ostentatiously flout them.[3]

Most governments in Islamic countries today are, in fact, secular in operation and practice, as has been most governance in Islamdom historically. The crucial and extremely important point, however, is that they are not supposed to be. By no means has the principle of *tawhid* been dismissed or reasoned away. It looms over Islamic countries as a constant presence that says this is not the way things should be. In political science terms, this means that as presently constituted they can have no tenable claim to legitimacy.

Of course, the polities in today's Islamdom are all careful to give great deference to Islam (more of this in the next section), but in only three of them—Sudan, the Saudi kingdom, and Iran—can a credible claim be maintained that they make an active attempt to formally base their justification for existence in Islam. As a result, the other regimes, fragile on other grounds, have the additional burden of being unable to legitimize themselves in the eyes of their peoples. (Incidentally, the three regimes mentioned have their own fragilities to contend with.)

In the last half-century, as the Islamic countries came to full political independence, finding another source of legitimacy—nationalism—seemed possible for a time. Nationalism came to Islamdom from outside. It is in origin a Western concept. And it is secular in nature, not deriving from divine revelation. Nevertheless, for some years it did seem to seize the Arab political mind, providing a rationale for the existence of Arab regimes, led by Nasser's Egypt.

There is wide agreement that nationalism as a unifying and motivating force in the Arab world declined sharply at the end of the 1960s. The trigger event was the loss of the Arab-Israeli war of 1967. Until then, Arab public opinion seems to have regarded the initial military success of the nascent Israeli state in establishing itself against the armed Arab opposition forces as some sort of fluke. The sudden and dismaying jolt of reality discredited the Arab leaders, especially Nasser, who had built their claim to rule on nationalism, encouraging their people in the belief that this was the way forward to glory, progress, and the restoration of Arab honor.

The god of nationalism having failed them, the Arabs (and the Iranians) turned to the God of their fathers. This reaction is perfectly familiar to us in Western politics: when you have just lost, say, an election where the stakes were particularly high, the tendency for the more ardent believers in the cause is to explain the disaster in terms of having wandered away from the home truths and pure principles that fired our efforts in our glorious—and successful—past. Among the Arabs, a wave of Islamic pietism swept away nationalism and its secular accoutrements—socialism, for example—and made way for the rise of political Islam, which was to be *the* ascendant force for the next three decades. The ideas of the Egyptian Sayyid Qutb (hung by Nasser in 1966), the Pakistani thinker A. A. Mawdudi, and the Ayatollah Khomeini were central to this movement.

These thinkers have to be understood as part of a conversation that has gone on in the Islamic world, and especially the Arabic part of it, since the beginning of the nineteenth century. Jolted into a consciousness of the outside world—meaning the European world—by Napoleon's foray into Egypt, Arabs awoke to the deeply disturbing realization that their societies were disastrously behind the Europeans in all those aspects of material culture that relate to state power. What to do about this is the question that has dominated Islamic thought ever since.[4]

Another way of putting it is, how can we Arabs modernize in a way consistent with Islam? Recall that separating the conduct of life in everyday affairs from the world of sacred knowledge is not an option (*tawhid*). The Arab polity in modern times (the last two centuries) has been very weak, but Arab culture and society are strong. The religion itself and the culture it has engendered were and are a mighty force. Arab society—meaning primarily the realm of social relations—is likewise solidly rooted, with strong and stable family and tribal relationships. But they are threatened by the forces of modernism, as Arabs see it, in the West. And that is how they feel today: *threatened* in their deepest social values.

They are right. They *are* threatened. The industrial society of modern times, of which the United States is the exemplar, is highly corrosive to traditional values, especially as they relate to social relationships: man/woman, parent/child, intergenerational, social and status hierarchies, and so on. Changes have always been a part of the human experience but never at such a fast pace as in modern times, a pace that forces the changes in values and behaviors into both the collective and personal consciousness. This is perfectly familiar to those of us who live in the Western world; uneasiness as to these matters is an important theme in contemporary U.S. politics and the subject of much tension and dispute.

All this is felt with particular acuteness in Islamdom. The Islamic religion—quite unlike Christianity—was born in triumphalism. Expanding rapidly, sweeping all before it, it quickly became the most powerful, most brilliant cultural and political force of its time. From its seventh-century beginning until the Mongol conquest of the thirteenth century, the culture of Islamdom was unmatched in intellectual achievement. Naturally, all this was taken by its adherents as affirmation of the truth of its claim to universal validity. The memory of this glorious past fires the imagination of Muslims to this day, the shining images burnished and savored over and over again.

Now, this is all very well and good while things are going your way. But when the currents of history are reversed, an acute problem arises. We are supposed to be winners—but we aren't winning. How can this be? Could it be that the master vision is not what it claims to be? Of course not! Muslims are no different than anybody else in this circumstance. The invariant response will be that since God has apparently withdrawn His favor from us, it can only be because we have fallen away from His guidance. The obvious and only solution to our woes is to find our way back to the true path from which we have wandered. Then the days of glory will come again.

This is the basic Islamist position. The best known and most persistent promulgation of this view has been undertaken by the Muslim Brotherhood.[5] Started by an Egyptian, Hassan al-Banna, in the 1920s, it has spread to other Arab lands. In its varied history, it has been sometimes persecuted, sometimes semitolerated. It has combined social service functions with social activism and sometimes, where possible, political activism. While the Muslim Brotherhood has usually not resorted to violence, some of its offshoots have. The Palestinian Hamas is one such offshoot. Today we might describe its position—at least in Egypt—as mainstream, nonradical Islamist.

This is the basic message of Qutb, Mawdudi, Khomeini, and their followers. Resist at all costs any notion that the way forward is to copy Western forms—"Westoxification," as the Iranian Ali Shariati put it. That notion was explored in the nineteenth century; much good it did us. To go forward, we must go back—back to the values and practices that were prescribed for us and that once made us great. In this line of thought, a particularly important figure Muslims turn to is the thirteenth-century thinker Ibn Tamiyya, who, like his twentieth-century heirs, was a reformer who called for return to the pure ways of the past. Another recurrent theme is a call to reinstitute shari'a as the guiding core for human affairs. Shari'a is the body of laws, edicts, and interpretations worked out by early Muslim scholars, based on the Koran and the collections of anecdotes and sayings attributed to the Prophet and his immediate successors. By now an immense codex of legal writings, with commentaries piled upon commentaries—actually, there are four different versions, though they largely overlap—our thinkers insist that shari'a is the only possible source of legitimacy for state and politics.

Go back to go forward. Here is a trap for the unwary Western observer. So often it is said that what these folk propose is to march back to the Middle Ages. This is simply not true. Even the most radical followers of the three writers mentioned here—even bin Laden himself—do *not* advocate giving up the airplane, the telephone, the microchip, or the pursuit of modern science. They do not reject modernity. What they reject is the Western version of it. They do not want to abandon the modern project—they want to tame it, to bring it within the scope of the received corpus of Islam.

That is, this is what they *want* to do. Indeed, the Islamists are joined in this by almost all the other voices in Islamdom today. The problem, of course, is just how to go about it.

The state of affairs in the majority of the world of modern Arab Islamdom is for the most part deplorable. The oil-rich states of the Persian Gulf are a partial exception, owing to their high per capita incomes (high by the standards of Islamdom, that is), but even they have their discontents, and in any case, they share many of the concerns of their less fortunate neighbors. Authoritarian governments maintain themselves often by brute force, widespread lack of fundamental human rights, sharply limited freedom of discourse in many parts, weak economic performance—the catalogue of miseries could go on and on. We do not have to rely on the testimony of outside observers in this. In July of 2002, some Arab intellectuals, acting through the United Nations, published "The Arab Human Development Report 2002." Their criticism of their own societies was unsparing. Among their points was that the gross national product (the measure of the total economic activity of a country) of all the Arab countries taken together did not exceed that of Spain. There are perhaps 275 million Arabs but only around 40 million Spaniards. Spain is not yet one of the richer Western countries. The authors of the report also note that if one excludes the export of petroleum from the calculation, the sum of the entire export trade of all the Arab countries is less than that of Finland. The authors include various social desiderata in their catalogue, to similarly dismal effect. And they are quite clear that in the words of Ziauddin Sardar, the report's authors "place the blame for these problems squarely on Arab states themselves" (Postrel 2002).[6]

Self-criticism of this kind is all too rare within the Arab world (and note that even the work just cited was not published within that world). Arabs voicing such views run a great risk of being denounced as traitors, depending on what they say and how and where they say it. The preferred—and safe—mode is to blame all their problems on somebody else. Some malign external force must be responsible for their many miseries. The usual culprit is, of course, the West and, principally, the United States. And first on the list of the catalogue of grievances is U.S. support for Israel.

The ocean of argument generated by the dispute between Israel and the Palestinian Arabs is too vast for the scope of this essay. But no discussion of the politics of Islamdom can avoid taking this problem into account. Israel, for the Arabs, is like Voltaire's God: if it didn't exist, it would be necessary to invent it. It is the great excuse, the all-purpose, emotionally charged issue that is called forth again and again to preempt the intellectual space that might otherwise have room for some serious self-examination.

This is not to say that the issue is contrived or artificial. There is a genuine grievance: some of Islamdom's own were pushed aside to make room for others from far away. The Arabs will say with justice that they have been made to bear the burden for the West's guilty conscience over its treatment of the Jews. The emotional charge of this issue in the collective mind of the mass public—and not only in the Arab world—has certainly escalated in the last few years because of the imagery of suffering, brought by television into people's homes, of the spiraling cycle of tit-for-tat violence that is going on. Naturally, the Arab media tend to show only one side of it—the Palestinians as the innocent victims of Israeli provocations—but innocent or not, the suffering is real.

Now, there can be no doubt that if some sort of solution could be worked out that would be seen by the Arabs as giving the Palestinians a modicum of fairness and hope for a better life, this would have a positive effect on public discourse in Islamdom. The Palestinian-Israeli issue would not so easily crowd out all others; reform-minded critics within Islamdom, those who are not radical Islamists, might well be emboldened to speak out a bit more. And the United States' rhetoric of democracy would carry more moral force. But no one should imagine that this would end the sense of resentment toward the West and toward the United States that resonates throughout Islamdom. The deeper problems, the quandary about the way to modernization and the fear of being culturally swamped by the powerful wave of Western culture, would still be there.

Such a solution would not mean an end to the prevalence of political violence that afflicts Islamdom, especially the Arab part of it. As previously noted, the Arabs have been struggling for two hundred years with the problem of how to come to terms with modernity. The values in conflict run deep; the most intense emotions are evoked, and feelings can run very high. Especially since the collapse of the nationalist idea as the solution, violence, killings, and assassinations have frequently been a part of this discourse.

Probably the worst example has been Algeria. As the regime that forced out the French sank into corruption and mismanagement, the attempt to replace the French with an Islamist regime, and the resistance to that attempt, provoked an orgy of killing on both sides that resulted in one hundred thousand deaths.[7] In Egypt, the assassination of Anwar Sadat was countered by the state with ruthless repression of the fringe groups responsible, followed by a counter response—and so the cycle has gone.[8]

The violence has not been limited to encounters between the state and those directly trying to bring it down. The struggle over the future is also a Kulturkampf; thinkers and intellectuals who dare to say controversial things have also been victimized. The Nobel laureate Naguib Mahfouz was the target of an assassination attempt and, of course, Nasser had the above-mentioned Qutb executed. These are but a few examples.[9]

The Soviet invasion of Afghanistan in 1979 gave rise to another dimension of politics-generated violence. Muslims flocked from all parts of Islamdom to training camps in Pakistan to receive training in arms so as to take part in the struggle to defend the Dar al Islam, the realm of Islam, against the Soviet infidel. These fighters, funded and encouraged by the United States and the Saudi kingdom, evolved their own vision of a radical Islamist future, a vision not limited simply to the Afghanistan episode. They came to see it as their mission to retrieve all the lost lands of Islamdom that had fallen to the infidel, including in this *al Andaluz* (Spain) and the Saudi kingdom itself, with its Two Holy Places now sullied by the presence of infidel military bases and soldiers. The French scholar Gilles Kepel—whose recent book *Jihad: The Trail of Political Islam* is both highly detailed and persuasively analytic and is essential reading for anyone wanting an overview of Islamist politics in Islamdom—has labeled this most radical variant of Islamism "jihadi-salafist" (Kepel 2002).[10]

The fact that the ultimate failure of the Soviet Afghan venture, in 1989, owed more to internal Soviet developments than anything else did not matter; the jihadi-salafists convinced themselves that it was their resistance that had not only defeated the infidel superpower but also induced the collapse of the very system itself. And as we now well know, they would shortly turn their attention to the remaining superpower. We did it once already, so why not again? The training and recruitment continued throughout the 1990s, with Afghanistan becoming a main base. Some of the fighters returned to their home countries to involve themselves with Islamist movements ongoing there. The jihadi-salafist voice has become one of the significant players in the ongoing conceptual struggle.

The traditional clerical establishment is another voice. Viewing itself as the guardians of Islamic orthodoxy, the clerisy (the ulema) has an uneasy relationship with the mostly secular rulers. The state patronizes the ulema with positions and often salaries. The religious scholars are given privileged access to mass communication, and in some cases they are allowed to censor all discourse that, in their opinion, touches on religious questions. The secular authority, ever anxious about its legitimacy in the eyes of the mass public, hopes, by allowing the ulema to direct and adjudicate social relationships, to deflect and discredit the taunts of the radical Islamists that the rulers and the existing social order are not truly Islamic at all and that they should be brought down. The Islamists also assail the ulema as sell-outs to the corrupt, un-Islamic state, made unwilling to lead the community (*umma*) along the true path because of the perquisites they receive from the state.

The interpretation of Islam offered by both the ulema and their Islamist challengers is in turn challenged by intellectuals and scholars who proffer fresh interpretations of the Islamic tradition, particularly as it relates to the position of women, human rights issues, the nature of shari'a, and other points. There are some impressive thinkers in this group. Unfortunately, with few exceptions, they are to be found mostly in Western universities (Postrel 2002).[11] The climate within Islamdom is so unfriendly to their discourse that they cannot operate there for very long before their position becomes untenable. This, of course, sharply limits their ability to contribute to the debate. Nevertheless, in the long run it is these thinkers who will have to work out some way of separating political identity from religious identity while still retaining some sense of a perhaps reinterpreted *tawhid.*

Incidentally, Muslim writers who challenge some of the interpretive traditions of Islam are not necessarily entirely safe even when living in the West. Threats have been made against some of them because of the alleged heterodoxy of their writings (Foer 2002). Indeed, there are even indications that some of the more aggressive Islamists may now consider it lawful to attempt to enforce shari'a in areas outside the political scope of Islamdom. It had been the usual under-standing that Islamic law did not apply in the Dar al Harb (realm of struggle), the parts of the world not under Muslim political control. However, because of the substantial Muslim populations outside the Dar al Islam (realm of Islam)—especially in Europe, where, for example, 11 percent of the population of France is now Muslim—there seems to be the beginning of an assertion that the realm of Islam now extends to these areas (Kepel 2002, 306–8). Apostasy and blas-phemy are punishable by death according to shari'a. The Ayatollah Khomeini's *fatwa* (legal dictum) condemning the author Salman Rushdie, a permanent resi-dent and citizen of a Western country, to death for his presumptive apostasy and blasphemy is an example of such an extension. According to this ruling, it would be lawful for a Muslim to kill Rushdie even though he had permanently estab-lished himself in the West. Note that the ruling was also evidently interpreted to apply to non-Muslims as well—those individuals presumably complicit in blasphemy against Islam because of their involvement in distributing Rushdie's works. Threats, and in some cases attacks, were made against non-Muslim pub-lishers and booksellers under the authority of this ruling.

To be sure, the lawfulness of the Shi'ite Khomeini's fatwa was disputed by voices from the orthodox Sunni ulema. And it has always been the case that it has been seen as lawful to conduct struggle (jihad) in the realm of unbelief so as to bring the true faith there. Even so, the assertion that the reach of Islamic law extends to these areas even *before* they have been converted to Islam seems to be a step beyond this traditional position.

So far we have stressed the centrality of the struggle over the interpretation of Islam in considering the turmoil in Islamdom. But there are also forces at work that can be understood in secular terms. The Arab population has grown rapidly, and there has been a rural to urban population shift. Most of all, there is the fact that the population profile in the Arab world shows a large bulge in the lower cohorts: up to two-thirds of the people are under thirty years of age. Detached from the rural status networks of their fathers and often poorly educated—but enough to know that others live well, while their own economic prospects are meager—this social element constitutes a powerful engine for discontent. The state is unable to provide either jobs to absorb the expanding labor supply or social services to meliorate conditions.

Add to this mix the expansion of modern communications, whereby the economically marginal become aware of the better life of the upper strata, and one can easily see why these societies have such volatile potential. The inability of the state to provide the promise of a solution creates a receptive audience for the Islamists. The latter provide social services that the widely despised state cannot along with their utopian message of return to the first principles of the religion—which, they stress, include a strong component of social justice.

Thus secular discontents become expressed within a religious idiom, gaining thereby great emotional power and apparent direction. At least, that is what the Islamists strive for and have at times achieved.[12]

WHAT CAN WE DO?

The argument presented here is that the violence that is so often a part of the politics of Islamdom is generated by unsettled internal conditions. The big questions are in contention: What kind of society do we want to be? How shall we arrange for the production of wealth and the fair distribution of the product? How can we do what needs to be done without betraying the tenets of the received religion and its cultural surround?

The terrorist violence that spills out of that world—the most dramatic, though by no means the only, example of which was the events of September 11, 2001—is a by-product of Islamdom's inner struggles. Only the Islamic peoples themselves can resolve these struggles. Although we in the West must, of course, vigorously pursue those who would project their discontents onto us, there is little we can do directly about their internal problems.

The radical Islamists who blame us for their troubles can hardly be expected to say that they hate us because they are afraid of us, afraid of what we represent to their future. To do so would come too close to acknowledging that their problems lie within themselves. So, of course, they recite a bill of grievances—starting with the Arab-Israeli question—that justify their anger and actions. But we can be skeptical about their specific complaints. Their real problem with us is existential—it has to do what we are, not with what we do.

Even supposing it were possible for us to withdraw from all involvement in the Middle East, the same unresolved problems that cause the current violent tendencies in the region's politics would still be there. The Palestinian Arab-Israeli matter would still be there. Israel stands on her own feet, has nuclear weapons, and would surely use them to defend her existence. Recall the anxiety produced a short time ago (2002) when Pakistan and India, two nuclear powers, appeared to be on the brink of war. Should there be a cataclysm in the Middle East, it is difficult to see how we could have any assurance of not being affected by it. Even leaving aside the matter of the area's vast energy reserves, imagining that we could isolate ourselves from events in the area is simply not realistic.

We must stay engaged with the politics of Arab Islamdom. There are some useful things we can do to address the conditions that give rise to political violence. We must widen our understanding of the area. To do that, we must make a clearheaded assessment of our cognitive assets. And the first step in this is to recognize that there are major disagreements within the various communities that study the area: the academics, the government experts, those in the communication community, and the interested public. For instance, the Middle Eastern Studies Association (MESA), to which many U.S.-based academics belong, has been subject to sharp criticism in Martin Kramer's 2001 book, *Ivory Towers on Sand: The Failure of Middle Eastern Studies in America*. The book's subtitle says it all. Naturally, those whose positions are attacked by Kramer have their own version as to who is right and who is wrong.

The earlier remarks about Edward Said referred to this controversy; many of the MESA scholars have been influenced by his ideas. The present essay is certainly not going to settle the question; readers will have to look at the arguments and make up their own minds. It should be noted that by no means are all U.S. Middle Eastern studies scholars associated with MESA or its viewpoints. In any case, the position here is not that we should exclude any voices from the discourse but rather that we should broaden it by encouraging new voices. The first problem is the language barrier. There are many people in the United States who have emigrated here from the Arab world (many came as students and graduate students and have remained, forming a sizable component of MESA membership, for instance). No doubt more use could be made of the language competency of these people—including the nonacademics—but it would be a mistake to rely on them alone. In the field of Soviet studies, sponsored by the U.S. government after 1945, émigrés made an important contribution, but it is well that a vigorous and successful effort was made to develop a native American body of Sovietologists. Émigrés have important insights to offer about their countries of origin, but they often arrive on our shores heavily freighted with various ideological baggage.

We clearly must widen the pool of those competent in Arabic. The U.S. government should increase the effort it already has under way, as it did in the case of Soviet studies.[13] It has in fact already proposed to do so but has encountered resistance from some MESA people.[14] This resistance should not be allowed to prevail.

The second thing we should do also draws on our experience of studying the former Soviet Union. A very important tool in that enterprise was the publication of a weekly bulletin, *The Current Digest of the Soviet Press.* The *Current Digest* translated and printed in English extracts and digests of the more important material from Soviet newspapers, journals, books, and official documents and statements. Well indexed and with short publication lead times, it made up-to-date information on current happenings in the USSR available to a broad non-specialist public in addition to serving the research community. Doing the same thing for the Arab world would be highly beneficial. It would enable nonspecialists to get a sense of the tone and texture of Arabic discourse, much of which is highly inflammatory. The responses that American readers and commentators would make could well impose a certain constraint on some of the more vicious rhetoric, since Arabs would quickly become aware of the impact of their words on the U.S. audience. Right now, there isn't much of an audience.

Such an enterprise would have to be subsidized by the U.S. government both in the translation and the distribution, which should be wide and of low cost to the end user so that every newspaper office and library would have it, and it should be posted on the Internet. The cost, compared to the costs of other aspects of the national security effort, would not be too large. Another highly useful and relatively cheap move would be to sponsor scholarly journals, in both English and Arabic, that could be vehicles for Islamic scholars—those resident in the West, and those in Islamdom who find it difficult to have their voices heard at home—who are doing interesting work in interpreting Islam in the light of modern conditions. Again, the experience of Soviet studies shows that the U.S. government can do this effectively: the bimonthly journal, *Problems of Communism,* published by the U.S. Information Agency, was for years an important venue for serious analysis of the Leninist world. Leading scholars were happy to publish in it.

In our encounter with Islamdom, we should mobilize the strengths that have made us powerful. Chief among these is the freedom and vigor of our internal discourse. We need to carry this over to our conversation with Islamdom. Herewith are some suggestions. Do not be apologetic about America. You will often hear hostile characterizations of our society from the other side: talk of drugs, crime, sexual license, and so on. The answer to this tactic is to firmly point out that they know of these things because we ourselves freely talk about them. Our Arab interlocutors need to be reminded that the capacity to talk openly about your problems is a necessary prelude to doing something about them. It is a sign of a society's strength, not its decadence—a lesson they might well apply to themselves.

Americans should not, of course, press the view that Arabs should blindly copy our example. But on the other hand, we need to make clear the relationship between some of the ways of a liberal society and the material and social progress desired by all. It is not an accident that we have achieved so much more than they in these areas. Further, we need to insist on reciprocity and fair play in regard to religious freedom. If Muslims are to be free to practice their religion in the West, it is only fair that elimination of restrictions on non-Muslim religious practice in Islamdom should also be the rule—to say nothing of eliminating outright persecution of non-Muslims there.

At some point in the conversation, Arabs will invoke the Crusades as a metaphor for present circumstances to prove the supposed continuing malevolence of the Western world toward Islamdom. Some of the charges are rather wildly imaginative: the British scholar Carole Hillenbrand (1999) observes that Sayyid Qutb, for instance, even characterized "Christian military opposition to the first Islamic conquerors in Syria and Palestine in the seventh century" as instances of "Crusade"![15] Americans encountering this move need to be aware, as Hillenbrand persuasively shows in Chapter 9 of her magisterial study, that this theme only began to be heard in Islamic discourse in the middle of the nineteenth century. Before then, Islamdom had often been in a position of superiority to the world of the Franks, having thus no reason to fear or resent it. Mostly, Arabs were simply oblivious to the West until Napoleon's intrusion forced it into their consciousness. The proper response to this is to remind anyone making the "Crusader" charge that the celebrated seventh- and eighth-century expansion of the Dar al Islam came at the point of the sword; those early jihadis were not invited in to the lands they conquered. So, as for bringing the doings of our ancestors into the current discussion, Muslims are simply in no moral position to complain about intruding in other people's territories and imposing their rule and their ways on others.

Supposing that the United States should be successful in increasing the amount and quality of our conversation with Islamdom, would that bring an end to the danger to us of terrorist acts of the kind we have suffered? In the short run, no. The jihadi-salafist element of the Islamist movement no doubt has a momentum of its own. It will never transform itself, and our only recourse is to fight it directly. Even so, the growth of more moderate voices in Islamdom would tend to shrink its base of support, shrink the supply of new recruits, and otherwise narrow its range of possibilities. It has happened before in the Arab world that effusions of political violence by radical Islamists have been met with revulsion by the Arab mass public.[16]

Indeed, according to Gilles Kepel, who appears to know political Islam better than anyone else in the Western world, there is at this time some reason to hope that the more radical versions of Islamism are beginning to fall into disrepute. Even some of the more moderate Islamists seem to have decided to take another look at such notions as democracy, civil rights, and so on (Kepel 2002, 368–75). Let us hope so, and let us also hope to do better than we have in understanding their world and helping those in it who share some of our values.

As these lines are being written, the United States has undertaken a massive intervention in the Arab world—one that far exceeds in scope and ambition the events of the Gulf War of 1991. The initial military phase of the engagement with Iraq—and Afghanistan—was quickly successful. But the next phase, winning the peace by fostering the establishment of a governmental system based on some form of democracy, has proved far more difficult. Progress has been made, but in both cases the question is still in the balance. In the wider Arab world, the U.S. intervention in Iraq has provoked deep nationalist resentment. It may also have produced some responses that could conceivably contribute to the project of encouraging democratic development as the long-term solution to the region's problems. Whatever the outcome, it appears that the United States has committed to a heavy investment and involvement in the future of Arab Islamdom as the Arabs continue their conflicted path to modernization.

NOTES

1. As used in this essay, Islamdom means those lands, and their practices and circumstances, where Islam predominates. Islam refers to the religion itself. This usage is borrowed from a televised talk by Bernard Lewis.

2. Except perhaps for exciting a certain romantic sympathy in a sector of the youth culture.

3. For a detailed study of Islamic political theory from the beginnings to modern times, see Black (2001).

4. The standard history of this conversation is Hourani (1983).

5. The standard scholarly account is Mitchell (1969).

6. Postrel (2002) gives an account of the U.N. Report.

7. For a full account of violence in Islamdom and of Islamist politics, see Kepel (2002).

8. For an excellent account of the struggles in Egypt, see Murphy (2002).

9. See Murphy (2002) for further examples of various kinds of repression directed against intellectuals who depart from somebody's notion of orthodoxy.

10. The term "jihadi" of course refers to struggle—one who fights. "Salafi" connotes a recovery of practices and positions past.

11. An exception is the Iranian writer Abdolkarim Soroush, an especially interesting thinker who is thoroughly familiar with Western philosophy, including the philosophy of science, but is also learned in the Islamic academic tradition. A collection of his essays has been recently published as *Reason, Freedom, and Democracy in Islam* (2000). Until now, he has been able to write and lecture in Tehran. However, as of the time of this writing, he seems to have been dismissed from his positions, so his ability to function may be tenuous.

12. Kepel (2002) describes the Islamists' target audiences with convincing clarity and detail.

13. Some steps have already been taken. Included in a recently passed bill providing for sharply increased spending on the U.S. intelligence effort are measures relating to translation and language training. See Associated Press (2002).

14. For an account of the politics of this, see Kramer (2001, 84–103). The stated objection is that if presently existing academic centers for Middle Eastern studies participate in a government-funded crash program to train more Arabic speakers, both they and the graduates of such programs would be regarded with suspicion in the Middle East as spies or perhaps government agents. This argument may or may not be pretextual. After all, some of these academic centers already receive funding from the U.S. government. It is no secret that many MESA people are hostile to U.S. policy toward the Middle East. And it is an objective fact that a major increase in the pool of those competent in Arabic would lessen our reliance on émigré scholars for our knowledge of what is being said in the Middle East.

15. This magisterial study will be definitive standard for many years to come.

16. Murphy (2002) illustrates this in some detail in various parts of her book.

REFERENCES

Associated Press. 2002. "Congress Approves Big Hike in Spending on Intelligence." *Portland Press Herald*, November 16, p. 6A.

Black, Anthony. 2001. *The History of Islamic Political Thought*. New York: Routledge.

Foer, Franklin. 2002. "Moral Hazard." *New Republic*, November 18.

Hillenbrand, Carole. 1999. *The Crusades: Islamic Perspectives*. Edinburgh: Edinburgh University Press.

Hourani, Albert. 1983. *Arabic Thought in the Liberal Age, 1798–1939*. 2d ed. Cambridge: Cambridge University Press.

Kepel, Gilles. 2002. *Jihad: The Trail of Political Islam*. Cambridge: Harvard University Press.

Kramer, Martin. 2001. *Ivory Towers on Sand*. Washington, D.C.: Washington Institute for Near East Policy.

MacKenzie, John M. 1995. *Orientalism: History, Theory and the Arts*. Manchester and New York: Manchester University Press.

Mitchell, Richard P. 1969. *The Society of Muslim Brothers*. Oxford: Oxford University Press.

Murphy, Caryle. 2002. *Passion for Islam*. New York: Scribner.

Postrel, Danny. 2002. "Islamic Studies' Young Turks." *Chronicle of Higher Education*, September 13, p. A14.

Said, Edward. 1978. *Orientalism*. London: Penguin Books.

Soroush, Abdolkarim. 2000. *Reason, Freedom, and Democracy in Islam*, trans. and ed. M. and A. Sadri. Oxford: Oxford University Press.

IRM HALEEM

8 Pakistan, Afghanistan, and Central Asia
RECRUITING GROUNDS FOR TERRORISM?

—Any analysis of terrorist groups and terrorism requires some very important qualifications. For a phenomenon that has existed for more than two thousand years, as Bruce Hoffman (2000, 314) notes, terrorism "owes its survival to an ability to adapt and adjust to challenges and countermeasures and to continue to identify and exploit its opponent's vulnerabilities." Be that as it may, the question remains as to the effective definition of terrorism and that of the "opponents" terrorism seek to exploit. Perhaps one of the most comprehensive definitions of terrorism is provided by Edward Mickolus (2002, 151–52): "The use, or threat of use, of anxiety-inducing extranormal violence for political purposes by any individual or group, whether acting for or in opposition to established governmental authority, when such action is intended to influence the attitudes and behavior of a target group wider than the immediate victims and when, through the nationality or foreign ties of its perpetrators, its location, the nature of its institutional or human victims, or the mechanics of its resolution, its ramifications, transcend national boundaries."

Two related and contradictory issues become immediately apparent in such a definition. The first is that terrorism may be perpetrated by either state or non-state actors. Thus, terrorism may either involve a government's repression of its own citizens through the instillation of violence and fear—some quintessential examples of this would include Nazi Germany, Pol Pot's Cambodia, and indeed Saddam Hussein's Iraq—or terrorism may involve the workings of domestic or supranational entities motivated by opposition to government and/or their own political agendas. Some examples to note in this latter context would include the Irish Republican Army (IRA) and Sri Lanka's Tamil Tigers as domestic terrorist groups opposed to the government and al Qaeda as a supranational

121

terrorist organization. In this manner, the definition of a terrorists' opponents becomes contingent on the particular context, so that "opponents" may either be citizens challenging government control, unrepresentative governments, or some abstract global enemy (such as "imperialism"), respectively. The second issue apparent in Mickolus's definition of terrorism is that of "ramifications" that "transcend national boundaries." This seems to exclude terrorist groups such as the IRA and the Tamil Tigers that have characteristically limited their attacks to their own domestic environments.

This chapter employs Mickolus's definition of terrorism with two very important qualifications. First, the term "terrorist groups" is used to refer to both domestic extremist groups as well as supranational (transnational or international) terrorist groups or movements. As such, terrorism is defined as a phenomenon with ramifications that may either be domestic or that may "transcend national boundaries." Such a definition beckons a further clarification of the controversial phenomena of "freedom fighters" (often domestic in nature, such as the Tamil Tigers, the Basque Nation in Spain, and the Kurds in Iraq). Should there be a distinction made between freedom fighters and terrorists? This leads to the second important qualification of the definition of terrorism as used here. To the extent that domestic rebellions and insurgencies—that is, domestic extremist groups—employ the same tactics as supranational terrorist organizations, they too are seen as part of the same rubric in this discussion. Such a qualification renders inconsequential any distinctions between terrorist groups and freedom fighters. Based on their modus operandi, one can therefore brand together groups seeking secession from perceived repressive governments (such as the Tamil Tigers in Sri Lanka), those seeking to expel what is perceived as the rule of an illegitimate external force (such as the IRA in Northern Ireland or the freedom fighters, or jihadis, in the Indian-administered Kashmir), and yet others seeking a broader ideological appeal to further their transnational aims (such as al Qaeda).

Having explicitly outlined the definition of terrorism as well as the needed qualifications as relevant to this discussion, a further qualification deserves mention—that of the moral or legal justifications of domestic rebellions and insurgencies. Of the many devastating consequences of the terrorist attacks on the United States on September 11, 2001—both immediate, as in the loss of thousands of lives, and long term, as in the subsequent fear instilled in societies worldwide—serious violations of human rights justified by the events of September 11 are noteworthy. *The Economist* presents a list of countries where the governments have pursued harsh extrajudicial policies against citizens and noncitizens suspected of domestic or international terrorist connections in the post-9/11 environment. These countries include, but are not limited to, Colombia, the United States, South Africa, Israel, Nepal, India, Malaysia, Russia, Jordan, the Philippines, Spain, China, South Korea, the United Kingdom, Canada, Yemen, and Egypt (*Economist* 2002, 19). The greatest danger emanating from the understandable increase of the fear of terrorism in countries worldwide is the increasing, but universal, rejection of the legitimacy of any kind of resistance or opposition to state terror. Domestic insurgencies and rebellions (or freedom struggles), when motivated by the repression of minority groups by their own governments, can not be seen as illegitimate in the context of liberal thinking that implies a right to rebellion against unrepresentative and repressive government—one might refer to the American Revolution as one illustration of this right. Jean Jacques Rousseau had even labeled this an absolute right of rebellion and the lesser of the two evils, namely violence and government repression. Given this, it is most important to note that it is not the freedom fighters' resistance against state terror that should be rejected on a carte blanche basis; it is instead the criminalization of these freedom fighters, and their subsequent use of indiscriminate violence, that ushers them into the category of terrorists.[1] In other words, domestic insurgencies and freedom fighters are a symptom of a problem, that of repressive and unrepresentative governments, that when left unaddressed becomes the problem itself—that is, terrorism.

A significant portion of this chapter discusses extremist terrorist groups based in Pakistan. It is most important to understand that this refers to the autonomous, often underground and increasingly antigovernment, militant Islamist groups in Pakistan and not the formal Islamist political parties that operate within the political and legal frameworks of the country. Thus, Ejaz Haider (2002) notes that the concern in the United States over the electoral victory of Pakistan's new Islamist coalition party—the Muttahidda Majlis-I-Amal (MMA)—during the country's most recent parliamentary elections (October 2002) is unfounded.[2] While it is indeed the first successful attempt at a coalition between different Islamist parties, Haider notes that the leadership of the MMA comprises highly educated and seasoned parliamentarians who are not extremists that one should fear.

This chapter is structured around two hypotheses. The first relates to the poverty-terrorism nexus in which the real threat to international and regional security comes from the persistence of extreme poverty and desperation in much of the Muslim Middle East, South Asia, and Central Asia, with a particular focus on Pakistan. The second hypothesis relates to the imperative of targeting domestic extremist groups in order to reduce the broader threat of international terrorist movements, particularly al Qaeda. Antidotes such as economic recovery through the disbursement of economic aid by international state or nonstate actors and policies targeted at institutionalizing government accountability that in turn reduce the legitimacy of domestic extremist groups are outlined as the domestic "micro targets," which are argued to give rise to a "macro impact," that is, the reduction in al Qaeda's regional and international threat.

Given that my micro target–macro impact hypothesis,[3] and to some extent the poverty-terrorism nexus, cannot easily be tested or substantiated in the short run, I shall borrow a disclaimer from Ahmed Rashid's recent book *Jihad: The Rise of Militant Islam in Central Asia:* "if . . . [this chapter] reads like a poor detective story, with clues that lead nowhere, mysterious evidence, and inconclusive theories, it is because the ending has yet to be written" (Rashid 2002, xi).

GHOSTS OF THE PAST

And then, the tail started to wag the dog.

—EJAZ HAIDER, "Pakistan's Transition to Democracy"

Various conflicting accounts exist in terms of the international complicity in facilitating regional and international terrorism.[4] The strictly military nature of the international commitment to Soviet-occupied Afghanistan (1979–89), Pakistan's economic national interests in post-Soviet Afghanistan,[5] and lawlessness spiraling out of control in Afghanistan during the early 1990s, facilitated by the ambivalence of outside observers, had inevitably to exact its price from neighboring Pakistan and, later, from the United States.

Between 1980 and 1991, the United States' commitment to the Afghan mujahideens in their struggle against Soviet occupation equaled approximately $5 billion. That this commitment was reflective of cold war politics and, as such, part of America's "Great Game" has already been exhaustively documented by numerous scholars. What is perhaps less known is that the American financial commitment was matched by the Saudis, with aid to Soviet-occupied Afghanistan totaling approximately $10 billion U.S. dollars, "most in the form of lethal modern weaponry" (Rashid 2000, 18). Pakistan had entered into the picture as the intermediary that distributed this aid to the mujahideens. It was Pakistan's infamous Inter-Services Intelligence (ISI) that carried out this role.

Perhaps the most significant historical fact in this context is that a part of the American-Pakistani anti-Soviet campaign involved the joint efforts of both the American Central Intelligence Agency (CIA) and Pakistan's ISI in a recruitment of the most "radical Muslims from around the world to come to . . . fight with the Afghan Mujahideen." Pakistan's vested interest in such a policy was to present itself as a solid Muslim state, interested in the furthering of Islamic causes, which the military leader of the time, General Zia ul-Haq, had considered important for his domestic and international legitimacy. The American vested interest for such a strategy was to give its cold war policy an added legitimacy by demonstrating "that the entire Muslim world was fighting the Soviet Union alongside the Afghans," a point that could most effectively be made by promoting the most radical and inevitably vociferous elements to Afghanistan. The Saudis also saw a political gain in promoting such a policy, as they saw an opportunity to promote their brand of Sunni Islam in Afghanistan and, more significantly, a chance to dump onto Afghanistan "its disgruntled radicals" such as Osama bin Laden. However, none of the actors involved in Afghanistan during the 1980s had "reckoned on these [radical] volunteers having their own agendas, which would eventually turn their hatred against the Soviets on their own regimes [as in the case of the mushrooming of extremist groups in Pakistan] and the Americans [as demonstrated by the events of September 11]" (Rashid 2000, 129).

The defeat of the Soviets in Afghanistan was attributed primarily to American military assistance in conjunction with the strategic planning of Pakistan's ISI. However, after the Soviet defeat and the collapse of the Soviet Union in 1991, much of the direct American interest focused in Afghanistan dwindled. While Afghanistan slipped into anarchy during much of the early 1990s, Pakistan's immediate interest continued, based as it was on Pakistan's desire to "open direct land routes for trade with the Central Asian Republics [and] . . . bring a Pakhtun group [such as the Taliban] to power in Kabul which would be Pakistan-friendly" (Rashid 2000, 26). Of significance here is the fact that more than 20 percent of the Pakistan army is comprised of ethnic Pakhtuns. Also of interest is the fact that Pakistan's Northwest Frontier Province (NWFP), which borders Afghanistan, is comprised mainly of ethnic Pakhtuns. Thus, Pakistan's desire to help in the consolidation of a predominately Pakhtun government in post-Soviet Afghanistan—namely, the Taliban—was understandable given national interests. However, after coming to power with the assistance of the Pakistanis, the "Taliban demonstrated their independence from Pakistan, indicating that they were nobody's puppet" (29). As the Taliban slowly consolidated its control over Afghanistan, it "declined to have anything to do with the other warlords whom they condemned as communist infidels" and continued to marginalize its Pakistani sponsors (44).

The ghosts of the past policies had finally come to haunt Pakistan when, during the late 1990s, the ISI revealed that the Taliban was providing safe haven and training camps for ultra-extremist sectarian groups that had begun to cause havoc in Pakistan (Mir 1999, 68). The Talibanization of Pakistan had thus become an unexpected by-product of the American-Pakistani Afghan policy of the 1980s, unleashing as it did radical elements that, after the withdrawal of the Soviets, had sought to find and fight another jihad in neighboring Pakistan and Kashmir. One cannot also ignore the policies of Pakistan's military leader during the 1980s, General Zia ul-Haq, who, in the interest of his legitimacy, promoted a strict Sunni sectarian Islamization of Pakistan, which further elicited radical sectarian elements from both within and without Afghanistan seeking to challenge the existence and influence of the Shias in Pakistan for the ends of their power games. In explaining this loss of control, one observer points out that "Pakistan could not have a Taliban victory, access to Central Asia, friendship with Iran and an end to Bin Laden-style terrorism, all at the same time" (Rashid 2000, 180).

The early 1990s saw the United States distancing itself ever farther from the Afghan issue. "For ordinary Afghans, the US withdrawal from the scene constituted a major betrayal," fomenting anti-American sentiments. Rashid notes that the loss of American interest in Afghanistan during the post–cold war era was less a product of design or betrayal and more a product of a "lack of strategic framework" in addressing the new Afghanistan. This haphazard policy was illustrated in a number of meandering moves that the Americans made vis-à-vis Afghanistan. "Between 1994 and 1996 the USA supported the Taliban politically through its allies Pakistan and Saudi Arabia, essentially because Washington viewed the Taliban as anti-Iranian, anti-Shia and pro-Western . . . [while naively ignoring] the Taliban's own . . . [Islamist] agenda" (Rashid 2000, 176). Such a policy ran completely opposite to the recommendations of Robin Raphel, the American assistant secretary of state for South Asia, who had begun warning the State Department as early as 1996 that "Afghanistan . . . [had] become a conduit for . . . crime and terrorism that . . . [could] undermine Pakistan, the neighboring Central Asian states and have an impact beyond Europe and Russia" (178). Warnings of the exportation of terrorism beyond the Afghan border fell on deaf ears, a mistake that both the Americans and the Pakistanis paid for.

The deteriorating economic conditions in Pakistan during 1997, as well as the Taliban's open support for bin Laden, finally provided reasons for the turnabout in the American stance toward the Taliban. The motivating fear was that the radical "threat which the Taliban posed could overwhelm its old and now decidedly fragile ally Pakistan" (Rashid 2000, 180). Here again, Rashid notes that the problem with Washington's obsession with bin Laden alone gave rise to a U.S. policy that was "again a one-track agenda, solely focused on getting bin Laden, rather than tackling the wider problems of Afghanistan-based terrorism." The "US policy appeared to have come full circle, from unconditionally accepting the Taliban to unconditionally rejecting them" (182). In a fate similar to that of Pakistan, the legacies of past policies exacted a toll from the Americans.

INCIDENCES OF TERROR

Before proceeding further, a chronology of the most recent terrorist attacks committed on Pakistani soil deserves mention. Pakistan has seen a marked rise in domestic terrorism in the aftermath of September 11, 2001, and the subsequent U.S.-led bombing campaign of Afghanistan. Domestic extremists groups in Pakistan appear to have taken on a new methodology that, experts argue, is reminiscent of the modus operandi of supranational terrorist organizations such as al Qaeda. Tactics such as suicide car bombings, which hitherto had not been reported in Pakistan, have now been recorded in a number of incidences. The collaborations of domestic extremist groups with al Qaeda are feared. The credibility of such fears lies in the knowledge that unlike the Irish Republic Army (IRA) terrorist group, al Qaeda "is not a traditional terrorist organization with a disciplined hierarchy. . . . [It is instead] a movement, almost amoeba-like, with varying degrees of support and contacts with other groups throughout much of the Muslim world" (Norton-Taylor 2002). This seems to imply that al Qaeda's threat comes not only from its immediate members—its nucleus if you may—but also from its broader reach, its ideological appeal, and the consequent emulation of its tactics by domestic extremists groups in various Muslim states from Pakistan to Indonesia.

The escalation of terrorist attacks on Pakistani soil is thought to be in part a backlash to the Pakistani government's alliance with the American antiterrorist campaign in the aftermath of September 11 and in part a reaction to the October 2001 U.S. bombing of Afghanistan. Terror incidents in Pakistan bring into question both the resilience of al Qaeda and the scope of its threat to Pakistan. Such fears are not entirely unfounded, as it is thought that as a result of the post–October 2001 dismantling of the Taliban government and its al Qaeda safe havens in Afghanistan, the "once middle level operatives have taken a bigger role in the organization and are cooperating with extremists across the world, from Southeast Asia to North Africa."[6] Whether terrorist attacks in Pakistan have intended to target Westerners or to destabilize General Musharraf's government as a form of retribution for his alliance with the United States is not immediately clear. What is clear is the vicious nature of such attacks. Examples of some most recent terrorist attacks on Pakistani soil include the March 2002 suicide attacker who killed four people and then himself in a Protestant International Church in Islamabad, Pakistan,[7] and the May 2002 suicide car bomb that exploded outside of a Sheraton Hotel in Karachi, Pakistan, killing some fourteen people, eleven of whom were foreign (French) nationals. This particular attack marked the "first incident of suicide bombing in Pakistan," and while no substantiated evidence has been found, experts have noted that the "attack's modus operandi resembled Al-Qaeda's" (Hussein 2002).

In light of the grim statistics of the incidences of terror in Pakistan, advancements made in apprehending those responsible for terrorism in Pakistan must also be noted. A senior police officer in Lahore, Pakistan, speaking on condition of anonymity, reported that the arrests of some fourteen suspected al Qaeda men were made in a township in the city (Shahzad 2002). In April 2002, sixteen suspected al Qaeda men, mostly Arab with links to Osama bin Laden, were arrested in Lahore.[8] In May 2002, more than four hundred people were arrested who belonged to various domestic extremist organizations thought to be sympathetic to al Qaeda, such as the Sipah-I-Sahaba Pakistan (SSP), Jaish-e-Mohammed (JeM), Lashkar-e-Tayyaba (LeT), and Tehrik-i-Jaffria (TiJ).[9] In mid-July 2002, twenty-one suspected terrorists of foreign origin (Arabs and Afghans) were arrested by Pakistan's paramilitary forces in the province of Balochistan. On July 12, 2002, Pakistan's *Daily Times* newspaper reported that the search for al Qaeda was being extended from Pakistan's tribal areas to the rest of its Northwest Frontier Province (NWFP) as well as the province of Punjab (*POT* 2002a, 3421).

The Poverty-Terrorism Nexus

For some, the call of the heart is greater than the capacity of the brain.

HUSSAIN ASKARI, "Cause and Effect"

Roots of radicalism can be traced to numerous causes, such as the political or economic alienation of the majority due to unrepresentative and unaccountable governance. While political alienation in the formation of and support for extremist groups is an important factor, equally important is rampant economic inequalities and poverty that provide explanations for the mushrooming of extremist groups in Pakistan. The phenomena of martyrdom in countries such as Pakistan, though somewhat different from the phenomena of extremist groups, must also be examined within this context. In his article "Cause and Effect," Hussain Askari (2001) documents interviews with wealthy young Pakistani men from Karachi who, despite their privileged lives, had made decisions to become jihadis (commonly understood as freedom fighters, or martyrs). To them, martyrdom was seen as a better alternative than defeat, where "defeat" is defined as succumbing to the imperialism and aggression of the West, in particular the United States. Zaffar Abbas (2001) notes that "imperialism" of the West is further understood as either "the West's support for highly repressive regimes in Muslim countries or the Israeli occupation of Palestinian land" (64). Most notably, the pride displayed by families of the deceased martyrs—such as the ones interviewed by Askari in Karachi, Pakistan—should shed light on the deeper causes of martyrdom and extremism. Askari notes that a sense of personal sacrifice for the possibility of a greater future collective benefit is one cause of martyrdom. Thus, while a desire for collective justice—in the face of actual or perceived imperialism—may form the allure for a martyr, personal desire for a better economic alternative appears to form the allure for joining extremist groups, which in turn creates the constituency bases for such groups.

What is crucial in understanding the poverty-terrorism nexus is that while extremist groups recruit from the impoverished masses, their leadership—not unlike revolutionary leadership—is often derived from the more privileged middle and upper classes. In fact, the estate of the head of al Qaeda, Osama bin Laden, is estimated at some $200 million (Ahmed 2001, 45). Similarly, the personal estate of Omar Sheikh—suspected as the mastermind behind the murder of American journalist Daniel Pearl and a member of the extremist organization 'Harkat-ul Mujahidin (HuM)—is calculated at $800,000 (Gunaratna 2002, 210). Thus, one can see the leaders of any extremist terrorist organization—national or supranational—as the "elite operatives" who subsequently recruit from the impoverished masses (offering them economic and/or political incentives) to provide the needed "foot soldiers" for the organization (*POT* 2002e, 3915).

Numerous economic surveys of Pakistan conducted since 1988 indicate that absolute poverty, measured in terms of calorie intake, has been on a steady increase in Pakistan since 1988. While absolute poverty had declined from 46.5 percent in 1969–70 to 17.3 percent in 1987–88, the survey notes its subsequent increase since 1988. Whereas 17.3 percent of the population lived below the poverty line during 1987–88, this number increased to 22.3 percent by 1992–93. Even more alarming is the fact that "independent estimates of poverty put the number in the range of 25 to 30 percent of the population" (Ali and Bari 2001, 35). Ironically, the year 1988, which marked the point of a steady increase in absolute poverty in Pakistan, also marked Pakistan's transition from a military regime to a decade of civilian governments (1988–99). Among other things, the rise in poverty during the tenure of the various civilian governments (from 1988 through 1999) indicates, at the very least, a lack of government accountability and brings into question the democratic nature of the civilian governments.[10]

TABLE 8.1 **Poverty and social condition indicators**

	Life Expectancy at Birth (1996)	Crude Death Rate per 1,000 (1996)	Underweight Children under 5 years of age (1990–97)
Pakistan	63	9	38%
Bangladesh	59	11	56%
China	71	8	16%
Sri Lanka	75	6	38%

Data compiled with information from Ali and Bari (2001, 37) and cross-referenced with the *World Development Report 1998–99* (Oxford: Oxford University Press, 1999).

Ali and Bari (2001) note that while some of the increase in poverty in Pakistan may be blamed on the economic recession in the country during the late 1980s and the 1990s, much of the blame rests on the civilian government's negligence. In particular, government policies that removed subsidies, allowed increases in the price of utilities, and, most significantly, reduced expenditure on areas of "health, education and social welfare" exacerbated the social condition of the millions of poor in Pakistan (35). In fact, according to the World Bank's "World Development Report 1998–99," Pakistan fared poorly on many of the human welfare indicators as compared to other less-developed states. Table 8.1 highlights Pakistan's realities with three human welfare indicators: life expectancy at birth, crude death rate per thousand, and percentage of underweight children under five years of age. Life expectancy in Pakistan (sixty-three years) was just a little higher than one of the world's poorest states, Bangladesh (fifty-nine years), in 1996. Sri Lanka, even with its ongoing Tamil Tigers insurgency, recorded a much higher life expectancy (seventy-five years) than Pakistan. In terms of crude death rates per thousand, Pakistan once again fared a little better than Bangladesh, nine as opposed to eleven deaths per thousand, respectively. As far as underweight children under five years of age, Pakistan and Sri Lanka fared second worst compared to Bangladesh, 38 percent as opposed to 56 percent, respectively.

Interestingly, the grim statistics in table 8.1 coincide with the sudden sharp rise in seminaries (or madrassahs) since 1996 in the province of Punjab, Pakistan, as depicted in appendix 8-A.[11] Civilian governments in Pakistan, in addition to their failure vis-à-vis welfare provisions, were further unaccountable in terms of their expenditures during the period 1988–99. Ali and Bari (2001, 35–38) note that excessive government expenditures were financed through maintaining huge budget deficits instead of through fair and appropriate taxation policies. In fact, an endemic problem in Pakistan during this decade was the policy of not holding the wealthy accountable for their tax liabilities at the expense of the poor. While the current military regime of General Pervez Musharraf (a product of the October 1999 coup d'etat) has introduced policies to address tax evasion and its resultant economic inequalities through the institution of the Accountability Bureau, the immediate success of these policies is hindered by decades of damage to the economic and social fabric of Pakistan. Ali and Bari note that the massive governmental corruption and tax evasion during the decade of 1988–99 saw an increase not only in poverty but also in inequality in Pakistan. Thus, while the income share of the "lowest twenty percent as well as the middle sixty percent has gone down . . . the share of the top twenty percent has gone up" (36). Facts such as these have left the poor feeling abandoned and have contributed, at best, to their sense of ambivalence and apathy toward government and, at worst, to their feeling of disgruntlement and their subsequent susceptibility to recruitment by extremist groups.

In the aftermath of the September 11 terrorist attacks on the United States, much of the Western media's attention focused on the phenomena of madrassahs (religious Islamic seminaries) as breeding grounds for terrorism. While most of these seminaries find a basis in tradition and religious observation in the Muslim world, and while most are not associated with violence or terrorism, exceptions unfortunately exist. Abbas (2002) notes that in Pakistan, the "phenomena of religious extremism and sectarian militancy is closely associated with the proliferation of seminaries" (50). While the extent of the misuse of seminaries may not be easily determined, what has in fact been determined is their great importance to the millions of poor in Pakistan. Quite aside from any negative affiliations, these seminaries have functioned as welfare institutions in a country where government has failed to address economic poverty and the welfare needs of the masses. Seminaries, or madrassahs, have provided "free food and shelter to a large number of students" in addition to education for those "who would otherwise not have any educational opportunities." As such, "families with few resources send their boys to the seminaries, secure in the knowledge that they will at least be well fed at someone else's expense." Not surprisingly, surveys conducted by private institutions as well as police departments in Pakistan indicate that "the possibility of the child being indoctrinated [in extremist ideology in the seminaries] does not figure largely on the poor man's horizon" (51).

The steady rise of seminaries in Pakistan, particularly in its largest province of Punjab, is illustrated graphically in appendix 8-A. In 2001, some 250,000 students were enrolled in the seminaries in Punjab alone. While this fact alone should not cause alarm given the religious, economic, and educational utility of the seminaries for the many poor in Pakistan, what is alarming is that in 1996, 750 of the 2,500 seminaries in the province of Punjab were involved in some kind of military training (Abbas 2002, 50). What is even more interesting is the direct relationship between the rise of seminaries in Pakistan and its financial endorsement from foreign governments. Abbas points out that in the 1980s, during the Soviet occupation of Afghanistan and the American as well as Muslim fears of the spread of communism, "funds . . . channeled into seminaries . . . helped create new institutions for whom the funds held more attraction than religion itself" (50). The suspected misuse of seminaries as forums for radical ideologies (packaged in religious rhetoric) thus appears to be rooted in the possible financial allure of the seminaries to the extremist groups. As such, Abbas's observation of seminaries and their foreign funding brings into question a number of issues: seminaries as forums for both genuine (religion and welfare) as well as corrupt (manipulation of religion by extremist organizations) aims; the allure of seminaries to extremist groups in search for both legitimacy and finances; and the manipulation of the many children, characteristically of economically improvised backgrounds, as pawns in the political aims of extremist groups.

In a special report titled "Sects and Violence," Amir Mir (2001) noted the "growth of foreign-funded deeni [religious] madrassahs . . . serving as recruitment and training centers for sectarian militants" in Pakistan. Even more alarming is the allegation that "most of the [foreign] funds [sent for the development of seminaries for genuine purposes] were used to recruit sectarian activists from the streets . . . by militant groups operating in the country" (70). If such reports are accurate, then they validate Abbas's observation that the funds sent to these seminaries have, at times, held more attraction than religion itself, thereby lending them to misuse by extremist groups. Such misuse of seminaries further validates the concern that some madrassahs have become avenues for extremist groups in search of both legitimacy (gained as a result of pulling the poor out of the streets and providing them free food and shelter along with religious teaching) and finances (gained, in particular, from foreign funding). The mobilization of support for extremism thus derives out of the economic allure of such attachments for the poor and destitute for whom the "projects and plans [of extremist groups] appear much better and worthier of support than the corrupt, [economically] unjust and unholy governments that attempt to rule them" (Gunaratna 2002, 239). "Hence, scores of innocent citizens are left at the mercy of terrorists on the rampage in the name of religion" (Mir 2001, 71).

The danger in the rise of seminaries in Pakistan comes not only from their misuse—what I refer to as the mushrooming of the politicized madrassahs—but also from their resistance to being regulated by the federal government (Abbas 2002, 50–51). In his pursuit of domestic extremist groups, General Musharraf promulgated an ordinance in August 2002 that sought to regulate and publicize the curriculum of the seminaries as well as ban their acceptance of foreign funding. The intention was to discourage extremist groups from using seminaries as forums for their own political agendas. However, not only was this regulation met with poor response, but, worse, religious leaders termed this effort a "Western conspiracy" aimed at destroying Islamic education (51). In fact, on July 24, 2002, "religious parties and clerics of all Islamic schools of thought unanimously rejected . . . the Madrasa Registration Ordinance 2002 and vowed to continue their efforts till its withdrawal by the government" (*POT* 2002d, 3494). The leaders of the Muttahidda Majlis Amal (MMA)—Pakistan's new Islamist political parties coalition—and "the heads of various madrasa boards said they would not compromise on the independence and autonomy of madrasas." Their criticism of the madrassah ordinance was based on their view that the madrassahs were crucial in protecting the true Islamic teachings and in "guiding the nation according to the Islamic teachings." Clearly, the issue of the misuse of madrassahs by radical factions with their own political agenda was not addressed in these criticisms of the government's madrassah-regulation ordinance.

In addition to the misuse of seminaries in Pakistan, Islamic charity organizations have also come under scrutiny in terms of their misuse. Charity to the poor and helpless—or zakat—is a central component of the pillars of Islam. Numerous genuine Islamic charity organizations exist in Pakistan as well as in general in the Muslim world. These are established to provide welfare to the needy given the fact that central governments have failed, or have neglected, this task. In its efforts to track the funding of terrorist organizations such as al Qaeda, the Bush administration, in the aftermath of September 11, focused its attention on the many Islamic charity organizations (or funds) in the United States and elsewhere. Among its blacklist of groups and organizations that the administration claims support terrorism is a little-known Pakistani charity organization, the Al-Rasheed Trust. In response to the American blacklisting of this trust, the State Bank of Pakistan froze its accounts. Mubashir Zaidi (2001, 46–47) notes that unlike other charity organizations, "Al-Rasheed Trust [created in 1996] is unknown to most Pakistanis." Its creation was motivated by the desire to "undertake welfare projects within Pakistan with the help of public donations." It is true, notes Zaidi, that since its creation the Al-Rasheed Trust has expanded its operations to "help Muslims in Chechnya, Kosovo and, above all, Afghanistan." In fact, its assets are compelling. "Last year, Al-Rasheed sent 750,000 dollars in cash to Chechnya alone. . . . [The trust] also sent 20 million rupees in cash to the Taliban and 2.1 million rupees to the Muslims of Kosovo." In addition to cash, its donations have also included tons of wheat and thousands of meters of cloth to the needy. These activities alone do not, and should not, implicate this trust for supporting any terrorist activities. However, to the extent that this trust also supports jihad, which the trust defines as the need to help the millions of poor Muslims that the international aid organizations have ignored, Zaidi notes that it therefore "treads a delicate path between traditional humanitarian work and support for militant Islamic causes." In other words, because the trust has expanded its mission from mere charity disbursements to calling for action, its deeper ideological stance, as well as the strings attached to its aid, come into question.

Maulvi Abdullah, the spokesman for the Al-Rasheed Trust, denies any allegations that the trust implicitly or explicitly supports terrorism of any kind. Critical of the U.S. list, Abdullah indicated that "the trust reserves the right to take legal action against the US for including its name in the list of terrorist groups" (Zaidi 2001, 47). However, Naziha Syed Ali (2001, 56–58) notes that perhaps the most damaging piece of evidence against this organization is the newspapers that it puts out, the weekly *Dharb-i-Mumin* and the *Islam Daily*. She includes these publications among the other so-called jihadi newspapers, most of which are published by known extremist groups such as the Jaish-e-Muhammad and Harkat-ul Mujahideen. Ali claims that the "content of these publications is a mixture of a call to arms, eulogies to those who have embraced 'shahadat' (martyrdom) and morale-boosting news items for the well-wishers of the mujahideen." Each page of one such publication, the *Jaish-e-Muhammad,* "displays the picture of two crossed Kalashnikovs," and according to Ali "there can be no more succinct statement of intent than that." She further points out that the news reported by these publications undergoes a "makeover" where facts are selectively reported and at times fabricated in order to compliment the ideological mission of the sponsoring organizations. In order to appeal to and mobilize the masses of the poor and uneducated, the "publications carry quotes from the Quran and the Hadith that reinforce the importance of jihad as a pillar of the faith." Thus, indoctrination in the name of religion, along with the allure of charity and welfare provisions, are the avenue through which some charity trusts and their publications seek to appeal to the improvised and desperate masses.

As in the case of Pakistan, the Central Asian states of Kyrgyzstan, Kazakhstan, Uzbekistan, and Tajikistan have also seen a rise in Islamic militancy that has found its constituency in the economic destitution of the masses. Unaccountable and unrepresentative governments, disinterested in the welfare of the majority, again present the dominant factor in understanding militancy in this region. In his analysis of the rise in Islamic militancy in Central Asia, Ahmed Rashid (2002) points to three prominent Islamist groups: the Islamic Renaissance Party (IRP), an Islamic political organization created in 1990 with branches in several Central Asian states; the Islamic Movement of Uzbekistan (IMU), a militant Islamic group created in 1999 by Tohrir Yuldeshev and Juma Namangani, motivated by their opposition to the Uzbekistan government; and the Hizb ut-Tahrir al-Islami (HT), a fundamentalist (and as such, an orthodox but strictly nonviolent) Islamic movement in Central Asian states. Rashid notes that "the IRP and IMU draw their main support from rural areas and farmers[, and] the HT finds most of its recruits amongst the . . . unemployed youth" (124). He notes that the "appeal of the HT in Kyrgyzstan appears to be growing because of the country's increasing poverty and public criticism that the government is incapable of solving the people's problems" (128). While the HT does not, at present, directly threaten any of the Central Asian states given its essentially nonviolent, "simplistic," and orthodox agenda, the fear is in its growing popularity among the masses (135). "For the desperate youth of Central Asia, the HT's single-minded, incorruptible activists, to whom in better times they might not have given a second thought, now appear to be saviors" (135). Of even more concern is the fear that the HT will eventually become militant because of the consistent government repression that it faces, and it is at that point that it will likely pose a terrorist threat (in the form of guerrilla warfare), amplified with its massive grassroots support network (132).

Politicized madrassahs, as in the case of Pakistan, also seem to have sprouted in Central Asian states, gaining legitimacy from the poverty of the masses and their disgruntlement toward the unrepresentative governments. The militant Islamist movement in Uzbekistan, the IMU, gained significant funding from Saudi Arabia in the 1990s with which it constructed madrassahs in Namangan (Rashid 2000, 138). The popularity of these madrassahs was obvious given their dual religious and economic functions. In fact, in Namangan, "madrassahs were so packed with young students—both boys and girls—that some ran three shifts a day to teach Koran and Islamic law and history" (139). The politicization of these madrassahs seems to have been a product of the political agendas of the founders of the IMU, Namangani and Yuldeshev. It is thought that in their personal struggle for power against President Karimov, by the end of 1991 "Yuldeshev and his men had attacked the CPU [Communist Party of Uzbekistan] headquarters and set in motion a movement that they claimed was a jihad to remove Karimov from the government of Uzbekistan" (138). In fact, the misuse of madrassahs—as forums for the political and ideological indoctrination of the unsuspecting masses—may be evident from the fact that "none of Namangani's former friends and allies credit him with much understanding of Islam" but that he is motivated instead by his hate for the Uzbek government (143).

SCOPE OF THE THREAT

Immediately after the US cruise missile attacks on Sudan and Afghanistan [in 1998], Osama's popularity among the [militant] Islamists [groups] reached a peak . . . [and] Islamabad [Pakistan] . . . realized it was a question of time before he would bring disaster on the Pakistani . . . people.

— ROHAN GUNARATNA, *Inside al Qaeda*

We have retreated from one front [Afghanistan] but that does not mean the cause is finished. We have plenty of other fronts—Kashmir, Palestine, Chechnya.

Unidentified Jihadi after the October 2001 bombing of Afghanistan, HUSSAIN ASKARI, "Cause and Effect"

Al-Qaeda . . . and their associate organizations continue to manipulate Islam as a weapon of politics.

ROHAN GUNARATNA, *Inside al Qaeda*

To analyze the relationship between the domestic ultra-extremist terrorist groups in Pakistan and the broader threat of al Qaeda to both Pakistan and beyond requires speculation regarding sympathies toward and alliances with al Qaeda from extremist groups, particularly in Pakistan and many Central Asian states, in the aftermath of October 2001 and the destruction of al Qaeda's bases in Afghanistan. In Pakistan, a list of domestic extremist groups—or the so-called jihadi outfits banned by the government of General Musharraf as of late—includes the following: Sipah-i-Sahaba Pakistan (SSP), translated as soldiers of the Prophet's companions, and its ultra-militant offshoot, Lashkar-e-Jhangvi (LJ), translated as the army of Jhangvi (the name of a town);[12] Lashkar-e-Toiba (LeT), translated as army of the pure; Hezb-ul-Mujahidin (Hezb), translated as the party of freedom fighters; Harkat-ul Mujahidin (HuM), translated as movement of the freedom fighters, and its militant offshoot Jayash-e-Muhammed (JeM), translated as army of Muhammed; and Sipah-e-Muhammed (SM), translated as soldiers of Prophet Muhammed and Tahrik-i Jafaria Pakistan (TJP) (Shia groups). The Pakistani government's efforts at targeting these extremist groups have been frustrated by the fact that most have gone underground after being banned. Ilyas Khan (2001, 27) notes that "according to some observers, this is the lull before the storm." In Central Asian states, a list of prominent Islamist groups include Hizb ut-Tahrir al-Islami (HT), a fundamentalist, nonviolent Islamic group in Central Asia; Islamic Movement of Uzbekistan (IMU), a militant Islamist group of Uzbekistan; and the Islamic Renaissance Party (IRP), an Islamist political party founded in Tajikistan.

Lieutenant General Dan McNeil, American commander of coalition forces in Afghanistan, speaking from the Bagram Air Base in Afghanistan in August 2002, noted that there might be more al Qaeda fighters in Pakistan now than in the original theater of war.[13] If this is true, then the danger of such al Qaeda infiltrations comes from the group's ability to collaborate with domestic-based extremist groups despite the fact that, as a U.S. intelligence official noted, they (al Qaeda) do not "operate with impunity there like they did in Afghanistan."[14] Given the hypothesis that al Qaeda's threat to Pakistan is a function of its collaborations with host domestic extremist groups, the strength of domestic extremist groups comes into question. Various reports suggest that hard-core militants number several thousand in Pakistan (Khan 2001, 28)—a statistic that reinforces the fact that only a small fraction of Pakistani society is radicalized and that "militancy or terrorism . . . [in Pakistan] is not approved of by most of the citizens" (Rehman 2001). The added danger from domestic extremist groups' collaborations with members of al Qaeda comes from the fact that members of such groups "are trained in the use of light and heavy weapons, explosives and urban warfare. They are also highly motivated and their suicide squads are considered extremely dangerous" (Khan 2001, 28).

In extrapolating the threat of al Qaeda by extension of its collaborations with domestic extremists groups in Pakistan, Gunaratna (2002, 206) notes that al Qaeda had already penetrated a number of extremist groups as early as the 1990s, "in particular, Harkat-ul Mujahidin (HuM), Jayash-e-Muhammad (JeM), Hezb-ul-Mujahidin (Hezb) and Lashkar-e-Toiba (LeT)." While these extremist groups were originally independent, Gunaratna notes that they "gradually came under the influence of Al-Qaeda" (209). In analyzing the broader al Qaeda networks, he further notes that "at the behest of Al-Qaeda, HuM [has] provided weapons to ASG [Abu Sayyaf Group] in the Philippines." While HuM is estimated to be five thousand strong, its ultra-militant offshoot faction, JeM, is estimated to be two thousand strong. More significantly, if, as speculated, HuM has been infiltrated by al Qaeda, it is very likely that JeM has followed the same fate. JeM poses a threat not only to Pakistan, but also to India through its jihad in Indian-administered Kashmir and its recruitment in India. Clearly, such information points to an operational reach of al Qaeda that was not limited to Afghanistan and that spans to Pakistan, India, and beyond. One must understand, however, that the failure of Pakistani or Indian governments in effectively reining in such terrorist groups does not implicate the government but, instead, points to the fact that such organizations are, in Gunaratna's words, "out of control" (213). In fact, "in response to the Pakistani government's crackdown on Islamists in Karachi, bin Laden wrote an open letter dated September 24, 2001," that sought to broaden the appeal of al Qaeda by portraying General Musharraf as an enemy of the "true believers" (216).

The disputed territory of Kashmir, according to Gunaratna (2002), offers another recruiting ground for al Qaeda. In fact, he notes, "immediately after the Soviet withdrawal, [al Qaeda] provided combat trainers and explosives experts to impart specialized training . . . [to] groups that participated in . . . [the Kashmir] war" (207). Then, in early "June 1999, the Taliban dispatched nearly 200 guerrillas of Al-Qaeda's 055 Brigade to fight in Kashmir." In addition, Gunaratna notes that "of the Pakistan based groups engaged in fighting in Kashmir, the three Harkat groups are ideologically and operationally intertwined with Al-Qaeda" (209). To broaden the scope of threat even further, it is thought that the Harkat forces, and by extension al Qaeda, are also fighting in "the Philippines, Bosnia and Chechnya" (214).

Perhaps the greatest threat to Pakistan from the domestic extremist groups, as well as from al Qaeda, comes from their bases or infiltration into Pakistan's most remote provinces, such as the Northwest Frontier Province (NWFP) and Balochistan. The threat here is twofold. First, these provinces are most remote and are areas where customary tribal law supercedes any constitutional law, which makes them beyond the effective control of the Pakistani central government. Second, these provinces constitute Pakistan's most economically impoverished areas where the majority of the population is likely easy target for recruitment by domestic or international terrorist organizations. In May 2002, the Pakistani army's elite special forces, the Special Services Group (SSG), moved into some remote tribal areas in the NWFP in the hopes of catching any Taliban or al Qaeda infiltrators. A botched raid that took place on a hideout in the Azam Warsak village. While some local tribesmen extended their support for the operations and goals of the SSG, there was an understanding that continued operations may offend the sensibilities of the local tribes, which may play into the hands of al Qaeda by portraying the Pakistani government as being at war with its own people.[15] The pursuit of any terrorist infiltrations in the closed tribal areas of these provinces thus poses a fundamental problem for the government of President General Musharraf.

Beyond South Asia, Central Asian states have also been speculated to be part of the broader reaches of al Qaeda. Gunaratna (2002, 169) goes as far as to note that "Al-Qaeda supported the Tajik Islamists' struggle to topple the Russian-backed Communist government" in the early 1990s. In fact, most Islamist groups in Central Asian states—both of a militant and nonmilitant nature—are thought to have sympathized with the erstwhile extremist Taliban regime (even if they had not agreed with the Taliban's particular interpretation of Islam). Rashid notes that while the HT denied receiving any funds or assistance from bin Laden, its members "clearly admired him" (Rashid 2002, 133). Further, he notes that the leader of IMU—the Uzbek's militant Islamist movement—is thought to have been "influenced by . . . Osama bin Laden" (143). Government officials in Kyrgyz and Uzbek, however, deny the moderation in these claims and point to a "meeting in Kabul in September 2000 when the Taliban, the IMU, the HT, Chechen separatists, and bin Laden held lengthy talks about future cooperation" (133). While such grandiose conspiracies seem unlikely, what is significant here is the ideological reach of bin Laden, and by extension al Qaeda, and the consequent possibility of new bases for al Qaeda in Central Asian states. Gunaratna (2002, 172) predicts that in the aftermath of the destruction of its bases in Afghanistan, "some Al-Qaeda members . . . are likely to retreat to Central Asia, where they may team up with Al-Qaeda trained associate members active in the Ferghana Valley, thereby leading to an improvement in the fighting capabilities of the Ferghana Islamists."

This offers an alarming insight to what Osama bin Laden may have meant when, in response to a question of what the United States could expect of him in the aftermath of the U.S. raids on his camp in Khost in southern Afghanistan on August 20, 1998, he replied, "For the American forces to expect anything from me, personally, reflects a very narrow perception of things" (Yusufzai 1999, 58). This statement brings to light the elusive nature of the al Qaeda terrorist organization. However, an analysis of the scope of the threat must be concluded with a mention of the limits of such a threat. In the post-9/11 era, Western media interest in Pakistan—as once again a frontline state—has given rise to questions as to the likelihood of Pakistan's nuclear arsenal falling into the hands of domestic or international terrorist groups. Perhaps the most reassuring counter to this speculated fear came from the most unlikely of all actors to offer such a reassurance, India (in light of the long historical animosities between India and Pakistan). In response to a question regarding the Pakistani government's ability to safeguard its nuclear arsenal, Indian defense minister George Fernandes, took a rather unusual stand when he stated, "A country possessing nuclear weapons does have checks and balances in place. . . . The fact is that the idea that Pakistan's nuclear assets may fall into the hands of extremists was misinformation that sought to create a panic" (Hasan 2001, 54).

MICRO TARGET, MACRO IMPACT

Gunaratna (2002) advocates three strategies for dealing with al Qaeda's threat. In the short term, he calls for better intelligence on the part of the United States as well as its international allies in the war against terrorism. In the midterm, he calls for a reevaluation, and perhaps a repudiation, of American foreign policy that has inadvertently supported repressive regimes in the Middle East, thereby providing ideological legitimization for domestic extremist groups and, by extension, al Qaeda, which seeks domestic extremist groups as surrogates. In the long-term, Gunaratna advocates the need to address what I refer to as the poverty-terrorism nexus that has provided the allure and justification for domestic terrorist groups in poverty-stricken states that, with reported collaborations with al Qaeda, broaden the threat to international security.

Gunaratna's short-term and midterm prescriptions, namely, better intelligence and the reduction of external support for repressive regimes, are already under way. His long-term prescription—namely, the need to address poverty—as it relates to effective reduction of al Qaeda's threat can only be achieved through first a crackdown on domestic extremist groups (the micro targets) in various Muslim countries. This micro target will have a macro impact—that of the reduction of al Qaeda's broader international threat in the long-term—by reducing the likelihood of al Qaeda finding new bases among existing domestic extremist groups. In the case of Pakistan, a successful crackdown on domestic extremist groups would require a two-pronged international assistance: economic and political. Economic assistance—referring to the imperative of continued international economic aid to Pakistan—would be needed to address the poverty-terrorism nexus. Political assistance—referring to the international mediation for the India-Pakistan Kashmir conflict—would be needed to reduce the legitimacy of extremist groups operating in Kashmir. With economic and political international assistance working in tandem, the constituency bases of the domestic extremist groups can be attacked, which, in the long-term, would also reduce al Qaeda's operational reach through the weakening or destruction of its surrogates (the domestic extremist groups).

Economic assistance, in the form of continued international economic aid—if used by the government to reduce the impoverishment of the masses—would have a dual impact. First, it would reduce the economic allure of joining extremist organizations (for example, in the form of free food, lodging, and education as discussed earlier) and thereby challenge the poverty-terrorism nexus. Second, it would assist President General Musharraf in his efforts at targeting domestic extremist groups by offering the masses an alternative to jihad[16] and martyrdom. In a statement verifying the importance of international economic assistance in Pakistan's crackdown on domestic extremist groups, Gunaratna (2002, 217) notes that "most Pakistanis perceive Musharraf . . . as an honest, strong and pragmatic leader who has the country's interest at heart, and they will most likely support his crack-down on extremism provided it benefits the population at large."

The United States appears to recognize the importance of continued economic assistance to Pakistan. In early 2002, the Bush administration announced an "economic package for Pakistan, including a proposal to Congress for $1 billion dollars in debt relief, [an] additional $100 million for education [absolutely crucial in order to offer the poor an alternative to the free education offered by the madrassahs] and $142 million dollars in increased market access for Pakistani apparel exports" (Mirza and Haider 2002).

Political international assistance to Pakistan would have to mean an international mediation for the Kashmir dispute, which has two dimensions: the Kashmiri struggle for independence from India, and the Pakistan-India dispute over territory that is Kashmir. If the justification for jihad in Kashmir can be removed—which currently is being provided by the Kashmiri struggle for independence—then the bases for the popularity and legitimacy of domestic extremist groups operating in Kashmir can be reduced or eliminated. Although the Kashmiri independence struggle became an important new theater of war for al Qaeda with the Soviet withdrawal from Afghanistan in 1989, scholars argue that Kashmir has become even more important for al Qaeda in the aftermath of the destruction of its bases in Afghanistan in October 2001 (Gunaratna 2002, 207–14). Gunaratna speculates that Kashmir will become the new, indirect recruiting grounds for al Qaeda through its penetration of extremist groups fighting alongside the Kashmiris. Thus, the speculation is that the war in Kashmir offers another jihad for both al Qaeda and its beneficiaries and sympathizers (domestic extremist groups) that will continue to be exploited, broadening the scope of al Qaeda's threat, unless the conflict is settled. Given this, the more difficult question is how to de-escalate the war in Kashmir and thereby de-legitimize the extremist groups operating there.

In terms of the dimension of the Kashmir conflict that is the India-Pakistan territorial dispute, Pakistan's stand has consistently been the need for a "meaningful dialogue between Pakistan and India to resolve the Kashmir dispute in line with the wishes of the Kashmiri people" (*POT* 2002c, 3393). Implied in this statement is the right for self-determination of the Kashmiri people as embodied in the UN resolutions that also provide for holding a plebiscite. Thus, the implication in Pakistan's statement comprises the second dimension of the Kashmir conflict: the desires of the Kashmiri people. Given the claims that "Kashmiris are waging a legitimate struggle for the implementation of UN resolution" and that India has been "trying to crush the Kashmiri struggle through brutal military might," the basis for the legitimacy of extremist groups, through their calls for jihad, becomes apparent (3393). In other words, while the Kashmiri struggle dates back more than fifty years, "the genuine Kashmiri resistance to Indian occupation has been eclipsed and, in some instances, tarnished by the outsiders who have done grave disservice to the Kashmiri cause by giving it a terrorist image" (*POT* 2002b, 3888). Cracking down on extremist groups operating in Kashmir, and consequently destroying any al Qaeda cells harboring within these groups, then becomes an issue implicit in the suggestion of the internationally sponsored resolution of the Kashmiri conflict. Such a resolution, by offering the Kashmiris some sense of a recourse, would likely take the fuel out of the extremist groups calling for jihad and, by extension, reduce their legitimacy in Kashmir. In a telephone conversation with President Bush, President General Musharraf noted that the "US must play an honest role to iron out differences between India and Pakistan over the Kashmir issue as a quid pro quo for its cooperation in the war against terrorism" (*POT* 2002f, 3430). In fact, even India, which has hitherto been averse to the idea of international mediation over the Kashmir dispute, has been reported as indicating an interest in such an idea.

CONCLUSION

Extreme poverty, particularly in Pakistan and Central Asia, is the crucial variable in the persistence of terrorism—domestic as well as international. The failure or inability of government to provide welfare to the masses of poor in these countries has enabled terrorist leadership to fill the void by offering economic incentives in exchange for radical political indoctrination. Thus, the (elite) leadership of domestic and international terrorist organizations, such as al Qaeda, continues to mobilize the impoverished, uneducated masses via essentially political rhetoric packaged in religious terms. Recent antiwar rallies in the United States, in particular in Boston, Massachusetts, in November 2002, carried the popular banner "War Is the Real Enemy," equating war with terrorism and war as the root cause of terrorism. However, pacifist arguments aside, the real enemy of peace is poverty.

Given the elusive nature of al Qaeda, its worldwide operational reach is extensive, forging networks and seeking new bases within already existing domestic extremist groups in Pakistan as well as in the states of Central Asia. The scope of al Qaeda's threat, both to Pakistan and beyond, is significant and requires long-term counter-terrorism measures. Among the most important long-term measures is international economic and political assistance to reduce the broader threat of supranational (transnational) terrorist organizations such as al Qaeda. An effective crackdown on domestic extremist groups (the micro targets) would ultimately reduce the broader threat from al Qaeda (the macro impact) by destroying new potential bases for al Qaeda within already existing extremist groups in Muslim states.

In the case of Pakistan, the targeting of domestic extremist groups would require both international economic and political assistance, particularly U.S. mediation in the Pakistan-India Kashmir dispute. While the nuances of the Pakistan-India Kashmir conflict and the Kashmiri struggle for independence from India are beyond the scope of this chapter, the conflict in Kashmir offers justification for extremist groups to expand their recruitment. Thus, international political assistance to resolve this conflict is imperative in reducing or eliminating the constituency bases for both domestic terrorist groups in Kashmir and, by extension, the operational reach of al Qaeda.

Putting these counterterrorist measures into action is likely going to be a challenge that may even bring into question the viability of some of the recommendations introduced here. Certainly, Pakistan does not stand alone with the presence of terrorist groups on its soil that it has been unable to effectively cripple. Other countries such as Sri Lanka, Israel, the Philippines, Colombia, Russia, India, Egypt, Algeria, and Spain have also been grappling with a similar problem. Thus, creating some sort of internationally recognized protocol for addressing terrorism seems much in need, as abstract as it may initially be. To this end, as Shakuat Qadir, a retired Pakistani soldier and a student of international terrorism, has said,

> If terrorism is to be eradicated from the world, a comprehensive strategy must be evolved. It must target those who are already terrorists and punish them. It must also resolve issues that create terrorists. It must address the three components—the head, torso and limbs—in a manner that prevents the birth of those who are compelled, for whatever reason, to join the swelling ranks of the terrorists (Qadir 2001, 49).

NOTES

I would like to thank Ayesha Jalal and Ejaz Haider for their most valuable comments on an earlier version of this chapter.

1. Ayesha Jalal brought this most important qualification to my attention in an informal email correspondence.

2. Ejaz Haider is the renowned columnist of the popular *Friday Times* (Lahore, Pakistan) and a current fellow at the Brookings Institute, Washington, D.C.

3. For more on the micro target–macro impact hypothesis, see Haleem (2004).

4. A detailed analysis of the Pakistani and American assistance of the mujahideens during the Soviet occupation of Afghanistan, and the intricacies of the facilitation of the Taliban in post-Soviet Afghanistan by Pakistan and its tacit support by the United States, cannot be outlined here given the scope of the chapter. Instead, the intension here is to highlight strategies and actions of the past that have contributed to regional and international terrorism.

5. This is not to imply that only the United States and Pakistan saw an opportunity to pursue economic interests in post-Soviet Afghanistan. One can add to the list Turkey, Israel, Russia, and the governments of Central Asian states. However, a comprehensive analysis of all the actors involved in post-1989 Afghanistan, and the impact they had in facilitating the Taliban and by extension Osama bin Laden, is beyond the scope of this chapter. For a detailed analysis, see Rashid (2000).

6. "Al-Qaeda Has Reorganized: NYT report," *Dawn* Internet Edition, June 17, 2002, www.dawn.com/2002/06/17/top16.htm.

7. "400 Held in Countrywide Crackdown," *Dawn* Internet Edition, May 11, 2002, www.dawn.com/2002/05/11/top4.htm.

8. "Police Arrest 16 Suspected Al-Qaeda Extremists," *Dawn* Internet Edition, April 2, 2002, www.dawn.com/2002/04/02/welcome.htm.

9. Salman Hussein, "Terrorist Attack Shakes Musharraf's Government," *Friday Times* Internet Edition, May 11, 2002, www.thefridaytimes.com. These extremist groups are discussed further in the section "Scope of Threat."

10. An issue to be discussed later as an antidote to the poverty-terrorism nexus in the section "Micro Target, Macro Impact."

11. The connection between seminaries and poverty is discussed later in this section.

12. It is interesting to note that Pakistani security agencies are currently investigating a possible link between India's intelligence agency, the Research and Analysis Wing (RAW), and this sectarian terrorist group, Lashkar-e-Jhangvi. For more information on the possible infiltrations of RAW into the ranks of LJ, for the purposes of destabilizing the Pakistani government and its relations with the United States, see "RAW-Pak Militant Bodies Link Being Probed," *POT* [Public Opinion Trends] *Analyses and News Service: Pakistan Series* 30(174) (July 30, 2002): 3432.

13. "More Al-Qaeda Men Now in Pakistan than Afghanistan: US," *Nation* Internet Edition, August 18, 2002, www.nation.com.pk.

14. "Al-Qaeda Regrouping in Pakistan," *Dawn* Internet Edition, June 18, 2002, www.dawn.com/2002/06/18.top14.htm.

15. "Tribesmen Held in Hunt for Al-Qaeda," *Dawn* Internet Edition, June 28, 2002, www.dawn.com/2002/06/28.top7.htm.

16. As defined (or misinterpreted) by extremist groups, that is, in terms of violence and terrorism.

REFERENCES

Abbas, Azmat. 2001. "The Real Battlefront." *Herald* (Karachi, Pakistan), November.
———. 2002. "Trail of Terror." *Herald* (Karachi, Pakistan), August.
Abbas, Zaffar. 2001. "Cause and Effect." *Herald* (Karachi, Pakistan), October.
Ahmed, Sanaa. 2001. "The Money Trail." *Herald* (Karachi, Pakistan), October.
Ali, Naziha Syed. 2001. "A Call to Arms." *Newsline* (Karachi, Pakistan), December.
Ali, Syed Mubashir, and Faisal Bari. 2001. "At the Millennium: Macro Economic Performance and Prospects." In *Pakistan 2000*, ed. Charles Kennedy and Craig Baxter. New York: Lexington Books.
Askari, Hussain. 2001. "Cause and Effect." *Herald* (Karachi, Pakistan), December.
Gunaratna, Rohan. 2002. *Inside al Qaeda: Global Network of Terror*. New York: Columbia University Press, 2002.
Haider, Ejaz. 2002. "Pakistan's Transition to Democracy: Internal Contradictions, External Implications." Paper presented at a forum of the Tufts University Fletcher School of Law and Diplomacy, sponsored by the Center for South Asian and Indian Ocean Studies and the Tufts Association of South Asians (TASA), Medford, Massachusetts, November 14.
Haleem, Irm. "Micro Target, Macro Impact: The Resolution of the Kashmir Conflict as a Key to Shrinking Al-Qaeda's Terrorist Network." *Terrorism and Political Violence* 16(1) (Spring 2004): 18–47.

Hasan, Syed Ali Dayan. 2001. "An Interview: George Fernandes." *Herald* (Karachi, Pakistan), December.

Hoffman, Bruce. 2002. "Rethinking Terrorism and Counterterrorism Since 9/11." *Studies in Conflict and Terrorism* 25(5) (September–October): 303–16.

Khan, M. Ilyas. 2001. "Waiting for the Storm." *Herald* (Karachi, Pakistan), October.

Mickolus, Edward. 2002. "How Do We Know We're Winning the War against Terrorists? Issues in Measurement." *Studies in Conflict and Terrorism* 25(3) (May–June): 151–60.

Mir, Amir. 1999. "Unholy Crusade." *Newsline* (Karachi, Pakistan), October.

———. 2001. "Sects and Violence." *Newsline* (Karachi, Pakistan), October.

Mirza, Tahir, and Masood Haider. 2002. "US Pledges $1 Billion Debt Relief: Linked to Antiterrorism, Fair Polls and De-escalation." *Dawn* Internet Edition, February 15. www.dawn.com/2002/02/15.top1.htm.

Norton-Taylor, Richard. 2002. "Bali Carnage Proves Saddam Is Wrong Target." *Dawn* Internet Edition, October 15. www.dawn.com/2002/10/15/int10.htm.

POT. 2002a. "Al-Qaeda Search in Fata to Reach Bannu, Kohat, Mianwali." *Public Opinion Trends Analyses and News Service: Pakistan Series* 30(173) (July 29): 3422.

———. 2002b. "Jehadis' Hijacking of Foreign Policy." *Public Opinion Trends Analyses and News Service: Pakistan Series* 30(193) (August 22): 3888–89.

———. 2002c. "Musharraf for Meaningful Dialogue on Kashmir." *Public Opinion Trends Analyses and News Service: Pakistan Series* 30(172) (July 27): 339–94.

———. 2002d. "Religious Parties Reject Madrasa Ordinance." *Public Opinion Trends Analyses and News Service: Pakistan Series* 30(177) (August 2): 3494.

———. 2002e. "Study Underlines Causes of Religious Extremism." *Public Opinion Trends Analyses and News Service: Pakistan Series* 30(195) (August 24): 3915–16.

———. 2002f. "US Mediator Role in Resolution of Kashmir Issue." *Public Opinion Trends Analyses and News Service: Pakistan Series* 30(174) (July 30): 3430.

Qadir, Shaukat. 2001. "Understanding Jihad." *Herald* (Karachi, Pakistan), October.

Rashid, Ahmed. 2000. *Taliban: Militant Islam, Oil and Fundamentalism in Central Asia.* New Haven, Conn.: Yale University Press.

———. 2002. *Jihad: The Rise of Militant Islam in Central Asia.* New Haven, Conn.: Yale University Press.

Rehman, Main Saifur. 2001. "A Moderate Country." Islamic Republic of Pakistan: Official Website. www.pak.gov.pk/public/A_moderate_Country.htm.

Shahzad, Asif. 2002. "2 More Al-Qaeda Men Arrested." *Dawn* Internet Edition, April 4. www.dawn.com/2002/04/04.top6.htm.

Yusufzai, Rahimullah. 1999. "Our Primary Targets Are the World's Infidels." Interview with Osama bin Laden. *Newsline* (Karachi, Pakistan), January.

Zaidi, Mubashir. 2001. "Charity or Terrorism?" *Herald* (Karachi, Pakistan), October.

FIGURE 8.1   Seminaries in Pakistan: 1947-71   —— Seminaries

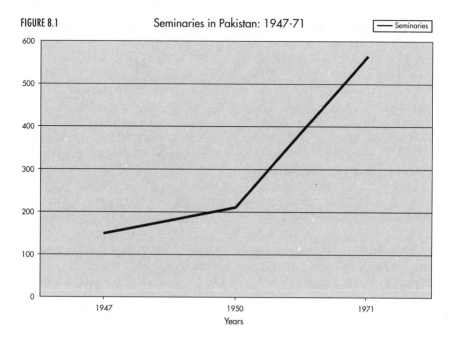

FIGURE 8.2   Seminaries in the Province of Punjab, Pakistan   —— Seminaries

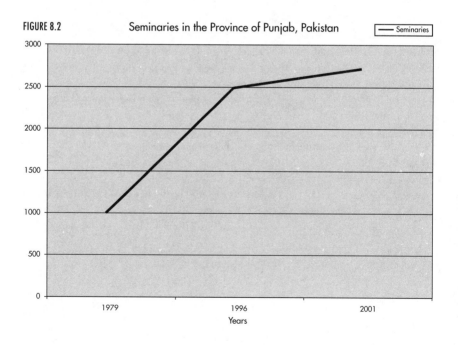

ABDULLAH AL-FAQIH

Promoting Democracy and Fighting Terrorism
A CONTRADICTION?

INTRODUCTION

The terrorist attacks on the United States in September 2001 brought to the forefront a small, impoverished, and otherwise obscure country on the southern tip of the Arabian Peninsula. Yemen (the formal name is the Republic of Yemen [ROY]), a country rarely mentioned in Western media, has become a frequent theme in the last few years. Its claim to fame is derived from the fact that Osama bin Laden—America's number one enemy—descended from a family that traces its roots to a remote region in the country. Yemen's is also derived from a mix of stereotypes, orientalist generalizations, and some valid observations. This scanty knowledge led many Western academics and officials to conclude that Yemen may very well serve as the successor to the Taliban's Afghanistan. The argument frequently presented is that the government of the ROY is weak and unable to extend its power to vast regions in the country where tribal chiefs still hold the final word, and, as the argument goes, those tribal chiefs are supporters of al Qaeda.

BACKGROUND

Historically, Yemen has been a complex place, not only for Americans and the West in general, but also for its people. For Americans, Yemen was for the most part too complex to comprehend and too marginal to invest time and money in to unravel its mysteries. When a revolution broke out in north Yemen on September 26, 1962, and established what would later be known as the Yemen Arab Republic (YAR), the Kennedy administration reluctantly recognized the new government.[1] It did so not to appease Nasser of Egypt, who backed the revolutionary change in Yemen. Nor did it want to upset the Saudis, who fiercely opposed political change in the country and saw in the creation of the YAR a serious threat to their national security.[2]

By recognizing the new political realities in Yemen, the Kennedy administration sought to present itself as a supporter of freedom at a time when many countries were struggling to break away from the control of colonists or despots. In addition, the Kennedy administration sought to block Soviet headway in the Arabian Peninsula. This latter goal was not totally achieved, because the Soviets did manage to find a foothold in the Arabian Peninsula after the new leadership in postindependence South Yemen adopted Marxism-Leninism as the ideology of the state.

During the 1960s, 1970s, and 1980s, the U.S. government chose to see Yemeni affairs through Saudi lenses, partially to appease the Saudis, who viewed Yemen as their own backyard, and partially to avoid the cost of a direct involvement in Yemen. The American officials' disinterest in Yemen resulted in a parallel attitude from corporate America, the rest of the West, and foreign investors in general. During the 1980s, American oil companies—worried by the prospects of a prolonged Iraq-Iran war and disruption of oil supplies—showed interest in exploration for oil in Yemen. It was this newfound interest in Yemeni oil that led George H. W. Bush, then vice president, to visit Yemen in 1986. This visit, however, did not mark a shift in U.S. policy toward Yemen. The U.S. government continued, as it had before, to ignore the attempts of Yemeni leadership to establish direct relations between the two countries.

When the two Yemens, the YAR and the People's Democratic Republic of Yemen (PDRY) decided to merge, the United States—again despite implicit Saudi opposition—blessed the move, hoping that it would bring stability and an end once and for all to the communist regime in the PDRY. Even when Yemen allegedly sided with Saddam Hussein and opposed the presence of foreign troops in the Gulf region in 1990, American officials were quick to forgive Sana'a for its miscalculation.[3]

The American position of selective and careful involvement was once again repeated during Yemen's 1994 civil war. When the leadership of the Yemeni Socialist Party (YSP)—the former ruling party in South Yemen—declared secession, the Clinton administration found itself in a very delicate position. On the one hand, the administration did not want to upset its number one ally in the Arabian Peninsula—Saudi Arabia—who tacitly supported the secession. On the other, the administration knew that secession would only trigger instability in a region where the United States had vital interests. Again, the U.S. government found itself on the side of Yemeni unity because it was the best way to avoid destabilization of the region and disruption of the flow of oil.

On the question of democracy, the U.S. government showed less enthusiasm from the beginning. While it welcomed the unification of Yemen and the adoption of democracy as a system of governance, it was keen not to send the wrong message to Yemenis or their neighbors in the Peninsula. For Americans, because of Yemen's location to the south of the Arabian Peninsula's archaic but friendly monarchies, supporting democracy in Yemen was more symbolic than real.[4]

The American difficulty in reconciling support for democracy and ensuring stability in the Arabian Peninsula was reflected in a comment made by David Mack, U.S. deputy secretary of state for Middle Eastern Affairs, during a visit to Yemen in the aftermath of the 1993 elections. While affirming U.S. support for democracy in Yemen, Mr. Mack implicitly warned Yemenis not to try to export democracy to their neighbors in the Peninsula (Watkins 1993).[5]

A SHIFT IN POLICY

Despite the setback in U.S.-Yemen relations in the early 1990s derived largely from Yemen's position on the Iraqi invasion of Kuwait,[6] relations between the two countries continued to grow after the end of the 1994 civil war. However, the U.S. shift in policy did not occur until the last half of the 1990s. While historically the U.S. government chose to let the Saudis filter its relation with Yemen the way they saw fit, U.S.-Saudi relations began experiencing difficulties during the second half of the 1990s.

This mishap in U.S.-Saudi relations was caused by the Saudi approach to building legitimacy and ensuring political survival. The Saudis, lacking the ideological leverage to counter Arab nationalism, communism, and other transnational ideologies, made it their duty to spread Wahhabism—an Islamic puritanical school to which the Saudi royal family subscribes. The United States found it in their interest to implicitly back the Saudi efforts to undermine the enemies of the West.[7] The fourfold increase in oil prices after the 1973 war between some Arab countries and Israel gave the royal family in Saudi Arabia the funding they needed to spread Wahhabism. This strategy backfired when Wahhabism broke ranks with the Saudi royal family and adopted a line of opposition to American presence in the land of the Muslims' two holiest shrines. With the religious elements resorting to violence, primarily targeting Americans in Saudi Arabia, the U.S. government grew leery of the Saudi royal family's policies in handling the Wahhabists. The Saudi denial of access to American investigators seeking to unravel the intricacies of attacks on Americans in Saudi Arabia in 1995 and 1996 caused a further rift between the two countries.

Deterioration in U.S.-Saudi relations led to a change in the U.S. approach to relations with Yemen. During the first half of the 1990s, the U.S. government had five objectives in its policy towards Yemen: (1) normalization of Saudi-Yemeni relations and the resolution of border conflict as an imperative for stability in the Arabian Peninsula, (2) normalization of relations between Yemen and Israel and an active Yemeni role in the Middle East peace process, (3) fighting terrorism, (4) economic reform, and (5) Yemeni domestic reconciliation and the solving of problems resulting from the 1994 civil war (Hudson 1997, 171–74).

In the last half of the 1990s, due largely to developments in U.S.-Saudi relations, the number one objective for America was to get a foothold in Yemen. Military and security cooperation became the dominant story, with top U.S. military personnel visiting Yemen frequently. In contrast, Yemen's interest in courting the United States revolved around economic interests. The Yemenis wanted the Clinton administration to support Yemen's economic growth directly by providing loans and grants and indirectly by propping up Yemen's position in international organizations (especially the International Monetary Fund and the World Bank). As far as security issues were concerned, the Yemeni officials tactically exploited the U.S. interest in strong security cooperation to pressure the Saudis to agree to a solution to disputes regarding the Saudi-Yemeni border.

The American goals in Yemen, in descending order, included military concessions, normalization with Israel, and the fight against terrorism. American military interests in Yemen started in the mid-1990s. As Alfred Prados states:

> Yemen has assumed increasing importance in U.S. strategic planning, as the
> United States faces a continuing requirement to maintain forces in the Persian
> Gulf region and expand command and logistics facilities in the area. At present,
> approximately 25,000 U.S. military personnel are deployed in the Persian Gulf region where they conduct overflights of Iraqi territory, interdict the flow of banned
> goods into or out of Iraq by boat, and help deter threats from Iraq (or possibly
> Iran) against Kuwait, Saudi Arabia, or other key U.S. allies. U.S. ties to Yemen,
> which lies athwart important waterways en route to the Persian Gulf, are designed
> to facilitate these missions, to support local counterterrorist efforts, and to contribute toward stability in the oil-rich Arabian Peninsula. (Prados 1999)

What made the United States more interested in Yemen in the last half of the 1990s were changes in U.S.-Saudi relations. With the growing discontent within Saudi Arabia and the desire of the Saudi royal family to distance itself from Americans, there was a feeling in Washington that Yemen, with its borders problem with Saudi Arabia, could serve an important American interest. "The issue of Saudi stability [had] been factored into Washington's strategic thinking for several years" even before the events of September 11. American concern with the stability of Saudi Arabia dramatically increased after the 1996 terrorist attack on the Khobar military barracks in Saudi Arabia, which killed nineteen Americans. The United States feared that Saudi Arabia—a close ally—might be lost in a similar fashion as Iran was lost to the Islamists in 1979. The rise of Crown Prince Abdullah—"regarded as a pious, incorruptible leader more responsive to the people and more willing than his predecessor, King Fahd, to take on Washington"—to power after deterioration of King Fahd's health set off an alarm in Washington (Sciolino 2001).

Yemenis welcomed the American interest and tried to use it to pressure the Saudis into solving the border disputes between the two countries. As a result, bilateral military activities increased after 1995. This was evident in the increase of the number of visits by senior U.S. military officers. It was also evident in the joint training exercises conducted by the two countries and in the U.S. participation in the establishment of a coast guard to help Yemen protects its borders. In addition, "Since 1997, U.S. special forces teams have trained 270 Yemeni Army personnel in de-mining operations" (Prados 2000).

The U.S. military also showed a greater interest in using the port of Aden because of its strategic location "at the crossroads of the Red Sea and Arabian Sea," and because it "is one of the world's largest natural harbors. . . . The convenience of Aden, increasing political or logistical problems at other nearby ports, and a desire to deepen defense relationships with Yemen, led U.S. officials to seek refueling privileges in Aden for ships en route to the Persian Gulf. In 1998, Yemen agreed to provide bunkering in Aden for 600,000 barrels of oil to support U.S. naval operations in the region" (Prados 2000).

In terms of normalization with Israel, the United States used its economic support for Yemen as leverage to push Yemen to establish relations with the Jewish state. However, because Yemen (unlike, for example, Jordan and Egypt) was not a frontier state, the U.S. government did not press Yemen as much, nor did it offer generous rewards for Yemen's subsequent moves. As a step in this direction, the ROY in December 1997 took part, along with other Arab countries, in a conference hosted by Qatar, the purpose of which was to discuss economic normalization with Israel. This event was highly controversial because it was boycotted by the United States's major allies in the Arab world, namely Egypt and Saudi Arabia (Fisk 1997). Furthermore, the Yemeni government under pressure from the United States started in early 2000 allowing Jews of Yemeni descent to visit Yemen. Although members of the group were carrying British and American passports, the visit attracted media attention and served

TABLE 9.1 **Major terrorist attacks against American targets since the end of the Gulf War (1990–91)**

December 29, 1992	Attacks on two hotels in Yemen where American troops en route to Somalia were staying; no American casualties
February 26, 1993	Attack on the North Tower of the World Trade Center in New York; 6 people killed and more than 1,000 injured
November 13, 1995	A bomb attack on a joint training facility in Riyadh; 5 killed, including 1 American
June 25, 1996	A truck loaded with explosives blew up at the Khobar military barracks in Dhahran, Saudi Arabia; 19 U.S. service personnel killed and 240 injured
August 7, 1998	U.S. embassies in Kenya and Tanzania were attacked; 213 people killed, including 12 Americans
October 12, 2000	Attack on the USS *Cole* in the port of Aden, Yemen; 17 U.S. servicemen killed
September 11, 2001	Attacks on the World Trade Center and the Pentagon; more than 3,000 people killed

Eleanor Hill, Staff Director, Joint Inquiry Staff, U.S. Senate, October 8, 2002. Hearing on the Intelligence Community's Response to Past Terrorist Attacks against the United States from February 1993 to September 2001. "Security Incidents in Yemen, 1990–1994," www.al-bab.com/yemen/data/incident94.htm. U.S. Department of State, "Significant Terrorist Incidents, 1961–2003: A Brief Chronology," www.state.gov/r/pa/ho/pubs/fs/5902.htm. Estimates of casualties vary among sources.

as an embarrassment for the Yemeni government. The Yemeni government also continued its policy of letting Yemeni Jews leave Yemen if they chose to do so (Gleit 2000).

Terrorism became a concern for the United States in its relations with Yemen, especially after the occurrence of attacks against American targets since the end of the Gulf War (table 9.1). However, as we will see, terrorism did not become the number one item on the U.S. agenda in Yemen until the attack on the USS *Cole*.

Current Yemeni president Abdullah Saleh received support from President Clinton on his 1999 presidential victory. He was also commended for his democratic views despite talks of his election being a sham.

TERRORISM IN YEMEN

The Yemeni connection started in the 1970s when the Saudis, in coordination with their security guarantor—the United States—decided to wage their war on communism by employing Islam. With South Yemen becoming the only communist country in the Arab world and with the threat it represented to the Saudi royal family and other monarchies in the Peninsula, Yemen was selected as a battleground in the fight against the evil empire. Throughout the 1970s and the 1980s, thousands of schools were created across Yemen to recruit and nurture a generation of young Yemenis who were as puritanical as the Saudis and Americans wanted them to be. In an impoverished country such as Yemen, Islamism became a profession, a career, and the only way to gain access to education and livelihood. During the 1980s, many Yemenis, with Saudi sponsorship, went to Afghanistan to join the jihad against the Soviets. Within Yemen itself, some top army officers and members of the ruling class became involved in the process of recruiting and preparing the mujahideen. As long as wealthy Saudis and leaders of jihad, such as Osama bin Laden, were paying the bills, jihad became a profitable trade for some Yemenis.[8]

By the late 1990s, Yemen had more jihadis than there were battles for jihad, and many of those jihadis turned toward their own country to liberate it from the infidel Yemenis! There are numerous stories of children in Saudi-sponsored madrassahs who turned against their own parents, friends, and relatives and accused them of being infidels. The veiling of women, which was common only in urban centers, became a countrywide phenomenon, and women failing to veil were subject to harassment and intimidation. Islamism, especially after the defeat of the leftist opposition to the regime in the north, became one of the pillars of the political order, with some relatives of the president coordinating the jihad efforts against the regime opponents. This was evident after Yemen unity when a wave of terror targeted the leadership of the Yemeni Social Party and led to the 1994 civil war.

When the jihad ended in Afghanistan by the late 1980s, many "Afghans" (Yemenis and non-Yemenis) returned to the country and were incorporated into civil and military institutions, especially the educational sector. Unlike other countries where the Arab "Afghans" faced detention, prosecution, and deportation, in Yemen they were welcomed. The main reasons for Yemen's behavior are its unity and the adoption of democracy. These two factors made Yemen very open, inevitably weakened political institutions, and created conflicting interests within the system.

Some of those returnees pursued a normal life; others had a radical agenda. Those belonging to the second group pursued a wave of terror that targeted members of the YSP as well as Americans and Britains. As table 9.1 illustrates, one of the early activities of this group was the attack on two hotels in the city of Aden on December 29, 1992. The target of the attack was a group of a hundred American soldiers serving as backup for U.S. military operations in Somalia. Reportedly, those who carried out the attack were acting in response to a fatwa issued by Osama bin Laden; they have not been captured (Leupp 2002).

In the 1994 civil war, the Yemeni "Afghans" (and as some alleged Arab "Afghans") played an important role in sustaining unity after the south attempted secession by siding with the northern faction (Smucker and LaFranchi 2002). Immediately after this war, the regime started a revisionist policy toward these groups and toward Islamists in general.

In mid-1997, the Yemeni government started a major operation of deportation of suspected Arab and foreign Islamists residing in the country. In this exodus, more than fifteen thousand Islamists were expelled from Yemen (Radwan 2002). This was partially in response to pressure exerted by the U.S. government and partially out of fear that those elements represented a threat to the regime.

THE USS *COLE* ATTACK

On October 12, 2000, a suspected al Qaeda suicide squad piloted a boat laden with explosives into the destroyer the USS *Cole* (Radwan 2002). The incident left seventeen American sailors dead and thirty-nine wounded. The incident caused an uproar both in the United States and in Yemen, and tensions arose between the two countries immediately after the incident because of the Yemeni government's hasty explanation attributing the incident to a fire. President Saleh initially denied that the attack was carried out by terrorists, and he suggested that the incident occurred inside (not outside) the ship.

In subsequent weeks and months, a chain of crises in U.S.-Yemen relations ensued. An interview in the *Washington Post* on December 10, 2000, with President Ali Abdullah Saleh of Yemen illustrates the issues of contention between the two sides. The following section in particular highlights the difficulties involved:

> WP: Can you talk about the agreement on the investigation guidelines that you signed [on November 29] with Washington? Do they allow the FBI to interview suspects?
>
> AAS: The agreement we signed organizes the cooperation between the U.S. and Yemeni investigators and gives the U.S. investigators greater access to information.
>
> WP: Can American investigators sit in on the interrogations of suspects and pass questions to your investigators?
>
> AAS: Yes, [the American] investigators can pass questions to the Yemeni investigators, who will ask the questions for them.
>
> WP: Will the U.S. investigators be able to sit in the same room as the suspects and the Yemeni investigators?
>
> AAS: Yes, they can sit with the Yemeni investigators, but not alone with a Yemeni suspect.
>
> WP: The United States wants to put on trial the people responsible for the attack on the *Cole*, but Yemeni law says suspects cannot be extradited. Will you let suspects go to the United States?
>
> AAS: [Extradition of suspects] is not allowed under our constitution.

WP: What about witnesses who are necessary to build a case against terrorists?

AAS: This depends on Yemeni law. A trial will be held here in Yemen in January and we will adopt all constitutional and legal measures.

WP: There have been reports that people high up in your government were involved in the bombing of the *Cole*—that such an operation couldn't have been done without high-level help.

AAS: These are weak stories aimed to create trouble with the U.S. side.

WP: To destroy the U.S.-Yemeni relationship?

AAS: They write about this as if it were a play. One opposition newspaper . . . even claimed my son was involved.

WP: Has the attack on the USS *Cole* set back U.S.-Yemeni relations?

AAS: No.

WP: Do you have any problem with the FBI being in your country? Have you and they been sharing information?

AAS: They are being treated as guests and given all facilities.

WP: There were stories after the bombing of the *Cole* in the Yemeni press that there had been a landing of U.S. tanks after the attack.

AAS: Actually there were two armored vehicles, which were brought to Aden and then taken back to the ship. . . .

WP: You told them to get them out of Aden?

AAS: We told them to take them back to the ships.

WP: Did you tell the FBI to go back to the ships, too?

AAS: We worked with them, [but] we had problems with the number of Marines at the hotel in Aden and we told them to go back to the ship, leaving only a few on shore.[9]

First, the Yemeni government, under pressure from opposition groups and fearing American intrusion, refused to allow FBI agents access to suspects. This was partially resolved when the two sides signed an agreement on November 29, 2000, that gave American investigators the opportunity to attend interrogations and submit written questions to suspects.

Second, the United States wanted to extradite suspects in the attack on the USS *Cole,* but the Yemeni government refused, citing a prohibition stipulated by article 44 of the Yemeni 1994 constitution, which states that "A Yemeni national may not be extradited to a foreign authority." Besides the president, Yemen's then prime minister (and close ally of Washington) Dr. Abdul Karim al-Iryani told *Newsweek* that the issue of extradition was "political dynamite" and that "maybe it is easier to punish them in Yemen than in the United States."[10] Worth noting is that thirteen of the suspected seventeen terrorists were Yemenis and the other three were Saudis of Yemeni descent.

Third, American investigators sought to expand the investigation to include high-ranking officials in the Yemeni government. The American side feared that the Yemeni investigators might conclude the case before solid evidence had been gathered. It appears also that Americans wanted to collect as much data as they could about possible organizations and persons in Yemen suspected of terrorism. The Yemeni side fiercely opposed such intrusive and unnecessary steps and sought to limit the investigation to the incident itself. Related to this was the issue of whether to expedite the investigation and send the suspects to court (the preference for the Yemeni side) or to postpone the trial and focus on collecting information. In the end, the Yemenis submitted to the American demand to delay the transfer of the case to court.

Fourth, the Yemeni government also felt uneasy with the presence of American investigators in the city of Aden and frequently asked them to retreat to the ships or to leave the city, citing security concerns and certain sensitivities.

Fifth, while American investigators were determined to link the incident to bin Laden, Yemeni officials were cautious in their conclusions. They did not want the incident to be used to justify an attack on a Muslim country similar to that carried out by the United States in 1998 targeting Sudan and Afghanistan. The target of the attack on Sudan turned out to be a pharmaceutical factory rather than a chemical plant. However, Yemeni officials, from time to time, made references to bin Laden. For example, Yemen's then interior minister Hussein Arab stated: "We think the *Cole* terrorists have strong links with Afghanistan and we can say, yes, there are links with bin Laden."[11]

Overall, U.S.-Yemen relations fluctuated during the investigation between steady but limited cooperation and short episodes of discord. At times, Yemen was calling the U.S. investigative tactics intrusive and the U.S. was calling Yemen uncooperative.[12] The road wasn't always smooth leading up to the September 11 attacks, but it wasn't always rocky, either. Contrary to what one may expect, the attack on the USS *Cole* appears to have strengthened (and not weakened) U.S.-Yemen relations. Not only had it brought Yemen under the American radar, but it also helped Yemen's leadership move aggressively to consolidate relations with Washington.

YEMEN'S RESPONSE TO SEPTEMBER 11

While the Yemeni government enjoyed a great deal of leeway to maneuver in its dealing with American investigators following the attack on the USS *Cole,* Yemen lacked that freedom after the horrific events of September 11. Looking back at the most recent history, the Yemeni leadership realized that neither its position on the

Iraqi invasion of Kuwait nor its handling of the investigation into the USS *Cole* incident met with U.S. expectations. President Ali Abdullah Saleh symbolized this when he acknowledged that Yemen paid a heavy price for its verbal support of Iraq in the Gulf War and that he was not going to make the same mistake again.[13] Equally significant has been the political scene in Yemen itself.

Yemen became a concern for the George W. Bush administration for many reasons. First, Yemen is the ancestral land of America's number one enemy, Osama bin Laden, and U.S. officials suspected and continue to suspect that bin Laden may move to Yemen. Second, Yemen's central government lacks effective control over vast regions in the country, especially to the north and northeast (Sachs 2002). In these regions, tribal chiefs, who are suspected of sympathizing with bin Laden, have more power than the central government. Third, as early as October 2001, a U.S. official described Yemen as having one of "the most significant" links to al Qaeda, "composed of mostly Yemenis who received military training in Afghanistan." Diplomatic sources in Yemen told CNN that "thousands of veterans of the Soviet-Afghan war are living in Yemen and were capable of launching 'uncoordinated or coordinated attacks.'"[14] The number of Yemenis joining the jihad in Afghanistan is hard to pin down, but experts put the number at somewhere between four thousand and forty thousand.[15] For Americans, the Afghanization of Yemen was a grim prospect.

The Yemeni government, in response to American concerns, acknowledges that thousands of so-called Arab "Afghans" live in the country. It stated, however, that it was carefully monitoring those returnees, that most of those Arab "Afghans" have been leading peaceful lives in the country, and that it had since 1998 deported about five thousand non-Yemenis—including the Arab "Afghans."[16] Yemen had started the deportation of Arab "Afghans" in 1998 to achieve two goals: appease the United States and other regional actors—in particular, Egypt—and minimize the risks those Arab "Afghans" presented to the country's political stability. Those Arab "Afghans" were viewed as socializing Yemenis into the opposition Islamic-oriented party—Islah.

On the question of Yemen's ability to expand the power of the central government to lawless regions, the Yemeni government repeatedly asked the United States for support. A key demand was for American help in building and equipping the Yemeni coast guard so that it could prevent infiltration of Yemen by al Qaeda elements. General Tommy Franks, during a visit to Sana'a in October 2002, confirmed Washington's commitment to help Yemen protect its coast by providing a number of boats and training the needed Yemeni individuals (Qadhi 2002).

In the aftermath of September 11, the Bush administration put Yemen under the microscope and, from time to time, there were signals sent through the media and diplomatic channels that Yemen could become the next target in America's war against terrorism. The Yemeni government did not miss those signals and acted in several ways to assure Americans that it was committed to the cause. Toward this end, the Yemeni government strongly condemned the terrorist attacks, carried out a swift wave of arrests among the Arab "Afghans," tightened the rope on the neck of its Islamist opponents, tried to expand state power and control to remote areas, and allowed Americans to carry out covert operations inside the country.

LETTERS AND STATEMENTS

In response to September 11, the Yemeni government released three separate correspondences. The first statement, issued on September 11, declared: "The Leadership, Government, and People of Yemen condemn and oppose strongly such vicious and terrorist acts." The second correspondence was a letter sent on September 12 from Yemen's foreign minister, Dr. al-Qarbi, to U.S. Secretary of State Colin Powell. In the letter, the Yemeni official wrote: "Our condemnation goes to all forms of terrorism which challenges our common vision towards peace and stability throughout the world." The third correspondence was a letter of condolence from President Saleh to President George W. Bush. In the letter, Saleh reiterated Yemen's position, adding that "such acts should not retract our efforts to curb and resist the perpetrators whoever they may be." [17]

CAMPAIGNS OF ARRESTS

Following September 11, the Yemeni government, under pressure from the United States and based on intelligence provided to it, carried out a massive campaign of arrests among the so-called Arab "Afghans." Those who were not Yemeni nationals were deported from the country, and Yemenis were kept in jail. The government also warned clerics in mosques of the danger of terrorism and its devastating impact on the economy. However, the U.S. government was pressing for the arrest of specific persons. When President Saleh of Yemen visited Washington on November 27, 2001, President Bush told him that the future of relations between the two countries (and the two leaders) would depend very much on Yemen's cooperation in the war against terrorism. Also, President Bush made it clear that the Yemeni government should without delay capture two of the most wanted al Qaeda operatives in Yemen—Qaed Sinan al-Harethi and Mohammad Ahmed al-Ahdel, who had been linked to the attack on the USS *Cole*—and if it could not, the U.S. government would send its own troops (Tyler 2002).

TARGETING ISLAH

The terrorist attacks on the United States coincided with a growing discord among political forces in Yemen. The ruling party—the General People's Congress (GPC)—was facing a growing challenge to its domination of power by the Yemeni Congregation for Reform (known also by its Arabic shorthand Islah, the Arabic word for reform). With Islah leading a coalition of opposition parties, the GPC leadership found itself in a defensive position while preparing for the upcoming elections of 2003. The events of September 11 presented Yemen with a dichotomy. All opposition parties on the left and the right outrightly rejected siding with the United States in the war against terrorism. At the same time, failing to cooperate with the United States would undermine Yemen's ruling party and make it more vulnerable to electoral defeat in 2003 elections.

Faced with this dilemma, the Yemeni government chose to side with the Americans and continues to try to crack down on its Islamists. Those who have followed the political evolution of Yemen since 1995 would see a deterioration of relations between the GPC and Islah. "The possibility of such cooperation precludes any chance that Islamists would come to power in Yemen in the foreseeable future."[18] This is also true for other parties, including the Yemeni Socialist Party and the nationalist and pan-Arabist groups.

EXPANDING STATE POWER

One of Yemen's illnesses is the stigma of lawlessness, which has been noted repeatedly in the Western media. This stigma emanates from the weakness of the central government and its inability to expand control to all areas, especially those in the north and northeast, that have become hotbeds for lawlessness and allegedly very attractive to al Qaeda remnants. Expanding state power over Yemen has been problematic. Although the United States (through the CIA) appeared to have channeled emergency aid to Yemen to deal with terrorism and train its antiterrorism forces, reports surfaced in the West that this funding might be misused. A case in point was the discovery of a North Korean shipment of Scud missiles while en route to Yemen on December 2002. As it turned out, Yemen claimed ownership of these missiles, promoting an uproar in some Western circles. As William Safire (2002) of *The New York Times* wrote, "U.S. officials were thunderstruck. Had Saleh not solemnly assured us 18 months ago, when we purchased his support in the war on terror, that he would no longer buy Scuds from North Korea? His disputes with the Saudis and Eritreans were long since resolved; the only logical explanation was that he planned to re-sell the secret shipment at a whopping profit to a nation or group that did not wish us well."

While it is not clear if the United States paid Saleh to purchase his support as Safire alleges, the missile crisis appeared to have provoked a great number of questions but offered no answers. Did the CIA offer money to the Yemeni side? If yes, how much? CNN reported that the United States had promised about $150 million to pay for security upgrades in Yemen.[19] The U.S. government also pressed Yemen to accept the presence of antiterrorism experts in the country to train Yemeni forces in counterterrorism and provide advice and assistance when needed.[20]

This move was very controversial in light of public resentment of American policy and public rejection of an American military presence. Opposition parties with the Islamists at the forefront have been trying to use this to mobilize people against the government.

AMERICAN COVERT OPERATIONS

On November 3, 2003, a CIA-operated unmanned spy plane fired a Hellfire missile at a car occupied by six suspected al Qaeda operatives—including Quaed Salim Sinan al-Harthi, whom the United States suspected of being the brains behind the attack on the USS *Cole*—in the province of Marib (Higgins and Cullison 2002). The initial explanation offered by the Yemeni government was that the car full of weapons exploded for no clear reason. Contrary to the Yemeni claim, the American government (just a few days before the November 6 midterm elections) quickly took credit for the attack. Under mounting criticism from opposition parties in regard to the Yemeni government's silence, the Yemeni government two weeks later released a statement in which it admitted that "This operation was carried out . . . as part of security coordination and cooperation between Yemen and the United States."[21]

This operation caused embarrassment for the Yemeni government, and one of the difficult questions concerns the issue of whether it knew about this operation or was surprised just like everyone else. Whatever the situation is, the Yemeni government has openly acknowledged knowing about the missile attack and said that the attack was part of a joint cooperation to combat terrorism. Not only that, but Dr. Iryani, who is now a political advisor to the president, stated in an interview with Fox News during a visit to Washington that his country would not hesitate in cooperating with the United States in the fight against terrorism even if that entails allowing Americans to carry out other covert operations against al Qaeda operatives in Yemen (Boustany 2002).

THREATS OF DISCORD

While U.S.-Yemeni relations witnessed improvement after the attack on the USS *Cole* and again after the events of September 11, the threat of discord is still present. For one thing, the Yemeni government still does not see eye to eye with the U.S. government on the question of Iraq. For another, the U.S. government continued to insist on investigating certain Yemeni individuals and has gone as far as trying to drag some Yemenis to other countries only to get them arrested. A case in point is that of Sheik Muhammad Ali Hassan al-Mouyad—a Yemeni cleric and philanthropist— who was lured by an undercover FBI agent to Germany (Lichtblau and Glaberson 2003). The U.S. government is accusing al-Mouyad of sponsoring terrorism, but the Yemeni government is denying any link between al-Mouyad and terrorist groups. Whether al-Mouyad's case or any other would develop into a crisis between the two countries is anyone's guess. It is worth noting, however, that the two countries have overcome many obstacles in the past few years, including those emanating from the investigation into the USS *Cole* and the September 11 attacks.

WHAT ABOUT DEMOCRACY?

In the early 1990s when the ROY was created and democracy was adopted as the political system of the country, the U.S. government was very shy in welcoming the move, fearing that a successful democratic experiment in Yemen might raise expectations in neighboring countries and lead to the destabilization of the friendly monarchies in the Arabian Peninsula and subsequently disrupt oil flows.

After the 1994 civil war that led to, among other things, the retreat on many democratization measures in the ROY, the U.S. concern in its dealings with Yemen was to gain a foothold in the country for its military. More democracy in Yemen was inducive to U.S. goals in the country since political parties and groups from all walks of life opposed any military concession to the United States. Therefore, the U.S. government's support for democracy in Yemen took the form of praising any measure taken no matter how modest that measure is. For example, President Saleh received support from President Clinton on his 1999 presidential victory. He was also commended for his democratic views despite talks of his election being a sham. Similar patterns were seen in the aftermath of Yemen's 2003 parliamentary elections when U.S. Secretary of State Colin Powell praised the Yemeni experiments despite widespread allegations of fraud.

In the aftermath of the September 11 attacks, and despite the rhetoric,[22] the U.S. government's policy seems to have adopted by default a cold war strategy whereby containing terrorist groups overrides any other goal. In practice, American officials appear to confuse containing terrorism with containing Islamism in its various social, political, and economic manifestations. Putting Islamism on the top of the list of America's enemies, which already includes (in the context of the Middle East) leftist, nationalist, and communist groups, leaves U.S. foreign policymakers with only one force to support, back, and ally with: that is, the current corrupt, inefficient, autocratic, and widely despised rulers.

The implications of this de facto policy are many. First, it enrages the masses in Arab/Muslim countries and deepens the anti-American feelings across the region. Second, in the long run it fosters radicalism and violence and legitimizes the use of violent means in the eyes of the masses. Third, it perpetuates the perception of the United States as a tyrannical, opportunist, unethical, anti-Muslim, and self-serving power.

For those in power in relevant countries, including Yemen, a U.S. support that is not linked directly to political and economic reforms will only exacerbate their legitimacy deficit and make their survival largely dependent on foreign support. It reduces their ability to be innovative and tackle the deteriorating social, economic, and political conditions. This in turn reinforces the power and attractiveness of radical groups that adopt terrorism as a means to achieve political ends.

Thus, a shift in policy is imperative. In the age of globalization and given the rise of terrorism as the number one threat, there is an urgent need for new thinking that overcomes the classical emphasis on national interest and power. The democratic approach to fighting terrorism is more likely to succeed and create stability in different countries and across the region. The democratic approach should focus on empowering the people through different mechanisms, including improving their living conditions and giving them full political, economic, and social rights. In the case of Yemen, terrorism is rooted in poverty, inequality, lack of economic opportunity, population explosion, and above all, weak to nonexistent state institutions. To uproot terrorism, one needs to address all these root causes. Democracy does not empower terrorists as some may argue, and there is no contradiction between promoting democracy and fighting terrorism. True, it is more expensive, but one need not forget that it is the surest approach to undermining radicalism.

CONCLUSION

U.S.-Yemeni relations in the last half of the 1990s and early years of the twenty-first century have developed rapidly. This was partially due to changing regional environments that forced the United States, fearing that old allies might have fallen under unfriendly regimes, to seek new allies in the region and partially due to the rise of terrorism as a threat to U.S. national security. Given that Yemen is one of the countries with the potential of becoming a hotbed for terrorist groups, the U.S. has moved to strengthen ties with Yemen in the hope of preventing it from becoming another Afghanistan. At the same time, the Yemeni leadership is seizing the moment to foster good relations with the United States so that it can increase political stocks internally and internationally. As it appears, the war against terrorism serves a common goal for both the Yemeni government, which seeks to expand its control on vast lawless regions, and the U.S. government, which seeks to suppress radical groups and movements and prevent them from gaining a foothold in Yemen.

NOTES

1. Yemeni-Saudi relations and U.S.-Saudi relations have been the major shaping force of U.S.-Yemeni relations. Historically, when U.S.-Saudi relations fall into despair, the United States comes closer to Yemen. And Yemen has followed a similar strategy. At times of crisis in Saudi-Yemeni relations, Yemen tends to emphasize its relations with the United States.

2. The British viewed political change in North Yemen as threatening to their presence in the South, especially in light of Nasser's support the revolutionary group in the North.

3. The U.S. government's immediate reaction to the Yemeni position, especially in the UN Security Council where Yemen happened to be a rotating member during the crisis, was to freeze all nonhumanitarian aid packages to Yemen.

4. The Washington-based National Democratic Institute (NDI)—a nonprofit organization largely funded by the American government—carried out many election-related activities in Yemen starting with the founding elections of 1993.

5. Mr. Mack stated, "It is important to remember that no country has a blueprint for democracy in another country. . . . So I don't think you should look on what you do here as a model for anyone else to follow" (Watkins 1993).

6. Another issue of concern to the American officials in the early 1990s was Yemen's reluctance to take concrete steps in joining the Arab-Israeli peace process and in normalizing relations with Israel.

7. During the 1960s, 1970s, and 1980s, consecutive American administrations found a great ally in the Saudis and Islam in their war against communism. This alliance between Saudi wealth and American warfare techniques came together in the Afghani war against the Soviets.

8. The activities of jihad and Yemen's involvement were part of organized CIA efforts (funded largely by the Saudi government and by charity groups within Saudi Arabia). Bin Laden, in particular, in his effort to mobilize people in the Muslim world for jihad in Afghanistan, drew on the wealth of his family.

9. "Yemen's President, Naming Names," *Washington Post*, December 10, 2000.

10. "Pieces of the Puzzle: A Break in the Case—But There's Not Enough Evidence Yet to Link the Cole Attack directly to bin Laden," *Newsweek*, December 18, 2000, p. 48.

11. Ibid.

12. "Yemen-Globalising under the US Umbrella," *APS Diplomat Fate of the Arabian Peninsula* 43(2) (August 26, 2002): 2.

13. "Could Yemen's Calm Be Threatened? Yemen and Its Islamists (Yemen's War on Terror)," *Economist*, February 16, 2002.

14. "Yemeni Forces Move on al Qaeda," CNN, December 18, 2001, www.cnn.com/2001/WORLD/meast/12/18/ret.yemen.qaeda0730/index.html.

15. "Could Yemen's Calm Be Threatened? Yemen and Its Islamists (Yemen's War on Terror)," *Economist*, February 16, 2002.

16. "Yemeni Forces Move on al Qaeda," CNN, December 18, 2001, www.cnn.com/2001/WORLD/meast/12/18/ret.yemen.qaeda0730/index.html.

17. "A Statement Concerning the Terrorist Attacks Carried Out in the United States" (September 11, 2001); "A Letter from the Minister of Foreign Affairs of the Republic of Yemen to the Secretary of the United States of America" (September 12, 2001); "A Letter of Condolences from Honorable President of the Republic of Yemen to the Honorable President of the United States of America" (September 11, 2001). Yemen Embassy, Washington, D.C., Press Releases, www.yemenembassy.org/welcome/pressrel/index.htm.

18. "Strategic Balance in the Middle East: The Situation of Yemen," *APS Diplomat Recorder*, January 17, 2000.

19. "Yemen, U.S. Increase Antiterrorism Cooperation," CNN, November 27, 2001, www.cnn.com/2001/WORLD/meast/11/27/yemen.us/index.html.

20. "U.S., Yemen Discuss Deployment of U.S. Forces," CNN, February 15, 2002, www.cnn.com/2002/US/02/15/us.yemen/index.html.

21. "Yemen Hunting Man Who Fled before CIA Hit," *Los Angeles Times*, November 20, 2002.

22. Amidst increasing criticism of Washington's role in supporting authoritarian regimes in the Middle East, Colin Powell declared in December 2002 that Washington would spend $29 million on promoting democracy across the Middle East. See "US Cash for Middle East Democracy," *BBC News*, December 13, 2002, www.news.bbc.co.uk/1/hi/world/americas/2571349.stm.

REFERENCES

Al-faqih, Abdullah. 2003. "From Liberalization and Democratization to Deliberalization and Dedemocratization." Dissertation, Northeastern University.

Boustany, Nora. 2002. "Yemeni Proclaims His Nation's Solidarity with U.S. in Fight against Terrorism." *Washington Post*, November 27.

Fisk, Robert. 1997. "Middle East: Arab Nations Stay Away from Talks in Snub to Clinton." *Independent* (London), November 14, p. 13.

Gause, F. Gregory. 1990. *Saudi-Yemeni Relations: Domestic Structures and Foreign Influence.* New York, Oxford: Columbia University Press.

Gerges, Fawaz A. 1997. "Islam and Muslims in the Mind of America: Influences on the Making of U.S. Policy." *Journal of Palestine Studies* 26(2) (Winter): 68–81.

Gleit, Heidi J. 2000. "Israelis in Yemen Have Foreign Passports." *Jerusalem Post*, March 30, p. 4.

Gordon, Michael R. 2002. "Cheney Asks Yemen to Join the Pursuit of al Qaeda's Remnants." *New York Times*, March 15.

Higgins, Andrew, and Alan Cullison. 2002. "The Story of a Traitor to alQaeda." *The Wall Street Journal*, December 20.

Hudson, Michael. 1997. "The Evolution of US Policy toward Yemen: Seeking Stability in Arabia." In *Yemen Today: Crisis and Solutions*, ed. E. G. H. Joffe, M. J. Hachemi, and E. W. Watkins. London: Carval Press.

Independent (London). 1994. "Protests in Yemen," January 6.

J.K.C.S and Yemen Times (Sana'a). 2001. "Seminar: Yemeni-American Relations, the Current Challenges," October 31. (In Arabic)

Joffe, George. 1997. "Yemen and the Contemporary Middle East." In *Yemen Today: Crisis and Solutions*, ed. E. G. H. Joffe, M. J. Hachemi, and E. W. Watkins. London: Carval Press.

Killio, David. 1994. "Saudi Meddlers in Yemen." *New York Times*, July 30.

Kostiner, Joseph. 1996. *Yemen: The Tortuous Quest for Unity, 1990–94*. London: Royal Institute of International Affairs.

Leupp, Gary. 2002. "The War on Terrorism in Yemen." *Counterpunch*, May 20.

Lichtblau, Eric, and Glaberson, William. 2003. "Threats and Responses: Financing Terror; Millions Raised for al Qaeda in Brooklyn, U.S Says." *New York Times*, March 5.

Lowrie, Arthur L. 1995. "The Campaign against Islam and American Foreign Policy." *Middle East Policy* 4(1–2) (September 1995): 210–20.

Nonneman, Gerd. 1997. "Key Issues in the Yemeni Economy." In *Yemen Today: Crisis and Solutions*, ed. E. G. H. Joffe, M. J. Hachemi, and E. W. Watkins. London: Carval Press.

Prados, Alfred B. 1999. "Yemen: Democratic Development and U.S. Relations." CRS Report for Congress, November 20.

———. 2000. "Yemen: U.S. Relations, Assistance, and the U.S.S. Cole Bombing." CRS Report for Congress, September 13.

Qadhi, Mohammed al-. 2002. "US Offers Nine Patrol Boats: Yemen Gets Help to Patrol Waters." *Yemen Times*, October 22.

Radwan, Amany. 2002. "An Unruly Backwater Tries Going Straight." *Time*, September 30, p. 8.

Sachs, Susan. 2002. "A Nation Challenged: The View from Iraq, Iran and Yemen." *New York Times*, February 6.

Safire, William. 2002. "Bush's Stumbles: The So San Affair." *New York Times*, December 20.

Schneider, Howard. 2002. "For Yemen, A Risk and an Opportunity." *Washington Post*, January 2.

Sciolino, Elaine. 2001. "U.S. Pondering Saudis' Vulnerability." *New York Times*, November 4.

Sharif, Abdu H. 2002. "Weak Institutions and Democracy: The Case of the Yemen Parliament, 1993–97." *Middle East Policy* 1(1) (March 2002): 82–93.

Smucker, Philip, and Howard LaFranchi. 2002. "Anti-US Strike Shakes Yemen." *Christian Science Monitor*, December 31. www.csmonitor.com/2002/1231/p01s04-wome.htm.

Tyler, Patrick. 2002. "Yemen, an Uneasy Ally, Proves Adept at Playing Off Old Rivals." *New York Times*, December 19.

Watkins, Eric. 1993. "Success of Yemeni Election Prompts Worries for the Saudis." *Financial Times*, May 14.

———. 1994. "Terror Main Weapon in Yemen War of Politics: The Arab Nation's Newfound Democracy and Unity Are under Threat." *Financial Times*, January 7.

Wenner, Manfred W. 1967. *Modern Yemen: 1918–1966*. Baltimore: Johns Hopkins University Press.

Whitaker, Brian. 1993. "Election Milestone." *Middle East International*, April 16.

———. 1994. "Fragile Union at Mercy of Outside Forces." *Guardian*, April 7.

Willems, Peter. 2002a. "An Uphill Battle." *The Middle East*, May, pp. 17–19.

———. 2002b. "Yemenis Resist US Pressure." *The Middle East*, July–August, pp. 15–16.

MEHRAN KAMRAVA

10 Repression, Fundamentalism, and Terrorism in the Middle East

Since the late 1970s, the Middle East has witnessed a reemerging convergence between two historically salient phenomena: continued repression by the state on the one hand, and a repoliticization of Islam on the other. Neither phenomena is particularly new or novel in the political history of the region. However, the particular context within which this latest convergence has taken place, in circumstances that are unique to the late twentieth and early twenty-first centuries, has resulted in the emergence of one strand of political Islam that is both highly violent and transnational in nature. This fundamentalist strand of political Islam competes with the two other strands of popular and reformist Islam. In a context of heightened political repression and continued political insecurity, Islamic fundamentalism's resort to violence has attracted a small but committed band of followers. As the conditions that originally heightened the popularity of Islamic fundamentalism continue to spread and deepen, so does the appeal of violence as a religio-political medium of expression at the expense of Islamic populism and reformism. In sum, political repression in the Middle East has pushed the oppositional phenomenon of political Islam into an increasingly radical and violent direction, in the process undermining the appeal of more tempered interpretations of the religion.

The emergence of Islamic fundamentalism as a source of radical domestic political opposition and international terrorism raises many questions. What led to the emergence of Islam as a viable forum for political opposition in the first place? What caused its steady radicalization and its resort to violence? Why and how has fundamentalism overshadowed other interpretations and strands within Islam? How does fundamentalism operationalize Islam as an ideology and violence as a means? And, more specifically, how did the Islamic concept

167

of jihad become one of the mainstays of global terrorism at the dawn of the twenty-first century? Only through answering these questions is it possible to gain insight into the underlying causes for the growth and spread of what is often conveniently, and frequently inaccurately, given the generic label of "Islamic fundamentalism."

THE POLITICAL HISTORY CONTEXT

Today, violent Islamic fundamentalism constitutes a potent, if small, strand within the larger world of Islam. The emergence of this radical strand is a product of the nuances that have taken place within Middle Eastern and Arab politics over the past few decades. In broad terms, a general background of political Islam has long been a salient feature of the region's political history. Up until the late 1960s and the early 1970s, and more specifically after the utter military defeat of the Arab nationalist project in the 1967 *nakba* (disaster) following the Six-Day War, political Islam faced serious competition from ostensibly secular ideologies such as nationalism and socialism as a viable medium for political expression. Whether part of the official ideology of the state (as in Algeria, Tunisia, Egypt, Syria, and the People's Democratic Republic of Yemen) or a platform of the state's more serious opponents (as in Iran and Turkey, and to a lesser extent in Jordan, Morocco, and parts of the Arabian Peninsula), the dominant ideological discourse remained essentially secular. This dominant discourse was often informed by some local variation of socialism if it was articulated by state elites or, alternatively, by socialism—usually Maoism—or by liberal democracy if articulated by state opponents.

Equally important was the existence of a series of highly charismatic political leaders throughout the Middle East, the most notable of whom was Gamal Abdel Nasser in Egypt, and many others who aspired to be like him, such as Ahmed Ben Bella in Algeria and later Moammar Khadafi in Libya. For each of these charismatic leaders, religion only informed a larger social and political background within which they articulated largely secular, nationalist agendas. While they could not afford to ignore religion altogether, they made no conscious efforts to portray themselves and their political projects as necessarily religious, nor did they see much political utility in manipulating religion for political purposes. In one way or another, Islam for them was never a central tenet of the populist polities that they were seeking to bring about. If anything, Nasser saw in the Egyptian Muslim Brotherhood (Ikhwan al-Muslimin) a dangerous opponent to both his personal power and his socialist project. In 1954, when the organization began calling for the implementation of Islamic law, the shari'a, the

Nasserist state arrested more than a thousand of its members and had many of them tortured. In 1966, Sayyid Qutb, a prominent figure within the organization and in many ways the spiritual father of Islamic fundamentalism, was hanged after enduring severe torture in prison (Sullivan and Abed-Kotob 1999, 43).

As it turned out, however, it wasn't Islam or the Muslim Brotherhood that unraveled Nasserism. It was, rather, Nasser himself, more specifically his penchant for repression and the facade of military prowess in which he had wrapped himself. When he died of a heart attack in September 1970, he was a broken man, a shadow of his former self. Ben Bella fared even worse. His fate was that of a child of a revolution devoured by the revolution itself. On June 19, 1965, he was overthrown in a bloodless coup, arrested, and sent to exile in Europe.

Beginning in the 1970s, secular discourses, both official and oppositional, steadily discredited themselves. Throughout the Middle East, in one form or another, largely secular projects such as nationalism, socialism, and Palestinian liberation proved themselves to be militarily incompetent, politically inept and repressive, economically hollow, and morally bankrupt. Not surprisingly, the discourses attached to each, also largely secular, underwent a similar loss of appeal and popular legitimacy. The fact that the primary architects of these secular doctrines were themselves defeated and dispirited, on the defensive, and, in many cases, politically suppressed did not help. Michel Aflaq, for example, who had originally articulated Ba'athist ideology in Syria under the banner of "unity, freedom, socialism," was expelled from Syria in 1966 and moved to Iraq, where "he imparted ideological legitimacy" to Iraq's Ba'athist regime (Virost 1994, 28–29). Aflaq, incidentally, happened to be Christian. Khalil Hawi (b. 1912), the renowned nationalist Lebanese poet, also a Christian, could not stand to further witness the downward spiral of everything that he and his generation had once hoped for. On the eve of Israel's invasion of Lebanon on June 6, 1982, Hawi committed suicide. As the Palestinian poet Mahmoud Darwish reflected in Hawi's eulogy, Hawi "was weary of the state of decay, weary of looking over the bottomless abyss" (quoted in Ajami 1998, 28). Another nationalist poet, the Syrian Nizar Qabbani, told an interviewer in 1985: "I don't write because I can't say something that equals the sorrow of this Arab nation. I can't open any of the countless dungeons of this large prison" (112).

Aflaq's exile, Hawi's suicide, and Qabbani's loss of words all symbolized a deeper malaise in the larger Arab nationalist project, a project whose genesis and flavor had long been secular. Secularism was being beaten and defeated, partly on account of its own failures and partly as a victim of circumstances beyond its control. Whatever the cause, its decline was steady and fast.

This loss of ground on the part of secular political projects and secular ideologies gave rise to and in turn reinforced the increasing ascendance of political interpretations of Islam, hitherto pushed into the background by a combination of state repression and lack of appeal among the urban middle classes. By the early to mid-1970s, the very class structure of Middle Eastern societies was being fundamentally altered—with expansive educational systems and bureaucracies giving rise to a salaried class of urbanites, and the lumpenproletariat growing to uncontrollable proportions due to rural-urban migration—and this only added to the ideological and practical appeal of political Islam. By the time the decade drew to a close, Islam had proven itself as a viable and powerful political force, emerging victorious in an Iran that had been ruled by a seemingly invincible monarch. To the majority of Sunni Muslims, initially at least, it seemed to matter little that Islam's political victory had been achieved under the banner of Shiʻism. What was important was the transcendence of political Islam from the realm of theory into practice. For the first time in more than a half-century, since the demise of the Ottomans, something remotely resembling the caliphate and calling itself an Islamic Republic had come to power. And, the new republic was not at all shy in seeking to inspire Islamists throughout the Middle East and beyond.

The 1980s brought new heights for political Islam. This was due to a convergence of three clusters of factors that included the failure of literally all Middle Eastern states to deliver the goods and services on which much of their domestic legitimacy depended, international conditions supportive of an increasingly radicalized Islam, and the increasing reemergence of Islam as a viable and potent source of collective and national identity. Combined, these factors not only increased the potency of Islam as a viable political solution but also led to its growing radicalization. By the time the decade was over, political Islam was well on its way to giving rise to an increasingly violent strand of fundamentalism.

One of the primary reasons for the deepening growth of political Islam had to do with the appearance of cracks in the "ruling bargains" that Middle Eastern states had been able to strike with their societies over the previous decades. As serious economic difficulties set in beginning in the early 1980s, many Middle Eastern states found it more and more difficult to fulfill their end of the bargain. Such bargains had been predicated on four primary premises designed to guarantee the state's legitimacy and resilience: defense of the motherland and its national interests; the provision of goods and services through patronage networks; fostering economic development through rent-seeking activities; and, to ensure the bargains' tenacity, state authoritarianism (Kamrava 2001). However, throughout the 1980s, Middle Eastern states faced multiple economic setbacks resulting from a decade-long recession, a serious decline in oil revenues, and the mounting costs of the Iran-Iraq War for literally all countries of the region.

Even Saddam Hussein, the new self-declared Nasser and Saladdin of his age, turned out to be a less than capable military leader, his supposed military victory over the Iranians in 1988 only skin-deep.

The ensuing void in state services was filled by a host of emerging Islamist organizations and associations in practically every Middle Eastern country. These Islamic organizations and charitable associations (*jam'iyyat khairiyya*) provide a slew of services, among them affordable health care, job training, infant day care for working mothers, and various forms of financial assistance such as money-lending and money transfers. Their size can vary from as few as four or five employees to scores of health care professionals, educators, or clerical personnel (Sullivan and Abed-Kotob 1999, 26–27). In Egypt especially, where the financial and structural limitations of the state have been particularly acute, there has been a proliferation of Islamic organizations of various types. In Palestinian Occupied Territories, the initial rise in the popularity of the Hamas organization was also a product of its sponsorship of a number of voluntary associations dedicated to preaching and guidance, health, education, sports, welfare, and charity (Mishal and Sela 2000, 20). A similar but slightly different development occurred in both Jordan and Egypt, where in many of the professional associations that were being established—belonging to physicians, pharmacists, engineers, dentists, and lawyers—individuals with strong Islamist convictions were being elected to leadership positions (Tripp 1996, 60–63).

The emergence and spread of Islamist organizations and professional associations with strong Islamist overtones have had two important, interrelated consequences. To begin with, although the services they provide by no means make the state redundant, they do serve as an important vehicle for addressing some of the needs of the more traditional strata of society. In Egypt, for example, there is a popular perception that "Islamic institutions have the concern for the poor that the public sector is supposed to have and the efficiency and quality attributed to the private sector" (Sullivan and Abed-Kotob 1999, 33). This has helped to further erode the legitimacy of the state while at the same time enhancing the credibility of Islamist alternatives. Related to this is a further development, namely the spread of a popular form of collective, communal identity that is heavily enmeshed with Islam and is distinct from the official identity that the state has been trying to articulate and spread among the masses.

Identity politics was, in fact, a second factor that directly contributed to the growing salience of an increasingly radical political Islam. Proliferating Islamist organizations provided ordinary people with an alternative source of identity—an Islamic sense of self, both at the individual and the national levels and, in some cases, even at the much larger level of the whole Muslim world. The fostering of a compelling sense of political identity, of being a part of and belonging to a body politic, was an endeavor in which the state had not only failed but, in fact, often seemed to be directly working against.

In the Palestinian territories and in Lebanon, where the state was either on the run (the Palestinian Liberation Organization [PLO] in the 1980s, if it could even be called a state) or in a condition of near-total paralysis, the Hamas and Hezbollah organizations respectively played especially crucial roles in fostering alternative, profoundly religious sources of identity. In Lebanon, years of neglect and institutional prejudice by the central government had created a pool of slum-dwelling Shi'ites living in the "belt of misery." When Israel invaded Lebanon in 1982, a conglomeration of armed Shi'ite groups, highly militant and with little to lose, joined to form the Hezbollah organization (Saad-Ghorayeb 2002, 10). As the invasion dragged on and turned increasingly bloody after the massacres of the Sabra and Shatila refugee camps, the Hezbollah, initially aided by Iran, became considerably more militant and developed deeper roots within Lebanon's Shi'ite community. For the first time, Lebanese Shi'ites had a group that actively represented them and defended their interests. As the war dragged on, and as the Hezbollah itself underwent a steady process of "Lebanonization," there was an increasing sense among the country's Shi'ites that they had earned their citizenship in their struggle against Israel and no longer belonged "on the edge" or "on the margins" (al-atraf) of the country (Dagher 2000, 43).

A somewhat similar development occurred for the Hamas in the Palestinian territories of Gaza and the West Bank, at a time when the PLO was bogged down in internal squabbles and was losing touch with many of its constituents in Palestine, having earlier been expelled from Lebanon by the advancing Israeli forces. In December 1987, when the spontaneous uprising known as the intifada erupted, "Hamas quickly attracted a large following. Young men joined up in droves, many of them already Islamic activists, others disaffected supporters of the PLO. . . . Of the young men who flocked to its ranks, many had refugee backgrounds and saw an opportunity for self-identity and esteem vis-à-vis the rest of society through their association with this religious organisation which put a mask of holiness on them" (Milton-Edwards 1996, 147).

A third set of factors revolved around the international and intraregional developments that were unfolding in the Middle East throughout the 1980s, not the least of which were the Iran-Iraq War of 1980–88 and the disintegration of Afghanistan as a viable national entity ruled by a sovereign state. The Iran-Iraq War prompted both of the belligerents—and on the Iraqi side its close allies in the Arabian Peninsula—to actively promote their own religious credentials and to court Islamist supporters. Fighting against a feverishly militant, brand

new *Islamic* Republic, Saddam Hussein was eager to emphasize his own religious credentials. The president frequently reminded his audiences that he
was a direct descendant of the Prophet Muhammad, and he often implied that
only Arabs could rightfully claim the mantle of Islam (Karsh and Rausti 1991,
151–52). Later on in 1991, in the midst of the Gulf War, the Arabic inscription
Allah Akbar (God Is Great) was added to the Iraqi flag. A similar official reemphasis of the state's Islamic credentials occurred in Saudi Arabia. For the Saudi
royal family, this reemphasis on Islam was given added urgency after the takeover in November 1979 of the Grand Mosque in Mecca by a group comprised
of several hundred Islamic fundamentalists. The takeover lasted more than two
weeks and ended only after close to three hundred militants and government
soldiers were killed in the ensuing firefight. Once the Grand Mosque was re-
claimed, the kingdom's official ulema (clerics), whose salaries were raised, were
told to emphasize the royal family's religious credentials during their sermons.
There was also a public campaign to clamp down on video stores selling movies
considered offensive to Islam (Wilson and Graham 1994, 589). Finally, in 1986,
King Fahd dropped the honorific "His Majesty" and instead adopted the title
"Custodian of Islam's Holiest Mosques." Even the self-avowedly Europeanizing
prime minister of Turkey at the time, Turgut Özal, found it prudent to undertake
a well-publicized hajj pilgrimage to Mecca in 1987.

The cumulative effects of the public embrace of Islam by these and other
states helped reinforce a general atmosphere of heightened Islamic identity
throughout the Middle East. Within each country, the state's belated championing of religion was often seen by the population, especially the urban middle
classes, as another sinister ploy to bolster its declining legitimacy. Domestically, therefore, such moves seldom succeeded in mollifying Islamist opposition. At a broader regional and international level, however, they did create a
larger atmosphere of heightened religious awareness, a sense that Islam was a
viable and powerful source of collective identity that demanded and received
the respect of successive governments in the region.

The 1980s started with Islam having entrenched itself within the dominant discourse and political atmosphere inside each Middle Eastern country and throughout the region. By the time the decade was drawing to a close, what was now
"political Islam" had given rise to a radical strand that embraced violence as a
tactical and strategic necessity. The underlying causes of this turn by a *subcat-
egory* of political Islam toward violence lay, on the one hand, in domestic political
dynamics within each Middle Eastern country and, on the other hand, in the larger
regional and international reverberation of events unfolding in three other Middle
Eastern countries, namely Lebanon, Palestine, and Afghanistan. More specifi-

cally, most states responded to the emergence of oppositional political Islam with reinvigorated authoritarianism and heightened levels of repression. This was especially the case in Iraq, Syria, Egypt, and Algeria, where state violence directed at Islamist groups helped pushed them underground and further in the direction of radicalism and violence. At the same time, the bloody course of the Lebanese civil war, the eruption of the Palestinian intifada in 1987, and the disintegration of Afghanistan during the prolonged struggle against Soviet occupation provided the backdrop against which the articulation of political Islam began to take shape in the late 1980s and early 1990s. More significantly, whereas Lebanon and Palestine starkly reminded Islamist groups of the plight of fellow Muslims and the perceived injustices meted out against them, Afghanistan provided the appropriate conditions and opportunities to put theory into practice, first by fighting against "godless invaders" and then by fighting for a truly Islamic state.

In Egypt, the Islamist opposition has long been divided between the more mainstream, largely reformist Muslim Brotherhood and the radical groupings collectively referred to as the Jama'at Islamiyya, or Islamic Groups. The Egyptian state's tolerance of the Muslim Brotherhood has ranged over time from begrudging tolerance and allowing it to partake in parliamentary elections to banning the organization altogether and throwing its members in prison. Egypt has, however, been consistent in its extremely harsh treatment of those suspected of being sympathetic to the goals and ideologies of any of the Jama'at groups. In September 1981, for example, following clashes between militant Islamists and Copts, Egyptian security forces rounded up some fifteen hundred religious activists and Jama'at sympathizers. Less than a month later, President Anwar Sadat was assassinated by members of one of the Jama'at organizations, the al-Jihad (Rubin 2002, 21–22). As the government's sweep of Islamist activists continued through the 1980s, so did intermittent terrorist attacks by Jama'at members on foreign tourists and former and current government officials.

Morocco also saw scattered terrorist attacks on foreign tourists in the 1980s and, to a lesser extent, in the 1990s, although the attacks were not anywhere close in magnitude to those in Egypt (Hughes 2001, 302–3). In Syria, the Syrian branch of the Muslim Brotherhood, long an opponent of President Hafiz Assad's regime, had agitated against the state for some time in the late 1970s and the early 1980s. In February 1982, after months of scattered attacks orchestrated by the Muslim Brotherhood, government forces attacked the city of Hama, which had been one of the Muslim Brotherhood's strongholds. In the three-week carnage that ensued, an estimated ten thousand to twenty-five thousand residents of the city were killed, countless homes were demolished, and entire neighborhoods and quarters were razed (Friedman 1989, 77–87).

Less than a decade later, Algeria witnessed a bloodbath of a different sort. In January 1992, the Algerian military stepped in and canceled the second round of parliamentary elections that had been scheduled a few months earlier. The first round of balloting, held the previous December, had resulted in an unexpected victory by candidates from a new Islamist party called the Islamic Salvation Front (Front Islamique du Salut [FIS]). What ensued was a bloody civil war that lasted for most of the remainder of the decade between FIS supporters on the one side and state security forces on the other. Altogether, during the next seven years or so, an estimated seventy-five thousand Algerians lost their lives and many more were wounded. Early in 1993, small armed gangs known as Armed Islamic Groups (Groupes Islamiques Armes [GIA]) began appearing throughout the country, especially Algiers. As one observer has noted, the GIA "seemed to be little more than gangs, but with the extra zeal that may have come from fighting in a religiously sanctioned campaign against a regime that was considered to be illegitimate and non-Muslim." The atrocities that were committed by both sides were equaled only by those committed during the country's national war of liberation from France from 1954 to 1962. During the thanatos of the 1990s, "the killing was often of the most intimate and grisly kind, the kind that perhaps only happens in civil wars where the enemy has to be totally demonized in order to legitimize the killing" (Quandt 1998, 66).

Such was the predicament of the Middle East by the end of the 1980s and the start of the 1990s. Syria's bloody uprising in Hama had been suppressed with unfathomable repression near the beginning of the decade, and an uneasy calm masked deeper Islamist resentment toward the secular regime in Damascus. Iran and Iraq were still smoldering from a violent conflict—the longest war of the twentieth century (Hiro 1991)—during which they had both sought to claim the mantle of Islam's leadership. Lebanon's sectarian-based civil war ended in 1990 only after the different sides had fought each other to exhaustion and the Syrian army intervened in the country with full force. Among the civil war's lasting legacies was the establishment and rise of a new political party calling itself the Party of God, Hezbollah, trained and supported by that other divinely inspired state, Iran's Islamic Republic. Meanwhile, Algeria's nightmare had only just begun as both the GIA and the government's security forces reigned terror on innocent civilians and bystanders. And Afghanistan was about to sink further into the abyss as the struggle against Soviet invaders gave way to fratricide among competing fanatical warriors.

Throughout the region, the state has been too insecure of its hold on power and too keenly aware of its unpopularity to allow any form of meaningful political opposition or even unfettered political participation. Instead, every attempt by even moderate political forces to carve out a space for themselves in the public domain is at best restricted by law and at worst crushed by violence. The experience of the Wassat Party in Egypt is instructive. Founded by a group of highly respected Islamist reformists in 1996, the party repeatedly applied to the Egyptian government for a permit to operate, but to no avail. Following each unsuccessful attempt, party leaders sought to allay government concerns by further moderating the party's already centrist ideological platform. But nothing seemed to satisfy the government, and the authorities even refused permission to party leaders to publish a newspaper (Baker 2003, 198–201).

Within such a context, when even moderate opposition is not tolerated, the radicalization of political dissent is all but inevitable. With mainstream ideologies shut out and moderate activism suppressed both legally and physically, the only recourse open to many political aspirants is to resort to extremism. The moderate opposition appears weak, at the mercy of a state that does not even recognize its right to exist, and advocates an accommodationist ideology that seems highly inadequate for tackling the harsh realities of the body politic. At the same time, through their binary vision of the world into good and evil, extremists offer a simple and compelling ideological framework that promises tangible results and immediate gratification. More importantly, extremism offers its adherents the conceptual and practical tools to combat the state on the uncompromising, violent grounds that state leaders themselves have laid out. Just as the demise of secular alternatives has pushed Middle Eastern political ideologies into the embrace of Islam, state repression has turned political Islam in an increasingly violent direction.

POLITICAL ISLAM AND ANTI-AMERICANISM

By the beginning of the 1990s, political Islam had found a new target: the United States. This identification of the United States as the real enemy was not necessarily a product of an ideological shift directed at battling the infidel enemy. Neither was it a manifestation of a larger civilizational clash in the making. Instead, it was a product of simple realpolitik. Facing unprecedented levels of repression and highly constricted environments at home, Islamist groups faced serious tactical and strategic challenges. Although they had been emboldened by the larger regional and international developments, and of course by the seemingly higher levels of piety among their own populations, many of the more radical Islamist groups appeared to have reached a tactical and strategic dead end. They had adopted armed struggle to overthrow the state and had dedicated much energy, manpower, and sacrifice to their endeavors. But the state, now more repressive than ever before, showed no signs of collapsing. Instead, many Islamist groups decided to embarrass the state internationally and to make cooperation with it costly in human terms. The Jamaʿat Islamiyya, for example, began targeting tourists in Egypt, and, at around the same time, the FIS started attacking foreign contractors and businessmen in Algeria. But the most spectacular attacks were directed at American targets and symbols.

The opening shot at America had been fired as early as 1979 by the Iranians, when on November 4 of that year street rioters attacked the U.S. embassy in Tehran and, with the blessing of Ayatollah Khomeini, took its diplomats hostage for 444 days. Then, on October 23, 1983, in the midst of the blaze and ruin of Beirut, came the first of a series of spectacular attacks on American might. A car laden with explosives drove through the barracks housing the U.S. Marines who had been stationed there to keep a nonexisting peace. Some 161 American soldiers were killed, another 75 wounded. Also dead were scores of French paratroopers stationed in the same complex. It took another decade for the United States to once again become the target of terrorism from the Middle East, which this time struck on American soil itself and in the heart of America's financial nerve center. On February 26, 1993, a car bomb went off in the garage of the World Trade Center in New York City, killing 6 and wounding nearly 1,000 people. Sheikh Umar Adbel Rahman, an Egyptian cleric who earlier had been linked to the assassination of Anwar Sadat and now lived in the United States, was convicted of being the primary force behind the attack. Then came two bombings directed at American forces stationed in Saudi Arabia, one in Riyadh in November 1995 and another on the Khobar Towers near Dhahran in July 1996. Five American soldiers were killed in the first attack and another 19 in the second, with hundreds more injured. Two years later, on August 7, 1998, the American embassies in Nairobi and Dar es Salaam were car-bombed by terrorists with Middle Eastern links, resulting in 258 deaths and more than 5,000 injuries. Finally, on October 12, 2000, the USS *Cole* was attacked off the coast of Yemen as it was docking in Aden to refuel. Seventeen American sailors died and many more were injured.

As daring and painful as these attacks were, they paled in comparison with what transpired on September 11, 2001, the tragic story of which is all too familiar and needs no repeating here. By the time that awful Tuesday morning was over, four jetliners full of passengers had been lost, the twin towers of the World Trade Center had crumbled, and the Pentagon itself was attacked. The mastermind behind the attacks, it was soon discovered, was none other than Osama bin Laden, long one of America's most determined and violent opponents in the Islamic fundamentalist camp. After 9/11, the landscape of New York City, and

America itself, was forever changed as a direct result of Islamic fundamentalism and its unbridled violence.

There was, of course, more to anti-Americanism than mere tactical and strategic convenience. The attacks on American targets and symbols by Islamic fundamentalists were the product of a larger, more complex phenomenon of pervasive anti-Americanism that had been simmering throughout the Middle East for some time. Middle Eastern anti-Americanism predated the reemergence of political Islam by a long shot, having grown out of a history of unconditional American support for Israel and for corrupt and repressive dictators who were seen to be doing America's bidding on its behalf. By the time Islam stepped in to fill the vacuum left by the discrediting of various secular "isms," anti-American sentiments were already widespread. For Islam, a powerful strand of which had already become politicized and radicalized, to also become anti-American was only natural.

What made the 1990s so deadly for the Americans in the Middle East was the dawn of what was seen as Pax Americana in the region following the end of the second Gulf War (Ajami 2001). Since the 1991 defeat and ejection of Iraqi forces out of Kuwait, the United States had made itself a permanent military presence in the Persian Gulf and the Arabian Peninsula. Through a series of bilateral and multilateral agreements with the states of the Gulf Cooperation Council, the United States steadily secured "access to naval and air bases, the prepositioning of war matériel, combined exercises, and vast arms sales" (El-Shazly and Hinnebusch 2002, 73). This level of American military and political penetration into the Middle East was unprecedented, and the angry reactions to it were swift and violent. Political Islam provided the available, and most viable and resonant, medium through which this anger and violence were expressed. Fouad Ajami's reflections in this regard bear repeating:

> There were men in the shadows pulling off spectacular deeds. But they fed off a free-floating anti-Americanism that blows at will and knows no bounds, among Islamists and secularists alike. For crowds in Karachi, Cairo, and Amman, the great power could never get it right. A world lacking the tools and the political space for free inquiry fell back on anti-Americanism. (Ajami 2002, 78–79)

Islam had stepped in at just the right time. First political, then radical, eventually violent, and always resonant, by the 1990s it offered the perfect blueprint for venting frustrations and for striking at enemies. Perhaps no other force or ideology could have mustered the level of commitment or the depth of violence that simmered throughout the decade and reached a crescendo on September 11, 2001.

Islam's journey from the political background in the 1950s and the early 1960s into the political limelight in the 1970s and the 1980s, and its resort to violence since the 1990s, has been a direct result of the evolving political context within which it found itself. Failed oppositional alternatives brought it to the fore, regional and international developments emboldened it, and state repression made it violent. As Ajami puts it, what we see is "a generational faultline between secular parents and their theocratic children" (Ajami 1998, xii). But the succession of Islam first by political Islam and then by Islamic fundamentalism was by no means a linear process. Neither did each successive layer of Islam completely overwhelm the previous one that had given rise to it. And, each of the three interpretations of the religion—Islam as a religion and a moral blueprint, Islam as a medium for political expression, and Islam as an inspiration for radicalism and political violence—is itself multilayered and far from being monolithic. Therefore, understanding the differences that mark one interpretation of Islam from another, and the precise role that Islam has come to play today in articulating cultural identity and offering political solutions for Muslims, is important. More specifically, what is the political ideology, if any, of Islamic fundamentalism?

ISLAMIST OPPOSITION

To better understand the essence and appeal of Islamic fundamentalism requires a clearer picture of the larger social and cultural milieu within which it operates. More specifically, since Islamic fundamentalism is a product of a larger social and political environment, one that it in turn effects, attention must be paid to some of the broader developments unfolding within Islam as a religion and a socially pervasive phenomenon. The reemergence of Islam as a medium for political expression, both peaceful and violent, and its rediscovery as a viable source of cultural identity have occurred at three levels. The first level, *popular* Islam, revolves around a general deepening of piety and religious convictions among a vast majority of Muslims in the Middle East and elsewhere. A second level, *intellectual* or learned Islam, is evident in a reemergence of Islam as a field of debate and theorizing by Islamic thinkers and academics throughout the Muslim world. The third level, Islamic *fundamentalism*, has its own worldview, ideal polity, and conceptual and actual tools for achieving political goals.

As a social phenomenon, the growth of popular Islam in Muslim societies is difficult to empirically quantify and measure. However, even casual, impressionistic observations in any Middle Eastern city quickly reveal the depth and magnitude of popular belief in and devotion to Islamic precepts. At the most observable level, one notices a far greater preponderance of men sporting beards and women wearing various forms of veil in a manner that, for both genders, represents their Islamic piety (Gaffney 1994, 88–90). This is the case not only in the more traditional quarters of cities in the Arab world, or in places where the observance of Islamic dress code is legally enforced, as in Saudi Arabia and Iran, but also in ostensibly Europeanized cities such as Istanbul and Tunis. In Turkey, what has come to be known as the "headscarf war" has been fought off and on since the early 1980s between the country's virulently secularist establishment and an expanding pool of urban women with Islamist sentiments. As one observer has noted, "an ultimate irony is the fact that many young Western-educated women are at the forefront of the headscarf movement, although Turkish women have acquired more legal rights than any women in the Muslim world" (Howe 2000, 104). There was a similar increase in the adoption of the Islamic dress by Tunisian women in the late 1980s, prompting the government to react by banning state agencies from hiring women wearing the hijab (Holmes-Eber 2003, 20).

There are two other equally revealing measures of increased levels of religious piety among average Middle Easterners. One has to do with the proliferation of formal and informal religious groups and societies, especially among the youth and university students. Beginning in the late 1970s, for example, as the number of Egyptian universities grew to more than double what it had been in the Nasser era, various Islamic societies were established on many campuses and became hotbeds of Islamist political activism (Choueiri 1997, 160). Throughout the 1980s, Islamist students gained ascendance on many Palestinian university campuses as well, a trend that was only accentuated in the 1990s (Abu-Amr 1994, 17; Milton-Edwards 1999, 132–34). In Algeria, students with Islamist tendencies became active in the so-called Student Mosque groups and other similar informal gatherings beginning in the 1970s, in turn paving the way for the explosion of Islamist sentiments in the late 1980s and the 1990s (Shahin 1998, 119–20). Similar developments took place on university campuses across the Middle East throughout the 1970s, 1980s, and 1990s. Even in the virulently secularist Turkey, the 1980s and 1990s saw a dramatic rise in the number and popularity of nongovernmental religious secondary schools, universities, and hostels. Most of these religiously based educational establishments are funded by the Islamist activist millionaire Fethullah Gülen and his charitable foundation, reportedly responsible for the founding of some one hundred schools in Turkey and another two hundred in Central Asia (Howe 2000, 37). Before long, many of the Gülen-funded hostels had turned into meeting places for sufi orders (*tarikat*) and informal Islamic discussion groups, much, of course, to the chagrin of the secular political establishment. By the early 1990s, official concern over the pervasiveness of Islamic sentiment on campuses prompted the zealous rector of Istanbul University to decree a ban on the observance of the Islamic dress code by female students (104).

Another indication of the rise of popular Islamist sentiment is the incredible increase over the last two to three decades in the number of mosques in practically all Middle Eastern countries and, for that matter, throughout the Muslim world. In the West Bank and Gaza, for example, the number of mosques jumped from 400 in 1967 to 750 in 1987, the year the intifada started (Abu-Amr 1994, 15). There have also been "galloping increases" in the number of mosques in Egypt even as there been a precipitous decline in the number of qualified professional preachers, with official estimates putting the total number of mosques in the country anywhere between 40,000 to 60,000 (Gaffney 1994, 265). In Tunisia, as more and more university students became attracted to Islam in the 1980s and the 1990s, many student organizations started opening small mosques on their university campuses (Hamdi 1998, 25). There has been a similarly discernible rise in Islamist sentiments among Moroccan university students (Entelis 1996, 99–100).

The general underlying causes for the popular resurgence of Islam are not that different from those responsible for Islam's politicization and eventual militancy. Repression and lack of responsiveness by the state, the successive failures of various secular ideologies and movements, and cultural alienation at the dizzying pace of social change, especially for recent arrivals to the cities, all combined to enhance the social resonance of Islam and its emergence as a viable source of identity. Two additional factors need mentioning. The first had to do with the initial courting of Islam by otherwise secular states for purposes of their own legitimacy. In addition to those mentioned earlier, Anwar Sadat's overtures to the Muslim Brotherhood and to Islam in general at the beginning of his tenure in office went a long way toward encouraging and emboldening Egypt's Islamist movement (Ansari 1986, 211).

A second factor revolves around the geographic concentration of a greater percentage of those with strong religious convictions in the provincial cities and towns instead of the capital city. In Egypt, for example, most of the members of the Jama'at Islamiyya are drawn from the southern cities of Upper Egypt, especially Asyut (Gaffney 1994, 82). In Turkey, similarly, political parties with vaguely religious platforms—the Refah, which was banned and resurrected as the Fazilet, and now its latest incarnation, the AK (Adalet ve Kalkınma) Party— have consistently done well in the eastern parts of the country and in other provincial towns. One of the primary reasons for this has to do with the state's diminished capacity to effectively penetrate society outside of the capital city, therefore eroding its ability to craft a political culture that supports its ideology and its overall position in relation to the larger society. Also, the provincial towns, with their less cosmopolitan and more conservative atmospheres, more easily lend themselves to the unfettered growth and spread of Islamist sentiments than do the larger cities, with their more complex, multilayered cultural context. Where alienation is more acute, so is the pervasiveness of the comforting cushion and worldview of religion.

The widespread social and cultural alienation of both the popular and the more learned classes in the Middle East has also resulted in the emergence of a more learned, intellectual Islam articulated by academics, intellectuals, and theoretician activists. In their analysis of contemporary Islamist discourse, Mansour Moaddel and Kamran Talattof (2000, 3) offer a division of Muslim thinkers into the two distinct camps of reformists and fundamentalists. There are five core issues, they maintain, that sharply distinguish the two groups from one another. They include (1) Islamic jurisprudence and its relation to the rational sciences and epistemology, (2) the relationship between Islam and politics and the proper form of government, (3) the nature of Western society and the larger idea of civilizations, (4) the status of women in society as prescribed by Islam, and (5) personal lifestyle and behavior.

While highly useful as a general signpost for distinguishing the two extremes of contemporary intellectual discourse within Islam, the sharp distinction offered by Moaddel and Talattof overlooks subtle differences among intellectuals in the moderate camp. In broad terms, as Moaddel and Talattof maintain, Islamist thinkers and activists may be divided into the fundamentalist and moderate categories. Equally important, however, are subtle differences among moderate thinkers on Islamic doctrine and jurisprudence. Nevertheless, there is widespread agreement among most activists and intellectuals belonging to this category on a number of key issues. For example, they generally bemoan the erosion of Islamic values in society, which they claim is largely due to the encroachment of Western materialism, and advocate a more authentic, indigenous vision of the ideal society. They seek to authenticate what they see as an imitative reality imported from the West. At the same time, they do not advocate or endorse retreat from the world of modernity or, for that matter, from active engagement in the global arena. They refuse to endorse violence as a viable political or social mean and, instead, advocate a gradualist, reformist strategy for achieving long-term objectives (Baker 2003). Not surprisingly, some of these Muslim thinkers have articulated highly complex and vibrant visions of an Islamic democracy. Representatives belonging to this category of thinkers include

Fethullah Gülen (b. 1938) in Turkey, Rachid Ghannouchi (b. 1941) in Tunisia, Mohsen Kadivar (b. 1959), Abdolkarim Soroush (b. 1945) in Iran, Abdelrahman Wahid (b. 1941) in Indonesia, and Anwar Ibrahim (b. 1947) in Malaysia.

Gülen's ideas are inspired by those of Said Nursi (1873–1960), who had earlier sought to foster a new Turkish national identity based on the construction of an Islamic consciousness and "a new map of meaning to guide *everyday* life" (Yavuz 1999, 588, emphasis in original). Through reading circles, *darshanes*, of which there are an estimated five thousand in Turkey today, Gülen and other followers of Nursi, generally referred to as the Nurcus, call for a remembering of the past rather than its erasure from the collective memory and a "rediscovery of the self." While he has been careful not to repudiate the secular legacy of Kemal Atatürk, Gülen has been the primary force behind the "construction of a 'new' national Islam of Turkey that is marked by the logic of a market economy and the Ottoman legacy" (593).

Rachid Ghannouchi similarly calls for a rebuilding and re-Islamization of Muslim societies. "We need to define ourselves," he maintains. "Tunisians are not tourists. They have a history and a background that forms their identity. The rules on which they live should come from that background" (quoted in Esposito and Voll 2001, 106). At the same time, while carving their own identity, Tunisians should "not refuse to interact and learn from other civilizations" (107). This neither excludes the possibility of political democracy nor implies blind imitation of the West. Islam itself, Ghannouchi maintains, has democratic foundations, giving people freedom of choice, education, property ownership, and participation in public life (Tamimi 2001, 91).

Anwar Ibrahim's arguments are quite similar, and he has tried to distinguish his position from both fundamentalism and Westernism: "We believe that a revitalization of tradition, with all its cultural and intellectual richness, is the most effective countervailing force against fanaticism and ethnocentrism. In the context of Islam, this process of revitalization comprehends the reassertion of the values of justice (al-adl), tolerance (al-tasamuh) and compassion (al-rahman)" (Esposito and Voll 2001, 195).

For his part, Mohsen Kadivar has devoted the bulk of his writings to examining the various aspects of religious government in general and religion's role in the Islamic Republic of Iran in particular. Kadivar's writings revolve around four main themes: a firm belief in religion as a viable, and in fact necessary, force in politics; the compatibility of religion and freedom; the political role and responsibilities of the clergy; and the nature and responsibilities of the *velayat faqih* (supreme jurisconsult). In relation to the last theme, the role of the *velayat faqih*, is where Kadivar's views come into sharp conflict with those of the official orthodoxy of the Iranian state. After a long and detailed analysis of Islamic political thought over the centuries, he delves into a detailed, critical analysis of the concept of *faqih* (Kadivar 1998). Although he never quite challenges Ayatollah Khomeini's seminal views on the notion of *velayat faqih*, he comes very close to doing so. After examining the concept as articulated in the Koran, in the sayings of the Prophet, and in Islamic and Shi'ite traditions, Kadivar comes to the conclusion that the concept has never been a central tenet of Islamic thinking and practice. More specifically, he maintains that absolute, religiously based *faqih* (*Velayat-e Shar'i Faqih*), used by Khomeini to justify theocratic authoritarianism, has no scientific and rational justification. That does not, however, necessarily rule out some modified form of jurisconsultancy that is subject to supervision and checks. The practical significance of this point, of course, has not been lost on the Iranian state. Nor, of course, has it gone undetected by the politically aware middle-class Iranians at large.

Despite the relative moderation of their arguments and their great reluctance to foment or be associated with extremist movements, literally all of these intellectuals have been subject to harassment and/or arrest by the authorities. Gülen has been living in self-imposed exile in the United States for years. Ghannouchi, currently in exile in France, has spent several years in prison off and on, and the political party he helped set up, al-Nahda (Renaissance), has been banned and driven underground. Ibrahim, who rose to become Malaysia's deputy prime minister, was later charged with sodomy and jailed after a sensational, politically motivated trial designed to embarrass and humiliate him. Kadivar has been arrested a number of times in Iran, and Soroush has been forced to spend long periods of time outside of Iran. Once again, in each of these cases, the state's active suppression of its moderate opponents has only served to polarize and radicalize political opposition and to push it in a radical direction.

Quite unlike the discourse of moderate reformists, there are no subtle nuances in Islamist fundamentalist ideology. Fundamentalist discourse is fundamentalist, whether articulated a hundred years ago or today. It stands in direct contrast to nearly every principle that moderate reformist discourse upholds. In broad terms, Islamic fundamentalism sees Islam besieged by an aggressive West that is determined to defeat and overwhelm it through its military might, its economic superiority, and its materialistic and decadent culture. The best defense against the West's aggression and against other similar conspiracies designed to destroy Islam is to base all social and political institutions and all cultural norms on Islamic precepts. Reform is insufficient; what is necessary is a reconstitution of the entire polity according to the norms laid out by the Prophet Muhammad when he was in Medina (Moaddel and Talattof 2000, 4). Only then can Islam be properly defended against the reemergence of the pervasive ignorance that proceeded it, that dark era known as the Jahiliyya.

In constructing a comprehensive political ideology, fundamentalism has found in Islam a series of convenient conceptual tools that can readily be interpreted to suit its purposes. The "modernists" have it all wrong, fundamentalists maintain, and their understanding of "true" Islam has been tainted by the incorrect interpretations of Western Orientalists. A correct understanding of true and pure Islam can only be acquired through reference to the Holy Koran, the application of Islamic law, the shari'a, and observance of the Prophet's deeds and traditions (*sunna*) as well as his sayings (*hadith*). Whether or not independent reasoning (*ijtihad*) is permissible or one should simply resort to imitation (*taqlid*) is a question that remains as yet unresolved (Esposito and Voll 2001, 10). This is largely a moot point, however, as doubt and uncertainty are not generally to be found in fundamentalist doctrines of any sort. With great certainty and self-assuredness, Islamic fundamentalist theorists such as the Egyptian Sayyid Qutb (1906–66) and Iran's Ayatollah Ruhollah Khomeini (1902–89) have constructed visions of the ideal Islamic polity, a general worldview, and Islam's place in it. At the same time, these and other theorists have pointed to the centrality of and the need for a struggle, a jihad, in defending Islam against conspiracies from within and from the outside.

Sayyid Qutb, one of the main figures within the Egyptian Muslim Brotherhood, subscribed to the notion that the world was divided into the binary arenas of the Abode of Islam (Dar al Islam) and the Abode of War (Dar al Harb). There are ever-occurring conspiracies against Islam and the Muslim world, at times carried out directly by hostile forces, namely European colonialists, and at times indirectly, through their domestic lackeys (Qutb 2000, 204). Secular ideologies such as liberalism, nationalism, and socialism have been incapable of defending the Muslims' interests, thus plunging Islamic societies into the darkness of Jahiliyya. Only Islam and an Islamic system could save Egypt and the larger Muslim world. Such a system would be based on a literalist interpretation of the shari'a, which "covers the entire scheme that God has devised for regulating human life. It includes within its sphere the regulation of thoughts and views, fundamentals of statecraft, principles and ethics of culture, laws of transactions, and regulations of knowledge and the arts" (198).

Seeking to dispel the notion that Islam in general and his arguments in specific were archaic and authoritarian, Qutb argued that the historical development and conduct of political systems claiming Islamic legitimacy should not be confused with the true essence of Islamic government. A truly Islamic state operates according to the principle of consultation (*shura*), does not practice tyranny, is not primitive but rather is forward-looking, and does not discriminate against minorities and the People of the Book (*ahl-e kitab*) (Choueiri 1997, 96–97). While not venturing into the specifics of the types of political action needed to bring about such a polity, Qutb called for the "organization of the masses and the promise of an updated Islam . . . [as] the ideal solution to the social crisis of his country. Social justice, rather than communism, was the national answer for a country proud of its unique history and independent character" (101).

There was no lack of detail in Ayatollah Khomeini's conception of the ideal Islamic polity. Similar to Qutb, Khomeini proclaimed that Islam is the solution and, interpreted properly, provides a thorough and ideal blueprint for a political system. "The nature and character of Islamic law and the divine ordinances of the *shari'ah*," he writes, "furnish proof of the necessity for establishing government, for they indicate that the laws were laid down for the purpose of creating a state and administering the political, economic, and cultural affairs of society" (Khomeini 2000, 253). In establishing such a government, Khomeini was unabashedly radical and revolutionary, his rhetoric incendiary:

> We have in reality . . . no choice but to destroy those systems of government that are corrupt in themselves and also entail the corruption of others, and to overthrow all treacherous, corrupt, oppressive, and criminal regimes.
>
> This is a duty that every Muslim must fulfill, in every one of the Muslim countries, in order to achieve the triumphant political revolution of Islam. . . .
>
> In order to assure the unity of the Islamic *umma* (community), in order to liberate the Islamic homeland from occupation and penetration by the imperialists and their puppet governments, it is imperative that we establish (an Islamic) government. In order to attain the unity and freedom of the Muslim people, we must overthrow the oppressive governments installed by the imperialists and bring into existence an Islamic government of justice that will be in the service of the people. (Khomeini 2000, 257)

As the leader of the Iranian Revolution and the founder of the Islamic Republican system, Khomeini is rather unique among theorists for his good fortune in putting his ideas into practice. The cornerstone of these ideas was the notion of rule by the *velayat faqih*, or a Supreme Jurisconsult, a position Khomeini himself occupied after the revolution's success until the time of his death in 1989. The Jurisconsult, Khomeini maintained, must have two essential characteristics: he must be learned in religion, and he must be just. "Should a meritorious person who has both qualifications emerge and establish a government, he has the same authority (*velayat*) in ruling the society as that of the Prophet, and it is incumbent upon the people to obey him" (quoted in Dabashi 1993, 443).

The arguments of Sayyid Qutb and Ayatollah Khomeini as well as others like them, such as the Indian Abul A'la Maududi (1903–79), have formed the theoretical backdrop against which one of Islam's central notions, jihad, has been used to legitimize violence against perceived enemies. Political repression at home and an unequal balance of power in the international arena formed the actual context of the radicals' operationalization of the concept. The concept itself has been subject to great debate and controversy among Muslim scholars, and its precise meaning has changed over time. In recent years, for many Westerners who have been on the receiving end of the wrath of Islamic fundamentalism, jihad has come to symbolize the very violent essence of Islam. Therefore, although a full treatment of the notion is beyond the scope of the task at hand, it is important to highlight some of the different definitions given to jihad at various times and to examine its use by Islamic fundamentalists as a legitimizing agent for violence.

Much of the ambiguity surrounding the notion of jihad arises out of the dual definitions that seem to be attributed to it in the Koran. This is largely a result of the concept's gradual transformation during the life of Muhammad's prophecy. Initially, as the Muslim community was beginning to form and the new religion's principles were being propagated in Mecca and later in Medina, jihad was used in the sense of striving to live a better life. As such, it was used to cement the bonding of the Muslim community through collective submission (Islam) to the only God (Allah). As John Esposito (2002, 30) explains, "Muhammad's prophetic call summoned the people to strive and struggle (jihad) to reform their communities and to live a good life based on religious belief and not loyalty to their tribes." The Koran 29:5 provides one such example: "For those whose hopes are in the meeting with Allah (in the Hereafter, let them strive); for the Term (appointed) by Allah is surely coming: and He hears and knows all things." Once the Muslim community was firmly established in Medina, it faced multiple challenges from the Meccan elite and from other nearby tribes, and jihad increasingly came to mean struggle against enemies for the preservation and benefit of Islam. Not surprisingly, therefore, a number of later Koranic verses employ the concept in a militaristic sense.

A careful reading of the Koran reveals very detailed guidelines for the conduct of warfare (Esposito 2002, 32). There are regulations concerning who is to fight and who is exempt from fighting (48:17, 9:92), when hostilities must cease (2:192), how prisoners should be treated (47:4), and the need for proportionality in warfare (47:7). At the same time, there are a number of what many consider "sword verses" in which the believer is enjoined to "slay the idolaters" (9:5), to "keep on fighting against (disbelievers) until the way prescribed by Allah prevails" (2:193), and to "fight against the followers of Satan" (4:76). As the Muslim community grew in size and military strength, especially after the Prophet's death, and as temporal concerns gradually equaled and even surpassed sacral ones for successive generations of Muslim rulers, the emphasis on the meaning of jihad shifted accordingly. Moreover, the eruption of the Crusades was not without significance. As time went by, through selective references to the Koran, both Muslim rulers and thinkers paid increasing attention to the militaristic meaning of jihad (Malik 1998, 63–71). Before long, the term had become synonymous with "holy war," its meaning as "inner struggle" (by both the individual and the community) for closeness to God more and more de-emphasized.

Not surprisingly, by the closing decades of the twentieth century, by the time Islam had once again become politicized and radicalized after decades of dormancy, jihad emerged as the Islamic fundamentalists' primary conceptual justification for resorting to violence. The very dynamics that propelled Islam into the political realm and pushed it in the direction of militancy and radicalism resulted in militaristic interpretations of jihad to gain supremacy over the other. The Osama bin Ladens of the Middle East, the self-declared warriors and defenders of Islam, have little patience with less activist, more introspective interpretations of jihad. They choose selective verses from the Koran, as well as selective hadiths from the Prophet, through which they construct a jihadist view of the world and their own place in it. For them, jihad is a viable means of defending Islam, and it must of necessity be violent. The Koran's injunctions on the rules of warfare, its prohibition on indiscriminate terror on noncombatants and on women and children, and the Prophet's preference for diplomacy over conflict are either ignored or forgotten. Under the banner of *jihad*, Islamic fundamentalists have vowed to unleash terror on their enemies. In the process, they have inflicted more harm to the religion than Islam's opponents could have ever hoped for. And, ironically, they have violated far more Islamic precepts than they have defended through their actions.

CONCLUSION

The historical evolution of Islamic doctrine from its inception until today is directly influenced by the evolving political circumstances in which Muslim rulers and thinkers have found themselves. This has been the case for every epoch in Islamic history, and the late twentieth and early twenty-first centuries have been no exception. In contemporary times, as in previous eras, we find a direct correlation between the larger national and international political contexts on the one hand and developments within Islamic thought and practice on the other. The political history of Islam since the middle of the twentieth century—its reemergence as a viable tool for political expression following the steady decline of various secular ideologies, and the ascendance within Islam of increasingly more radical strands due to the proportionately higher levels of state repression directed at it—clearly shows that politics pushed Islam to become first political and then radical.

There are three highly interrelated, yet still distinct, strands within the latest incarnation of political Islam. They include what may be broadly labeled as popular, intellectual, and fundamentalist Islam. While quite different and in some respects diametrically opposed to each other, these three strands have developed a symbiotic, reinforcing relationship with one another. Each trend has had a deepening and reinforcing effect on the others. For obvious reasons, fundamentalist Islam has generated the greatest degree of attention and controversy, as it has managed to inflict terror on its victims with considerable success. However, developments occurring within the other two strands, especially within intellectual Islam, are just as likely to shape the course of the future trajectory of Islam as is the case with Islamic fundamentalism.

To determine with any degree of certainty the likely future course of Islamic theory and practice is difficult. Nevertheless, there are strong indications that radical fundamentalism will remain part of the Islamic landscape, and by extension that of the global landscape, for the foreseeable future. The conditions that originally gave rise to Islamic fundamentalism have not disappeared, and, in fact, in many ways they have become far more pronounced in the post-9/11 environment. In some ways, as the United States has invaded and occupied Afghanistan and Iraq under the banner of "fighting terrorism," Islamic fundamentalism's premise that there is an ever-present conspiracy against Islam has become a self-fulfilling prophecy. At a time when the American military's presence in the Middle East is more extensive than at any other point in the past, and when many Middle Easterners feel that America's "war against terrorism" is in reality a war against Islam, religiously inspired anti-Americanism is only likely to deepen in the Middle East. The American invasion of Afghanistan might have overthrown the Taliban and its fanatical brand of Islam, and the U.S. military did dismantle Saddam Hussein's "republic of fear" with speed and resolve. In the long run, however, such enterprises will only strengthen the resolve and popular appeal of Islamic fundamentalism. In the Arab street, anger against the United States and its domestic allies is at an all-time high. For the foreseeable future, all indications point to the continued ascendance and popularity of Islamic fundamentalism and the violence to which it frequently resorts.

REFERENCES

Abu-Amr, Ziad. 1994. *Islamic Fundamentalism in the West Bank and Gaza: Muslim Brotherhood and Islamic Jihad.* Bloomington: Indiana University Press.

Ajami, Fouad. 1998. *The Dream Palace of the Arabs: A Generation's Odyssey.* New York: Pantheon.

————. 2001. "The Uneasy Emporium: Pax Americana in the Middle East." In *How Did This Happen? Terrorism and the New War,* ed. James E. Hoge and Gideon Rose, 15–30. New York: Council on Foreign Relations.

————. 2002. "The Sentry's Solitude." David Makovsky, et al. In *The Middle East in Crisis,* ed. David Makovsky et al., 72–86. New York: Council on Foreign Relations.

Ansari, Hamied. 1986. *Egypt: The Stalled Society.* Albany, N.Y.: SUNY Press.

Baker, Raymond William. 2003. *Islam without Fear: Egypt and the New Islamists.* Cambridge: Harvard University Press.

Choueiri, Youssef M. 1997. *Islamic Fundamentalism.* London: Pinter.

Dabashi, Hamid. 1993. *Theology of Discontent: The Ideological Foundation of the Islamic Revolution in Iran.* New York: New York University Press.

Dagher, Carole H. 2000. *Bring Down the Walls: Lebanon's Postwar Challenge.* New York: St. Martin's.

El-Shazly, Nadia, and Raymond Hinnebusch. 2002. "The Challenge of Security in the Post–Gulf War Middle East System." In *The Foreign Policies of Middle East States,* ed. Raymond Hinnebusch and Anoushiravan Ehteshami, 71–90. Boulder, Colo.: Lynne Rienner.

Entelis, John P. 1996. *Culture and Counterculture in Moroccan Politics.* Lanham, Md.: University Press of America.

Esposito, John L. 2002. *Unholy War: Terror in the Name of Islam.* Oxford: Oxford University Press.

Esposito, John L., and John O. Voll. 2001. *Makers of Contemporary Islam.* Oxford: Oxford University Press.

Friedman, Thomas. 1989. *From Beirut to Jerusalem.* New York: Farrar, Straus and Giroux.

Gaffney, Patrick D. 1994. *The Prophet's Pulpit: Islamic Preaching in Contemporary Egypt.* Berkeley: University of California Press.

Hamdi, Mohamed Elhachmi. 1998. *The Politicisation of Islam: A Case Study of Tunisia.* Boulder, Colo.: Westview.

Hiro, Dilip. 1991. *The Longest War: The Iran-Iraq Military Conflict.* New York: Routledge, Chapman, & Hall.

Holmes-Eber, Paula. 2003. *Daughters of Tunis: Women, Family, and Networks in a Muslim City.* Boulder, Colo.: Westview.

Howe, Marvine. 2000. *Turkey Today: A Nation Divided over Islam's Revival.* Boulder, Colo.: Westview.

Hughes, Stephen O. 2001. *Morocco under King Hassan.* London: Ithaca Press.

Kadivar, Mohsen. 1998. *Nazariye-haye Dowlat dar Feqh-e Shi'a* [Perspectives on Government in Shi'a Theology]. Tehran: Ney.

Kamrava, Mehran. 2001. "The Middle East and the Question of Democracy." In *Towards Sustainable Development in the Third World*, ed. Jeff Haynes, 187–216. London: Palgrave.

Karsh, Efraim, and Inari Rausti. 1991. *Saddam Hussein: A Political Biography*. New York: The Free Press.

Khomeini, Ruhollah. 2000. "The Necessity of Islamic Government." In *Modernist and Fundamentalist Debates in Islam: A Reader*, ed. Mansoor Moaddel and Kamran Talattof, 251–62. New York: Palgrave Macmillan.

Malik, Iftikhar H. 1998. "Islamic Discourse on Jihad, War and Violence." *Journal of South Asian and Middle Eastern Studies* 21(4): 47–78.

Milton-Edwards, Beverley. 1996. *Islamic Politics in Palestine*. London: I. B. Tauris.

Mishal, Shaul, and Avraham Sela. 2000. *The Palestinian Hamas: Vision, Violence, and Coexistence*. New York: Columbia University Press.

Moaddel, Mansoor, and Kamran Talattof. 2000. "Contemporary Debates in Islam: Modernism versus Fundamentalism." In *Modernist and Fundamentalist Debates in Islam: A Reader*, ed. Mansoor Moaddel and Kamran Talattof, 1–21. New York: Palgrave Macmillan.

Quandt, William B. 1998. *Between Ballots and Bullets: Algeria's Transition from Authoritarianism*. Washington, D.C.: Brookings.

Qutb, Sayyid. 2000. "Islam as the Foundation of Knowledge." In *Modernist and Fundamentalist Debates in Islam: A Reader*, ed. Mansoor Moaddel and Kamran Talattof, 197–206. New York: Palgrave Macmillan.

Rubin, Barry. 2002. *Islamic Fundamentalism in Egypt Politics*. London: Palgrave Macmillan.

Saad-Ghorayeb, Amal. 2002. *Hizbu'llah: Politics and Religion*. London: Pluto.

Shahin, Emad Eldin. 1998. *Political Ascent: Contemporary Islamic Movements in North Africa*. Boulder, Colo.: Westview.

Sullivan, Denis J., and Sana Abed-Kotob. 1999. *Islam in Contemporary Egypt: Civil Society vs. the State*. Boulder, Colo.: Lynne Rienner.

Tamimi, Azzam S. 2001. *Rachid Ghannouchi: A Democrat within Islam*. Oxford: Oxford University Press.

Tripp, Charles. 1996. "Islam and the Secular Logic of the State in the Middle East." In *Islamic Fundamentalism*, ed. Abdel Salam Sidahmad and Anoushiravan Ehteshami, 51–69. Boulder, Colo.: Westview.

Virost, Milton. 1994. *Sandcastles: The Arabs in Search of the Modern World*. Syracuse, N.Y.: Syracuse University Press.

Wilson, Peter W., and Douglas F. Graham. 1994. *Saudi Arabia: The Coming Storm*. Armonk, N.Y.: M. E. Sharpe.

Yavuz, M. Hakan. 1999. "Toward an Islamic Liberalism? The Nurcu Movement and Fethullah Gulen in Turkey." *Middle East Journal* 53(4): 584–605.

PART THREE

Asia

LAWRENCE C. REARDON

 Interpreting Political Islam's
Challenge to Southeast Asia
INTERNATIONAL TERRORISM, NATIONALISM,
AND RATIONAL CHOICE

POLITICAL ISLAM AND THE THREAT TO DEMOCRACY

Following the tragic events of September 11, 2001, the United States and its allies conducted dramatic counterterrorism operations around the world. Coalition forces defeated the Taliban forces governing Afghanistan, and captured or eliminated several top al Qaeda leaders in the Middle East and Asia as well as confiscated millions of dollars of its monetary assets. The American, British, and Australian governments furthermore approved the invasion, occupation, and rebuilding of Iraq to fight global terrorism and to promote a more democratic Middle East.

Yet on October 16, 2003, U.S. Secretary of Defense Donald Rumsfeld admitted that the United States had not made "decisive progress" in counterterrorism (Moniz and Squitieri 2003). Western intelligence organizations estimated that between twenty-five thousand and seventy thousand al Qaeda members continued to operate in cells scattered throughout the world (Benjamin 2003, 3). In 2003, these cells reportedly were responsible for bombing the British consulate, the Hong Kong Shanghai Banking Corporation headquarters, and Jewish synagogues in Turkey; foreign housing compounds in Saudi Arabia; and the Jakarta Marriott in Indonesia, and for two attempts to assassinate Pakistani President Pervez Musharraf. With the failure to find neither weapons of mass destruction nor definitive links between Saddam Hussein and al Qaeda, the United States lost a degree of legitimacy in its global counterterrorism efforts (Cirincione, Mathews, and Perkovich 2004, 46; Marquis 2004; Kessler 2004). The United States' occupation of Iraq and the December 2003 capture of Saddam Hussein provided greater legitimacy to radical Islamic leaders such as Osama bin

Laden, who sought to radicalize political Islamic movements, attract a new generation of jihadi recruits among the world's 1.5 billion Muslims, and implement a global jihad against "Zionists," "crusaders," and secular Islamic states (Leser 2003; Priest 2003).

To prevent the radicalization of political Islam and to implement a successful "forward strategy" of democracy (Bush 2003), the United States and its coalition allies must learn from its past "war" on global communism. While the forty-year struggle with the Soviet Union eventually was successful, Western leaders exacerbated and perhaps prolonged the conflict by misperceiving the actual threat. Initially, the Truman administration used the perception of a national and international security crisis to persuade a reluctant Congress to fund anticommunist operations in Greece and Turkey in 1947. Promoting a Manichaean worldview, American policy elites enacted unprecedented domestic and foreign policy changes to prevent total political chaos (Halle 1967).

Unfortunately, the Manichaean strategy became the dominant mind-set among policymakers during the 1950s and 1960s. Domestically, investigations of communist infiltration during the McCarthy era threatened the democratic ideals embodied in the U.S. Constitution. Internationally, the Manichaean view transformed an insular foreign policy into a multilateral, interventionist strategy. By viewing the world as divided between good and evil, American leaders did not recognize the differences between the communist regime in the Soviet Union and those in Eastern Europe and China. In the developing world, American policymakers misinterpreted nationalist independence movements because of a monolithic communist conspiracy, resulting in direct and indirect military involvement in the Middle East, Indochina, Africa, and Latin America. Most importantly, the United States overlooked human rights abuses and democratic development to support anticommunist regimes.

In conducting its counterterrorist campaign in the post-9/11 period, some American policymakers and their advisors have reverted to simplistic Manichaean interpretations of Islam that fail to differentiate between political and radical Islamic movements (Mylroies and Woolsey, 2001; Mylroies 2003).[1] Similar to anticommunist campaigns of the post–World War II era, basic constitutional rights have been threatened by the USA Patriot Act and the incarceration of "enemy combatants," who are denied due process of the law (Hamblett 2003). Internationally, the United States has de-emphasized multilateral intervention justified by international law to promote unilateral intervention based on a self-determined, preemptive strategy. Osama bin Laden of al Qaeda, Sheik Omar of Afghanistan, Saddam Hussein of Iraq, the fundamentalist mullahs of Iran, and Abu Bakar Ba'ashir of Jema'ah Islamiyah are increasingly seen as part of an

Islamic monolithic threat to global democratic regimes. Thus, there is a tendency to interpret any Islamic movement as the consequence of monolithic Islamic radicalism; political Islam is thus indistinguishable from radical Islam. In short, Islam has become the new communism.

ISLAM AND SOUTHEAST ASIA

Proponents of a nonsecular Islamic state (Islamists) played a larger political role in the 1970s and 1980s throughout the Muslim world (Esposito 1995, 11). According to the Sudanese Islamic leader Hassan al-Turabi, socialist secular states in Asia, the Middle East, and Africa had proven to be failures. While successfully ousting the previous colonial rulers, the new nationalist leaders did not provide "a sense of identity and a direction in life." Government elites, the military, and the people called for the reestablishment of an Islamic civil society —sometimes violently as in the Iranian case or gradually as in Malaysia (al-Turabi 2002). During this same period, the Saudi Arabian government used its petrodollars to propagate Wahhabi doctrines throughout the Islamic world. By financing the building of mosques and Islamic schools (madrassahs), the Saudis propagated a literal interpretation of the Koran that promoted the establishment of a true Islamic state (Desker 2002, 384–85).

To establish an Islamic civil society, most Islamists promote *political Islam*, which advocates the state's transformation into a pure Islamic state based not on secular but religious authority. Political Islam rejects the notion of a modern secular state, which promotes a barbaric and decadent society bereft of morality and the laws of Allah (shari'a). Such an Islamic state would

> bring about spiritual upliftment and lead to the development of a more just,
> democratic, moral, principled, and socially conscious society, devoid of repressive legislation and unhealthy activities such as gambling. Democratic ideals
> . . . are only acceptable within a secular context, since such ideals would automatically be a feature of a system which is inherently just within an Islamic
> theocratic state. [It possibly would] reject the concepts of majority rule and
> individual choice, since the former allows for the possibility of morally wrong
> tenets being implemented, and the latter involves the assumption that individuals are all-knowing. (Gomez and Sundaram 1999, 243)

While divided among themselves over strict or more liberal interpretations of the Koran (Desker 2002), political Islamists work within the existing political system. They form political parties that participate in local and national elections, such as the Turkish election of 2002 or the Indonesian and Malaysian elections of 2004. They form extensive grassroots organizations that provide a variety of social services by establishing schools, hospitals, orphanages, and even institutions for microfinancing; such "good works" not only increase the parties' political legitimacy but also spread the faith (dawa). They are supported abroad by governmental and nongovernmental organizations, such as the Muslim World League and the Organization of the Islamic Conference (OIC), which is composed of fifty-six Islamic nations around the world. Political Islamists thus are vibrant members of an emerging civil society in the developing world whose ultimate goal is to establish an Islamic "civil" society, which varies according to local conditions (*Economist* 2003; al-Turabi 2002, 37–40).

A minority of Islamists promote *radical Islam*, which shares the same long-term goal of political Islam but considers that the secular attack on Islamic society must be overcome with decisive power. Perhaps the best known theorist of contemporary radical Islamists is the Egyptian scholar Sayyid Qutb. Qutb justified the use of violence to transform the "ignorant" state (jahiliyya), which is the result of rationalist ideas adopted by Westerners and Muslims alike (Euben 1999). By potently combining religious and political goals, radical Islamists call upon individual Muslims or those organized as domestic or transnational organizations to carry out violent holy struggle (jihad)—including military action, terrorism, and suicide terrorism—for the purpose of either seceding from or transforming the state (Gearson 2002; Barkan and Snowden 2001). The distinction between these two categories can become blurred, as political and radical Islamists are free to adopt peaceful or terrorist strategies. Yet such distinctions are useful in analyzing the motives of Islamic organizations (Emmerson 2002, 122; Mirskii 2003, 30).[2]

Southeast Asia in the past has not been considered a hotbed of political or radical Islam. Although containing one-fourth the world's Muslims, postcolonial Southeast Asia was dominated by secular leaders who instituted strong authoritarian governments primarily focused on economic development (World Bank 1993; Blondel, Inoguchi, and Marsh 1999).

However, in the 1990s Southeast Asian states encountered several unforeseen phenomenon. First, the March 1997 implosion of the Thai financial sector spread throughout Southeast and Northeast Asia. The resulting Asian financial crisis created a high degree of economic instability and dislocation, which put into question the legitimacy of the governments' development philosophies. Second, the authoritarian development state was increasingly under attack. Thailand and the Philippines joined South Korea and Taiwan in establishing liberal democratic states. In 1998, the Indonesians overthrew the Soeharto government and established a nascent democratic state; Malaysia and Singapore also were under increasing domestic pressure to liberalize politically. Finally, the Southeast Asian states had to deal with a rising tide of cultural and religious animosity. While continuously dealing with separatist movements in the post-colonial period, the Southeast Asian states especially in the post-9/11 period have encountered a renewed call for the establishment of an Islamic civil society that is supported by both political and radical Islamists.

INDONESIA

Political Islam

With a population of more than 210 million people, 87 percent of whom profess Islam, Indonesia is the world's fourth most populous nation and the largest Muslim country. Although a founding member of the OIC, it is not officially an Islamic state—but it also is not a secular state. Shortly after Queen Juliana of the Netherlands recognized the Republic of Indonesia on August 17, 1950, President Soekarno implemented Pancasila, or the Five Principles of State, whose fifth principle was to unite the multiethnic, multireligious state by promoting a "Belief in God and mutual respect for the belief in others." As the "third rail" of Indonesian politics, Soekarno's vision continues to be challenged by Islamists who desire to establish a pure Islamic state based on shari'a (Hamayotsu 2002, 365–66; Zainu'ddin 1980, 273).

In 1945, Islamists hoped to enshrine Islamic principles in the constitution. The Jakarta Charter of 1945 mandated "the obligation for adherents of Islam to practice Islamic Law" and also mandated that the president should be a native Indonesian and a Muslim (Johns 1987, 210–11). While Soekarno eventually abandoned this promise, the Masyumi (Modernist Islamic Party) continued to promote the idea of an Islamic state in the 1950s. As a major political movement with a solid grassroots organization composed of civic and educational institutions, Masyumi garnered one-fifth of the popular vote during the first national elections in 1955. However, Masyumi's unwillingness to criticize radical Islamic movements and their continued support for the establishment of an Islamic civil society were thwarted by Soekarno, who with the support of the military and the communist party (PKI) implemented his Guided Democracy form of authoritarian government by 1959. By 1960, Masyumi was banned (Zainu'ddin 1980, 213–54; Cheong 1999, 78–80).

Following his gradual rise to power in the late 1960s, President Soeharto and his military allies concentrated on establishing his New Order form of authoritarian rule that placed heavy emphasis on economic development (MacIntyre 1999, 261–86;

Aspinall and Berger 2001, 1009). According to the electoral law of 1969, restraints were placed on organized political parties; Masyumi was again forbidden to organize (Zainu'ddin 1980, 273). Instead, Soeharto promoted representation by functional groups (Golkar), in which the state appointed party members composed of "civil servants, the armed forces, intellectuals, women, youths, workers, farmers, veterans, and even pedicab drivers" (Cheong 1999, 107). Throughout the New Order period, Soeharto and the military continued to restrict the number of political parties and suppress outside political activities, especially political Islamic activities.

While the resignation of Soeharto and the collapse of the New Order regime on May 21, 1998, ushered in a new era of political freedom in Indonesia, most of the newly formed political parties continued to adhere to Soekarno's strategy of promoting a multiethnic, multireligious nation. In the parliamentary elections of June 7, 1999, Soeharto's Golkar still won 22 percent of the vote; during the 2004 election, Golkar transformed itself into a more Islamic-friendly party (Donnan 2003a; Hamayotsu 2002, 369–70). The PDI-P (Indonesian Democracy Party of Struggle) won 34 percent of the parliamentary vote in 1999; its leader, Megawati Soekarnoputri (Soekarno's daughter), eventually was appointed president of Indonesia in 2001. Even the PKB (National Awakening Party), which was established in 1926, continued to promote a secular agenda (10 percent of the 1999 vote). As the political arm of the Nahdatul-Ulama (Revival of the Ulama), which is Indonesia's largest moderate Islamic nongovernmental organization with more than forty million members, PKP manages an extensive educational network of Islamic schools and other institutions (International Crisis Group 2003, 13; Johns 1987, 207).

Perhaps realizing that the promotion of an Islamic state would be rejected by the Indonesian military, the two remaining Islamic political parties indirectly support the establishment of an Islamic state. Following the 1999 vote, the PPP (United Development Party) and PAN (National Mandate Party) controlled 15 percent of the Indonesian parliamentary seats. The PPP originally was composed of four Muslim parties that participated in New Order general elections from 1977; in 1999, the PPP won 12 percent of the parliamentary vote. Its general chairman, Hamzah Haz, was appointed vice president of Indonesia in 2001 and subsequently became its most internationally controversial leader. While traditionally not supportive of the establishment of an Islamic state, the PPP promoted the introduction of shari'a law. Hamzah also strengthened dialogue with radical Islamic groups such as Jema'ah Islamiyah and Laskar Jihad, arguing on May 29, 2002, that there were no terrorists in Indonesia. Hamzah became internationally famous in April 2003 after calling George W. Bush the "king of terrorists" (Malley 2003, 137; Donnan 2003b; Moore 2003).

PAN traces its origins to the Muhammadiyah, which had been formed in Java in 1912 to revive the Islamic religious training under attack by the Western education system; it is the second largest moderate Islamic nongovernmental organization in Indonesia (Zainu'ddin 1980, 143–44; Johns 1987, 206–7). Amien Rais, who is the PAN party leader and chairman of the Indonesian parliament's upper chamber, has continued PAN/Muhammadiyah's multicultural transformation; they support a multireligious society and urge the adoption of a non-Islamist platform in order to gain long-term political influence (International Crisis Group 2003, 11; Desker 2002, 384).[3] Rais has publicly stated, "It's impossible to change a Pancasila nation into a shari'a nation." He would not promote an Islamic state because he "wanted to be a national figure, not just an Islamic figure" (Deutsche Presse-Agentur 2003). Thus, PAN hoped to expand its legislative presence in the 2004 election by moving to the center.

The majority of Indonesian people are devout Muslims who are critical of Hollywood values and hypocritical Western governments. Yet they reject radical Islamic groups and the establishment of an Islamic state based on the shari'a. The Indonesian parliament and the largest Islamic groups demonstrated this sentiment most recently in 2002, when they opposed a constitutional amendment to establish shari'a law (Malley 2003, 139).

Radical Islam

The radical Islamic movement in Indonesia has its origins in the Darul Islam (Islamic Domain) movement, whose membership in part consisted of Indonesian military and civilian combatants demobilized after the establishment of the republic. Rejecting Soekarno's Pancasila strategy, Darul Islam advocated the establishment of a separate Islamic state. The Indonesian army finally defeated the small-scale guerrilla operations in west Java, Aceh, south Sulawesi, and Kalimantan in 1962. As a result, the Indonesian army remained highly suspicious of political and radical Islam as well as all communists (Zainu'ddin 1980, 228; Cheong 1999, 79; Hamayotsu 2002, 366; van Dijk 1981).

While the Soeharto era was distinguished by rapid economic development that substantially raised the overall living standards of Indonesia, it was not until the post-Soeharto era that Indonesia enjoyed a new era of democracy. Yet democratic change was accompanied by a new era of ethnic strife as well as by secessionist movements in Indonesia's exterior islands of East Timor, Aceh, and Papua (Irian Jaya) as well as Islamic terrorism (Bhakti 2000). After decades of suppression, radical Islam has reemerged in the post-Soeharto era, funded in part by Saudi proponents of Wahhabism who believe in a literal interpretation of the Islamic texts. Like its Southeast Asian neighbors, Indonesia continues to engage Islamic-related separatist movements in Aceh and Ambon. Unlike its neighbors, it has suffered the most from recent radical Islamic terrorist operations, which resulted in 250 deaths between August 2000 and 2003.

Several radical Islamic movements vie to claim Darul Islam's role of promoting an Islamic state through separatist operations. Fourteen years after Darul Islam's defeat, Aceh's Islamic radicals once again organized to form the Free Aceh Movement (GAM), whose purpose was to reinstate Aceh's sovereignty lost in the late nineteenth century and to establish a free Islamic state (Chalk 2001, 254–56; Zainu'ddin 1980, 80–83, 132–33). By the late 1980s and early 1990s, the Soeharto government transformed Aceh into a military operations area and utilized twelve thousand military troops to carry out an extensive military campaign that eliminated three thousand Acehnese. Not surprisingly, the military occupation fueled GAM's separatist zeal (Aspinall and Berger 2001, 1017; Sulistiyanto 2001, 441–43). In the post-Soeharto era, GAM agreed to a cease-fire in May 2000. However, the negotiations broke off on May 18, 2003, when the Indonesian government declared martial law in the Aceh province. Initiating the largest military operation since the East Timorese invasion of 1975, President Megawati sent forty thousand troops to engage approximately five thousand GAM separatists (Sipress 2003a, 2003b). Desiring to defend the integrity of Indonesia in the post-East Timor era, the Megawati government also was motivated to retain Aceh's abundant resources of petroleum, natural gas, gold, and lumber, as well as its strategic location on the Strait of Malacca.

Beginning in 1999, violence increased in Ambon, Maluku, whose population is almost evenly divided between Christians and Muslims. By June 2000, the newly established Laskar Jihad sent three thousand members to Ambon. With the support of some Indonesian military, Laskar Jihad hoped to establish control over Ambon, thus thwarting the establishment of a separate Christian state. Its long-term goal was to institute shari'a law and establish an Islamic state throughout all of Indonesia (Schulze 2002, 58–59; Desker 2002, 387–88). While a settlement was reached on February 12, 2002, and a zone of neutrality established between the two sides, five thousand people were slaughtered and seven hundred thousand people became refugees. Following the settlement and the Bali bombing, Laskar Jihad disbanded its fifteen thousand-member organization, although there is some question whether it has been reconstituted in Papua (Malley 2003, 140–41; *PNG Post-Courier* 2003; Go 2002).

Perhaps the most infamous radical Islamic group operating in Indonesia has been Jema'ah Islamiah (JI) and its alleged leader Abu Bakar Ba'ashir. Originally using a pirate radio station and an Islamic boarding school in Solo to promote the teaching of shari'a law in the 1960s and 1970s, Ba'ashir escaped to Malaysia in 1985 to avoid continued imprisonment by the Soeharto government.

Returning to Indonesia in 1999, Ba'ashir established the Indonesian Mujaheddin Council (MMI), which essentially was the radical Islamic equivalent of the more liberal Nahdatul-Ulama and the Muhammadiyah Islamic civic organizations. According to Ba'ashir, "The MMI is an institution where a lot of people from a lot of Muslim groups including the NU and Muhammadiyah gather at one table to discuss how to get our vision of shari'a implemented into national laws. . . . As long as Muslims are the majority, the country should be ruled by shari'a" (Abuza 2002, 451). Allegedly, Ba'ashir also assumed the leadership of JI after 1999 and approved the subsequent terrorist campaign (Ministry of Home Affairs 2003, 6).

The bombing rampage started on August 1, 2000, when a car bomb exploded, killing two people and wounding several, including the Philippine ambassador. The following month, a car bomb exploded inside the Jakarta Stock Exchange building's garage, killing sixteen people; nineteen more died when bombs were ignited outside Christian churches in ten different Indonesian cities during the 2000 Christmas Eve services. During 2002, a series of bomb attacks occurred in Jakarta, including attacks in shopping centers, supermarkets, nightclubs, and in front of an unoccupied U.S. government building.

The most spectacular bombing occurred on the second anniversary of the attack on the USS *Cole* in the Yemeni harbor. On October 12, 2002, three bombs exploded simultaneously in Bali: one ton of explosives packed inside a Mitsubishi L300 van exploded outside the Sari Club, five kilos of TNT were contained in a "vest bomb" worn by a suicide bomber at Paddy's Bar, and a third smaller bomb was placed outside the American consulate. Known as the "island of the gods," Bali's pristine beaches and rakish nightlife transformed the island into Indonesia's most important tourist destination; it also is regarded by radical Islamic groups as demonstrating the corrupting influence of Western society. Altogether, 202 people died, including Indonesians, Australians, Canadians, Britons, and Swedes, in the worst terrorist attack in Indonesia's history and the most deadly terrorist attack since the World Trade Center disaster. Eerily reminiscent of the Bali bombings, another minivan exploded outside the Marriott Hotel-Jakarta on August 5, 2003, killing 16 people and injuring 150. The attack was justified as a "fatal slap in the face of the United States and its agents in Muslim Jakarta that has been desecrated by the dirty U.S. and the insolent racist Australian presence" (*Al-Quds al-Arabi* 2003; Nakashima 2003a).

While the Indonesian military leader General Sutarto acknowledged that Indonesia had become a hotbed for foreign terrorist organizations, the Bali bombings finally changed the attitude of many Indonesians. Ba'ashir was eventually arrested and, in September 2003, tried and convicted for the attempted overthrow of the Indonesian government, although the Jakarta superior court overturned the sedition charge in November 2003 (Go 2003).

Impact on the Transition to Democracy

Indonesians astonished most of the world after 1998 for not devolving into chaos but, rather, evolving into a vibrant, growing democracy. Yet there are questions as to whether their newfound freedoms are threatened by the global and domestic war against radical Islam (Freidman 2002). Some of these problems are shared with many other developing democracies. Amnesty International and Human Rights Watch reported that forty-six politically motivated arrests and detentions were made between the release of all prisoners of conscience in 1998 and 2003. Some of those arrested had insulted the Indonesian leadership; others were arrested promoting Aceh's independence (Amnesty International 2003a). In addition, a series of legal prosecutions was carried out in 2003 that severely restricted press freedoms (Amnesty International 2003b).

While it is the responsibility of governmental and nongovernmental organizations to bring light to such violations, other trends are more serious. With the dramatic increase in criminal and terrorist activities following the collapse of the Soeharto government, the military and the security organizations have regained a degree of legitimacy. Since 9/11, the United States has reestablished limited ties with the Indonesian military, intelligence, and police organizations by providing training and financing to support antiterrorist actions. As a result, Indonesia continues to be the largest recipient of U.S. foreign assistance funds in East Asia (Lum 2002, 9). The close connection between Indonesia and the United States has prompted the former Laskar Jihad commander to claim that the United States was directing the detention of any Islamic activist who has ever been to Afghanistan or Ambon (Purdum 2002; *BBC Monitoring Asia Pacific* 2003c). Following the Bali bombing, the Indonesian parliament partially reinstated the intelligence and security services' domestic powers of surveillance and apprehension; they thus again detained suspects without trial. The Indonesian police continued to arrest JI suspects, some of whom were brought to trial (Donnan 2003c; Nakashima 2003b). Discussions continue over the adoption of an internal security act similar to those enjoyed by Malaysia and Singapore (Malley 2003, 135–36; Donnan and Kazmin 2003, 4). On May 19, 2003, martial law was declared in the Aceh province that ended negotiations with the Free Aceh Movement. While the Indonesian military argued that its new offensive in Aceh might last a decade, some outside observers argue that the Indonesian military is repeating its tactics of rape, kidnapping, and murder practiced in East Timor (Perlez 2003, A3; Donnan 2003d).

Signaling a reversal of post-Soeharto reforms, the military appears to be increasing its influence over the civilian government. While the major political parties have agreed to its increased role in society, the military could threaten the stability of Indonesian democracy. The former defense minister Juwono Sudarsono has already argued that the events of May 2003 leading to the reimposition of martial law in Aceh "was open defiance" of the civilian leadership in Jakarta (Sipress 2003a; Mietzner 2002).

MALAYSIA

Political Islam

With more than half of its 24.5 million population professing Islam, Malaysia is the second largest Muslim country in Southeast Asia. Gaining its independence from Great Britain in 1957, nearly a decade later than Indonesia, Malaysia has enjoyed a longer period of political and economic stability. Such stability is partially due to the continued strength of the authoritarian development state under the "tutelage" of the United Malays National Organization (UMNO).

However, in September 2001 a controversy arose as to whether Malaysia is an Islamic state, and this has continued to plague Malaysian politics (Martinez 2001). Following the electoral successes of the major Islamic opposition party in 1999 and the 9/11 incident of 2001, the Mahathir/UMNO regime used the controversy to equate political and radical Islam. The opposition parties cried foul but found it difficult to disentangle themselves from the radical Islamic movements. With the end of the Mahathir regime in 2003 and elections in the spring of 2004, the role of political Islam continued as an explosive political and religious issue in Malaysia.

Malaysia is a model authoritarian development state with the facade of democratic institutions but in reality is highly controlled by the government (Gomez and Sundaram 1999). While Chinese (24 percent) and Indian (7 percent) minorities traditionally dominated the local economy, the Malay majority (50 percent) instituted an "affirmative action" program in 1971 known as the New Economic Policy (NEP). NEP and succeeding policies used a quota-type system to raise the economic and social standing of the Malays as well as the indigenous peoples (10.9 percent), which together were the so-called sons of the soil (bumiputera). Under the leadership of UMNO, the sons of the soil successfully co-opted the Chinese and Indian minorities by adopting long-term goals to develop a strong economy and establishing a multiracial, multireligious, and multicultural state. They also utilized long-standing fears of communism (the enactment of a state of emergency to fight local Chinese communists until 1960) and Indonesia (President Soekarno's policy of confrontation until 1966). In this way, UMNO merged the ideals of modern economic growth and Islam to develop a new Islamic path of modernization (Fuller 1998, 44–45).

To this end, the various ethnic groups entered into a National Front in 1973— the Barisan Nasional (BN) (Gomez and Sundaram 1999, 234–36). Led by the Malays (UMNO), the BN is a coalition of several ethnically based parties including the Chinese (Malaysian Chinese Association [MCA]) and the Indians (Malaysian Indian Congress [MIC]). In reality, UMNO was the ruling party. Mahathir Mohamad led the Barisan Nasional coalition government as prime minister from 1981 to 2003. By guaranteeing consistent economic growth, monopolizing the media, and skewing the electoral system to support UMNO constituencies, Mahathir's control was unquestionable as long as he maintained control over UMNO factions (Crouch 1996, 74–75; Gomez and Sundaram 1999, 237–41, 255–57). He relentlessly used the Internal Security Act (ISA) and other laws to monopolize regional and national elections and affect complete control over the state, including the opposition parties and political Islam.

Malaysia's primary opposition parties are allied as the Barisan Alternatif (BA), which primarily includes the Party Islam SeMalaysia (PAS); the Democratic Action Party composed mostly of ethnic Chinese; and the Parti KeADILan Nasional, founded by Anwar Ibrahim's wife in 1998. With the severe economic recession caused by the Asian financial crisis and the imprisonment of several political leaders in 1998 (Lim Guang Eng of the Chinese Democratic Action Party; Deputy Prime Minister Anwar Ibrahim, who was subsequently convicted of corruption and sodomy), the Reformasi movement arose in Malaysia (Funston 2000, 9; Gomez and Sundaram 1999, 242–43). Focusing on the elimination of KKN (corruption, cronyism, and nepotism) and promoting a more open, democratic system, Reformasi became an effective rallying cry supported by political parties and nongovernmental organizations, such as the Islamic Malaysian Youth Movement (ABIM) (Weiss 1999).

With nearly half a million members, the Islamic party PAS is the largest and most important opposition party in BA. With the revival of Islam in Malaysia in the early 1980s, UMNO's leader Mahathir adapted progressive Islamic ideas to Malaysia's secular modernization program, which included convincing the Islamic activist leader Anwar Ibrahim to join UMNO. In this light, PAS argued that it represented the true Islamic path and promoted the establishment of a pure Islamic state. Because of its willingness to cooperate with the Chinese and Indian "infidel" (kafir) political parties, PAS questioned UMNO's suitability to rule an Islamic state (Kamarulnizam 1999). Although Malaysia has proclaimed

Islam as the official state religion, PAS maintains that shari'a law first must be enshrined within the constitution in order for Malaysia to be considered a true Islamic state.

The core of PAS support is located in the northern Malay states of Kelantan, Terengganu, Kedah, and Perlis; PAS ruled Kelantan from 1959 to 1978 and again after 1990. In the watershed election of 1999, PAS not only captured 27 of the 193 seats in the federal parliament but also gained control of the northeast state of Terengganu. On July 8, 2002, the PAS-controlled state assembly of Terengganu approved the adoption of shari'a law, including Hudud and Qisas punishments such as stoning or hand amputation (McCawley 2002; Ahmad 2002). In the lead-up to national elections occurring in spring 2004, PAS put forward a fifty-three-page Islamic state document in which PAS stated its intentions to amend the constitution to promote "religious freedom, economic rights, and the rights to conduct business, political rights, educational rights including the use of mother tongue, rights to practice own culture, rights to assemble, and to set up organizations" (Bernama 2003).

UMNO's response was predictable: Prime Minister Mahathir viewed the Reformasi movement and the 1999 elections as being similar to the events in Indonesia that brought down President Soeharto (Funston 2000, 25). Thus, Mahahtir tried to constrain PAS's control of the two state governments by recentralizing government financial outlays (June 2001) and ending government financing of six hundred private Islamic schools, which are called the Sekolah Agama Rakyat (February 2003) (Pereira 2003a). Mahathir also claimed to be a true Islamic leader by undertaking the hajj to Mecca, criticizing U.S. actions in the Middle East, assuming leadership of the OIC, and severely criticizing the international "Jewish conspiracy." Most importantly, he proclaimed in September 2001 that Malaysia was already an Islamic state, with the 1957 constitution enshrining Islam as the religion of the federation (von der Mehden 1987, 186–90). The implication was that Malaysia did not need PAS and that its shari'a law was unnecessary.

The response of PAS's coalition partners in Barisan Alternatif was also predictable. The BA had never formally advocated the adoption of an Islamic constitution but had promoted the freedom of religion (Funston 2000, 13). DAP (Democratic Action Party), which traditionally supported a democratic, multiethnic society, withdrew its political participation in PAS's Kelantan and Terengganu state governments (Gomez and Sundaram 1999, 242). DAP and many of the coalition partners feared that the PAS initiative would have a detrimental effect on BA's chances in the 2004 election and, more importantly, in the long-term viability of the BA coalition (*BBC Monitoring Asia Pacific* 2003b).

Radical Islam

Using the ISA, the Malaysian Home Ministry successfully contained twelve radical groups that attempted to overthrow the Malaysian government between 1967 and 2003, including the radical Islamic groups Jema'ah Islamiyah (JI) and Kumpulan Militan Malaysia (KMM) (*New Straits Times* 2003).[4] Malaysia has been used as a peaceful haven for the radical Islamists in Southeast Asia. Abu Bakar Ba'ashir fled to Malaysia in 1985, where he and other Islamic radicals such as Riduan Isamuddin (Hambali) established JI in the late 1990s. Focusing on the establishment of a pan-Islamic state in Southeast Asia, Ba'ashir and Hambali recruited new JI members throughout Malaysia, Indonesia, and Singapore (Ministry of Home Affairs 2003, 6).

In Malaysia, JI's alleged accomplice was KMM, whose purpose was to bring about the violent overthrow of the Malaysian state and to install a radical Islamic government. With membership cells located in nine Malaysian states and its operation center in Selangor, KMM allegedly carried out bank robberies and terrorist activities in Malaysia. More importantly, it hosted meetings between al Qaeda and other regional radical Islamic groups—possibly including the first meeting to sketch out the 9/11 attacks. KMM also provided support for Zacarias Moussaoui, the alleged twentieth member of the 9/11 suicide mission (Bernama 2001). By 2003, Malaysia had arrested and detained indefinitely nearly eighty KMM members, including Nik Ahdli, the son of PAS spiritual leader Nik Aziz Nik Mat. Nik Adli is accused of having developed a close relationship with al Qaeda while training in Afghanistan and leading the KMM (Pereira 2003c; Abuza 2002, 444).

Impact on the Transition to Democracy

Although the Malaysian government remains highly critical of U.S. actions in Afghanistan and Iraq, the Bush administration has praised Malaysia's crackdown on terrorist activities since 9/11, including the freezing of terrorist assets and the arrest of KMM members indirectly connected to the 9/11 attacks (Hashim 2002). In his May 2002 official visit to the United States, Mahathir signed a bilateral Declaration of Cooperation to Combat International Terrorism; he also agreed to establish the Southeast Asian Regional Centre for Counter Terrorism in Kuala Lumpur (Searcct) in July 2003, which was funded by the United States and managed by Malaysia. Malaysia is thus engaged in closer antiterrorist operations with its ASEAN neighbors and the United States, although it continues to rebuff Australian intelligence agencies (Vaughn 2003, 13; Lau 2003).

Despite these actions, the U.S. State Department remained concerned about severe human rights violations such as the lack of due process that continues to define the "Asian values" of the Malaysian government (Vaughn 2003, 9). The Internal Security Act (ISA) has been the primary weapon used to combat terrorism in Malaysia since 1960, when it was first adopted to combat communism. The ISA enables the government to detain any suspicious individual for up to twenty-six months; with court approval, ISA allows indefinite detention (Fritz and Flaherty 2003, 1355–59). Directly after the 9/11 incident, Prime Minister Mahathir renewed his accusation that PAS was directly linked with JI/KMM; the government has since relied on the ISA, the Police Act, the Sedition Act, the Official Secret's Act, and the Education Act to jail JI/KMM members as well as opposition party members and other dissidents (Funston 2002, 14). The request by the Human Rights Commission of Malaysia in December 2003 to replace the ISA has prompted some discussions of reform (*BBC Monitoring Asia Pacific* 2003; Darshini 2003). However, revisions of the ISA should be viewed pessimistically, as the government continues to emphasize the war against terrorism, citing the ISA as Malaysia's equivalent to the USA Patriot Act as well as the war against Western ideas.

The newly appointed prime minister of Malaysia, Abdullah Badawi, took initial steps in 2004 to transform the Malaysian political system by initiating in-depth investigations on corruption, graft, and police brutality. Coming from a prominent family of Islamic scholars, Prime Minister Badawi hopes to bolster UMNO's legitimacy and reduce the PAS's electoral appeal in the 2004 elections. Whatever the case, Malaysia remains a global model for Islamic economic growth and a prime example of secular Islamic authoritarianism.

THE RESPONSE OF THE PHILIPPINES, THAILAND, AND SINGAPORE TO RADICAL ISLAM

While nearly 95 percent of its seventy-seven million people profess Christianity, the Philippines also enjoys a sizable Muslim minority (5–8 percent) located mostly on the southern islands of Mindanao, Basilan, Sulu, and Palawan. For four centuries, these Muslims fought the Spanish and American colonial powers and, more recently, the Philippine government for greater autonomy (Che Man 1990, 46–73; Islam 1998, 444–46, 448–51). Enjoying a separate language, religion, and culture, the Muslim peoples recently were threatened by the southern migration of Filipino Christians, which has prompted fears of a "Christianization" of the south. Following a series of massacres and President Ferdinand Marcos's imposition of martial law in 1972, the Moro National Liberation Front (MNFL) was established to defend the "free and independent" Islamic republic. Although gaining political, financial, and military support from the OIC, Malaysia, and Libya, the MNFL succumbed to fifteen years of political and ethnic infighting, resulting in the MNFL's agreement to relinquish its goals of independence by 1987 (Noble 1994; Che Man 1990, 138–57). By November 6, 1990, President Corazon Aquino agreed to establish an autonomous region in Muslim Mindanao (ARMM) in four southern provinces; President Fidel Ramos in 1996 agreed that the MNFL should undertake managerial responsibility for economic projects conducted in Mindanao.

While the MNFL was effectively co-opted by the 1990s, other groups with more radical Islamic agendas supplanted the MNFL, including the Moro Islamic Liberation Front (MILF). With between twelve thousand and fifteen thousand members, the MILF includes a number of core members trained in Afghanistan during the 1980s (Abuza 2002, 435). According to JI's second-in-command, who was captured by Filipino forces in October 2003, the MILF established several safe houses and training camps in the southern Philippines in which Indonesian and other JI terrorist recruits continued their training after the fall of Afghanistan (Jones 2003, 16–18). Although the Filipino military destroyed some of these camps in mid-2000, other camps led by rogue MILF leaders took their place. The leadership of the MILF has disavowed responsibility for the camps; in summer 2003, the MILF leadership agreed to a cease-fire and began negotiations for a comprehensive peace agreement with the Philippine government in 2003 (Che Man 1990, 193–95; Sipress and Nakashima 2003; Bonner 2003; Abuza 2002, 437–39).

Internationally, the most notorious radical Islamic group in the Philippines is the Abu Sayyaf Group (ASG). The United States has declared the ASG, unlike the MILF, as a terrorist organization. Established in 1991 and led by Filipino veterans of the Afghan wars, ASG reportedly enjoyed strong links with al Qaeda. Having launched a series of attacks on Christian settlements in the south and initiating a wave of kidnappings and extortion attempts, the Filipino military engaged Abu Sayyaf in a series of counterassaults (Tan 2000, 272–77; Banlaoi 2002, 300–302; Perez 1995). Fearing Abu Sayyaf's close connections with al Qaeda, including its involvement with the 1993 and 2001 World Trade Center attacks, the attempts on Pope John Paul II's life, and the plot to blow up U.S. airliners flying over the Pacific (Abuza 2002, 441–43), the United States provided millions of dollars for helicopters, patrol boats, military advisors, and other security assistance. Starting in February 2002, the United States initiated the short-term joint Filipino-U.S. military exercises Balikatan 2002 and Balikatan 2003. In 2003, 350 U.S. counterterrorist advisors were sent to the southern Philippines to help destroy Abu Sayyaf forces (Banlaoi 2002, 304–5). Despite the U.S. designation of Abu Sayyaf as an international terrorist group, it is questionable whether Abu Sayyaf is an al Qaeda affiliate or is purely a band of kidnappers and extortionists.

While living in one of the most autocratic and densely populated states in the world (Khong 1999), four million Singaporeans, 77 percent of whom are of Chinese descent, were stunned to hear in December 2001 that thirteen JI terrorists were operating in their own backyard (Snitwongse 2002, 8). According to the authoritative 2003 Singaporean *White Paper* produced by the Ministry of Home Affairs, the Singaporean branch of JI had been established in the late 1980s by local Muslim cleric Ibrahim Maidin. Besides attacking all "infidel" operations, the JI's ultimate goal was to establish a pan-Islamic state, whose core would be Indonesia and that would include Malaysia, Singapore, Brunei, and the southern Philippines.

Returning from terrorist training in Afghanistan in 1993, Ibrahim Maidin planned but did not implement the bombing of U.S. military personnel at a Singaporean subway station and attacks on the U.S. and Israeli embassies as well as on U.S. naval vessels in Singaporean anchorage. Following the December 2001 arrests, the Singaporean Internal Security Department (ISD) initiated a second series of arrests in August 2002 and captured nineteen additional JI members. By February 2003, the Indonesians arrested Mas Selamat Kastari, who had been appointed the Singaporean JI cell leader in 1999. During the summer 2003 trial, Mas Selamat confirmed that JI planned to fly a hijacked plane into Singapore's airport control tower as well as bomb Singapore's petrochemical refineries, water supply system, and the ministry of defense (Pereira 2003b). All JI operatives remain in custody in Singapore, and the ISD continues to strengthen its surveillance of Singaporean citizens.

Finally, Thailand's quiet war against radical Islamic terrorists became world news on August 11, 2003, when Thai officials arrested Hambali, one of the most wanted JI leaders in Southeast Asia. Having lived in Thailand for more than eighteen months, Hambali was apparently plotting to attack foreign embassies and possibly the 2003 APEC summit meeting in Bangkok. In light of a series of recent bombings and assassinations, the Thai government admitted publicly to the existence of a separatist movement along the Malaysian border (Lyall 2003, 9; *Nation* 2004).

The ongoing arrests of JI terrorists are just a continuation of a long-term struggle against radical Islam (Agence France Press 2003; *Nation* 2003a). By successfully implementing an education and cultural assimilation program in the 1920s and 1930s, the Thais successfully assimilated Chinese, Indian, and Malaysian minorities into Thai society. However, many of Thailand's approximately six million Muslims living in the southern provinces of Patani, Yala, and

Narithiwat that border northern Malaysia retain a Malay identity and language. They are proud of their heritage as successors of the seventeenth-century Islamic kingdom of Patani. Since 1968, they have supported the radical Islamic group the Patani United Liberation Organization (PULO), which emphasizes the improvement of education as well as the bombing of Thai government offices, schools, and Buddhist temples (Che Man 1990, 32–43; Islam 1998, 443–44). Established in 1995, the New PULO adopted a less violent agenda to achieve Patani self-autonomy. Receiving financial support from the opposition PAS party in Malaysia, both groups were responsible for an increase in separatist attacks in the late 1990s (Chalk 2001, 242–43).

By July 2003, Thai news sources stated that PULO had "ceased its armed operations, opting instead for diplomacy and propaganda campaigns" (*Nation* 2003b). Yet, a new group, the Mujahideen Pattani, continued to attack Thai security personnel, forty of whom were killed between 2000 and 2003 (*Nation* 2003c; Che Man 1990, 67). Following the torching of twenty schools that masked the theft of small arms from a local military depot, Thailand in January 2004 imposed martial law in the Yala, Patani, and Narithiwat provinces (Ghosh 2004). However, tensions continued to escalate as the Thai military reacted forcefully to the continued assassination of Thai government officials and Buddhist monks.

The Philippines, Thailand, and Singapore have strengthened antiterrorist measures, including the improvement of border security forces and domestic intelligence agencies. They have also increased cooperation with the United States, resulting in Hambali being turned over to the CIA in August 2003, as well as with their ASEAN allies (Nakashima and Sipress 2003). Questions remain as to whether these measures are designed to deter terrorism or are an excuse to return to authoritarianism. The adoption of draconian antiterrorist measures by the democratically elected Prime Minister Thaksin Shinawatra of Thailand has drawn criticism not only from opposition party members in Thailand but also from Western observers (*Washington Post* 2003). Of course, this is not a problem for Singapore, which is not a democratic state.

THREE EXPLANATIONS: INTERNATIONAL TERRORISM, NATIONALISM, AND RATIONAL CHOICE

Three different approaches—or, in international relations jargon, levels of analysis—can be used to understand the radicalization of political Islam in Southeast Asia: (1) a transnational terrorist threat explanation; (2) an indigenous national movement explanation; and (3) a rational choice explanation (Waltz 1959, 16–41). Each approach has certain explanatory strengths and weaknesses.

International Explanations for Islamic Terrorism in Southeast Asia

The most popular method for understanding the radicalization of political Islam is the transnational terrorism approach, which de-emphasizes importance of the political, economic, and social conditions of the countries as well as the mindset of religious and political leaders. Peter Chalk interprets the international terrorist problem as a "grey area phenomena" (GAP), which he defines as

> threats to the stability of sovereign states by non-state actors and non-governmental processes and organizations. Although many GAP problems come to involve violence, not all do. Those that manifest themselves in an aggressive manner are typically associated with the activities of non-state actors such as international crime syndicates, drug trafficking organizations, and terrorist groups. . . . All GAP issues, whether violent or not, represent a direct threat to the underlying stability, cohesion, and fabric of the modern sovereign state. . . . Issues such as terrorism, drug trafficking, and environmental degradation may emanate from within states; however, their effects are generally not contained, typically having an impact that is truly transnational in nature. (Chalk 2000, 127)

Radical Islamic terrorism thus is viewed as a transnational phenomenon that had been transformed from a local to a regional or global phenomenon.

When applied to terrorism in Southeast Asia, this type of analysis focuses on the relationship of al Qaeda and regional Islamic groups such as Jema'ah Islamiyah. Such an approach is common in the popular press, scholarly works, and private consulting groups and among officials in the U.S. and Southeast Asian governments (Desker and Ramakrishna 2002). According to this approach, al Qaeda considers Southeast Asia its second global front. Al Qaeda thus has forged strong links with thousands of Southeast Asian Islamists who underwent training in the Afghan camps between 1985 and 1995, fought side by side with Osama bin Laden during the battle of Jaji in 1987, and studied the Wahhabi interpretation of the Koran in Pakistani Islamic schools (madrassahs) (Jones 2003, 4; Abuza 2002, 429–34). These groups are not primarily motivated by local political, ethnic, or religious problems but rather by a common desire to establish a pan-Islamic state in Southeast Asia and to implement a global jihad against all "infidels."

As the primary trans-Southeast Asian radical Islamic organization, the JI is the key to al Qaeda's success in Southeast Asia. Its core leadership includes an emir (Adbullah Sungkar and later Abu Bakar Ba'ashir) who is advised by four councils (governing, religious, fatwa, and disciplinary). To manage the Islamic revolution effectively, JI broke up Southeast Asia into four regional areas (*mantiqis*).

Mantiqi I covered Singapore and Malaysia and was seen as providing the economic wherewithal for JI operations; Hambali was its head until early 2002, according to the testimony of detained JI members, when he was replaced by Mukhlas. Mantiqi II covered most of Indonesia and was considered the target of jihad efforts; it was reportedly led by Abdullah Anshori, alias Abu Fatih, who remains at large. Mantiqi III covered Mindanao, Sabah, and Sulawesi and was responsible for training. It was led by Mustopa, the man arrested in a raid in mid-July 2003 outside Jakarta. Mantiqi IV, covering Papua and Australia, was responsible for fund-raising and was led by a man called Abdul Rohim. Hambali was the overall head of the mantiqis, according to one of the Singapore JI detainees. (Jones 2003, 11)

To solidify ideological control, JI established a large network of Muslim boarding schools (*pesantrens*) to promote radical Islamic thought as well as JI military training. In addition, JI members seeking a spouse were persuaded to marry relatives of other JI members; reportedly, Hambali acted as matchmaker.

The approach sees little distinction between the transnational terrorist groups and political Islam, which are publicly supported and privately connected.[5] Besides establishing close relations with other radical Islamic groups, radical Islamic groups such as JI have infiltrated political Islamic parties in order to promote a more radical Islamic agenda. CNN reporter Maria Reesa sees this as a particular threat to the developing democracies in Southeast Asia that are holding elections in 2004, such as Indonesia, the Philippines, and Malaysia (Ressa 2003).

Because these groups constitute a global threat to democracy, analysts thus promote a global response through bilateral and multilateral means. For Jones and Smith, members of the Association for Southeast Asian Nations (ASEAN) must admit their failure in the 1980s and 1990s to recognize the growing threat of radical Islam (Jones and Smith 2002, 351). Justine Rosenthal argues that the United States thus must "sleep with the enemy" and develop stronger alliances with countries that are nondemocratic and frequent violators of international norms of human rights. "Over the short-term this is bearable; crises often call for states to put aside nominal differences to accomplish more important goals. . . . [The United States] will need to make some gestures of enforcing standards of political and human rights by errant coalition partners if it hopes to maintain policy consistency" (Rosenthal 2003, 482). Thus, while the United States cannot ignore Malaysia and Singapore's use of the ISA to suppress democratic activities or ignore the Indonesian military's human rights abuses, it must acquiesce in order to confront global terrorism.

The international environment approach is a clear and simple explanation for the rise of radical Islam in Southeast Asia. Clearly, it makes sense for al Qaeda to view Southeast Asia as a natural target following the fall of Afghanistan to "infidel" forces. Al Qaeda undeniably has taken advantage of the decades-long Saudi promotion of Wahhabism in various Islamic schools to develop a dedicated core of believers in the establishment of an Islamic state based on shari'a law. These converts to radical Islam subsequently were processed through the Afghani terrorist training camps and returned to Southeast Asia to implement change. By viewing the problem from a global and regional perspective, the international terrorism approach thus uncovers a recurring pattern of infiltration and deception that has been duplicated throughout Southeast Asia.

Analysts relying solely on the international environment approach must be careful not to be overpredictive. As in the analysis of the communist threat during the cold war era, it is dangerous to assume that monolithic Islamic terrorism can exist. Undeniably, al Qaeda and JI have some degree of influence over all the political and radical Islamic movements in Southeast Asia. Yet, the international environment arguments have yet to demonstrate the degree of control of al Qaeda, starting with the alleged relationship between al Qaeda and Iraq. Are Abu Sayyaf in the Philippines, the KMM of Malaysia, or the New PULO radicals in Thailand actually being directed by al Qaeda and part of a vast regional conspiracy to establish a pan-Islamic state in Southeast Asia? Or are they just local bandits or phantom terrorist organizations? As John Gershman has pointed out, al Qaeda does not enjoy the same control over radical Islamic groups in Southeast Asia as it did over the Taliban in Afghanistan (Gershman 2002, 61; Chalk 2001, 245–46).

Second, it is in the interest of the United States and regional governments to treat Islamic terrorism as a monolithic threat. Not only are monolithic explanations simpler to explain to their domestic constituents (i.e., the Manichaean good versus evil explanation), but such explanations reduce the legitimacy of opposition parties, especially political Islamic parties. During the forty years of confrontation with global communism, the United States and some of its allies were willing to push aside many human rights concerns in order to achieve the "greater good." By not recognizing the difference between political and radical Islam, the United States and its Southeast Asian allies would repeat the mistakes of the past and impede the development of civil society. If the United States or its Southeast Asian allies take advantage of the terrorist crisis to undermine the political Islamic parties, political Islamists will seek support from the radical Islamists, thus prolonging the global war on radical Islamic terrorism. Therefore, studying the past to avoid repeating mistakes of the past is wise.

State-Centric Explanations for Islamic Terrorism in Southeast Asia

State-centric explanations accept the important role of pan-Islamic groups such as al Qaeda and JI as well as the influence of individual leaders but argue that the state plays an even more important role in the radicalization of political Islam. Such explanations thus focus on the political, economic, ethnic, and/or religious milieu of each state. In other words, some countries are more democratic than others; some countries are more prosperous; and some countries have successfully assimilated ethnic and religious groups. Instead of subsuming local similarities and differences, the state-centric approach argues that they are the primary determinant of Islamic radicalization.

The state-centric approach also is sensitive to the long historical tradition of political and radical Islamic movements in Southeast Asia that predate Osama bin Laden and Abu Bakar Ba'ashir. All the countries studied have a shared colonial experience: Malaysia and Singapore were ruled by Great Britain; Indonesia was controlled by the Dutch; and the Philippines was ruled by Spain and the United States. While Thailand escaped direct rule by foreign countries, Malays living in the south consider the Thai kingdom as a colonial occupying power following the defeat of the kingdom of Patani in the seventeenth century. Unlike homogeneous societies of Korea and Japan, these nations are an amalgam of peoples of various ethnicities, languages, and cultures who initially were forced to accept a common heritage and subsequently developed a sense of nationalism based on their struggle for independence (Hoston 1994, chap. 1). Yet, this sense of nationalism is not shared by all peoples, especially in areas where borders have been drawn arbitrarily that cross ethnic and religious boundaries (Weiner 1971).

State-centric analysts consider such differences as important. One of the primary differences among Islamists is the view of Islam itself. In interpreting Indonesia's Laskar Jihad, Kristen Schulze argues that the movement is

> essentially a homegrown rather than an international jihadist organization. It is the product of a very specific Indonesian situation—the conflict in Ambon— and the Indonesian government's inability to manage the violence. Its emergence was the result of the turmoil of democratic transition and economic crisis that allowed for suppressed social, ethnic, and sectarian conflicts to resurface. . . . However, despite the organization's links to the Taliban and alleged ties to Abu Sayyaf, the organization's threat is not one of international terrorism. Rather, it is an internal threat to the mainstream interpretation of Islam in Indonesia and, crucially, the Indonesian state's monopoly of force. (Schulze 2002, 57–58)

Thus, Schulze, like Desker, focuses on the conflict within Indonesian Islam over the traditional syncretistic and the more fundamentalist view; Ambon was only a test to understand the degree of support within Indonesia for changing the syncretistic status quo. Gershman and Mirskii similarly point out that a monolithic Islam does not exist in Southeast Asia; the diversity of SEA Islamism mitigates the control of one pan-Islamic group (Gershman 2002, 62; Mirskii 2003, 37).

Other scholars such as Peter Chalk see the rise of Islamic radical movements as the result of the "insensitivity to local concerns, regional neglect, military repression, and the contemporary force of militant Islam" (Chalk 2001, 241). Andrew Tan (2000) argues that many Southeast Asian states are multiethnic states with weak political integrity, resulting in strong religious and ethnic clashes that are aided and abetted by outside influences. Aspinall and Berger argue that separatist movements, including radical Islamic movements, were "all fueled by brutal and indiscriminate state violence against them during the Soeharto era and this violence goes a long way towards explaining high levels of support for independence in each territory" (Aspinall and Berger 2001, 1004). Kikue Hamayotsu (2002) puts forward a similar argument but adds that the post-Soeharto period of emerging democracy in Indonesia has allowed a greater role for political Islam and restrained the government's ability to suppress radical Islam.

State-centric explanations are sensitive to both the uniqueness of the individual state and the characteristics shared among states. While not as parsimonious as international terrorist explanations, patterns of behavior can be derived through comparative analysis. The distinction between political and radical Islam is emphasized as are other historical, political, economic, or sociological differences. As such, the approach is more useful in understanding the impact of counterterrorism on the democratic transition and development of civil society in Southeast Asia. However, by its very nature, state-centric explanations of Islamic radicalization underemphasize the larger threat posed by al Qaeda, JI, and other pan-Islamic movements.

Rational Choice Models of Islamic Terrorism in Southeast Asia

One model not prevalent in the current literature on Southeast Asian terrorism is the application of rational choice theory. Since Herbert Simon (1947) first proposed a rational-comprehensive approach in the late 1940s, rational choice models of decision-making have become increasingly popular in American social science. Such models focus on the individual decision maker or assume that hierarchically ordered organizations can function as unitary rational actors. Actors attempt to adopt the most efficient strategy to achieve long-term goals.

Based on these assumptions, analysts can deduce decision-making behavior unencumbered by complicated variables such as values, norms, or other culturally defined characteristics. Analysts using the rational choice paradigm thus believe they can develop more broad-ranging, parsimonious theory to understand decision-making dynamics.

Rational choice models of decision making arguably are based at the individual level of analysis. Decisions are taken by individuals rationally pursuing their long-term goals; their pursuit is influenced by variables exogenous of the individual that are located within the state or the international environment. Herein is the power of economic theories of decision making, as social scientists can more readily develop universal theories of policy behavior based on the assumption that all actors are motivated in a similar fashion. Yet the endogenous nature of rational choice analysis does not preclude individuals from acting as a group when it is in their rational interest to do so. While demonstrating the difficulty of coherent interest-group action, Mancur Olson (1982) has also shown that individuals can and do find it rational to act as a collective force to obtain agreed-upon objectives; this in turn can prohibit states from obtaining their long-term goals. Thus, actors are not only individuals but also firms and sectors. In other words, hierarchically ordered political parties and interest groups as well as ruling elites act as unitary rational actors who possess a certain degree of autonomy to formulate and carry out decisions (Geddes 1995, 92, n19; Gill 1998, 10–11, 199–200).

Rational choice approaches assume that unitary rational actors seek to achieve long-term goals of survival and prosperity. These so-called first-order preferences[6] for a businessperson might be the pursuit of long-term economic growth for the company that provides stock options for its employees; for the politician such goals could entail a successful reelection, the maintenance of a ruling coalition, or the continued domination of the preeminent leader. To achieve these long-term goals, the model assumes that actors are primarily motivated to achieve their goals at the lowest possible cost. However, actors are confronted by a world of finite resources. The choice of strategies is thus influenced by certain exogenous variables: interactions with other actors pursuing their long-term goals; access to production inputs such as capital, land, and labor; and access to the marketplace. Actors are also not all-knowing, and they attempt to gather as much information as possible to estimate potential cost and benefits of each policy option, especially when confronted by important decisions. In cases when actors are repeatedly confronted by a similar problem, they can learn from previous actions—successful and unsuccessful—that they or others have made (Geddes 1995; Gill 1998; Reardon 2002; Levy 1994). In sum, actors make decisions based on utility maximization.

In applying rational choice theory to explain the radical Islamic terrorism in Southeast Asian states, the focus is on Islamic terrorist leaders and the ruling state elites. Each hierarchically ordered Islamic terrorist organization is considered a rational unitary actor. The rational choice approach minimizes the differences within the terrorist organization, whether they are between the elites or the membership. Considering the hierarchical, nondemocratic nature of terrorist organizations, such aggregation is considered plausible as long as the terrorist elites and membership realize the importance of maintaining a unified hierarchical organization. Ruling state elites also are assumed to enjoy a certain degree of autonomy to formulate and implement decisions. This assumption is valid considering the high degree of governmental intervention in the Southeast Asian states, which in the 1960s would have been considered bureaucratic-authoritarian but now have been promoted to "developmental states" or "emerging democracies." Analysts thus can aggregate behavior and deduce policy behavior.

One possible approach is to adapt the arguments proffered by Anthony Gill's (1998) *Rendering unto Caesar: The Catholic Church and the State in Latin America*. According to Gill, states attempt to minimize the cost of ruling. When compared to coercive tactics and patronage, it is far cheaper to gain the support of the people by creating a supportive ideology. In countries such as Indonesia and Malaysia where Islam is the dominant religion, mosques offer the state a ready source of ideology that can legitimate the role of the state's leaders. As such, there are strong incentives for the state to engage in a cooperative relationship with Islam. Because of their unstable political footing, the post-Soeharto leaders sought legitimacy through support from Islamic leaders and did not wish to offend them by investigating radical Islamic movements. In Malaysia's case, Mahathir did not want to cooperate with the mosques as much as transform the state into an Islamic religious entity; he thus desired to gain legitimacy by having Malaysia become an Islamic state.

A rational choice explanation also can explain why political Islamic groups, such as PAS in Malaysia, the PPP and PAN in Indonesia, or the MNFL in the Philippines, chose to collaborate with the state. According to Gill's paradigm, political Islamic parties desire to maximize their membership and their resources. Yet, because of the low cost of establishing an Islamic party, Islamists theoretically could join a plethora of Islamic parties. Thus, it is in the political Islamic party's interest to develop strong relations with the state, which can provide direct state support for its activities. If it can maintain a stable relationship with the state, the political Islamic party is more capable of recruiting and retaining new members. Similarly, radical Islamic groups are motivated to curtail terrorist actions against the state and engage in cease-fire talks, such as occurred with the New PULO in Thailand or the MILF in the Philippines.

Yet, when the opportunity cost of cooperation exceeds the benefits, either the state or the political Islamic party will defect from the cooperative relationship. State actors initiate conflict with Islamic groups when the opportunity costs exceed the benefits of cooperating with the Islamic group. This occurred after the Bali bombing in Indonesia when state authorities realized that the costs of cooperating with radical Islam exceeded the benefits. It could explain President Megawati's imposition of martial law and reengagement with GAM in Indonesia's Aceh province in 2003. Political Islamic actors support radical Islamic initiatives when the opportunity costs of cooperation exceed the benefits. Following the Christians' success in establishing an independent state in East Timor, Islamic separatists in Aceh and Ambon took advantage of the weakened Indonesian state to increase Islamic separatist activities.

Rational choice analysis provides a solid deductive explanation for the dynamics of cooperation. While de-emphasizing the "grey area phenomena" and the specific ethno-religious characteristics of individual states, the assumption of rationality is a potent tool to analyze decision making across Southeast Asia. There are two caveats. The first is that empirical evidence must be found to justify deductive reasoning. The second relates to Gill's (1998) rational choice approach applied in countries dominated by Roman Catholicism to understand the cooperative behavior between the state and the Catholic Church. Gill's reasoning can be readily adapted to Indonesia and Malaysia, where Islam is the dominant religion. His assumptions would need to be altered in understanding the relationship between the state and a minority religion, such as Islamic groups in the Philippines, Thailand, and Singapore.

CONCLUSION

There are various ways to understand the radicalization of political Islam in Southeast Asia. Academics have published a smorgasbord of arguments based on state-centric explanations. While most literature accurately explains the individual characteristics of Southeast Asian countries, a systematic analysis must be undertaken to determine whether a particular state-centric explanation applies to all Southeast Asian countries. The rational choice analysis is a particularly powerful explanation of cooperative behavior between states and Islamic groups. Further testing is needed to see whether deductive reasoning accurately describes the empirical evidence.

Without a doubt, the most parsimonious analysis of the radicalization of political Islam in Southeast Asia is the international terrorist explanation. Blaming al Qaeda or JI dominates the mass media and often is the explanation of choice for the less democratic nations in the area, such as Malaysia and Singapore. Yet the explanation's simplicity is also its weakness. Without concrete evidence of collaboration, international terrorist explanations can collapse into Manichaean arguments of good versus evil. Besides sacrificing the truth, Manichaean arguments can threaten the newly emerging civil societies throughout Southeast Asia.

NOTES

I am very grateful to Din Zainu'ddin, Ailsa G. Thomson Zainu'ddin, Rosemary Reardon, and Bernard Gordon for reading earlier versions and making many insightful suggestions. I also sincerely thank my research assistants Hans Olsen and Sid Whitaker.
    1. For the neoconservative influence on the Bush administration, see Bergen (2003).

    2. Although agreeing with the basic dichotomy of meaning, authors disagree about specific terminology. Political Islam is called "fundamentalism," "Islamism," and "defensive fundamentalism." Radical Islam is called "jihadism" and "offensive fundamentalism."

    3. For an interesting discussion of Nahdlatul Ulama, Muhammadiyah, and the liberal Islamic movement in Indonesia, see Desker (2002, 386–87).

    4. The other ten groups include Tentera Sabillullah (1967), Golongan Rohaniah (1971), Koperasi Angkatan Revolusi Islam Malaysia (1972), Kumpulan CRYP-TO (1977), Kumpulan Mohd Nasir Ismail (1980), Kumpulan Revolusi Islam Ibrahim Mahmood@ Ibrahim Libya (1985), Kumpulan Jundullah (1987), Khumpulan Mujahiddin Kedah (KMK) (1988), Kumpulan Perjuangan Islam Perak (KPIP) (1998), and Kumpulan Al-Ma'unah (2000).

    5. Prime Minister Mahathir would agree with Abuza, who argues that Malaysia's opposition PAS party "has covert linkages [to al Qaeda] through an underground and extremist faction that has been linked to Kumpulan Mujaheddin Malaysia (KMM)" (2002, 445); see also Jones and Smith (2002). Barry Desker adopts a far more sophisticated view of political and radical Islam, stating that Islamists in Southeast Asia are divided between secularists, fundamentalists, and radicals. Yet, he still views al Qaeda as the "major security threat to governments in the region over the next decade" (Desker 2002, 391).

    6. This chapter adopts Barbara Geddes' (1995) clarification of rational choice terminology by substituting "first-order preferences" for "goals" and "second-order preferences" for "strategies."

REFERENCES

Abuza, Z. 2002. "Tentacles of Terror: Al-Qaeda's Southeast Asian Network." *Contemporary Southeast Asia* 24: 427–65.
Agence France Press. 2003. "Trial of Four Alleged Thai JI Members Opens in Bangkok." November 18.
Ahmad, A. 2002. "Bill Does Islam No Honor." *New Straits Times* (Malaysia), July 10.
Al-Quds al-Arabi. 2003. "Abu-Hafs al-Masri Brigades Claim Responsibility for Jakarta Attack," August 8.

al-Turabi, H. (2002). "The Islamic Awakening's Second Wave." *New Perspectives Quarterly* 19: 36–41.

Amnesty International. 2003a. *Indonesia: New Prisoners of Conscience in the Post-Suharto Era*. July 9. http://web.amnesty.org/library/eng-idn/index.

———. 2003b. *Indonesia: Press Freedom under Threat*. October 1. http://web.amnesty.org/library/eng-idn/index.

Aspinall, E., and Berger, M. T. 2001. "The Break-up of Indonesia? Nationalisms after Decolonisation and the Limits of the Nation-State in Post–Cold War Southeast Asia." *Third World Quarterly* 22: 1003–24.

Banlaoi, R. C. 2002. "The Role of Philippine-American Relations in the Global Campaign against Terrorism: Implications for Regional Security." *Contemporary Southeast Asia* 24 (August): 294–312.

Barkan, S., and Snowden, L. 2001. *Collective Violence*. Boston: Allyn and Bacon.

BBC Monitoring Asia Pacific. 2003a. "Malaysian Human Rights Commission Wants Internal Security Act Replaced," December 15.

———. 2003b. "Malaysia's Anwar Urges Opposition Leaders to Remain Unified," November 19.

———. 2003c. "Radical Indonesian Muslim Leader Accuses US of Order Abductions," September 26.

Benjamin, D. 2003. "Two Years after 9/11: A Balance Sheet." *United States Institute of Peace Special Report* 111: 1–12.

Bergen, P. 2003. "Armchair Provocateur: Reading Laurie Mylroie, the Neocon's Favorite Conspiracy Theorist." *Washington Monthly* 35 (December): 27–31.

Bernama [Malaysian News Agency]. 2001. "Government Has Documentary Proof of KMM-Taliban Links, Says Mahathir," September 28.

———. 2003. "PAS Launches 'The Islamic State Document,'" November 12.

Bhakti, I. 2000. "Indonesia after the Fall of President Soeharto: A 'Case Study' in Human Security." In *Asia's Emerging Regional Order*, ed. W. Tow et al., 230–60. New York: UN University Press.

Blondel, J., T. Inoguchi, and I. Marsh. 1999. "Economic Development v. Political Development." In *Democracy, Governance and Economic Performance*, ed. I. Marsh et al., 1–19. Tokyo and NY: UN University Press.

Bonner, R. 2003. "Threats and Responses: Southeast Asia." *New York Times*, May 31, p. A1.

Bush, George W. 2003. "Remarks by the President at the 20th Anniversary of the National Endowment for Democracy." November 6. 2003. www.whitehouse.gov/news/releases/2003/11/20031106-3.html.

Chalk, P. 2000. "'Grey Area Phenomena' and Human Security." In *Asia's Emerging Regional Order*, ed. W. Tow et al., 124–41. New York: UN University Press.

———. 2001. "Separatism and Southeast Asia: The Islamic Factor in Southern Thailand, Mindanao and Aceh." *Studies in Conflict and Terrorism* 24: 241–69.

Che Man, W. K. 1990. *Muslim Separatism: The Moros of Southern Philippines and the Malays of Southern Thailand*. Singapore: Oxford University Press.

Cheong, J. 1999. "The Political Structures of the Independent States." In *Cambridge History of Southeast Asia*, Vol. 2, Pt. 2, ed. N. Tarling, 59–199. New York: Cambridge University Press.

Cirincione, J., J. Mathews, and G. Perkovich. 2004. *WMD in Iraq: Evidence and Implications.* Washington, D.C.: Carnegie Endowment of International Peace.

Crouch, H. 1996. *Government and Society in Malaysia.* Ithaca: Cornell University Press.

Darshini, S. 2003. "Najib: Procedural Aspects of ISA Can Be Reviewed." *New Straits Times* (Malaysia), December 20.

Desker, B. 2002. "Islam and Society in South-East Asia after 11 September." *Australian Journal of International Affairs* 56: 383–94.

Desker B., and K. Ramakrishna. 2002. "Forging an Indirect Strategy in Southeast Asia." *Washington Quarterly* 25 (Spring): 161–76.

Deutsche Presse-Agentur. 2003. "Presidential Aspirant Says Political Islam 'Not Selling' in Indonesia." November 20.

Donnan, S. 2003a. "Asia-Pacific: Suharto's Party Looks to Reinvent Itself." *Financial Times,* July 5, p. 5.

———. 2003b. "Asia-Pacific: US Dubbed 'King of Terrorists' by Indonesia's Vice-President." *Financial Times,* September 5, p. 10.

———. 2003c. "Indonesian Police Foil New Terror Offensive." *Financial Times,* July 12, p. 7.

———. 2003d. "Indonesians Text Messages of Support for Aceh Clampdown." *Financial Times,* July 21, p. 8.

Donnan, S., and A. Kazmin. 2003. "Indonesia Seeks Access to Detained Terror Suspect." *Financial Times,* August 19, p. 4.

Economist. 2003. "Two Theories." *Economist* 368 (September 13): 8–11.

Emmerson, D. K. 2002. "Whose Eleventh? Indonesia and the United States Since 11 September." *Brown Journal of World Affairs* 9(1): 1–12.

Esposito, J. 1995. *The Islamic Threat: Myth or Reality.* 2d ed. New York: Oxford University Press.

Euben, L. 1999. *Enemy in the Mirror: Islamic Fundamentalism and the Limits of Modern Rationalism.* Princeton: Princeton University Press.

Friedman, T. 2002. "The War on What?" *New York Times,* May 8, p. A31.

Fritz, N., and M. Flaherty. 2003. "Unjust Order: Malaysia's Internal Security Act." *Fordham International Law Journal* 26 (May): 1355–1359.

Fuller, G. 1998. "Does Islam Have an Alternative to Globalization?" *New Perspectives Quarterly* 15 (Spring): 44–45.

Funston, J. 2000. "Malaysia's Tenth Elections: Status Quo, Reformasi or Islamisation?" *Contemporary Southeast Asia* 22 (April): 23–59.

Gearson, J. 2002. "The Nature of Modern Terrorism." *Political Quarterly* 73: 7–24.

Geddes, B. 1995. "Uses and Limitations of Rational Choice." In *Latin America in Comparative Perspective,* ed. P. H. Smith, 81–108. Boulder, Colo.: Westview.

Gershman, J. 2002. "Is Southeast Asia the Second Front?" *Foreign Affairs* 81 (July/August): 60–74.

Ghosh, N. 2004, January. "Army Takes Control in Three Thai provinces." *Straits Times* (Singapore), January 6.

Gill, A. 1998. *Rendering unto Caesar: The Catholic Church and the State in Latin America.* Chicago: University of Chicago Press.

Go, R. 2002. "Laskar Jihad Dispands in Face of Blast Outrage." *Straits Times* (Singapore), October 16.

———. 2003. "Cleric Cleared of Treason, Jail Term Cut." *Straits Times* (Singapore), December 2.

Gomez, E., and J. Sundaram, J. 1999. "Malaysia." In *Democracy, Governance and Economic Performance*, ed. I. Marsh et al., 230–60. Tokyo and New York: UN University Press.

Halle, L. 1967. *Cold War as History.* New York: Harper & Row.

Hamayotsu, K. 2002. "Islam and Nation Building in Southeast Asia: Malaysia and Indonesia in Comparative Perspective." *Pacific Affairs* 75: 353–75.

Hamblett, M. 2003. "Panels See Limits in Bush's Antiterror Authority: Second and Ninth Circuits Rule against Government in Handling of U.S., Foreign Detainees." *New York Law Journal*, December 19, p. 1.

Hashim, S. 2002. "US Understands Reason for ISA, Says Rais." Bernama (Malaysian National News Agency), May 11.

Hoston, G. A. 1994. *The State, Identity, and the National Question in China and Japan.* Princeton: Princeton University Press.

International Crisis Group. 2003. "Indonesia Backgrounder: A Guide to the 2004 Elections." *International Crisis Group Asia Report No. 71* (December 18): 1–36.

Islam, S. S. 1998. "The Islamic Independence Movement in Patani of Thailand and Mindanao of the Philippines." *Asian Survey* 38 (May): 441–56.

Johns, A. 1987. "Indonesia: Islam and Cultural Pluralism." In *Islam in Asia: Religion, Politics and Society*, ed. J. Esposito, 202–29. New York: Oxford University Press.

Jones, D. M., and M. L. Smith. 2002. "From *Konfrontasi* to *Disintegrasi*: ASEAN and the Rise of Islamism in Southeast Asia." *Studies in Conflict & Terrorism* 25: 343–56.

Jones, S. 2003. "Jema'ah Islamiyah in Southeast Asia: Damaged but Still Dangerous." *International Crisis Group Asia Report No. 63* (August 26): 1–60.

Kamarulnizam, A. 1999. "National Security and Malay Unity: The Issue of Radical Religious Elements in Malaysia." *Contemporary Southeast Asia* 21 (August): 261–83.

Kessler, G. 2004. "Arms Issue Seen as Hurting U.S. Credibility Abroad." *Washington Post*, Jaunary 19, p. A1.

Khong C. 1999. "Singapore." In *Democracy, Governance and Economic Performance*, I. Marsh et al., 287–304. Tokyo and New York: UN University Press.

Lau, L. 2003. "Anti-terrorism Centre Opens in Kuala Lumpur." *Straits Times* (Singapore), July 2.

Leser, E. 2003. "Endless War on Terrorism." *Le Monde*, November 15.

Levy, J. S. 1994. "Learning and Foreign Policy: Sweeping a Conceptual Minefield." *International Organization* 48: 279–312.

Lum, T. 2002. "U.S. Foreign Aid to East and South Asia: Selected Recipients." *Library of Congress, CRS Report to Congress*, April 10, pp. 1–28.

Lyall, K. 2003. "Hambali Talks under Grilling." *Australian*, August 21.

MacIntyre, A. 1999. "Indonesia." In *Democracy, Governance and Economic Performance*, ed. I. Marsh et al., 261–86. Tokyo and New York: UN University Press.

Malley, M. S. 2003. "Indonesia in 2002: The Rising Cost of Inaction." *Asian Survey* 43: 135–46.

Marquis, C. 2004. "Powell Admits No Hard Proof in Linking Iraq to Al-Qaeda." *New York Times*, January 9, p. A1.

Martinez, P. A. 2001. "The Islamic State or the State of Islam in Malaysia." *Contemporary Southeast Asia* 23 (December): 474–503.

McCawley, T. 2002. "Jakarta May Declare Civil Emergency in Aceh." *Financial Times*, July 10.

Mietzner, M. 2002. "Politics of Engagement: The Indonesian Armed Forces, Islamic Extremism, and the 'War on Terror.'" *Brown Journal of World Affairs* 9 (Spring): 71–84.

Ministry of Home Affairs. 2003. *White Paper: The Jema'ah Islamiyah Arrests and the Threat of Terrorism.* Singapore: Ministry of Home Affairs, Republic of Singapore, 1–54.

Mirskii, G. 2003. "'Political Islam' and Western Society." *Russian Politics and Law* 41: 29–44.

Moniz, D., and T. Squitieri. 2003. "Defense Memo: A Grim Outlook." *USA Today*, October 22, p. 1A.

Moore, M. 2003. "Fall of the Extremists." *Age* (Melbourne), April 12, p. 7.

Mylroies, L. 2003. *Bush vs. the Beltway: How the CIA and the State Department Tried to Stop the War on Terror.* New York: HarperCollins.

Mylroies, L., and R. Woolsey. 2001. *The War against America: Saddam Hussein and the World Trade Center Attacks: A Study of Revenge.* 2d ed. New York: HarperCollins.

Nakashima, E. 2003a. "Lethal Blast Hits Jakarta Hotel." *Washington Post*, August 6, p. A1.

———. 2003b. "Militant Convicted in Bali Bombings." *Washington Post*, August 8, p. A13.

Nakashima, E., and A. Sipress. 2003. "Tips, Traced Call Led to Capture of al-Qaeda Suspect." *Washington Post*, August 16, p. A14.

Nation [Thailand]. 2003a. "Agencies Acted on Their Own," July 30.

———. 2003b. "Attacks on Police Done by Muslim Separatists," July 18.

———. 2003c. "Police Hail Arrest of Senior PULO Suspect," December 20.

———. 2004. "Iron-fisted Response May Worsen the Crisis," January 6.

New Straits Times [Malaysia]. 2003. "Takeover Attempts by 12 Groups," September 26.

Noble, L. G. 1987. "The Philippines: Autonomy for the Muslims." In *Islam in Asia: Religion, Politics and Society*, ed. J. Esposito, 97–124. New York: Oxford University Press.

Olson, M. 1982. *Rise and Decline of Nations.* New Haven: Yale University Press.

Pereira, B. 2003a. "Bid to Put Squeeze on Religious School." *Straits Times* (Singapore), February 14.

———. 2003b. "Leader Admits US Base in Singapore Targeted." *Straits Times* (Singapore), June 12.

———. 2003c. "Malaysia Extends Blitz on Home-grown Terror Suspects. *Straits Times* (Singapore), September 24.

Perez, L. 1995. "Ramos Orders Police Operations against Terrorist Groups." *Straits Times* (Singapore), April 9.

Perlez, J. 2003. "Indonesia Says Drive against Separatists Will Not End Soon." *New York Times*, July 9, p. A3.

PNG Post-Courier. 2003. "Fears of Armed Islamic Activist in Papua," May 2.

Priest, D. 2003. "Hussein's Capture Not Likely to Harm Al-Qaeda." *Washington Post*, December 26.

Purdum, T. S. 2002. "US to Resume Aid to Train Indonesia's Military Forces." *New York Times*, August 3, p. A3.

Reardon, L. C. 2002. *The Reluctant Dragon: Crisis Cycles in Chinese Foreign Economic Policy*. Seattle: University of Washington Press.

Ressa, M. 2003. *Seeds of Terror: An Eyewitness Account of al-Qaeda's Newest Center of Operations in Southeast Asia*. New York: Free Press.

Rosenthal, J. A. 2003. "Southeast Asia: Archipelago of Afghanistans?" *Orbis* 47 (Summer): 479–93.

Schulze, K. E. 2002. "Laskar Jihad and the Conflict in Ambon." *Brown Journal of World Affairs* 9: 57–69.

Simon, H. A. 1947. *Administrative Behavior*. New York: Free Press.

Sipress, A. 2003a. "Indonesian Army's Upper Hand." *Washington Post*, June 26, p. A10.

———. 2003b. "War on Separatists Leaves Aceh in Turmoil." *Washington Post*, August 19, p. A12.

Sipress A., and E. Nakashima. 2003. "Al-Qaeda Affiliate Training Indonesians on Philippine Island." *Washington Post*, November 17, p. A18.

Snitwongse, K. 2002. "Southeast Asia in 2001: A Paradigm in Transition?" In *Southeast Asia Affairs*, ed. Daljit Singh et al., 3–25 (Singapore: Institute of Southeast Asian Studies).

Sulistiyanto, P. 2001. "Whither Aceh?" *Third World Quarterly* 22: 437–52.

Tan, A. 2000. "Armed Muslim Separatist Rebellion in Southeast Asia: Persistence, Prospects and Implications." *Studies in Conflict & Terrorism* 23: 267–88.

van Dijk, C. 1981. *Rebellion under the Banner of Islam: The Darul Islam in Indonesia*. The Hague: Martinus Nijhoff.

Vaughn, B. 2003. "Malaysia: Political Transition and Implications for U.S. Policy." *Library of Congress, CRS Report to Congress*, October 21, pp. 1–17.

von der Mehden, F. 1987. "Malaysia: Islam and Multiethnic Polities." In *Islam in Asia: Religion, Politics and Society*, ed. J. Esposito, 177–201. New York: Oxford University Press.

Waltz, K. N. 1959. *Man, the State and War*. New York: Columbia University Press.

Washington Post. 2003. "Our Man in Bangkok." December 26.

Weiner, M. 1971. "The Macedonian Syndrome: An Historical Model of International Relations and Political Development." *World Politics* 23 (July): 635–664.

Weiss, M. L. 1999. "What Will Become of Reformasi? Ethnicity and Changing Political Norms in Malaysia." *Contemporary Southeast Asia* 21 (December): 424–50.

World Bank. 1993. *The East Asian Miracle: Economic Growth and Public Policy*. New York: Oxford University Press.

Zainu'ddin, A. G. T. 1980. *A Short History of Indonesia*. 2d ed. Stanmore: Cassell Australia.

SUZANNE OGDEN

12 Inoculation against Terrorism in China
WHAT'S IN THE DOSAGE?

INTRODUCTION

China has had relatively few terrorist incidents, almost all of which are carried out by members of only one minority group, the Uyghurs. The Uyghurs live primarily in the northwestern border province of Xinjiang Uyghur Autonomous Region. Compared to terrorism worldwide, China's conditions, culture, and identity within the international system as well as the state's security measures have led to a low level of terrorism and to the state's own lack of interest in supporting terrorism outside of China.

Terrorism is defined here as the unlawful use of force or violence against civilians or property for politically motivated objectives. Such objectives are politically motivated in the sense that the goal of violence or force is to compel a government, or a civilian population, to address a political, social, religious, or ideological concern of the terrorists. Terrorists generally believe that their cause is just and that their use of violence is a last resort against a repressive and unresponsive state, ethnic group, or international order. The purpose of the violence is to instill terror in an audience far wider than the immediate victims for the objective of bringing about broad systemic change that will ameliorate the injustice. Terrorist acts are not those carried out in order to achieve personal, individual goals, such as a common criminal would do (Whittaker 2001, 3–9).

Terrorism must be distinguished from purely political acts that, under international law, are not considered offenses as well as from acts that are intended to challenge or destroy a regime but do not deliberately harm or terrorize innocent civilians. In short, the use of violence against a regime, and even the assassination of government officials as part of a revolution, fight for indepen-

227

dence, or secessionist movement, would usually not be considered offenses under international law. On the other hand, using random terror against innocent people would be, regardless of the legitimacy of the cause. The problem is that although the "right to self-determination" is recognized by the United Nations Charter, a minority ethnic, religious, or national group that wants to challenge a state in possession of a large military force often resorts to either guerrilla warfare or terrorism (Combs 2000, 11–13, 35, 37). Although the dividing line is contested, international law draws a distinction between the violence used by revolutionaries, "freedom fighters," secessionists, or anticolonial nationalist political movements and the violence used by terrorists.

These distinctions as they regard China are important to keep in mind. There is plenty of violence in China, but according to this definition, except for two terrorist attacks by Uyghur separatists in Xinjiang in 1992, two in Beijing in 1997, and one in Chengdu in 1999, this violence would not usually be labeled as terrorism. Nor is violence in China seen as an extension of international terrorism. Most of the Uyghurs' efforts to achieve independence have involved armed clashes with Chinese soldiers and police or attacks on state property (railroads, telephone poles, buildings) rather than terrorism against the civilian population. Their antigovernment riots in the 1990s were largely in response to religious restrictions, publications that offended Islamic values, and the testing of Chinese missiles in Lop Nor, Xinjiang.[1] Nor is violence in China likely to be converted into terrorism, unless the conditions or motivations for terrorism become more compelling. Not knowing what those conditions or motivations might be, we would be forced to engage in rather useless speculation; however, the very fact that terrorism is becoming so common internationally may itself increase the likelihood that one group or another will consider terrorism as an option in China.

CONDITIONS, ENVIRONMENT, AND MOTIVATION FOR TERRORISM

The general conditions, context, and motivations for terrorism worldwide are listed below. Real conditions may vary from perceived conditions, but, like everyone else, terrorists take action on the basis of perceptions, not reality.

 • There is a perceived unjust and exploitative treatment of an ethnic, national, or religious (sub)group, often resulting in absolute poverty, or at least comparative poverty, for the victim group. Minimally, the exploitation has led to a decline in the standing, power, and status of the victim group.

The exploiters may be the majority, a regime, international actors, or even the international system.

♦ The regime or a group within the population is oppressive to the point that the victim group feels it will (or has) lost land, its language, and/or the right to continue its religious and ethnic practices. Indeed, the victim group worries that if policies do not change, its very existence as a distinct cultural, national, or religious group will be threatened. The concern is about (cultural) genocide.

♦ Members of the victim group are not allowed to speak freely by the regime or dominant majority, and they are often jailed or even executed as a means of control.

♦ Alternatively, but sometimes in combination with the above, terrorists believe their group's beliefs should be viewed by others as superior. Instead, they are ignored or even pushed around by those whom they consider their inferiors or even their enemies.

♦ Terrorists believe in a greater cause than themselves. It is usually political or religious and is often based on a messianic or millenarian view of the world. Usually, there is a charismatic leader who motivates others to be followers so that they can achieve their rightful place. Self-sacrifice is called for within the victim group, and innocent civilians outside the victim group are expendable in the struggle to achieve its goals.

♦ The country suffers from what is called "structural violence": racism, ethnic oppression, xenophobia, and the extreme polarization of wealth. This often creates fertile ground for the rise of movements that endorse extreme measures, including terrorism, to achieve their vision of a better world. These groups are often classified as "right wing," in part because they rely on political, ideological, religious, or ethnic prejudice to justify their goals and means. They tend to divide the world into good and evil and to dehumanize the enemy, so that using violence against the faceless enemy is easy and justifiable. Thus, in the United States, the Aryan Nation and the many groups it has sprouted use violence and even terrorism against the enemy, who are viewed as the children of Satan. The Irish Republican Army has used terrorism against the Protestants, and fundamentalist Islamic groups, often in the name of jihad, use terrorism against the evil infidels. In each of these cases, religion, or even religious fanaticism, justifies terrorism.

♦ Religious fanaticism, underlain by a claim to the righteousness and superiority of the group's beliefs, has been a key factor in causing groups to turn to terrorism. But even when not fanatical, religion has often lain at the root of terrorism for the reasons stated above. Political fanaticism has likewise often rooted itself in religious beliefs.

♦ Today's would-be terrorists tend to live in urban areas. The higher density of an urban population makes it easier for terrorists to organize, move about, and remain anonymous within the population. In addition, terrorist acts are more likely to occur in cities, where large numbers of urbanites can witness them. As the mass media are concentrated in cities, terrorist events occurring there are more likely to be covered. Coverage by the mass media means that far more people, and even the state itself, may feel fear and terror. Terrorists don't want to waste time, money, and lives being no more than trees falling in a forest, where no one hears the sound.

♦ Although the conditions motivating terrorism are more likely to exist in the more authoritarian or dictatorial states, the actual terrorist acts tend to occur wherever the state's capacity and willingness to control terrorism is limited. This is as likely to occur in the more open and liberal democratic states, where the protection of civil liberties and individual rights allows terrorists to operate more freely, as it is in societies where social conditions allow violence to flourish. For related reasons, acts of terrorism are more likely to be publicized in the mass media of the more democratic states, whereas authoritarian states may not report terrorist acts at all, thus depriving terrorists of their audience. Of course, the policies of the liberal democratic states may themselves be the reason for terrorism striking them.

♦ Most terrorists are fairly well educated and usually have some level of technical and scientific expertise. This enables them to organize and communicate in a sophisticated network, to carry out terrorist actions that require technological know-how, and to evade the ever-tighter security and counterterror measures of the state.

♦ Terrorists are usually frustrated because no one is paying attention to their needs and requests. They see no alternative way to get attention and mitigation of unjust treatment than through terrorist actions.

♦ Internationally, terrorist movements have had a wide variety of motives: the largely middle-class Brigate Rosse, which in its first ten years (1970–80) carried out some fourteen thousand terrorist attacks, believed that Italy had become a bourgeois dictatorship and that only force could be used to overthrow it. Brigate Rosse was unhappy with Italy's domestic policies, a rigidified social structure, and governance by one party in power for a long time. These issues hardly appear to be the stuff of terrorism, but the Brigate Rosse did not feel that the parliamentary process was addressing their concerns, in part because the Italian Communist Party relinquished its commitment to revolution.[2] In the United States, the Weathermen's motivation for terrorism was even less compelling: a "crisis of identity" and "suburban boredom" as well as, perhaps, a remedy for personal problems (Whittaker 2001, 26–32). In short, terrorists do not necessarily need some grand cause as a motivation, but without it they are unlikely to gain the sympathies of large numbers of people.

♦ Terrorists are believed to have a psychological need to belong to a group, to be accepted (Whittaker 2001, 19). If such people choose to become involved with terrorists, then they are likely to carry out the demands made on them by the group. That theory, of course, assumes that such individuals would have failed to have their needs for group acceptance fulfilled by belonging to nonterrorist groups.

CHINA'S CONDITIONS AND CONTEXT

How, then, does China fit into this picture of the conditions and context that have provided fertile ground for terrorism elsewhere? It must be said right at the start that given the limited terrorism in China, my inclination is to examine why it is limited. (I mean limited in the sense that it pales in comparison with, say, Middle Eastern terrorism, IRA terrorism, or the terrorism committed by Italy's Brigate Rosse from 1970 to 1980.) But I do this with the understanding that if tomorrow major groups of terrorists began to emerge, I would be looking at different aspects of Chinese culture, state policy, and the international situation to explain why terrorism had taken root in China. There are countless variables that could factor into the appearance of terrorism, but we are unlikely to know which ones matter until it happens.

Among the factors that might explain why terrorism is limited in China is, first, the ethnic, religious, and racial composition of the People's Republic of China. Ninety-two percent of China's population is ethnically Han. Most of China's minorities, including those who might wish to secede from China, tend to live in remote and inhospitable places. The vast majority (75 percent) of China's national minorities live in self-governing (autonomous) regions. Their populations are small compared to the size of territory that they inhabit. The 8 percent of the population classified as national minorities[3] (about one hundred million people, spread out among fifty-five minorities) inhabit close to 60 percent of China's land, much of it in the vast hinterlands along less-developed borders. So they are fairly well dispersed, and there are relatively few large urban concentrations of ethnic minorities. This is in part because cities within minority areas are usually dominated by the Han culture. Minorities in the cities have tended to be assimilated into Han culture. There is, in any event, a considerable Han population in these autonomous regions due to assimilation policies before the 1980s that encouraged, or forced, Han Chinese to move to minority areas. One of the primary reasons for this forced migration was Beijing's concern that given the existence of populations just across China's borders with the same ethnicity as China's own national minorities, the latter might be tempted to secede to join in a state with their ethnic cousins. In Kazakhstan alone there are two hundred thousand Uyghurs, most of whom emigrated from Xinjiang in earlier years.

The result is that in the politically volatile province of Xinjiang (bordered by India, Pakistan, Afghanistan, Tajikistan, Kyrgyzstan, Kazakhstan, Mongolia, Tibet, and China proper), about 37 percent of its population of 19.25 million is Han Chinese,[4] while Uyghurs comprise between 8 and 9 million, under half the population. The rest of the population is a mix of Kazakhs, Kyrgizs, Uzbeks, and other national minorities. The Han Chinese are the majority population in the cities (the capital, Urumqi [Ulumuqi], with a population of 1.4 million, is 80 percent Han), but most of the Uyghurs live in oases in crowded, dense communities, reinforcing their identity as both Uyghurs and Muslims. Finally, Uyghurs have a stronger territorial concentration than most of the other minorities (including Tibetans and Mongols), which also reinforces their ethnic solidarity. The administrative boundaries of minority autonomous regions do not, in any event, correspond entirely with the cultural zones where people live.

The Uyghurs have off and on for centuries (and certainly since the 1870s) been under the control of China's rulers, but they have resisted assimilation. Twice before the Chinese Communist Party (CCP) victory in 1949, they established an East Turkistan Islamic Republic in Xinjiang and carried out dozens of armed revolts against Chinese military rule. Those seeking independence today hope to reestablish East Turkistan.[5] Ethnic conflict with the local Han, ineffective policies for Xinjiang's development, and incompetent Han cadres in the party and state leadership (few of whom ever bother to learn the Uyghur language)[6] are at the root of Uyghur antagonism toward the Chinese state and the desire for independence. Uyghurs also resent the fact that the income of the Han is so much higher than their own, that the Han enjoy advantages denied to the Uyghurs, that there are so many Han migrants, and that Beijing is exploiting Xinjiang's considerable mineral wealth to develop the rest of China without enriching Xinjiang itself. But it is clear that Beijing is determined not to allow Xinjiang, China's largest province at one-sixth of China's total geographical expanse, to become independent.

Intermarriage of Uyghurs with the Han is rare, and the Uyghur and Han communities are not well integrated with each other. In particular, conservative public sexual mores and distinctive dress distinguish Uyghur women, who tend to cover their entire faces and hair with purdahlike head scarves (Gladney 1994). The CCP regime's earlier assimilation policies had promoted Han migration to Xinjiang and severely curtailed the Uyghurs' practice of Islam and the teaching of the Uyghur language in schools. With the abandonment of these policies in the reform period that began after 1979, mosques and religious schools have proliferated, and separate schools for Han and Uyghur students have been established so that the Uyghurs could learn in their own language. The rationale for the change in Beijing's policy was to preserve and respect national minority language and culture, thereby quelling the tension generated by the policy of assimilation. However, the switch from a policy that discriminated against the Uyghurs to one that segregates them in education (as well as in housing) may be creating a stronger sense of ethnicity and difference that is itself fueling ethnic tensions (Lee 2003).

On the other hand, there are few signs of ethnic conflict between the Zhuang people and the Han. The Zhuang are China's largest national minority (thirteen million), 90 percent of whom live in China's southeastern province of Guangxi Zhuang Autonomous Region. Over hundreds of years, they have assimilated Han culture and intermarried with Han Chinese. In the capital city, Nanning, Zhuang are indistinguishable from the Han, although Zhuang in the countryside have maintained their traditions, dress, customs, and language.

The same is true of the Mongolians, a smaller minority (about 4.8 million), most of whom live in the Autonomous Region of Inner Mongolia and practice Buddhism (Lamaism). Inner Mongolia lies on the southern side of Mongolia, which is an independent state. Beijing's concern that the Mongolians in China would want to unite with Mongolia led to a policy that diluted the Mongol population with what has grown to be an overwhelming majority of Han Chinese. According to the 2000 national census, the national minority (largely Mongol) population was only 4.93 million—a mere 20.76 percent of the total population of 23.76 million.

As it turns out, because Inner Mongolia's economy has done better than that of the neighboring state of Mongolia, secessionism has not had significant appeal. Inner Mongolia's capital, Huhhot, is, like Urumqi, essentially a Han city. In contrast to Urumqi, however, assimilation of Mongols into Han culture in the capital is almost complete. As a result, there are fewer tensions between the Han and the Mongols than between the Han and the Uyghurs. Mongolians are dispersed throughout the vast countryside as shepherds, herdsmen, and farmers and retain many of their ethnic traditions and practices; however, because their population is so thinly spread out and many remain nomadic, it is harder to get

Mongolian nationalism whipped up as a foundation for secessionism, much less terrorism.

Tibetans number about 4.6 million, many of whom actually live in the provinces abutting the Tibetan Autonomous Region in China proper. Within the Tibetan Autonomous Region, close to 90 percent of Tibetans live in rural and mountainous areas. As in other autonomous regions, most Han Chinese are found in the capital city of Lhasa, but Tibetans, like Uyghurs, have resisted assimilation into Han culture. So Lhasa, even though the Han population is now in the majority, is not a Han city. Instead, the two cultures live beside each other—uncomfortably. Although Tibetans would like more autonomy, if not independence, they only intermittently engage in violence against the regime and rarely engage in anything that could be labeled terrorism. Like other ethnic activists in China, Tibetans tend to act pragmatically rather than as fanatics dedicated to a cause regardless of the consequences. This is in part because Beijing's policy toward politically motivated violence directed toward undermining China's control over Tibet has been swift and brutal. The Tibetan rebellion against Chinese rule in 1959 was summarily quashed, and there have only been sporadic efforts since then to challenge Chinese rule. One reason is that there is a powerful Chinese military presence in Tibet. Another is that the Dalai Lama, Tibet's spiritual leader who is living in exile, has strongly advised Tibetans against the use of violence to achieve greater autonomy. Further, although Tibetan history is full of violence and cruelty to others, especially other Tibetans, Buddhism itself emphasizes peace and abjures violence.

Nevertheless, some Tibetans (largely those who reject the Dalai Lama's leadership of Tibetan Buddhism) do believe they are living in an occupied territory and endorse violence as the only way to gain independence from Chinese rule. But it is clear to any would-be terrorists that, at least at this time in history, and under the conditions of underdevelopment and relatively low levels of education and technological expertise in Tibet, terrorist actions against the Chinese state would bear little fruit.

Since the reform period began in 1979, the Chinese state has mitigated many of its harsher assimilation policies toward all minorities. Tibetans benefited from this change as well, although demonstrations that erupted in 1987, and grew still larger in 1989, led to the reimposition of martial law and a clampdown on the monasteries (lamasaries), the religious schools, and the teaching of Tibetan in schools.

Nevertheless, Beijing is determined to develop Tibet and raise the standard of living substantially. In the last twenty years, Tibet has received more state subsidies for poverty reduction and infrastructure development than any province in China. As a result, Tibetans are better fed and clothed than they were, but Tibet still remains China's poorest administrative area. Generous state subsidies and a growing tourist industry seem unable to generate development. This is largely because of disastrous centrally conceived policies, a bloated administrative structure, a large Chinese military presence to house and feed, and incompetent Han cadres who have little understanding of local issues and rarely speak Tibetan (Dreyer 2003).

Regardless of what the Chinese do to develop Tibet, it is viewed with suspicion. New roads or railroads? The better for the Chinese to exploit Tibetan resources and even to invade. Encouraging tourism in Tibet or sending Tibetans to higher-quality Chinese schools outside of Tibet? The better to destroy Tibetan culture. Allowing Chinese entrepreneurs to do business in Tibet or permitting desperately poor youth from neighboring provinces to go to Tibet for work? The better to take away jobs from Tibetans. Projects to develop Tibet's infrastructure for development? The better to destroy its environment. China's large military presence (primarily in Lhasa and along the border with India), tight party control over the urban Tibetan population, and disdain for Tibetan culture do little to alleviate these suspicions. Nevertheless, like the Chinese, many young Tibetans in Lhasa are swept up in efforts to make money (a pleasure somewhat reduced by the fact that the increasingly large number of Chinese entrepreneurs in Lhasa usually make higher profits than they do) and to become part of the modern world—surfing the Internet, playing computer games, listening to rock and pop music. They are less interested in retaining traditional Tibetan cultural values than their elders would wish.

Finally, in the case of both the Tibetans and Uyghurs, since their land has long been under the control of the Chinese, the issue is not as much the loss of territory as the extinction of their culture. The policy of forced migration of Han to the minority areas has decidedly diluted the ethnic base of the national minorities, yet it has simultaneously reinforced the we-they dichotomy in Tibet and Xinjiang—a sort of cultural division of labor and of living. Assimilation policies that required minorities to learn standard Chinese rather than their own languages and that severely restricted the practice of their religion and any cultural practices that were considered superstitious or "antisocialist" (meaning backward) have been perceived by the Tibetans and Uyghurs as threats to cultural survival.

Amongst China's fifty-five national minorities, significant percentages of the Miao, Yao, and Yi are adherents of Protestantism and Catholicism. To wit, substantial numbers of Han Chinese are followers of formal religions, including Islam and Christianity. Indeed, although China's nearly nine million Hui (Han

Chinese who practice Islam) are classified as a "national minority," in fact over many centuries the vast majority became integrated into mainstream Chinese culture, with their only remaining distinct characteristics being their practice of Islam and related dietary restrictions. Reforms in China's minorities policy since the 1980s have, however, allowed the Hui to restore many of their customs, festivals, education, and even Middle Eastern Islamic architecture. The call to prayer occurs over the loudspeakers in Hui villages, and almost all Hui villagers show up for prayers five times a day. In recent years—no doubt because their primary identity is religious rather than ethic—they have come to identify more with the world Islamic community, with some even making the hajj to Mecca. This reflects the fact that there are greater contacts and more interaction with Muslims both inside and outside China. Nevertheless, most Hui continue to speak standard Chinese and to view themselves as both Chinese *and* Muslim. They are widely dispersed throughout every province and a majority of counties in China, and they live together with non-Muslim Chinese. In general, in spite of shared Islamic beliefs, they do not identify with Uyghur nationalism, which is seen as particular to Uyghur ethnicity and not to a broader Islamic religious identity (McCarthy 2003).[7]

Besides Islam, Han Chinese are also practitioners of Taoism and various branches of *qigong*, Protestantism, Catholicism, and Buddhism. The vast majority engages in ancestor worship at one level or another. Superstitions and animistic practices abound among the less well-educated Han Chinese, so charlatans have rich fields to plow. Religious sects, such as Falun Gong, spring up overnight and appeal to millenarian instincts, which have a long history in China. In short, China is a hodgepodge of religious beliefs and practices. And if, as Karl Marx averred, religion is the opiate of the masses, then China is completely doped.

It is in this context that two elements—the dominant Han Chinese culture and state policies—are of importance for understanding why terrorism has been so limited in China.

HAN CHINESE CULTURE

Why do China's minorities, or even Han Chinese who live with the national minorities, not engage in more terrorism? Apart from the success of Chinese policies of assimilation and repression in containing terrorism, Han Chinese culture is relevant to the issues of (1) Han Chinese terrorism against minorities, (2) Han Chinese terrorism against the regime, and (3) state-supported terrorism against other countries.

First, Han Chinese tend to feel superior to the national minorities, whom they have traditionally disdained as "backward," "barbarian," and even worse. (Before the CCP regime banned such terms, the national minorities were usually referred to as "dogs.") Minimally, to the degree they have not adopted Han mainstream culture, they are not considered as "civilized" as the Han. But, because policies have so overwhelmingly favored the Han, and because the Han do not feel that Chinese culture is threatened by the national minority cultures, the Han have little reason to resent China's minorities. Of course, like other communist regimes, the CCP regime has not permitted racism or ethnic hatred to be expressed in the media, and there is undoubtedly considerable dislike boiling beneath the surface.[8] During the Cultural Revolution (1965–75), when "attack the four olds" (customs, habits, ideas, things) was policy, young Chinese were all too happy to destroy any artifacts of minority cultures as remnants of "feudalism," but since they exhibited equal enthusiasm in destroying artifacts of Han culture, it is hard to use this as evidence of ethnic hatred.

Beijing's continual efforts to showcase national minority culture is not just to placate the minorities enough for them to want to remain under the control of China, or because they want to promote tourism in minority areas. Beijing also seems to be fighting an uphill battle to convince Han Chinese that the national minorities' cultures are truly worthy of respect. The point here is that as long as the press is controlled enough to suppress the expression of ethnic hatred, and as long as the government can prevent the emergence of groups motivated by ethnic hatred, we are unlikely to see terrorism aimed at the minorities emerging from amongst a Han majority.

Finally, because China's national minorities have historically inhabited the same land and are therefore not viewed as people who have stolen Chinese land and because they do not encroach on the jobs of the Chinese, there are fewer factors generating ethnic hatred.

What about Han Chinese terrorism against a repressive CCP regime? In some societies, a transfer of power only occurs by violence, but this has not been the case in China since the death of Mao Zedong in 1976. Since that time, the leadership has changed peacefully three times (1978–79, 1997, and 2002–2003). Further, since 1979, expertise has come to matter more than "redness" in the choice of China's leaders, so anyone who is talented has a good chance of moving into political or economic leadership at the various administrative levels or in their work units. Elections at the village level since the mid-1980s in most of China's villages have also opened up the possibility of a truly representative leadership. (This is not an assertion that elections are always free and fair, but in many of China's 930,000 villages, they are definitely making a difference.) (Ogden 2002).

In short, although at the highest level power is still transferred behind closed doors, there are many other levels at which it is now possible for true political leaders to emerge and to express their frustrations, demands, and concerns as well as to share in the benefits of being part of the elite. In addition, with capitalism in full swing, many Chinese who otherwise might have been frustrated with their poverty have opportunities to improve the material aspects of life. The result of these conditions (and others to be addressed) is that the use of terrorism to overthrow the state is less likely today than it ever has been. But, of course, stagnant economic growth and social instability could change those conditions overnight.

An additional mitigating factor is that Chinese culture does not readily lend itself to the mind-set of terrorism. Chinese are, for example, socialized into non-violence. Chinese children are punished by their parents if they get into a physical fight—regardless of who started the fight. Moreover, there is from the Chinese perspective a clear line between, on the one hand, verbal protest and dissent and, on the other hand, violence. Thus, worker protests and demonstrations usually receive social support, but if protestors cross the boundary by damaging property or physically attacking people, they usually lose social support.[9]

Although the regime is considered corrupt and repressive by many Chinese, this does not segue into a belief that terrorism would be a way to address issues of governance. Moreover, for more than twenty years, the period in which terrorism has sprouted worldwide, China's government has been able to claim credit for dramatic strides in social development and economic growth. And even though growth and capitalism have spawned problems of massive unemployment and the polarization of wealth as well as social instability, the continual growth offers hope to many of those who are doing poorly that eventually they too will prosper. There is, in short, not the sense of hopelessness and pessimism that tends to characterize societies prone to terrorism.

Nor does Han culture sanction violence to address problems such as unemployment. Instead, demonstrations, or rather remonstrations, in front of the offices of the relevant officials, blocking traffic on roads in the countryside and towns, or presenting petitions to the relevant offices are considered the appropriate methods to seek redress. Needless to say, these efforts often fail and violence does occur, but it is usually directed against individual officials or offices. Seeking revenge, on the other hand, is endemic in Chinese culture. In the countryside, arson, murders, and beatings of officials against whom individuals have grievances—such as corrupt officials who exploit villagers, collect excessive (and illegal) taxes, carry out forced abortions, and so on—are common. Again, however, violence tends to be directed against individuals, not the state as such, and the purpose of violence is not to instill terror in the general population but to rectify wrongs or seek revenge.

As was noted above, terrorists are usually frustrated because no one is listening, or responding, to their concerns. But China's central government has managed to portray itself as the ally of the peasants by providing them with many avenues of redress: encouraging letters and visits to local officials to vent their grievances, institutionalizing village elections, and allowing collective protests, media investigations, and lawsuits. Although their burdens may have continued in spite of these outlets, the rural poor still have the sense that at least the central party-state is listening and cares (Bernstein and Lu 2003). Measures such as these have meant that, thus far, violence by the Han Chinese has tended to be engaged in by individuals with specific grievances, not by terrorist networks, and they have attacked individuals who are neither faceless nor anonymous. There is no greater cause motivating them than that of the redress of an individual, family, or small group grievance.

Terrorism worldwide is, as noted, usually carried out by fairly sophisticated and well-educated individuals. Country people, even if educated, are unlikely to have access to the technology, training, or ability to organize the complex cell structure so necessary for a sophisticated terrorist action. This would not preclude a peasant from driving a truck full of fertilizer (rigged as an explosive) into a government building, but this rarely occurs in China's countryside because the infrastructure, motivation, and culture for terrorism are lacking.

This said, it should be noted that historically almost all of China's major rebellions and revolutions have started in the countryside, and in Nepal widespread terrorism has arisen in the countryside among a people (including an aboriginal group called the Tharus) who are generally described as "meek" and certainly poorly educated and without access to high-level technology. The guerrilla insurgency and terrorism that began in Nepal in 1995–96 and has been led by the Maoists (no connection with China and Maoists there) has already led to the deaths of more than eighty-five hundred people, and the Nepalese state has essentially abandoned control in those areas where the Maoists are strongest. The Maoists have appealed to the sense of injustice and exploitation that pervades Nepal's peasantry, which has suffered from a long history of discrimination and impoverishment at the hands of the dominant castes in this feudal Hindu kingdom (Waldman 2004). Nepal is a good example of what could happen in China if polarization of wealth in the countryside becomes entrenched and optimism about the future disappears.

Worldwide, organizing terrorism is easier in cities because of the concentration of people; the higher levels of education of prospective terrorists; access to technology, computers, and weapons; and the ability to melt in with the crowds. But in China's cities, except in the large migrant communities, the party-state is itself still well organized. Although the party is far less meddlesome and less effective than in the past, party cells in each work unit (*danwei*)—the main organizational unit remaining in the cities—still meet regularly in small groups with all the work unit's members. For example, in the crackdown on Falun Gong that began in 1999, China orchestrated a well-structured campaign to locate Falun Gong leaders (and members) in the work units. Combating superstition and Falun Gong is "ideological" work—the setting of moral values, which falls to the CCP officials in work units. Whereas CCP officials used to enforce the morality of Marxism-Leninism-Maoism, they now enforce the morality of the modernizing state on the one hand and the morality of being "civilized" on the other. To be civilized is, in part, to be modern and scientific. Civilized Chinese reject participation in organizations based on superstitions. Those who are not civilized are not really Chinese. Although followers of Falun Gong teachings are not necessarily punished, they are encouraged to relinquish their practices. Leaders, when found, are interrogated and will likely be imprisoned.

In mainstream Chinese culture, which is still based on enormous pride in the long history of China and its extraordinary accomplishments, to be civilized is an important concept. Today, the regime successfully appeals to the need to be civilized (in the past, it appealed to the importance of being "red") to gain compliance with basic regime values among the majority Han. Although many nationalities proclaim their superiority in one form or another, China's discourse on identity is one geared perfectly to reject those who engage in violence. Chinese culture uses shame, shunning, and isolation of individuals as a way of punishing those who deviate from the group norms.[10] But the broader point is that although individuals may find acceptance within a small group of terrorists in China, they would be fully rejected by society at large for engaging in terrorism.[11]

Thus, Falun Gong may have millions of adherents among Han Chinese, but for most urbanites the fact that Falun Gong is now publicly decried as a superstitious, unscientific cult (and that the party-state has targeted it) is enough to ensure they will not join it. Falun Gong, like most groups rooted in the Han population, does not actually espouse violence. Its actions have been limited primarily to peaceful demonstrations in protest of the government banning the organization as a sect in the first place and to several individuals who carried out self-immolations in public. Thus far, then, their motivation for political protests has not been their very own millenarian beliefs but rather their conviction that the government has unfairly labeled Falun Gong as a sect and not allowed its adherents to practice their religion freely. With some restrictions, China now allows freedom of religion for followers of mainstream religions, but groups that engage in superstitious practices are considered "sects," which are illegal. The Chinese are ever mindful that sects, such as the Aum Shin Rikyo (Aum Supreme Truth) in Japan, have used terrorism in the pursuit of their cause.[12] Just as important, in Chinese history, sects (such as the White Lotus sect in the nineteenth century) brought about large-scale rebellion and chaos in the country, so the government is determined to suppress any sect that is able to organize and mobilize large numbers of people.

Moreover, the willingness of the CCP in the last twenty-five years to allow mainstream religions and even some popular local cults to flourish does not extend so far as to allow them to use trickery (or intimidation) to persuade people to convert, such as by frightening them with horrible consequences (on earth or in the afterlife) if they resist conversion.[13] Falun Gong's appeal to fear was one of the reasons the party gave for outlawing the group, even though it was arguably no more guilty of this than the mainstream religions. And, of course, the CCP was not about to allow any religion to suggest that it, rather than the party itself, had claims to an "absolute truth" or "infallibility."[14]

POLITICAL AND RELIGIOUS FANATICISM IN THE NAME OF A HIGHER CAUSE

So the question is, then, who would be both motivated and capable of being a terrorist? Terrorists are often motivated by what we term religious or political "fanaticism." This term suggests that those who are terrorists are not truly rational, or at least are motivated by goals that are not rational from our own perspective, and are willing to sacrifice the lives of innocent people for those goals. This has not been the case in China since the communists took over in 1949. Political dissidents have rarely been true fanatics, even if their goal has been to establish another political party or to overthrow the regime.[15] Indeed, if we look to Chinese (Han) political dissidents, especially those who are classified as intellectuals, we know why. They tend to be interested in political issues that can be addressed through policies and reforms, and out of concern for their own livelihoods they tend to be self-censoring, rarely pushing beyond boundaries acceptable to the party-state.

Although dissident Han intellectuals have at times been motivated by nationalism, they are almost never motivated by an ethnic or religious cause. With rare exceptions, China's students and intellectuals, whether or not they are dissidents, are the most privileged segment of the entire population, have the greatest opportunities to succeed, and are revered in the society and the culture. Today they are the group least likely to throw away their future by becoming political fanatics in their advocacy of, say, democracy.[16] Were they to use violence, much less terrorism, to achieve this goal, it would likely prove counterproductive and alienate the sympathies of the broader population. Chinese act in a here-and-now, pragmatic manner. If they use violence, it is to redress an injury against a known offender, not to create terror among the innocent. Being pragmatic, students and intellectuals, like most Chinese these days, just want to make money, get promoted, and make their families proud of them.[17]

Finally, intellectuals, the vast majority of whom still work for, and are paid by, state institutions, have not yet been able, or willing, to create an effective leadership for a social movement with a greater cause than themselves. When they have tried, the government has quickly suppressed them. Because the Chinese people embrace the party-state's argument that those who attempt to form social movements to challenge the government are likely to create chaos (*luan*) and thwart China's economic development—often evoking images of Red Guards and the chaos of the Cultural Revolution (1966–76)—the Chinese have not been inclined to join such movements. Although there was much sympathy for the Tiananmen Square demonstrators in 1989, the combination of effective state coercion and fear of chaos among ordinary people prevented these events from subsequently spiraling into greater violence.

On the other hand, some dissidents are not intellectuals. For example, workers sometimes have tried to form independent political parties or autonomous trade unions. Their actions are limited less by a concern for being civilized or creating chaos than by other matters, such as the state's use of force to control them, and by society's hostility toward those who use violence. Even well-educated members of the national minorities belong to a privileged sector and are unlikely to risk their good fortune in moving up the narrow funnel to success in China for the sake of risky gains. Thus far, only the Uyghurs' desire for an independent Republic of East Turkestan has provided a powerful enough motivation to outweigh all that could be lost by engaging in terrorism.[18]

One could argue that terrorists are not likely to engage in rational cost-benefit calculations about the consequences of their actions, as they are often motivated by religious ideas that are not necessarily "rational" to begin with (e.g., concepts of Satan, heathens, a fiery hell, divinely ordained missions that may require that heathens be killed, etc).[19] As noted above, many Han Chinese practice religion across a wide spectrum of ideas, but only the sects appeal to ideas that are the millenarian, messianic, and apocalyptic type that might give rise to a charismatic Han leader calling for violence and even the use of terrorism.

In Chinese culture, moreover, popular Buddhism shapes the concept of "immortality" of the soul, of divine sanctions and an afterlife, in which the virtuous enjoy an afterlife in some form of Heaven and the evil are condemned to a hell or the nether world. The idea of an endless cycle of death and rebirth, with individuals carrying their bad (and good) karma with them to their next life, is something to be escaped, not embraced. One thing is certain: killing innocent human beings would earn only bad karma, and rebirth would be in a degraded status. Better, in the view of popular Buddhism, to engage in meditation or reci-́ tation of the scriptures than to redress wrongs through violence.

Thanks to the introduction of the scientific viewpoint and, later, Marxism, ancestor worship slowly lost hold in China during the twentieth century. Nevertheless, to honor the dead remains an integral element in popular religion in the countryside. Apart from Muslims, and perhaps Christians (who tend to ignore the contradictions set up between worshipping a Christian God on the one hand and popular Buddhism and ancestor worship on the other), most Chinese hope that once they are deceased and become ancestors, their descendants will take good care of them. If they do not, the ancestors may be condemned to being ghosts who haunt the living, an unhappy afterlife. So it is ancestor worship, not divine intervention, that determines a person's life after death. This worldview takes away the incentive for performing acts to earn a person merit in the eyes of an all-powerful God. In fact, apart from monotheistic Muslims and Christians, those Chinese who are religious at all tend to be polytheistic, which means they lack moral certainty as to which action, if any, would earn them merit for going to Heaven—if they believed in Heaven in the first place!

Finally, the moral certitude that comes from a belief in divine sanctions, and that characterizes more fanatical Christians and Muslims in other countries, is rarely evident in China—even if the Chinese are, arguably, among the most morally self-righteous peoples in the world (on political and social issues, not religious ones). Although Chinese Muslims (the Hui) and non-Chinese Muslims (such as the Uyghurs), Protestants, and Catholics believe deeply in their own religion's principles, they tend to be quite tolerant of the religious practices of others in China. This is so in part because these mainstream religions in their Chinese variants have had to deviate from religious orthodoxy in order to graft religion onto their own culture and customs.

Of course, China has historically had its share of charismatic types claiming absolute truth, such as the leader of the Taiping sect in the nineteenth century who claimed to be the second coming of Christ. In the 1990s, the charismatic leader of Falun Gong likewise claimed special spiritual powers. As with charismatic leaders of religious groups elsewhere, these Chinese leaders have claimed supreme truth and knowledge, and they have combined this with a mixture of the occult and various religious elements (and often some physical exercises and medicinal panaceas as well). They talk of the coming of Armageddon and recruit those who are alienated from society, lonely, emotionally unbalanced, unemployed, and down on their luck, but individuals who merely seek better physical, and spiritual, health also find Falun Gong appealing.

As for those Uyghurs who have engaged in terrorism, they are not motivated by religious fanaticism but, rather, a desire to achieve a concrete, pragmatic goal: Xinjiang's secession from China. This is in spite of the fact that they have in the last decade received funding from the Islamic world, including, it is believed, from terrorist groups located therein. Uyghurs do not, however, accept the tenets of Islamic fundamentalists, nor do they view their struggle against Chinese rule as a struggle of good against evil. (Indeed, as has often been noted, Islam is much more moderate, tolerant, and progressive as it spreads eastward.) It is an out-and-out political struggle for independence from Chinese rule.

Nevertheless, in December 2003, when the Chinese government issued its first terrorist list, the four groups and eleven individuals on it were all from the Uyghur community. Two of the groups, the World Uygher Youth Congress and the East Turkestan Information Center, are based in Germany. Their supporters claim that they are not terrorist groups but, rather, advocates of direct dialogue with the Chinese government for greater autonomy and rights for the Uyghur people. The Chinese government blames the other two groups, the East Turkestan Islamic Movement (banned for more than a decade) and the East Turkestan Liberation Organisation, for much of the violence and terrorism in Xinjiang before 2000. The government admits that there have been no terrorist incidents in Xinjiang since 2000.[20] Beijing claims that the East Turkestan Islamic Movement has ties to al Qaeda and points to the detention in U.S. facilities in Guantanamo Bay of twenty-two Uyghurs caught in Afghanistan as confirmation of their links to international terrorism. Nevertheless, as Gladney notes, although the Xinjiang Uyghurs are becoming more conservative, it is "not the kind of Hasbullah, Taliban type of Wahabist Islam that the government seems to be very much afraid of" (Australian Broadcasting Company 2003).

STATE POLICIES

Terrorism is more likely to occur in states whose governments are either unable or unwilling to undertake strong counterterrorist actions. As noted above, liberal democratic states have a more difficult time cracking down on terrorism because of a concern for violating civil rights, and many less-developed countries lack the financial, technological, and human resources to control terrorist organizations and activities within their borders.

China has never been tolerant of violence, much less terrorism, against the state. The CCP regime has always been concerned with politically motivated violence, in no small measure because when the CCP took power in 1949, it still faced considerable efforts to overthrow its rule. Any efforts to undermine the power of the state by violence have been quashed. Owing to the strong organizational capabilities of the party-state, perpetrators of politically motivated violence have usually been caught quickly and dealt with summarily. Their actions have always been defined as criminal activity. Before the term was dropped in the mid-1990s, such actions were called "counterrevolutionary." Although the term "counterrevolutionary" certainly included many politically motivated *nonviolent* activities aimed at overthrowing the party-state, counterrevolutionaries, like terrorists today, were by definition *criminals* and as such were punishable according to the Criminal Law.

The preservation of stability and public order in China, even if at the expense of other rights, seems generally acceptable to the population. So China's policies aimed at suppressing politically motivated violence have not been constrained either by the public or by lawyers demanding protection of individual or civil rights. And, in any event, Chinese police have greater powers for interrogation, detention, wiretapping, and other matters than are found in liberal democratic states. Viewing terrorists as criminals bent on destabilizing society leads most Chinese citizens to be predisposed to cooperating in ferreting out terrorists.

The pursuit of terrorists is, moreover, not hampered by a lack of human, technological, and financial resources. The pervasive party cell network throughout China's cities and countryside helped establish an organizational framework to root out enemies of the regime. So did the state policy of requiring household registration for everyone living in the cities[21] and a policy that essentially locked most Chinese into one locale for their entire lives. This policy, maintained until the 1980s, made mobility virtually impossible and thereby diminished the abilities of would-be counterrevolutionaries to organize and gather in large numbers to overthrow the regime. Reform policies and liberalization since the early 1980s have, however, made it far easier for citizens to move about and escape the watchful eye of the public security system. As a result, China has witnessed a surge in criminal behavior, including the smuggling of arms across its porous borders. There has also been growing evidence of Muslim extremists from Inner Asian, South Asian, and Middle Eastern countries crossing into Xinjiang Province, possibly to help fund and organize terrorist activities.

Nevertheless, China is still more successful in controlling migrants, immigrants, and foreign residents than are liberal democratic countries. Isolation in living compounds reserved just for foreigners in cities and the restrictions on foreigners traveling in the interior of China have helped the central government keep tabs on potential troublemakers. Moreover, although some of China's national minorities have widely varying racial characteristics, foreigners tend to be highly visible in China; non-Chinese speakers also are sometimes identified as foreigners and inherently suspect. So, although the reforms and liberalization of the last twenty years have made tracking foreigners in China's largest cities increasingly difficult, tracking is still easier in China than in most states.

China's capacity as a state to crack down on terrorism has been aided by Interpol and the international community. When considering the international dimension, it is important to remember that terrorism as defined in today's world, in which politically motivated violence against the state victimizes innocent civilians, did not occur in China until the 1990s. This was almost twenty years after terrorism began occurring worldwide on a broadening scale. As a result, China has benefited from international counterterrorist organization, knowledge, and technology—especially since it joined with the United States in the war against terrorism after the terrorist attacks on the United States on September 11, 2001. This has given China the upper hand in countering violence by the Uyghurs. It has also meant that China's efforts to crack down on Uyghur violence have not been hampered by the protests of the international human rights community.

The Uyghur actions against unarmed anonymous civilians allowed the regime to condemn the perpetrators as terrorists. Once this happened, it was easier to convince both the Chinese public and the international community that they were not "freedom fighters" who had merely engaged in a "political crime" protected by international law.[22] Once the authorities caught the Uyghurs allegedly culpable for several concrete acts of terrorism in Beijing in 1997–98, they undertook a major crackdown on the Uyghur community in Beijing and restricted and monitored Uyghurs traveling or living outside of Xinjiang. Since then, there has not been further terrorism in the heartland of China. In the wake of the September 11 attack on the United States, the state has been even more assiduous in monitoring the activities of Uyghurs traveling outside of Xinjiang.

In short, the state's attention to eliminating politically motivated violence, its policies of household registration, and a pervasive party cell structure have limited the *opportunities* for terrorism. But, the end of controls on internal migration and the increasing porosity of China's borders as it becomes more integrated into the international community have contributed to the deterioration of the state's ability to control the population. The smuggling of weapons, technology, and equipment useful to terrorists into China has become increasingly difficult to control. Nevertheless, compared to most countries in the developing world, and even compared to the United States, there are relatively few weapons (especially guns) available to ordinary citizens in China.[23]

What, then, of the impact of authoritarianism on terrorism, or even on low levels of politically motivated violence? When the People's Republic of China was the most authoritarian, from 1949 to 1979, the CCP regime effectively eradicated violence against the party-state. Authoritarian controls were effective in maintaining law and order, and the Chinese populace, which had suffered from more than a century of internal chaos and wars, generally accepted these controls as in their best interest. In other words, once the CCP was firmly in power, the Chinese people did not resort to terrorism to confront authoritarianism.

What has seemingly offended those Uyghurs who have become terrorists is not authoritarianism per se. Rather, it is the incompetence, and corruption, of party-state cadres, ill-conceived policies laced with Great Han chauvinism, and poorly executed policies. One can postulate that if the cadres and the policies had been better, the Uyghurs might not be attempting to secede from China. What we do know is that terrorist attacks in Beijing did not occur until China had allowed its citizens far greater freedom, including the right to move more freely around the country. Today, would-be terrorists can move to cities and live anonymously outside traditional work units, among the unregistered millions. In short, reforms, liberalization, development, and the internationalization of China have given terrorists opportunities they previously lacked.

Thus, in the case of China, connecting the form of government, whether it be democracy or authoritarianism, with terrorism or the lack thereof reveals little. Rather, *cultural values* and *demographic conditions* (urban-rural, Han-minority, rich-poor), as well as the specific policies that create the *conditions, opportunities*, and *motivations* for terrorism, are the more relevant variables in explaining terrorism.

AUDIENCE AND MASS MEDIA

In China, in spite of the proliferation of the mass media and expanding parameters for new ideas and perspectives, the state still exercises control over such matters as reporting of violence. Apart from not wanting to publicize terrorism and other forms of violence against the state because this might play into the hands of others who sense its weakness, the Chinese government has traditionally insisted that the media (and the arts) present good role models and be morally uplifting.[24] But Beijing is clearly in a quandary as to how to present the situation in Xinjiang. Since September 11, 2001, it has wanted to portray the Uyghurs as terrorists; yet, at the same time, it wants foreign investors to consider Xinjiang a good investment opportunity (Australia Broadcasting Company 2003). So it cases the situation as one in which there are potential terrorists but that the Chinese government has prevented them from acting. The crackdown on crime and terrorism since the mid-1990s has required that reporters expose unflattering aspects of China, but the stories are usually reported in a "the bad will be punished and the good will prevail" format. Newspaper stories highlight successes, good news, victories for individuals, and so on. Reports on violence, then, often take the form of morality plays: a crime is committed, the perpetrators (especially those labeled as "terrorists") are evil, the cause is unjust, the victim is innocent, and the offenders have already been caught and punished.

While some may decry the Chinese controlling the press in this manner, many share their view about the impact of reporting terrorism. Some theories hold that it will lead others to act violently, to feel less inhibited, or even to engage in copy cat crimes. Social learning theory posits that people learn behavior by observation. Although there is yet no hard evidence to suggest that reporting terrorism actually causes terrorism, the media do "present models, stimulate aspirations, and indicate goals for terrorists." Further, the media appear to lead terrorists to commit increasingly "bizarre and cruel acts to gain media attention" so that the world will know about their grievances and the legitimacy of their cause (Combs 2000, 137–39). Indeed, if the media publicize terrorists' grievances and demands, they are toeing a fine line between news and propagandizing on behalf of the terrorists.[25]

CHINA'S POSITION IN THE INTERNATIONAL COMMUNITY

One of the primary motivations for terrorism against the United States and other Western countries today is believed to be their support of Israel and of Middle Eastern dictators who rule fundamentally repressive societies with massive poverty. Resentment of American hegemony on a global scale is also believed to be a motivating factor. These issues have not, however, motivated the Chinese government to support international terrorism. As for the Uyghurs, although they are Muslims, they likewise seem not to identify with these concerns in the Middle East. Nor do they identify with the tenets of Islamic fundamentalism that are interpreted to call for a jihad against the "infidels," the United States in particular. The concept of the Han Chinese government as made up of "infidels" is an idea whose time has not come. In short, these are not the Uyghurs' issues.

But what about the anger that the United States has provoked within China by, say, its role in blocking Beijing from integrating Taiwan under Beijing's administration? With Taiwan, as with most of its other issues with the United States, China's government is hoping that diplomacy, its own evolving political system, economic integration, and military strength will ultimately get it what it wants. If Beijing were to resort to force, in all likelihood it would take the form of a traditional military confrontation, not terrorism.

China is a status quo power that is simply not interested in jeopardizing its recognized role as a valuable player in the international system by adding terrorism to its repertoire. China uses traditional means of diplomacy, trade, aid, and military power—the tools of a strong state actor—to get what it wants. Although the United States, and others, have frequently upset China with their actions, the Chinese government and people have far more confidence than they did just twenty years ago. They no longer see themselves as "victims" of imperialism or the developed states. Their pride in China's civilization, remarkable economic performance, and their many other accomplishments have brought China international respect and recognition in the last twenty years,[26] undercutting what might otherwise be a more compelling motivation for state terrorism.

Finally, China does not want to give other countries an excuse to attack it. When Bush said after September 11, 2001, that, in effect, you are either for us or against us, China was quick to join with America in the war on terrorism. Thus, China is unlikely to engage in international terrorism as part of its foreign policy.

STATE TERRORISM AND MASS TERRORISM

Is Beijing overseeing a system of state or mass terrorism within China? The answer is no. There is a difference between an authoritarian state such as China today—which attempts to gain complete control over its population through a well-organized party cell system, household registration, and an internal security system directed toward maintaining social stability—and a system such as that of the former USSR (or Argentina during its "dirty war" in the late 1970s) that relied heavily on secret police to eliminate opponents of the regime. Of course, the Chinese party-state has not permitted antiregime dissidents and, in its worst periods when Mao Zedong controlled policy, has sent them (and many others whose ideas the regime found threatening, or at least unacceptable) to labor camps.[27]

The Great Proletarian Cultural Revolution (1966–76) is often described as a period of "mass terror." Until the state lost control of it, this was a state-directed terrorism against the alleged enemies of the regime, or at least against those who were in some respect "reactionary." It involved the state-sanctioned use of violence against civilians and property for politically motivated objectives. Although the young Red Guards carried out wanton violence and roamed the country looking for things to destroy, the targets of political attacks and violence were usually known individuals, people in the same work unit or neighbors of the victimizers who were allegedly "class enemies" or guilty of "crimes" against the people in the Byzantine world of political struggle that evolved in that period. The "terror" was in the unpredictable and arbitrary nature of "mass justice" and the violence of the young Red Guards, and it was often directed by the rotating, temporary agents of the party-state apparatus. The violence also reflected efforts to attack one's potential attackers first, thereby preempting their legitimacy. Like much of the violence in China even today, it was often directed toward specific individuals as a means of personal revenge. The Cultural Revolution shows how easily a culture can be transformed from "peaceful" to "terrorist," but it is also important to remember that the Cultural Revolution ended almost thirty years ago.

CONCLUSION

China's growing pluralization and increased rights for its people, as well as the introduction of a free market and the internationalization of China's economy, have created conditions that could have either positive or negative effects on the growth of terrorism. On the positive side, these rights and policies have provided the Chinese with greater capabilities to improve their livelihoods and articulate their grievances. China's economic policies have led to an average annual growth rate of more than 8 percent since 1980. As long as economic growth continues, the same optimism and hope for the future that has fueled willingness among the Chinese people to work hard and see if they, too, can get rich will probably be the best prophylactic to terrorism. Chinese socioeconomic and demographic conditions in this respect are in stunning contrast to those in the Middle East, which have proven fertile ground for terrorism. On the negative side, China's reforms have led to the polarization of wealth, large-scale unemployment, and social instability, conditions that have in other countries provided a breeding ground for violence and the anger that fuels terrorism. Finally, we can only speculate as to whether an increasingly competitive mass media market in China will create the conditions so valued by terrorists—full coverage of terrorist actions—or, alternatively, provide those with grievances with a channel for addressing their issues and putting pressure on the government to change its policies.

NOTES

I am indebted to Peter Perdue and Amílcar Barreto for their criticisms and suggestions on an earlier draft of this paper.

1. In 1992, Uyghur separatists planted a bomb on a public bus in Urumqi, killing six and injuring many. They also planted a bomb in a Kashgar hotel in 1992 and are believed to be

responsible for planting a bomb on a bus in Chengdu, Szchuan Province, in 1999. "Turkmen (Uighurs and Kazakhs) Chronology," University of Maryland Minorities at Risk Project, www.cidcm.umd.edu/inscr/mar/data/chiturkchro.htm.

2. Many, if not most, of the attacks were against civilians, but they also attacked police and police stations as well as leading government, financial, and business figures.

3. According to Dru Gladney (1995, 5), in the 1990s there was a rush toward "reclassification" or "category shifting" as individuals redefined their nationality, moving either from Han to minority or from identity in one minority to another. Gladney speculates that this may have resulted from "affirmative action" policies that favored the minorities and allowed them to have more children, pay fewer taxes, gain greater opportunities in becoming officials, speak and learn their own minority's language, and practice their own religion. They were also encouraged to display their cultural differences in the arts and popular culture. Although "ethnic chic" is still very much on display in China, there has been some retreat from these policies since the mid-1990s, especially in Tibet and Xinjiang.

4. National Population Census of 2000. Only 6 percent of the population was Han in 1949.

5. Uyghur and Chinese accounts of the history of Xinjiang vary dramatically. Suffice it to say that the Uyghurs reject Chinese claims to having controlled Xinjiang since antiquity; they accuse the Chinese of burying Chinese ancient artifacts in Xinjiang and then "discovering" them later for the media. See, for example, Erkin Alptekin, "Falsification of Turkic History, Culture and Civilization," www.uighur.org/turkistan.asp?inc=tarihd&numara=18.

6. In the Han population, 49.7 percent cannot speak any Uyghur and 33 percent speak it poorly, with only 3.2 percent speaking it well, whereas only 14.2 percent of the Uyghurs cannot speak Chinese at all and 47.9 percent speak it well (Lee 2003, 436).

7. Of course, not all Hui are the same, but many Hui in Yunnan Province—bordering on Myanmar (formerly Burma), Laos, and Vietnam—are increasingly likely to see themselves as Islamic. That is, they are taking what they think is Middle Eastern Islam (the Saudi version) as the model for religious practice, education, customs, architecture, food, and even dress. Some of the Islamic schools in Yunnan are now focusing exclusively on Islam, Islamic history, and Arabic in order to provide a supplement to the state-run schools, which provide the math, Chinese language, science, and so on. Still other Chinese Muslims want to be religiously "correct" (the Islamic element) yet modern and progressive (the Han Chinese element). Differences of opinion over Hui practices and the role of Islamic education appear regularly in articles in Hui journals. Although the most authentic version of Islam (isolationist vs. integrationist) is contested, there appears to be a consensus that an "authentic" Hui is both a Chinese Muslim and a Muslim Chinese (Susan K. McCarthy, personal correspondence, January 2004).

8. When materials such as photos of Muslims worshipping beside pigs or articles suggesting deviant sexual practices in Muslim communities have been published that demean those of the Islamic faith, the authorities have been quick to withdraw the materials and punish those responsible for them. However, the government, now far less puritanical than it was twenty-five years ago, does not seem to consider the pictoral portrayal of seminude minority women in magazines as racist.

9. What is remarkable is that the Chinese tend to be so individualistic, competitive, and aggressive, yet at the public level they tend to conform on the question of violent behavior.

This is not to say that the Chinese show a great concern for other sorts of public and social goods. Instead, they tend to divide the world into *nei* and *wai* (inside and outside). Thus, while many Chinese will spit on streets, they will not spit in their home, and while they will be kind to an old lady they know, they will not necessarily be kind to strangers (Catherine Yeh, personal discussion, April 2003). One could hypothesize that the Chinese respect public goods, such as order and nonviolence, that are supported and enforced by the state but that they do not respect those public goods for which the state does not demand respect.

10. In China, a child who is being punished is thrown *out* of the house (symbolically out of society), in contrast to the United States, where a child is sent to her or his room *inside* the house (Catherine Yeh, personal discussion, April 2003).

11. This is, of course, true for most societies, but in those societies that produce the most terrorists, terrorism tends to be accepted as legitimate by larger segments of the population.

12. The Aum Supreme Truth sect made a sarin nerve gas attack on the Tokyo subway in 1995, killing twelve and injuring almost six thousand people.

13. For example, telling people that they will not be permitted to get on the spaceship, with limited seating capacity, to Heaven if they do not convert.

14. Although the party relinquished such claims after the death of Mao in 1976, it still does not allow others to claim infallibility or absolute truth. This is at the heart of why the Chinese government does not allow Chinese Catholics to embrace the infallibility of the Pope by regarding him as the head of the Catholic Church in China.

15. One could, of course, argue that the Great Proletarian Cultural Revolution would be an exception to this, but the fanaticism was channeled into an intense power struggle that ultimately turned violent. Participation in this struggle was encouraged, indeed demanded, from the leadership. It did not emerge naturally from below. When we speak of this period as one of mass terror, we are usually talking about the psychological struggle among various factions, which did indeed terrorize people—even those who were not being directly attacked—and also led to the deaths of many. But, this is a different sort of terrorism as the term is being used today.

16. This said, it should be remembered that the primary leaders of the many groups (except the workers) in the Tiananmen demonstrations in the spring of 1989 were students and intellectuals. To wit, one of the main leaders of the student movement was a Uyghur, Wuerkaixi. But, the students and intellectuals in these protests against the government were hardly fanatics, and they engaged in peaceful protests, remonstrations, and the presentation of petitions. Only toward the end, when the workers joined in, did violence erupt, but it was not directed against innocent civilians and could not be labeled as terrorism. The key incidents of violence by the participants were the burning of empty buses, but when Chinese troops tried to enter Beijing to end the occupation of Tiananmen Square, ordinary citizens, many of whom had not even marched in the demonstrations, attacked them in an effort to stop them.

17. The bombs set off in Qinghua University and Beijing University cafeterias in early 2003 were the work of a single disgruntled worker who had no political motivation.

18. According to Lee (2003, 449), thousands of Uyghur youths who have been educated in colleges and universities are unemployed, yet Han graduates can easily get a job in the government sector in Xinjiang. This could provide both a motivation and a basis in the population for terrorism.

19. As Hoffman (1998, 169) notes, religious terrorists, unlike secular terrorists, "do not seek to appeal to any constituency or authority other than their own god or religious figures, and therefore feel little need to regulate or calibrate their violence."

20. Gladney's research indicates there have not actually been any violent (terrorist) incidents in Xinjiang since the spring of 1998 (Australia Broadcasting Company 2003).

21. One of the reasons the household registration system made it exceedingly difficult for anyone to move to another city, much less migrate from the countryside to the city, was because until the reform period that began in 1979, all grain in the cities was rationed. Each person needed a coupon in order to buy grain where they lived, so any outsider really had no access to the basic grain ration. Once free markets were introduced and grain was no longer rationed, this element of control over migrants was lost.

22. The Uyghurs had engaged in local demonstrations and riots in Urumqi and Kashgar, the two major cities in Xinjiang, in previous years, but the government's condemnation of them as terrorists was dismissed by most observers, including the international community.

23. Of course, there are many factories that make fireworks, whose raw materials could easily be converted into explosives if they fell into terrorists' hands, and fertilizer as the basis for bombs is an obvious alternative in the countryside. But as noted earlier, effective terrorism is not likely to occur in the countryside.

24. For similar reasons, the state tightly controlled the media coverage of Falun Gong incidents. The state did not want Falun Gong to get publicity about their grievances or how successfully they could organize and thus perhaps inspire others to join with them.

25. In the wake of the events of September 11, 2001, even the United States curtailed the mass media because, allegedly, it would hurt government efforts to find the terrorists or stop terrorist activities. The government also "squeezed" those journalists who spoke too sympathetically about terrorists and their goals by suggesting, for example, that the United States might bear some responsibility for causing the terrorist attacks of September 11.

26. To mention only a few: The choice of Beijing for the 2008 Olympics, China's positive role in the United Nations and its agencies, and its lead role in bringing about negotiations over nuclear weapons with North Korea, the United States, and Japan.

27. Another example of mass terrorism would be the Reign of Terror (1793–1794), when Robespierre, as head of the Jacobin Party, ruled France.

REFERENCES

Australia Broadcasting Company. 2003. "China: Muslim Uighurs Top New Terrorist List." Interview with Dru Gladney, University of Hawaii, and Alim Seytoff, President, American Uigher Association, December 19. www.abc.net.au/ra/asiapac/programs/s1013806.htm.

Bernstein, Thomas P., and Xiaobo Lu. 2003. *Taxation without Representation in Contemporary Rural China*. New York: Cambridge University Press.

Combs, Cindy C. 2000. *Terrorism in the Twenty-First Century*. 2d ed. Englewood Cliffs, N.J.: Prentice Hall.

Dreyer, June Teufel. 2003. "Economic Development in Tibet under the People's Republic of China." *Journal of Contemporary China* 12(36) (August): 411–30.

Gladney, Dru C. 1994. "Representing Nationality in China: Refiguring Majority/Minority Identities." *Journal of Asian Studies* 53(1) (1994): 92–123.

———. 1995. "China's Ethnic Reawakening." *AsiaPacific Issues* 18 (January): 1–8.

Hoffman, Bruce. 1998. *Inside Terrorism*. New York: Columbia University Press.

Lee, Herbert S. 2003. "Ethnic Relations in Xinjiang: A Survey of Uyghur-Han Relations in Urumqi." *Journal of Contemporary China* 12(36) (August): 431–52.

McCarthy, Susan K. 2003. "Chinese Islamic Revival and the Post-Mao State: The Challenge of Invented Traditions." Paper presented at the International Studies Association, International Convention, CEU, Budapest, June 26–28.

Ogden, Suzanne. 2002. *Inklings of Democracy in China*. Cambridge: Harvard University Press and Harvard University Asia Center.

Waldman, Amy. 2004. "Maoist Rebellion Shifts Balance of Power in Rural Nepal." *New York Times*, February 5, p. A3.

Whittaker, David J., ed. 2001. *The Terrorism Reader*. New York: Routledge.

DAN G. COX

13 Political Terrorism and Democratic and Economic Development in Indonesia

In light of the attacks against the United States on September 11, 2001, political leaders may easily forget that protests can take many forms and that varying forms of violence should elicit different responses from national governments. There is a predisposition, lately, on the part of governmental leaders to label every act of violent dissent as terrorism. There is good reason for this. Terrorism is working in that it is engendering terror. But there is a danger in treating all forms of violent protest the same—mainly, that nonterrorist protesters might turn into terrorists if they are consistently treated as such. Further, successful terrorist attacks can damage the economy and endanger the democratic freedoms in even the most robust democracy. When terrorism strikes a fledgling industrial democracy, the results can be even more devastating.

Years of human rights abuses on the part of the Indonesian government have already led to a secessionist movement on the island of East Timor. This movement culminated with successful secession from Indonesia on August 30, 1999, when 78 percent of the East Timorese population voted to leave the republic. Secessionist movements in the Indonesian provinces of Aceh and Irian Jaya threaten similar results. However, the Indonesian government is unlikely to allow either of these provinces to secede. There are many reasons underlying the Indonesian government's reticence, chief among them the fact that allowing Aceh and Irian Jaya to defect could have a cascading effect that would tear the fragile republic of island cultures apart at the seams.

As if secessionist movements were not pressure enough on the young democracy, the government has also had to deal with terrorist attacks from the militant Islamic

255

group Jema'ah Islamiyah (JI). While JI and similar militant Islamic groups do not enjoy widespread popular support, the ramifications of successful terrorist attacks in Indonesia, such as the October 12, 2001, Bali nightclub attacks, have had a deep impact on the government's response to secessionist movements in Aceh and Irian Jaya. Whether it is violence resulting from secessionist movements or terrorist attacks, the ramifications for the future of democracy and economic development are great.

DEFINING TERRORISM

One of the most troubling aspects of terrorism is its definition. There is currently no agreed-upon international definition of terrorism and few international treaties on the subject. As a result, there is a great deal of contention over both the definition of and enforcement against terrorist acts. There are several areas of contention in any definition of terrorism that deserve some discussion. The first area of contention lies in defining who might commit terrorist acts. The possible actors can be lumped into two main categories: state and nonstate.

State actors would include the government, the military, and police forces. Nonstate actors could range from large, amorphous organizations such as al Qaeda all the way down to a single individual who does not belong to any organized terrorist group but acts in sympathy with an overall movement. The area of question lies with state actors, as there is no dispute that nonstate actors can commit acts of terrorism. Can state actors commit acts of terrorism? Few articles examine this question very thoroughly and fewer authors make the argument that state actors can commit acts of terrorism. Nevertheless, the contention that state actors can commit acts of terrorism deserves some attention here.

Peter Sproat argues that states can indeed commit acts of terrorism. He notes that the word "terrorism" was first used to describe violent acts carried out by the French government in 1793 and 1798 (1997, 117). While Sproat does acknowledge that most scholars reject the idea of state-sponsored terrorism, he finds the arguments against to be lacking. He begins by dismissing out of hand the argument that there must be a definitional barrier between human rights abuses committed by state and nonstate actors. He also quickly dispatches contentions made by international legal scholars that no legal definition of terrorism includes the state as an agent of terrorism on the grounds that he himself is mainly interested in the political aspects (119–20). One could counter that politics and law are not so easily separated, as politics is mainly the business of making and administering laws to govern citizen behavior.

But even if one accepts that state actors cannot perpetrate terrorist acts, the definition of terrorism is still ambiguous. In fact, one author questions whether the word "terrorism" should be used to describe the World Trade Center attacks. Chibli Mallat postulates that these attacks were different from attacks normally conceived as terrorist. "By its sheer size, its wantonness, its ferocity, its callousness, its suddenness, the means used, the thousands of innocent civilians destroyed in minutes, September 11 qualifies as a crime against humanity." He quite rightly goes on to argue that crimes against humanity carry a good set of precedents for punishment (2002, 246–47). But this only illustrates the underdevelopment of the definition and international norms surrounding terrorism. It is not a good reason to lump a large-scale terrorist action under a more developed international legal term such as "crimes against humanity."

Problems also occur with regard to the application of the term "terrorism." Even when there is common agreement regarding what does not constitute a terrorist act, political considerations often allow politicians to define acts that are clearly not terrorist as such. For example, Peter Weiss notes that violent anticolonial movements after World War II were often portrayed as terrorist movements by the colonizing nations and their allies (2002, 11). A more recent example of misapplication of the term "terrorism" for political ends comes from Operation Iraqi Freedom. Loyalists to Saddam Hussein were labeled terrorists when they attacked U.S military personnel as forces were invading the city of Baghdad. These actions more clearly fall under the rubric of armed resistance or guerrilla warfare, as the attacks were generated against a clearly aggressive, invading military force. But because U.S. officials wished to cast supporters of Hussein in the worst possible light, administration officials successfully labeled these actions as terrorist.

In order to avoid some of the confusion surrounding the designation of terrorist acts, some time must be devoted to choosing as accurate a definition of terrorism as possible. One of the earliest modern attempts to define terrorism comes from Raymond Aron: "An action of violence is labeled 'terrorist' when its psychological effects are out of proportion to its purely physical results" (1966, 170). This is not a great definition, because one could argue that the psychological effects of certain military actions, such as mining a public road during a time of war, could be out of proportion to the physical results produced thereby. However, it is an important starting point—once one concedes that terrorism can only be committed by nonstate actors, the core point of psychological disproportionality is cogent.

International legal attempts to define terrorism are few and far between. One recent example offers some insight into a possible definition. In 1999, the United Nations offered a first attempt at an international definition of terrorism. Under the proposed *International Convention for the Suppression of the Financing of*

Terrorism, terrorism is defined as "any . . . act intended to cause death or serious bodily injury to a civilian, or to any other person not taking an active part in hostilities in a situation of armed conflict, when the purpose of such act, by its nature or context, is to intimidate a population, or to compel a government or international organization to do or abstain from doing any act" (United Nations 1999, Article 2, Section 1, Subparagraph B).

Paul Pillar prefers the more precise interpretation put forth by the U.S. State Department, which defines terrorism as any act that is "premeditated, politically motivated violence perpetrated against noncombatant targets by subnational groups or clandestine agents, usually intended to influence an audience" (2001, 13). Pillar makes one slight modification to this definition by noting that a lone individual can be politically inspired to commit an act of terrorism without being a formal member of a subnational group or clandestine organization. Pillar also emphasizes that terrorism cannot be perpetrated by a "government's duly uniformed or otherwise identifiable armed forces" (14). He argues that any formal attack by a government's military must be interpreted as some sort of warfare or human rights abuse. This is an important reinforcement of the notion that only nonstate actors can commit acts of terrorism.

A trend has emerged, noticeable in both the UN's and the U.S. State Department's definitions of terrorism, that emphasizes terrorism as acts perpetrated only against noncombatants. This is a very important point to consider in analyzing terrorism in Indonesia. If one accepts this tenant, then any violent act against a government's military or duly uniformed law enforcement agents must be defined as something other than terrorism.

One proviso should be added to the discussion of an appropriate definition of terrorism. Peter Weiss argues that most definitions fail to consider nonviolent forms of terrorism such as "blacking out an electricity grid or a cyber network" (2002, 13). This is an important point to consider, and any thorough definition of terrorism should include provision for nonviolent acts of terrorism. Therefore, for the purposes of this analysis, terrorism is defined as any premeditated, politically motivated violent or nonviolent act perpetrated against noncombatants by subnational groups, clandestine agents, or individuals sympathetic to larger terrorist groups and movements, with the intent to influence an audience toward or against an action.

ACEH AND THE FREE ACEH MOVEMENT

Aceh, located on the northern tip of Sumtara, is an industrial province with abundant natural resources and shares a rich history of anticolonialism with the rest of Indonesia. These characteristics should have led to harmonious relations between Aceh and the Indonesian national government. Unfortunately, this has not occurred, and the result has been human rights abuses on the part of the government and a secessionist response in the form of the Free Aceh Movement or Gerakan Aceh Merdeka (GAM).

To understand the formation of GAM, one must understand the historical interaction of Aceh with the Indonesian government. Aceh boasts vast supplies of oil, natural gas, and timber (Crow 2000, 92). Arun, the second largest city in Aceh, is home to two of the largest natural gas reserves in all of Asia. These two deposits are largely responsible for the estimate that Indonesia has over two billion cubic meters of proven natural gas reserves.[1] One field in Arun alone translates into an estimated $1.5 billion worth of natural gas production a year, and the total natural gas production in Aceh is chiefly responsible for making Indonesia the largest exporter of natural gas (Murphy 2001b, 6). The financial importance of Aceh to Indonesia has been present from the first days of the formation of the Republic of Indonesia. In the early years of Indonesian independence, Aceh helped finance the purchase of Indonesia's first aircraft, funded diplomatic outposts, and helped fund the national government during a financial crisis (Sulistiyanto 2001, 438). The embarrassment of riches in Aceh should have translated into an affluent and politically potent populace. But this did not occur.

Why the population of Aceh failed to profit from the natural resources present is rooted in the historical relationship between Aceh and Indonesia. Most of the provinces that now comprise the archipelago nations of Indonesia were under Dutch and Japanese colonial rule, while a few areas were under Portuguese rule, such as the newly independent East Timor. Aceh is unique in that this province resisted Dutch colonization longer than any other part of Indonesia. As Priyambudi Sulistiyanto argues, it was Islam that united the Acehnese against foreign incursions and helped sustain a war against Dutch invaders starting in 1873 and lasting until 1903 (Sulistiyanto 2001, 438). The tenacity of the Aceh people is demonstrated by the fact that more than one hundred thousand Acehnese citizens lost their lives during this war with the Dutch colonizers (Crow 2000, 92).

After the Japanese colonizers were expelled in 1945, the Dutch came back to Indonesia. But the fierceness and resolve shown by the Acehnese during their previous war with the Dutch caused the Netherlands to refrain from attempting to recolonize Aceh. Aceh considered itself to be an independent nation at this point, but this independence was short-lived. Because of the shared history of resistance to Dutch and Japanese colonizers and as a result of the strategic and resource importance of the province, President Sukarno extended an invitation to Aceh in 1947 to join the Indonesian Republic. President Sukarno promised to give Aceh governmental autonomy. However, in 1950, President Sukarno lifted Aceh's special autonomy, and three years later this resulted in a declaration by the Achenese governor, Teungku M. Daud Beureu'h, that Aceh had become an independent Islamic state (Sulistiyanto 2001, 438–39). During this crisis, President Sukarno introduced his notion of guided democracy that expanded the power of Sukarno's authoritarian regime through the use of emergency military powers (Aspinall and Berger 2001, 1006). The rebellion in Aceh had the unfortunate negative effect of legitimizing the use and expansion of authoritarian force. In 1959, Sukarno offered again to make Aceh a special semiautonomous region; this offer was eventually accepted, and the rebellion officially ended in 1962.

But tensions continued, and Sukarno and his successor, Suharto, continued to treat the citizens of Aceh poorly. Despite the fact that by 1980 Aceh was contributing two to three billion dollars annually to the Indonesian economy, the government was only sending eighty to ninety million dollars back for economic development. As Sulistiyanto argues, "Given its wealth of natural resources, Aceh could be a prosperous region similar to the small but wealthy kingdoms of Kuwait and Brunei, but it remains, instead, one of Indonesia's less-developed provinces" (2001, 439). This only helped to foster an environment ripe for continued animosity.

The economic facts coupled with human rights abuses by the Indonesian military (TNI) fueled rebellion. On December 4, 1976, Teungku Hassan di Tiro, a political activist, declared Aceh's independence and established the Free Aceh Movement (GAM), the most prominent lasting manifestation of the secessionist movement. The movement almost collapsed immediately, and in 1979 Teungku Hassan di Tiro was forced into exile in Sweden (Sulistiyanto 2001, 440). Not much was heard from GAM during most of the 1980s, as few people had joined the open rebellion. Fewer than two thousand freedom fighters are estimated to have existed during this time period, and the military was experiencing great success in suppressing the rebellion. President Suharto replaced President Sukarno and ratcheted up the pressure on all dissident movements by declaring that any opposition to governmental directives or actions would be interpreted as an attack on the state and considered treasonous (Aspinall and Berger 2001, 1009).

While GAM was not experiencing much success during most of the 1980s, it remained disruptive and a constant thorn in the side of President Suharto. By the end of the decade, Suharto was becoming so frustrated with GAM that he doubled the number of troops in Aceh to twelve thousand and declared it a militarily occupied area, or Daerah Operasi Militer (DOM). The DOM lasted from 1989 to 1998. During this period, Suharto abused his emergency powers and gave power to the military and police forces in Aceh to arbitrarily arrest without cause, interrogate using torture, and kill anyone suspected of supporting GAM

(Sulistiyanto 2001, 401). Thousands were tortured and killed during the 1980s and 1990s, fueling the movement and resentment toward the Indonesian government and its occupation. Suharto never released his authoritarian grip on the region, and it was not until President Habibie was elected, after Suharto was forced from office, that the military occupation ended.

THE CURRENT STATE OF ACEH

Despite the removal of President Suharto and the subsequent presidencies of Habibie and currently Megawati, the situation in Aceh has not improved. During President Habibie's short reign, conflict spread to areas of Aceh that had previously been untouched by violence (Sulistiyanto 2001, 446). In 2000 alone, an estimated twelve hundred people were killed in Aceh (Murphy 2001a, 6).

In recent months, President Megawati has had little success in engendering peace. When peace talks break down, the response is harsh and very reminiscent of the Suharto regime. A peace agreement had been reached with GAM in December of 2002, but the cease-fire soon collapsed. Some, including the U.S. government, blamed GAM for the collapse (*Economist* 2002a). However, many locals in Aceh claim that the ceasefire negotiations broke down because the government increased its military campaign against GAM while simultaneously offering concession to GAM (*Economist* 2002b). Recent evidence indicates the TNI is committing widespread human rights abuses. In one incident in May of 2003, eight young males, ages eleven to twenty years old, were shot in the head at close range when soldiers ran across them at a local fishing pond (Andrew 2003, 19). On May 2, 2003, after renewed peace talks collapsed, President Megawati ordered immediate rocket attacks on rebel positions (Wiener 2003, 42). Reaction to these and previous attacks perpetrated by the government can be summed up by the remarks of one man living in Aceh: "If we hadn't hated Indonesia before, we would now" (Murphy 2001a, 6).

The use of force is only serving to galvanize opposition against Indonesian rule. Rebel fighters in GAM numbered only two thousand in the 1980s and 1990s but have now swelled to more than five thousand. On May 19, 2003, President Megawati responded by deploying forty thousand troops to Aceh with the express purpose of suppressing GAM and the Free Aceh Movement (Shari 2003, 47). This troop movement coincided with a declaration of martial law by the Megawati government. Aceh is once again an occupied region. What is most disturbing about this occupation are reports that the crackdown is attacking all forms of free expression in Aceh. The TNI is reportedly attacking governmental activists, and the military has apparently razed more than 350 public schools

(Hinman and Schamotta 2003, 8). Attacks on democracy and democratic activists will do little to create democracy in Indonesia. The recent occupation of Aceh by TNI has some observers worried that one hundred thousand people will soon be displaced, creating a large-scale human rights crisis (Barker 2003, 62). The situation has become so grim that the U.S. government has warned the Indonesian government against continuing its military occupation, arguing that a war with GAM cannot be won militarily (Perlez 2003).

For most of the conflict, GAM has been involved in some sort of rebellion or guerrilla warfare against what many in Aceh see as unfair governance and occupation. There is some question as to whether or not some recent civilian deaths at a factory in Aceh were the result of GAM or the military dressed in civilian clothing. But most of the hard evidence points to a freedom movement that has shied away from creating civilian casualties. Despite this fact, there will be an ever-increasing temptation to lump GAM in with other terrorist groups operating in Aceh. The benefits of doing so include legitimizing the use of force and the current military occupation of Aceh, the greater possibility of receiving military and economic aid to fight this war (especially from the Untied States), and the greater leniency with which abuses of civil liberties will be viewed.

There is also the very real possibility that as the Indonesian government ratchets up its oppressive techniques, an actual terrorist campaign will ensue. The lack of success by GAM may force leaders to choose alternative terrorist paths. If this happens, the Free Aceh Movement will become synonymous with terrorism, and even the nonterrorist activists will lose international legitimacy.

There are cogent reasons explaining why Indonesia is reluctant to allow Aceh to secede. Aceh has been a part of Indonesia since Indonesia became a nation-state. Further, many Indonesians have an affinity for Acehean history and its long struggle against Dutch colonial rule (Aspinall and Berger 2001, 1016). As mentioned earlier, Aceh is a resource-rich area, and the natural gas and oil in the region help boost the Indonesian economy but also fuel industrial growth.

Some might argue that Aceh should be allowed to secede since East Timor was allowed to do so in 1999. But there are major differences between the situation in East Timor and Aceh. First, East Timor was not colonized by the Dutch, and therefore it does not have a large place in Indonesian history or national pride (Aspinall and Berger 2001, 1015). East Timor was also forcibly annexed by Indonesia while, in contrast, Aceh freely accepted an invitation by President Sukarno to join the Indonesian nation. East Timor also did not contribute as heavily to the Indonesian economy and, as a separate island, was more easily removed from the Indonesian nation-state. The secession of Aceh could also encourage other regions, such as Irian Jaya, to secede.

TERRORISM AND MILITANT ISLAM IN INDONESIA

On October 12, 2002, Indonesia suffered one of the deadliest terrorist attacks in recent history. More than two hundred people were killed and hundreds more injured in a Bali nightclub bombing. Two other bombs went off that night—one near the U.S. consulate in Bali and one near the Philippine consulate in Manado—but no casualties were attributed to these two smaller bombings (Malley 2003, 135). The group linked with these and some more recent attacks is Jema'ah Islamiyah (JI), which represents a vociferous minority view that Indonesia should become a Muslim theocracy. The rhetoric from leaders of JI is not only aimed at moderate secularists such as President Megawati but is also commonly leveled against the United States and other Western nations. Imam Sumudra, the alleged mastermind behind the October 12 events, is being charged with the bombings and also with planning to wage a larger war against the United States (*Taipei Times Online* 2003). Bali itself was probably targeted because the Hindu-dominated island had escaped the ethnic violence present in other parts of Indonesia. Another argument for attacking Bali is that if the terrorists could strike here, then no place was safe for the Indonesian citizens and tourists visiting the country (Ratnesar et al. 2003, 35).

There was some warning of the possibility that JI would engage in a vicious terrorist campaign, as many Asian and Western intelligence agencies had established links between al Qaeda and JI (Malley 2003, 136). There may also be a regional link between militant Islamic groups such as JI in Indonesia and similar groups in the Philippines, such as the Abu Sayyaf Group (ASG) and Moro Islamic Liberation Front (MILF) (Murphy 2001d, 7). The location of the third bomb on October 12, 2002, near the Philippine consulate building adds further circumstantial credibility to such a claim.

JI has followed the October 12 attacks with two other major attacks on Indonesian noncombatants. On July 14, 2003, the group allegedly set off a high-explosive bomb in the Indonesian House of Representatives and People's Consultive Assembly complex. There were no casualties, as ample warning was given. Government officials speculated that this action was a warning to the government to cease the military crackdown against JI (*Jakarta Post Online* 2003).

A more recent attack occurred on August 5, 2003, and resulted in at least 10 deaths and 150 wounded in a Marriott business hotel. The bombing coincided with Indonesian court decisions that were to be handed down in subsequent days against members of JI (Bradsher 2003). Most consider this bomb, too, to be the handiwork of JI.

The attacks that are most likely being carried out by JI are clearly terrorist in nature. All have been perpetrated by a subnational organization, JI, against noncombatants, usually civilians. Their goal is to terrorize the Indonesian and American governments into changing their policies. These terrorist incidents have had a devastating impact on Indonesia's economy. The Bali bombings alone caused a 10 percent decline in the Indonesian stock market and sent the Indonesian rupiah into a tailspin (Shari, Balfour, and Crock 2002, 57). These attacks have had a negative effect on democracy and have pushed President Megawati to "pursue a more aggressive policy against possible terrorist threats" that includes year-long detention of suspects without trial (Malley 2003, 137). Unfortunately, secessionist movements in Aceh and Irian Jaya are slowly being labeled as terrorist threats. There is a link being created between terrorism and secession by the Indonesian government. Such a link is dangerous and may, in the end, only create more true terrorist opposition.

POTENTIAL CONSEQUENCES FOR INDONESIA

There are clear contrasts that can be drawn between the secessionist operations of GAM and the terrorist acts of JI. Nevertheless, both movements have, and will continue to have, detrimental consequences for Indonesia. The main concern is that if the problems that secessionist movements pose aren't dealt with properly, fairly, and justly by the Indonesian government, then these movements could merge with more militant Islamic movements.

In regard to economics, continued international terrorism from JI carries the potential for a protracted downturn in the Indonesian stock market, devastation for the tourism industry, and reticence to invest global capital on the part of transnational corporations. Failure to successfully deal with GAM will result in diminished production from that region and, most importantly, slow or stop the flow of oil and natural gas from Aceh. All outcomes could be devastating as Indonesia attempts to recover from the 1998 Asian recession.

In terms of the democratic process, terrorism and armed resistance to human rights abuses in Aceh are having a detrimental effect on civilian control of the military and the development of democratic norms. These are very important considerations for Indonesia, as the democratic experiment there is only a few years old. Further, the TNI has historically enjoyed a dual role, playing a pivotal part in both civilian and military affairs. There is clear evidence that TNI has taken this role to mean, at times, that it does not have to listen to the directives of the civilian government. For example, the TNI perpetrated human rights abuses against the people of East Timor despite President Habibie's disapproval (Kingsbury 2000, 303).

This paints a particularly disturbing picture for a number of reasons. First, this incident is recent and shows that not much has changed in Indonesia.

Second, as R. William Liddle argues, "Establishing civilian supremacy over the military is a top priority for any democratizing regime" (2000, 11). Third, the vast majority of Indonesian history falls under the Sukarno and Suharto dictatorships in which the military either acted autonomously or was directed to perpetrate human rights abuses. Fourth, the current terrorist threat has pushed President Megawati to use the military in a very undemocratic fashion.

Indonesia is moving farther away from the goal of civilian control of the military because of the current terrorist threat. But the actions of governmental officials, from police officers abusing human rights in Aceh to President Megawati suspending civil rights to fight terrorism, send the wrong message to citizens in Indonesia. How can political leaders in Indonesia convince the populace to embrace democracy when they are themselves limiting democratic freedoms and infringing individual rights? Given the authoritarian history of Indonesia, such actions could easily lead to a revival of popular support for some form of authoritarian rule.

THE BIGGER PICTURE FOR SOUTHEAST ASIA

The situation regarding terrorism and secessionist movements in not unique to Indonesia. One need only look north to the Philippines to see a similar example.

In the Philippines there is a clear religious split (unlike in Indonesia). The Philippines, because of its Spanish colonial history, is predominantly Catholic. But the southern island of Mindanao is almost 80 percent Muslim. The Muslim populace has attempted for almost three decades to forcibly secede from the Philippine Republic with no success. Several groups have fought with the government, and today these groups have evolved to produce divergent groups.

The Moro National Liberation Front (MNLF) is a purely secessionist group that most resembles GAM. The MNLF's main goal was to secede from the Philippines and establish a separate Islamic state. However, in 1996, a peace was reached when the Philippine government offered MNLF an autonomous region in Muslim Mindanao. The government was to allow this semiautonomous region to institute Muslim practices in schools and, to a limited extent, in the legal system (*Economist* 2003b).

The agreement did not sit well with the far more militant Moro Islamic Liberation Front (MILF) and the Abu Sayyaf Group (ASG). Both groups' leaders said they would settle for nothing less than an independent Islamic state. However, MILF and ASG, despite having clear ties to Osama bin Laden and al Qaeda, are not overly similar with JI. The main difference lies in what MILF and ASG have become. These groups are now more criminal rather than secessionist or even terrorist in nature.

The ASG has found funding opportunities through a kidnap-for-ransom scheme that often has little or nothing to do with the group's stated goals of secession or spreading Islam (Murphy 2001c). Both groups have lost at least some control over parts of their organizations that have become "more interested in gangsterism than negotiations" (*Economist* 2003b). Despite the lost focus, international events, such as the U.S. war with and current occupation of Iraq, have swelled the ranks of these groups and caused new groups to form (*America* 2003).

The result of the terrorism, criminal activity, and secessionist movements among these groups is similar to what has happened in Indonesia. President Gloria Arroyo will receive ninety-two million dollars from the United States to fight terrorism and to fight local insurgents (Banlaoi 2002, 295). The military will be unleashed, and human rights will probably be violated despite several sources (*Economist* 2003a; Murphy 2001d) arguing that peace will best be engendered through nonmilitary and, most importantly, economic development. The alleviation of poverty in any region tends to have a calming effect on the people. When people are deprived and feel that this deprivation is due to unfair governmental practices, more citizens are likely to join a secessionist movement.

IMPLICATIONS FOR SOUTHEAST ASIA

The main implication for Southeast Asia is that terrorism and secessionist movements will continue to plague many nations in the region for years to come. The key is to delineate between rational and irrational dissenters. Unfortunately, no blanket policy can be used against all groups perpetrating political violence. Sometimes, violence is justified. Such is the case in Aceh where years of governmental abuse have resulted in a popular uprising. The current Indonesian governmental policy of fighting GAM with harsh military intervention only deepens the conflict. A better, albeit unlikely, approach would be to come to the bargaining table as equals.

Meanwhile, a universal definition of terrorism needs to be developed and justly applied without political motivation. To allow countries to lump every dissenter and secessionist group under the broad umbrella of terrorism is a recipe for disaster.

Further, not all terrorists are alike. There will be an overriding compulsion on the part of Western nations and Southeast Asian leaders to treat all terrorists equally. But if GAM decides tomorrow to engage in clearly recognizable terrorist acts, the underlying moral justification for secession would not cease to exist. The Indonesian government would be well advised to negotiate fairly, this time, with GAM and allow Aceh to exist as a truly semiautonomous region before the convoluted quagmire of terrorism, secession, and criminality emerges as it has in the Philippines.

Indonesia can ill afford to lose Aceh. But forcing Aceh to heel will not prevent secession. No matter how distant and different militant Islamic groups of Southeast Asia are, they all share a bond and a growing interconnectedness. If the governments of Southeast Asia overreact militarily, this bond will grow tighter and more national secessionist movements, such as GAM and MNLF, will have a compelling reason to join as well. There is a short window of opportunity, while militant Islam remains a relatively small and isolated movement in Southeast Asia, before this region of the world becomes as inhospitable to the West and as chaotic as the Middle East is today.

Finally, the United States must take a strong leadership role in order to help Indonesia in its quest for democratic governance and economic development. The United States could intervene in Indonesia and insist that President Megawati deal with the people of Aceh fairly instead of continuing to abuse human rights in the region. The United States, Australia, and other international players need to take an active part in ensuring that Indonesia, a crucial challenge in the war on terrorism, does not continue to stray from the path of democratic development.

NOTES

The author wishes to thank Stephanie Cox for her helpful comments and insights.

1. The estimates and location of natural gas reserves were taken from "Indonesia: Economy, Politics and Government," *World of Information Business Intelligence Reports* 1(1) (2001): 1–53.

REFERENCES

America. 2003. "Iraqi War Causes More Radicalism in Southern Philippines." Vol. 188: 4.

Andrew, Marshall. 2003. "Bloody Days in Indonesia." *Time* 161 (2 June): 19.

Aron, Raymond. 1966. *Peace and War*. London: Weidenfeld and Nicolson.

Aspinall, Edward, and Mark T. Berger. 2001. "The Break-Up of Indonesia? Nationalisms after Decolonization and the Limits of the Nation-State in Post–Cold War Southeast Asia." *Third World Quarterly* 22: 1003–24.

Banlaoi, Rommel C. 2002. "The Role of Philippine-American Relations in the Global Campaign against Terrorism: Implications for Regional Security." *Contemporary Southeast Asia* 24 (August): 294–312.

Barker, Geoffrey. 2003. "Quiet Diplomacy in Aceh." *Australian Financial Review*, May 19, p. 62.

Bradsher, Keith. August 2003. "Indonesia Bombing Kills at Least 10 in Midday Attack." *New York Times*, August 6, p. A1.

Crow, Karim D. 2000. "Aceh—The 'Special Territory' in North Sumatra: A Self-Fulfilling Promise?" *Journal of Muslim Minority Affairs* 20: 91–104.

Economist. 2002a. "Ceasefire in Aceh?" Vol. 365 (November 22): 40.

———. 2002b. "In Aceh, 'Indonesian' Is a Synonym for Foreigner." Vol. 364 (October 8): 39.

———. 2003a. "No Peace, No Peace Talks." Vol. 367 (May 10): 36.

———. 2003b. "War without End." Vol. 367 (May 3): 46.

Hinman, Pip, and Justin Schamotta. 2003. "Legally Lethal: Indonesia Military Get the Go-Ahead to Gun Down Human Rights." *New Internationalist*, July, p. 8.

Jakarta Post Online. 2003. "Bomb at DPR/MPR Compound Act of Terrorism: Police," July 15. www.thejakartapost.com/Archives/ArchivesDet2.asp?FileID=20030715.@01.

Kingsbury, Damien. 2000. "The Reform of the Indonesian Armed Forces." *Contemporary Southeast Asia: A Journal of International and Strategic Affairs* 22: 302–21.

Liddle, R. William. 2000. "Indonesia in 2000: A Shaky Start for Democracy." *Asian Survey* 41: 208–20.

Mallat, Chibli. 2002. "The Original Sin: 'Terrorism' or 'Crime against Humanity'?" *Case Western Reserve Journal of International Law* 34: 245–48.

Malley, Michael S. 2003. "Indonesia in 2002: The Rising Cost of Inaction." *Asian Survey* 43: 135–46.

Murphy, Dan. 2001a. "Aceh Civilians Caught in the Middle." *Christian Science Monitor* 93 (January 12): 6.

———. 2001b. "Indonesia's War over Riches." *Christian Science Monitor* 93 (March 9): 6.

———. 2001c. "The Philippine Branch of Terror." *Christian Science Monitor* 93 (October 26): 4.

———. 2001d. "U.S. Pushes Southeast Asian States on Islamic Radicals." *Christian Science Monitor* 93 (October 12): 7.

Perlez, Jane. 2003. "U.S. Steers Indonesia Away from War against Separatists." *New York Times*, May 31, Sec. A, p. 4.

Pillar, Paul. 2001. *Terrorism and U.S. Foreign Policy*. Washington, D.C.: Brookings Institution Press.

Ratnesar, Ramesh, et al. 2003. "Al-Qaeda's New Proving Ground." *Time* 160 (November 28): 35–36.

Shari, Michael. 2003. "Global Wrap-up." *Business Week*, June 2, p. 47.

Shari, Michael, Fredrick Balfour, and Stan Crock. 2002. "Fallout from Bali May Clobber Southeast Asia." *Business Week*, October 28, p. 57.

Sproat, Peter Alan. 1997. "Can the State Commit Acts of Terrorism? An Opinion and Some Qualitative Replies to a Questionnaire." *Terrorism and Political Violence* 9 (Winter): 117–50.

Sulistiyanto, Priyambudi. 2001. "Whither Aceh?" *Third World Quarterly* 22: 437–52.

Taipei Times Online. 2003. "Bali Bomber Goes on Trial for His Life," June 3. www.taipeitimes.com/News/world/archives/2003/06/03/2003053766.

United Nations. 1999. *International Convention for the Suppression of the Financing of Terrorism*. December 9. United Nations General Assembly Resolution 54/109.

Weiner, Eric. 2003. "Déjà Vu." *New Republic* 228: 42.

Weiss, Peter. 2002. "Terrorism, Counterterrorism and International Law." *Arab Studies Quarterly* 24 (Spring/Summer): 11–24.

PART FOUR

Africa

JOHN W. HARBESON

14 Perspectives on Terrorism and African Democratic State Formation

Balancing the pursuit of terrorists with the preservation of personal civil and political liberties while maintaining democracy is difficult enough for mature democratic states. How are new, fledgling democracies supposed to surmount this hurdle? The problem is complicated by the proliferation of international regimes that mandate the protection of human rights and sanction terrorism. How are new democracies to honor these regimes while also responding to domestic exigencies that may both reflect and exacerbate their weakness?

In the course of my recent research, I have become increasingly aware of the inadequacies of contemporary empirical political theory. In an effort to identify minimally essential properties of key political phenomena such as the state and democracy in order to establish their universal meanings, scholars have in fact often excluded the essential properties of those phenomena. The experiential base underlying the formulation of those definitions has not been correspondingly universal. These definitions have continued to be grounded primarily in the experience of mature industrialized and democratic states of Europe and North America. For that reason, they may satisfy the *necessary* but perhaps not the *sufficient* standard for working, universally applicable empirical definitions. This important flaw in empirical political theory fundamentally diminishes its applicability and utility in regard to the problem of combating terrorism in poor countries where the state is weak and democracy only nascent and partially consolidated, as in much of sub-Saharan Africa. Flawed theory, in turn, obscures essential policy priorities necessary to achieving the goal of ending terrorism in these environments.

Everyone recognizes the importance of the rule of law to both the health of the state and the realization of democracy. Most ironically, however, received working theories of both the state and democracy have been formulated and perpetuated in such a way as to obscure the interdependence of parallel processes of state-building and democratization in generating the fundamental rules of the political game upon which the health of each depends.[1] An important corollary is that existing working theories of the state and democracy jointly obscure the critical processes of citizenship participation in building political firewalls against terrorism.

TERRORISM, DEMOCRACY, AND STATE WEAKNESS IN SUB-SAHARAN AFRICA

Contemporary literature testifies to the complexity of the phenomenon of terrorism.[2] One central aspect of terrorist behavior is that it disregards law. In this sense, it is a form of criminal behavior, but criminal behavior that attacks not just individuals but the foundations of political society as a whole. For example, as one recent work, "A description and understanding of terrorism is easy. It is the *unlawful* or threatened use of violence against individuals or property to coerce and intimidate governments or societies for political, religious, or ideological objectives" (Cilliers and Sturman 2002, 4, emphasis mine).

As a starting point, this is a serviceable, probably broadly acceptable definition up to a point. Its limits become apparent when one moves from a definition that is presumptively of universal applicability in the abstract and in normative terms to establishing a comparably universal *empirical* working definition. Definitions of terrorism are problematic for many reasons, not least because of the difficulty of establishing a clear distinction between legitimate and illegitimate political contestation. As more than one commentator has observed, one person's terrorism is another's political liberation struggle. This observation points to the difficulty of defining what political insurgents may do to advance their cause and what regimes may do to quell political contestation that may appear to threaten political order.

In mature, established, and democratic states, those who threaten or use violence are almost by definition defined as criminals or as a fringe element arrayed against an established political order accepted unequivocally by an overwhelming majority of citizens. The limits of acceptable political behavior can safely be left to adjudication by the courts in terms of constitutional and legislative provisions adopted by nearly universally accepted democratic processes.

The determination of what is legitimate political behavior and what is not, and therefore to be denoted as "terrorism," is a far deeper problem in weak, embryonically democratizing states that have become prevalent in the post–cold war world. In practical terms, governments are presumed to have the coercive power to determine and certify what is and is not legitimate political behavior. However, many states in

Africa have been widely characterized as hybrids, partially democratized governments that nonetheless display important residual manifestations of authoritarian rule. At the same time, this ambiguity, manifested in the limited and uncertain extent to which their writs run effectively within the territorial boundaries each purports to control, serves to exacerbate the weakness of African states themselves. In such circumstances, therefore, the question of what is legitimate has not been definitively established. Rival understandings of what is legitimate coexist at best uneasily with one another while the question of who has what capacity to define and enforce what is legitimate remains in dispute to varying and uncertain degrees. What constitutes illegal and illegitimate political behavior also remains in question. What is terrorism to one person is a legitimate liberation struggle to another because the underlying rules of the game defining legitimate and, therefore, legal behavior in weak states have not been definitively established.

Therefore, the campaign against terrorism depends not only, or perhaps even primarily, on attacking the terrorists directly. Rather, it demands great emphasis on strengthening the state, where the state is understood as a political community based on shared adherence to fundamental rules of the game as a foundation for adherence to the rule of law. Substantively, however, acts falling within the foregoing capsule definition of terrorism are *intrinsically* illegitimate, and in the abstract few would dispute such a claim. But the foregoing working definition itself makes clear that abstract normative principles about what constitutes legitimate and illegitimate political behavior must be codified in law established by sovereign polities in order to distinguish and isolate terrorist as well as common criminal behavior empirically from that which is lawful.

There is a deeper issue here, however, that harks back to the founding literature of modern political philosophy. It is an issue hinted at but only lightly explored in the analogous context of African states being under pressure to accept World Bank/International Monetary Fund structural adjustment medicine in order to stimulate their economies. The phenomenon of weak states whose laws and policies have enjoyed at best limited, conditional, opportunistic acceptance conjures up the specter of a return to the state of nature whose characteristics the early liberal political philosophers specialized in exploring. To the extent that a polity is unable to cause its writ to run compellingly and universally within its internationally recognized boundaries, *what other rules, if any, apply to the extent that polity's rules don't, that is, where and to the extent that a state of nature has reappeared?* Will Reno's (1998) work on warlord capitalist states in West Africa is instructive in detailing the extent to which not only state institutions but also the public sector itself, in Habermasian terms, is cannibalized and all but disappears. What rules apply in such a modern manifestation of philosophically hypothetical state of nature?

On this point, liberal theory offers at least two different broad scenarios. First, there is the Lockean state of nature. Locke believed the state of nature to be one of a peaceful enterprise governed by "natural" rules limiting acquisitiveness that are accessible to rational individuals. The state of nature remains viable until, on the basis of popular consent, money is introduced that sets aside those natural rules, causing conflicts requiring the formation of civil society and a state pledged to protect life, liberty, and property. Applied to contemporary circumstances, a Lockean perspective on a stateless order would depend on individuals determining that what we understand as terrorist behavior is irrational and contrary to their interests. Thus, on that basis, international regimes protecting both individual rights and sanctioning terrorist behavior are grounded in the interests of rational individuals. From this perspective, the actions of terrorists in the context of weak African states are not only reprehensible but irrational.

Second, however, a Hobbesian state of nature envisages a war of all against all where rational actors are preoccupied with accomplishing their self-preservation by whatever means are at hand. A precivil society Rousseauian variant hypothesizes a less egalitarian set of circumstances than in the Hobbesian scenario in which the strong rule with or without color of law. In contemporary circumstances, Hobbes might be expected to argue that the definition of what is lawful and what is not depends entirely on the capacity of a state to enforce its rules. Conversely, to the extent that the state's writ has ceased to run or rival pretenders to sovereign power offer conflicting rules of the game, what constitutes "lawful" political behavior and how it differs from what is "unlawful" becomes problematic. State weakness and/or incomplete transitions between two contrasting governing regimes, therefore, critically undermine the task of isolating terrorist behavior in order to proscribe and attack it.

One might claim that the rules and definitions set forth in applicable international regimes substitute for what Locke regarded as "natural," that is, that international regimes back up states and substitute for them when their authority is weak or has been undermined. On this basis, a Lockean scenario trumps a Hobbesian one, and acts made unlawful by those international regimes outlaw for everyone the use or threat of political violence even where a state empirically lacks the sovereign authority to enforce its laws. Clearly, for example, the international community has established that it has the resolve and the capacity to launch peacekeeping missions to make those rules effective, at least in certain circumstances.

At least two further fundamental problems present themselves, however. First, the international community has fashioned peacekeeping missions primarily only in post–civil war circumstances as a step in restoring or replacing a state that has collapsed. It has resisted intervening where states are merely weak and/or are in uncertain transitions from one domestic regime form to another. Second, international regimes have been the creation of states, while those resorting to terrorist behavior, as specified in the working definition, can be said to have made themselves effectively stateless by their actions. Individuals and groups who by their actions have made themselves effectively stateless can and do elevate alternative religious, political, and ideological norms of their own construction to levels at least commensurate with the place that functioning states and their citizens may assign to international conventions. In effect, therefore, they postulate a war of all against all at the level of universal political norms as well as in more practical terms.

In short, international regimes upholding basic human rights and proscribing terrorist behavior supply a basis for sanctioning the behavior of errant state behavior, rebuilding collapsed states, or strengthening the legitimacy of weak but compliant states. But they are no *substitute* in and of themselves, empirically, for strong rule-based states. The question, then, becomes how and on what basis to strengthen states so that they possess the legitimacy as well as the coercive capacity to resist and combat terrorism. To pose this question is to expose a fundamental and pervasive problem with the working operational understanding of what a state is that undermines efforts to strengthen them against terrorist depredations.

The root of the problem is a nearly universal practice in the academic literature as well as in the real world of reducing the state to a government's bureaucratic structures. One primary effect of blurring this distinction is to obliterate the idea of the state as a body of fundamental rules of the political game to which governments are answerable and to which citizens have assented. In its place, the working meaning of the state in most academic and practical usage is implicitly a bureaucracy that undertakes to govern a subject population. A second equally important consequence of this reductionism is to diminish greatly the idea of *citizen ownership* of the state, understood as a body of fundamental rules of the political game to which citiens have explicitly or implicitly assented. To be sure, normal usage of the idea of the rule of law implies basic standards of fair enforcement and adjudication. However, absent a pervasive understanding that this bureaucracy is accountable to underlying fundamental rules of the game accepted by the citizens to which they apply, the bureaucracy *per se* becomes the authoritative source of making, implementing, and adjudicating rules. Thereby, a fundamental feature distinguishing legitimate and strong state-based governance from the depredations of terrorists becomes blurred and diminished.

Democracy is a critical factor in this equation in a way that has tended to be overlooked in the continuing preoccupation with its electoral dimensions. A considerable volume of printer's ink has been expended recently in puzzling over the coexistence of partial democracy and persistent manifestations of authoritarian rule in what have been described as hybrid or "gray" democracies, sometimes rationalized as "democracy with adjectives." Authoritarian regimes have exhibited some adroitness in accommodating even reasonably free and fair elections and yet remaining in power. An equally widespread recognition in the literature that elections alone do not a democracy make has somehow not led to a clearer understanding of why and how hybrid regimes persist. What has been missing is an appreciation of the importance of democratic processes in state formation, understood as the formation and acceptance by citizens of fundamental rules of the political game, as well as in securing regime electoral accountability to its citizens.

The implication is that participatory processes of formulating, building popular acceptance of, and diffusing understanding of fundamental rules of the political game constitute the essence of state strengthening. Several corollaries follow. First, state strengthening in this way is the key to distinguishing, marginalizing, and ultimately defeating terrorism as antistate behavior. *Citizen ownership* of the fundamental rules of the game, promoted in this fashion, may constitute the strongest and most important bulwark against terrorism.

Second, democratic processes are essential in state strengthening thus defined. Even if the drafting of fundamental rules of the political game, normally in the form of constitutions, is a task for political elites, citizen input in their formation, acceptance, and diffusion of their understanding necessarily democratizes the process. Third, the phenomenon of hybrid partially democratic, partially authoritarian regimes may have been encouraged to the extent that initial multiparty elections have been permitted to assert both temporal and de facto logical priority over state reformation and strengthening as understood here. Fourth, unlike elections, the processes of diffusing understanding, building acceptance, and modifying as needed fundamental rules of the political game are ongoing ones by contrast to the periodic, finite events that are national elections.

Fifth, if international regimes cannot *substitute* for democratic state strengthening or what has been recommended here, extensive and sustained international support has been invaluable, perhaps even indispensable in some instances (Harbeson 1999). The question of the *justification* for international support for democratic state-building points to a hypothesis that scholars have only recently begun to explore in any depth. The evidence that al Qaeda and other major terrorist networks have flourished primarily in weak, fractured, or collapsed states such as Sudan, Somalia, and the Condo has suggested broadened recognition that the persistence of such dysfunctional states are not in the interests of the state system as a whole. Prior to the end of the cold war, there existed widespread recognition that for legitimacy weak states depended in large measure on recognition and inclusion in the family of nations symbolized by UN membership (Jackson 1990). Less apparent at the time was the extent to which those states were held together by authoritarian and corrupt rulers propped up by the cold war superpower rivalries. Increasingly apparent since the end of the cold war, and with the emergence of powerful nonstate-based terrorism, is that the integrity of the global state system is also dependent on individual states building the capacity to resist terrorism that potentially threatens all states. That is, the state system is only as strong as its weakest link.

IMPLICATIONS FOR THEORY AND POLICY

A particularly important implication of the foregoing review of some interconnections of terrorism and weak, partially democratizing states in sub-Saharan Africa is that these circumstances are important in broadening the existential bases upon which empirical political theory rests. The circumstance of weak states and nascent, partial democracies drives home the importance of building theory on more than the experience of states and democracies at the point where they have become durable and stable. Theory must reflect and speak to the experiences of the many states and democracies that still fall well short of realizing that objective. To fail to broaden the experiential foundations of theory in this way is to risk missing the importance of factors that may be critical to the strengthening of states and democracies.

The brief exploration of the problem of weak states and embryonic democracies in the context of strong nonstate-based global terrorist networks suggests a number of hypotheses concerning needed modifications of applicable theory. First, while democratic theory typically regards a stable state as a prerequisite for democratization, post–cold war African circumstances have suggested that democracy may be important in the process of state formation as well as a beneficiary of it. Second, a prevalent tendency to reduce the state to coercive bureaucracies has often diverted attention away from what should be the proper focus on state-building, at least in the early stages, namely, the state as fundamental ruler of the political game.

Third, as centrally important as free and fair elections are to democracy, democratic processes of formulating, adopting, amending, and diffusing understanding of fundamental rules of the political game may be both logical and temporal prior to initial elections. Fourth, for weak states and nascent democracies of the late twentieth and early twenty-first centuries, external support in facilitating their proper alignment with applicable international regimes may be essential in ways that existing democratic and state theories all but ignore. Fifth, the prominence of strong nonstate-based global terrorist networks may have brought to light a new post–cold war reality that strong states are as much in the interests of a healthy state system as legitimization by the state system is crucial to the durability of new and weak states.

The last point suggests some important policy directions that have a quality of going "back to the future." Condoleezza Rice suggested in congressional hearings following 9/11 the importance of "draining the swamps" that can and do incubate terrorism in weak African states (U.S. House of Representatives 2001). Rice's testimony brought home the reality that terrorism feeds on every aspect of the ongoing crisis of the human condition in sub-Saharan Africa. She warned that poverty, social and cultural oppression and discrimination, and grave weakening of the continent's human resources through HIV/AIDS, educational deprivation, and denial of adequate health care are not only unacceptable per se but contrary to the interests of the United States and other wealthy countries as well.

For two decades or more, however, the economies of industrialized states have become increasingly interdependent, carrying as a corollary the further marginalization and increasing relative impoverishment of African countries in the global economy. Multilateral and bilateral assistance has been employed to oblige or entice African states to adhere to political and economic norms asserted by industrialized states and stable democracies. The "implicit bargain," held out by the Washington consensus, that increased foreign investment would reward compliant states has been forthcoming at best at modest levels. Perhaps equally serious in the era of non-state-based global terrorist networks is the prospect that powerful states may oblige weak states to comply with their global antiterrorist campaigns in ways that may be antithetical to those states' efforts to strengthen their democratic institutions.

All these post–cold war realities are strikingly reminiscent of those that occurred during the early and middle years of the cold war. At that time, the fear and threat of communism prompted U.S. and other Western powers to hypothesize that impoverished newly independent states could be tempted by the blandishments of communism, thereby threatening the West's global military and political strategic interests. They therefore deemed generous foreign assistance to ameliorate third world poverty and strengthen weak states to be advantageous to themselves as well as, they hoped, the newly independent countries. The obvious potential tension between donor and recipient countries in the foreign assistance relationship was recognized but regarded as of secondary importance given the overarching raison d'être for both sets of parties. In the first years of the post–cold war era, one prominently cited rationale for sharply diminished levels of foreign assistance to combat African poverty was that such aid was, after all, no more than an artifact of the now-concluded cold war. The implications of the preceding analysis are that global terrorism has supplied a new rationale for extensive foreign assistance once provided by global communism.

The political rationale for foreign assistance has thus come full circle—almost. The fundamental difference is that weak states in Africa and elsewhere are not likely once again to be propped up by military and political alliances as they once were in the cold war era. The strengthening of weak states must be a project of those states themselves to a much greater extent than earlier, albeit with external assistance in support of an array of international regimes upholding human rights and democracy and proscribing terrorism. The strengthening of African states, however, appears to hinge on an amended understanding of what constitutes the essence of stateness and of democracy's role in its cultivation. These lessons of African experience represent important contributions to political theory that may redound to the benefit of all the members of the family of nations.

NOTES

1. I explore this in a paper entitled "Resurrecting Political Community: Democratization and the State in Sub-Saharan Africa" for the 2003 American Political Science Association meetings and am presently preparing the paper for publication.

2. Among the key recent and relevant works on which the chapter relies are Cilliers and Sturman (2002), Mogthaddam and Marsella (2004), Laqueur (2001), Walker (2002), Rotberg (2003), and U.S. House of Representatives (2001).

REFERENCES

Cilliers, Jakkie, and Kathryn Sturman, eds. 2002. *Africa and Terrorism*. Pretoria, South Africa: Institute for Security Studies No. 73.

Harbeson, John W. "Rethinking Democratic Transitions: Lessons from Eastern and Southern Africa." In *State, Conflict and Democracy in Africa*, ed. Richard Joseph, 39–57.

Jackson, Robert H. 1990. *Quasi-States: Sovereignty, International Relations, and the Third World*. Cambridge and New York: Cambridge University Press.

Laqueur, Walter. 2001. *A History of Terrorism*. New Brunswick, N.J.: Transaction Publishers.

Reno, Will. 1998. *Warlord Politics and African States*. Boulder, Colo.: Lynne Rienner Publishers.

Rotberg, Robert, ed. 2003. *State Failure and State Weakness in a Time of Terror*. Washington, D.C.: Brookings Institution.

U.S. House of Representatives. 2001. *Africa and the War on Global Terrorism*. Hearing before the Subcommittee on Africa of the Committee on International Relations of the U.S. House of Representatives, November 15.

Walker, Clive. 2002. *Blackstone's Guide to the Anti-Terrorism Legislation*. Oxford: Oxford University Press.

15 Resilient Authoritarianism, Uncertain Democratization, and Jihadism in Algeria

INTRODUCTION

The Algerian complex crisis (1992 to the present) has claimed thousands of lives, mostly innocent civilians.[1] Many an observer has been puzzled by the level of brutality of the armed Islamist[2] groups. Anthropologists, sociologists, and political scientists alike have been bewildered by the degree of violence and sheer barbarity that Islamist extremists have used in the fratricide conflict. This violent behavior can be traced to a variety of factors: failure of state policies, lack of democratic political culture, the elite's simplistic version of the war of national liberation (1954–62), manipulation of Islam by both the state and Islamist groups of all persuasions, and external factors such as the drop in oil prices, ramifications of the East-West confrontation in Afghanistan, and the collapse of the Soviet bloc.

Among the endogenous factors, one can cite, for example, how postindependence rulers propagated the view, with a degree of success, that Algeria owed its victory against colonial France to armed struggle alone. While armed struggle is only a moment, albeit inevitable, in the march toward national independence and nation- and state-building, Algeria's rulers glorified violence against the enemy at the expense of politics, which played a critical role in the denouement of the savage war. Combined with the absence of democratic channels and the suppression of an autonomous civil society after independence, that vision helped create among the young generations, who did not experience the anticolonialist war, belief in violence as the ultimate alternative to resolving conflict.

While the responsibility of successive regimes for the crisis is indisputable, that of the Islamists, even those who did not necessarily resort to violence, is even greater. Indeed, the responsibility of the Islamists consisted of falsifying history and claiming that the Algerian war of liberation was a jihad, a holy war against the enemy, to reestablish Islam in the country. It is therefore no wonder—despite the absurdity of their allegation—that the armed Islamist factions fought for the overthrow of the "infidel" [taghut] state. Thus, killing even of innocent civilians was justified since the struggle was conducted in the name of God for the establishment of a never-defined Islamic state and society. The redemption of society required all means, including the most atrocious.

A brief examination of the place of Islam in contemporary Algerian society may shed some light on recent events. Furthermore, in analyzing Algeria, one should be aware of the successful propaganda that radical Islamist groups (RIGs)[3] and salafi (fundamentalist) jihadist groups[4] (SJGs) have used to manipulate public opinion to such a degree that the state rather than the groups that have committed the atrocities appeared as the culpable party. Although state repression in the last decade has been robust, there is no doubt that RIGs and SJGs are responsible for most of the killings.

ISLAM AND POLITICS

Politics and religion in Algeria have always been intertwined. The Islamic religion and traditions permeate both civil society and the state. In fact, Islam in Algeria, more than in any other Middle Eastern society, has come to constitute the basis of identity and culture. Islamic beliefs regulate social behavior and, to a large extent, also govern social relations. The Algerian state has, since independence in 1962, despite its secularist inclinations, always resorted to Islamic symbols to establish and reproduce its legitimacy. Paradoxically, social movements and the religious opposition have used Islam not only to wage their struggle against the established regimes but also to challenge the religious claims of the state. In sum, these groups have sought to de-legitimize the state and the elites in charge of governing the country.

Radical Islamism emerged as the most important and potent protest movement in the years following the death of Houari Boumediene in December 1978. Although authoritarian and populist, the regime of Boumediene (1965–1978) had succeeded in creating a substantial level of legitimacy and support among the masses. The success of the regime stemmed mostly from the overall socioeconomic performance it achieved. Regardless of one's opinion of the Islamist movement in Algeria, neither Islam nor the Islamist phenomenon can be dissociated from the country's history and from the nationalist movement. Thus, to assert that the Islamist movement, not necessarily in its violent form, is one of the belated progeny of colonial rule is no exaggeration. While the movement is the product of a combination of factors, including the socioeconomic failure of the 1980s, particularly after the drop in oil prices in 1986, the doctrinal underpinnings draw partly from the crisis of identity caused by 132 years of colonial domination. The brutality of French rule in Algeria is legendary. The colonial authorities did not content themselves with killing, pillaging, plundering, and exploiting the entire natural and human resources. They also expropriated the principal local religious institutions: mosques and religious schools were closed, religious lands were expropriated, and Islamic culture was projected as inferior to Christian/Western civilization. Thus, French colonial domination in Algeria went beyond the monopolistic control that French capitalism exerted over commerce, banks, industry, and agriculture. The colonial state operated a systematic uprooting of Arab and Islamic culture. The French administration exercised almost full control over the cultural and religious activities of indigenous Muslims, who made up the overwhelming majority of the population. Unlike the European minority, Muslims lived in poverty and were denied basic religious, cultural, political, and economic rights. Because France resorted to extremely coercive ways to establish its cultural hegemony, and because French colonialists treated the native population and values with contempt, Algerians had no other recourse but to cling to Islam. Not surprisingly, Islam became— and still is—the most salient component of Algerians' national identity. Although secular in nature, the nationalist movement, too, used Islamic values as symbols for popular mobilization against colonialists. Most of the leaders of the nationalist movement, whose struggle culminated in the War of National Liberation (1954–62), were French-educated and held a secular vision of politics and society. Yet, the war against the French was conducted as jihad, and fighters were designated as mujahideens (holy warriors). The nationalist movement was not homogeneous; an important component came from religious associations.

ISLAM AND NATION- AND STATE-BUILDING

After independence, Algeria established an authoritarian regime characterized by the absence of political pluralism in which a small group, backed by the military, held power. The single party, the Front de Libération Nationale (FLN), which led the revolution, controlled civil society. The state drew its legitimacy not from any democratic process, but from the war of liberation and a developmentalist strategy in which Islam held a privileged position. The references to Islam and socialism rested on the notion of social justice, which Algerians were deprived of during the colonial years. Yet, the clientelist system that the authorities instituted did not correspond to the socialist discourse or to Islamic morality, because ultimately only small segments of the population truly benefited from development policies despite some initial successes. Undoubtedly, the original achievements of industrialization in the 1970s and the tangible social benefits it provided (free medical care, free education, and the little taxation made possible by the oil rent) did preserve the consensus and save the tacit social contract for a time. In the 1970s, promises for a better future were indeed credible. But when the state failed to deliver on its promises in the 1980s, its legitimacy was inevitably undermined and the whole edifice, painstakingly put together, began to crumble. The question of Islamism, therefore, cannot be dissociated from the process of nation- and state-building and its failures (Zoubir 1994, 1995).

Early on, Algerian authorities used Islam for political and ideological purposes. In order to build a modern identity and to gain legitimacy, successive regimes sought to integrate what they defined as a modern type of Islam into revolutionary, vanguard perspectives. Thus Islam, understood in its modernized form, was decreed the religion of the state in the 1963, 1976, 1989, and 1996 constitutions and was conceived as the foundation of identity of Algerian citizens. In the so-called socialist era (1962–80), the role of the state consisted not only of bestowing upon citizens the material benefits of the modern world (work, education, and all kinds of services) but also of promoting Islamic principles and morality. The authorities hoped to achieve this objective through the construction of mosques, the teaching of the Arabic language, and the creation of a multitude of religious institutions. The state established its monopoly over religious life and stifled interpretations which deviated from the official norms that the state propagated.

ISLAMIST CHALLENGE TO THE STATE

Various Islamist organizations have challenged the regime at different times and to different degrees since 1962. Thus, to attribute the emergence of Islamism to socioeconomic factors alone, though the latter have undoubtedly contributed to its eruption, would be erroneous.

The first Islamist association, El-Qiyam al Islamyya (Islamic values), founded in 1963, enjoyed a practically legal existence until 1970. The organization's aversion to the socialist and secular policies adopted by the country's single-party system mobilized a few religious figures. The association included individuals such as Abassi Madani, future leader of the Islamic Salvation Front (FIS). Opposition to socialism was only one aspect of El-Qiyam's slogans. The organization also put forth other demands that future Islamists would in due course include in their agendas: full implementation of the shari'a (Islamic law); closing of stores during Friday prayers, a demand satisfied in 1976 by the Houari Boumediene regime; a ban on the sale of alcohol; exclusion of non-Muslims from public jobs; separate beaches for men and women; introduction of religious teaching in schools, which was instituted in 1964; and interdiction for women's participation in sports as well as parades celebrating national holidays. The "cultural" association sought the banning of all non-Muslim organizations (secularist, Marxist-socialist, or nationalist).

Foreign ideologues, such as Jamal ul din al Afghani, Mohamed Abduh, Shakib Arslan, Hassan al Banna, Sayyid Qutb, Mohammed al Ghazali, and Abu 'ala al Mawdudi, exerted a certain degree of influence on the association. El-Qiyam paved the way for future Islamist organizations in Algeria; its members remained anchored within the system, thus exerting pressure to extract further concessions from the state on moral, socioeconomic, and cultural issues.

El-Qiyam was not unique in using Islam as an instrument of opposition to the regime. A traditional current linked to the jamaat al 'ulema (Association of Religious Scholars), successor of the preindependence "reformist" association founded by Sheikh Abdelhamid Bin Badis in 1931, expressed on several occasions its opposition to government policies. Jamaat al 'ulema was actually close to the El-Qiyam. The association criticized what it perceived as Westernization of Algerian society and degradation of Islamic values. Bitter attacks against Boumediene's socialist policies and alleged degradation of morals in Algeria came from one of the forefathers of Algerian Islamism, the imam Abdellatif Soltani, who criticized socialism as a foreign ideology incompatible with Islam, for Islam does not prohibit private property. Sheikh Soltani also attacked the alleged atheism that resulted from secular teaching in public schools. He saw shari'a as the response to all problems that society faced, a perspective still prevalent within most Islamist factions.

THE RADICALIZATION OF POLITICAL ISLAM

Most commentators argue that jihadist Islam emerged in Algeria following the interruption of the electoral process in January 1992 or that state policies alone were responsible for the emergence of a violent movement. This is an inaccurate and simplistic view for several reasons. Violent RIGs—though quite small until the emergence of the FIS and not yet constituting a movement properly speaking

—have operated in the country since the 1960s. Islamism as a powerful social movement emerged in the late 1970s and early 1980s; its radicalization intensified in the 1980s. The rise of the movement resulted from a variety of factors of which failure of state policies, especially those related to welfare, constituted only one aspect. Given that the state established its almost total domination over the public sphere and hindered blossoming of the private domain, only the mosque could offer an existential refuge. The mosque also became a moral substitute for alcohol, drugs, and violence, which had constituted the main pursuit hitherto. The state ceased to be seen as the provider; instead, society, especially its youth, felt betrayed by an elite who seemed oblivious to the predicament of the youth. Thus, not only did the youth communicate with the state through violence, expressed in the form of cyclical riots, but they also rejected all the founding myths and symbols of the Algerian nation. In other words, the state lost its legitimacy and its raison d'être in the eyes of this disenchanted population.

In sum, although the question of Islam in the political system has always been central, the recent phenomenon of radical Islamism resulted from a combination of factors. Failure of social, economic, and cultural modernization is one major cause. The secularist elites, like those in many other Arab-Islamic countries, understood modernization in its material sense only. Thus, they failed to take into account the necessity for a process of secularization, which, despite Islamist or fundamentalist claims to the contrary, is not necessarily antithetical to Islamic values. The regime failed in its attempt to reconcile a Western model of modernization, without its democratic values to be sure, with a traditional, patriarchal society. In many ways, the state helped strengthen Islamism because it perpetuated neopatriarchy that rests on demagogic and equivocal positions of religious and cultural issues. Moreover, the corruption and inefficiency of the regime, which hampered genuine development policies, led to intolerable stagnancy. Evidently, the blame for failure of the developmentalist strategy cannot be put solely on the state. Demographic explosion contributed a great deal to the worsening socioeconomic problems. Worse still, the trauma that followed chaotic urbanization, which resulted from the dislocation of traditional society, debilitated the diffident modernization programs, especially in the sociocultural realm. The result was an identity crisis, with disastrous consequences. The failure of Arab nationalism and concomitant defeats suffered by Arab regimes against Israel, success of the Iranian Revolution, and humiliations by the West, such as the war against Iraq in 1991 and in 2003, provided additional ingredients for continued radicalization of the Islamist movement.

Another factor that facilitated the growth and rapid expansion of Islamism was the state's loss of control over the thousands of mosques that the state had built since independence. The "volunteers," often self-proclaimed Islamist imams, with little or no theological training, progressively took control of mosques from which they propagated their radical ideology. The mosque was no longer a place of prayer; it became the political base of the Islamist movement and the place where future emirs of the RIGs and SJGs were formed. By then, of course, state-appointed imams had lost their credibility because of their pacifist, apolitical inclinations and their identification with the regime. After the 1988 uprising, the FIS, founded in March 1989 following the liberalization process, was already in control of practically all mosques in the country.

The most violent, albeit small, RIGs rallied around Mustapha Bouyali, who founded the Armed Islamic Movement (MIA) in 1982 and served as its emir until his violent death in 1987. Bouyali's actions epitomized the impulsive response that some Algerians used against the state because of a lack of democratic channels to express frustrations and disenchantment with modernization. The 1979 Iranian Revolution also bolstered Algerian RIGs, who were persuaded that no matter how strong a state was, it could be brought down. The forerunner of the MIA was an organization, also created by Bouyali, known as the Group for the Struggle against the Illicit, which had conducted attacks against bars and individuals. The organization had little influence, and soon Bouyali was forced to search for more effective means—armed struggle—against the regime. Even though many Islamists were in agreement with Bouyali regarding the foundation of an Islamic state in Algeria, other Islamist activists did not share the violence he and his followers, such as Ahmed Merah, advocated. Bouyali believed that a small, well-disciplined organization, made up of determined individuals committing political assassinations and acts of sabotage, could seize power and hold on to it until they succeeded in swaying the population to their cause. That belief was strengthened following the 1982 arrest of Islamist figures with no links to the MIA, such as Abdelatif Soltani, Ahmed Sahnoun, and Abassi Madani, over incidents that took place at the University of Algiers. The authorities dismantled Bouyali's organization rather quickly. However, security forces were unable to trap and kill Bouyali and a handful of his followers until 1987. In 1989, President Chadli Bendjedid pardoned Bouyali's hard-core disciples in the hope of preventing further radicalization of the movement. But many of them eventually joined the guerrilla war waged in the 1990s and led by well-equipped RIGs who were more extremist and better organized.

In the 1990s, domestic and international events unleashed RIGs, which nearly swept away the Algerian state. Indeed, the botched liberalization process initiated after the riots of October 1988 was mainly beneficial to the most radical within the Islamist movement under the banner of the FIS, which, in opposition to the Algerian constitution, was nonetheless legalized by the authorities.

THE FIS: THE UMBRELLA FOR RIGS/SJGS

From its creation in February 1989 until its ban in March 1992, the FIS consisted of a diversity of groups and ideological currents.[5] The heterogeneous leadership of the FIS, combining radicalized salafists and new activist militants who never really agreed on the means to achieve power—their principal preoccupation—vowed to establish a vaguely defined Islamic state. The aspirations of the various groups integrated in the FIS diverged greatly. Some upheld a millenarian vision; hence, recourse to violence, whose major aim was dismantling the nation-state in its current design, was an intrinsic part. For others, the objective was limited to a mere substitution of the Islamist elite for the one currently in charge of the state. Still others had no clear strategy whatsoever; nihilism best characterizes their mind-set. What is certain, though, is that the chief objective within the FIS was the appropriation of the state by legal (electoral) means for some or through violence for others. Yet, in spite of its heterogeneous nature, the FIS articulated a dominant ideological discourse that addressed important political and social issues. But, because of the ideologization of Islam, which unavoidably shifted the core of the debate from theological concerns to norms and values of the sociopolitical domain, core beliefs of Islam were either retrograded or entirely cloaked. Like many other Islamist movements in the Middle East and North Africa, a number of FIS leaders came under the influence of Egyptian and Indo-Pakistani Islamists, such as Hassan Al-Banna, Sayyid Qutb, Abul A'la Mawdudi, and Mohammed Ghazali. The major components of the discourse were around those "ills" that have plagued modern society and led to its "decadence." In their view, contemporary secular ideologies—such as liberalism, socialism, communism, and feminism—have replaced religion and corrupted societies. In the vein of the principal Islamists who inspired them, many FIS leaders believed that the evils of the *jahilyia* (pre-Islamic society) have not only plagued the Western world but also have been blindly emulated in Islamic societies. Islam, in their opinion, is the only solution to such grave problems. The state in Islamic societies has failed to carry out its duties and thus has deviated from the divine commandments and in fact contributed to the *jahilyia*. The regimes should be considered infidels and must therefore be fought through a jihad. By the same token, the assassination (*qital*) of rulers would be perfectly lawful (*halal*) from a religious perspective.

RIGs in Algeria developed an interpretation of Islam that refuted any liberal reading. They bitterly opposed any attempt to justify the separation of politics from religion. *Laïcité* (secularism), the separation of state and religion, constitutes in their eyes the biggest threat to Islamic societies. The objective underlying such interpretation was quite functional. The appeal from RIGs derived particularly from a critique of the secular state, which, in their view, failed in its tasks precisely because it had stayed away from Islam. One can easily see how Islamists could successfully use similar arguments against the democratic forces that based their position on secular principles. Consequently, democratic values become, in the RIGs' conception, sacrilegious and totally antithetical to Islam. Secular values, upon which democracy is said to rest, lead to disharmony (*fitna*) within Islamic societies. The irony is that these conclusions regarding secularism and democracy do not derive from any theological or serious political analysis of the concepts. The whole discourse regarding those concepts serves one purpose: propaganda within the context of a strategy of conquest of power. But there is evidence, which derives from their own speeches, that had radical Islamists been allowed to take power in 1992, they would almost certainly have discarded the republican constitution and outlawed secular political parties altogether.

The radicalism of the FIS and the perceived threat it posed to the regime and armed forces resulted in annulment of the legislative election in January 1992. Following that interruption and the banning of the party, the slow decomposition of the FIS and imprisonment of its political leaders led eventually to the preponderance of RIGs and SJGs that threatened the very fabric of Algerian society. In fact, the state itself was on the brink of collapse during 1993–95.

While the origins of Islamism in Algeria are undoubtedly domestic, external factors played a considerable role in the reinforcement of the movement. Because so much focus was on the FIS, many analysts failed to investigate the various extremist RIGs and SJGs within its structures. In essence, they failed to see the control of the Algerian "Afghans" over many autonomous SJGs and the support that they received from abroad to destroy the state. Not until 9/11 did analysts begin to study the connection between Algerian RIGs and the international jihadist Islamist network.

RIGS/SJGS, THE IRANIAN REVOLUTION, AND THE AFGHAN CONNECTION

The 1979 Iranian Revolution had an important impact in Algeria. Several Islamists revealed that the MIA was in fact born in 1979. The first jihadist appeals appeared in 1982. Sheik Othman's Jamaát al Jihad in western Algeria supported Bouyali's call for a jihad against the "tyrannical and impious regime." Various groups had planned the assassination of important political figures. The attempts failed only because the security services succeeded in dismantling a number of RIGs.

The other external event related to the war in Afghanistan during 1978–90. Bouyali's group threatened to assassinate Soviet citizens in Algeria unless the Soviet Union stopped meddling in Afghanistan's domestic affairs. The war in Afghanistan infuriated Islamist militants the world over, who perceived Soviet involvement in that country as a communist war against Islam. Thus, Mahfoud Nahnah, the representative in Algeria of the Muslim Brotherhood organization, helped in the recruitment of young Algerians—even those living in France— eager to fight the Soviets in Afghanistan. Approximately three thousand Algerian volunteers received military training, mostly in Peshawar, to fight the Soviets. The Peshawar-based Palestinian salafi militant Abdallah Azzem exerted a strong ideological influence on these "combatants of Islam." Several local and foreign organizations, such as *daáwa wa'l tabligh* (predication and transmission) or *daáwa wa'l irshad* (predication and orientation) helped these young volunteers, many of whom were unemployed, make their journey to Pakistan. Many of the jihadists eventually joined the Armed Islamic Group (GIA), the most ruthless RIG in Algeria. In fact, some sources claim that Nacereddine Ouahabi (alias Qari Saïd al-Jazaïri), an adherent to the *al hijra wa'l takfyir,* was the principal founder of the GIA in Pakistan in 1991. Given that most Arab "Afghans"—who made up Osama bin Laden's al Qaeda organization—considered that democracy was *kofr* (blasphemy), it is no wonder that the GIA condemned the FIS for participating in elections and for not rejecting democracy. For the Arab "Afghans," the establishment of the Islamic state would come only through jihad.

Upon their return to Algeria in the late 1980s, the "Afghans" established contacts with salafi leaders in the FIS as well as with Bouyali's old companions—for example, Abdelkader Chebouti and Mansour Miliani. Their objective was to launch the jihad in Algeria. The interruption of the electoral process in January 1992 provided the justification—not that they needed one—to begin the assault on the state, its institutions, and its representatives. A spectacular commando action occurred in February 1992 against the Amirauté naval base in Algiers. This, however, was not the first such attack—a deadly action had already taken place in December 1991 against a military base in Guemmar in the southeastern part of the country. The "Afghans" brutally murdered young conscripts and seized automatic weapons. From 1992 onward, the RIGs launched countless other bloody operations. Various armed organizations, such as Chebouti's Movement of the Islamic State (MEA) or Qam'r Eddine Kherbane's *al baqyun al a'hd* (those loyal to the oath), and many other RIGs would for a time join under one umbrella organization, the GIA. The experience that the "Afghans" acquired in Pakistan and Afghanistan proved quite useful not only militarily but also in helping those "Afghans" take command, as emirs, over the SJGs. They managed to produce simple explosives and weapons (e.g., the *hebhab*, an archaic rocket launcher) that were devastating. According to intelligence sources in Algeria, the GIA received financial support as well as weapons from a variety of foreign sources. Morocco constituted a secure logistical base for the GIA; the weapons that were acquired in Europe and elsewhere transited through Morocco. Apparently, the seven thousand-strong Salvation Islamic Army (AIS), the armed branch of the FIS that surrendered in 1997,[6] did not receive the same support from abroad as did the GIA. Perhaps the explanation lies in the connection to the "Afghans" enjoyed by the GIA. Members of the GIA, who surrendered in the late 1990s, testified that the GIA received financial aid and sophisticated transmission equipment from bin Laden. The latter provided the jihadists with offices in Yemen, the Sudan, and other countries.

RIGS, SJGS, AND THEIR IDEOLOGICAL REFERENTS

Despite the presence of groups that shared similar views to the SJGs, the ideological referents of the FIS were rather straightforward. The demands were mostly socioeconomic and political, even if the party's discourse was political discourse wrapped in religious cloak. However, the ideological referents of the SJGs were less clear and created lots of confusion because they were alien to most Algerians. This is why understanding the role that the "Afghans" played within the Islamist movement and the beliefs that foreign ideologues propagated and communicated to the various *katibat* (phalanges)[7] helps shed light on the horrible acts the SJGs committed against innocent civilians regardless of sex, age, or profession. It also helps to explain the deadly infighting among different armed groups and why many individuals preferred to surrender to the state authorities rather than carry on the jihad.

The cancellation of the electoral process in January 1992 led to the fragmentation of the FIS into a number of SJGs, which fought a fierce struggle for power and/or the unification of the various groups under one umbrella. Although calls for jihad were made before 1992 by few individuals or were used as a threat to extract concessions from the regime, from 1992 onward such calls became widespread. The celerity and effectiveness with which commando operations were conducted proved beyond a doubt the SJGs' longtime preparation. Mustapha Bouyali's old companions—Mansour Meliani, Abdelkader Chebouti, Rabah Gettaf, and Baa Azzedine as well as "Afghans" such as Mustapha Suni and Abdenacer El Eulmi—multiplied the operations of the MIA, which they had resurrected the previous year. Successful attacks were launched against military barracks to steal weapons. The El Muwahidun group and hijra wal takfyir also initiated commando operations to rob explosives. In February 1992, Chebouti and Said Makhloufi created the Movement for the Islamic State (MEI) to replace the MIA, which in 1993 became the AIS. The MEI's proclaimed objective was the organization of the jihad throughout the country, and even within the barracks, and the overthrow of the secular state. The Saudi-trained member of the FIS, Sheik Yekhlef Cherati, had pronounced a fatwa (religious edict) that made licit the killing of the security forces and their families.

A collection of individuals finally decided to consecrate the GIA with the aim of intensifying the armed struggle to establish the Islamic state. Abu Adlan (whose real name is Abdelhak Layada) took over the leadership of the GIA from October 1992 until July 21, 1993. Benameur Benaissa, known as the "executioner," succeeded him for a month. Mourad Sid Ahmed (alias Jaafar el Afghani) ruled over the GIA from August 1993 until his death on February 27, 1994. Another "Afghan," Gousmi Cherif (alias Abu Abdullah Ahmed) took command of the GIA in March until his death on September 26, 1994. From 1992 until Gousmi's death, the GIA targeted individuals (state employees, security forces, intellectuals, and foreigners) for assassination. The GIA also undertook major operations of sabotage against factories, railways, roads, and bridges as well as attacks against banks, public offices, clinics, and, of course, military garrisons. Unlike what occurred in subsequent years, the GIA spared civilian populations in the hope that they would support and adhere to the organization's projects. There was an obvious attempt to discredit the state and demonstrate the latter's incapacity to guarantee public safety. The GIA also sought to create an atmosphere of fear and paralysis so that the state structures would stop functioning, thus leading to the collapse of the state, a goal that the GIA nearly achieved. Whatever the other objectives, the GIA aimed at seizing the maximum weapons and ammunition to wage war against an infidel state.

Under the leadership of Jamel Zitouni (October 27, 1994–July 16, 1996), the GIA witnessed consequential changes. Zitouni launched a campaign against not only the Jaz'arists (Algerianists), whom he accused of treason for trying to take over the leadership of the GIA, but also against the "Afghans" so the local leaders of the movement could control the organization. The bitter struggle within the GIA's leadership also derived from Zitouni's decision to attack civilians. Mustapha Kertali, for instance, emir of Katibat Errahman, claims that he broke away from the GIA because he could not find a religious argument to justify the killing of the families of the security forces. Although it lost the support of many local leaders and religious figures, the GIA benefited from the backing of the Egyptian Ayman

Al-Dhawahri and the London-based Palestinian exegete Abu Qutada, whose fatwas justified the horrendous atrocities that the GIA committed; he enunciated the fatwa, which justified the killing of the spouses and children of security forces.

The GIA witnessed tremendous dissidence under Zitouni's leadership. The reasons for the dissidence revolved around religious interpretations concerning the methods of the jihad—*jaz'arist* and salafi dissidents accused him of having only limited theological knowledge—but also over power issues, with the influential emirs accusing him of being incapable of leading the GIA. Gradually, the GIA lost most of its outside support and began splintering into a multitude of groups owing allegiance to self-proclaimed emirs, all claiming to be true to the salafi tradition. Among the most notorious groups is the Islamic Front for Armed Jihad (FIDA), created in 1992, that specialized in the assassination of intellectuals; the *katiba* of Sid Ali Belhajar, which became in 1997 the Islamic League for Predication and Jihad (LIDD); the *katiba* of Mustapha Kertali, who, following his dissidence from the GIA, created the Islamic Movement for Predication and Jihad (MIPD); *jama'at humat al Daáwa al salafyia* (Guardians of the Salafi Predication [DHDS]), also known as *katiba al Ahwal; El Jama'a el salafyia lil daáwa wa'l jihad* (Salafi Group for Predication and Jihad [GSPD]); *El jama'a el salafyia el mukatila* (Salafi Combatant Group [GSC]); and many others.

The atomization of the jihadist groups coincided with Zitouni's decision to attack French interests in Algeria.[8] This period was also characterized by deadly struggles among various autonomous groups, leading to the assassination of important emirs, including Zitouni, who was killed by Sid Ali Belhajar. In addition, this period witnessed horrendous crimes against all segments of Algerian society and the near collapse of the state.

The accession of Antar Zouabri (alias "Abu Talha"), an illiterate criminal, to the head of the GIA on July 18, 1996, marked yet another period in the jihadist struggle in Algeria. Zouabri's reign, which lasted until his violent death in February 2002, was marked by further dissidence within the GIA, the most noteworthy being that of Hassan Hattab, who eventually founded in 1998 Salafi Group for Predication and Combat (GSPC) as an alternative to the GIA. Hattab advocated a "clean jihad," a decision that led Zouabri to use even more barbaric methods to demonstrate his control over the jihadist movement. While the GSPC allegedly targeted mostly military objectives, the GIA directed its attacks against entire civilian communities.

To outside observers, the crimes that the jihadist groups have committed are incomprehensible; however, the jihadists have always sought to provide religious endorsement for their crimes. For instance, the London-based Egyptian self-proclaimed exegete Abu Hamza el Misri, an "Afghan" veteran who preached at the mosque in Finsbury Park, legitimated Antar Zouabri's actions. In fact, in

1997 Abu Hamza allowed the publication of the newspaper *Al-Ansar*, which had been suspended during Zitouni's reign. Most jihadist groups find justification for their violent acts in the teachings of the *al-salaf al-salih* (virtuous or pious forefathers), such as Ibn Hanbal, Ibn Abdelwahab, and Ibn Taymia.[9] The SJGs, who use self-proclaimed imams who barely hold any theological knowledge, seek to legitimize jihad by apostatizing entire populations. Thus, in order to justify the massacres on a large scale, Abu Al-Mundher (real name Mahfoud Assouli), Zouabri's "legal officer,"[10] apostatized all those who fought, even through their writings, the mujahideen (i.e., the SJGs) as well as those opposed to the jihad. Of course, those who provide logistical support are spared from the massacres. But the families of members of the AIS, which had agreed in 1997 to a cease-fire with the authorities, were also branded as apostates and thus their killing was religiously justified. Members of the GIA never hesitate to distort or provide fallacious interpretations of verses of the Koran or the hadiths (Prophet Muhammad's sayings) to justify their odious crimes.

The most important salafi group is the GSPC, which has a membership of about 350 individuals and is concentrated in the eastern part of the country. The GSPC, led by Hassan Hattab, formerly a prominent figure of the GIA—he headed three phalanges and later commanded the GIA's Zone II—is also a salafi jihadist organization. Hattab claims that he left the GIA because he refused to condone the excommunication of the Algerian people by Zitouni and Zouabri. However, in the twenty-four-point document in which he lays out his thinking, Hattab states unequivocally that the fight against apostates will continue. Any regime in Algeria can be considered a tyranny if it opposes Muslims, which incidentally is a position similar to that advanced by the FIS during its legal existence. In sum, the difference between the GIA and the GSPC concerns the target: for the former there was no discrimination between civilians and military, whereas for the latter the main target is security forces.

The GSPC, whose membership includes a great number of "Afghans," has benefited, according to Algerian security officials, from bin Laden's support since its creation. According to a former member of the organization, bin Laden himself suggested the name of the GSPC. Undoubtedly, the support that the GIA and the GSPC have received from abroad has prolonged the conflict in Algeria.

Like the GIA and the multitude of small phalanges, the GSPC has refused to give up the jihad despite the law of the Civil Concord, which basically grants amnesty for those who have taken arms against the government. Though this is not the place to provide a sociological analysis, suffice it to say that these groups, whatever their ideological pretensions, are today groups of bandits rather than religious zealots. The kidnapping of foreign tourists in the Sahara desert in February 2003 is a case in point, even if the $80 million ransom paid by the German government in August 2003 to secure release of the hostages will supposedly be used for the purchase of weapons to continue the struggle against the "apostate" regime. The fatwas that justify racketeering of the populations as well as the bank robberies are merely a subterfuge that helps militants gain a modicum of credibility among a population that has rejected them. Undoubtedly, socioeconomic and political reforms coupled with better governance will be the best answer to bringing an end to the existence of such groups.

THE GOVERNMENT MEASURES TO COMBAT TERRORISM

The Armed Islamist insurrection took the security forces by surprise. The authorities never imagined the formidable organization and the armament of the jihadist groups. The level of uncontrolled destruction that the armed groups inflicted upon the state structures, personnel, intellectuals, journalists, moderate Islamists, and various strata of society was such that few doubted the demise of the Algerian state. The question that analysts asked was not whether but how soon the state would collapse and the Islamists would take over, thus compelling many governments, including the United States, to contemplate the possibility of an Islamist regime. Whether out of fear of Islamist reprisals or other considerations, many governments refused to assist Algerian authorities in the fight against terrorism. Indeed, not until December 2002, during William Burns's visit to Algeria, was it decided that the United States would provide nonlethal military equipment to Algerian security forces to combat terrorism.

In the period 1994–95, the Algerian authorities realized that unless they mobilized all the resources at their disposal, including the civilian population, they would fail to confront the Islamist armed groups. The armed forces were not ready for an antiterrorist struggle. The National Popular Army (ANP), which took up the task of confronting the armed groups, was organized as a modern army prepared to defend the territory against foreign forces, mainly Morocco, Libya, or France. In fact, most of the ANP's 130,000-strong forces, 80 percent of whom consisted of young conscripts, were concentrated along the border with Morocco. The police and gendarmerie services, supposed to cover a country five times the size of France, were fewer than those in neighboring Morocco or Tunisia. The public industrial sector and other state structures had little protection. In sum, in the early 1990s, the state in Algeria was weak, almost nonexistent. The situation was worsened by the country's dreadful financial situation. Aware of the near-collapse of the state and its institutions, the civilian and military authorities took some measures to preserve the survival of the state. The first action was to remove elected Islamist officials from the municipalities and replace them with state-appointed officials; many of those officials were eventually assassinated by Islamists. The state removed Islamists from the municipalities for fear that the elected Islamist officials would provide logistical support for the insurgents. The state also decided to arm thousands of people throughout the country to serve as auxiliaries to the regular troops. These security agents, known as *gardes communaux*, played a critical role in preventing the insurgents from fulfilling their goals. Of course, many *gardes communaux* were unemployed youths; their enrollment was often motivated by economic considerations.

In order to protect public infrastructures, the authorities compelled companies to set up *services de sûreté interne d'établissements,* which were basically specially trained security services within those establishments. According to Algerian officials, within one year of the creation of such services, the number of acts of sabotage against social and economic structures was reduced by 75 percent. The state also created *détachements de protection et de sûreté,* brigades entrusted with the protection of industrial projects.

Because jihadists targeted isolated villages and the suburbs of most cities, the authorities set up the *groupes de légitime défense* [GLDs], which, though sometime deficient, did much to reduce terrorist attacks on innocent civilians. Although a few GLDs committed atrocities against families of Islamists or collaborated with jihadists, overall the existence of GLDs, in partnership with regular state security forces, helped protect villages against terrorist incursions.

In addition to these and other measures, the state authorities sought to remove from various institutions individuals whose sympathy with radical Islamists was proven. Furthermore, the government increased the police force and provided the new recruits with more efficient antiterrorist training both in Algeria and abroad. The police force acquired some adapted equipment imported from the former Eastern bloc, South Africa, and elsewhere.

More recently, measures have been taken in the 2003 Financial Law to combat the funding of terrorism and money laundering. The law now allows authorities to track down the financial sources of the terrorist networks. A variety of means permits officials to freeze suspicious assets and to use intelligence methods to thwart suspicious financial operations.[11]

Undoubtedly, despite the violation of human rights and other reprehensible acts, Algerians did remarkably well in preventing the state from collapsing and in combating the most violent jihadist groups.

Although the government did not take adequate political measures, the civil concord that was finalized and implemented in 1999 bore its fruit, since more than six thousand armed insurgents laid down their weapons. This policy and the measures the state has undertaken since the mid-1990s proved to be relatively successful. Indeed, in January 2003, General-Major Mohamed Lamari revealed that the number of insurgents was brought down from twenty-seven thousand to around one thousand.[12] While the number of jihadists cannot be known for certain, there is no doubt that it has been greatly diminished and that the security forces have forced the jihadists to move and operate in remote areas, even though they continue to cause damage.

DEMOCRATIZATION: SHIELD AGAINST JIHADISM

The Algerian case is somewhat unique in Middle Eastern and North African (MENA) countries in that the rise of the jihadist was more complex than elsewhere. The colonial legacy, exploitation of religion by the authorities, failure of development policies, mismanagement of the economy, demographic explosion, lack of democracy, collapse of oil prices, breakup of the Soviet Union—whose political and military ties were very close with Algeria—and the return of the "Afghans" all combined to give rise to an unprecedented insurgence against the regime in place. Radical Islamism exploited the chaotic liberalization to weaken the state. Failure of the regime to negotiate a political pact with the Islamists before the December 1991 elections resulted in a catastrophic scenario that neither had anticipated. The overwhelming victory of the FIS at the legislative elections stunned even the FIS leaders. Objectively, the leadership of the Armed Forces had warned that they would not tolerate any political party jeopardizing the country's republican constitution. Although the Islamist armed insurrection against the regime took a radical turn after the cancellation of the second round of the election scheduled for January 16, 1992, Islamists had used violence throughout the 1980s and even during the period of liberalization when the FIS had a legal existence. Once the electoral process was canceled, forces within the FIS, a mass party composed of heterogeneous groups, launched an armed insurrection to topple the regime. Jihadist forces, led by "Afghans," directed the uprising; they resorted to the most brutal means to achieve power. In the first few years, jihadist forces benefited from voluntary or forced support from many segments of the population opposed to the regime. However, the bitter power struggle between various groups had terrible consequences for the civilian populations, when some groups decided to massacre the families of rival groups or those populations that withdrew their support from certain jihadist groups. The decision of the jihadist groups to carry out massacres against civilians at large was taken following the overwhelming participation of the population in the presidential election of November 1995. In 1996, the government provided arms to populations that wished to defend themselves against terrorist attacks. These new forces played a considerable role in reinforcing the effectiveness of the security forces.

The international networks established in Europe and elsewhere did undoubtedly contribute to the prolongation of the Algerian tragedy. Had it not been for the resistance of the population at large and civil society, the main victims of the SJGs, the whole state edifice would have crumbled. At the moment, SJGs receive little voluntary support amongst the population. Whether the regime will carry out the necessary reforms in the country that will eradicate the roots that gave rise to SJGs in the first place remains to be seen.

Although the causes for the rise of RIGs and SJGs in Algeria are domestic, these groups have become part of a global network. Undoubtedly, the U.S. government did not calculate the consequences of the policy pursued in Afghanistan in the 1980s and 1990s—what some scholars and intelligence specialists have called "blowback." Indeed, the return of the "Afghans" and their integration into rising SJGs in various Arab countries, including Algeria, has had consequential effects not only on the respective governments but also on the weaving of the international network, such as the Jihadi Salafi International and al Qaeda.

In Algeria, not only should the economic problems that resulted in the rise of radical Islamism be tackled (through genuine reforms), but the educational, judicial, and cultural systems also need to be reformed. There is currently heated debate between those such as President Abdelaziz Bouteflika, who wishes to achieve the policy of "National Reconciliation" through a rehabilitation of the FIS, and those who believe that a general amnesty would only vindicate the Islamist movement and its armed insurrection against the state. In fact, what is needed in Algeria, and most MENA countries for that matter, is genuine democratization within, of course, the Muslim world's own specificities. Two major factors have given rise to extremist versions of Islam. The first has to do with the authoritarian policy that various governments have pursued since their independence from colonial rule. The second stems from U.S. policies in the region—not only blind support for Israel but also support for dictatorial Arab regimes.

In Algeria, as in other MENA countries, widespread corruption, the lack of democratic freedoms, the marginalization or sheer exclusion of large segments of society (especially young people), arbitrary rule, clientelism, nepotism, and human rights violations caused ruling elites to lose their legitimacy, which explains the appeal of the Islamist wave. The severe socioeconomic crises caused by inflation, soaring international debt, high unemployment, and mismanagement of resources, coupled with no means of redress through democratic institutions, resulted in the repudiation of the tacit social contract that rulers had established with the ruled following independence from colonial domination. Such factors laid the grounds for the new social groups, which have challenged the authority and the legitimacy of the state with an intensity and on a scale never previously witnessed. Although RIGs and

SJGs were the leading force opposing the state, others, including cultural groups, human rights organizations, student organizations, moderate Islamists, business associations, and women's associations are now political forces to reckon with. Tens of thousands of autonomous groups have surfaced, and citizens are eager to and capable of playing a positive role in the modernization of society. Obviously, the Algerian regime is still resistant to genuine change and will oppose any meaningful reform movement or the growth of a consequential civil society.[13] The recurring crackdown on the independent press is a clear indication of how far the regime is willing to go in allowing civil society to participate actively in the shaping of state policies. This is precisely why secular and moderate Islamist political parties must continue to oppose strong challenges to the regime. Certainly, a degree of civility and dedication to democracy must exist within society at large, because—as the Algerian case well illustrates—without tolerance and acceptance of the other, the political and social struggle would turn violent.

Ultimately, the old rulers will have to make up for their lack of legitimacy and the fragility of their rule by negotiating honorable pacts with civil and political society. Controlled or tutelary democracy might be the first step toward liberalization and democratization in Algeria, as well as in the rest of MENA. Without a doubt, the process will be slow and shaky because democracy itself is a process, not an end. The real brake to democratization in Algeria is not the cultural factor but rather the resistance of the old rulers to allow sweeping change to take place. As Albert Schnabel correctly points out about MENA, "what is required is not the immediate (or even eventual) adoption of full-fledged Western-style liberal democracy, but a gradual process toward more participation in the political and economic life and governance of the country, in harmony with religious norms and teachings respected throughout society" (Saikal and Schnabel 2003, 2). Beyond doubt, unless such changes are inaugurated, Algeria will continue to generate RIGs and SJGs, and the sacrifice that Algerians paid to stop their takeover of society would have been in vain. All the security measures to combat terrorism would amount to naught, and a return of social instability with unforeseen consequences will continue to haunt the state and Algerian society.

NOTES

1. Figures diverge as to the number of casualties, but most agree that more than one hundred thousand people were killed.

2. The term "Islamist" is used here to refer to those groups and parties that exploit Islam for political means. Islamists are more concerned with power than with religious issues; thus, politics is cloaked in religion.

3. RIGs are politico-religious groups who reinterpret Islamic tenets and use radical means to bring about change within their societies. The objective is purportedly the establishment of an Islamic state based on RIGs' peculiar interpretation of Islam and Islamic tenets.

4. These groups are in essence similar to RIGs; however, in addition to adopting a literal, strict version of Islam, SJGs have made the holy war paramount in the struggle to return to the ideal, original Islamic society—that is, the one of the time of the Prophet Muhammad, again, according to their peculiar version.

5. For a convincing analysis of the FIS as an umbrella for terrorist groups, see Issami (2001).

6. Major-General Mohamed Touati, the president's advisor on national security affairs, told me in an interview in Algiers in late October 2002 that the AIS did in fact surrender in 1997 and that there was no negotiated secret agreement, as was reported in the press.

7. Among these phalanges one can cite the following: *Errahmane, El Ghoraba, El mawt, El Feth, El Forkan, El Khadra, El Ahwal, A'Talaba,* and others.

8. Apparently, the FIS representative to the United States, Anwar Haddam, who was also a member of the GIA, is the one who urged Zitouni not to attack U.S. interests in Algeria.

9. Salafism is a ninth-century movement, which was resurrected under Saudi Wahhabism in the nineteenth century. Salafism advocates a return to the origins of Islamic tradition as articulated by Prophet Muhammad and his closest companions. In sum, Salafism advocates a return to life in the city of Medina, where a pure, unadulterated Islam was practiced. Ibn Taymia advocated jihad, which he claimed constituted the sixth, hidden pillar of Islam!

10. The GIA found exegetes within it own ranks; it also formed its own. The imams who refused to provide fatwas to justify the killings were executed, as was the case of well-respected theologian Mohamed Bouslimani of Nahnah's Movement for a Peaceful Society.

11. See *Le Quotidien d'Oran* (2003). See also Algeria's National Report, "Mise en œuvre de la Résolution 1373 (2001) Adoptée par le Conseil de Sécurité des Nations-Unies le 28 septembre 2001," which describes at length the actions taken by the Algerian government to implement UN Resolution 1373 on terrorism.

12. See *Le Point* (2003).

13. On the importance of civil society in MENA, see Zoubir (1999, 2003).

REFERENCES

Issami, Mohamed. 2001. *Le FIS et le Terrorisme-Au Coeur de l'Enfer.* Algiers: Editions Le Matin.

Le Point. 2003. "Interview, Le général de corps d'armée Mohamed Lamari, Chef d'état-major de l'Armée nationale populaire (ANP) algérienne," 1583 (January 17): 44–45.

Le Quotidien d'Oran. 2003. "Lutte contre le financement du terrorisme et le blanchiment d'argent. La fin du secret bancaire pour l'argent suspect," January 8.

Saikal, Amin, and Albrecht Schnabel, eds. 2003. *Democratization in the Middle East: Experiences, Struggles, Challenges.* New York: United Nations University Press.

Zoubir, Yahia H. 1994. "Algeria's Multi-Dimensional Crisis: The Story of A Failed State-Building Process." *Journal of Modern African Studies* 32(4): 741–47.

————. 1995. "Stalled Democratization of an Authoritarian Regime: The Case of Algeria." *Democratization* 2(2): 109–39.

————. 1999. "State and Civil Society in Algeria." In *North Africa in Transition: State, Society, and Economic Transformation in the 1990s*, ed. Yahia H. Zoubir, 29–42. Gainesville, Fla.: University Press of Florida.

————. 2003. "The Rise of Civil Society in Arab States." In *History in Dispute: The Middle East Since 1945*, ed. David Lesch, 81–85. Farmington Hills, Mich.: St. James Press/ Manly Publishers.

MOHAMMED M. HAFEZ

16 A Tragedy of Errors
THWARTED DEMOCRATIZATION AND ISLAMIST
VIOLENCE IN ALGERIA

In 1989, Algeria embarked on a democratization experiment that
ended in a tragic failure. After years of authoritarian rule characterized by an
imperious executive, a domineering military, and single-party rule, Algerians
witnessed an unprecedented opening up of the political system and the beginning of elections, pluralism, and individual and collective freedoms. The process
of liberalization gave rise to numerous political contenders, including parties
based on ethnicity, ideology, and religion. It was the latter, however, that seemed
to benefit the most from the transition to democracy. The Islamic Salvation Front
(*Front Islamique du Salut* [FIS]) became the premier party to challenge the ruling National Liberation Front (*Front de Libération Nationale* [FLN]). The rise of
the FIS and its success at the polls led, initially, to restrictions on the substance
of democratization and, ultimately, to the cancellation of the entire process in
1992. A bloodless military coup put an end to national elections that promised
to bring the FIS to power and began years of unmitigated regime repression and
Islamist violence. More than one hundred thousand Algerians have been killed
since 1992, and there appears to be no end to the bloodshed.

What went wrong? Why did the process of democratization give way to a protracted civil war between the Islamists and the state regime? What lessons can
we learn from Algeria's failed experiment? How might we apply those lessons to
other Muslim countries contemplating political liberalization?

The concept of political opportunity structures, which refers to the opportunities and constraints for peaceful and militant activism within a political environment (Tarrow 1994; McAdam, McCarthy, and Zald 1996; McAdam, Tarrow,

and Tilly 1997), is useful for exploring the Algerian tragedy. The violence in Algeria was not an inevitable outcome of Islamist participation in the political process but, rather, a product of failed channeling of the opposition toward conventional institutional politics. The political opportunity structure created incentives for militant activism during the opening phase of the democratization process and disincentives for moderation at its peak. *Had the state elite combined political openness with a measured policy of repression during the critical phase of transition to democracy, the violence could have been averted.* Instead, the regime applied an ill-fated mix of political inclusion and almost no repression against radical Islamists during the first two years of political liberalization and switched to complete political exclusion and indiscriminate repression against Islamists after nearly three years of political participation and resource mobilization. By that time, repression was not only perceived as illegitimate, it incited violence instead of deterring it. Simply put, the state created a monster that it could not slay.

POLITICAL OPPORTUNITY STRUCTURES

Sociologists and political scientists interested in explaining the rise of social movements developed the concept of political opportunity structures (POS), which was initially equated with "the degree to which groups are likely to be able to gain access to power and to manipulate the political system" (Eisinger 1973, 25). Subsequent formulations expanded the concept to include electoral realignments (Piven and Cloward 1977), the availability of elite allies and support groups (Gamson 1975; Jenkins and Perrow 1977), the instability of elite alignments (Tarrow 1996), low levels of state repression (Tilly 1978; McAdam 1982; Brockett 1991), and the institutional strength of the state (Kriesi et al. 1992). All these studies, at their core, contend that the rise, expansion, and behavior of social movements depend on the opportunities and constraints generated by the broader political environment, which structures the cost-benefit calculations of different movement organizations within a political context.

Two dimensions of the POS are of particular importance to movement strategies—the degree of access to the institutionalized political system and the nature of state repression. These two aspects explain the strategic orientation of Islamists in Algeria during the democratization process. Specifically, the manner in which the state combines its political inclusion policy with its repression policy in the formative stages of the movement will channel movement behavior toward moderation or militancy in the ascendant phase of the movement.[1]

ACCESS TO THE INSTITUTIONALIZED POLITICAL SYSTEM

The institutionalized political system refers to the set of formal institutions of the state—parliaments, government ministries, policy-implementing agencies—and informal mechanisms, procedures, and "policy styles" by which the state elite governs (Kitschelt 1986, 63). Meaningful access to the institutionalized political systems refers to the degree to which groups can participate in state institutions both *procedurally*, through direct access to formal and informal policymaking mechanisms, and *substantively*, by exercising influence through access to these mechanisms.

Under completely accessible systems, movement organizations encounter few restrictions on their ability to form parties, compete in elections, lobby state officials, hold public office, engage in policy formulation, appeal to judicial review through courts, and challenge state policies through formal and informal channels of conflict mediation. Conversely, completely inaccessible systems make illegal any attempt by movement organizations to engage in formal policymaking and, instead, opt to repress them. Between these two poles lies formal access to the political system, whereby challengers can count on procedural access to the political system but not substantive influence. A state that only provides formal access to the system often intends to give the appearance of political inclusion without ever intending to cede consequential access to the levers of power.

How does the degree of system accessibility influence the strategic orientation of Islamist movements? The more accessible the system, the more likely Islamist movements will adopt accommodative strategies over time. On a basic level, open access to the system means that the movement has an option beyond disruption or revolutionary struggle to affect change. Open access creates the possibility for debate between moderates and radicals within the movement over whether to pursue institutional strategies or a clandestine path to change. Closed or formal access, on the other hand, while not necessarily precluding debate over strategies and tactics between radicals and moderates, is likely to narrow the range of options from which moderates can draw.

This possibility for debate between moderates and radicals in the Islamist movement has important consequences for collective action. First, the option of pursuing "proper" channels of conflict resolution will entice many Islamists to shun disruption and violence and choose the path of institutional bargaining and competition, resulting in a movement divided between two strategies. A divided movement, in turn, is likely to reduce the material and organizational resources of the militant wing, which will likely reduce the scale of its militant activities.

Many studies of revolutionary movements have substantiated the claim that the more inclusive the state, even an inclusive authoritarian state, the less likely it is to unify opponents behind a revolutionary strategy (Skocpol 1979; Goodwin and Skocpol 1989; Parsa 2000; Goodwin 2001). Revolutionary movements in Colombia, Venezuela, Peru, and Bolivia in recent history were unable to forge unified movements partly because elected governments "contributed greatly to the weaknesses of the revolutionary opposition since the reformist option seemed to provide the opposition with an alternative path" (Wickham-Crowley 1992, 170).

Just as important, open access to the political system is likely to amplify the voices of moderate Islamists by giving credence to the idea that change could be achieved through extant state institutions. Open access allows moderates to argue that participating in conventional politics could offer a less costly path to social change. Closed or circumscribed access, on the other hand, makes arguing for disruption and violence easier for radicals by highlighting the inability of moderates to affect change through conventional politics. As Goodwin (1997, 18) explains, access to the institutionalized political process "discourages the sense that the state is unreformable or an instrument of a narrow class or clique and (accordingly) needs to be overhauled." Piven and Cloward (1977, 91), for example, attribute the demise of the unemployed workers' movement in the United States during the New Deal era to institutional channeling that "encouraged faith in the possibility of national electoral influence" and "destroyed the incentive of the leaders of the unemployed to exacerbate disorder."

Finally, open access to the political system could potentially increase the institutional resources of Islamists—political recognition, free public platform in parliaments, elite patronage, and bureaucratic and ministerial positions. These resources, in turn, allow the movement to exert influence through elite ties, negotiate concessions with the authorities, put new issues on the political agenda, publicize the demands of the movement through the parliamentary platform, and solidify the role of the movement in society by working to undermine state repressive policies against the movement. Movement access to the political system, as Oberschall (1993, 56) explains, "shifts some of the costs of obtaining resources onto institutionalized politics." The acquisition of institutional resources is important in the long run if the movement wishes to stabilize its resource base. Consequently, militant activities that endanger institutional resources will be rejected.

While open access to state institutions is a necessary condition for political accommodation on the part of the emerging opposition, it is not sufficient to produce accommodative strategies. Open access to state institutions without any constraints on extrainstitutional militancy may encourage the movement to rely on street militancy to bolster its influence in the political process. The nature of state repression is equally as important as the degree of system accessibility in shaping the strategic orientation of Islamist movements.

State repression refers to any action taken by the authorities that "raises the contender's cost of collective action" (Tilly 1978, 100). Comparable to the degree of institutional accessibility, state repression is a palpable way for a movement to gauge the tolerance limits of the system. There are at least two dimensions of repression that deserve careful attention: timing and consistency. The manner in which the state combines the timing and consistency of repression is a primary determinant of a movement's strategic calculations. Certain combinations will push the movement toward militancy and violence, while others will pull it toward accommodation.

THE TIMING OF STATE REPRESSION: PREEMPTIVE VERSUS REACTIVE

The *timing* of state repression refers to whether repression is applied preemptively or reactively. Repression is *preemptive* when it is applied before aggrieved activists are able to organize and mobilize disparate supporters and sympathizers around a common goal. Repression is *reactive* when it is applied after activists have had an opportunity to organize otherwise small and isolated political forces. Preemptive repression seeks to strike at the movement before it has had an opportunity to gain organizational momentum, while reactive repression seeks to demobilize an already organized and mobilized segment of the population (Brockett 1995).

Preemptive repression predisposes the movement toward nonmilitant strategies for two reasons. First, preemptive repression denies activists the opportunity to rapidly expand material and organizational resources for extrainstitutional collective action. A movement encountering repression at every attempt to acquire material and organizational resources might garner a great deal of sympathy and tacit support from a large segment of the population; however, preemptive repression also makes acting out of anger difficult because it creates uncertainty as to the size and nature of commitment in the movement. Uncertainty as to the power of the movement will force activists to become cautious and will deter supporters from backing radical groups who may appear overzealous or "ahead of their time."

Reactive repression, on the other hand, predisposes the movement to rebellion for three reasons. First, activists will have had a chance to acquire material resources, mainly through expansion of membership contributions. This means that activists encountering repression after a series of mobilizations will not only become more aggrieved but will also command resources with which to fight back. Second, in contrast to preemptive repression, reactive repression allows the movement to expand its organizational resources by allowing sympathizers and supporters to gauge realistically the level of support and commitment in the movement. If commitment and support is deemed high, then supporters will feel empowered to join insurgent organizations, act on their grievances, and take a chance to bring about change (Klandermans 1984; Opp, Voss, and Gern 1995; Lichbach 1995; Kurzman 1996).

Finally, reactive repression that seeks to eradicate an organized and mobilized movement is more likely to induce rebellion than preemptive repression because activists and supporters will seek to halt the loss of resources accumulated over time. In other words, movements will not only act because they are empowered, but also because they may view inaction as a cost in terms of the loss of hard-earned movement resources and threats to the lives of family, friends, and cadres (Loveman 1998, 481–82). As Kriesi et al. (1995, 40) points out, when repression threatens to considerably worsen the challenger's ability to exert influence in the future, movement organizations might choose to fight back "even though it may be expected to accomplish little more than a continuation of the present situation or even a mere reduction of the expected deterioration."

THE CONSISTENCY OF REPRESSION: CONSISTENT VERSUS INCONSISTENT

The consistency of repression, following Lichbach (1987), Rasler (1996) and Moore (1998), refers to the mix of repressive and accommodative state policies toward a movement. If a state repeatedly applies repression to certain movement activities without ceding any concessions to these activities, then the repression policy is deemed *consistent*. For example, if the state repeatedly imprisons demonstrators demanding reforms and refuses to adopt any of their demands, then repression is consistent. If, however, the state applies repressive measures against demonstrators but at the same time seeks to placate them by offering concessions, then the repression policy is deemed *inconsistent*. In other words, inconsistent repression involves the simultaneous punishment and rewarding of a singular strategy, while consistent repression involves the repeated application of sanctions against one strategy deemed inappropriate while rewarding others deemed permissible.

Consistent repression of militant activities in an Islamist movement will likely produce nonmilitant strategies in the movement, while inconsistent repression of militant activities will likely encourage militant strategies. Consistent repression that does not reward rebellious activities will signal to potential supporters that additional militancy will not produce concessions and, therefore, is futile. Islamist militancy under consistent repression only entails costs and no benefits. Such a repressive policy is likely to strengthen nonmilitant voices that wish to shift to a less costly strategy. If the system offers moderate Islamists meaningful access to conflict mediation, then consistent repression of militant strategies will more likely strengthen the position of the moderates, who will be able to argue that accommodation offers a less costly and more rewarding path to exert influence. In contrast, inconsistent repression that punishes and rewards militant Islamist activities simultaneously will produce mixed signals to the movement and result in mixed interpretations of the political environment. Militant Islamists will be able to argue that state concessions are the direct outcome of militancy. Therefore, while militancy may incur costs, it also promises to result in benefits.

In sum, the preceding analysis suggests that if a state provides Islamists meaningful access to state institutions and preemptively and consistently represses militant behavior, then the movement will adopt accommodative strategies. Conversely, a state that denies Islamists access, or provides them mere formal access to the system, and applies repression against the movement reactively and inconsistently will almost certainly push the movement toward militancy and even mass insurgency.

OPPORTUNITY STRUCTURES AND ISLAMIST STRATEGIES DURING ALGERIA'S DEMOCRATIZATION PROCESS

From 1989 to 1992, the years of political liberalization and aborted democratization, Islamist strategies went through four phases: accommodation and limited militancy (1989–91), escalating militancy (May–June 1991), moderation and retreat from confrontation (June–December 1991), and violent insurgency (1992 and beyond).

Accommodation and Limited Militancy: 1989–91

Prior to 1989, Islamists hardly engaged in any overt political opposition or extrainstitutional activities such as demonstrations, marches, assassinations, or armed attacks against the state.[2] This quietism was largely a product of political exclusion and persistent repression of any form of political opposition, whether ethnic, confessional, or ideological.

Algeria's exclusionary political system prior to 1989 featured a form of authoritarianism characterized by a military-dominated executive branch, a system of single-party rule, and an imperious state bureaucracy that administered the daily lives of Algerians but lacked substantial power over policymaking. Most observers agree that the locus of power was the military-dominated executive and that the sole party, the FLN, was a legitimating device for the regime. It mobilized public support for state policies and served a supervisory role over "civil society" by incorporating various functional organizations—the National Organization of Guerrilla Fighters (ONM), General Union of Algerian Workers (UGTA), National Union of Algerian Women (UNFA), and National Union of Algerian Youth (UNJA) (Entelis 1986; Hermassi 1987; Rakhila 1993; Yefsah 1994; Korany and Amrani 1998). The Algerian state also relied on a secret police to monitor and repress opposition, and the secret services (*sécurité militaire* or *mukhabarat*) "became the centerpiece of the system's control over political life" (Quandt 1998, 24).

Public policy was the domain of a state-based elite commanded by the military in alliance with technocrats and historic figures from the war of liberation (Ruedy 1992). Those outside of the regime had little effective power to influence public policy through institutional strategies. As Roberts (1996, 6) explains, "only those civilians with powerful patrons in the army high command, and against whom the security services have had no objections, have been realistically able to aspire to ministerial office."

In October 1988, the Algerian regime was rocked by five days of rioting, whereby youth attacked symbols of the state including city halls, police stations, courts, post offices, and state-owned businesses. The riots reflected growing economic discontent with the inept and corrupt state regime. According to unofficial sources, approximately five hundred people were killed (Wanas 1996). The October riots and the heavy hand with which the rioters were dealt with led to a legitimacy crisis. President Chadli Benjedid called for major political reforms that sought, at least ostensibly, to make the system more inclusive. These reforms began in October 1988 when Chadli announced that the FLN would no longer participate in direct management at any level of state government. Subsequently, the FLN was separated from the ruling government and was no longer in a position to oversee elections and appoint candidates. Other reforms were instituted in the 1989 constitution, including freedom of expression, association, and assembly (Article 39); the right to unionize (Article 53) and strike (Article 54) in the public and private sectors; a limited role for the military (Article 24); and an independent judiciary (Article 153). The most significant reform was the right to form associations of a political nature (Article 40), thus officially abandoning one-party rule (Ali 1996; Amar 1996; Kharfallah 1996).

Reforms were not limited to constitutional matters. Algerians witnessed palpable changes in their political life in the aftermath of the October riots. The press was given tremendous freedom to publish; the number of newspapers and newsmagazines increased from 37 to 137 from 1990 to 1992 (Entelis 1996, 57; Kharfallah 1997). In addition, Algeria witnessed a significant expansion in the number of workers' strikes—an average of 2,148 strikes for each year between 1989 and 1991 compared with an average of 877 strikes for each year between 1979 and 1988. "During spring 1990, marches, demonstrations, and rallies became virtual daily occurrences" (Mortimer 1991, 583).

There were additional developments in 1989 that signaled greater openness in Algeria. In March, the military withdrew from the FLN central committee; in April, the national assembly abolished state security courts; and in October, licenses to demonstrate and hold rallies were no longer necessary. These reforms signaled a significant opening in the system and appeared to have ushered in a new era in Algeria. As Entelis (1992, 19) put it, "in only nine months, from October 1988 to July 1989, the Algerian political system was fundamentally transformed from a single-party authoritarian state to a multiparty, pluralistic nation of laws."

The Islamists took advantage of almost every aspect of reforms. In March 1989, Islamists came together to form the FIS as a political party that mobilized myriad personalities and groups to take advantage of party pluralism. Islamist organizing extended into the early 1990s as other Islamist political parties were formed. The most notable of the new parties were *Harakat al-Mujtama al-Islami* (Islamic Society Movement [Hamas]) and *Mouvement de la Nahda Islamique* (Islamic Renaissance Movement [MNI]). The former was established and led by Mahfoud Nahnah, while Abdullah Jaballah established the latter. Both were preachers and senior activists in the movement. Along with these official Islamist organizations and parties emerged a number of small groups with a radical Islamist orientation. These groups carried titles such as *Amr bil M'arouf wal Nahi 'an al-Munkar, Takfir wal Hijra, Jama'at al-Sunna wa al-Shari'a,* and *Ansar al-Tawhid* (Ayyashi 1993; Burgat and Dowell 1997; Tawil 1998).

Although the Code of Associations prohibited the formation of political parties based exclusively on a confessional basis, the FIS was licensed as a political party and participated in local government and national elections.[3] The FIS published its own newspapers (*al-Mounqidh, al-Hidaya,* and *al-Forkane*), formed its own union in 1990 (*Syndicate Islamique du Travail* [SIT]), and, most important of all, was allowed to legislate and enforce some Islamist reforms in the local councils it controlled after the June 1990 elections. There is general agreement that Chadli facilitated the inclusion of Islamists in the political system as a way to counter recalcitrant opposition figures who have retaken key positions within the FLN following the 1988 riots and spoken against his economic liberalization measures since the mid-1980s (Roberts 1992, 1994a, 2003; Entelis 1994; Rasi 1997; Shahin 1997).

The prevailing strategy of the movement from 1989 to 1991 combined political accommodation with extrainstitutional militancy. The most prominent Islamist force from 1989 to 1991 was the FIS. Led by Abassi Madani and Ali Belhaj, two Islamist activists who gained notoriety in the 1980s, the FIS succeeded in drawing many Islamists into its front.[4] Although the FIS was a political party that sought to work within the system, it was also a populist movement that organized rallies, marches, and demonstrations to highlight its demands and exhibit its popularity to the larger public. Its rallies and demonstrations easily mobilized thousands of supporters and at times brought out hundreds of thousands. Its most effective medium for publicity, however, was the mass Friday prayers around key mosques in Kouba and Bab el-Oued, where Abassi and Belhaj preached on alternate weeks. The mosques would regularly overflow onto adjacent streets, where worshipers would lay down their prayer rugs to pray.

The FIS presented the public with two faces, one moderate and the other radical. In its 1989 political program, the FIS described its method as that of "moderation, centerism (*al-wasatiyya*), and comprehensiveness." According to the document, the FIS pursues its goals through "persuasion not subjugation." Abassi, the principal leader of the FIS, sought to reassure the public of FIS's good intentions and moderate message, particularly when it came to issues of democracy and individual liberties. Although Abassi declared his preference for *al-shura* (Islamic tradition of consultation) over democracy, he defined the former as a system that permits freedom of expression, encourages self-criticism and accountability, and precludes political monopoly. In contrast to those who argue that "only God legislates," Abassi maintained that "it is the people that rule and no government should exist without the will of the people; Islamists are not enemies of democracy" (Ghanim 1992, 33–34).

His deputy Belhaj, however, did not hesitate to give fiery speeches in which he denounced democracy, the state, and opponents in vitriolic terms. To Belhaj, democracy is "an un-Islamic institution" and "a system that permits prostitution." Any victory for Islamists through the polls is "not a victory for democracy but a victory for Islam." He promised that the FIS "will not exchange *al-shura* with democracy," which he portrayed as "poison that leads to heresy" (Ahnaf,

Botiveau, and Frégosi 1991, 97; Jasour 1995, 46; Ali 1996, 268). Although Belhaj repeatedly declared his abhorrence for autocratic rule, he rejected the notion of majority rule by maintaining that "the truth is not measured by counting the proponents or opposing voices, but with the authoritative proof that the creed presents. . . . The truth is not decided by the majority even if the latter were Muslims . . . but is represented by adopting the divine truth, even if we alone do so" (Ali 1996, 269).[5] This rejection of majority rule strongly suggests that Belhaj did not believe in the alternation of rule if it entailed turning over power to those who did not represent the "truth."

FIS's tactical repertoire from 1989 to 1991 also vacillated between militancy and moderation. In addition to having freedom to pursue institutional activities, the FIS was unhampered in its extrainstitutional conduct. Islamists took to the streets time and again, in rallies or public prayers, with relatively few impediments from the authorities. The FIS did not hesitate to challenge the regime, and it often thrived on confronting opponents, especially the FLN. This populist militancy is best exemplified in two episodes: a march in April 1990 and the demonstrations against the Gulf War in 1991.

On April 20, 1990, the FIS held a landmark demonstration that brought together between six hundred thousand and eight hundred thousand people to march in silence. The sheer size of participation and the discipline with which it was conducted was impressive enough, but what made the march significant was the fact that it was scheduled on the same day the FLN was scheduled to hold its own march against the political use of mosques by Islamists. This move by the FIS was clearly intended to embarrass the FLN, who would have had difficulty matching the participation levels reached by the FIS.

The boldness of the FIS was repeated during the Gulf War of 1990–91. Although the FIS condemned the Iraqi invasion of Kuwait, it adopted a pro-Iraq stance as the U.S.-led international force prepared to liberate Kuwait. The FIS, along with other parties, organized a mass demonstration of approximately four hundred thousand people on January 18, 1991. Other parties participated, but it was the FIS that was vociferous in its calls against the West. Its leaders called for jihad and demanded that the state open up training camps for volunteers to fight the "new crusaders" in Iraq. Belhaj, in his usual truculent style, declared that "we do not want power . . . we leave the thrones to you. We want *jihad*, only *jihad* and to meet *Allah*." President Chadli Benjedid condemned the "demagogy" and "blackmail" of the FIS but this did not stop the latter from organizing another demonstration that was equally belligerent in its tone. On January 31, 1991, the FIS mobilized about sixty thousand supporters, some of whom carried signs that read "There is no God but Allah, Chadli is the enemy of Allah" (Ayyashi 1993, 103–6).

While these two examples highlight the populist militancy of the FIS, a closer examination of the period 1989–91 will indicate the extent to which the FIS was willing to accommodate the state and limit its militancy to remain a legitimate actor in the political process. The April 1990 demonstration, while intended to confront and embarrass the FLN, was also intended to counter charges of Islamist violence, hence the silent and disciplined march.[6] During the Gulf War, the FIS never went beyond vitriolic rhetoric, and its demonstrations were within the boundaries of legality and generally peaceful (Qawas 1998, 98).

Between the April 1990 demonstrations and May 1991, the FIS participated in local government elections as a political party. It appointed candidates and ran an election campaign that resulted in the FIS winning the majority of communal and departmental assemblies.[7] Its preelection rallies and marches were largely intended to give publicity to the Islamist party, not to denounce the system of party politics. After the June 1990 election, Abassi declared the willingness of the FIS to cooperate with other parties and guaranteed individual freedoms in FIS-controlled departments and communes.

Politically, the FIS limited its demands to national elections and did not call for presidential elections. Instead, Abassi declared his willingness to form a government under Chadli in case of an FIS victory in the parliamentary elections (Rasi 1997, 335–36). In 1990, when asked if "it [was] possible to anticipate cooperation between the FIS and the President," Abassi responded that "if [the president] stays the course he began with, then that will result in our support for him." He added that "we believe that our future relations will be good."[8] FIS's disposition to work with the president and its noninsistence on immediate presidential elections are significant, because institutional power was largely vested in the presidency.[9] This highlights FIS's willingness to work gradually within the system. Moreover, the FIS did not challenge the unpopular economic reforms of Chadli and Hamrouche but limited its demands for social reforms, including prohibition on coeducation, expansion of Arabization programs, and cancellation of laws deemed contrary to Islam (Ayyashi 1993, 26–27; Roberts 1994b, 459–65; Willis 1996, 128–29).

Moreover, although militancy played an important role in winning public support, the FIS also sought to win adherents through the provision of social services — market cooperatives, medical clinics, youth clubs, and football teams. These measures were intended to highlight the prowess of Islamists through palpable examples (Mortimer 1991, 579; Bekkar 1997, 286–87; Vergès 1997; Qawas 1998, 116–18). Its communes and departments were not turned into Islamist states, although in some of them Islamists did impose their morality on others (Ahnaf, Boutiveau, and Frégosi 1991, 142–43; Willis 1996, 158–62).

In sum, between 1989 and 1991, the FIS adopted a strategy of political accommodation (or "cohabitation"), limited extrainstitutional militancy to generally peaceful marches and rallies, and engaged in a populist discourse that sought to appeal to various audiences within and outside of the movement. What explains FIS's relatively moderate, limited, and nonviolent militancy on the one hand and, on the other, its contradictory and sometimes radical discourse during the opening phase of political liberalization from 1989 to 1991?

From 1989 to late 1990, the system seemed to offer Islamists both procedural and substantive access to state institutions. The limited nature of FIS's militancy in this period made sense given that it was offered the opportunity to organize and participate in state institutions with few restrictions. Revolutionary (anti-institutional) militancy would have only given its opponents inside and outside of the state reason to call for its repression. Furthermore, the fact that the military did not repress FIS's limited militancy—rallies, marches, and demonstrations—meant that the FIS was not risking its legality or legitimacy by engaging in peaceful extrainstitutional activities.

But why did the FIS adopt a contradictory, often undemocratic discourse when it thrived within an emerging democratic system? Why did it not unequivocally embrace democracy and pluralism as it did later in the 1990s and as did Hamas and MNI? Part of the answer is that the FIS sought to appeal to various audiences in the Islamist movement, including those who viewed democracy as a Western and, more importantly, un-Islamic "innovation." To maintain its front, the FIS did not wish to take a clear position that may have driven some of these activists and supporters away but instead opted for an "intelligent double-act" (Roberts 1991, 144) that allowed it to mobilize many Islamists behind it. FIS's leadership allowed the various tendencies in the movement to express themselves publicly (during sermons and demonstrations) and avoided language that implied a single position or a stance from which it could not retreat at a later time, hence its preference for *al-shura* over democracy in its 1989 political program.

This is only part of the answer, however. The FIS was able to conduct a double-act because it was permitted to do so by the state. Its contradictory rhetoric was not punished through repression or threat of dissolution in this period. Despite numerous antidemocratic statements by Belhaj and others, the FIS was allowed to preach and publish its message with impunity. Its marches and sermons were not interrupted when FIS leaders began to engage in vitriolic rhetoric. In other words, the FIS was able to exercise the double-act option because the structure of political opportunities favored an ambiguous discourse and only punished violent actions, not militant rhetoric. Therefore, the FIS could afford to pursue a policy that earned it popular support without threatening to bring about its political exclusion. As we shall see below, when the state began to impose sanctions on the FIS for its radical rhetoric in June 1991, the party moderated its discourse.

Escalating Militancy: May–June 1991

The height of FIS's militancy came in May and June 1991 when the FIS called for a "general and unlimited" strike. The strike was in response to an electoral law that was blatantly intended to benefit the ruling FLN. Although many opposition groups condemned the law, the FIS took its opposition further by calling for a general strike on May 25. Some parties portrayed the strike as "dangerous" and antidemocratic. The interior ministry issued a communiqué denouncing it as adventurism that could harm the democratic process and national security. The military deployed forces two days before the strike was to commence, signaling the potential for violence. Despite the bad publicity and threat of a clampdown, the FIS went ahead with the strike (Tahiri 1992, 94; Charef 1994, 148).

The strike began with demonstrators calling for an Islamic state and presidential elections. Demonstrators carried signs that read "Down with Chadli" and chanted slogans denouncing democracy. When the strike failed to halt work, many Islamists took it upon themselves, either by threat or by force, to prevent workers from entering factories, shopkeepers from opening their shops, and school teachers and university professors from teaching (Rasi 1997, 344–46). Just as important, some Islamists distributed a tract entitled "The Principles and Objectives of Civil Disobedience" in which the author, Said Makhloufi, a member of the FIS consultative council, argued that political work has reached an impasse and civil disobedience is necessary to bring about an Islamic government.

The strike, which extended into June, turned into a series of rallies and occupations of public squares in the capital. The military finally decided to dislodge the demonstrators by force, producing a series of clashes and escalations that lasted throughout June and resulted in mass arrests and numerous deaths and injuries.[10] The confrontations also resulted in the dismissal of Prime Minister Mouloud Hamrouche and a "state of siege." The state-movement confrontation culminated with the arrest of Abassi and Belhaj on charges of fomenting, organizing, and conspiring against the state.

In sum, after a period of relative moderation and limited militancy (1989–May 1991), the FIS escalated its militant rhetoric and activism to press its demands. However, FIS's militancy was not revolutionary in nature. It sought to flex its muscles, not topple the regime. The question is, what explains this escalation in nonrevolutionary militancy on the part of the FIS?

The answer lies in the structure of political opportunities—the degree of system accessibility and the nature of state repression. As indicated earlier, President Chadli permitted the inclusion of Islamists as a way to counter the political weight of traditional leftist elites who were opposed to his economic reform program. The political inclusion of Islamists, however, was not intended to allow the FIS to dominate the electoral process or empower it to establish an Islamic state. On the contrary, once Islamists exhibited the potential to dominate the newly instituted system of party pluralism, the state began to take measures to deprive the FIS of substantive power.

Following FIS's victory in local elections in June 1990, the central government passed additional laws that encumbered FIS governors. As Shahin (1997, 139) explains, "According to the new laws, the right of the municipalities, particularly at main cities, to appoint their staffs was relegated to the Interior Ministry. The municipalities were also deprived of their authority to distribute land, allocate housing opportunities, and carry out development programs without the approval of the central authorities."

These impediments posed a serious challenge to the FIS because they threatened to discredit the movement for its seeming inability to fulfill its election promises. In addition to legal and bureaucratic obstacles, the government enacted new electoral laws in April 1991 that prohibited the use of mosques for "electoral propaganda." The new laws also redrew voting districts so as to artificially increase the representation of cities in the southern region, where the FLN was dominant, to give the latter more votes than it would have otherwise.[11] This new law was clearly intended to prevent the FIS from using its network of mosques (estimated at about nine thousand) to mobilize supporters and sought to preclude a landslide victory for the FIS during the national elections. The new law was widely denounced by the opposition, but the FIS in particular saw it as "high treason" (Mortimer 1991, 588).

Thus, while the state initially offered the FIS both procedural and substantive access to state institutions, in late 1990 and early 1991 the state took measures to diminish its substantive power without denying it procedural access to state institutions altogether. This shift in the opportunity structure affected the strategic orientation of the FIS, which sought to bypass the increasingly hostile state by relying on its mobilization capacity to simultaneously discredit the regime and expand its own popularity in preparation for parliamentary elections (scheduled for June 1991). When the government sought to further curb the power of the FIS through electoral reforms, the party decided to further escalate its militancy by calling for a general strike in May 1991.

Relaxed government repression prior to June 1991 facilitated FIS's decision to escalate its militancy. As indicated earlier, government repression since 1989 was largely limited to those who engaged in violence. As long as the FIS did not advocate and engage in violence, it was given leeway in the streets. This was the case during the April 1990 march, mass prayers in the streets, and Gulf War demonstrations. Interestingly, despite the vitriolic rhetoric of FIS's leadership during Gulf War demonstrations, these demonstrations did not produce major arrests by security forces. In other words, up until June 1991, FIS's experience gave advocates of escalation little reason to think that if they engaged in nonviolent militancy they would induce heavy repression. Indeed, the idea for the general strike came to Abassi by observing a successful general strike by UGTA in the previous March (Charef 1994, 119–20). Simply put, advocates of escalation within the FIS thought they could get away with nonviolent, extrainstitutional militancy. Escalation was calculated to put pressure on the state to abandon legal measures that sought to limit the power of the FIS without inducing repression that will deprive the FIS of access to the system altogether.

Moderation and Retreat from Confrontation: July–December 1991

After the arrest of its principal leaders, the FIS took measures to ensure that it remained a legitimate actor in the system. In July 1991, it held an *al-Wafa'* (Loyalty) conference in Batna to sort out its strategy in the aftermath of the June events. A group led by a moderate provisional leader, Abdelkader Hachani, did not want the withdrawal of the FIS from the political arena or a boycott of the elections. Instead, it wanted to continue with the electoral path. Following the conference, the FIS issued a public communiqué announcing the decision to freeze the membership of two advocates of radical protest—Said Mekhloufi and Qameredin Kharban—who wanted to boycott the elections and proceed with protest to exert pressure on the regime to release FIS leaders and repeal the biased electoral laws. In doing so, the moderate FIS leadership signaled to the regime that it would not tolerate those who advocate militancy and violence (Charef 1994, 117–18; Tawil 1998, 40–41; Qawas 1998, 107–10).

In addition to these measures, the FIS provisional leader Hachani moderated the tone of the party after June and did not organize rallies until it was made legal to do so again.[12] When armed (non-FIS) Islamists killed three policemen in November 1991 in an attack on a border post in Guemmar, the FIS was quick to condemn it. Hachani affirmed that "the FIS operates within legality" (Charef 1994, 221; Tawil 1998, 44). Finally, the FIS participated in the national elections in December 1991 and won 188 seats out of 430 national assembly seats in the first round of the elections and was poised to win an overwhelming majority of seats in the second round. However, a military coup in January 1992 put an end to the electoral process.

In sum, the aforementioned analysis suggests that the FIS was not simply a moderate or militant party. The strategy of the FIS in May–June 1991 can be best characterized as calculated tactical militancy within an overall accommodationist orientation. The FIS escalated and de-escalated its militancy to gain both procedural and substantive access to political institutions. It was not a revolutionary party that aimed to build an Islamist state at any cost and irrespective of the means. In other words, unlike the radical groups that wanted to overthrow the system through armed struggle and shunned democracy as un-Islamic, the FIS was clearly against revolutionary violence in this period. The FIS used its populist militancy to ensure the proper working of a newly instituted system of party politics that benefited it the most; it did not wish to overthrow the system. When the state regime began to manipulate the rules of the emerging system to deny the FIS substantive access to political institutions, the FIS escalated its militancy to reverse the manipulation. However, when this militancy threatened to lead to intensive repression, the FIS began to accommodate the regime.

Why did the FIS not engage in more militancy as opposed to seeking accommodation with the regime after June 1991? The FIS did not shy away from confrontation before, and it certainly had the capacity and support to mobilize more demonstrations. There were those inside the FIS who were advocating more militancy, and the June events highlighted the presence of radical activists who did not hesitate to clash with the military. The FIS, however, chose to accommodate the regime by not engaging in further demonstrations and by promising to abide by peaceful means. Why?

The answer, again, has to do with the nature of political inclusion and state repression. The FIS had access—albeit circumscribed access—to state institutions and was in position to expand its substantive access to the levers of power during parliamentary elections (rescheduled for December 1991). Further confrontation with the military risked FIS's access to the system while not guaranteeing success. As Quandt (1998, 63) explains, "the FIS could flood the streets with demonstrators, but the military had the tanks." The promise of national elections in six months meant that the FIS had something to lose if further militancy proved ineffective in the face of repression.

The consistency of state repression toward militancy and the relatively selective nature of its repression after the June events further reinforced the accommodationist inclination of the FIS. During and after the June 1991 events, the military set new boundaries of permissible opposition in the system. Greater restrictions on FIS's extrainstitutional activities were imposed. After the military refused to allow Islamists to continue with their demonstrations and forced them to disperse, it began to arrest the radical elements who were in the forefront of confrontations. More significantly, it arrested Abassi and Belhaj for making "seditious" remarks to their supporters. Mass prayers that spilled over into the streets were no longer permitted, and worshipers were prevented from praying in mosques outside of their areas. In August, the military shut down FIS's newspapers for purportedly advocating civil disobedience. In September, the authorities detained Hachani, the provisional leader of the FIS, for a month (Willis 1996, 182; Shahin 1997, 145). All along, the authorities refused to concede to FIS's demand for the release of Abassi and Belhaj. These measures made it clear to the FIS that sustained extrainstitutional activities and militant rhetoric would no longer be tolerated.

The fact that the moderate Hamas and MNI were not repressed gave indication that the state would only tolerate those who maintain their opposition off the street. In other words, the state distinguished between Islamists who engage in party politics only (Hamas and MNI) and those who supplement their electoral strategy with militancy (FIS). The former were spared repression, while the latter were the target of repression. Furthermore, despite the provocative measures taken by the army, such repression was not far-reaching. After the June events, only a few thousand Islamists were arrested despite the fact that tens of thousands engaged in demonstrations.[13]

Consistent and relatively selective repression meant that the option of militancy was dangerous and less promising than the option of accommodation. Further militancy would have threatened to negate all the accomplishments of the FIS; accommodation promised the possibility of expanded institutional access and resources. The FIS opted for accommodation from July 1991 to January 1992.

Violent Insurgency: 1992 and Beyond

The relative moderation and nonviolent militancy of the Islamist movement gave way to a full-scale insurgency in Algeria following the coup that put an end to the electoral process in 1992. The FIS was poised to win a major electoral victory, but the military stepped in to halt the process. The FIS leadership initially sought a political solution to the crisis and rallied the FLN and the Socialist Forces Front (SFF) to challenge the constitutionality of the coup. When the FIS was banned a few months later, it appealed to the Supreme Court to reverse the ban. In the first half of 1992, some FIS leaders—Abdelrazak Rejjam, Rabeh Kebir, and Anwar Haddam—made appeals for a political solution based on, inter alia, the release of prisoners, relegalization of the FIS, and return to elections.[14]

Many of FIS's activists, however, did not share the moderation of the leadership and began to clash with security forces all over the country. Initially, these clashes took the form of dispersed confrontations with security forces. Over the course of time, insurgents organized themselves into numerous armed groups, including the Armed Islamic Movement (Mouvement Islamique Armé [MIA]), Islamic State Movement (Mouvement pour l'Etat Islamique [MEI]), and Islamic Front for Armed Jihad (Front Islamique du Djihad Armé [FIDA]). But the two most prominent armed groups to emerge in the post-coup era were the Armed Islamic Group (Groupe Islamique Armé [GIA]) and Islamic Salvation Army (Armée Islamique du Salut [AIS]).

The GIA was constituted by the most radical elements of the movement in October 1992. It brought together former activists in the Bouyali group, Algerian "Afghans," and new recruits from the Algiers, Medea, and Blida regions. These groups opted to stay outside of the FIS apparatus from 1989 to 1991 largely because they did not believe in democracy and the electoral process. The GIA waged a total war that sought to displace the regime and construct an Islamic state in its stead. Its famous slogan of "no dialogue, no cease-fire, no reconciliation, and no security and guarantee with the apostate regime" highlighted its intransigence and dedication for an all-out war against the state. In its total war against the regime, the GIA spared few people from the threat of violence. It attacked policemen, soldiers, government officials, state employees, journalists, intellectuals, foreigners, and ordinary civilians. Its tactics included assassinations, armed attacks, bombings, sabotage, massacres, mutilations, and throat cutting (Tawil 1998; Martinez 2000; Hafez 2003, 2004).

The other armed group, the AIS, was officially formed in July 1994 as an armed wing of the FIS. It existed in the eastern and western regions of Algeria as early as 1993. The AIS declared its official formation after the GIA appeared to have united other armed groups in the middle of the country under its banner in May 1994. In contrast to the GIA, the AIS waged a limited war against the state as a way to force the military regime to release FIS leaders, rehabilitate the FIS as a legitimate political party, and reinstitute the electoral process. Moreover, the AIS was not opposed to dialogue with the regime and at times initiated negotiations to end the insurgency. In contrast to the expansive violence of the GIA, the AIS limited its violence to security forces and government officials. The AIS opposed and denounced attacks on intellectuals, foreigners, and anyone who was not directly involved in the persecution of Islamists. Similar to the GIA, the AIS relied on assassinations, armed attacks, bombings, and sabotage (Hafez 2000).

The military regime failed to halt the Islamist insurgency throughout the mid-1990s, despite repeated attempts at negotiations with the armed insurgents and international support for a peaceful settlement of the crisis. In 1997, the AIS declared a unilateral cease-fire. However, the GIA and other splinter groups rejected this initiative. Instead, it began to engage in more brutal violence and outright massacres against ordinary civilians.[15]

In sum, the coup of 1992 was the impetus for a shift in strategy from calculated extrainstitutional militancy to anti-institutional violent insurgency. This shift raises two important questions. First, why did FIS activists turn to violence? Prior to 1989, Islamists were excluded from politics and repressed, but they did not turn to violence then. What changed? Second, why did Islamists adopt the strategy of armed insurgency as opposed to mass demonstrations? The FIS was able to organize mass collective action in the recent past. Why did it not do so again?

The political system after 1992 became completely exclusionary vis-à-vis Islamists from 1992 to 1995 and only partially inclusive of non-FIS Islamists thereafter. At no time during this period were Islamists provided substantive access to the levers of power, and state repression was reactive, indiscriminate, and initially inconsistent. State repression came after three years of Islamist organizing and mobilization, and it did not distinguish between moderates and radicals or among leaders, activists, supporters, and sympathizers.

The military coup of 1992 did not just seek to deny the FIS the ability to dominate the national assembly; it also sought to exclude the party from politics altogether. After the dissolution of the national assembly and cancellation of the elections, the High State Committee (HCE) declared a state of emergency, suspended the FIS, and closed down its headquarters. In March, the FIS was formally dissolved; this decision was confirmed by the Supreme Court the following month. In July, a military court sentenced Abassi and Belhaj to twelve years in prison. In November, the state empowered authorities to close down charitable and cultural organizations associated with the FIS, and more than three hundred councils controlled by the FIS were dissolved.

In addition to banning the FIS, the military struck at its mobilization capacity. In February, it opened five detention centers in the Sahara desert to hold Islamist activists rounded up since the coup. Thousands of Islamists, including five hundred FIS mayors and councilors, were detained between January and March 1992. In October, special courts that were banned under the 1989 constitution were brought back, and tougher sentences for "terrorists" were instated. Finally, in December, the Ministry of Religious Affairs ordered the destruction of all unofficial mosques.

State repression in the 1990s was reactive; it came after three years of Islamist organizing and mobilization, which culminated with a landslide victory for the Islamist party. The cancellation of the elections and dissolution of the FIS were seen as blatantly unfair by Islamists, thus making moderation less likely to resonate with activists and supporters after the coup. Although the state was exclusionary and repressive toward Islamists in the 1980s, exclusion did not come after such a clear victory for the movement. Just as important, repression targeted the institutional and organizational resources of the movement—its party, union, local government councils, and mosque networks—after three years of mobilization. Thus, the movement had a great deal to lose if it did not fight back.

Reactive state repression facilitated Islamist militancy in other ways. Three years of organizing and mobilization allowed activists in various parts of the country to develop bonds and trust in the movement. In the communes, for instance, the FIS organized functional cells and neighborhood committees that organized activities related to mosques, relief and emergency, and schools. Moreover, the FIS organized a trade union that included a number of professions—education, tourism, telecommunications, and transportation. The FIS also organized a number of associations such as "The League of Islamic Universities and Intellectuals," "The Islamic Youth Association," and "The Association of the Children of Martyrs" (Lamchichi 1992, 102; Labat 1995, 186).[16] The discipline with which Islamists conducted some of their marches and mass prayers indicates the extent of coordination that developed within the movement since 1989.

Furthermore, Islamist-organized social services—medical clinics, youth clubs, market cooperatives—not only allowed Islamist activists to regularly work together but also put them directly in touch with their communities, which facilitated the development of links with potential recruits. These links also meant that Islamists could draw political and material support from their communities in times of need.

Moreover, state repression came after Islamists were allowed to gauge their numerical support time and again. Elections, rallies, and demonstrations empowered Islamists because it allowed them to measure their popular support repeatedly and realistically. The fact that the FIS could bring out hundreds of thousands to march under its banners and millions to vote for it meant that the Islamists commanded legitimacy and could rely on the active participation of their members and supporters.

In addition to being reactive, state repression was initially inconsistent. In the immediate aftermath of the coup, the authorities arrested Islamists *en masse* irrespective of whether they were violent militants or mere supporters of the movement. Accurate arrest figures are unavailable, but estimates range from six thousand to thirty thousand interned in desert camps. However, after arresting thousands of Islamists and detaining them under harsh desert conditions, the state let many of them go free as a conciliatory measure toward the movement in 1992 and 1993. In June 1992, twelve hundred detainees were freed in the run-up to the Islamic holiday 'Aid al-Adhha and, more significantly, eight thousand were released in the beginning of 1993 (Willis 1996, 309). It is difficult to know whether many of the released Islamists joined the underground, but the links formed and experiences shared with militants under intense prison conditions undoubtedly facilitated the recruitment of some of them into armed groups.

Moreover, state repression after the coup did not distinguish between peaceful demonstrations and violent militancy. The state of emergency imposed on February 9, 1992, forbade all forms of protest. FIS supporters were prohibited from organizing demonstrations and gathering outside of mosques before or after prayers. Riot police were stationed in Islamist strongholds every Friday following the cancellation of the elections to prevent after-prayer demonstrations. Consequently, when Islamists attempted to organize marches, especially after Friday prayers, they were not allowed. A march scheduled by the FIS for February 14, 1992, was canceled after the authorities forbade it and deployed heavily armed paratroopers along the proposed route of the march. FIS supporters were also prevented from demonstrating after Abassi and Belhaj were sentenced to twelve years imprisonment in July 1992. As Abdelkarim Ghamati, a member of the FIS Provisional National Executive Bureau, explained, "The crisis cell in the [FIS] discussed the issue of demonstrations and the possibility of rallying people, as happened in Iran, to take to the streets, confront the military and remain in its face until it returned to the people its choice by reversing the coup. But the cell rejected this idea because lives were going to be lost. We recognized that the regime would not hesitate to kill the people if they conducted demonstrations or gatherings."[17]

Heavy police presence in Islamist strongholds signaled the state's resolve to prevent Islamists from protesting. The harsh conditions under which Islamists were likely to be imprisoned if they engaged in protest gave them added incentive not to fall prey to government arrests. Thus, all conditions converged to make Islamists favor hit-and-run violence over peaceful civil disobedience.

In sum, the beginning of Islamist insurgency in Algeria coincided with political exclusion combined with reactive and inconsistent repression. The perceived injustice of the coup combined with extensive organizational networks, activist and community links, and realistic self-assurance to give Islamist grievances material force. Reactive and inconsistent state repression made these conditions possible.

THE LESSON OF ALGERIA

The attacks of September 11, 2001, on the United States and the subsequent war on terrorism and Iraq have brought to the forefront the perennial debate about the desirability and feasibility of democracy in the Muslim world. The official policy of Western governments is that democracy is urgently needed in the Muslim world and a potential solution to the protracted conflicts and terrorism stemming from that part of the globe. The question is, what type of democracy should this be and is there a place for Islamic movements in it? The Western camp is divided between the accommodationists, who want to include Islamists in the political process, and the confrontationalists, who see Islamists as a threat to democratization (Gerges 1999). To the accommodationists, inclusion of Islamists based on a political pact that delineates the parameters of proper political conduct could lead to moderation, pragmatism and, ultimately, a genuine democratic process (Esposito and Voll 1996). To the confrontationalists, inclusion of Islamists, who are inherently antidemocratic and deeply anti-Western, could lead to theocracy, regional instability, and international terrorism (Rodman 1994; Pipes 1995, 2002; Kramer 1997). Each side may point to Algeria as evidence for their perspectives, but both would be in error.

The choice between moderation and violence in Islamist movements during a democratization process is shaped by the structure of political opportunities, defined as the degree of system accessibility and the nature of state repression. If the democratic process grants Islamists substantive access to state institutions, and if it preemptively and consistently represses extrainstitutional militancy, the opposition will be channeled toward conventional political participation and shun violence. If, on the other hand, the state denies Islamists access and if the state applies repression inconsistently—punishes both moderate and radical strategies of political opposition—Islamists will be channeled toward militancy. This likelihood increases if repression is applied reactively—after an extended period of resource and organizational mobilization on the part of Islamists.

The lesson of Algeria is that neither unencumbered inclusion nor political exclusion is sufficient to produce moderation or militancy, respectively. In addition to inclusion/exclusion, we need to take into account the type of repression policies that could spark rebellion or deter them. In Algeria, the state failed to channel the emerging Islamist movement into conventional political participation and state institutions because it combined the wrong inclusion-repression policy during the ascendant phase of the movement and during its height of power. During the ascendant phase, the state gave Islamists uncircumscribed access to state institutions and permitted Islamists to engage in unhindered extrainstitutional mobilization of resources and people repeatedly. In other words, the Islamists were rewarded when they participated in institutional politics, and they were rewarded when they mobilized in the streets. This allowed the Islamist movement to build up cadres, resources, and organizations with which to exert pressure on the regime and fight back when encountering restrictions and repression.

During the Islamists' height of power—as they were on the verge of national victory—the regime engaged in complete political exclusion and in reactive and inconsistent repression of Islamists. In other words, the regime did not seek to contain Islamists or negotiate the terms of power sharing. On the contrary, it closed all the movement's peaceful options by dismantling its organizations, canceling its earlier victories in local elections, and prohibiting all Islamists from participating in the political process. Not only did it deny a popular party its right to rule, but it also denied it the right to challenge these decisions through peaceful protest. Finally, the state applied repression harshly and then let some eight thousand Islamists go free by early 1993. After three years of political and organizational mobilization, the Islamists had much to lose and, more importantly, had the resources with which to fight back.

The tragic mistakes of the regime were matched by grave mistakes on the part of the Islamist movement. The contradictory rhetoric concerning democracy, the threatening declarations toward the Francophone elite, and the anti-Western discourse, especially during the Gulf War protests, all alienated large segments of the Algerian population, terrified entrenched elites, and gave succor to those in the West who prefer the authoritarian status quo over an Islamic government. As Maddy-Weitzman and Litvak (2003, 69) concluded, "The FIS failed to build a broad anti-government coalition, as Khomeini had done in the Iranian revolution, because its secular partners did not trust its declared adherence to political pluralism." Subsequent attacks on intellectuals, journalists, and foreigners lend credence to the view that Islamists are inherently undemocratic, anti-Western, and intolerant of secular dissent. Governments that normally would not oppose democratic transfer of power—that is, France and the United States—ended up either actively supporting the Algerian putschists (France) or were completely silent with regard to its repression (the United States). Had the Islamist movement presented itself as a genuine political force that seeks to replace authoritarian rule with democratic governance, and had Islamists not opposed the war on Iraq with such anti-Western rhetoric that called for jihad against the new crusaders, domestic and international support for the Algerian regime would have been substantially reduced and may have even precluded the military from acting in the way that it did, as happened in the Philippines in the mid-1980s and Eastern Europe a few years later.

Recent history from the Muslim world suggests that a number of Islamists and governments have internalized some of Algeria's lessons already. During the 2002 parliamentary elections in Morocco, the Party of Justice and Development refrained from overtly religious rhetoric, avoided threatening declarations against the established order or secular parties, and went so far as to limit the number of parliamentary candidates to avoid an overwhelming victory that could possibly frighten the ruling regime (Willis 2002).

As for governments, Jordan has successfully institutionalized its Islamic opposition through a mix of political inclusion and preemptive and consistent repression of extrainstitutional activism. The state allows the Muslim Brotherhood to organize a party, participate in elections, and even hold large numbers of seats in parliament and key positions in state ministries. However, it prohibits mass protests and demonstrations and strictly monitors its activities in civil society—charities, mosques, and professional associations—to prevent it from establishing a social base outside of conventional political channels. As Wiktorowicz (2001, 31) explains, "the [Jordanian] state only permits organized political parties, which are regulated at the Ministry of the Interior. Political content in other venues of organizational work is suppressed." Turkey also allowed Islamists to come to power in the mid-1990s and in 2002. To be sure, political inclusion is often short-lived and is rife with threats of military intervention. Nonetheless, Islamists have learned to negotiate the boundaries of their political opportunity structure (Heper 1997; Narli 2003).

The Moroccan, Jordanian, and Turkish models are far from perfect, but they are feasible given the precariousness of transitioning from authoritarianism to democracy in a world where democratic ideals and advocates are sparse. Institutional inclusion and a policy of preemptive and consistent repression of extrainstitutional strategies will facilitate political institutionalization of Islamists. The success or failure of democratization in the Muslim world will likely depend, at least in part, on astute leaders—both within the state and the Islamist opposition—who have studied and taken to heart the lesson of Algeria.

NOTES

1. The concept of channeling movement strategies comes from Jenkins and Eckert (1986) and McCarthy, Britt, and Wolfson (1991).

2. The only exception to this general trend was the rise of an armed Islamist group called the Mouvement Algérien Islamique Armée but better known as the Bouyali group, after its founder and leader Mustapha Bouyali. This group emerged in 1979 but began to take organizational form in 1982 after a merger of several smaller groups under the leadership of Bouyali. The latter sought to build a militant organization by soliciting moral support from Algeria's preachers and by drawing supporters from various mosques in the middle of

Algeria. Although this group did muster the support of approximately six hundred activists (mainly south of Algiers), it never posed a serious challenge to the Algerian state and was largely shunned by other Islamists and preachers at the time (Khelladi 1992, 73–80; Ayyashi 1993, 192–207; Charef 1994, 27–35; Burgat and Dowell 1997, 265–68).

3. The FIS was licensed in September 1989. Both Chadli and his prime minister, Mouloud Hamrouche, justified the legalization of the FIS as necessary for the democratic process.

4. Abassi was an activist in the al-Qiyam movement in the 1960s and one of three leaders to be arrested for organizing the November 1982 demonstration. He was subsequently imprisoned for two years. Ali Belhaj was imprisoned from 1983 to 1987 for supporting the Bouyali group. He was also an imam (prayer leader) in the al-Sunna mosque at Bab al-Ouad in the capital and organized the October 10 demonstration during the 1988 riots (Shahin 1997, 129–32).

5. For more on the views of Belhaj on democracy, see al-Ahnaf, Botiveau, and Frégosi (1991, 85–99).

6. Islamists were accused by critics of violently imposing their morality on others, especially women. On April 11, 1990, during the month of Ramadan, Islamists in Algiers attempted to forcibly prevent a concert from taking place. This incident, among others, put the FIS on the defensive.

7. In the communes the FIS earned 54.3 percent of the votes, while in the departments it earned 57.4 percent of the votes (Willis 1996, 393–95).

8. Interview with Abassi Madani in al-Hayat, June 28, 1990.

9. The 1989 constitution hardly touched presidential powers. The president headed the Council of Ministers, which allowed him to supervise governmental programs and laws. The right to revise the constitution remained the prerogative of the president. Finally, article 120 allowed the president to dissolve the parliament at any time (Korany and Amrani 1998, 22–23).

10. Prime Minister Sid Ahmed Ghozali put the figures at 55 killed, 326 injured, and 2,976 arrested.

11. Law 91–06 prohibited proxy voting and the use of mosques as a political campaign platform (African Contemporary Record 1990–1992, B440). The new laws also allowed for single-member constituencies and increased the number of parliament seats from 290 to 542.

12. In August 1991, Hachani publicly reaffirmed that only through free elections could the FIS come to power. The state of siege was lifted on September 29, and the first FIS rally since the June events was on October 4. Another peaceful march of three hundred thousand was held on November 1, and a rally was held on December 22. The FIS did not organize demonstrations after July, despite the incarceration of its leadership, and dispersed its rallies and mass marches over three months.

13. Approximately thirty thousand people participated in a mass demonstration on May 27, 1991.

14. It was not until late 1992 that some FIS leaders began publicly calling for jihad and not until 1993, after the emergence of the GIA, that it began to organize seriously an armed wing (Willis 1996; Tawil 1998; Martinez 2000). Rabeh Kebir, in an interview with al-Hayat on January 11, 1993, stated that the FIS had yet to declare jihad but would do so if the regime maintained its repressive policy.

15. It is beyond the scope of this chapter to discuss the reasons behind the failed negotiations, cease-fire, and subsequent violence. For more information and analysis on this aspect of the conflict, see Martinez (1997, 2000) and Hafez (2003, 2004).

16. In 1989 there were about twelve thousand voluntary associations. By 1991, there were forty thousand, many of which were religiously oriented. Although these numbers may appear high, other observers have noted the expansion of voluntary associations throughout Algeria during this period (Qawas 1998; Charef 1994).

17. Interview with Ghamati (Tawil 1998, 93–94). Mustapha Karatali, the emir of al-Rahman militia, which joined the GIA in 1994, confirms Ghamati's remarks. In an interview with *al-Hayat* (February 8, 2000, p. 8), he states that on February 7, 1992, the FIS organized a peaceful demonstration but the regime responded with brutality. Many people were killed and arrested.

REFERENCES

Ahnaf, M. al-, B. Botiveau, and F. Frégosi. 1991. *L'Algérie par ses islamistes*. Paris: Karthala.

Ali, Haider Ibrahim. 1996. *Al-Tiyarat al-Islamiyya wa Qadhiyat al-Dimuqratiyya*. Beirut: Markaz Dirasat al-Wihda al-Arabiyya.

Amar, Mon'am al-. 1996. "al-Jazair wal-Tadidiyya al-Muklifa." In *al-Azma al-Jazairyya: al-Khalifiyyat al-Siyasiya wal-Ijtimaiyya wal-Iqtisadiyya wal-Thaqafiyya*, ed. Sulieman al-Riasni, 39–91. Beirut: Markaz Dirasat al-wihda al-Arabiyya.

Ayyashi, Ahmeda. 1993. *al-Haraka al-Islamiyya fi al-Jazair: al-Joudhour, al-Rumouz, al-Masar*. Casablanca, Morocco: al-Dar al-Biydha.

Bekkar, Rabia. 1997. "Taking up Space in Tlemcen: The Islamist Occupation of Urban Algeria." In *Political Islam*, ed. Joel Beinin and Joe Stork, 283–91. Berkeley: University of California Press.

Brockett, Charles D. 1995. "A Protest-Cycle Resolution of the Repression/Popular-Protest Paradox." In *Repertoires and Cycles of Collective Action*, ed. Mark Traugott, 117–94. Durham, N.C.: Duke University Press.

Burgat, François, and William Dowell. 1997. The *Islamic Movement in North Africa*. Austin: University of Texas Center for Middle Eastern Studies.

Charef, Abed. 1994. *Algérie: Le Grand Dérapage*. Paris: éditions de l'aube.

Eisinger, P. K. 1973. "The Conditions of Protest Behavior in American Cities." *American Political Science Review* 67: 11–28.

Entelis, John P. 1986. *Algeria: The Revolution Institutionalized*. Boulder, Colo.: Westview Press.

———. 1992. "Introduction: State and Society in Transition." In *State and Society in Algeria*, ed. John P. Entelis and Phillip C. Naylor, 1–30. Boulder, Colo.: Westview Press.

———. 1994. "Islam, Democracy and the State: The Reemergence of Authoritarian Politics in Algeria." In *Islamism and Secularism in North Africa*, ed. John Ruedy, 219–51. London: Macmillan.

———. 1996. "Civil Society and the Authoritarian Temptation in Algerian Politics: Islamic Democracy vs. the Centralized State." In *Civil Society in the Middle East*, vol. 2, ed. A. R. Norton, 45–86. Leiden: E. J. Brill.

Esposito, John L., and John O. Voll. 1996. *Islam and Democracy*. New York: Oxford University Press.

Gamson, William A. 1975. *The Strategy of Social Protest*. Homewood, Ill.: Dorsey Press.

Gerges, Fawaz A. 1999. *America and Political Islam: Clash of Cultures or Clash of Interests*. New York: Cambridge University Press.

Ghanim, Ibrahim al-Biyoumi. 1992. *al-Haraka al-Islamiyya fi al-Jazair wa Azmat al-Dimuqratiyya*. Paris: Umat.

Goodwin, Jeff. 1997. "State-Centered Approaches to Social Revolutions: Strengths and Limitations." In *Theorizing Revolutions*, ed. John Foran, 11–37. New York: Routledge.

———. 2001. *No Other Way Out: States and Revolutionary Movements, 1945–1991*. New York: Cambridge University Press.

Goodwin, Jeff, and Theda Skocpol. 1989. "Explaining Revolutions in the Contemporary Third World." *Politics and Society* 17(4): 489–509.

Hafez, Mohammed M. 2000. "Armed Islamist Movements and Political Violence in Algeria." *Middle East Journal* 54(4) (Autumn): 572–91.

———. 2003. *Why Muslims Rebel: Repression and Resistance in the Islamic World*. Boulder, Colo.: Lynne Rienner.

———. 2004. "From Marginalization to Massacres: A Political Process Explanation of GIA Violence in Algeria." In *Islamic Activism: A Social Movement Theory Approach*, ed. Quintan Wiktorowicz, 37–60. Bloomington: Indiana University Press.

Heper, Metin. 1997. "Islam and Democracy in Turkey: Toward a Reconciliation?" *Middle East Journal* 51(1) (Winter): 32–45.

Hermassi, Muhammed Abdelbaqi. 1987. *al-Mujtama wal-Dawla fi al-Maghrib al-Arabi*. Beirut: Markaz Dirasat al-Wihda al-Arabiya.

Jasour, Nazim Abdelwahed al-. 1995. "al-Mawqif al-Faransi min al-Islam Asiyasi fi al-Jazair: Ab'aadih al-Iqlimiyya wal-Dawliyya." *al-Mustaqbal al-Arabi* 202 (December): 43–59.

Jenkins, J. Craig, and Charles Perrow. 1977. "Insurgency of the Powerless: Farm Worker Movements (1946–1972)" *American Sociological Review* 42: 249–68.

Jenkins, J. Craig, and Craig M. Eckert. 1986. "Channeling Black Insurgency." *American Sociological Review* 51(6): 812–29.

Kharfallah, al-Tahir bin. 1996. "al-Huriyyat al-Umoumiyya wa Huquq al-Insan fi al-Jazair min Khilal Destour 1976 wa 1989: Dirasa Muqarana." In *al-Azma al-Jazairyya: al-Khalifiyyat Asiyasiya wal-Ijtimaiyya wal-Iqtisadiyya wal-Thaqafiyya*, ed. Sulieman al-Riyashi, 93–108. Beirut: Markaz Dirasat al-wihda al-Arabiyya.

———. 1997. "Mu'ana al-Sahafa al-Mustaqila fi al-Jazair." *Shuoun al-Awsat* 59 (January–February): 81–95.

Khelladi, Aïssa. 1992. *Les islamistes algériens face au pouvoir*. Algiers: Alfa.

Kitschelt, Herbert. 1986. "Political Opportunity Structures and Political Protest: Anti-Nuclear Movements in Four Democracies." *British Journal of Political Science* 16: 57–85.

Klandermans, Bert. 1984. "Mobilization and Participation: Social-Psychological Expansions of Resource Mobilization Theory." *American Sociological Review* 49: 583–600.

Korany, Bahgat, and Saad Amrani. 1998. "Explosive Civil Society and Democratization from Below: Algeria." In *Political Liberalization and Democratization in the Arab World:*

Volume 2, Comparative Experiences, ed. Bahgat Korany, Rex Brynen, and Paul Noble, 12–35. Boulder, Colo.: Lynne Rienner.

Kramer, Martin. 1997. "The Mismeasure of Political Islam." In *The Islamism Debate*, ed. Martin Kramer, 161–73. Tel Aviv: Moshe Dayan Center for Middle Eastern and African Studies.

Kriesi, Hanspeter, Ruud Koopmans, Jan Willem Duyvendak, and Marco G. Giugni. 1992. "New Social Movements and Political Opportunities in Western Europe." *European Journal of Political Research* 22: 219–44.

————. 1995. *New Social Movements in Western Europe*. London: University College London Press.

Kurzman, Charles. 1996. "Structural Opportunity and Perceived Opportunity in Social Movement Theory: The Iranian Revolution of 1979." *American Sociological Review* 61 (February): 153–70.

Labat, Séverine. 1995. *Les Islamistes algériens: entre les urnes et le maquis*. Paris: Seuil.

Lamchichi, Abderrahim. 1992. *L'Islamisme en Algérie*. Paris: L'Harmattan.

Lichbach, Mark Irving. 1987. "Deterrence or Escalation? The Puzzle of Aggregate Studies of Repression and Dissent." *Journal of Conflict Resolution* 31: 266–97.

————. 1995. *The Rebel's Dilemma*. Ann Arbor: University of Michigan Press.

Loveman, Mara. 1998. "High-Risk Collective Action: Defending Human Rights in Chile, Uruguay, and Argentina." *American Journal of Sociology* 104(2): 477–525.

Maddy-Weitzman, Bruce, and Meir Litvak. 2003. "Islamism and the State in North Africa." In *Revolutionaries and Reformers: Contemporary Islamist Movements in the Middle East*, ed. Barry Rubin. Albany: State University of New York Press.

Martinez, Luis. 1997. "Les enjeux des négociations entre l'AIS et l'armée." *Politique Étrangère* 62(4) (Winter 1997–98): 499–510.

————. 2000. *The Algerian Civil War, 1990–1998*. New York: Columbia University Press.

McAdam, Doug. 1982. *Political Process and the Development of Black Insurgency, 1930–1970*. Chicago: University of Chicago Press.

McAdam, Doug, John D. McCarthy, and Mayer N. Zald, eds. 1996. *Comparative Perspectives on Social Movements: Political Opportunities, Mobilizing Structures, and Cultural Framings*. New York: Cambridge University Press.

McAdam, Doug, Sidney Tarrow, and Charles Tilly. 1997. "Toward an Integrated Perspective on Social Movements and Revolution." In *Comparative Politics: Rationality, Culture and Structure*, ed. Mark Irving Lichbach and Alan S. Zuckerman, 142–73. New York: Cambridge University Press.

McCarthy, John D., David Britt, and Mark Wolfson. 1991. "The Institutional Channeling of Social Movements by the State in the United States." In *Research in Social Movements, Conflicts, and Change*, ed. Louis Kriesberg, 45–76. Greenwich, Conn.: JAI Press.

Mecham, R. Quinn. 2002. "Out of Virtue, a Promise of Light: The Transformation of Political Islam in Turkey." Conference paper presented at the Islam and Political Institutions panel of the Middle East Studies Association Annual Meeting held in Washington, D.C., November 23–26.

Moore, Will H. 1998. "Repression and Dissent: Substitution, Context, and Timing." *American Journal of Political Science* 42(3): 851–73.

Mortimer, Robert. 1991. "Islam and Multiparty Politics in Algeria." *Middle East Journal* 45(4) (Autumn): 575–93.

Narli, Nilufer. 2003. "The Rise of the Islamist Movement in Turkey." In *Revolutionaries and Reformers: Contemporary Islamist Movements in the Middle East*, ed. Barry Rubin, 125–40. Albany: State University of New York Press.

Oberschall, Anthony. 1993. *Social Movements: Ideologies, Interests, and Identities*. New Brunswick, N.J.: Transaction Publishers.

Opp, Karl-Dieter, Peter Voss, and Christine Gern. 1995. *Origins of Spontaneous Revolution: East Germany, 1989*. Ann Arbor: University of Michigan Press.

Parsa, Misagh. 2000. *States, Ideologies, and Social Revolutions: A Comparative Analysis of Iran, Nicaragua and the Philippines*. New York: Cambridge University Press.

Pipes, Daniel. 1995. "There Are no Moderates: Dealing with Fundamentalist Islam." *National Interest* 41 (Fall): 48–57.

———. 2002. *In the Path of God: Islam and Political Power*. New Brunswick, N.J.: Transaction Publishers.

Piven, F. F., and R. A. Cloward. 1977. *Poor People's Movements: Why They Succeed, How They Fail*. New York: Vintage.

Qawas, Muhammed. 1998. *Ghazwit "al-Inqaz": M'araket al-Islam al-Siyasi fi al-Jazair*. Beirut: Dar al-Jadid.

Quandt, William B. 1998. *Between Ballots and Bullets: Algeria's Transition from Authoritarianism*. Washington, D.C.: Brookings Institution Press.

Rakhila, Amer. 1993. *al-Tatawur al-Siyasi wal-Tanzimi li-Hizb Jabhat al-Tahrir al-Watani, 1960–1980*. Algeria: Diwan al-Matbouat al-Jamiya.

Rasi, George al-. 1997. *al-Islam al-Jazairi: min al-Amir Abd al-Kader ila Umara al-Jama'at*. Beirut: Dar al-Jadid.

Rasler, Karen. 1996. "Concessions, Repression, and Political Protest in the Iranian Revolution." *American Sociological Review* 61 (February): 132–52.

Roberts, Hugh. 1991. "A Trial of Strength: Algerian Islamism." In *Islamic Fundamentalism and the Gulf Crisis*, ed. James P. Piscatori. Chicago: The Fundamentalism Project, University of Chicago Press.

———. 1992. "The Algerian State and the Challenge of Democracy." *Government and Opposition* 27(4) (Autumn): 433–54.

———. 1994a. "Doctrinaire Economics and Political Opportunism in the Strategy of Algerian Islamism." In *Islamism and Secularism in North Africa*, ed. John Ruedy, 123–417. London: Macmillan.

———. 1994b. "From Radical Mission to Equivocal Ambition: The Expansion and Manipulation of Algerian Islamism, 1979–1992." In *Accounting for Fundamentalism: The Dynamic Character of Movements*, ed. Martin E. Marty and R. Scott Appleby, 428–89. Chicago: The Fundamentalism Project, University of Chicago Press.

———. 1996. "The Zeroual Memorandum: The Algerian State and the Problem of Liberal Reform." *Journal of Algerian Studies* 1: 1–19.

———. 2003. *The Battlefield: Algeria 1988–2002, Studies in a Broken Polity*. New York: Verso.

Rodman, Peter W. 1994. "Co-Opt or Confront Fundamentalist Islam?" *Middle East Quarterly* 1(4) (December): 61–64.

Ruedy, John. 1992. *Modern Algeria: The Origins and Development of a Nation*. Bloomington: Indiana University Press.

Shahin, Emad Eldin. 1997. *Political Ascent: Contemporary Islamic Movements in North Africa*. Boulder, Colo.: Westview Press.

Skocpol, Theda. 1979. *States and Social Revolutions*. New York: Cambridge University Press.

Tahiri, Nur al-Din al-. 1992. *al-Jazair: Bayna al-Khiyar al-Islami wal-Khiyar al-Askari*. Casablanca, Morocco: Dar al-Bidha.

Tarrow, Sidney. 1994. *Power in Movement: Social Movements, Collective Action and Politics*. New York: Cambridge University Press.

———. 1996. "States and Opportunities: The Political Structuring of Social Movements." In *Comparative Perspectives on Social Movements*, ed. Doug McAdam, John D. McCarthy, and Mayer N. Zald, 41–61. New York: Cambridge University Press.

Tawil, Camille al-. 1998. *al-Haraka al-Islamiyya al-Musalaha fi al-Jazair: min al-Inqadh ila al-Jama'a*. Beirut: Dar al-Nahar.

Tilly, Charles. 1978. *From Mobilization to Revolution*. Boston: Addison-Wesley.

Vergès, Meriem. 1997. "Genesis of a Mobilization: The Young Activists of Algeria's Islamic Salvation Front." In *Political Islam*, ed. Joel Beinin and Joe Stork, 292–305. Berkeley: University of California Press.

Wanas, al-Munsaf. 1996. "al-Dawla al-Wataniyya wal Mujtama al-Madani fil Jazair: Muhawala fi Qirait Intifadhit Tishreen al-Awal/October 1988." In *al-Azma al-Jazairiyya: al-Khalfiyyat Asiyasiyya wal Ijtimaiyya wal Iqtisadiyya wal Thaqafiyya*, ed. Sulieman al-Riyashi, 195–209. Beirut: Markaz Dirasat al-Wihda al-Arabiyya.

Wickham-Crowley, Timothy P. 1992. *Guerrillas and Revolution in Latin America: A Comparative Study of Insurgents and Regimes Since 1956*. Princeton, N.J.: Princeton University Press.

Wiktorowicz, Quintan. 2001. *The Management of Islamic Activism: Salafis, the Muslim Brotherhood, and State Power in Jordan*. Albany: State University of New York Press.

Willis, Michael. 1996. *The Islamist Challenge in Algeria: A Political History*. Reading, UK: Ithaca Press.

———. 2002. "'Beards and Ballots': Morocco's Islamists and the Legislative Elections of 2002." Conference paper presented at the Islam and Political Institutions panel of the Middle East Studies Association Annual Meeting held in Washington, D.C., November 23–26.

Yefsah, Abdelkader. 1994. "L'armée et le pouvoir en Algérie de 1962 à 1992." *Revue du monde musulman de la Méditerranée* 65: 74–94.

17 Human Rights Treaties and Their Influence on Democratization

GHANA, UGANDA, AND ZAMBIA

INTRODUCTION

International treaties and regimes have value if and only if they cause states to do what they would otherwise not do (Mitchell 1994, 425). The proliferation of human rights treaty law reflects a widely held assumption that international treaties are an effective remedy against states' violations of human rights. Although hundreds of international and regional human rights treaties enjoy wide state participation, many countries, including most African states, comply poorly. The persistent problem of making states consistently comply with their international agreements makes compliance an important area of study. Aside from Oran Young's (1979) and Roger Fisher's (1981) seminal works on compliance theory more than twenty years ago, compliance has, until recently, been neglected as a focus of study.[1] Scholars have now begun to revisit the issue of compliance in theoretical debates and through empirical studies.

Here, the focus is on three African countries—Ghana, Uganda, and Zambia —and how they have responded to the United Nations (UN) Convention on the Rights of the Child (CRC) and the UN Convention on the Elimination of Discrimination against Women (CEDAW).

COMPLIANCE IN INTERNATIONAL RELATIONS THEORY

The trend in the theoretical literature is to analyze compliance through the prism of international relations theory (Kingsbury 1998; Krasner 1983; Mitchell 1994; Chayes and Chayes 1993). The theoretical debate on compliance is built on the framework of major contending schools of international relations theory with each theory explaining compliance in a significantly different way (Kingsbury 1998, 350). One's answer to the question of why states comply is therefore dependent upon one's understanding of international relations at the broadest level. Hence, various explanations have been postulated based on realism, where the determining factor is power and self-interest (Greico 1988; Morgenthau 1973; Waltz 1979); rational choice theory, where a system of incentives can provide benefits to outweigh the costs of a state not acting in its immediate self-interest (Ruggie 1983; Krasner 1983; 2000); liberalism, where the determinative factors are found in domestic politics (Abbot 1989; Hurrell 1990; Slaughter 1995; Moravcsik 1992, 1998; Koh 1997); or constructivism, where social structures shape actors' identities, interests, and behavior (Wendt 1999).

Because realists and rationalists take self-interest as constant and exogenously determined, their analyses are relegated to enforcement or incentive structures to induce desired state behavior, which are of limited relevance in areas such as human rights. Although liberal theories focus on domestic factors, liberal assertions linking the democratic nature of a government to its likelihood of compliance with international law do not explain how domestic changes make a state more likely to comply. This is problematic in the human rights debate, because how to bring about domestic change is at the heart of the matter. The constructivist approach does recognize the potential for positive transformational effects through interactions in the international system; however, how norms and more specifically how international laws become internalized is not adequately addressed (Klotz 1995; Finnemore 1996). Although each approach raises some important issues, none provide an adequate framework to comprehensively explain the empirical realities of compliance.

In response to the theoretical interest in compliance, empirical studies have sought to flesh out the theoretical debate. Although these studies begin with a discussion of compliance theory, the variables found to substantially impact compliance were not rooted in these theories. For example, Harold Jacobson and Edith Brown Weiss (1998), in a large environmental study explored hypotheses derived from rational choice assumptions, regime theory, and international law, concluded that the most important variables to compliance were domestic leadership, domestic administrative capacity, and the level of activity of local environmental NGOs (nongovernmental organizations). In contrast with the predictions of international relations theory, issues such as power, interests, and the nature of the domestic political system were found to have only an indirect impact upon compliance. Similarly, other studies by Chayes and Chayes (1993), Mitchell (1994), and Victor, Raustiala, and Skolnikoff (1998) found that the variables identified by international relations theory were not determinative in state compliance with the international treaties analyzed.

COMPLIANCE WITH HUMAN RIGHTS TREATIES IN COMMONWEALTH AFRICA

There have been few rigorous attempts to empirically identify the causes of compliance with respect to human rights treaties (Hathaway 2002, 6). In Commonwealth Africa, despite overall low compliance with human rights treaties, some things on the ground have clearly changed.[2] More substantial changes are still necessary, but a better understanding of how these states comply is a precondition for promoting more positive change.

INTERNATIONAL HUMAN RIGHTS LAW: THE UNITED NATIONS TREATY SYSTEM

Treaties are the primary mechanism through which international and regional organizations try to establish universal human rights standards. UN human rights treaties, a major part of the broader human rights regime, create specific binding legal obligations for state parties with each treaty establishing its own mechanism to oversee the compliance process.

UN ENFORCEMENT OF HUMAN RIGHTS STANDARDS

There are a variety of mechanisms available for inclusion in a UN human rights treaty, and each treaty contains some combination of the following: state party reporting procedures, individual complaint procedures, interstate complaint procedures, and inquiry procedures. All UN human rights treaties contain oversight provisions that are similar in form and function. In reality, despite such mechanisms, the UN plays only a weak monitoring and supervisory role, and the implementation of these treaties is left to the state parties.

With respect to the monitoring and supervision provisions of the CEDAW and the CRC, each treaty establishes its own committee to supervise implementation.[3] Although committee members are elected by and are nationals of state parties, they serve in their individual capacities.

State parties are obliged to provide reports to these committees, detailing progress with regard to legislative, judicial, administrative, and other measures to implement the treaty.[4] This reporting obligation requires each state to submit a report after treaty ratification and then every few years thereafter.[5] The reports are considered and discussed at a meeting between the Committee and a government representative. The committees may also invite UN specialized agencies to submit additional reports and attend these meetings. In the case of the CRC, the committee can request that the UN secretary general initiate studies on specific issues relating to children's rights. In addition, NGOs will often submit unofficial "shadow" reports providing detailed information from interested domestic groups to augment or refute a government's report. Although committee members normally read these reports, these reports are not part of the formal process.

At the end of this process, the committees draft "Concluding Observations" that consist of an acknowledgment of the positive aspects of the report, the identification of subjects of concern, and suggestions and recommendations for improvement for that state. The committees do not purport to measure state compliance or determine if and where violations have occurred. This procedure is not a meaningful judicial or enforcement proceeding.

In 1999, an optional protocol to the CEDAW enabled individuals and groups to lodge complaints before the committee, granting individuals and groups in the states that have ratified the protocol direct access to the committee. As with other UN treaties and protocols granting direct access to a human rights committee, decisions made with respect to these complaints are not binding upon the state. No specific individual complaints provision exists within the CRC treaty or in either of the two CRC optional protocols.[6]

DOMESTIC COMPLIANCE PROCESSES

When a state ratifies a treaty, it becomes subject to a treaty's supervision and monitoring mechanisms. Although UN mechanisms are weak, they nonetheless potentially expose state parties to the scrutiny of interested parties, most notably international NGOs that are able to draw international attention to violators. For this reason, governments do consider measures for compliance. However, because UN supervision processes do not pierce the shield of state sovereignty, states can choose either to make an effort at real compliance or to merely adopt measures of ostensible compliance for the benefit of the international community.

Real compliance with UN human rights treaties requires extensive domestic changes. First, the state party must amend its domestic legal framework to cohere with treaty obligations.[7] This involves the enactment of new, appropriate legislation and the repeal of laws that conflict with the treaty. Second, the state party must ensure that the institutions, agencies, and manpower necessary to implement and enforce the new legal standards exist. Third, although these treaties do not make reference to the judiciary, access to the judicial system or some quasi-judicial body is a vital component to protecting and enforcing individuals' legal rights domestically. Fourth, state parties must commit the maximum resources possible given their available resources to implement these laws. Finally, domestic norms in consonance with the treaty's focus must be cultivated. This means that the state must establish a common understanding of the standards of behavior established by the treaty within that society.

While real compliance entails significant commitment and effort by a state, ostensible compliance entails superficial measures such as law and policy documents drafted to merely satisfy UN supervision mechanisms that are never intended to be implemented.

THE INCORPORATION OF HUMAN RIGHTS TREATIES INTO THE DOMESTIC ARENA

The fact of ratification does not provide insight into how a country will respond to meeting treaty obligations. The weak UN supervision and monitoring processes mean that, in practice, implementation and compliance is essentially a domestic process.

UGANDA AND THE CRC

The CRC has had a significant impact on law and policy in Uganda. Uganda ratified the CRC in 1990. The government created the Child Law Review Committee to review the legal system and change all laws not in compliance with the country's treaty obligations. The result was a restructuring of the law and the judicial system.[8] Specifically, the 1995 constitution included a provision that specifically protected the rights of children.[9] The legislature also enacted the Children's Statute, which incorporated all child rights and protection laws into one domestic statute. The statute's content follows the CRC closely.

The new law articulates all the children's rights embodied in the CRC and overhauled both government and judicial structures in order to implement the statute. The salient provisions are the following: First, the law requires that all local governments appoint a secretary of Children's Affairs to be responsible for children's welfare in each district.[10] Second, the existing Village Resistance Committee Courts are to act as courts of first instance for minor criminal offenses with powers to grant limited remedies.[11] Third, the law creates a family and children's court system to deal specifically with all criminal matters (excluding capital offenses) and civil matters involving children. Fourth, the law creates stringent rules for special, protective treatment of children charged with criminal offenses. All courts must apply the Children's Statute, including the obligation to protect children from harmful cultural or social practices.[12]

The CRC has also had an impact on how new laws are framed. For example, the Land Act (1998) now provides for the consent of a child in the sale of the land upon which the family resides, and the penal laws have also been amended to make child protection laws more stringent.[13]

In 1996, the National Council for Children Act established the National Council for Children (NCC). The NCC's mandate is to coordinate and implement all aspects of children's welfare, including implementation of the Children's Statute and the National Program of Action for Children (a strategy paper on how to reach stated goals, including the necessary budget allocations). The NCC operates in conjunction with various government ministries, local government, NGOs, and international organizations. The NCC has ensured that there is a child rights dimension in the various government sector policy papers, particularly with respect to education and health (the Universal Primary Education Policy and the National Health Policy, respectively). There have been significant increases in resource allocation to social services.

UGANDA AND THE CEDAW

The legal reforms to women's rights are enshrined in the constitution. The 1995 Uganda constitution goes further than to simply prohibit discrimination against women. First, the constitution provides for affirmative action in favor of marginalized groups on the basis of sex, age, disability, or any other reason created by history, tradition, or custom to redress inequities that exist. The constitution itself mandates that there be a female representative for every district in the parliament and that one-third of the membership of each local government council be reserved for women.[14] The Local Government Act reiterates this constitutional provision. These affirmative action provisions have been implemented to significantly improve the representation of women in the public sector.[15]

Second, the constitution prohibits any laws, customs, or traditions that are against the dignity, welfare, or interests of women or that undermine their status.[16] This obviates the problem of customary law (in law but not always in practice) by making any discriminatory customary laws unconstitutional.

Third, the constitution reforms the laws of marriage. Prior to the new constitution, there were various pieces of legislation governing marriage that contained provisions in conflict with the CEDAW.[17]

Fourth, the constitution provides that the parliament must enact laws to remove any discrimination in the workplace and must ensure equal pay for equal work.

In 1988, the government created the Ministry of Women in Development, charged with women's affairs. The ministry has made some notable achievements, which include the formulation and implementation of a National Gender Policy, gender dimensions to sector policy frameworks such as education and health, data collection on the basis of gender, research in the area of women's rights, legal education for women, gender sensitivity training within the government, and advocacy and awareness in the general public.

The National Gender Policy framework calls for the reform of gender-neutral laws to incorporate a gender dimension. For example, the newly reformed Land Act not only deemed all customs preventing women for inheriting land null and void but also has created land committees to administer and protect the interests of women. At least one member of each land committee must by law be a woman.

ZAMBIA AND THE CRC

Despite its ratification of the CRC, Zambia has not changed any of its legislation vis-à-vis children or made any serious effort toward complying with its treaty obligations. The 1996 constitution does not specifically provide for the protection of children's rights; instead, children's rights are subsumed under the general bill of rights. Moreover, the constitution provides that laws with respect to adoption, marriage, divorce, other matters of personal law, and customary law are exceptions to the bill of rights.[18] This means that the failure to provide adequate legal protection for children is constitutionally sanctioned. This constitutional provision combined with a customary court system to apply traditional or customary laws exclusively makes the effective implementation of children's rights impossible.[19]

Several statutory laws are also inconsistent with the CRC. For example, the Employment of Young Persons and Children's Act, the primary piece of legislation addressing child labor, was amended in 1989 but not in coherence with the restrictions on child labor in the CRC. The act does not provide a comprehensive child labor legal framework or adequate protection for the children the law does cover. For example, the statute regulates children working in industry but does not apply to commercial, agriculture, domestic, or any other area of the informal sector where child labor is endemic.[20] Furthermore, the few protections provided by this law are not enforced. The Labor Office does not monitor child labor or seek the prosecution of offenders, and even if this statute were to be enforced, its limited scope and lenient penalties would not discourage child employment.[21] As a result, child labor in urban and rural areas continues unabated.[22]

After the ratification of the CRC, the government drafted the National Program of Action for Zambian Children (NPA) that delineates its plans to address the issue of children's rights. The policy paper addresses strategies to improve access to child education and health services as part of the broader development effort. The document is devoid of any rights language; access to education and health services is not addressed as a matter of rights; and civil, political, or social rights for children are not included. Disaggregated expenditure on children specifically is not available; however, the budget allocation for both health services and education in real terms has declined every year in the last decade.[23] The NPA paper does acknowledge Zambia's ratification of the CRC, but its framers consider the CRC more a loose set of guidelines than a legally binding international treaty.[24]

Thus far the government's efforts to implement its legal obligations under the CRC remain minimal. The several laws that need to be amended or replaced to comply with CRC have not been changed.[25] Moreover, there has been no constitutional amendment to remove the customary law exception discussed above, which is crucial for the effective implementation of children's rights.

ZAMBIA AND THE CEDAW

The 1996 constitution prohibits all forms of discrimination, including gender discrimination. As with children's rights, the constitutional exception with respect to adoption, marriage, divorce, burial, devolution of property on death, and other matters relating to personal law as well as in the application of customary law also negatively impacts the realization of women's rights (Sampa et al. 1994).[26]

There have, however, been some legal reforms. Many other overtly discriminatory pieces of legislation have been amended. For example, the Employment Act, the Tax Act, and the Land Act were amended to remove provisions that overtly discriminated against women. In addition, the Intestate Succession Act was passed to end the customary practice of relatives rather than a female spouse and children inheriting the family property.[27] There has nevertheless been little success in the campaign to change the constitution, which, as discussed above, is fundamental to the realization of women's rights. Furthermore, there remain problems of effective implementation and the weak enforcement of these protective laws.

The national machinery to implement the CEDAW is the Gender In Development Division (GIDD) in the Cabinet Office. Although ostensibly in a good position to influence decisions, the GIDD has not had a significant impact regarding legal or administrative reforms. The GIDD produced the National Gender Policy but has not been able to effect implementation.[28] The GIDD has acknowledged that the government does not take gender issues seriously and that implementation is not a priority.[29] As one example, the Gender Policy's affirmative action program has not been executed, and the government had made no effort to address the gender gap.[30]

Other policy frameworks, such as health and education policies, do not have gender dimensions. The statistical data shows that with respect to almost all economic indicators, women are worse off than men and that the gap continues to grow as the economy declines.[31] The few gender programs that exist rely heavily on donor support with little budgetary or other logistical assistance from the government.

GHANA AND THE CRC

In Ghana, prior to the ratification of the CRC, many of the laws relating to children had not been amended since colonial times. When the 1992 constitution was established, a few articles from the CRC were incorporated into its provisions—specifically, the child's right to be protected from work that constitutes a threat to his health, education or development; from torture or other cruel, inhumane, or degrading punishment; and from social economic benefits by reason only of religious or other beliefs. The constitution also stipulated that parliament must enact new legislation to ensure adequate care by parents and to provide special protection against exposure to physical and moral hazards.[32]

These constitutional provisions were clearly not an effort to incorporate all the obligations articulated in the CRC but marked the beginning of the process of legal reform in children's rights. In 1998, the Children's Act was enacted into law. This statute created a comprehensive legal framework for children that corresponded to the provisions of the CRC in many respects and repealed or amended several contravening laws.[33]

The CRC did result in a change in the laws and policy framework; however, the government has generally not implemented or enforced these laws and policies. In many cases, these laws provide for the creation of new agencies or the allocation of additional resources for effective implementation. As the examples cited indicate, the government has made no effort to either implement or enforce the legislation.

The Children's Act mandates the restructuring of the juvenile justice system. It creates Child Panels, nonjudicial bodies with limited jurisdiction and powers, to grant remedies in civil and criminal cases involving children. These panels, however, have not been created, and as a result children continue to go through the adult criminal system and are still routinely imprisoned with adults.[34] The Criminal Code (Amendment) Act that criminalizes female genital mutilation is not enforced. Despite widespread practice, only seven people have been arrested under this law passed in 1994 and none have been prosecuted (UNICEF 2000, 94). With respect to child labor, all forms are prevalent and highly visible in both rural and urban areas in spite of legislative restrictions. There is no effort to monitor child labor or to enforce the existing labor laws.[35]

The government also adopted various new policy frameworks that refer to the CRC (National Program of Action, Ghana Vision 2020, The Child Cannot Wait, and The Program for Free Basic Education by the Year 2005), yet the government continues to address education and health much the same way as it did before. Government spending on education has not significantly increased since 1988, and per capita spending per child is low, even for sub-Saharan standards.[36] In the area of health, the overall budget allocation seems low; however, evaluating access to and standard of health facilities for children is difficult without adequate data.[37]

The Department of Social Welfare is charged with responsibility for social rights for children. This department has not been allocated additional resources to address children's rights and remains one of the most underfunded government departments in Ghana. As a consequence, the department has no capacity to implement the rights articulated in the treaty.[38] These examples demonstrate Ghana's failure to meet the treaty's "maximum possible" resource allocation standard for economic, social, and cultural rights.

GHANA AND THE CEDAW

The 1992 Ghanaian constitution prohibits discrimination on all bases, including gender.[39] It further allows for, but does not require, affirmative action to redress social, economic, and educational imbalances in Ghanaian society.[40] The constitution's women's rights section contains three articles providing for prenatal and postnatal care for mothers, maternity leave, day care for preschool children, and equal training for and promotion of women.[41] The government excluded many of the other proposals favorable to women's rights recommended by the Committee of Constitutional Experts for the new constitution.[42]

There have been few other legislative changes. Parliament has passed new legislation on inheritance to protect women from being disinherited when their spouses die and, in criminal law, outlawing female genital mutilation.[43] However, there remain several overtly discriminatory statutes on the books. For example, Ghanaian law accords different rights to marriages under the marriage ordinance, customary marriages, and marriage under the Mohammedans ordinance. Aside from the inferior position of women in general in customary marriages, the latter two allow polygamous marriage that, by definition, contravenes the CEDAW's mandate of equality in marriage and family relations.[44] Other examples include an article in the constitution that makes obtaining citizenship more difficult for spouses of female Ghanaians than for spouses of male Ghanaians and the Labor Decree of 1997 that prohibits the employ of females in mines, underground work, or any industrial work at night.

The primary government body for the role of achieving gender equality is the National Council on Women and Development (NCWD). The NCWD does not have the power, influence, or resources to implement gender policies, push for legislative changes, or ensure that existing laws are implemented. The government has drawn up a draft National Gender Policy and a draft Ghana Plan of Action; however, these policies have not been implemented.[45] No new additional government machinery has been established to protect and promote women's rights at the policy level.

EXPLAINING THE DIFFERENCES

Although both the CRC and the CEDAW induced some changes in each country, the extent and quality of these changes were significantly different. In Zambia and Ghana, the changes have been superficial and relegated to the low-cost exercise of enacting laws and empty policy documents that were not accompanied by logistical support or the resources necessary for implementation and enforcement. In contrast, Uganda has made an effort at real compliance and has made progress beyond simply enacting laws and drafting policy documents. The legal framework in each case was a more complete reflection of the provisions of the CRC (essentially reproduced in the Children's Statute) and the CEDAW. Furthermore, the government provided adequate and appropriate government machinery with real powers and resources to implement the law and propel women and children's rights in Uganda.

The difference in results between Ghana and Zambia on the one hand and Uganda on the other was not that they had significantly different domestic political systems; they do not. In each country, power is consolidated in the presidency such that the president, virtually independently, sets all important national laws and policies. This overwhelming presidential power has become institutionalized and has persisted despite regime changes and dramatic economic reforms in all of the three countries studied. The implication of this for treaty compliance is that the president rather than a spectrum of domestic actors determines the domestic treaty implementation and compliance processes.

In each case, the president decided when a treaty would be ratified, what laws and policies would be drafted, and the extent to which government agencies worked to implement these laws and policies. Thus, the president determined whether compliance would be real or ostensible, and this was clearly reflected in the comprehensiveness of the laws and policies, the motivation of government machinery to implement these laws and policies, the allocation of resources, and the state's willingness to allow the NGO community to work effectively. President Museveni's personal interest in the promotion of women and children's rights (which does not extend to general civil and political rights) explains the remarkable progress in Uganda.

If the key to treaty compliance in these countries is the interest of the president, general recommendations to improve compliance are difficult to make. This notwithstanding, there are currently important changes under way that loosen the president's grip on political power and may bode well for treaty compliance and human rights in general. In Ghana and Zambia, the systemic change from one-party to multiparty states has eased primary party political domination over the legislature, thus reducing the ability of the president, who controls the party, to independently dictate law and policy. With respect to real compliance, this could mean that in the future the legislature and an unencumbered judiciary are able to assume important roles in the process. The potential impact of these institutions in the compliance process is an interesting area for future study.

These changes have already had an impact in enabling NGOs unaffiliated with the government to operate and proliferate.[46] In Zambia and Ghana, this occurred with the change from a one-party to a multiparty state system; in Uganda, this occurred with the institution of the Museveni government. The proliferation of NGOs has not yet made a substantial impact independently because of stringent political controls, but the reduction of presidential power and increased influence of other government institutions expands the capacity for NGOs to assume greater influence. Paradoxically, in countries such as Uganda, democratic changes in the political regime, particularly if combined with a change in president, may have a negative impact on treaty implementation with the CRC and the CEDAW. If, however, the changes made thus far can become institutionalized, the laws and policies should become internalized as domestic norms such that reversal is no longer conceivable.

CONCLUSION

Empirical studies demonstrate that compliance is always a highly complex process of separate but related international and domestic processes. The UN human rights treaty process articulates universal standards but does little to propel domestic implementation and compliance. The domestic process occurs largely independently of the international process, with a state's domestic political system having crucial implications for compliance. A state's political system essentially determines if and how the state will respond to the human rights treaty it has ratified, but the treaties themselves have not, as yet, had significant impact on the process of democratization. This can only occur with change in the international treaty system that will enable the international system to impinge upon the domestic system.

In the countries examined, all three states responded to the treaty by, at a minimum, making superficial changes to satisfy the noninvasive UN supervision procedures and, at a maximum, making a real effort to comply. Which way it went was determined by the interest of the president in the treaty subject matter. This interest provided the stimulus for action by government institutions and, moreover, made possible the government-NGO collaboration vital for effective change. This is not to imply that the interest of the president can overcome all obstacles to compliance. Other factors such as national poverty, weak institutions, inadequate manpower, and HIV/AIDS, which affect both government and NGOs, still undermine treaty implementation. However, without presidential interest, state machinery does not become engaged in the implementation process, and NGOs are unable to independently propel the process beyond superficial compliance.

Human rights treaty law can and has worked to transfer international legal standards into the domestic legal arena. In Ghana, Uganda, and Zambia, real compliance with these legal standards depended on domestic politics but did little to independently impact the democratization process. Without significant changes to the UN international treaty system that allow treaty law to impinge on sovereignty to engender compliance, the level of compliance will depend on the domestic political situation but will not impact it or positively influence the domestic democratization processes. This notwithstanding, even ostensible human rights treaty compliance in the form of new legislation and policies holds the potential to provide a platform for progress realized in the future. The laws and policies that are already on the books could provide a focal point for domestic pressure groups and NGOs so that as they gain strength, they can leverage international support to engender significant domestic change in both human rights implementation and democratization.

NOTES

1. Young (1979) explains the problem of compliance in the context of the decentralized international system and makes suggestions to strengthen compliance mechanisms through formal and informal International institutions. Fisher (1981) argued that the best way to foster compliance was through the enforcement of legal judicial decisions of domestic and international legal institutions. He rejected the argument for general enforcement of standing rules and contended that the compliance problem should be addressed in the framework of ensuring compliance with the legal decisions made in the application of those laws—second-order compliance.

2. Almost all countries sign and ratify at least some human rights agreements; almost all countries are willing to pay lip service to the idea of human rights; and almost all countries (excluding countries involved in civil wars) have experienced some positive changes in areas of human rights practice.

3. The Committee on the Elimination of Discrimination against Women and the Committee on the Convention on the Rights of the Child.

4. Article 18 of the CEDAW and Article 44 of the CRC.

5. Every four years for the CEDAW and every five years for the CRC.

6. There are two optional protocols to the Convention on the Rights of the Child: the Optional Protocol on the Involvement of Children in Armed Conflicts, and the Optional Protocol on the Sale of Children, Child Prostitution and Child Pornography.

7. The study of the implementation of domestic implementation of international treaties is generally undertaken by domestic lawyers studying compliance within a specific area of the law. There are few comparative analyses; one example is Lutz and Sikkink's (2000) study of international human rights law and practice in Latin America. These authors, however, focus upon normative change in broad categories of human rights and not change in response to specific human rights treaties.

8. The Children's Statute repealed or amended the following inconsistent laws: the Penal Code (amended), the Probation Act (amended), the Approved Schools Act (repealed), the Reformatory Schools Act (repealed), the Adoption of Children Act (repealed), the Affiliation Act (repealed), the Magistrates Court Act (amended), the Judicature Act (amended), and the Resistance Committees (Judicial Powers) Statute (amended).

9. Article 34.

10. Part III of the statute and also included in the Local Government Act of 1997.

11. These include reconciliation, compensation, restitution, apology, caution, or a guidance order.

12. Article 8.

13. For example, defilement—sexual relations with an individual below the age of eighteen—is a capital offense.

14. Article 32(1), Article 78, and Article 180, respectively.

15. Thus in 2000, the vice president is a woman, and women constitute 13 percent of the cabinet, 18 percent of the national legislature (of the fifty-three female members of Parliament, thirty-nine were elected as a result of the affirmative action program that reserves these seats for women, and five are the result of seats reserved for disadvantaged groups), 45 percent of the local government councilors, 21 percent of the top decision makers in the civil service, and 23 percent of judicial officeholders.

16. Article 33(6).

17. Article 31 of the constitution provides that only men and women over the age of eighteen have the right to get married, that all marriages must be consensual, and that widows' inheritance from a spouse are constitutionally protected.

18. Article 23.

19. The customary court system is the most accessible to the general population in the judicial system. These courts have wide jurisdictional powers in family law, including the adjudication of cases relating to property, inheritance, marriage, and maintenance. Customary

law does not have a strict legal definition of a child, and children (arbitrarily determined by an adjudicating court) are generally not recognized as having enforceable rights per se. This has serious consequences for any effort to protect children's rights. For example, under the customary law of marriage, an individual is generally considered old enough to marry once puberty has been reached. The customary law exception to the constitution's bill of rights means that the customary marriage of an underaged person is both legal and constitutionally sanctioned.

20. According to a survey by the International Labor Organization and the Central Statistical Office, 87 percent of all working children are engaged in agriculture and not in industry. See Government of the Republic of Zambia and the International Labor Organization (1999).

21. The Labor Office states that it cannot respond to reports of child labor abuse because of the lack of resources. The fines levied in penalties are stated in currency that has been devalued several times since the enactment of the law.

22. In Zambia, 58.6 percent of all children ages five through fourteen and 41.6 percent of children ages fifteen through seventeen worked in the twelve months preceding a 1999 survey by the ILO and Central Statistical Office (Government of the Republic of Zambia and the International Labor Organization 1999).

23. See Government of the Republic of Zambia (2000b, 7).

24. The last page of the document addresses the issue of children's rights and acknowledges the problems with the current legal system but makes no proposals to change the laws.

25. See Zambia's initial report to the CRC Committee (Government of the Republic of Zambia 2002).

26. Customary law is based on the idea of fundamental differences in the roles of the sexes in society, and therefore, in most cases, women are considered subordinate to men.

27. In contrast, upon the death of a wife, the property automatically devolves to her husband.

28. The Gender Policy was drafted in 1996 and was only adopted in 2000 with pressure from women's groups on the eve of a UN conference.

29. See Government of the Republic of Zambia (2000a).

30. In the year 2000, women constituted 11 percent of the members of parliament, 9 percent of the cabinet, 5 percent of the deputy ministers, 18.5 percent of High Court and Supreme Court judges, and 5 percent of local government councilors. See Non-Governmental Organizations Coordination Committee (2000).

31. See Men and Women in Zambia: Facts and Figures. 1996. Central Statistical Office.

32. Article 28.

33. The bill revised, amended, or repealed the following legislation that contravened the CRC: the Marriage Ordinance (amended), the Adoption Act (repealed), the Labor Decree of 1967 (amended), the Scouts and Girl Guides Decree (amended), the Maintenance Decree (repealed), the Day Centers Decree (repealed), the Intestate Succession Law (amended), the Social Security Law (amended), the Courts Act (amended), the Maintenance of Children Act (Commencement) Instrument of 1965 (revoked), the Maintenance of Children Decree (Commencement) Instrument of 1978 (revoked), and the Day Care Regulations of 1979 (amended).

34. There are only five institutional homes. Detention in an industrial school or institution is a mandated period of three years—often longer than an adult prison sentence for a similar

offense. This is a further disincentive for a child to go through the juvenile system and raises additional child rights issues.

35. The closest estimates are from the 1992 census survey that puts the percentage of working children between the ages of ten and fourteen at 39 percent. Also see Van Ham, Blavo, and Opoku (1993).

36. The average expenditure in sub-Saharan Africa is 3.6 percent for education and 1.5 percent for health. Ghana is considered one of the richer nations, and its allocation in 2000 was 3.1 percent.

37. Aside from data on under-five mortality rates, disaggregated data with respect to children's access to health and the standards of health facilities is not collected. In 2000, the budget allocation was 1.3 percent of GDP.

38. See UNICEF (2000).

39. Articles 12(2).

40. Article 17.

41. Article 27.

42. See Ghana Committee of Experts (Constitution) (1991).

43. The Intestate Succession Law 1985, the Interstate Succession (Amendment) Law 1991, and the Criminal Code (Amendment) Act.

44. Article 16.

45. Within the government itself, there are still very few women in positions of influence. In the last election, women formed only 9 percent of Parliament and 2.9 percent of the District Assembly and were only 10 percent of the cabinet ministers, 8.5 percent of the ministers, 16 percent of the members of the Council of State, and 11 percent of magistrates and judges.

46. See Keck and Sikkink's (1998) tabulation of the increase in overall number of NGOs.

REFERENCES

Abbot, Kenneth. 1989. "Modern International Relations Theory: A Prospectus for International Lawyers." *Yale Journal of International Law* (14): 335.

Alston, Philip. 1992. *The United Nations and Human Rights: A Critical Appraisal.* Oxford and New York: Clarendon Press and Oxford University Press.

Chayes, Abram, and Antonia Handler Chayes. 1993. "On Compliance." *International Organization* 47(2): 175–205.

Finnemore, Martha. 1996. *National Interests in International Society.* Ithaca, N.Y.: Cornell University Press.

Finnemore, Martha, and Kathryn Sikkink. 1998. "International Norm Dynamics and Political Change." *International Organization* 52(4): 887–917.

Fisher, Roger. 1981. *Improving Compliance with International Law.* Charlottesville: University of Virginia Press.

Ghana Committee of Experts (Constitution). 1991. *Proposals for a Draft Constitution of Ghana.* Accra: Ghana Publishing Corporation.

Government of the Republic of Zambia. 1996. *Women and Men in Zambia: Facts and Figures.* Central Statistical Office. Lusaka: Government Printers.

————. 2000a. *Gender, Population, and Development in Zambia: A Review of the Laws and Policies.* Gender Development Division. Lusaka: Government Printers.

————. 2000b. *Report on the Follow-up to the World Summit for Children.* Lusaka: Government Printers.

————. 2002. *Zambia Report to the UN Committee on the Rights of the Child.* Lusaka: Government Printers.

Government of the Republic of Zambia and International Labor Organization. 1999. *The Child Labor Survey Country Report.* Lusaka: Government Printers.

Greico, Joseph. 1988. "Anarchy and the Limits of Cooperation." *International Organization* 32(3): 485–508.

Hathaway, Oona. 2002. "Do Treaties Make a Difference? Examining Compliance with Human Rights Treaties." *Yale Journal of Law* 111(8): 1935–2039.

Hurrell, Andrew, and Benedict Kingsbury. 1990. *The International Politics of the Environment.* Oxford: Clarendon Press.

Jacobson, Harold, and Judith Weiss. 1998. *Engaging Countries.* Cambridge, Mass.: MIT Press.

Keck, Margaret E., and Kathryn Sikkink. 1998. *Activists Beyond Borders: Advocacy Networks in International Politics.* Ithaca, N.Y.: Cornell University Press.

Kingsbury, Benedict. 1998. "The Concept of Compliance as a Function of Competing Conceptions of International Law." *Michigan Journal of International Law* 19(2): 345–73.

Klotz, Audie. 1995. *Norms in International Relations: The Struggle against Apartheid.* Ithaca, N.Y.: Cornell University Press.

Koh, Harold Hongju. 1997. "Why Do Nations Obey International Law?" *Yale Law Journal* 106: 2598–2659.

Krasner, Stephen D., ed. 1983. *International Regimes.* Ithaca, N.Y.: Cornell University Press.

————. 2000. *Sovereignty: Organized Hypocrisy.* Princeton, N.J.: Princeton University Press.

Lutz, Ellen, and Kathryn Sikkink. 2000. "International Human Rights Law and Practice in Latin America." *International Organization* 54(3): 663–59.

Mitchell, Ronald B. 1994. *International Oil Pollution at Sea: Environmental Policy and Treaty Compliance.* Cambridge, Mass.: MIT Press.

Moravcsik, Andrew. 1992. *Liberalism and International Relations Theory.* Cambridge, Mass.: Center for International Affairs.

————. 1998. *Explaining the Emergence of Human Rights Regimes: Liberal Democracy and Liberal Uncertainty in Postwar Europe.* Cambridge, Mass.: Weatherhead Center for International Affairs, Harvard University.

Morgenthau, Hans J. 1973. *Politics among Nations.* 4th ed. New York: Knopf.

Non-Governmental Organizations Coordination Committee of Zambia. 2002. *Report on the Current Legal and Socio-Economic Status of Women in Zambia.* Lusaka: NGOCC Publications.

Ruggie, John. 1983. "Continuity and Transformation in the World Polity: Towards a Neorealist Synthesis." *World Politics* 35(2): 261–85.

Sampa, Annie, et al. 1994. *Gender Bias in the Zambian Court System.* Lusaka: Women in Law and Development in Africa Publications.

Slaughter, Ann-Marie. 1995. "International Law in a World of Liberal States." *European Journal of International Law* (6): 503–38.

UNICEF. 2000. *The Situation Analysis of Children and Women in Ghana.* Accra: UNICEF Publications.

Van Ham, Nana Apt, E. G. Blavo, and S. K. Opoku. 1993. *Street Children in Accra: A Survey Report.* Accra: UNICEF Publications.

Victor, David, Kal Raustiala, and Eugene B. Skolnikoff. 1998. *The Implementation and Effectiveness of International Environmental Commitments: Theory and Practice.* Cambridge, Mass.: MIT Press.

Waltz, Kenneth. 1979. *Theory of International Politics.* Reading, Mass.: Addison-Wesley.

Wendt, Alexander. 1999. *Social Theory of International Politics.* Cambridge and New York: Cambridge University Press.

Young, Oran. 1979. *Compliance and Public Authority: A Theory with International Applications.* Baltimore: Johns Hopkins University Press.

PART FIVE

Western and Eastern Europe

LADA PARIZKOVA

18 European Counterterrorism Lessons for U.S. Policy

European nations have had significantly more experience with international terrorism than has the United States. They have handled terrorism in various ways—sometimes through mutually cooperative action and sometimes through the initiatives of individual countries. The threat of terrorist acts is real enough, and destructive weapons and chemicals are relatively easy to come by. The experiences of Germany, Spain, France, the United Kingdom, and Italy and the response by the European Union to acts and threats of terrorism provide useful information on how best to meet the challenge.

BACKGROUND: THE EVOLUTION OF THE EUROPEAN UNION AND ITS POLICIES

During the cold war, European security had been assured by the North Atlantic Treaty Organization (NATO) and, more precisely, by the United States, whose priority was the deterrence of the Soviet Union and the stability of Europe. Today, the situation has changed, not only due to the end of bipolarity and subsequent disintegration of the Soviet Union, but also due to the differing perceptions of the threat and of the necessity of military power in Europe. Robert Kagan (2003) describes such perceptions as the European strategic culture, which emphasizes negotiation, diplomacy, commercial ties, and international law over the use of force; seduction over coercion; and the preference of multilateralism over unilateralism. The basis for such a strategy is in the rejection of the balance-of-power principle after WWII. The proof of the success of such a strategy can be said to be the contemporary integration of Europe. It is, in fact, a unique example of reconciliation between nations at war.

In such an environment of cooperation and eventual integration of national policies—starting with the coal and steel industries along with trade and customs cooperation, and including common policies and funds for agriculture, regional development, unemployment, and other social policies—the Europeans moved beyond the old system of power politics and discovered a new system for preserving peace. These compromises within the European community require intense cooperation and negotiation. The essence of the European Union (EU) is in subjecting the interstate relations to the rule of law. By demonstrating comprehensive multilateralism, the EU exemplifies one solution to the world's conflicts and the creation of an enduring peace.

The European commitment is usually described as a temple with three pillars. The first pillar is the various treaties that contributed to European integration, such as the Rome Treaty, the Single European Act, the Maastricht Treaty, the Amsterdam treaty, and so on.

The second pillar is the common foreign and security policy together with defense policy, all still partly under national control. The speed of integration of these very sensitive fields has been increased after the attacks on the United States in September 2001. Even though there had been some cooperative procedures installed prior to this date, the necessity of coordination of national foreign and security policies became evident in the face of the threat of international terrorism. The military action taken against Iraq by the United States has tested these policies.

The third pillar of the EU involves internal national policies—mostly judiciary and internal affairs, including asylum, immigration, and the like. Following 9/11, substantial efforts to coordinate these policies and facilitate cooperation among the national polices, intelligence agencies, and judicial institutions have been accelerated.

The EU adopted a number of specific measures for the fight against terrorism prior to the attacks of September 11. In October 1996, the European Council decided to create a register of competence, knowledge, and specific experience in the field of antiterrorist fighting in order to facilitate cooperation between the member states of the EU. On the basis of a common action in June 1998, the council decided to create the European judicial network, which would have jurisdiction in the matter of terrorist offenses. In December 1998, the Council of Ministers decided to assign Europol with responsibilities for offenses committed or suspected to have been committed in the framework of terrorist activities. In December 1999, the council recommended cooperation relative to the financing of terrorism. But Europe's history with terrorism is far more extensive than the past ten years.

HISTORICAL EXPERIENCE WITH TERRORISM IN EUROPE

Even though cooperation among the member states concerning terrorism is improving, security is still the sovereign responsibility of individual member states. Some European countries, such as France, Germany, Great Britain, and Spain, have long-term experience with these phenomena; some have limited experience, which leads to different national institutional structures in the fight against terrorism. In some countries, there are specific statutes concerning terrorism; other countries rely on a criminal code. This means that in some countries membership in terrorist organizations is illegal and punishable under law. Before the adoption of mutually cooperative antiterrorism statutes, tracking down terrorists was difficult due to the poor extradition laws and different conceptions of what constituted "terrorism" in some countries.

The European countries have also reacted to the September 11 attacks by adopting tactical measures, including crisis management plans, operational measures such as freezing financial assets, and strategic measures such as making changes in the organizational structure of the national security systems.

GERMANY

Germany's experience with terrorism has been relatively recent. One could argue that the 1968 student protests that turned into riots may be the first example. The best-known example of a terrorist group is the Rote Armee Fraction or Red Army Faction (RAF), which became known as the Baader-Meinhof Gang. The RAF is an example of an antiestablishment domestic terrorist group that sought to change domestic policy through revolution and subsequent terrorist activity. At the beginning of its activism, RAF appealed to a significant segment of the German population (10–15 percent). When it moved from merely robbing banks to murder, support vanished. Most of the leaders of this group were captured in mid-1972, but RAF's followers would kidnap and murder close to a dozen people in the next five years in an effort to secure the release of its leaders.[1] The German government used these events to approve new laws giving it broader powers to combat terrorism, a move supported by the majority of the German population.

An example of international terrorism that took place on German soil was the 1972 anti-Israeli terrorist attacks at the Munich Olympic Games, when eight Palestinian Black September terrorists seized eleven Israeli athletes in the Olympic Village. In a failed rescue attempt by West German authorities, nine of the hostages and five terrorists were killed. There was also the 1986 bombing of the La Belle nightclub in Berlin, frequented by U.S. soldiers stationed in the city. During this attack, two U.S. soldiers were killed and seventy-nine American servicemen were injured. When Libya's involvement in the attack became known, U.S. military jets bombed targets in and around Tripoli and Benghazi.

Germany has been an important staging point for the al Qaeda network in Europe, serving as a center for propaganda, recruitment, fund raising, investment, procurement, and shipping. Al Qaeda operated within large Muslim communities and established its own cells in Hamburg, Frankfurt, Dusseldorf, and Duisburg. Due to the limited power of police restricted to each Land (a German administrative district), security service surveillance was not continuous. The result was a lack of knowledge of the scale of terrorists' activities in the country. One of the major planners of the September 11 attacks, Mohammed Atta, had been based in the Hamburg cell. Following the attacks, German intelligence worked closely with American counterparts and stepped up surveillance operations and arrests. The results of the investigations concerning the al Qaeda cells in Germany proved that the structure of al Qaeda was more free form than country based, amorphous rather than centralized.

Measures needed to combat terrorism were adopted by the German government. These included new legislation defining terrorism and enabling the monitoring and prosecution of terrorists and persons or organizations supporting terrorists; initiatives leading to the improvement of intelligence searches of different databases; and a program that may lead to improved accessibility to biometry and, most importantly, fingerprints. The German government created an additional budget for security measures through the increase on cigarette and insurance taxes. In the security area, it created 2,320 additional positions within the various agencies aimed at improving both internal and external security measures. Additionally, Germany adopted very strict procedures relating to financial monitoring and money laundering.

SPAIN

Spain has a long history with domestic terrorism, requiring the government eventually to respond by creating a semiautonomous region. The terrorist group Euskadi ta Askatasuna (Basque Fatherland and Liberty [ETA]) has killed more than eight hundred people since the early 1960s when it began its lethal attacks. The ETA was founded in 1959 with the aim of establishing an independent homeland based on Marxist principles in the northern Spanish provinces of Vizcaya, Guipuzcoa, Alava, and Navarra, and the French departments of Labourd, Basse-Navarra, and Soule. It has been primarily involved in bombings and assassinations of Spanish government officials, security and military officers, and politicians and judicial figures. The ETA finances its activities through kidnappings, robberies, and extortion. In the past, some ETA members have received training in Libya, Lebanon, and Nicaragua. Many of them have been put on the list of suspected terrorists following the September 11 attacks and are actively sought out by security forces. While some have been arrested, others have allegedly received sanctuary in Cuba and South America.

Another group aiming to change Spain's domestic policy is the First October Antifascist Resistance Group (GRAPO), formed in 1975 as the armed wing of the illegal Communist Party of Spain. It calls for the replacement of the Spanish government with a Marxist-Leninist regime and for the removal of all U.S. military forces from Spanish territory. It has about a dozen hard-core activists but has killed approximately ninety people and injured more than two hundred. Thanks to the periodic arrests of GRAPO members by both Spanish and French police, the organization's activities have been disrupted and its violence erratic.

Spain has a well-developed counterterrorist infrastructure spanning from elite autonomous police forces to specialized judges with far-reaching capabilities. An important figure with an international reputation is the judge Baltasar Garzon, a member of the Audiencia Nacional who became famous by bringing charges against General Pinochet for human rights violations in Chile. During the time of the September 11 attacks, the EU was under a Spanish presidency and the fight against terrorism became a top priority. Spain proved to be for greater cooperation and coordination at the EU level, as exemplified by the role of the National Center of Intelligence located in Madrid. Although bureaucratically the center is under the Ministry of Defense, it is directly accountable to the prime minister's office. A number of other agencies exist under the Ministry of the Interior—for example, the Civil Guards (the equivalent of the French Gendarmerie), the National Police, and special security groups. The Foreign Intelligence Brigade is the part of the organization whose task is to investigate international terrorism aimed at Spain. Apart from tactical and operational measures adopted by the government, such as anti-money laundering procedures and a biochemical emergency plan, the Spanish Ministry of the Interior has launched in-depth reform of antiterrorist intelligence services.

A large Muslim population and the proximity to North Africa made Spain attractive for setting up several al Qaeda cells. Important al Qaeda members such as Ressam (the millennium bomber) and Mohammed Atta (the organizer of the 9/11 attacks) visited Spanish cells in Alicante and Castellon. Other al Qaeda members residing in Spain provided support operations for al Qaeda's branches in Europe, including recruiting prospective terrorists. The Algerian members of the Spanish cells specialized in forging and adapting documents, obtaining high-tech equipment, and raising funds via credit card fraud. However, there is no link between the ETA and al Qaeda, since, according to one al Qaeda member, the ETA had nothing to offer. The difference between national and global terrorism in this case is clearly obvious. While the ETA has only limited and specifically defined goals, al Qaeda has a worldwide network and support structure as well as global goals aiming to change the world order. These two groups utilize similar tactics but have completely different objectives, networks, targets, and outcomes. The connecting link is their effort to oppose a symmetrically stronger enemy and through violence influence its policy. The stronger the enemy, the more drastic the tactics. Power, in this case, has a negative effect; it does not deter but rather encourages the adversary to adopt increasingly dangerous tactics such as suicide bombings in places with a high density of civilian populations.

Traditionally, terrorists choose symbols of power as their targets. In the case of the ETA, the symbols are typically state employees; in the case of al Qaeda, the symbols are either institutions such as embassies, administrative buildings, or property belonging to the group's political enemies. In the case of attacks on warships or military barracks, or even the Pentagon, the majority of experts agree that these are, in fact, legitimate military targets for an attack, which could exclude them from being defined as acts of terrorism (should the war on terrorism be actually classified as war).

FRANCE

The French experience with terrorism dates back several decades. Both national as well as international terrorism was present in French territories, especially during the 1980s and the 1990s. Terrorist groups present on French soil could be classified into three general types. There were those under the influence of radical leftist philosophies aimed at the overthrow of capitalist systems and the downfall of American-led "imperialism." One example is Action Directe, which was similar to the Red Army Faction in Germany. The evolution of the fight was also similar—first attacking only material targets and then adopting the tactics of political assassinations.

The second category of terrorist organizations use regional separatist groups that advocate independence or autonomy for specific areas in France, such as the Basque Country, Brittany, and Corsica. The ETA, so prominent in Spain, is also present in France but is less visible. The Breton Liberation Army (ARB) used terrorist tactics only once, in April 2000. Since then, it has lost most of its supporters. Corsican terrorist groups had popular support, but with the assassination of the prefect Claude Erignac in 1999 by Yvan Colonna, son of a former Corsica deputy, its popularity waned. The arrest of Colonna in July 2003 was important for police and security forces, whose reputations suffered as a result of a drawn-out and strangely unresolved affair.

The most important type of terrorist group is that involved in international terrorism aimed at changing the foreign policy of states, mostly in regard to change of French policy either in the Middle East or in Algeria.

The early mistake of the French counterterrorist policy was that it adopted the so-called sanctuary doctrine, hoping that offering a neutral ground would assure the inactivity of terrorist groups on French soil. The problem was that once the groups created their infrastructure, planning attacks against French targets became even easier. The sanctuary doctrine was replaced by the accommodation policy. This might have contributed to the fact that from 1987 until 1994 there were no international attacks on French soil. However, the accommodation policy did not prevent the next wave of attacks in the mid-1990s. The French government, in the face of the threat of terrorism, adopted several important measures, some involving legislation to help combat terrorism on another level of organizational coordination. Strong government agencies were further strengthened and significantly improved. Agencies with overlapping responsibilities charged with fighting against terrorism had been a serious block in effective cooperation.

One example of the French approach is the position of investigating magistrate, in particular Jean-Louis Bruguiere, which provides inside information with which the French system can work. The famous judge Bruguiere has been involved in many international terrorism cases. His post authorizes him to conduct impartial investigations to determine whether a crime worthy of prosecution has been committed. Afterwards, he turns the case over to a prosecutor and a defense attorney. He can open judicial inquiries as well as authorize search warrants and wiretaps and issue subpoenas. He is not answerable to any political authority and is granted a wide range of powers. His powers can be dangerous as well as advantageous. In the French case, the personal integrity of the judge has given this post a special meaning.

Infiltration of the French Muslim communities by al Qaeda (and other terrorist organizations) was part of the strategy to form a European network. France had gained experience with Islamic terrorism during the mid-1990s when the main terrorist groups—the Armed Islamic Group (GIA), the Islamic Salvation Front (FIS), and the Salafist Preaching and Combat Group (GSPC)—targeted France in retaliation for its involvement in the suppression of the election results in Algeria in 1991 where the fundamentalists claimed victory. The GIA's campaign of violence, beginning in September of 1993, involved killing French citizens, taking hostages, and kidnapping. The violence culminated in 1995 with the bombing of the Paris subway. The terrorists fulfilled one goal by bringing international attention to the political situation in Algeria. However, the GIA did not stop its campaign of terror. Becoming brutal, it began targeting the Algerian rural population. Tens of thousands of villagers were massacred.

The September 11 attacks reminded many of one of the GIA's actions in France. On December 24, 1994, the GIA hijacked an Air France flight from Algiers to Paris, with the intention of crashing the fully fueled plane into the Eiffel Tower. The attack did not succeed. French authorities duped the terrorists into believing that the aircraft did not have sufficient fuel to reach Paris and diverted it to Marseilles. Upon arrival in Marseilles, an elite French antiterrorist force stormed the plane and ended the threat. The international community should have been alerted to the possibility of this tactic being readopted, but as in the case of Tokyo's chemical attacks, it was not taken seriously enough. French authorities stepped up operations against the GIA, but its highly mobile terrorist cells simply began to disperse to Italy, Belgium, Germany, and Spain.

The antiterrorist policy of France is based on a combination of factors. First, there is the legislation enabling the pursuit of terrorists and their supporters (September 9th Act of 1986). There is also the operational and repression plan called Vigipirate. This plan was conceived in 1978 during the first wave of terrorist attacks in Europe. The goal was to strengthen security through the mobilization of all police and military units. There are two stages to the plan—Vigipirate Simple and Vigipirate Reinforced, in which the armed forces participate. It was first activated during the Gulf War in 1991 and has not been deactivated. It was used in 1995 and 1996 as well as during the 1998 World Cup when there was a real threat from Algerian extremists. Apart from this, France also has the emergency plans Piratox for chemical attacks, Piratome for nuclear attacks, Piratair for airplane hijackings, and Pirate-mer for ship hijackings.

There is no single authority responsible for the fight against terrorism. Instead, there are a number of agencies and departments under the Minister of Defense and the Minister of the Interior. Among the most important are the General Directorate for External Security (DGSE) and the Directorate of Territorial Security (DST). An unusual but important part of the structure is Gendarmerie Nationale, which is similar to the Civil Guards in Spain and polices some 95 percent of France. The cooperation among independent agencies under different ministries is a result of many years of practice and efforts aimed at producing greater efficiency and more information sharing.

UNITED KINGDOM

The United Kingdom has been dealing with domestic and international terrorism for decades. First, during the period of decolonization between 1950 and 1970 and again in the late 1960s, it confronted the threat of Irish terrorist activities, both Catholic and Protestant, directed against British interests (see chap. 19 in this volume). The conflict has its roots in the 1920s when Ireland had been partitioned; Catholics in the northern counties felt discriminated against, and many in the Republic of Ireland felt the country needed to be unified. At the same time, Protestants believed that Northern Ireland was theirs and that it was part of Great Britain. Both felt victimized. Disagreement between the two ethnic and religious countries continues to this day. In 1968, citizens of Northern Ireland, inspired by civil right movements in the United States and in the rest of Europe, took to the streets to protest for equal treatment. Their demands for rights regarding work, housing, voting, impartial policy, and improved educational opportunities were ineffective. Even though the marches continued for several years, the British government did not change its discriminative policies. The end of peaceful marches and the beginning of overt terrorism began with the Bloody Sunday massacre in January of 1972, when the British army overreacted and killed demonstrators who tried to attack them. The beginning of popular support for the Irish Republican Army (IRA) originates from this period. The leaders of the IRA suffered. Their families were deported or imprisoned by the British. Their decision to use terrorist tactics against the British army was based on despair, hatred, and humiliation. Although eventually negotiations with the leaders of the IRA became possible, the more time it took, the more radical some members of the organization became, refusing to make any concessions at all. The creation of the radical wings of the IRA, such as Continuity Irish Republican Army (CIRA)[2] or Real Irish Republican Army (RIRA)[3] proves how difficult controlling a once-united group can be when it becomes a divided movement with uncompromising terrorist elements. Again, as with other countries, terrorism appears as a consequence of a nonfunctioning political dialogue.

The domestic terrorism targeted mainly at changing British policy in Northern Ireland has recently been combined with the international and global terrorist networks that had a base in London. Some of London's mosques (such as the one in Finsbury Park) became centers for al Qaeda recruitment in Europe. Its strategy was to recruit Muslims of European or American nationality. The United Kingdom, due to its reputation as a country with expansive civil liberties and tolerance toward immigrants, became, and partly still is, the major sanctuary for many terrorist groups. These include al Qaeda, the Algerian GIA, and the Egyptian Islamic Jihad. Measures taken after September 11 were aimed at improving cooperation with the United States as well as the rest of Europe. The antiterrorist law adopted in December 2001 has been criticized for being discriminative toward foreigners. It enables police and security forces to imprison a foreigner suspected of participating in terrorist activities without any judgment day. The British adopted the most severe security measures in Europe. This might have contributed to the rapid development and support of preventive actions in the United Kingdom. The revelation of plans similar to those in the New York attacks, this time aimed at the Houses of Parliament, served to prevent the potentional attacks from occurring. Immediately after the New York attacks, authorities grounded all domestic and international flights. The planned British Airways flight from London to Manchester, intended to be hijacked and crashed into the British parliament, never took place.

ITALY

Italy has its own experience with domestic terrorism, beginning in the 1970s with the Red Brigades and continuing until this day. The Red Brigades, who had a similar radical leftist ideology as did the RAF in Germany or Action Directe in France, based on the hatred of capitalism and strong anti-Americanism, engaged in a large number of assassinations and bombings, targeting high-level civil servants and politicians. The most famous of its assassinations was that of former prime minister Aldo Moro in 1978. Today, a new generation of terrorists keeps alive the original ideology of the Red Brigades. It has been responsible for the assassination of an advisor to the Minister of Labor, Marco Biagi, in March 2002. This return of the Red Brigades, as it has been called, has been a shock for many Italians as well as terrorist experts. The domestic terrorists still use the tactics of the 1970s, such as car bombings, and target only politically active and important officials.

Al Qaeda has set up bases in Italy in order to provide safe haven for its members hunted elsewhere in Europe and to serve as a transit point for Islamists going to fight in the Balkans and Caucasus. The center of al Qaeda recruitment and planning has been traditionally in a mosque in Milan.

The arrests of suspected terrorists started early in Italy. In April 2000, Italian authorities arrested members of an al Qaeda-linked cell preparing to bomb the U.S. embassy in Rome. The arrests followed in March 2001 with suspects preparing chemical attacks on European targets. Since the September 11 attacks, there has been increased attention to the possibility of further attacks. During Easter of 2002, warnings were issued to Florence, Milan, Venice, and Rome of the threat of attacks against American targets and interests.

The search for al Qaeda terrorists in Italy has focused also on all those who might help or support the terrorists. These included false document suppliers, such as those arrested in July 2002.[4] Actions take against insurgent populations have shown results. Five Moroccan men suspected of planning attacks on NATO bases in Verona and London were taken into custody in January 2003. The suspects were found with the maps of London and kilograms of explosives during a routine police search for illegal immigrants in an abandoned building near Venice.[5] A similar search for illegal immigrants by the Italian police uncovered traces of another al Qaeda cell near Naples. At the end of January 2003, security forces arrested twenty-eight Palestinians with maps of NATO installations as well as explosives, detonators, and forged documents. However, given that Northern Italy is a hub for al Qaeda activities in the Balkans and Southern Europe, the number of detained suspects is not overwhelming. There are many critics of the Italian police and legal system, which seems to be unprepared to fight terrorism. An example of inactivity of the Italian authorities is the case of the Turin al Qaeda cell, which has been under surveillance by the Italian intelligence service since June of 2001. The Turin mosque has been a recruiting center since the beginning of the 1990s and has sent al Qaeda members to fight in Bosnia and Chechnya. This cell in fact obtained substantial assistance from an officer of the Pakistan embassy in Rome to help al Qaeda members obtain false Pakistani passports. Pakistan's position in the fight against terrorism is a delicate one for the Italian authorities. In spite of knowledge about the cell, no action has been taken.

MEASURES ADOPTED BY THE EU

The EU reacted to the September 11 attacks as it would have had the United States been a member state. The EU focused on supporting the United States, morally and materially. It strengthened security in air travel and introduced new proposals to locate and detain alleged terrorists. The EU expressed sympathy for the victims of the barbaric acts of 9/11 and confirmed its support for the government of the United States in the fight against terrorism.

The decision to follow a coordinated approach, decided on September 21, has established a series of measures in areas concerning external relations, police and judicial cooperation, air travel, and humanitarian, economic, and financial aid. The majority of the measures adopted for cooperation were under way before September 11 and were waiting adoption. The European Council summit that took place in December 2001 in Laeken succeeded in making real progress in the field of cooperation between the police and judicial authorities, especially in harmonizing the response to terrorism.

EUROPOL

Europol, created in 1999, serves as a central data bank on terrorism. To perform its tasks, Europol maintains a computerized information system directly accessible for consultation by designated users. Every member state has a liaison to represent its interests. However, the liaison is not involved in the exchange of intelligence data or information concerning terrorism. To protect the civil rights of citizens, any individual wishing to obtain self-related data stored within Europol may make a request free of charge. In case of disinformation, individuals have the right to request that Europol correct or delete incorrect data. An independent joint supervisory body is responsible for monitoring the activities of Europol to ensure that the rights of the individual are not violated by the storage, processing, and utilization of its data.

Europol's primary function is to coordinate and encourage cooperation among the member states' police forces. Europol's role has been expanded since 9/11 to create common investigation groups for terrorism, drug trafficking, and human slave trading. Along with combating terrorism, Europol is now mandated to fight against illicit trafficking of nuclear materials and radiological sources as well as arms, ammunition, and explosives and any crimes related to these activities. To fulfill the tasks as given in its mandate, Europol has combined its activities in a Counter Terrorism Program (CTP) and a Counter Proliferation Program (CPP). It has also developed supporting programs such as the Networking Program, the Preparedness Program, and the Training and Education Program. One of the greatest weaknesses of Europol is that it has no power over Central and Eastern Europe, where false identities and credit cards are fabricated in bulk. Another weak point is the insufficient number of language experts in Arabic, Pashto, and Urdu, essential for translations of intercepted communications and especially for network infiltration.

EUROJUST

In the face of transnational criminal and terrorist activities, the EU created a cooperative body in the field of judicial affairs to coordinate the efforts of member states. Eurojust was created by a council decision in February of 2002 to fulfill a unique role. Its mission is to enhance the development of European-wide cooperation on criminal justice matters. This means that Eurojust plays a key role in interactions with European institutions such as parliament, the EU Council, and the EU Commission. It also works with liaison magistrates, the European Judicial Network, the European police office (Europol), and the European Anti-

Fraud Office (OLAF). Eurojust is the legal starting point by which subsequent developments to strengthen the European judicial area will be defined.

The scope of Eurojust is broad. It covers areas such as computer crime, fraud and corruption, money laundering, environmental abuse, and participation in criminal organizations. In execution of its tasks, Eurojust acts through its national members, or as a college consisting of all national members, each with one vote.

Coordination of the information services relating to terrorism includes a number of forums. The most important is the group Terrorism, Radicalism, Extremism and International Violence (TREVI) created in 1975. TREVI is divided into six working groups and is responsible for information exchange and coordination of European legislation. A second forum is the Bern Club with nineteen countries represented, fifteen of which are EU members. The organization provides an opportunity for meetings of informal groups on a case-by-case basis.

THE EUROPEAN ARREST WARRANT

An important step in the coordination of European police actions was the adoption of the European arrest mandate. Drafted in the Laeken treaty and adopted in Seville in June 2002, its main asset is that it abolished the formal extradition procedure among the member states and replaced it with a system of surrender between judicial authorities. This introduction of a new, simplified system of surrender is designed to remove the potential delays in extradition procedures. It is the first concrete measure in the field of criminal law implementing the principle of mutual recognition, which acts as the cornerstone of judicial cooperation on the European level. This council decision was based on previous efforts in the field, including the European Convention on Extradition in December of 1957 and the European Convention on the Suppression of Terrorism in January 1977. A number of other conventions adopted recently have also dealt with this issue: a convention implementing the Schengen Agreement in 1990 (gradual abolition of checks at the borders of the member states) and two other conventions (in 1995 and 1996) simplifying extradition procedures among member states.

The European arrest warrant together with Eurojust should be major elements in the European antiterrorist fight. Even though major progress has been made toward the creation of common judicial and police cooperation within the EU, a greater integration of legislation and the creation of more commonly accepted procedures is needed. Progress in these areas has been held back, in large part due to member states wishing to maintain jurisdiction in critical areas. Integration in these policy and institutional areas of concern has a long way to go.

THE EU AND PREVENTIVE ACTIONS

The EU traditionally emphasizes the importance of preventive actions in fighting terrorism and stresses the role of economic, social, cultural, and security cooperation with developing countries. It provides large amounts of humanitarian aid to countries suffering from economic breakdown, natural disasters, or internal conflicts that often lead the population to the edge of radicalism. Apart from material aid, the EU supports the strengthening of political and cultural dialogue with the Arab and Islamic worlds.

Cooperation between EU member states and Mediterranean countries has been developed within the framework of the Barcelona Process (also known as the Euro-Mediterranean Partnership). The decision to launch such a partnership followed twenty years of increasingly intensive bilateral trade and development cooperation. Its key objectives are to establish a common Euro-Mediterranean area of peace and stability based on such fundamental principles as respect for human rights and democracy, the creation of a free-trade area between the EU and its partners, the development of human resources, and promotion of understanding between cultures.

Most Mediterranean countries have programs for the development of weapons of mass destruction (WMD), and some of them have already used or tested these weapons. Libya employed chemical weapons in 1987 in its war against Chad. Egypt used mustard gas in Yemen during the 1963–67 civil war and sold chemical agents to Iraq, which were used during the Iran-Iraq War during 1980–88.[6] Chemical and biological weapons were also used in 1987 and 1988 against the Iraqi Kurds.

An important factor in the Middle East security environment is the Arab-Israeli conflict, which needs to be resolved in order to achieve any progress in the nonproliferation policy. The nuclear capacity of Israel is increasing the security dilemma as other countries in the region attempt to match Israel in this area. Some countries work alone on their programs or seek cooperation from other Middle Eastern countries. Some have links with Russia, North Korea, and China, who supply production technologies.[7] For Europe, this is a sensitive area that directly affects security.

The EU policy toward the developing countries has always included humanitarian assistance, viewed by the community as its true success story. A division of labor exists between member states' bilateral humanitarian aid and community humanitarian assistance, which is represented by the European Commission Humanitarian Aid Office (ECHO), created in 1992. The EU is the largest humanitarian donor in the world; as a whole, it supplies 50 percent of global humanitarian aid annually, with ECHO alone supplying 25 percent of it. The EU contributes aid to the so-called forgotten crises—that is, areas that are targets of concern largely ignored by the member states. Following the war in Afghanistan, the EU donated more than 310 million euro to address the crisis affecting the civilian population. The commission released 5.5 million euro in emergency aid and an additional 6 million euro to the World Food Program. In Iraq, between 1992 and 2003, ECHO provided aid worth 157 million euro, making it the largest single external donor of humanitarian assistance. Programs included support to hospitals in Baghdad, mobile water treatment units, and therapeutic soy milk for children. A contribution of more than 100 million euro was announced as an immediate response at the outbreak of war.[8]

An important factor in the field of aid is cooperation between humanitarian and military forces, which is being discussed within the EU. One risk is that a multitude of nonhumanitarian actors delivering relief can lead to confusion of roles and a waste of resources. If military forces were to deliver aid directly and control the operational activities of humanitarian organizations, there would be a serious risk for relief workers perceived as auxiliaries of the military and potentially as enemies. One example of blurred roles was the U.S. Special Forces using humanitarian relief as a cover during initiatives in Afghanistan. There is a need to respect international norms, meaning that the development of military and civil defense assets for humanitarian purposes should be made at the request of, and not imposed on, the people involved and should be done within strict rules of engagement.

There are both national and common activities in the EU relating to security causes. An example of a rational action is the British participation in the Enduring Freedom operation in Afghanistan. In others, the EU develops common strategies for all member states. In the first weeks after the September 11 attacks, there was a strong sense of unity among the member states, who all expressed their solidarity with the United States. An illustration of their cooperation was the adoption of a joint EU-U.S. statement on measures to combat terrorism, issued on September 20, 2001. It recognized the legitimacy of a U.S. response to the attacks on the basis of UN Security Council Resolution 1368 and called for the broadest possible global coalition against terrorism to be developed under the aegis of the UN. Additionally, the EU has expressed its willingness to play a greater part in bringing an end to regional conflicts, particularly in reference to the Middle East. The EU has stressed that it also rejects any equation of terrorism with the Arab and Muslim world.[9]

THE ISRAELI-ARAB CONFLICT: THE EU VERSUS THE U.S.

Concerning the Middle East, there are fundamental disagreements between Europe and the United States. The United States has concentrated its efforts on Iraq and Saddam Hussein, claiming that the destruction of this despotic regime, and consequentially the emergence of democracy in this country, should have a positive effect on other nations in the region. This would lead, in turn, to a resolution of the Arab-Israeli conflict. The European view, on the other hand, is that there is an urgent need to find a solution to the Arab-Israeli conflict first, after which bringing peace and democratization to the other Middle Eastern countries would be possible.

The divergent strategies marked post-9/11 discussions between the United States and Europe and finally led to opposition from some European leaders to the U.S. plans to attack Iraq. This opposition did not stem not from an unwillingness to destroy Saddam Hussein. Rather, it reflected the fundamental disagreement about the strategy of peacemaking in the Middle East, where the Arab-Israeli conflict seemed a much more urgent task to resolve than initiating a war in Iraq. The hesitation of the U.S. administration in involving itself in the Arab-Israeli peace process, accompanied by indications of President Bush's sympathy toward Ariel Sharon and his hawkish tactics, led European countries in other directions. The U.S. and Israeli strategy for removal of Yasser Arafat appeared counterproductive since it reinforced his authority among Palestinians. Developments such as the collapse of the Palestinian government of Mahmoud Abbas, who was favored by Washington, and slow movement toward a new one under his successor Ahmed Qurei, a long-time Arafat associate, returned Arafat to center stage. It appears that those who most helped Arafat to regain his position are those who tried to force his removal. President Bush and Ariel Sharon (who voiced his willingness to launch an operation aimed at killing the Palestinian leader) may have strengthened rather than weakened Arafat's leadership.

THE EU AND CRISIS MANAGEMENT

Within the European Common Foreign and Security Policy, a particular emphasis has been put on the strengthening of civil-military coordination in EU crisis management. The first crisis management exercise (CME 02, conducted in May 2002) tested the security and defense structures, procedures, and arrangements of the EU. The intention is to develop a rapid response for emergency relief operations and accelerated decision-making and deployment. This was intended to be the first of several such exercises.

The EU's first operation in this regard was the creation of a European Union Police Mission (EUPM) in Bosnia and Herzegovina and its takeover of security responsibilities from the UN International Police Task Force (IPTF) in January of 2003. This was only one of the EU's contributions to support the rule of law and democratic structures in Bosnia and Herzegovina. All EU member states and eighteen third-party states contributed personnel to this mission, comprising five hundred police officers and more than three hundred international civilian and local staff. The EU has also declared its readiness to take over military operations in the Balkans, as has NATO.

In its effort to prevent diamond conflicts in certain African states, the commission has conducted negotiations on an agreement establishing an international certification scheme for rough diamonds based on the control of exports and imports. The plan adopted was first declared at a Kimberley Process ministerial meeting. The principle is that shipments of rough diamonds will be sealed in tamper-resistant containers and that for each shipment a Kimberly Process certificate will be issued.

The core focus of the external action of the EU is support for the reinforcement of global nonproliferation and disarmament. Its measures focus on multilateral approaches, export controls, international cooperation, and enhanced political dialogue. The EU initiated a multilateral process to establish an International Code of Conduct against ballistic missile proliferation (November 2002); it is the first step in the process to construct global nonproliferation norms on missiles. Ninety-four states subscribed to the code. The EU Code of Conduct on Arms Exports, operating since 1998, has consolidated its position as the most comprehensive international arms export control pact.

Apart from arms exports control, the EU remains committed to the goal of total elimination of antipersonnel land mines worldwide and repeated its invitation to all states to join this effort. In the area of weapons that may be considered excessively injurious or have indiscriminate effects, the EU points out the importance of the Convention on Certain Conventional Weapons, which regulates or prohibits the use of such weapons. One example of the active policy was the continued support for nonproliferation and disarmament projects in the Russian Federation, where the EU in 2002 allocated an additional 6.1 million euro, of which 2.8 million was for the destruction of chemical weapons. The EU stresses the importance of participation in multilateral forums and plays an active role at the UN, in particular in the fields of security, terrorism, and human rights. With the development of the EU's civilian crisis management program, there will be an even greater opportunity for interaction between EU and international organizations such as the OSCE (Organization for Security and Cooperation) in

Europe and the Council of Europe. Following the enlargement of the EU in May 2004, EU-OSCE relations are solid. Out of the fifty-five participating states in OSCE, twenty-five are EU members. Concerning the fight against terrorism, the priorities are in developing a common evaluation of the terrorist threat against member states, exploring the possibility of using military or civilian capabilities to protect civilian populations, and continuing with the implementation of EU pilot projects of technical assistance. Pilot projects include providing technical assistance to third world countries such as Indonesia, the Philippines, and Pakistan.

The protection of civilian populations is particularly important in case of the threat of chemical, biological, radiological, or nuclear (CBRN) weapons. This topic has been of concern to European governments for several years, but it took the events of September 11 to give CBRNs priority. There was the possibility of the dissemination of WMD after the end of the cold war, which states tried to limit by signing the Non-proliferation Treaty (NPT) in 1995. A new stage began when nonstate actors, not bound by any treaties, became a threat. Biological and chemical weapons had become popular among the Afghani mujahideen. Videotapes captured by the coalition showed their experiments with such weapons.

Many al Qaeda members are in fact chemical weapons experts, which is not surprising given that most of their supporters are graduates of technical universities. The accessibility of the main components for the production of such weapons is one of the reasons for their popularity. The others include low cost, small production units, ease of hiding, low possibility of detection while being transported, and the massive effects they can have. A small amount of anthrax, sarin, tabun, or smallpox can harm large populations. The anthrax attacks in the U.S. killed five people and appeared to paralyze Congress for several months. No such cases appeared in Europe, but the population has been as terrified as in the United States and is obsessed with any suspicious white powder.

The danger from the disintegrated former Soviet chemical factories, where more than seventy thousand experts worked in the development of biological weapons, is a reality. Difficult living conditions in Russia after the dissolution of the Soviet Union (inflation in the thousands of percent, loss of jobs resulting in high unemployment) led many of these scientists to states or groups searching for technology and knowledge relating to the production of WMD. Even though the official policy of Russia after the September 11 attacks included full support for the United States, the Russian president continued to keep a certain level of independence in foreign policy, maintaining close ties with several of the U.S. enemies referred to by President Bush as the "Axis of Evil." For example, Russia supports Iran's civil nuclear power program. A need for cooperation exists among Europe, Russia, and the United States in their approach to Iran. Better international supervision needs to be maintained in order to control its nuclear facilities. The International Atomic Energy Agency (IAEA) reported that Iran was not cooperating with inspectors. The danger of the Iranian nuclear program is clear. Its midrange missile, called Shabab 3 or "Shooting Star," has a range of more than eight hundred miles, enough to reach Israel or Turkey, and there are concerns that it could be equipped to carry a nuclear warhead. Iran has claimed that its nuclear program was strictly for energy purposes, not weapons, but has refused to sign an additional protocol to the nuclear Non-proliferation Treaty that would allow more detailed inspections of its nuclear facilities.

The weapons are available. They are hard to detect. Terrorists will use them.

NOTES

The author wishes to thank William Crotty, Yvonne Ramsey, Ben Lampe, Brooke Trahan, Amy Huffman, Paul Lehnus, and Lindsay Ford, all with the Center for Democratic Study at Northeastern University, for their assistance in the preparation of this analysis.

1. Apart from other actions, on June 27, 1976, members of the Baader-Meinhof Group and the Popular Front for the Liberation of Palestine (PFLP) seized an Air France airliner and its 258 passengers. They forced the plane to land in Uganda, where on July 3 Israeli commandos successfully rescued the passengers. This affair is known as the Entebbe Hostage Crisis.

2. CIRA is a radical terrorist splinter group formed in 1994 as the clandestine armed wing of the Republican Sinn Féin (RSF), which split from Sinn Féin in the mid-1980s. Its goal is to force the British out of Northern Ireland. The RFS use bombings, assassinations, kidnappings, extortion, and robberies to achieve its goal.

3. The RIRA was formed in early 1998 as a clandestine wing of the 32-County Sovereignty Movement. It calls itself a "political pressure group" dedicated to removing British forces from Northern Ireland and unifying Ireland. The RIRA uses various terrorist tactics, including bombings and assassinations. Its leaders opposed Sinn Féin's adoption of the Mitchell principles of democracy and violence in 1997.

4. Seven North Africans and one Rumanian have been arrested for supplying false documents to al Qaeda members living in Europe. The Italian police also seized false passports, driving licenses, and official seals that could be used to issue papers giving foreigners permission to live in Italy.

5. "Suspected Moroccan Terrorists 'Had Map of London,'" Anova, January 24, 2003, www.ananova.com/news/story/sm_742928.html?menu=.

6. In terms of fatalities, one of the largest conflicts since WWII.

7. Syria has been supplied with Soviet missile technology as well as Chinese missile technology. Libya is engaged in missile cooperation with Iran, North Korea, and China. Egypt is regularly suspected of transferring Western technology to North Korea in exchange for ballistic technology. Iran maintains cooperation programs with Russia, China, and North Korea.

8. "Assisting the Iraqi Population," ECHO Humanitarian Aid Office, http://europa.eu.int/comm/echo/field/iraq/index_en.htm.

9. "Action by the European Union Following the Attacks on 11 September," DG External Relations, Common Foreign and Security Policy, MEMO/01/327, Brussels, October 15, 2001, http://europa.eu.int/comm/external_relations/cfsp/news/me01_327.htm.

REFERENCE

Chan, Sylvia. 2002. *Liberalism, Democracy, and Development*. Cambridge: Cambridge University.

Davies, Barry. 2003 *Terrorism: Inside a World Phenomenon*. London: Virgin Books.

Dinan, Desmond. 1999. *Even Closer Union*. Palgrave: New York.

Dryzek, John. 1996. *Democracy in Capitalist Times: Ideals, Limits, and Struggles*. Oxford: Oxford University Press.

Elshtain, Jean Bethke. 2003. *Just War Against Terror: The Burden of American Power in a Violent World*. New York: Basic Books.

European Union. "Official Journal" of the EU is available online.

Gilpin, Robert. 2000. *The Challenge of Global Capitalism: The World Economy in the 21st Century*. Princeton: Princeton University Press.

Guanaratna, Rohan. 2002. *Inside Al Qaeda: Global Network of Terror*. New York: Columbia University Press.

Held, David, Anthony McGrew, David Goldblatt, and Jonathan Perraton. 1999. *Global Transformations: Politics, Economics, and Culture*. Stanford, Calif.: Stanford University Press.

Kagan, Robert. 2003. *Of Paradise and Power: America and Europe in the New World Order*. New York: Knopf.

Nugent, Neil. 1999. *The Government and Politics of the European Union*. Durham: Duke University Press.

Pinder, John. 1998. *The Building of the European Union*. Oxford: Oxford University Press.

Rummel, R.J. 2002. *Power Kills: Democracy as a Method of Nonviolence*. New Brunswick, N.J.: Transaction Publishers.

Sbragia, Alberta M. 1992. *Euro-Politics*. Washington: Brookings Institution.

Stern. Jessica. 1999. *The Ultimate Terrorists*. Cambridge, Mass.: Harvard University Press.

Stern, Jessica. 2003. *Terror in the Name of God: Why Religious Militants Kill*. New York: Harper Collins.

Stiglitz, Joseph E. 2003. *Globalization and Its Discontents*. New York: W. W. Norton & Company.

Whittaker, David J. 2004. *Terrorists and Terrorism in the Contemporary World*. London: Routledge.

DAVID E. SCHMITT

19 The Impact of September 11 on Terrorism and Peace Processes in Northern Ireland

INTRODUCTION

The tragic attacks of September 11, 2001, had far-reaching impacts on American politics and society as well as significant consequences for the international community. The horrific consequences for the victims of this assault as well as the negative impact on New York and, to a lesser extent, Washington, D.C., and the country at large is well known. The events of 9/11 have also had an ongoing impact on the Northern Ireland peace processes, particularly in regard to U.S.-British relations and to pressures placed on republicans (those who have supported the armed struggle for the unification of Ireland and the end of British control).

Almost any crisis has some positive consequences, however tragic the results in human terms. There appears to have been an increased sense of national cohesion in the United States after the attacks as well as higher levels of commitment to public service. Had the initial attacks occurred at a much later date, it is possible that al Qaeda might have by then acquired weapons of mass destruction (WMD). Of particular relevance for the Northern Ireland conflict is that September 11 created a level of revulsion against terrorist violence in the United States and the democratic world that made all but the most ardent supporters of the republican movement likely to view future Irish Republican Army (IRA) bombings and terrorist attacks as unacceptable. Additionally, the dramatic increase in suicide bombings in Israel, such as the bomb at Hebrew University in July 2002 that killed four Americans, adds to a strong climate of animosity toward this kind of violence.

BACKGROUND TO THE NORTHERN IRELAND CONFLICT AND PEACE PROCESSES

Although history is not the only important variable explaining the development of the Northern Ireland conflict, the conflict does have strong historical roots. The seventeenth century was especially significant in setting some of the basic parameters of the current struggle. After the defeat of native Irish leaders in the north of Ireland by English forces in the early seventeenth century, the plantation of settlers from the island of Britain helped create a dominant Protestant settler group. These settlers reinforced the Protestant population that had emigrated earlier to Ulster, the northeastern province of Ireland. The subjugated native Irish, who were mostly Catholic, launched a violent, short-lived rebellion in 1641 against the Protestant community. Retaliation by English forces under Cromwell, and later victory by the Protestant King William of Orange against the Catholic forces of King James II at the Battle of the Boyne in 1690, secured British dominance of Ireland that lasted until the twentieth century (Curtis 1968, 221–71).

As a means of securing the political control and stability of Ireland, the Act of Union of 1800 merged Ireland into the United Kingdom of Great Britain and Ireland. During the nineteenth century, the British government implemented significant political reforms giving Catholics political rights, but the nineteenth century also produced sources of grievance. The famine of the 1840s provided a powerful anti-British symbol for later Irish revolutionaries. Agrarian unrest over the exploitation of tenant farmers contributed to continuation of the revolutionary strand to Irish politics. By the late nineteenth century the Irish Party, backed mostly by Catholics, held the balance of power in the British House of Commons. A Home Rule bill introduced in 1886 failed in the House of Commons, but a Home Rule bill was passed in 1893 only to be defeated in the House of Lords. Demonstrations and rioting by Protestants and Catholics in Northern Ireland over the issue fueled distrust and hostility between the two communities. It was only in the latter part of the nineteenth century that Northern Ireland became polarized into relatively distinct Catholic and Protestant communities. Prior to that time, each group was not yet unified (Ruane and Todd 1996, 23–43).

In the 1890s, a cultural revival emerged that sought the restoration of the Irish language and a return to Irish literature, music, and culture. In response to Irish demands, a Home Rule bill was passed in 1914 that would have granted Ireland limited autonomy. This might have assuaged the strong feelings of many of the more radical Irish nationalists. However, implementation was delayed

DAVID E. SCHMITT

because of the First World War. In 1916, frustrated Irish nationalists launched a rebellion that culminated in the Anglo-Irish War of Independence and the partitioning of the island in 1920. Protestant unionists in the northern province of Ulster had sought and were granted by the British Government of Ireland Act a six-county political unit in the north. With two-thirds of the population in the new region of Northern Ireland, unionists believed they had the means to ensure that Northern Ireland would never become a part of a united Ireland (Hennesey 1997, 3–10).

Thus, Northern Ireland remained within the United Kingdom and acquired its own parliament and system of local government, while the rest of Ireland became an independent country in 1921. During the early 1920s, riots as well as attacks on Catholics to drive them into ghetto areas produced many deaths in Northern Ireland (Budge and O'Leary 1973). However, viewing the conflict between the Protestant and Catholic communities of Northern Ireland as a tribal confrontation is simplistic. Some leaders of the movement for home rule and independence had been Protestants. Additionally, there have been many instances of cooperation between Catholics and Protestants in Northern Ireland, and relations between the two communities in the Republic of Ireland have been good (Harris 1972; Coakley 1998).

Also, the development of the conflict in Northern Ireland has many dimensions resulting from economic, political, psychological, and other conditions. Catholics as a group were poorer and had higher unemployment levels than Protestants. The IRA and Protestant paramilitary groups in Northern Ireland are based in working-class areas and draw their support mainly from these sectors of the population. The conflict can also be analyzed from the viewpoint of external versus internal factors or as the result of conflict processes themselves (Feldman 1991). For example, Irish Americans in the United States have been an important source of support for revolutionary activity from the nineteenth century to the present.

Although different scholars emphasize different viewpoints, clearly a variety of causes underlie the contentious history of nationalist and unionist politics in Northern Ireland, and the core issue is the division between the two communities themselves (Whyte 1990). Most basic is the fact that the Protestant majority is in favor of remaining a part of the United Kingdom. A majority of Catholics, on the other hand, favor unification with the Republic of Ireland, although many view this as a long-term aspiration (Ruane and Todd 1996, 66).

The Northern Ireland political system was dominated from the beginning by the Protestant community, which overwhelmingly supported the Unionist Party. Catholics were represented by the Nationalist Party and later by the

Social Democratic and Labour Party (SDLP), founded in 1970. Catholics did have basic political freedoms. They could practice their religion, had freedom of speech, could vote in elections, and, at their insistence, maintained a separate school system. Nevertheless, discrimination against Catholics was significant and impacted negatively on their lives as well as undermined any chance that the government could acquire legitimacy among the minority community. Property qualifications for voting in local elections fell more heavily against Catholics, who were less likely to own property. Discrimination in employment in both the public and private sectors was a serious problem for a community with high rates of unemployment. An overwhelmingly Protestant auxiliary police force (the B-Specials) and a seldom-employed Special Powers Act that permitted internment also served to alienate Catholics. Although there is debate about the degree of discrimination in public housing, clearly this also constituted a source of discontent (Hennesey 1997, 129–30).

A civil rights movement emerged in the 1960s that sought to end these forms of discrimination. Although moderate Protestant leaders were willing to make concessions, the fears of a united Ireland enabled radical leaders such as Ian Paisley and others to mobilize support against reform. From the point of view of many unionists, the argument that the civil rights movement was a plot to undermine the Northern Ireland link with the United Kingdom was compelling. Riots and attacks on Catholic areas by Protestant mobs ultimately caused the British government to deploy its army personnel, who were at first welcomed by Catholics as protectors. Law enforcement measures impacted most heavily on the Catholic community, however, and the British government's handling of law enforcement and security issues was often ill informed and heavy handed; also, there were instances of collusion by some in the security forces with loyalist paramilitaries. These undermined efforts by the British government to build trust in the minority community (Stevens 2003).

One of the most counterproductive decisions occurred in 1971 when the British government participated in an internment operation that involved a large-scale sweep into Catholic areas and the arrest, and sometimes maltreatment, of suspects who in most cases had no credible link to the IRA. Another serious law enforcement error occurred on Bloody Sunday in January 1972, when thirteen Catholic demonstrators were killed by British paratroopers. Gradually a low-intensity guerrilla war emerged, led by the Provisional IRA (hereafter referred to as the IRA). In March 1972, the British government suspended the Stormont government and parliament and began a period of direct rule of Northern Ireland. Although many positive reforms occurred throughout the conflict, the British government's sometimes harsh handling of security issues created great discontent among the Catholic population. Part of this strong military and police response to terrorism and a low-intensity war is understandable in the face of an IRA campaign that targeted British and Northern Irish officials, security force personnel, and civilians. In July 2002, the IRA apologized for the people killed and injured by its military campaign. The apology specifically mentioned one of its most destructive multiple bombing attacks, often referred to as Bloody Friday (*Irish Times* 2002).

British policy toward ending the conflict can be viewed as having three principal dimensions. First, many reforms have been implemented over the years since the troubles began (Cunningham 2001). These included fair housing, fair voting, and political representation measures. Also, major efforts were undertaken to secure fairer public and, later, fair private employment practices (Schmitt 1980). Second was the vigorous military campaign involving the police, military, intelligence services, and other personnel. The third and most fundamental goal of the British government has been to establish a fair system of government for Northern Ireland that would have the support of both communities. The major constitutional-level reform prior to the Good Friday Agreement (GFA)[1] was the Sunningdale Agreement of 1973 that established a power-sharing assembly and executive comprised of unionist and nationalist politicians. This government was brought down, however, by a strike of loyalist workers in May 1974. Also, the British government reaffirmed in 1973 its policy that if by a majority vote the people of Northern Ireland chose to leave the United Kingdom and unite with the Republic of Ireland, it would honor that choice. The major policy goal of the British authorities has been to create a government for Northern Ireland that would permit the meaningful participation of both communities in the decision-making process and that would have the support of the two communities.

THE PEACE PROCESS

The decision of the Sinn Féin party (the political wing of the IRA) and the leadership of the IRA to enter the peace process in the early 1990s was brought about by many factors. Some scholars emphasize causes internal to Northern Ireland, such as the IRA's realization that it could never militarily coerce Britain into leaving Northern Ireland (Tonge 2002). Other scholars emphasize international variables such as the end of the cold war (Cox 2000).

The GFA accord was reached under considerable pressure by the Irish and British governments as well as substantial intervention by the United States, including President William Clinton and former Senator George Mitchell, who chaired the peace process (Finnegan 2002). A reasonable conclusion is that both internal and external forces contributed to the peace process that culminated in the signing of the GFA in April of 1998 (Guelke 2002). The GFA was an achievement of historic and international significance. After more than thirty years of violent conflict, most key political parties in Northern Ireland, including Sinn Féin as the effective representative of the IRA, reached an accord that established a power-sharing government in Northern Ireland. The loyalist Democratic Unionist Party (DUP) led by Ian Paisley did not sign the agreement, but two minor parties representing loyalist paramilitary organizations also signed the accord. The British and Irish governments, who had worked together to achieve the accord, were also signatories. Among the other forces crucial to the signing of the GFA were the political skills of John Hume, leader of the moderate, nationalist SDLP; David Trimble, leader of the moderate Ulster Unionist Party (UUP); and Gerry Adams, leader of Sinn Féin. Trimble and Hume won Nobel prizes in 1998 for their efforts.

The voting mechanisms established for the new legislative assembly assured that both communities would have to agree before key legislation could be passed. Specifically, key votes would be on the basis of parallel consent (an overall majority as well as a majority of both the unionist and nationalist members voting) or weighted majority (60 per cent of members voting plus at least 40 percent of unionist and nationalist members voting). In an important innovation, the executive committee (cabinet) was established on the basis of proportional representation within the assembly, assuring that members of all important parties would hold cabinet-level positions. The first ministers and deputy first ministers are elected on a cross-community basis to ensure that these two leadership positions are held by members of the two respective communities.

A North/South Ministerial Council was also created. Although it lacked significant powers, this body constituted a significant concession to republican and nationalist sentiment. Partly to assuage the unionist and loyalist communities, a British-Irish Council was established that included representatives of the British and Irish governments as well as the devolved governments, including Northern Ireland, Scotland, and Wales. Thus, there was an east-west dimension to the accord. A British-Irish Intergovernmental Conference was also created; this provided an ongoing mechanism for the British and Irish governments to discuss issues regarding Northern Ireland (Good Friday Agreement 1998). Thus, the GFA combines both consociational (power-sharing) and confederal features (O'Leary 2001).

That an accord could be reached at all is remarkable given the extreme gap in the goals of the participants as well as the intense distrust among the leaders and their respective communities. Approximately thirty years of low-intensity conflict had resulted in more than thirty-three hundred deaths, many more injuries, and a much more segregated society than had previously existed. The SDLP supported the unification of Ireland by democratic means, while Sinn Féin and the IRA had seen violence as the key to achieving British withdrawal and a united Ireland. All unionist and loyalist parties and the vast majority of the Protestant community supported retention of the link to Britain. As part of the strategy for garnering support from the paramilitary organizations, IRA and other prisoners convicted of terrorist crimes were released from prison if they renounced violence. This caused great upset among those in the unionist community because they had been victims of IRA violence. This policy, however, was consistent with peace processes in some other conflict situations. In Lebanon, for example, members of the paramilitary organizations were integrated into the regular army as a result of the Ta'if Agreement of 1989 (Schulze 2001).

Part of the logic behind the power-sharing approach is that all groups get to participate in governing and in the benefits of government employment as well as receive more equitable treatment in society (Lijphart 1977, 1984). Power sharing is a kind of quota system based on the percentages of groups within the population as reflected by party-line voting, which is usually along ethnic lines in deeply divided societies. It is intended to be a least-bad option for creating a government system that is capable of functioning and surviving. A major successful model of power sharing is Switzerland, which has a stable democratic system based on power sharing among its language groups.

Yet power sharing has a number of liabilities. It always limits the power of groups that may have a majority of the population because it increases the power given to minorities. In Northern Ireland, this means that the unionists and loyalists have given up significant power. To be sure, they employed their power from 1920 to 1972 to the detriment of the Catholic minority. But from the unionist/loyalist perspective, they are fighting for their cultural and national survival, which many see as lost if Ireland becomes united. The loss of unionist majority control of the political system allows, from their point of view, for policies supportive of eventual unification and reduces the ability to enforce the law against republican enemies who have subjected the unionist community to a decades-long violent assault.

Also, by allowing minority groups to block legislation, there is a potential for the government to become immobilized. If power-sharing arrangements freeze majority status or if majorities are able to prevent the taking of censuses or delay or manipulate voting, they may break down in chaos when the population growth of minority groups propels them into majority status and they cannot achieve power. This later problem is unlikely to occur in Northern Ireland, however, because the British government has the ability to guarantee fair elections and accurate census counts.

Perhaps most basic of all is that power sharing can perpetuate a system of political division along ethnic lines and prevent majoritarian politics from developing, that is, limiting the ability of cross-community parties and voting to become the norm. As Donald Horowitz (1990, 2001) has pointed out, it may be possible to design political processes and structures in such a way that parties not ethnically based can emerge as the most attractive to political elites and voters. But given the highly polarized character of Northern Ireland politics, cross-community organizations such as the Alliance Party have been unable to draw anywhere near a majority of voters. The core issue is the existence of the border coupled with the violent campaign to erase it and create a united Ireland. This means that unionists fear not only cultural survival but physical survival as well. For nationalists and republicans seeking a united Ireland, a moderate party such as the Alliance Party is seen as supporting the status quo (union with Britain) or as being incapable of protecting the Catholic minority, many of whom have also been concerned with cultural and physical survival from a regime that has a past record of discrimination and harshness in law enforcement. Yet, power sharing may be the best option for some deeply divided societies (O'Leary 2001). The ability of the Northern Ireland GFA to survive over the long term will be an important indication of what may be possible in more contentiously divided societies with higher levels of violence. Those systems have many important differences from Northern Ireland. They may not have a democratic tradition or literate population, for example. Nevertheless, Northern Ireland constitutes a useful test of the power-sharing approach to conflict resolution.

The Northern Ireland case also illustrates an important difficulty with international efforts to create power-sharing arrangements that work, namely the problem of political legitimacy. There is no question that the GFA would never have occurred without the strong intervention of the British, Irish, and American governments. But from the perspective of some in the unionist, loyalist, and republican communities, the compromises were forced upon them. The issue of decommissioning was so contentious that the matter was deferred. The SDLP was probably the most receptive group to the idea of power sharing and compromise, but, overall, key groups were unhappy with various aspects of the accord. None of this is to suggest that an alternative course would have worked. Given the deep cleavages in Northern Irish society, the GFA may well have been the best possible alternative. Certainly the leaders and groups inside and outside Northern Ireland who worked toward the settlement deserve enormous credit for their efforts.

As noted, by postponing a decision on the crucial question of decommissioning of IRA (and Protestant paramilitary group) weapons, final agreement on the accord became possible. The term "decommissioning" was employed to avoid giving the impression that the IRA was surrendering. An international panel led by General John de Chastelain of Canada was charged with overseeing the process of decommissioning. There were other contentious issues that have not been entirely resolved during the peace process, such as the reform of the Royal Ulster Constabulary (police), now the Police Service of Northern Ireland. But it has been the decommissioning issue that was most responsible for the precarious existence of the government institutions of Northern Ireland created by the GFA. From the standpoint of the democratic politicians of Northern Ireland and the Republic of Ireland as well as Britain and the United States, there could be no real democracy until decommissioning occurred, for the basic reason that the armed parties would have the implicit threat of violence whenever their wishes were not met.

POLITICAL IMPACT OF SEPTEMBER 11 ON THE REPUBLICAN MOVEMENT

The attacks of September 11 on New York and Washington, D.C., radically altered the playing field for the IRA. Bombing had been one of the IRA's main strategies during the conflict, with many attacks on civilian and security force targets, particularly during the 1970s. In addition to numerous explosions within Northern Ireland, the IRA also carried out bombings outside Northern Ireland, especially in England. Among the more recent instances were the bombings at Canary Wharf in London and in Manchester in 1996, with approximately three hundred people wounded in these attacks.

September 11 so profoundly altered the international political environment for the IRA that a bombing attack anywhere in Northern Ireland, on the island of Britain, or elsewhere would produce far more hostility than sympathy from most quarters, including the American government and Irish-American community. Indeed, any significant form of terrorism such as the assassination of British officials would spark widespread condemnation and erode the support and goodwill that Sinn Féin and its leaders have acquired since committing to the peace process. This is especially so after British participation with the United States in the attack on Iraq in 2003.

From the standpoint of Sinn Féin and the IRA, too-rapid movement on decommissioning could create a threat of defections by more militant members into offshoot groups such as the Real IRA, which is continuing the armed struggle.

The republican leadership appears to believe that an excessively rapid accommodation could even motivate dissidents to take over the IRA, perhaps sparking an internal war and threatening the lives of IRA and Sinn Féin leaders. Also, republican leaders undoubtedly see the retention of weapons as a bargaining chip. Indeed, prior to September 11, there had been no decommissioning of weapons by the IRA. September 11 put great pressure on the IRA to begin the process of decommissioning. In October, in the presence of international inspectors, the IRA decommissioned some of its weapons, and another decommissioning took place in April 2002.

In sum, the events of September 11 have placed serious constraints on IRA military operations and have made a major return to violence by the IRA unlikely. Should a major excess by British or Northern Irish security forces occur against members of the Catholic community, the number of Irish Americans who would support such measures might increase. Nevertheless, in the environment of the war on terrorism, the majority of Irish Americans would condemn such measures. Also, given the likelihood that negotiations would at some point continue over settlement issues, Sinn Féin and the IRA would need the goodwill of the Irish and American governments. Leaders in Washington are unlikely to be as tolerant toward Sinn Féin and the IRA while waging the war on terrorism as was the Clinton administration. A resumption of a full-fledged terrorist campaign of the IRA would virtually assure that President George W. Bush or any future president would follow the wishes of the British government concerning any contacts with the republican movement. Should further attacks on the United States occur, the ability of the IRA to attack targets in Britain would be still more constrained. Nevertheless, dissidents could take over the IRA or defect to paramilitary organizations such as the Real IRA. If the IRA were to return to a violent campaign, Loyalist paramilitary organizations would undoubtedly expand their operations, with the major efforts directed at targets identified as republican. Mounting violence could bring the return of larger-scale attacks on Catholic citizens.

A RENEWED STRATEGIC RELATIONSHIP BETWEEN THE UNITED STATES AND BRITAIN

The British government has considered its "special relationship" with the United States as a center pin of its foreign policy (Drumbell 2001). In return, the United States has regarded the United Kingdom as its most loyal and important ally from the standpoint of consistent support on a range of international issues around the world. As one illustration, during the Reagan administration the British allowed American attack aircraft to be launched from the British mainland in 1986 for a counterterrorist attack against the Khadafi government of Libya. The importance of this support from a political as well as military perspective is indicated by the fact that the French government would not allow these aircraft to fly over French territory, necessitating an inefficient circuitous route to the target. British support for the American position in international politics and especially its support on military and national security matters have been of enormous benefit to several American presidents. During the cold war, the United States could ordinarily depend on British support and assistance from a variety of perspectives. Despite the loss of empire and its declining status as a world power, British diplomatic, military, and intelligence resources were of excellent quality and in many ways provided support for U.S. efforts vis-à-vis the Soviet Union and its allies. The U.S. Department of State maintained a particularly close relationship with its British counterparts, and the British government could ordinarily depend on the support of the United States in its antiterrorist campaign against the IRA.

Of course, American support for the British government and the peace process was neither cohesive nor consistent. The U.S. Congress, for example, has had radical as well as moderate pro-Irish factions. The "four horsemen" (Speaker of the House Thomas P. O'Neill, Senators Ted Kennedy and Patrick Moynihan, and New York governor Hugh Cary) were an especially effective team in arguing for the rights of the Catholic minority of Northern Ireland from the standpoint of a constitutional and nonviolent perspective (Finnegan 2002, 100–102). Private Irish-American organizations such as NORAID (Irish Northern Aid) raised money for the republican cause. Other Irish-American organizations and individuals backed democratic reform and a fair system of government for the North. Financial assistance for economic development and other projects in Northern Ireland has been significant.

There was a subtle but fundamental shift in British/American relations after the end of the cold war (Cox 2000, 249–62). The British government appears to have lost influence over the United States regarding its handling of the Northern Ireland problem, because U.S. need for British backing was much less intense. President Clinton would likely not have allowed Gerry Adams into the United States over the vociferous objections of the British government had he needed British support in his management of the cold war. Adams's visit to the United States and his meetings with President Clinton and other officials established important links that contributed to the signing of the GFA. It should be noted that Clinton and other government officials also met with David Trimble as well as other politicians from Northern Ireland.

The intensity of the U.S. government's resolve on security issues results from its belief that terrorism is a threat to the survival of the American way of life. The symbolic impact of September 11 was far greater than the considerable harm caused by the attacks themselves. The collapse of the World Trade Center towers, the assault on the Pentagon, and the crash of the hijacked airplane in Pennsylvania disrupted business, especially in New York; cost the lives of approximately three thousand people; set back economic recovery from a recession; and seriously damaged specific economic sectors such as tourism. Tragic as the human consequences were, the much greater impact of these attacks was the transformation of the American view that wars happen elsewhere to the realization that this time the war was being brought to U.S. soil. Indeed, the main target of al Qaeda and similar organizations is the United States.

Furthermore, there was an immediate validation of the view of many public officials and scholars that the United States was vulnerable to attack by weapons of mass destruction, including chemical, biological, and nuclear devices (U.S. Commission on National Security/21st Century 1999, 2000, 2001). The problem of Russia's control over thousands of nuclear weapons, the existence of poorly guarded weapons-grade materials around the world, and the relative ease of manufacturing some biological and chemical warfare agents all create a realistic fear of a cataclysmic attack on the United States.

The concern is not that the United States is going to be taken over by a foreign power or that a huge percentage of the population is going to be killed. The threat of takeover does not exist, and the country is too large in physical size as well as population for such a catastrophic loss of population to be possible in all but the most extreme scenarios. But the potential for the loss of hundreds of thousands if not millions of lives is real, and the economy could be crippled for decades. Despite Russian assurances, some nuclear weapons and weapon-grade materials may possibly have been stolen, and the possibility exists that terrorists will acquire nuclear devices. Even more possible is that terrorist organizations may possess or obtain chemical or biological weapons.

After September 11, then, the United States found itself in a quite vulnerable situation. It was suddenly in a new and unique war in which its traditional military assets were of limited value in protecting the American homeland. Although there had been earlier terrorist attacks in the United States, these were of relatively limited consequence. The United States itself had now become a significant battleground and the main target of the enemy. The stakes in the war on terrorism were now the maintenance of the American way of life. The U.S. government needed every available resource, and international support for its fight against terrorism has become crucial. British support for U.S. policy has been consistently strong since September 11, and Britain appears to have again acquired its former influence with the U.S. government. The extent of British support is indicated in a variety of ways, most notably in its backing of President George W. Bush's attempt in 2002 to build support for the U.S. attack on Iraq and its subsequent participation in the invasion of Iraq. However, many politicians and citizens in Britain did not agree with these decisions.

During the cold war, Americans recognized the threat posed by the Soviet Union and its allies, but the conflict remained abstract and distant. The Berlin and Cuban missile crises never resulted in open warfare, and the fighting in places such as Korea and Vietnam were faraway conflicts that did not threaten the American homeland. The threat of a nuclear holocaust was real, as indicated by the Cuban missile crisis of 1962 when the Soviet Union and the United States almost went to war (Allison and Zelikow 1999). But for the most part, this threat was so apocalyptic that it seemed rather remote.

In contrast, the U.S. homeland was directly attacked in 2001 in a brutal and highly symbolic way. The World Trade Center towers and the Pentagon were core symbols of the economic and military power of the United States. There is a general recognition by the America citizenry that the United States will almost certainly be hit again, probably repeatedly. The enemy is illusive and widespread around the world; it has the tacit and probably direct support of some world leaders, not to mention many citizens of some Arab and Muslim countries. Moreover, there are many serious gaps in security arrangements within the United States (O'Hanlon et al., 2002). There are, of course, limits to British influence over the United States. Each country has its own economic agenda and political realities to confront. In particular, membership in the European Union means that many of Britain's basic economic interests are linked to those of the EU.

POLITICAL FALLOUT WITHIN THE UNITED KINGDOM

If September 11 gave the British government greater clout with the United States because of its staunch support for the American war on terrorism, it also created difficulties for Prime Minister Blair in his dealings with the unionist community. The fact that Blair was strongly condemning international terrorism and insisting on harsh measures against al Qaeda and its supporters meant that the unionist community of Northern Ireland could charge him with hypocrisy when he appeared to take an insufficiently strong stand against the republican movement in Northern Ireland. Blair faced a dilemma. He had to be accommodating to Sinn Féin and the IRA to enable the GFA to be achieved in the first place, but this required private assurances to the unionists that he would insist on decommissioning. Blair also recognized the problem for Sinn Féin and the more moderate IRA leadership that a too-compliant approach to decommissioning by the IRA leadership ran the risk of major defections. But the British government also faced the wrath of the unionists, who saw a double standard in Blair's tough line taken against international terrorism and an accomodationist approach to the IRA and Sinn Féin. Indeed, there were increasing demands by unionists for the IRA to disband, a goal strongly advanced by the British, Irish, and American governments especially after the suspension of the Northern Ireland government in 2002.

Because of IRA foot-dragging on decommissioning and the undemocratic behavior of republicans, the majority of the unionist community turned against the agreement, and David Trimble came very close on several occasions to being defeated for leadership of the Ulster Unionist Party by members opposed to the agreement. Such a defeat would have brought down the new government of Northern Ireland, because his replacement would have withdrawn from the executive committee. Within the republican community, September 11 facilitated the ability of Gerry Adams and other more moderate members of the republican movement to pressure the IRA to begin the decommissioning process.

The credibility of Sinn Féin and the IRA were seriously undermined by the capture of two IRA and one Sinn Féin member by the government of Colombia in August 2001. These individuals were charged with providing training to Revolutionary Armed Forces of Colombia (FARC) terrorists. In April 2004, the Colombian court found the accused guilty of traveling under false passports rather than training terrorists, but the prosecution has appealed the case. Also, the visit by Gerry Adams to Cuba in December 2001 antagonized U.S. politicians and many Irish Americans. During the visit, Adams called upon the United States to lift its embargo and to seek normal relations with Cuba. Having allowed Gerry Adams to visit the United States over the objections of the British government and having placed substantial pressure on unionist leaders to agree to include Sinn Féin in the new executive committee in Northern Ireland, the United States viewed the visit as at the least a lack of gratitude. The U.S. ambassador to Britain diplomatically referred to the trip as "unhelpful" (*BBC News* 2001). These acts by the IRA and Sinn Féin strengthened the position of the British in their dealings with U.S. leaders and the American public. The conviction of three men in Florida in 2000 of illegally exporting arms, probably to the IRA, suggests that the IRA may also have been attempting to rearm while making limited concessions on decommissioning.

Furthermore, the IRA has continued its pattern of vigilante justice, although in 2002 the number of such cases appears to have declined (*Irish Times* 2002).

Rather than relying on the criminal justice system to punish wrongdoers, it continued to employ beatings and other punishments against alleged offenders (Knox and Monaghan 2002). This fundamentally undemocratic behavior and violation of the rights of the accused to an orderly and fair legal process offended democratic politicians throughout Northern Ireland and the republic. Sinn Féin and the IRA had committed themselves to a democratic solution to the conflict, and Sinn Féin held important leadership roles in the government of Northern Ireland. In October 2002, the IRA and Sinn Féin were implicated in a spying operation within the Northern Ireland Office of the British Government. This is the body responsible for implementing British policy in Northern Ireland and for directing aspects of the northern Irish political system not under a Northern Ireland government's authority. This agency has been intimately involved in security measures during the existence of the assembly and during periods of direct rule. Especially ominous was the taking of data on security guards and other officials who could some day be considered as targets for the IRA in the event of renewed hostilities.

If undemocratic behavior discredited the republican movement and strengthened the position of the British government with the United States, it had the more serious consequence of further undermining the peace process by making it far more difficult for David Trimble to maintain the support of his own party. Largely because of Sinn Féin's continuing involvement with violence and undemocratic practices as well as its reluctance to implement decommissioning, the leaders of the principal political parties in the Republic of Ireland, which is heavily Catholic, stated that they would not serve in a coalition government with Sinn Féin candidates elected in the republic's national elections held in May 2002. Although their actions were understandable, their decision made David Trimble's position all the more difficult in confronting dissidents in his own party. How could he justify continuing to serve in the executive committee with Sinn Féin politicians when even the Republic of Ireland's leaders would not form a government with Sinn Féin? With David Trimble planning to resign from the executive committee in the aftermath of the spying incident, the British government had no alternative but to suspend the Northern Ireland executive committee and Assembly. After the suspension of the government on October 15, 2002, the British and Irish governments stated their joint intention to make the GFA succeed. President Bush issued a statement in strong support for the British action (Bush 2002). All three governments emphasized the need to fully decommission. In the November 2003 Northern Ireland elections, the DUP, which is opposed to the agreement, displaced the more moderate UUP. Sinn Féin won more seats than the SDLP. Of course, the electoral success of the DUP and Sinn Féin makes the future success of the GFA more problematic.

The republican movement and some nationalists believe there has been insufficient movement toward demilitarization, that is, a reduction in forces, facilities, and operations by the British military and security forces. From the British point of view, they have already demilitarized to a significant degree, and the U.K. government is responsible for security in Northern Ireland in a situation where the other side has failed to live up to its promises to disarm. But the question of demilitarization is an important symbolic and quality-of-life issue for republicans and some nationalists, and possibly more could be done in this area. Additionally, from the viewpoint of the IRA and Sinn Féin, the GFA calls for decommissioning in the context of the implementation of other aspects of the agreement. Republicans claim, for example, that the police reform mandated by the GFA has yet to be fully achieved. Democratic parties and many leaders throughout Ireland, and, of course, the U.S. government and many Irish-American citizens, see this as an excuse for unjustifiable stalling.

Additionally, opposition by unionists to the implementation of some aspects of the agreement greatly complicated the peace process. The Patton Commission, a body with international representation, recommended a series of changes to policing in Northern Ireland designed to legitimize the police and law enforcement processes to alienated sectors of the minority community. The ultimate aim was to have a system of policing acceptable to all sectors of society. Many unionists and, of course, loyalists adamantly opposed the change of name from Royal Ulster Constabulary to the Police Service of Northern Ireland. This change as well as other reforms have now been implemented. As indicated above, Sinn Féin continues at this writing to find some aspects of police reform to be unacceptable.

THE PROBLEM OF LOYALIST VIOLENCE

Violence by loyalist paramilitary organizations and individuals constitutes a serious threat to the peace process. These organizations are far less constrained by the impact of September 11 than is the republican movement. Whereas Sinn Féin and the IRA have depended significantly on the financial and political support of Irish Americans, the paramilitary movement within the Protestant community has had no such important dependencies. It is more fragmented than its republican counterparts as well as less disciplined. Loyalist paramilitaries, for example, have been implicated in various kinds of crimes such as drug dealing within their own communities to a much greater extent than has occurred among republicans. Punishment beatings and other vigilante-type actions are more likely to be related to criminal activity than in areas subject to IRA influence. In addition, whereas the IRA is seeking a revolutionary change in the political status of Northern Ireland, loyalist paramilitary groups are fighting a defensive action against change. This is less likely to provide a cohesive, dedicated, and disciplined following committed to an ideological cause and subject to strong leadership.

Additionally, unlike the leadership of Sinn Féin, the leaders of loyalist organizations representing paramilitary groups have not had significant political interactions with leaders in the American and Irish governments. Of course, there were two small political parties representing loyalist paramilitary organizations during the negotiation phase of the GFA. The Ulster Democratic Party represented the Ulster Defense Association (UDA) and the Progressive Unionist Party represented the Ulster Volunteer Force (UVF). Only the Progressive Unionist Party won seats in the legislative assembly established by the GFA, and it won only two seats. The UDA has been heavily involved in violence in recent years. Unionist politicians and citizens as well as constitutional loyalists have been opposed to the violence committed by loyalist paramilitaries.

One of the most serious aspects of loyalist attacks is the potential for serious retaliation by members of the republican community. At some point, the IRA could engage in major counterattacks against loyalist targets. Escalating violence would necessarily involve government police and security forces attempting to arrest perpetrators and restore order. In brief, there is a risk that loyalist violence could not only undermine the peace process but also, in a worst case scenario, bring about a renewed armed struggle for the unification of Ireland. Yet September 11 constitutes an important restraint on republican leaders, who understand the long-term importance of retaining positive links with the United States and with democratic politicians in the Republic of Ireland. In this important regard, the tragic events of September 11 have produced some positive consequences in making far less likely a return to full-scale armed combat by the IRA.

THE REPUBLIC OF IRELAND

The most significant impact of September 11 on the Republic of Ireland has been the decrease, for reasons discussed above, in the possibility of a return to a full-scale armed struggle in Northern Ireland. For the Irish government, this conflict has consumed enormous political and administrative resources and, more significantly, has confronted government leaders with the potential for increased violence and political instability within the republic itself. Although the Irish government has sometimes challenged British security and human rights policy in Northern Ireland, in general it has worked closely with the British in an effort to find a solution to the problem and has cooperated on security matters (O'Halpin 2002). Indeed, it enacted its own emergency legislation to deal with the crisis and has sought to prevent the republic from being used as a safe haven for republican paramilitaries. The Irish government has also made clear its position that any future unification of the two political systems on the island would have to occur through a process of consent. This commitment to democratic procedures was reaffirmed in the GFA.

For most of the period since 1970, the leadership of the IRA and Sinn Féin have viewed the government of the republic as illegitimate and as a lackey of Britain. At the founding of the state in 1922, a brief civil war broke out between members of Sinn Féin and IRA supporting the treaty with Britain for a new southern state and those who viewed the compromise settlement as unacceptable. The insurgents lost, and most ultimately chose to participate peacefully in the politics of democratic southern Ireland. Both treaty and antitreaty forces joining the new political system adopted new party names. But a small remnant continued, sporadically and ineffectively, to resist the new state. The contemporary republican movement sees itself as the legitimate heirs of the original independence movement and the war of independence and has continued to employ the Sinn Féin and IRA labels.

Until the peace process began in the 1990s, the goal of contemporary republicans has been militarily to drive the British out of Northern Ireland and to set up an all-Ireland government based on republican principles that emphasized socialism. Given the authoritarian and violent nature of the republican movement, the long-term prospects of the political system after any IRA victory were, of course, uncertain. Among other things, such a military victory against the British would probably have provoked a civil war in Northern Ireland. Of course, during the 1990s the mainline republican leadership made clear its recognition that there was no hope for a military victory, and they have been committed to gaining a place in a devolved northern government, implicitly accepting unification as a long-term goal (Patterson 1997). After the peace process began in the early 1990s, Sinn Féin has worked somewhat cooperatively with Dublin governments, which were pushing for an Irish dimension to any settlement. The Irish government has also exerted significant pressure on Sinn Féin during the peace process to compromise and to decommission.

After the outbreak of violence in Northern Ireland, the southern government had to contend with such security challenges as IRA robberies within the republic, the killing of southern police officers in confrontations with the IRA, high-profile kidnappings, and the assassination of the British ambassador in 1976.

The greatest threat to security to the republic was retaliatory attack by loyalist paramilitaries from Northern Ireland. Although there have been few instances of such violence, bombings in Dublin and the town of Monahan in 1974 produced thirty-three deaths and numerous casualties, illustrating the potential difficulty. The loyalist paramilitary UVF claimed responsibility for these attacks. It remains uncertain whether the UVF acted in collusion with the UDA or even with members of the security forces within Northern Ireland (Mullan 2000). The point is that the Republic of Ireland is vulnerable to terrorist attacks organized by northern loyalist militants. And such endeavors would not take great technological and organizational capacity, although the fact that the three 1974 bombings in Dublin occurred almost simultaneously suggested the need for some coordination in that assault. Multiple attacks in the future remain a possibility, and the republic, with relatively limited military and police resources, could face a serious problem were prolonged, full-scale hostilities in Northern Ireland to resume. In brief, from several security perspectives, the Republic of Ireland has a profound stake in encouraging the success of the peace process. As indicated earlier, the government of the republic has also been concerned about other issues regarding Northern Ireland, such as discrimination and human rights matters.

CONCLUSION

From several perspectives, September 11 clearly has had a significant impact on the Northern Ireland peace process as well as on the relationship between the United Kingdom and the United States. Most fundamental have been the constraints placed on Sinn Féin and the IRA. While these constraints are not limitless, they create a strong disincentive for the IRA to reinstitute its campaign of bombing. Attacks on the island of Britain or other external targets would produce especially intense reaction, and even a return to bombing in Northern Ireland would erode substantial support for the IRA and Sinn Féin. Bombing and other forms of terrorism are now seen in a far less legitimate light among both Irish-American supporters of the republican movement as well as leaders and citizens throughout the democratic world.

The republican movement continues to engage in undemocratic actions and behaviors that constitute a major threat to the success of the peace process. Of course, the leadership of the republican movement faces the problem of defections from members upset at the idea of disarming, but they committed themselves to the building of democracy in Northern Ireland and can be reasonably held to account for their failure to deliver in this area. Most basic is the point that the IRA has not fully decommissioned its weapons.

September 11 increased the influence of the United Kingdom with the United States. The fact that America was now in a fight that was in some ways more dangerous and difficult to prosecute than the cold war meant that British support once again became a primary resource for the United States in its military and diplomatic strategies. The staunch support of the British government on issues such as military action on Iraq makes it a particularly important ally and gives the British the credibility and stature to advise and to quietly disagree where necessary. Although this influence is not limitless and the two countries will continue to differ on some economic and other issues, the importance of British support for the United States is difficult to overstate. Depending on leadership changes in the United States and Britain, the degree of cooperation as well as British influence on America could, of course, recede. Yet from the perspective of American leaders, the United States is in a life-and-death struggle, where the use of nuclear weapons and other WMD on American soil is a real possibility. The British government gains influence on international politics to the extent that it can help influence the politics of the world's only superpower. Thus, continued cooperation could bring benefits to both the United States and Britain. Some critics argue that American/British cooperation on Iraq has been unfortunate from the standpoint of world stability and the security of the United States and Britain.[2]

Loyalist paramilitary organizations continue to engage in vigilante practices as well as other forms of undemocratic behavior. Like the IRA, they have also failed to decommission their weapons, although most probably would do so if the IRA were to decommission its weapons. Particularly troublesome would be a major resurgence of loyalist paramilitary violence against Catholics. A significant violent response by members of the republican community could create major levels of fighting and lead Northern Ireland back into armed struggle. Because loyalists are not dependent on aid from the United States and have far less need to placate supporters outside of Northern Ireland, they are much less constrained by September 11 than are the republicans.

Overall, the impact of September 11 on the peace process in Northern Ireland has been largely positive, contributing to pressures on the IRA to refrain from returning to full-scale military action and strengthening the hand of the British government in supporting democratic forces within Northern Ireland. Yet it also complicated the position of the British prime minister in his dealings with the unionist community, among other things because of the apparent inconsistency in his tough position on international terrorism and his much more accomodationist position vis-à-vis the republican movement. A broader lesson of the dilemmas confronting the British government is that terrorism unleashes forces that are very difficult to constrain. The higher the levels of violence and the longer the duration of the conflict, the more difficult it becomes to build trust and to achieve compromise.

The United Kingdom and the Republic of Ireland are viable, respected democracies. If the peace process is so difficult in this setting, the complexity of bringing peace and stability, not to mention democracy, to places such as Afghanistan, Iraq, and Pakistan should be apparent. Although Northern Ireland presents a set of circumstances and constraints very different from those in less modern societies, the Good Friday Agreement can be an instructive case for international efforts to create viable political systems in war-torn and deeply divided societies. In the struggle against international terrorism, this quest is fundamental to the establishment of a safer and more stable world.

NOTES

A preliminary version of this chapter was presented at the thirty-fourth annual meeting of the Northeastern Political Science Association, Providence, Rhode Island, November 8, 2002. The author wishes to thank Adrian Guelke of Queen's University, Belfast, and Joshua Spero of Merrimack College, North Andover, Massachusetts, for suggestions on a draft version of this chapter. Any remaining errors of fact or interpretation are, of course, the responsibility of the author.

1. The Good Friday Agreement is also sometimes called the Belfast Agreement, or simply the Agreement. The use of the term "Good Friday Agreement" is more common in the nationalist community, but this more familiar designation has no political connotation as used in this chapter.

2. The question of whether the American and British decision to invade Iraq was wise or justified or whether this action reduced or increased the risk of attacks against the United States, Britain, and the West is beyond the scope of this chapter.

REFERENCES

Allison, Graham, and Philip Zelikow. 1999. *Essence of Decision: Explaining the Cuban Missile Crisis*. 2d ed. New York: Longman.
BBC News. 2001. "Adams' Cuba Trip Comes under Fire." Northern Ireland, December 19, 2001. http://news.bbc.co.uk/1/hi/northern_ireland/1718864.stm.
Budge, Ian, and Cornelius O'Leary. 1973. *Belfast: Approach to Crisis*. London: Macmillan.
Bush, George W. 2002. "Statement by the President on Northern Ireland." White House, Office of the Press Secretary, October 14.
Coakley, John. 1998. "Religion, Ethnic Identity and the Protestant Minority in the Republic." In *Ireland and the Politics of Change*, ed. William Crotty and David Schmitt, 86–106. London: Longman.

Cox, Michael. 2000. "Northern Ireland after the Cold War." In *A Farewell to Arms? From "Long War" to Long Peace in Northern Ireland*, ed. Michael Cox, Adrian Guelke, and Fiona Stephen, 249–62. Manchester: Manchester University Press.

Cunningham, Michael. 2001. *British Government Policy in Northern Ireland: 1969–2000*. Manchester: Manchester University Press.

Curtis, Edmond. 1968. *A History of Ireland*. 6th ed. London: Routledge.

Drumbell, John. 2001. *A Special Relationship: Anglo-American Relations in the Cold War and After*. London: Macmillan.

Feldman, Allen. 1991. *Formations of Violence: The Narrative of the Body and Political Terror in Northern Ireland*. Chicago: University of Chicago Press.

Finnegan, Richard B. 2002. "Irish-American Relations." In *Ireland on the World Stage*, ed. William Crotty and David E. Schmitt, 95–110. London: Longman.

Good Friday Agreement. 1998. *The Agreement: Agreement Reached in the Multi-Party Negotiations*. Belfast: Northern Ireland Office.

Guelke, Adrian. 2002. "The International System and the Northern Ireland Peace Process." IBIS Working Paper #2002. Dublin: Institute for British-Irish Studies, University College.

Harris, Rosemary. 1972. *Prejudice and Tolerance in Ulster*. Manchester: Manchester University Press.

Hennesey, Thomas. 1997. *A History of Northern Ireland*. New York: St. Martin's Press.

Horowitz, Donald. 1990. "Making Moderation Pay: The Comparative Politics of Ethnic Conflict Management." In *Conflict and Peacemaking in Multiethnic Societies*, ed. Joseph V. Montville, 451–76. Lexington, Mass.: Lexington Books, D. C. Heath.

———. 2001. "The Northern Ireland Agreement: Clear, Consociational, and Risky." In *Northern Ireland and the Divided World: The Northern Ireland Conflict and the Good Friday Agreement in Comparative Perspective*, ed. John McGarry, 89–108. Oxford: Oxford University Press.

Irish Times. 2002. "Apology Could Be a Damage—Limitation Exercise," July 18, p. 6.

Knox, Colin, and Rachel Monaghan. 2002. *Informal Justice in Divided Societies: Northern Ireland and South Africa*. New York: Palgrave Macmillan.

Lijphart, Arend. 1977. *Democrocy in Plural Societies: A Comparative Exploration*. New Haven: Yale University Press.

———. 1984. *Democracies: Patterns of Majoritarian and Consensus Government in Twenty-One Countries*. New Haven: Yale University Press.

Mullan, Don. 2000. *The Dublin and Monaghan Bombings*. Dublin: Wolfhound Press.

O'Halpin, Eunan. 2002. "Ireland and the International Security Environment: Changing Police and Military Roles." In *Ireland on the World Stage*, ed. William Crotty and David E. Schmitt, 140–52. London: Longman.

O'Hanlon, Michael, Peter R. Orszag, Ivo H. Daalder, I. M. Destler, David L. Gunter, Robert E. Litan, and James B. Steinberg. 2002. *Protecting the American Homeland*. Washington, D.C.: Brookings Institution Press.

O'Leary, Brendan. 2001. "The Character of the 1998 Agreement: Results and Prospects." In *Aspects of the Belfast Agreement*, ed. Rick Wilford, 49–83. Oxford: Oxford University Press.

Patterson, Henry. 1997. *The Politics of Illusion: A Political History of the IRA*. 2d ed. London: Serif.

Ruane, Joseph, and Jennifer Todd. 1996. *The Dynamics of Conflict in Northern Ireland: Power, Conflict and Emancipation*. Cambridge: Cambridge University Press.

Schmitt, David. 1980. "Equal Employment Opportunity as a Technique toward the Control of Political Violence: The Case of Northern Ireland's Fair Employment Agency." *Current Research on Peace and Violence* 3: 33–45.

Schulze, Kirsten E. 2001. "Taking the Gun out of Politics: Conflict Transformation in Northern Ireland and Lebanon." In *Northern Ireland and the Divided World: The Northern Ireland Conflict and the Good Friday Agreement in Comparative Perspective*, ed. John McGarry, 253–75. Oxford: Oxford University Press.

Stevens, John. 2003. "Stevens Enquiry: Overview and Recommendations, 17 April 2003." CAIN Web Service, University of Ulster. http://cain.ulst.ac.uk/issues/collusion/stevens3/stevens3summary.htm.

Tonge, Jonathan. 2002. *Northern Ireland*. 2d ed. London: Prentice Hall.

U.S. Commission on National Security/21st Century. 1999. Phase I: *New World Coming: American Security in the 21st Century*. Washington, D.C.: U.S. Government Printing Office. www.nssg.gov/Reports/NWC.pdf.

———. 2000. Phase II: *Seeking a National Strategy: A Concert for Preserving Security and Promoting Freedom*. Washington, D.C.: U.S. Government Printing Office. www.nssg.gov/PhaseII.pdf.

———. 2001. Phase III: *Road Map for National Security: Imperative for Change*. Washington, D.C.: U.S. Government Printing Office. www.nssg.gov/PhaseIIIFR.pdf.

Whyte, John. 1990. *Interpreting Northern Ireland*. Oxford: Oxford University Press.

20 Political Violence and Organized Crime in Serbia
THE IMPACT ON DEMOCRATIZATION

If someone believes he will stop the implementation of laws by getting rid of me—then he is very wrong, because I am not the system.
—ZORAN DJINDJIC, Prime Minister of Serbia (February 24, 2003)

I personally liquidated Zoran Djindjic. . . . For me this is a political murder because I believed it would stop further extraditions of Serbian warriors to The Hague [Tribunal].
—ZVEZDAN JOVANOVIC, detained assassin (April 7, 2003)

INTRODUCTION

The most challenging impediment to democratic transition in Serbia during the period from 2000 to 2004 was the persistence and consequences of the violent criminality that had burgeoned conspicuously for more than a decade under the previous authoritarian regime of Slobodan Milosevic. From the collapse of the Milosevic regime in the fall of 2000 through the first two and a half months of 2003, the work of Serbian reformist politicians to consolidate democracy was undermined by organized criminal networks, composed in part of former and active paramilitary and security forces. Those networks were also indirectly or directly linked to the state apparatus and influential political figures of the ostensibly post-Milosevic regime. The bulk of those criminal-paramilitary-security networks had been established or stimulated by the Milosevic dictatorship during the 1990s against the backdrop of the political and societal turbulence associated with Yugoslavia's violent dissolution. Indeed, the assassination of the reformist prime minister of Serbia, Zoran Djindjic, in mid-March 2003, was a desperate act of self-protection by criminal and former paramilitary elements who had been closely linked to the former dictatorship. The primary motivation of those who murdered Djindjic was, as they named their plot, to "Stop [extradition to the] Hague," that is, to avoid prosecution by the International Criminal Tribunal for the Former Yugoslavia (ICTY). Thus, there is a direct association between the violence and criminality that occurred on the Balkan political landscape during the 1990s and the daunting challenges to democratic change in the years since the technical collapse of the Milosevic regime.

The criminal clans and warrior bands of veterans who were behind the assassination of Djindjic succeeded in removing their immediate target, but the murder of the prime minister precipitated an antiterrorist campaign by his successors in the ruling Democratic Opposition of Serbia (DOS) coalition (an eighteen-party grouping) and opened a new phase in Serbia's political evolution. Initially, the post-Djindjic assault on terrorism had considerable success in dampening violence and crime in Serbia. But by the end of 2003, when some of the self-proclaimed and alleged assassins of Djindjic were put on trial, the reform coalition that had inherited the slain prime minister's mantle had politically disintegrated, and the official policy of ridding Serbia of its recent pattern of nationalism, criminality, and defective legal culture effectively lost its momentum. Indeed, the December 28, 2003, parliamentary elections in Serbia resulted in remarkable electoral success for some of the very political forces that had significantly contributed to laying the groundwork for political violence and turbulence in the Balkan region over the previous fifteen years.

In this exploration of the origins of political terrorism in Serbia under Milosevic's authoritarian regime, the initial failure of democratic reform forces to reverse the impact of the criminality-terrorism nexus in Serbia, and the course and consequences of the 2003 campaign against crime and political violence in the wake of the Djindjic assassination, terrorism is understood as the systematic use of violence designed to intimidate, coerce, or murder noncombatants (civilians and political officials) in order to advance certain goals or policies. Defined as such, terrorism may be state-sponsored or a method used by nonstate forces on behalf of, or against, the state. Terrorism can be distinguished from warfare, but it is frequently associated with a wartime environment or its aftermath. Moreover, terrorism may be differentiated into political or nonpolitical (e.g., criminal terrorism to advance economic goals) dimensions, although the two facets can become closely linked. It is violence that persistently and intentionally (not collaterally) targets noncombatants that is at the core of terrorism in the sense used throughout this essay.

MILOSEVIC'S CRIMINAL STATE

During the late 1980s, Slobodan Milosevic abandoned the policy injunctions and political rhetoric, albeit not the total mind-set and traits, of the stagnant communist (Titoist) regime he had served for many years as a high official. Milosevic would acquire power at the summit of Serbia's political hierarchy, first endorsing covertly, and then more openly, a blatant nationalist program. He also employed populist and demagogic methods that were unconventional for Yugoslavia's communist officialdom. Milosevic, whose only political goal was the pursuit of power, would use nationalism whenever and to the extent that it served his interests (Cohen 2002). During the early 1990s, as Yugoslavia violently disintegrated—due in large measure to Milosevic's policies—and as savage warfare, international sanctions, and economic deterioration enveloped the former Yugoslavia, the Serbian dictator increasingly relied on organized criminality and state-sponsored terrorism, both as an instrument of policy and as a methodology to maintain his power. The quest by Milosevic to become the "new Tito" and assume unbridled control of Serbia and then socialist Yugoslavia—an ambition stoked by his scheming and closely collaborating wife—did not initially involve the use of organized criminal assistance and terrorism. But the underpinning for the criminalization of the Milosevic regime and its use of terror are evident even prior to the collapse of socialist Yugoslavia. For example, during the period between 1987 when he assumed power in Serbia and Yugoslavia's dissolution in 1991, Milosevic had not only established firm control over the party system, the media, and the economy in Serbia and Montenegro but also firmly dominated the police apparatus and the administration of justice.

Inheriting political management of Serbia's police operations in the late 1980s, Milosevic quickly built up a strong and politically loyal internal security service. By 1993, fifty thousand people were employed by the Ministry of Internal Affairs, and at least another twenty thousand police reservists had been recruited. By 1995, the police force was estimated to be around one hundred thousand strong, or larger than the combined military forces. Disciplined, generously financed, and well trained and equipped, including units with antiaircraft cannons and heavy mortars and artillery, the police also received better salaries than most other sectors of the state apparatus, including the military. The conspicuous differences between the police and military apparatuses in Milosevic's Yugoslavia became strikingly apparent in the early 1990s as the Belgrade regime strove to acquire political control over the Serbian communities in Croatia and Bosnia and to ensure the political stability of Serbia and Montenegro.

The professional and political weakening of the army and the militarization of the police apparatus allowed Milosevic to guide the course of events in the Croatian and Bosnian Serb communities in a more surreptitious, personalized, and extraconstitutional manner. During and after the wars in Croatia and Bosnia, the Serbian police-state nexus would also function as an internal shield, a praetorian guard, protecting the authoritarian regime and its elite from its own citizens. In 1993, the Police Academy of Serbia was founded with a substantial budgetary allocation. The school's curriculum included courses on military doctrine and the use of heavy armor and artillery. Though the media may have served as the primary vehicle used by the Milosevic regime for promoting the officially acceptable ideological and political line, including a steady diet of nationalist themes, the existence of a strong police apparatus was used selectively against nonconforming segments of the Yugoslav population. As such, the police constituted a central pillar of an outwardly "soft" authoritarian system.

The politicization of the judicial system was also a part of Milosevic's "technology of domination." Judicial appointments were firmly in the hands of the regime, as pro-regime judges headed all judicial election committees. The poor material position of judges and cutbacks in the number of judicial appointees also increased the insecurity of judges and enhanced political control over the courts. As in the previous communist regime, "moral-political suitability" as interpreted by the ruling party was critical in deciding eligibility for the bench (Stefanovic 1992, 8). Legislative oversight of judicial appointments was negligible because of the powerless position of the opposition parties in the Serbian Assembly and the overall impotence of parliamentary institutions in the structure of power. Political intervention in judicial decision-making also became the norm during the early 1990s (Mrsevic 1998). The arbitrary and politicized nature of the prosecutorial and judicial sectors allowed the regime to protect its supporters and punish its opponents. With the growing criminalization of the economy and growth in quasi-legal practices by the state's economic sector and state-linked private companies during the early 1990s, the politicization of justice was especially valuable to managerial subelites within the ruling establishment. "Financially insecure judges can be bribed very easily and it often looks as if they are," claimed one Serbian lawyer specializing in criminal law. "The first thing my clients want to know is how much money is needed for the judge. . . . Without hard currency or influential friends you have to wait a long time for justice, and the results are unpredictable" (Milinkovic 1993). Thus, by the early 1990s, the ruling establishment in Serbia had a well-developed security network and a pliant justice system to protect both their legal and illegal operations, not to mention their privileges, perks, and positions.

The impact of the wars of the Yugoslav succession on Serbia, and particularly the breakdown of routine economic activity under the pressure of UN sanctions, contributed to the growing criminalization of society in Serbia and Montenegro during the first half of the 1990s. The most representative example of this trend was the rise of Zeljko Raznjatovic, better known as Arkan, from a minor figure in Belgrade's underworld to a high-profile actor in Serbian political life. Wanted by Interpol and a dozen European countries in connection with bank robberies during the 1970s and 1980s, Arkan emerged as a prominent figure on the Belgrade scene when, with the help of the Serbian Ministry of the Interior, he organized paramilitary units to fight for Serb interests in Croatia and Bosnia (and later in Kosovo). Arkan's Serbian National Guard, popularly known as the "Tigers," became notorious for their brutal "ethnic cleansing" campaigns. But the Milosevic-controlled media turned Arkan into a "hero of the Serbian nation." As most normal business activity was curtailed or disappeared owing to international sanctions, Arkan's companies and his Obilic football club were permitted to flourish. In exchange, Arkan expressed admiration for Milosevic. "Milosevic woke up the Serbs," he remarked in one interview. "He woke me up as a Serb too" (Zimonjic 2000). When a Croatian diplomat conducting secret negotiations with Milosevic asked about Arkan in 1993, the Serbian president only laughed and said, "I too must have someone to do certain kinds of work for me" (Sarinic 1999, 46). The most violent and ultranationalist supporters of Arkan made an easy transition from football hooliganism to full-blown terrorism on behalf of the Milosevic regime. In part, such hooliganism derived from the aggressive "football anticommunism," or a popular breaking free from state control. Indeed, Milosevic used Arkan to control and channel hooliganism on behalf of the state. Violence at sporting events against teams from outside Serbia became a training ground for later state-sponsored violence against targeted ethnic "enemies."

Wrapping himself in the Serb struggle of epic tradition—including the myth of the Battle of Kosovo and the history of Serb brigandage against Turkish occupation (the *hajduk* tradition)—Arkan claimed that his activities demonstrated a commitment to the "defense of Serbs" throughout the former Yugoslavia (Colovic 2000). The "heroization" of mafia activity in Serbia made a mockery of the regime's claim of upholding the rule of law and transformed the climate in Milosevic's soft dictatorship into a dangerous environment where selected wild and arbitrary justice became increasingly routine.

Another Serbian ultranationalist whom Milosevic would manipulate was Vojislav Seselj, a vocal anti-Titoist dissident who, in the early 1990s, would become one of the most enigmatic, controversial, and extremist figures in Serbian political life. In early 1990, Seselj's small Serbian Freethinkers Movement had joined with supporters of the writer-politician Vuk Draskovic to form the Serbian Movement of Renewal (SPO). But Seselj soon broke with Draskovic (who was the godfather of Seselj's eldest child) and in June 1990 launched the Serbian Chetnik Movement (SCP). Seselj then ran as an independent candidate in the 1990 presidential election but received only 1.9 percent of the vote. In early 1991, Seselj established the Serbian Radical Party (SRS), drawing together several disparate ultranationalist groups. Seselj employed various brutish, belligerent, and often clownish maneuvers to gain publicity. In 1990, for example, he assaulted one of his comrades in the SCP with a baseball bat, and the same year he was involved in the forcible expulsion of Croatian families in a number of Vojvodina villages. During the wars in Croatia and Bosnia, Seselj led paramilitary volunteer units against "anti-Serb" forces and promised to use "rusty spoons" to mutilate his Muslim enemies. An ardent Serb nationalist and anticommunist who opposed monarchism, Seselj's right-wing populist program consisted of an eclectic admixture of themes from traditional European fascism and newer ideas borrowed from Western Europe's current radical right.

By the time that socialist Yugoslavia disintegrated, Milosevic had already consolidated his regime based on a blend of old state socialist ideas, Serbian nationalism, and dictatorial methods. But it was only during the wars of the Yugoslav succession in the 1990s that the Serbian regime really began to resemble the character of a criminalized state willing to extensively utilize political terrorism. Indeed, in the conflicts that the Serbian dictator helped to orchestrate in Croatia and Bosnia from 1992 to 1995, and later in Kosovo in 1998 and 1999, Milosevic—through stealth and a network of loyal henchman such as Arkan, Seselj, and many others in order to mask his direct involvement—promoted the use of systematic violence against combatants and noncombatants alike. The now relatively well-known and notorious ethnic cleansing campaigns conducted in Croatia, Bosnia, and Kosovo were carried out by a network of Belgrade-directed state security forces and paramilitary units. A substantial portion of the paramilitary fighters came from the republic of Serbia within Milosevic's new two-unit Federal Republic of Yugoslavia (Serbia and Montenegro), and especially from smaller communities outside Belgrade. Recruits were also drawn from the large Serbian communities in the neighboring republics of Croatia and Bosnia. Those attracted to paramilitary service came from varied social backgrounds. Some were motivated by dedication, misguided or otherwise, to Serbian patriotic ideals. However, some former convicts and individuals with serious psychological and social problems were also attracted to service in the paramilitary formations. The various official and quasi-official paramilitary forces often worked directly alongside regular Serbian military personnel from the Yugoslav army or its "successor" armed forces that came under the control of local Serbian authorities in Croatia and Bosnia.

Throughout the wars following Yugoslavia's breakup, Milosevic tried to conceal his willingness to employ terror against non-Serb populations by essentially contracting out the direct responsibility or systematic violence and intimidation. Much of the evidence for Milosevic's command responsibility would gradually emerge in his subsequent trial for crimes against humanity that would be held at the International Criminal Tribunal for the Former Yugoslavia at The Hague (and which was still taking place at the time of this analysis). Most of the groups were formed between 1990 and 1993 and included Arkan's Serbian Volunteer Guard (the "Tigers"), Seselj's SCP, Frenki Simatovic's Special Operation Units (JSO, or "Red Berets" or "Frenkijevci"), Dragoslav Bokan's White Eagles, and Captain Dragan's Knindzas, among others.[1] These groups were recruited, supported, and assisted, not to mention controlled directly or indirectly (depending on the unit or group), by Serbia's Ministry of the Interior (MUP). The MUP acted through agencies such as the Serbian State Security Service (SDB, later RDB, the Division of State Security), headed by Jovica Stanisic beginning in March 1991 (Frenki Simatovic, an ethnic Croat, was his deputy) and by Radovan Stojicic "Bazda," the head of Serbian Public Security Forces, beginning in 1992. Rade Markovic succeeded the assassinated Bazda in mid-1997 and then succeeded Stanisic in October 1998. The State Security Service of Serbia also worked with its equivalent agencies in the Bosnian Serb republic and the Republic of the Serbia Krajina (a breakaway part of Croatia until 1995). Stanisic coordinated a group of key officials in Yugoslavia's security and intelligence services, known as the military line, that was essentially a parallel chain of command that linked Serbian paramilitary forces outside Serbia with the Belgrade regime. Mihalj Kertes (a former high official in Yugoslavia's Security Service and in the MUP), who, as Milosevic's minister for the Serb diaspora was in charge of supplying weapons to Serbian communities outside Serbia and later was the head of the Custom's Administration for the Milosevic regime, worked closely with Stanisic and the network of paramilitary forces. The close wartime links that were established among the police, paramilitary forces, and criminal groups and clans were often built on personal connections and joint illegal activities that went back as early as the 1970s. Milosevic consolidated these links in order to terrorize population groups during the warfare in Serbia's neighboring republics and also to repress political officials and groups targeted by the Belgrade regime within Serbia.

Disagreements still remained in 2004 concerning the degree of Milosevic's personal knowledge regarding all the activities carried out by Serbian paramilitaries in Croatia, Bosnia, and Kosovo and to what extent Milosevic may have given direct orders for their nefarious activities. However, there is more certainty about the operations that paramilitary forces conducted and also that they had considerable support or organizational direction from Serbian security officials who were undoubtedly under Milosevic's direct control. Many of the nationalists involved in "special" police and paramilitary formations established or exploited by Milosevic were products of a culture of hatred and violence that enveloped the disintegrating Yugoslav state, and especially Serbia, during the late 1980s and early 1990s. Such a cultural underpinning for political terror was especially apparent in the sports hooliganism and in certain areas of popular culture, such as ultranationalist folklore and folk music. The Serbian paramilitary groups also drew upon—at least in their nomenclature, insignia, and self-proclaimed goals—a long-established Balkan mythology regarding the heroism of irregular forces and warrior bands. Most members of the paramilitary forces operating in Croatia and Bosnia returned to Serbia at the conclusion of the war in Bosnia (November 1995). Many such veterans would again play paramilitary roles and be involved in terroristic and violent activities in Kosovo in 1998 and 1999, and some would continue to be active in both the last stages of Milosevic's rule and in post-Milosevic Serbia.

During late 1999 and the first half of 2000, as opposition elements began to coalesce, the Milosevic regime became increasingly repressive. In mid-2000, this was increasingly reflected in the preparation of draconian "antiterrorism" legislation. For example, the draft bill envisioned long-term prison sentences for those convicted of publishing information deemed a threat to the state. The underlying purpose of the antiterrorism legislation went well beyond control of the media; the regime was particularly interested in stifling the activity of the student resistance organization Otpor, which had been a thorn in Milosevic's side since 1998. The political radicalization of student activity was, in part, a reaction to the regime's stringent use of the University Law adopted in late May 1998. Otpor had been formed five months later as a "cell" of resistance to the regime's crackdown on self-governing autonomy and free expression at the university. One Otpor leader, Ivan Marovic, claimed that from March 1999 to March 2000, 190 activists from the movement had been beaten and had sustained slight injuries (ONASA News Agency 2000). The police were also used to prevent Otpor demonstrations in a number of cities.

Milosevic had never taken lightly the threat to his regime from the traditional opposition parties, but the simultaneous appearance of unconventional forms of dissidence by the student radicals now made matters far more serious. The unexplained murder in late April of the state airline's chief executive (Zika Petrovic, who had been a friend of Milosevic's from their teenage years in Pozarevac) and the assassination on May 13 of a high official of the Socialist Party of Serbia (SPS) from Vojvodina (Bosko Perosevic)—two incidents in a string of similar acts of violence in Serbia over the preceding year—were quickly labeled by the regime as terrorist acts that were engineered by Otpor. Between May 13 and late June, the police maintained open files on some 640 activists from Otpor (BBC Monitoring 2000). Most members of Otpor, which was banned as a terrorist organization, were held for only a short time. But other members of the movement were beaten by the police for handing out antigovernment posters or simply drawing graffiti or wearing T-shirts with the Otpor symbol—a clenched fist. Itself a terroristic regime, Milosevic officials tried to smear all its political foes, whether they were using militant or moderate methods, by characterizing them as part of a so-called terrorist bloc.[2]

In late July 2000, when Slobodan Milosevic called for elections in Yugoslavia —for the federal presidency, the legislature, municipalities, and the province of Vojvodina—his political position, though weakened compared to earlier years, was still quite secure. The major levers of power that had sustained his regime for some thirteen years were still under his control, and perennially fragmented opposition appeared to be living up to its reputation and record of disarray. It was this situation, and the continued rift between the two major opposition leaders, Zoran Djindjic and Vuk Draskovic, that emboldened Milosevic to call for early elections on September 24, 2000.

As the electoral campaign in the autumn of 2000 unfolded, the routine violence that had taken the lives of scores of underworld and political figures in past years continued. The disappearance of Ivan Stambolic, Milosevic's one-time political mentor, while jogging in Belgrade on August 24, 2000, added a new name to the list of famous and infamous individuals who appeared to be the victims of violence. It also raised the question once again of whether such murders were ordered by a dictator intent on removing individuals who knew too much or who might even become alternative candidates for high office. Moreover, all the political machinations and brutality in Serbian politics were occurring within the context of a deteriorating economy, which itself was a major source of potential instability and violence. With an isolated economy, a steadily falling gross domestic product, an industry in ruins, and for the first time fear that the country might face a food crisis (in the winter of 2000) owing to drought and drastically lower yields of agricultural products, the possibility of some kind of mass expression of protest against the regime increased.

During the fall of 2000, Serbia experienced—over only a three-month period —a profound political realignment and transfer of power from Slobodan Milosevic to moderate and centrist opposition forces. A dictatorial leader and his political elite were replaced by a counter-elite committed to democratic development. In order to oust Milosevic, Serbia's opposition parties had first coalesced into the eighteen-party DOS coalition and had advanced an attractive and fresh candidate for the presidency of Yugoslavia who could, and did, successfully challenge the tottering and weakened dictator. This new candidate, Vojislav Kostunica, proved appealing to the majority of Serbian voters, not because he was a particularly telegenic or charismatic figure, but because of his basic modesty, honesty, and innate "grayness," not to mention his relative marginal position on the existing Yugoslav political stage. Indeed, Kostunica, who headed the small Democratic Party of Serbia (DSS), was considered a democratic nationalist. He also had the distinct advantage of never even having met, let alone brokered any deals with, Slobodan Milosevic.

The decision to advance Kostunica and thereby temporarily circumvent the two major established and long-standing opposition figures—Zoran Djindjic and Vuk Draskovic—was a gamble that paid off. Kostunica quickly took the lead over Milosevic in public opinion polls and won the presidential election of September 24, 2000. Clearly, in retrospect, when Milosevic had called the election in July he had seriously underestimated the intensity and scale of popular antipathy toward his regime and his family. That fatal miscalculation was probably due to hubris, in this case an unfounded belief that the majority of Serbian citizens would remain politically obedient as they had during and immediately after the 1999 NATO attack against Yugoslavia.

But despite having lost the September election, Milosevic refused to acknowledge Kostunica's victory and tenaciously clung to power for ten days following the election. The fallen leader was finally ousted only as a result of a domestically coordinated, but largely externally funded, "spontaneous eruption" of post-election popular demonstrations, or what amounted to a relatively peaceful and nearly bloodless "democratic revolution." The final phase of the Milosevic regime began when protestors at the center of the demonstrations, in front of the Federal Assembly, tried to storm that building. Initially a lone man in a tracksuit rushed the police line. He was followed by dozens and soon hundreds of protestors. When a confused and halfhearted effort by riot police to prevent entry into the building by using tear gas, stun grenades, and clubs failed, the protestors surged into the legislature and began setting fires and looting offices. Other police inside and outside the building fled. The crucial decision by the police to ignore Milosevic's orders to crush the demonstration resulted from secret negotiations the night before between Zoran Djindjic and Milorad Lukovic-Ulemek (widely known as Legija), the Serbian secret police commander in charge of Milosevic's JSO. Legija had close links to the network of paramilitary and security forces that had served the Milosevic regime throughout the 1990s. Legija explained his decision to Djindjic: "I'm not a politician, I'm a professional. I see that Milosevic lost the election" (CNN 2002). Legija's promise to Djindjic that the JSO would not intervene to obstruct the October 5 demonstration was an important signal that emboldened the antiregime activists in DOS and helped end Milosevic's rule. As demonstrators poured into the federal parliament building on October 5, Legija called Djindjic on his cell phone to announce: "It is all over" (Bujosevic 2001, 47–48).[3] Vojislav Kostunica was sworn in as president of Yugoslavia on October 7, 2000. For his part, Milosevic, in another example of his political unpredictability, chose neither to take his life, as a great many observers had hoped or calculated, nor to flee to some safe haven (e.g., Belarus, Libya, Cuba, or China), as others expected. Instead, he decided to remain in Yugoslavia; this decision would have a profound short-term impact on the country's political life, well beyond the technical fall of the dictatorial regime.

Despite Milosevic's continued presence on Serbia's political landscape, the collapse of support for the old regime in October 2000 and the extent of the DOS victory were unquestionable. In the September 24 municipal elections, for example, Milosevic forces suffered an ignominious defeat as DOS swept to power in more than 90 cities. In Belgrade, DOS took 96 of the Citizen Assembly's 100 seats. When, on December 23, 2000, republic-level elections were finally held in Serbia, the full extent of popular support for DOS and the post-Milosevic regime became fully apparent, with the coalition winning 64 percent of the vote in Serbia and 176 of the 250 seats in Serbia's legislature.

Vojislav Kostunica's popularity had undoubtedly helped DOS achieve an even more impressive victory in the December 2000 republic-level elections than it had in the September federal-level contest. But the DOS electoral campaign in Serbia had been led by Zoran Djindjic—an old arch rival of Kostunica's from the democratic opposition ranks—and it was Djindjic who was installed in December as Serbia's new prime minister. Thus, alongside the important Milosevic question, there was now new uncertainty in Yugoslavia's post-Milosevic transition, namely, whether the seasoned, highly pragmatic, Western-oriented, and very ambitious Djindjic would be able to cooperate successfully with the incrementalist, legally oriented, and decidedly anti-American Vojislav Kostunica. More broadly, could the unwieldy eighteen-party DOS coalition transcend the Kostunica-Djindjic rivalry, and how would this dysfunctional duumvirate affect the new government's ability to deal with both the thorny Milosevic question and the even more daunting economic and territorial problems faced by the country?

THE DAWN OF "DEMOCRACY": DISCONTENT AND CONTINUITY IN THE INITIAL TRANSITION (OCTOBER– MARCH 2002)

Regrettably, the strong political influence of the symbiotic alliance between war criminals and organized criminal gangs that had been inspired by the Milosevic regime was not impaired by the dictator's formal departure from power and the electoral victory of a democratic opposition. Indeed, leading members of the paramilitary groups, who had maintained close contact with leaders of the democratic opposition during the fall 2000 election, and who had played a crucial role in the collapse of the Milosevic regime, would emerge as key players following Milosevic's departure from power. For example, Legija and his JSO comrades would again assist the new regime when Prime Minister Djindjic, at the end of March 2001, ordered the arrest of Milosevic. However, the informal working arrangements—ranging from a temporary standoff to direct and sometimes corrupt ties in the case of certain members of the ruling coalition—between Djindjic's democratic reform government and criminal elements within Serbia began to seriously deteriorate after Djindjic extradited Milosevic to The Hague tribunal near the end of June 2001. At the same time, Djindjic also became more assertive in attacking crime and corruption within Serbia. It was even rumored that Djindjic was planning a crackdown on members of the police services involved in illegal activities (in November 2001, a Belgrade news magazine claimed that more than 360 Serb police officers were targets of an investigation by the International Tribunal for the Former Yugoslavia).

In early November 2001, Legija's Red Berets were directed to arrest two police officers pending their extradition to the Netherlands. This provocative order sparked a police rebellion, with scores of Red Berets—whose members had operated in Bosnia and Kosovo and had a reputation for brutality—deploying armored personnel carriers to block the Belgrade-Budapest highway (from November 9 to November 16) and demanding a halt to all extraditions for war crimes until a Yugoslav law was passed on the issue. They also demanded the sacking of Serbia's MUP. The JSO protest ended only after a compromise was reached involving the reorganization of the state security leadership and an agreement by the government not to hold Red Beret commandos criminally responsible for their participation in earlier military operations. During the dispute, President Kostunica, who had been a vocal critic of extradition to The Hague, supported the demands of the JSO officers. For his part, Prime Minister Djindjic harshly criticized Kostunica's approach to the JSO rebellion as "inappropriate" and ordered the restructuring of the JSO into a nonsecret antiterror unit within the regular police chain of command. The JSO rebellion illustrated the vulnerability of the new regime to pressure from the former and current paramilitary forces. The JSO action also underlined the obstacles to democratization that resulted from the ongoing tug-of-war between Kostunica and Djindjic over control of the security services, and more broadly over the country itself.

The salience of the "Milosevic question" in Serbian political life during 2001, together with the Djindjic-Kostunica rivalry (which only intensified after

Milosevic's extradition), impeded the momentum of democratic reform in Serbia and also allowed the war criminal–organized crime nexus to perpetuate its resources and power. Djindjic, although a pragmatist, and predisposed to accommodate international pressure for taking action against criminal elements in Serbian society and in the security apparatus, found it extremely difficult and potentially dangerous to become involved in a direct confrontation with his former "allies" from the paramilitary and crime network. Meanwhile, the federal president, Vojislav Kostunica, favored a more incremental approach to reform than Djindjic and advocated a philosophy of "legalism" rather than a rapid wholesale purge of old regime elements. Moreover, Kostunica was also a political animal and very aware of Djindjic's longstanding contacts in the Serbian republic's police apparatus (not to mention the prime minister's technical authority over those services). In order to compensate for Djindjic's hold on the levers of power in Serbia, Kostunica found it expedient to permit former members of Milosevic's regime to maintain their positions in the federal-level military and security services. A belief widely held, if somewhat simplistically but also with considerable accuracy, in Serbia was that, to a large extent, Djindjic controlled the Serbian police and Kostunica the federal military machine and that this duality created a political stalemate, which impeded the fundamental reforms necessary to eliminate remaining war criminals and organized criminal gangs on Serbia's political landscape.

The Kostunica-Djindjic face-off continued throughout 2002. Meanwhile, Serbia lost valuable time and energy that should have been focused on critical issues such as economic restructuring, creating a rule of law, and fighting corruption. Clearly, the Milosevic regime's officially sanctioned linkage between political officialdom and criminal structures had left his political successors with entrenched problems of lawlessness and political violence that they proved incapable of overcoming. There was an abundance of rhetoric concerning reform and also incessant discussions about reform policies, but in practice reforms were more "simulated" than real (Anastasijevic 2003). In July 2002, Serbian Interior Minister Dusan Mihailovic claimed he had information that "certain power centers" were planning to destabilize the country through "liquidating prominent politicians" in the ruling DOS coalition (*SEE Security Monitor* 2002). Mihailovic had earlier warned that Serbian leaders, including Djindjic, had been receiving death threats from illegal groups (Agence France-Presse 2001). At the time, in early 2001, Mihailovic had suggested that there were between sixty thousand and seventy thousand undeclared arms in Serbia, including automatic rifles, rocket launchers, grenade launchers, mortars, and bazookas.

Speculation in the press during July 2002 put the number of organized crime groups in Serbia between 150 and 300, with a dozen powerful crime groups

located in Belgrade and 5 prominent bosses contending for the position of supreme mafia leader in the capital of the country. After an investigation into the
assassination of a police general, Bosko Buha, in June 2002, Interior Minister
Mihailovic had claimed that Serbia's "criminal heritage" was the result of a
"criminal pyramid" that included "individuals in the custom's administration,
state security service, this or that state institution, close to drug dealers and
hard currency dealers, murderers and racketeers in the streets . . . this pyramid
has two faces. One face is war crimes committed in our [Serbia's] name and the
other face is organized crime" (BBC Monitoring 2002a).

As a rule, Prime Minister Djindjic, who had been clashing with Mihailovic
over the handling of organized crime during 2002 and who was very sensitive
to accusations about his own involvement with criminal elements, tended to
play down the difficulties with organized criminal groups and even insisted that
the mafia "has been systematically defeated because there is no longer a connection between it and the authorities" (BBC Monitoring 2002b). But near the
end of 2002, Djindjic had to admit that in his republic "internal security is at a
very low level, and [that] is how a state's credibility is measured." Djindjic also
added that at times the police were "not the only force in Serbia which has force
at its disposal. . . . I would say that it is still more risky to be a policeman or a
judge in Serbia than a criminal. The system is less capable of protecting its officials than the mafia is capable of endangering them" (BBC Monitoring 2002c).

At the end of 2002, an amended law on criminal protection went into effect that contained special provisions to fight organized crime. For example, a
witness protection program was introduced. But Interior Minister Mihailovic
admitted that the police had "many moles in their ranks" and that "there is a
great danger that the criminals will learn about these protected witnesses" (BBC
Monitoring 2002d). As of early 2003, Mihailovic had still not been able to solve
the prominent cases of political assassination that had occurred toward the end
of the Milosevic regime—such as the murders of the journalist Slavko Curuvija
and the former politician Ivan Stambolic. The perpetrators of at least fifteen
major mafia killings also remained at large.

Not one of the fifty-two organized crime groups included in a police "White
Book" compiled during the summer of 2002 had been broken up, nor had their
activities been curtailed. It was widely believed and frequently reported in the
media that the major crime clans—such as those in the localities of Zemun and
Surcin around Belgrade—had a close working relationship with officials in the
police, the judiciary, and the political parties. The Zemun clan was reported to be
heavily involved in drug trafficking and the abduction of people for ransom. The
Surcin clan had begun with car thefts, and with petrol and cigarette smuggling

that flourished in the 1990s, and moved on to heroin and cocaine trafficking. Before falling out with one another, the two clans cooperated and were allied in armed clashes and assassinations with other members of the underworld. The high-profile assassination of the paramilitary and political leader Arkan in January 2000 resulted from such interclan violence.

During the first two months of 2003, a number of factors converged that would culminate in a tragic and major blow to Serbia's reformist coalition and open an entirely new phase in post-Milosevic political development. Paradoxically, as 2003 began, Prime Minister Djindjic's political prospects seemed brighter than at any point since the fall of Milosevic just over two years earlier. First, Djindjic's old rival, Vojislav Kostunica, was about to leave his position as president of the Yugoslav Federation because of an EU-brokered accord that essentially reconfigured the country into a loose confederal union named Serbia and Montenegro. That accord—which Kostunica had helped negotiate—required the establishment of a new constitution and the selection of new officials for the union. The reorganized state, inaugurated on February 4, essentially gave the top political leaders of the two republics—Zoran Djindjic of Serbia and Milo Djukanovic of Montenegro—the greatest influence in guiding the affairs of the new two-unit union. Kostunica, Djindjic's old political rival, stepped aside quietly in early March, as required by the terms of the accord. Second, Djindjic seemed to be quite adept at exploiting the dominant Serbian nationally oriented constituency that Kostunica (and before him Milosevic) had more or less relied upon as a political base. Indeed, Djindjic seemed to be openly courting nationalist sentiments by suggesting that Serbia must continue to play a prominent role in Kosovo—which was still technically part of Yugoslavia, but a UN protectorate since 1999—where the predominantly Albanian population and political elite were firmly focused on the attainment of political independence. Djindjic even hinted that should Kosovo be granted independence by the international community, a review of the terms of the 1995 Dayton Accord on Bosnia would be necessary and the Bosnian Serbs should be allowed to pursue their own state-seeking goals. During February, Djindjic also mentioned the possibility of partitioning Kosovo or even federalizing it in order to accommodate Serbian concerns. Djindjic's comments irritated international officials who, in the main, wished to postpone discussion of Kosovo's future status and certainly opposed any talk of partition or territorial reconfiguration in the region as a whole. But by the end of February 2003, Djindjic was already planning to have talks with Albanian leaders in Kosovo to discuss future arrangements.

At the same time, Djindjic was under strong international pressure to finally remove the antireform remnants of the Milosevic regime, to extradite indicted war criminals to The Hague, and to end the persistent influence of organized criminal groups in Serbian society and political life. Until such policies were adopted, most Serbian reformers and foreign officials believed that Serbia, and its union partner Montenegro, could not move substantially forward with authentic democratization. In January and February 2003, Djindjic appeared to anticipate the drying up of international funds if he hesitated too long with the matter of extraditing war criminals (for example, the U.S. Congress's decision to certify aid for Serbia and Montenegro was scheduled for March 31 but then moved to June 15). Djindjic signaled that he was willing to cooperate more effectively with the ICTY and finally take measures against the "criminal pyramid." In January, a Belgrade court jailed Milosevic's former secret police chief, Rade Markovic, for seven years because of his role in the 1999 murder of four of Vuk Draskovic's aides (the so-called Ibar Highway case).

Indicted war criminals and members of organized crime clans became especially anxious when Milosevic's crony, former Serbian president Militunovic, surrendered to The Hague tribunal and also after the SRS leader and former paramilitary chief, Vojislav Seselj, announced in an act of bizarre bravado that he would depart for The Hague on his own volition and attempt to use the tribunal as a soapbox for his views. These events together with Djindjic urging the indicted Bosnian Serb general Ratko Mladic to surrender to The Hague and a visit to Djindjic by The Hague prosecutor Carla del Ponte, who was pressing for Serbian cooperation with the ICTY, created an atmosphere of considerable anxiety in the ranks of Serbia's crime networks. On February 21, just days after meeting del Ponte, Djindjic was the target of an attempted assassination. In a manner reminiscent of the attempted assassination of Draskovic and his aides in 1999, an oncoming freight truck suddenly swerved into the path of Djindjic's car. The prime minister narrowly avoided a high-speed collision. The driver, who had a long criminal record and close ties to the Surcin clan, was apprehended, although the police were initially unable to establish any direct links to the group or to find the individuals who may have ordered the assassination. But suspicion immediately focused on the Serbian underworld and particularly on Legija, the former commander of the Red Berets. It was, after all, veterans of the Red Berets, the Interior Ministry's Special Operations Unit, who had committed atrocities in Croatia, Bosnia, and Kosovo (and who were rumored to have carried out the Ibar Highway attack on Vuk Draskovic in 1999), and thus had a good deal to fear from the ICTY.

Djindjic brushed aside the attempt on his life. On February 27, he indicated that action against organized crime lay ahead in Serbia and that he expected results within two weeks. Thirteen days later, on March 12, the assassins struck again. Djindjic was killed by a sniper as he walked in front of the Serbian government building in Belgrade. The assassination—at least the third and possibly the fifth attempt on Djindjic's life, as was later learned—was carried out by individuals from the Red Berets and coordinated by the infamous Colonel Legija, working from an apartment rented by the Zemun crime clan.

It was later revealed that Legija, having sided with Djindjic and the democratic forces to overthrow Milosevic, came to deeply resent the prime minister's plans not only to distance himself from his earlier associations with indicted war criminals and paramilitary figures but also to facilitate extradition of top leaders from these interlinked groups to The Hague tribunal.[4] Djindjic was reputed as having said that because members of the Red Berets had been fighting against an armed enemy during their service in Kosovo and had not killed civilians, they would not be extradited to The Hague. But Legija and his co-conspirators no longer trusted Djindjic. Indeed, the plot to kill the prime minister was entitled "Stop [extradition to the] Hague." But Legija's falling out with Djindjic probably began in November 2001 after the JSO mutiny and the prime minister's decision to place the elite commando unit under stricter control. Legija, a former street criminal and French legionnaire, had begun his paramilitary career working with Arkan's notorious Tigers and then headed the Red Berets (the JSO after 1995) during the wars of the Yugoslav succession, before moving (as a result of his expulsion from the JSO after several serious acts of insubordination and violence) directly into the work of organized crime. He had once indicated, referring to his days in the paramilitary forces in Croatia, Bosnia, and Kosovo, that he did not fight against other Serbs. Yet in coordinating Djindjic's assassination, Legija had not only eliminated a major Serbian political leader who was in the prime of his life but had also committed a brazen act of political terrorism designed to reverse Serbia's potential reform and obstruct Serbia's adherence to international law regarding the extradition of war criminals. Djindjic did not enjoy widespread personal popularity in Serbia, and his pragmatism was often seen as excessively opportunistic, but he was respected by most Serbs as a man who had paid his dues in the trenches of opposition to authoritarian rule and was dedicated to reforming and modernizing Serbia. The assassins had expected Serbia's so-called healthy patriotic forces to pour into the streets to support a radical change in the policies of the regime. But on the day of Djindjic's funeral, hundreds of thousands of saddened and disgusted citizens walked through Belgrade in complete silence. The Serbian government immediately ordered a state of emergency and launched a comprehensive campaign to apprehend those who had conspired to assassinate Djindjic and began a general crackdown on organized crime.

POST-DJINDJIC DEMOCRATIZATION:
PLURALISM VERSUS TERRORISM

In the wake of the Djindjic assassination, the key challenges for his successors were whether they would be able to successfully manage the serious political crisis faced by Serbia and move ahead with Djindjic's vision and reform program. Unfortunately, although Serbia's reform leaders were able to arrest many of those implicated in the prime minister's assassination and temporarily break up some of the major criminal networks in the country, they were not successful in effectively overcoming the fragmentation and inertia within the party system and political class that had impeded reform momentum throughout the post-Milosevic period. Illegal activities suffered a setback, but real progress in establishing a rule-of-law system was very limited.

Following the assassination, the reform-minded forces in the ruling DOS coalition were able to maintain order in the country and to select one of Djindjic's close associates, Zoran Zivkovic, to become prime minister. In that sense, the assassins' plans of destabilizing the country and ending democratic governance failed in the short run. Moreover, the state of emergency declared by the Serbian authorities, which lasted forty-one days (March 12 to April 22), did considerable damage to the grip of the criminal pyramid that had survived during the first two and a half years of the post-Milosevic transition. During the anticrime campaign known as Operation Sabre, the police by early April, with help from the military, had apprehended roughly ten thousand people, of whom forty-five hundred were still in detention. A wide range of individuals were arrested, including former secret police officials such as Jovica Stanisic and Frenki Stamenkovic as well as the former chief of the military, General Nebojsa Pavkovic, and Arkan's wife, Svetlana Ceca-Raznjatovic. Criminal charges were filed against some thirty-two hundred persons. The sweep of criminals also allowed police to solve fifteen murder cases—a dozen of which were committed by members of the Zemun clan—as well as a large number of kidnappings and drug-related cases. By the end of June 2003, the police claimed to have solved twenty-nine murder cases committed in earlier years and thirty murders during 2003 alone. It was quickly discovered that a one-time deputy commander of the Red Berets, Zvezdan Jovanovic, had fired the bullet that killed Djindjic. Jovanovic and other JSO operatives had comprised the team assembled by Legija to murder the prime minister. The assassins had apparently received vital information on Djindjic's movements from inside the Serbian security apparatus.[5] Information acquired during the crime sweep also enabled the police to find the body of Ivan Stambolic and link his murder to the JSO. The JSO was disbanded as a unit, and those members cleared of criminal activity were transferred to the gendarmerie. Although most of his key associates were apprehended, Legija remained at large. (Legija surrendered to authorities on May 3, 2004, and was to stand trial for his alleged role in Djindjic's assassination.)

Opinion surveys initially revealed broad public support for Operation Sabre and the hope in the country that organized crime could finally be contained. In order to carry out the government's emergency campaign, the police and investigating authorities in Serbia were granted broad powers. For example, by mid-April, the Serbian legislature had passed amendments to six judicial laws that would provide the police and judiciary with powers that went beyond the state of emergency. The new legislation included the extension of pretrial detention, broader provisions for confiscation of property held by suspected criminals, and the introduction of rules allowing sentences for different crimes to be served consecutively. Stiffer provisions were also introduced regulating the possession of weapons and ammunition as well as for the extortion of evidence, robbery, cover-up, false testimony, and other "security threats." In addition, the Serbian government banned the publication of information in connection with the reasons underlying the state of emergency, with the exception of official state releases, and stopped the distribution of several newspapers as well as broadcasting from a few radio and television stations. Government authorities suggested that some media outlets were directly owned or under the influence of criminal elements and had created a climate designed to destabilize the Djindjic regime.

Prime Minister Zivkovic would later claim that the crackdown on organized crime and the JSO had actually been planned well before Djindjic's assassination and that it was because such a campaign was to be launched that the assassins had rushed to strike. Police activity as part of the government's postassassination anticrime campaign was closely coordinated with the Yugoslav military. As part of the reconfiguration of the country into the state union of Serbia and Montenegro, which had already been implemented when Djindjic was murdered, the army and police were placed under closer civilian control. Former President Kostunica's military intelligence chief, General Aco Tomic, was also ousted from the military and then arrested on suspicion that he was linked to Djindjic's assassination. Milosevic's former chief of the military establishment, General Pavkovic, who had served Milosevic and remained in his post throughout the Kostunica presidency, was also placed in custody. The changes in the military sector initially facilitated a shift in the post-Djindjic government toward greater cooperation with the ICTY, and several leading indictees were extradited to The Hague. The new minister of defense for Serbia and Montenegro, Boris Tadic, also ordered military officers to report any information they might possess on the location and activities of ICTY indictees, such as General Ratko Mladic.

The Serbian government's decision to broaden police powers, introduce stronger punishment for crimes, and regulate the media evoked strong criticism, particularly from domestic opposition and nongovernmental bodies within Serbia but also from some foreign officials and international groups. Overall, however, particularly in view of the circumstances, the measures taken to deal with criminals seemed justifiable, and the restrictive steps with respect to the media were relatively mild and short-lived. By the summer of 2003, the crisis atmosphere in Serbia seemed to have abated. Unfortunately, as Serbian elite circles and the public awaited the results of a formal inquiry into the forces and motives behind Djindjic's assassination, the political controversies and infighting within the ruling DOS coalition and between DOS and its opponents continued to dominate and debilitate political life and, particularly, the cause of further reform. Members of the ruling coalition, including some of Djindjic's closest associates, implicitly or explicitly blamed Kostunica for having prevented the full implementation of the DOS reform program and for coddling the individuals and groups, in and outside government, who had conspired to assassinate Djindjic. More extreme members of the ruling coalition, such as Vojvodina's Assembly speaker Nenad Canak, even implied that Kostunica and a "demonic plan" were directly responsible for the murder of the prime minister. Kostunica, for his part, reminded observers that the JSO had actually been under the authority of Djindjic's government and had earlier cooperated with the murdered prime minister and his closest associates. It is probably fair to conclude—and to necessarily emphasize a major weakness of post-Milosevic Serbia—that both Djindjic and Kostunica, at different points, had established lines of communication and different forms of accommodation with various organized crime figures. Thus, both political leaders, who were contending for political supremacy in the country after Milosevic's departure from power and were attempting to prudently navigate the political shoals, sought to avoid a direct confrontation with the murky and powerful parallel criminal power structure that was deeply entrenched in Serbian society (i.e., gangs, clans, war criminals, rogue paramilitary figures, and corrupt political officials).

After Djindjic's death, Kostunica and a number of other political leaders outside the slain prime minister's Democratic Party maintained that the state of emergency was misused and expanded by the ruling coalition in order to settle accounts with the government's political opponents. Clearly, as the shock of the assassination and the initial momentum of the anticrime campaign waned, political leaders in the country began positioning themselves for the next elections. Arguments also began to focus on the drafting of a new constitution for Serbia. The tenuous state union of Serbia and Montenegro continued, but elite discussions began to concentrate on when Serbia and Montenegro, together or each on their own part, would become members of the European Union. The grip of war criminals and organized crime members on the country had definitely been weakened as a consequence of the assassination. Greater civilian control over the army, police, and intelligence services also represented a significant step forward in democratization. For example, in July 2003, the chairman of the Serbian Assembly's Security Committee pointed out that in the ten previous years the committee had met only nine times, while in 2002–2003 there had been seventeen sessions. But real civilian oversight of the security sector was still a very new facet of the Serbian political landscape, and a good deal of work remained before there could be any real oversight or transparency. The state of emergency had ended, but the campaign against organized crime remained active and quite imperative.

The group of economic reformers around Zivkovic, all former Djindjic appointments, continued to maintain that the struggle against organized crime was actually stimulating economic development in Serbia and was a precondition for further democratic progress. Unfortunately, during the last six months of 2003, there was mounting popular disenchantment in Serbia with the country's bleak economic situation, the seeming ineffectiveness of the republic's squabbling politicians and parties, and the revelations about corruption on the part of several top officials in the ruling coalition. By mid-November 2003, the ruling DOS coalition had disintegrated, and for a third time in fourteen months an election to choose a new president for Serbia failed to attain the required minimum of 50 percent of the electorate necessary for a valid contest. Early parliamentary elections to deal with the political stalemate in Serbia were finally held on December 28, 2003, but the parties most closely associated with Zoran Djindjic's brand of post-Milosevic reform did very poorly in comparison to the front-running Serbian Radical Party of Vojislav Seselj (who was incarcerated at The Hague awaiting trial) that took roughly 27.7 percent of the vote and received 82 seats in the 250-person Assembly. In contrast, Djindjic's Democratic Party only received 12.6 percent of the vote. Despite, and partially because of, international pressure and the previously mentioned difficulties perceived by the electorate, Serbian politics had shifted to the right of center, for the moment at least. Even the Socialist Party of Serbia, led by the incarcerated Slobodan Milosevic, was able to garner 7 percent of the vote. When considered together, the parties broadly committed to reform had a relative majority in the Serbian Assembly, but the various reformist parties were deeply divided between and among themselves.

The late 2003 electoral outcome did not mean a return to the terrorism and violence of the Milosevic era, or even the type of rampant corruption, criminality, and violence of the initial post-Milosevic years (2001–2003). Indeed, the more moderate right-of-center and nationally oriented Serbian Democratic Party of Vojislav Kostunica was expected to rally the reform forces around its banner and organize a new reformist bloc to prevent SRS control of the country (a task that was still proving very difficult at the end of January 2004).[6] But the election results did not bode well for stability and reform momentum or, in the short run at least, for the ability of Serbian elites and citizens to make real progress in eradicating the root causes and legacy of terrorism and violence that remain in the country. Indeed, there was a serious likelihood that continued disunity within the ranks of the democratic and moderate forces would permit the substantial nondemocratic and criminal elements in society to survive, possibly regroup, and even expand their activities. Organized crime syndicates in Serbia appeared to be less well organized than before Djindjic's assassination, and thus the facets of "state capture," or the control of the regime by illegal groups and networks employing violence, seemed less prevalent in Serbia at the onset of 2004 compared to the situation in the first two and a half years after the Milosevic regime. But Serbia remained a very weak state in many respects, that is, in terms of its legitimacy, accountability, transparency, and the effectiveness of its governmental institutions. The ability of the majority of decision-makers to establish boundaries between their private interests and the public interest also remained one of the most serious concerns. In such an environment, organized criminality and corruption can flourish, and the potential is considerably reduced for institutionalizing a genuine rule-of-law system that can ensure a relatively honest and fair system of governance.[7] Political research indicates that although most Serbian citizens want a "normal life" without wars and also reject the "warrior mentality," they have serious difficulty facing the issue of who is responsible for the events of the recent past. Serbian public opinion also exhibits a strong rejection of The Hague tribunal, a desire of Serbia to try its own war criminals, and a rejection of the idea that crimes were committed by Serbs during the 1990s on a "systematic basis."[8] Regrettably, Djindjic's vision for a fully modern, prosperous, and authentically democratic Serbia, which has put the negative facets of its past behind it, remains a challenging and somewhat distant goal.

NOTES

1. A good overview of these groups can be found in Gow (2003, 77–89).

2. The regime was also involved in a second assassination attempt on June 15, 2000, against Vuk Draskovic of the Serbian Renewal Party. Draskovic was slightly wounded. In the first attack on Draskovic in 1999, several of his associates had been killed.

3. Legija would continue in his police post until February 2001.

4. The Hague's chief prosecutor, Carla del Ponte, has claimed that on February 17 Djindjic confided to her that "they're going to kill me."

5. Even after his expulsion from the JSO, Legija continued to have close ties with members of Serbia's Security-Information Agency, the BIA (the successor to the SDS). For example, Milorad Bracanovic, Legija's former deputy commander in the JSO, was appointed deputy director of the BIA in November 2001 and only removed in January 2003. Bracanovic was arrested not long after Djindjic's death.

6. When the new Serbian Assembly convened on January 27, 2004, the "democratic bloc" of parties still had not reached agreement on a government. Meanwhile, eighty-two deputies of the Serbian Radical Party appeared in the Assembly all wearing T-shirts with Vojislav Seselj's picture and the inscription "Seselj-Serb Hero."

7. On the continued difficulties of combating organized crime in Serbia, see United Nations (2003a, 61–77; 2003b).

8. See Spasic (2003) and Pavicevic (2003).

REFERENCES

Agence France-Presse. 2001. "Death Threats against Serb and Yugoslav Leaders, Minister." April 26.

Anastasijevic, Dejan. 2003. "Vecni plamen." *Vreme 666* (October 9).

BBC Monitoring. 2000. "NGOs Report 640 Cases of Detention Since 13th May." June 27.

BBC Monitoring. 2002a. "Serbian Interior Minister Explains 'Two Faces' of Country's 'Criminal Pyramid.'" November 11. www.csees.net/news_more.php3?nId=10150.

BBC Monitoring. 2002b. "Serbian Police, Politicians Disagree on Existence, Strength of Organized Crime." July 9. www.csees.net/news_more.php3?nId=5372.

BBC Monitoring. 2002c. "Serbian Premier: Politicians Slowing Down Reforms, but not Blocking Them." December 26.

BBC Monitoring. 2002d. "Undercover Agents Introduced in Serbia to Combat Organized Crime." December 28.

Bujosevic, Dragan. 2001. *5. Oktobar, Dvadest ceteri sata prevrata*. Belgrade: Medija centar.

CNN. 2002. "People vs. Slobodan Milosevic." February 9, transcript #020900CN.V79.

Cohen, Lenard J. 2002. *Serpent in the Bosom: The Rise and Fall of Slobodan Milosevic*, rev. ed. Boulder: Westview Press.

Colovic, Ivan. 2000. "Kriminalci kao ratni junaci." *Danas*, February 1–2.

Gow, James. 2003. *The Serbian Project and Its Adversaries: A Strategy of War Crimes*. Montreal: McGill-Queen's University Press.

Milinkovic, Branko. 1993. "Yugoslavia: Legal System Crumbles As Hard Up Judges Quit." *Inter Press Service*, December 9.

Mrsevic, Zorica. 1998. *Izazovi sudske nezavisnosti*. Belgrade: Uprava za zajednicke poslove republickih organa.

ONASA News Agency. 2000. "Regime Fights Its Opposers, Serbian Opposition." March 3.

Pavicevic, Djordje. 2003. "Zlocina i odgovornost." In *Politika i svakodnevni zivot: Srbija 1999–2002*, ed. Zagorka Golubovic, 146–48. Belgrade: Institut za filozofiju i drustvenu teoriju.

Sarinic, Hrvoje. 1999. *Svi moji tajni pregovori sa Slobodanom Milosevicem: Izmedju rata i diplomacije, 1993–1995 (1998)*. Zagreb: Globus International.

SEE Security Monitor. 2002. "Beta Sources Confirm Belgrade Police Found Plans to Murder DOS's Jovanovic." July 4. www.csees.net/news_more.php3?nId=5253.

Spasic, Ivana. 2003. "Secanje na nedavnu prolost." In *Politika i svakodnevni zivot: Srbija 1999–2002*, ed. Zagorka Golubovic, 124–25. Belgrade: Institut za filozofiju i drustvenu teoriju.

Stefanovic, Nenad. 1992. "Judicial System in Serbia: The Notorious Footprints." *Vreme News Digest* 20 (February 10): 8.

United Nations. 2003a (October). *Common Country Assessment for Serbia and Montenegro*. Belgrade: United Nations.

———. 2003b (November). *Republic of Serbia, Ministry of Justice and Ministry of Interior Policy Paper for Donor Co-ordination Meeting*. Belgrade: United Nations.

Zimonjic, Vesna Peric. 2002. "Arkan 'Was Murdered for Knowing Too Much': The Death of a Warlord—Serbia Ripped by Speculation that Order for Assassination in Belgrade Hotel Came Right from the Top of the Regime." *Independent*, January 17, p. 10.

21 State-Building and the Final Status in Kosovo

The complex of factors that play havoc with efforts today to find a final status for Kosovo also generate a foundation for the type of political and economic system that the international community imagines. State-building, a generic label for the full range of efforts that will be reviewed, had been a central feature of the behavior of powerful political systems throughout the colonial period of the nineteenth and twentieth centuries. The consequences of these efforts provide numerous and conflicting signals about the viability of such strategies. The twenty-first century adds still further complications to the task, owing largely, if not solely, to issues related to pace and costs. Moral and philosophical issues abound. Kosovo watchers certainly ask: Is the state-building task designed to serve the patron or the client? Is the motive economic or security? Is the transition respectful of endogenous culture or manipulative? In the abstract, these are matters of such scope as to befuddle analysis. Defenders of state-building diligently insist that the answer to all of the questions above is "both." Academic skepticism prevails. In the context of specific examples, we approach some understanding of the dynamics of regime change and the state-building enterprise that stems from it. Kosovo takes its place among those places in the world that present ongoing evidence of the importance of these questions.

Crucial to the examination of this process is the *prescriptive* nature of the replacement system. In today's terms, do the "established" systems in our world anticipate a *corporate* state or a *democratic* state? Lost in the rhetoric is the question of whether the objective is functional (that is, the possibility of short-term delivery of goods, services, jobs, and material well-being) or cultural and long-term evolutionary transition (involving the foundation elements—values and behaviors—that can support the democratic processes). While not mutually exclusive, the key texture is distinguishable and the patterns of institution-alization are different.

One basis of controversy over policies, management, and directions for Kosovo is likely a function of noncongruent views of the major powers involved in Kosovo on this central question. Why does Kosovo matter to the international community? The United States Institute of Peace (USIP) shares its perspective:

- Balkans regional stability, including prevention of terrorism and organized crime
- Potential for democratic governance in a largely Muslim context
- Credibility for the US, UN, OSCE, EU and NATO
- US military readiness and availability to other missions
- Impact on relations with Europe and Russia
- Avoiding and alleviating humanitarian disasters (United States Institute of Peace 2002, 5)

On the one hand, Kosovo is a small and potentially manageable case for exami-nation. On the other, it has many thorny features that make a simple linear case impossible. The reader will certainly notice that the elements included here lead powerfully away from optimism. One can draw from this analysis a sense that, with dramatic rethinking of the process, headway is possible.

CHALLENGES FOR THE INTERNATIONAL COMMUNITY

International Administration

Michael Steiner (former) and Harri Holkeri (current) have served as the UN sec-retary general's special representative to Kosovo. This innocuous-sounding title in reality has given them unchallenged power in the territory. The United Nations Mis-sion in Kosovo (UNMIK) is functionally a ruling authority with massive military backing. Akin to a colonial governor, Steiner and Holkeri encourage low-level po-litical institutions to form and retain a veto over the substance and direction of their policies. The rationale for frequent vetoes is always that the Kosovar "authorities" have ignored or violated a political principle that is essential to the development of a democratic and progressive political system. De facto, this is the exercise of ultimate authority backed by the Kosovo Force (KFOR). The UNMIK self-image is one of protector. The preparedness for violence, and in many cases the eagerness for it among local groups, validate the international claim. The UN special representa-tive is joined by Pascal Fieschi, the accomplished career diplomat, who is the head of mission for the Organization for Security and Cooperation (OSCE) in Kosovo. The OSCE role is centered on the education and socialization relating to political development. It assesses, informs, and nurtures, thereby avoiding day-to-day exercise of authority. KFOR is the NATO-sponsored muscle that is ever-present, highly visible, and in the faces of Kosovars and Serbs. They represent the apparent (publicly acknowledged) authority in Kosovo.

The delicate point, however, is that the approach being exercised seems to validate just one premise: military power prevails. There is no real political design in place that would or could generate public confidence or that would point to anything other than authoritarian power. The Kosovar public has no political architecture that they can examine, think about, or critique. The prevailing Kosovar political thought is that *somebody* will dictate its future; better it be one of its own people. To be clear, the current institutional arrangement has no *publicly perceived* division of labor, no allocation of power with prescribed limits, and no avenue for public recourse. The OSCE mission makes the aggressive case that it is working on reframing attitudes and perceptions.

The unusual quality of the Kosovo dilemma is that the international authorities are approaching the issues in a conventional and responsible way but are working with a self-declared, unconventional time frame. By setting time limits and specifying goals and dates, the UNMIK and other administrative authorities have bound themselves into a highly charged and pressurized corner.

The proliferation of European- and American-based NGOs in Kosovo has created a basic fabric for civil society though altogether dependent upon external funding. The relationship between the always small and deeply engaged NGOs and the "big guys" on the block—UNMIK, KFOR, and OSCE—who have formidable resources of all sorts is classically unsynchronized. However, to claim that they are working at cross-purposes would be wrong. In analytical perspective, one is drawn to the conclusion that resources have been used without generating maximum results. This is especially clear if one focuses on the nurturing of service, administration, and control functions that can survive and continue after the international elements depart. This is the much-expressed goal of sustainability and/or capacity-building.

The political reality in Kosovo today is that there is a three-headed management framework where two of the elements are working intently but are marginalized by the equally hard-working third. NGOs and Kosovar authorities work in the margins where UNMIK authority allows. Given the current power imbalance weighted heavily toward the UNMIK, the imminent withdrawal of the most significant UNMIK contingents will most certainly create instability and fear in the population. There are signs that violent spasms could erupt, not when the forces leave but rather when the forces announce their departure. In this important way, the case could be made to prolong the UNMIK administration.

The Melos Phenomenon

The ancient Athenians proclaimed their dedication to "democracy" and its pro-liferation. They too used force to subdue systems they perceived as anathema. Athenians forced conquered subjects to adopt this particular form of government. The leadership of the island of Melos, once conquered by Athens, articulated a desire to remain neutral. The Athenian leadership responded by denying the Melians that choice. The Melian government argued that the Athenians were being unfaithful to their own principles. History quotes the Athenian retort: "You know as well as we do that right, as the world goes, is only in question between equals in power, while the strong do what they can, and the weak suffer what they must."

While in Iraq state-building is currently characterized by fast-talking am-biguity, Kosovo represents a more clear record for evaluation. The "evidence" (rather the data we have on Kosovar attitudes) appears to indicate that Kosovars will not support the international community's effort to frame Kosovar politics in the context of a decentralized Serbia (or Yugoslavia). The international ad-ministration in Kosovo faces the same dilemma faced by the ancient Athenians: the indigenous people do not share their vision of the future. If brought to a plebiscite, Kosovars would most likely support an intolerant theocracy because it would ensure non-Muslim discomfort and rationalize crystallizing the second class status of non-Muslims/non-Albanians.

Self-Determination of Peoples

The moral and political dilemma here is intrinsic to "freedom," which one can only assume means "self-determination of peoples." It really is a simple no-tion. Do *all* groups have the right to self-define? And having done that, are they entitled to draw lines that selectively delineate a constituency and, finally, to gauge public sentiment and decide by majority support on any form of political authority they might imagine or favor?

Cost-Effectiveness of Protectionism

If Kosovars, as suggested, are disinclined to opt for liberal, democratic institu-tions, is it possible to make the case that, to achieve even short-term humanistic goals, the actions of the international community were rational and just? As with the other episodes of international intervention in the former Yugoslavia, it is certainly true that the international military's presence saved lives and froze the conflict, thereby preventing more dislocation and human tragedy. But is this action cost-effective? Specifically, will history write that the UNMIK and KFOR were efforts well and effectively made given the cost and the outcome?

The delicacy of such a question is obvious. Normative views will draw one to think differently about answers. Nonetheless, there are a couple of observations we can make that shed some light on potential answers. First, one might wish to examine the ratio of military personnel to civilians in contemporary Kosovo. Officially, there are thirty-eight thousand troops (from thirty-seven countries in 2003) in Kosovo under the KFOR umbrella. Beyond that, more than four thousand additional UNMIK police officers are monitoring and training more than four thousand Kosovo police recruits. There are at most two million people living in Kosovo and one soldier for every fifty persons, conservatively calculated. Second, let us examine the ratio of foreign nationals to Kosovar civilians. At its peak, there are more than two thousand NGOs with activities in Kosovo. There may have been as many as eight thousand internationals employed by these NGOs in (or in and out of) Kosovo. UNMIK personnel number around five thousand, not counting contractors. Combined, this suggests roughly one "international" for every forty Kosovars. What these numbers could suggest is poignant. Rather than question the administrative effectiveness of the international community (indeed a supersensitive subject), highlighting how small the population being served actually is may be more meaningful. Other areas of postconflict are larger and on that basis, many will argue, should warrant the attention of the international community and its resources.

Actual costs are very hard to research definitively. The UNMIK alone is spending between $400 million and $500 million per year. The cost of KFOR is purposively not accessible. Apart from the "raw" cost to international agencies and supporting countries is the economic and political anesthesia of foreign presence and administration. In Kosovo, the absence of a functional banking system or anything like a balanced economy are veiled by the international military and administrative and NGO personnel constantly infusing externally sourced income into the local economy. The euro is the active currency. Kosovar income is generated by commercially servicing internationals and reselling consumer products. The universal dependency on this service-sector economic activity suggests, at best, a fragility. It has distracted or dissuaded investors (precious few to begin with) from primary or secondary production. It has also given rise to significant (for Kosovo's size) black market activity. These are unhealthy costs and ones that are likely to outlive the much more evident and impressive amounts of money injected into Kosovo by the international community. Unemployment is roughly 50 percent, and if jobs directly related to international administration and international agencies including NGOs were to evaporate, the number would be closer to 70 percent. The much-feared pullout (or diminished role) of the international administration is being accelerated by the timetable for the final solution driven by political considerations very distant from Kosovo.

At the end of 2003, the UNMIK had reported 101 KFOR deaths and 26 UN-MIK deaths over the period since the operation began (June 1999). Down the road, a final analysis will certainly gauge the costs in the context of the political result. If Kosovo *and* Serbia do not ultimately move toward an apparently constructive relationship with the United States and the EU, the cost will be judged to be too much. If, however, the outcome sets a platform for inter-ethnic conciliation and political compromise built on general principles of participation, civil society, and tolerance, the verdict will be positive. It will be hailed as evidence that U.S. and EU relationships with a Muslim society are workable and compatible. In either event, the cost will be high.

REQUISITES: THE BIG 3

State-building conjures up notions of a *process* that can serve different goals and render quite different outcomes. Recognizing the wide range of activities that are possible under this generic label, it may be useful to identify specifically what requisites this analysis is searching for in Kosovo. Three sets of variables are crucial to the creation of a political system that can function in the twenty-first century. If Kosovo is to have independence or a high level of autonomy, these will be key indicators of democratic viability and political health. The first is an emerging value consensus. The second is an elaborated political architecture, and the last is effective executive and legislative leadership.

In brief, until or unless a consensus about the most central values emerges, it will be impossible for a leader or leaders to be genuinely democratic. This consensus can be imagined as a *direction* for the society. Short of a consensus emerging, leaders will be unable to take people where they want to go simply because so much disparity exists in that public sentiment. Established democracies have the luxury of institutionalized and deeply embraced values that point in a direction, albeit with many differences and nuances of difference.

Kosovo is a classic example of a phenomenon seen widely with the challenges to communism in the 1980s. Movements evolved (Solidarnosc, Civic Forum, Democratic Forum, etc.) that coalesced public support around what it was that folks were against. The consensus quickly revealed itself inadequate as populations began to disagree (dialogue) about what it was *they want to work toward*. Kosovo will most certainly have this experience if it gets past the immediate political issues drawn by the international intervention there.

If Kosovars did share a vision of the future—that is, *where* they want their leaders to take them—the aforementioned problem for the international community might be that it is not a direction compatible with UNMIK designs. From my own not-rigorous-enough data collection in Kosovo (circa 2002), one could suggest that Kosovars *do not* subscribe to democracy-supporting value sets but *do* support capitalism-supporting values.

The viability of Kosovo will definitely be conditioned on its ability to produce public policies and administer basic services. In essence, a political machinery would need to be assembled that could politically produce. This could be conceived as the system's *vehicle* for moving the society toward its destination. Problems of a system-threatening kind persist here. The legislature has, to date, demonstrated little efficacy or vision. This has been well documented by Michael Steiner and his staff over the course of his last two years in Kosovo and reported to the Security Council. Law and order prescribed in terms that protect and enhance only the majority have been the norm. Uniform application of rules and a general ineffectiveness in terms of addressing criminal activity (or aggressively entrepreneurial businesses in the absence of commercial codes) has caused both internationals and locals to become deeply skeptical.[1] Educational policies and resources have not been mustered. Security forces (Kosovo Protection Corps [KPC]) have made very little progress in eclipsing the power of the Kosovo Liberation Army (KLA) in the countryside. The administrative components are a mere shell of what they will need to be before they can function in minimally adequate ways. Where competent officials do exist, an absence of resources castrates their efforts. A report from late 2003 concludes that "the civil service shows a general lack of professionalism in implementing transparent, non-politicized and ethnically balanced procedures in such areas as recruitment and procurement. Furthermore, municipal regulations, once adopted, are often not implemented" (UN Security Council 2003, 3).[2]

Finally, if a value consensus identified a direction and a functional political vehicle existed, the remaining element would be the *driver*. This would suggest that astute leadership would be required to "drive" the society toward its goals in a confidence-engendering manner. Leadership in yet-to-be-institutionalized political environments ironically needs to be much more skilled and adept than counterparts in institutionalized systems. The grooves in the patterned, established political systems guide policy and politics in ways that limit the range and constrain the mistakes of leaders. But in new and forming political systems, leaders are driving on ice, meaning that the leader faces uncertain challenges and unanticipated consequences with every decision. The executive and diplomatic leadership of the Kosovars has, on balance, been unimpressive. This should be understood in context. The challenges and sophistication required are mammoth. The elected and intellectual leadership has been lacking and *understandably* substandard. Where would we expect leadership to come from in a situation of the Kosovar type? President Rugova, to be kind, has a Ph.D. in literature and is an amateur geologist. Prime Minister Rexhepi is a general surgeon. Perhaps more damning still is the lack of a clear and resounding commitment of either of them to democratic and tolerant directions for Kosovo. They endorse elections because *they were elected,* not because they have confidence in the political institution.[3]

Reflecting on the degree to which Kosovo measures up against the simple model, the international community must definitely have deep-seated qualms about Kosovo's readiness for independence or its ability to engage itself in the political dynamics of a decentralized system led by Serbia. Its value consensus is limited to negative values, its political machinery is disassembled and missing parts, and its leadership is without special qualities.

Elections as Political Art

The salience and sheer weight ascribed to elections by political analysts is formidable. This is surprising given the voluminous literature on election irregularities and manipulation in established as well as new political states (Ottaway 2003). Nonetheless, the mainstream argument is that any alternative is less constructive. Perhaps so, but the reality that must be acknowledged in Kosovo and similar political environments is that elections are more clearly *art* than *science.* They reflect the normative and prescriptive thinking of those *managing* the "transition." There is an inventory of dimensions characterizing the electoral system that sketch the artistic elegance. What the world sees and what Kosovars see certainly does vary with the experience and political sensibilities of each population.

First among these is the designation of the "constituencies." Where and how the boundaries are drawn and how the electorate is defined or "qualified" in Kosovo predestines the outcome. Post-Dayton elections in Bosnia come to mind as keen examples. Even in classic, established democracies, the preelection identification of constituencies is a partially visible process at best and is a locus of significant power struggles.

Second are the choices. The range and representativeness of the candidates and/or the policy options color the attractiveness or acceptability of the elections. Given the absence of civil society or rooted pluralism, the menu is, at very least, directed by those with power. War-validated political groups (most often paramilitary groups) and externally sponsored groups (necessarily KFOR/ UNMIK-endorsed) tend to generate the electoral choices.

Third, in the absence of pluralism, political parties have abbreviated and uncompromising platforms. They are ideological parties that reject pragmatism and the mass appeal that could generate. The texture of these political elements is intimidating and aggressive. The general public retains a distance from these organizations and often views them as other than embracing. The tone is polarizing rather than accommodating. The strident elements of political parties in Kosovo portray an "only truth" aura that will serve democratic development very poorly.

Fourth, voter turnout is problematic. Aside from common boycotts of the sort seen in recent Montenegrin and Kosovar elections, a more elemental issue exists. Elections are understood as the *moment* when the people's voice identifies *the* direction and the authority-laden elite for Kosovo's future. While not absurd, the missing perception is of elections as a *process*. The region has a record of electing persons who behave postelection in an authoritarian way. What emerges is a political psychology where successful candidates imagine themselves as "supertrustees" as opposed to "delegates," which would imply continuous links to the constituency. This perception draws policymaking away from compromise and real dialogue.

Fifth, following from the above point, the gaps between elections (assuming a commitment to hold elections again) are characterized by closed or narrowly constrained input mechanisms in the system. There is a view that a voter by voting buys a ticket and sits back and experiences the ride. A more constructive view, but one that is hard to find in Kosovo, is the notion that elections are one kind of input but that democracy requires *regular* elite-mass interaction and significant efforts by leadership to account for both popular and minority interests.

The overarching point here is not that elections are counterproductive. To the contrary, they do forge some support. But without evolving awareness of the limits and imperfections of democratic processes and without genuine leadership interest in unpopular views, elections remain a less central feature of politics than the commitment to developing civil society. Elections are *art* in the real sense that Kosovars will see what they want to see in them—positive and negative. They will not assuage political anxiety. One man's masterpiece is another's ugly picture.

None of the above argues for ignoring elections. Rather, it suggests an approach that anticipates the limits of elections and the likely public response to them. If the electoral choices are to be managed by external forces in the name of state-building, the implication is that this should be done in a way that favors elites who understand and stand committed to the broader notions of democratic development.

U.S. Deputy Defense Secretary Paul Wolfowitz, after a May 2003 trip to Bosnia and Kosovo, suggested that these places hold lessons for American efforts to bring postwar stabilization and the transition from dictatorship to democracy in Iraq and Afghanistan. He concluded, "The experience in Bosnia shows the danger of rushing to hold elections . . . simply as a show of democracy taking root. The threat is that dangerously divisive leaders may be the first to take power." He went on to say that the peacekeeping missions in Bosnia and Kosovo convince him that forces need to be "so big and strong that nobody would dare pick a fight with us. . . . By holding elections so early, it became impossible to remove some bad actors, because they now had electoral authority." He claimed that Bosnia and Kosovo remain channels for terrorist networks to move money and people. Wolfowitz concluded, ominously I think for Kosovo, by saying that "Iraq has this advantage, which is that we are there . . . and with an enormous commitment to help get it right" (Shanker 2003). The ominous part is what he did not say about Kosovo and what that implies.

MICROSTATE VIABILITY AND RESPONSIBILITY

As Kosovars and the international community look to the future, all must recognize that an independent Kosovo would assume the place of a microstate in our twenty-first-century world. As a part of the confederation whose name has not yet been established (Serbia, Montenegro, Kosovo), it would still be beset by some issues facing microstates. The sea change in Europe is already clearly in the direction of the congealing of the macrostate we know as the European Union. It is interesting to speculate about which near-term step would likely lead most quickly to Kosovo's inclusion in the EU. In either case, the prospects are distant and improbable given current EU criteria. It is essential that one recognize that far more developed and established European sovereign states have, upon careful analysis, concluded that their futures are more assured as a part of the macrostate—the incumbent sacrifice of sovereignty notwithstanding.

What then can be said for Kosovar prospects? The inventory of infrastructure and related issues is intimidating. A précis of those challenges follows.

Economic Factors

REVENUE PICTURE: Unlikely foundations for collecting tax revenues of any sort; 32 percent of all government revenue from international "donor" grants; energy, water, and waste infrastructure near end of useful life.[4] Seventy-nine percent of total revenue was collected from "border and boundary taxes."[5] Four hundred fifty-four UNMIK staff function as the Customs Service.

UNEMPLOYMENT: Very high and edging upward; withdrawal of internationals would exacerbate. By the highest estimate, 50 percent employed but only 30 percent full-time; ninety-seven thousand who paid into pension funds receive nothing.[6]

CURRENCY: Status of euro unclear if injections from international community diminish; return to dinar broadly objectionable.

FOREIGN DIRECT INVESTMENT: Virtually insignificant; environment is uncertain given politics and legal voids.

BUSINESS ECONOMICS: Experiencing illusions owing to temporary infusions from multiple external actors; disinclined to assess "permanent" foundation of economy; 50 percent of businesses state-owned; 78 percent of all businesses are "microenterprises" with zero to four employees.[7]

Infrastructure and Social Services

TRANSPORTATION: Rail system defunct; busses and taxis partially restored; external air service supported by internationals; secondary roads only.

COMMUNICATIONS: Fuzzy infrastructure; current phone service provided via Monaco in tenuous partnership.

HEAT, POWER, WATER: Severely diminished capacity; Pristina experiences daily cutoffs, and the situation declines throughout the towns and countryside. In 2002, only the four days of Kofi Anon's visit to Kosovo were interruption-free.

EDUCATION: Six percent illiterate (83 percent of those are women); average teacher salary is equivalent to $150 per month; 23,000 teachers for 476,000 students; one university with 18,500 students and 3 political scientists.[8]

HEALTH: Twenty-one hundred doctors; only Albania in Europe has fewer doctors and nurses for its population; hospitals suffer from electricity, water, heating, and waste problems; 50 percent of births at home with no professional assistance.[9]

Political Factors

SECURITY FORCES: Untested and barely organized; response to challenge from corruption and gray-area businesses patently unclear; major crimes include arson, assaults, murders, and kidnappings; total crimes recorded average five hundred per week; prison population has exceeded capacity. Average salary is $150 month.[10] The presence of "extremists and criminal elements" in the KPC has prompted numerous indictments and "disciplinary action" by UNMIK and KFOR monitors. The KPC's current strength is 2,954 active and 1,735 reserve members.[11]

LEGITIMACY: Ethnic platform with little concern for political routines or institutions. So-called parallel structures, including rump courts established by Kosovar and Serbian would-be authorities, complicate the creation of broadly supported institutions.[12]

DIPLOMATIC AND TRAVEL CREDENTIALS: Nonexistent; KFOR and UNMIK issue some identity cards that can pass for travel documents on a selective basis.

The factors above represent a short list of elements that will require direct, immediate, and purposeful remedy. Clearly, these are some of the problems faced by the state-building process. Certainly the international administrators are consistent in their sense that most of these problems need to be resolved, though a few could be selectively carried over if progress on the bulk of these is evident.

For the international players in Kosovo, the matter of responsibility for the rectification of these ills is center stage. Does the international community, having stepped in and assumed control, have responsibility to ensure the modernization and operation of these elements irrespective of the political disposition of Kosovo?[13] The question is also asked in dramatic fashion in Afghanistan and Iraq. Kosovo, however, is a case that stands apart from these other examples. It is a Muslim territory that imagines the United States in very positive terms and has a clear, though not well defined, appreciation for American efforts in Kosovo. This is *broad* support but not very deep. If U.S. policy stands by its posture that Kosovo is to remain a part of Serbia, the tide of public opinion could and will turn very quickly.

In reality, the question of external responsibility is likely to hinge on the sophistication of the rhetoric of the new Kosovo. If the sounds and symbols emanating from Pristina are warm and fuzzy with due lip service to democratic slogans and mechanics, the United States and Europe will sustain their commitment. If Pristina exercises real independence and articulates the strident nationalist positions that are popular, the Kosovars will find themselves summarily and abruptly abandoned—not an enviable position in which to find oneself. This matter of "responsibility," then, will turn on the mechanics of self-interest as defined in the global environment by the powerful Western players.

Sincerity, conscience, and wishful thinking aside, Kosovo faces life as a microstate (independent or otherwise) and will have no stand-alone viability by any twenty-first-century measure or standard. The hard reality is that Kosovars need a heavy dose of uncomfortable, practical, forward-facing analysis about who they are and who they want to become.

Minimalism and Democracy

Democracy, in its most elaborated sense, is a robust, complex, full-bodied political system of constant strains and managed conflicts. It does not lend itself to rapid institutionalization, high levels of public certainty, or to piecemeal construction. If the international community genuinely seeks state-building with a democratic texture, the process cannot be abbreviated or summarized. However, apparent pressures are building, which indicates that partial results *will* be acceptable and long-term outcomes *will* be abandoned in Kosovo.

First, consider a number of rather unsettling realities with which Kosovo must contend. Public expectations among those living in Kosovo are narrow, short-sighted, and not elaborated. Economic competitiveness is undetermined because no real productive sectors are functioning. It is very unlikely that exports would be possible in any foreseeable term. The capacity to attract investment and thereby to create earnings via exports is altogether unclear and, at best, problematic. Political inexperience is the norm, and a kind of political naïveté, especially when dealing with democratic dynamics, is evident even among the "leadership." Perhaps most crucial and, in spite of serious efforts by NGOs in Kosovo, the rudiments of civil society and grassroots initiative are a long way from the point of sustaining active roles in a postconflict Kosovo.

Second, consider the degree to which Kosovo has been eclipsed by regime change and "state-building" in other parts of the world. The key difference is that in those more recent areas of overt action by the Western powers, a case has been made that intervention was required by the nature of the threat posed by those places to the West. In Kosovo, the motive was always humanitarian and never justified by the argument that we were at risk from inaction. This results in thinner resolve and commitment to the Kosovo project.

Third, the issue set out at the beginning of this chapter is uncomfortably revisited. Is the international community invested in creating a democratic Kosovo or a corporate state that remains at least minimally pro-American or pro-West? It is possible that we will achieve neither, but the question is one focusing on our *aim*. In the case of Kosovo, there are so many ways to avoid the issue. One common response is that we intend to see Kosovo returned as a respected part of Serbia and that our effort to nurture democracy will be directed to *Serbian* democratic development. Still another is to market the thesis that *democracy lite* is indeed a partial step toward democracy. Critics will counter that it is a poor, terminal substitute for democracy.

In the final analysis, one is drawn to suggest that there is little if any evidence to support the idea that intervention in Kosovo will be sustained to the point of making real institutional change. The powers that have engaged there, the UNMIK and KFOR in particular, have contributed to a *kind* of stability that is appreciated and necessary. To the extent they recognize that an elaborate political architecture is required, they also recognize that they are not likely to have the resources and time to build that structure. Noble and impressive people-to-people efforts have been made to create a platform for quality-of-life improvements for Kosovars. However, it is an appropriate concern for all those working in Kosovo today that sustainability is a far-off reality.

Kosovar Credulity?

The UNMIK "government" functioning as protector and mentor is deeply engaged in the process of assessing Kosovo's readiness for the next step. Pressure is coming from UN headquarters to move to that next stage with a clearer view of the end game. In response, Michael Steiner reported to the UN Security Council citing three dimensions of preparedness that should preclude any change in political status. He made the case that Kosovar political credibility is contingent on its capacity and performance to (1) protect, (2) administer, and (3) construct.

FINAL SOLUTION/FINAL STATUS

The USIP has dedicated a great deal of its recent energies to the search for options for the future of Kosovo. They have even run a number of simulations for the anticipated negotiations with real-world experts and diplomats to anticipate the process and outcome. The USIP has generated no less than eight studies and impressive analyses of the situation. The OSCE's Department of Democratization working with its commission in Kosovo has published a substantial report entitled "Kosovo's Concerns: Voters' Voices" that contributes still more to our knowledge of the political landscape. Coupled with extensive UN reports and studies vintage 2003, the literature has developed impressively. This is perhaps the appropriate place to review some of their conclusions.

UN and UNMIK

The UN Security Council is technically the key player in the management of Kosovo. The reports and statements emanating from the Security Council at its sessions in February[14] and April 2003[15] took up the Kosovo situation. The key themes were (1) the UN remains committed to the creation of a multiethnic and democratic Kosovo; (2) it endorses the "primacy" of standards to ensure the needs of people over determination of Kosovo's final status; and (3) UN Resolution 1244, establishing the mission, remains fully valid in all aspects.[16] The second theme is elaborated a bit further on.

Steiner himself appealed to the Security Council to understand how crucially important it is for the UN to "remain in charge" in Kosovo until the main objectives of Resolution 1244 are fulfilled. He reported that Belgrade and Pristina had agreed that *quality of life* and *meeting benchmarks* were the most crucial objectives. Steiner recommended against the "status first" position that claims the region is ready for a final status agreement between Serbia and Kosovo. The Security Council pointed warily to the June 21 meeting of the EU in Greece, which advanced the commitment to push along issues of "self-government" and decentralization in Kosovo. The UN Security Council went to the point of condemning and rejecting "all attempts . . . that are inconsistent with Resolution 1244" and any other unilateral initiatives. The resolution commits the UN to managing postconflict Kosovo until it achieves eight benchmarks. At that point, the resolution calls for Kosovo to return to its status as a part of Serbia "with substantial autonomy." The "standards before status" position endorsed in the winter of 2003 is built around the following inventory of benchmarks:

1. Establishment of functioning democratic institutions
2. The rule of law in place
3. Freedom of movement guaranteed
4. The return of refugees and internally displaced persons[17]
5. Basic economic institutions in place and economy functioning
6. Property rights guaranteed
7. Dialogue with Belgrade routinized
8. Integrity for the Kosovo Protection Corps (police independent of the KLA)

With much more *anticipation* than *reality* reflected in this list, the Security Council added the "responsibility of the majority to make the minority communities feel that Kosovo is their home too, and that the laws apply equally to everyone. The minority community representatives must join and work within the institutions to benefit from them."[18]

Having established that tone and apparent commitment, the Security Council, *nonetheless,* endorsed Steiner's recommendation that "all remaining competencies" be transferred to the Provisional Institutions of Self Government by the end of 2003.[19] This notwithstanding, a report covering the period through the end of 2002 in the wake of Kosovo's second municipal elections stated that

> Kosovo is still a considerable way from reaching the individual benchmarks and targets set out in the benchmark matrix. A year after the formation of the Provisional Institutions of Self-Government, much remains to be done to build effective representative, transparent and accountable institutions with meaningful participation of minority community representatives in the civil service. At the start of 2003, it is clear that both the majority and the minority communities must make renewed efforts to inject new momentum into improving inter-ethnic dialogue and promoting the reconciliation process. Courageous steps are now needed on all sides. . . . Kosovo is still a long way from having truly functioning democratic institutions and a society where minorities could fully participate. Sixty percent of positions designated for multiethnic candidates remain unfilled.[20]

Steiner observed that the UNMIK should focus on what was required for a "decent life in Kosovo, on what people actually wanted." He warned that ethnically defined interest politics prevails and added that municipalities now had two years of experience at running local affairs but had still not (1) committed to fair treatment for minorities and (2) that local extremists could still act with impunity.[21] Steiner concluded that 2003 was *not* the year for finally solving Kosovo's status. The Spanish member of the Security Council added, "Any attempts to pre-judge the final status of Kosovo now are ill-timed and counter-productive."[22] Many other members suggested that not only was capability required but the will as well. They noted that tolerance and mutual respect were essential attitudes for the benchmarks to be met. And still others warned against the scheduled troop reductions, warning that the consequences would be unacceptable.

When the Security Council revisited the Kosovo situation, its evaluation was constructed around a report by Hedi Annab, assistant secretary-general for Peacekeeping Operations. His report was mixed but underlined the frailty of the UN timetable for disengagement from Kosovo. His overall assessment was that planned transitions had been "hampered by political inter- and intra-party struggles." He examined the so-called *Constitutional Framework* and observed that "the Kosovo Assembly remained unable to bridge political and ethnic differences. Ethnic violence and crime seemed to be on the increase. Minority issues . . . remained problematic." He underscored the complex and mixed situation, adding that the UNMIK was under "steadily increasing pressure" to violate the letter and spirit of Resolution 1244. He warned that acts and statements of extremism had increased in the first part of 2003 while voices of moderation had been "weak and muted."[23]

The crushing reality to the Security Council members seems to be that while the UNMIK and KFOR restored a kind of order, peace, and security to Kosovo, avoiding a human catastrophe, "the situation today is characterized by hatred, rejection, violence and a continuation of domination."[24]

United States Institute of Peace

No other entity has devoted as much effort to finding a way out of the malaise in Kosovo than the USIP. There are three reports that all have focused on the next step for the international community in Kosovo. One dates from February 2002, the second from July 2002, and the last from February 2003. The content and the utility of that content are impressive.

The USIP reports, based on the 2002 simulations, suggest that the negotiations will be especially difficult and the status will take the next five years to work through. Other conclusions suggest that the U.S. government must take the leading role as power broker. The *United States* should define what is an "acceptable" solution. UN Resolution 1244 is now the "problem" rather than a basis for a solution. Modalities of the negotiations will be crucial to their success. The overriding goal of the Albanian ethnics is independence. A formal timetable will lead to failure. Both Kosovars and Serbs might be willing to partition territory in an agreement but with the objective of creating ethnic homogeneity. This option was unacceptable to the international players. European delegates played secondary roles. EU membership and economic incentives were useful. Implementation of a final status agreement will require prolonged international presence—military and civilian. Ominously, none of the three rigorous simulations generated a definitive conclusion on final status (United States Institute of Peace 200b).[25]

The second report is valuable because it identifies and assesses the full range of options for final status. By the analysis of the task force there are eight options:

* Kosovo remains a protectorate indefinitely
* Cantonization/decentralization
* Loose federation
* Commonwealth
* Decision by an international panel by a certain date
* Conditional independence
* Independence with existing orders at a certain date
* Independence with partition (United States Institute of Peace 2002a)

These are primarily options that begin with the political architecture of the future status of Kosovo. USIP scholars and diplomats concluded only that two options were to be ruled out as "unrealistic": the immediate independence for Kosovo and the simple return of Kosovo to Belgrade's control. Ironically, these are the two options most stridently supported by the Kosovars and Serbs, respectively. A third option—to rearrange borders to create ethnic homogeneity—was rejected as moving away from long-term international peace and security.

The last special report modifies some of the ideas in its earlier analyses. However, it does emphasize the growing problems with Kosovo's unresolved status. Among these are damage to any search for investments, slow Serb returns (repatriation), and growing Kosovar unrest and distrust of the international community. The USIP now advocates negotiations between Pristina and Belgrade with strong U.S. *and* EU guidance. The United States is to provide regional security guarantees, and the EU is to create economic incentives. It endorses UNMIK benchmarks but recognizes that the unfulfilled ones are the most crucial: democratic self-governance, return of refugees and displaced persons, and respect for the law and related mechanics (United States Institute of Peace 2003).

The negotiations are to have two phases: "dialogue" between Pristina and Belgrade starting now and "proactive consultations" engaging the United States, the EU, the UN and Russia starting by 2005. Following an agreement, the USIP report prescribes that the EU "should take over responsibility for Kosovo" and that the final status should be approved by the UN Security Council (United States Institute of Peace 2003, 1).

While acknowledging how much effort the USIP has invested in the challenge that Kosovo presents to the international community, the USIP does suffer from what might be called commitment anxiety. It comes close to prescribing a scenario, then backs away. In its conclusions and recommendations in its most recent report, it waffles. The report, counter to the USIP's own findings, claims that "with democratic regimes in both Belgrade and Pristina, the international community will expect Serbs and Albanians to come to a negotiated solution for Kosovo final status" (United States Institute of Peace 2003, 6). Its formula provides that the UNMIK should:

+ Continue with the benchmarks process
+ Convene Belgrade-Pristina dialogue on other than final status issues
+ Conduct consultations with the EU, the United States, and Russia on final status

The United States should:

+ Determine its own position on final status
+ Play a key role in regional security
+ Obtain support in the UN Security Council
+ Engage Russia in the process

The EU should:

+ Develop economic incentives to build into negotiations
+ Determine its position on final status

And Belgrade and Pristina should:

+ Prepare for discussion of mutual interest other than final status
+ Establish initial negotiating positions for final status
+ Begin to socialize populations on economic imperatives, wisdom of minority rights, and rule of law (United States Institute of Peace 2003, 6–7)

These recommendations appear to make a very modest contribution to the search for a final solution and appear to reflect diplomatic caution more than constructive direction.

OSCE

The OSCE's mission statement is a sophisticated and refined description of goals and objectives. It touches on all of the necessary issues and sets out a range of activities that in a neutral, hypothetical setting could generate quick and impressive results. But it lacks a strong sense of realism. It is built exclusively on the ideological presumptions of developed capitalist and democratic systems. As a point of departure for any system's attempt at establishing such functional and modern behaviors and institutions, it is hard to criticize (OCSE 2002, 2003).

Nonetheless, OSCE faces the most daunting task: to create from very little legacy a set of attitudes and perceptions that could frame democratic behavior and weather the inevitable reversals that will come with the search for a final status. As the "institution-building pillar" of the UNMIK administration, OSCE needs the heaviest dose of realism it can internalize.

With this clearly in the minds of the Department of Democratization in Kosovo, a comprehensive effort was made to survey Kosovars and Serbs about their political opinions. The surface rationale was to create an opportunity for the public to speak out and send clear signals to the candidates and political parties facing elections in Kosovo (circa November 2001). The study, entitled "The Kosovo Concerns: Voters Voices," was printed in a booklet and widely distributed, as promised, to candidate-politicians. The strategy was to challenge politicians to respond to those public interests. Accountability was also part of the object lessons implied in the exercise. The survey was managed to the extent that it provided options to speak out *only* on those matters ("competencies") articulated in the *Constitutional Framework*.[26] The survey involved more than one hundred local meetings and more than thirteen thousand residents. It adeptly represents the range of views in the general public. Not surprisingly, the key finding is that majority and minority participants order priorities quite differently.

Overall, bearing in mind the overwhelming Kosovar majority, the order of priorities suggested by the study was:

1. Law and order (identified as "urgent")
2. Education, science and technology
3. Health (especially creation of a health care system)
4. Kosovo Protection Corps (expectation of it being the *army* of Kosovo)
5. Economic and financial policy
6. Good governance, human rights, and equal opportunity
7. Youth and sports (more than half of population under age twenty-six)
8. Environmental protection
9. Rights of communities (read: minorities)
10. Culture

On the fifth priority—economics and financial policy—those surveyed did point to the devastating impact of unemployment. The solution articulated most often was state-owned property and entities. Some challenged that direction with arguments favoring privatization. "Everyone was unanimous that the uncertainty regarding the political direction of Kosovo impeded foreign investment." All agreed that foreign investment was needed to facilitate reconstruction of the "current destroyed economy" (Arrigoni, Broadbent, and Valier 2001, ix). The point to be made here is the naive assumption that with a final status established, the logic for and quantity of capitalist investment in Kosovo from foreign sources would appreciably change.

Naturally, such efforts to establish the opinion landscape of the Kosovo population are of great value. Yet they point to perplexing realities as much as to neat strategies. For example, law and order (the top priority) is not necessarily democracy-supporting, and with "good governance" well down the list, one is left to speculate that Kosovars are not aware of the centrality of politics to the future of any system. Figure 21.1 reproduces the graphic presentation from that report.

Another View from Within

A preliminary survey of the very small number of "political scientists"[27] working in Kosovo in 2003 probed their perceptions of the Kosovo reality. None have Serbian heritage, so what is represented is the view from the mainstream majority in ethnically Albanian-dominated Kosovo. When the scholars were queried about "preferred outcome," the uniform response was that Kosovo should be a sovereign, independent country. When asked what the *popular* view on this question would yield, the answer was that this was also the popular view. These answers claimed that more than 90 percent of Kosovars equate "solving" the Kosovo problem with full independence. Pressed for what the outcome would, in fact, likely be, the scholars' thrust was that it would be closer to Resolution 1244 (Kosovo returned to Serbian control). Specifically, one scholar predicted a "Dayton 2 Model." Kosovo becomes a part of a Union of Serbia, Montenegro, and Kosovo in which Kosovo has nearly complete autonomy in domestic affairs and virtually no role in foreign affairs. He called this a "para-state" and saw a parallel with the reality in Bosnia today.

Responses to other questions were also illuminating. Answers are synthesized below.

QUESTION: What party/player/country/organization would be most effective at organizing and directing the negotiations?

ANSWER: Only with heavy U.S. involvement can there be any hope of a sustainable peace. Analysts cannot "imagine" a situation in which the UN, OSCE, or EU have the status to lead the way.

QUESTION: Will the likely political outcome be accompanied by (a) migration and (b) violence?

FIGURE 21.1 **Kosovo's Concerns: Priorities (Ranked 1 to 10)**

Law and Order, 6.53
Education, Science and Technology, 5.97
Health, 5.53
Kosovo Protection Corps, 4.35
Economic and Financial Policy, 4.21
Good Governance, Human Rights and Equal Opportunity, 4.18
Youth and Sport, 3.42
Environmental Protection, 3.25
Rights of Communities and Their Members, 3.15
Culture, 3.04
Labor and Social Welfare, 2.60
Domestic and Foreign Trade, Industry and Investments, 2.41
Development of relations with Euro-Atlantic Comm., 2.19
Judicial Affairs, 1.67
Agriculture, Forestry and Rural Development, 1.59
Family, Gender and Minors, 1.56
Transport, Post, Telecomm. and Info Technologies, 1.48
External Relations, 1.11
Administrative and Operational Customs Activities, 1.06
Fiscal and Budgetary Issues, 1.04
Local Administration, 0.93
Tourism, 0.90
Public Administration Services, 0.6
Non-resident Affairs, 0.6
Emergency Preparedness, 0.6
Mass Media, 0.2
Spatial planning 0.1
Statistics 0.1

Note: During the meetings the participants received the questionnaire with the 28 areas of responsibilities of the *Constitutional Framework for a Provisional Self-Government.* They had to indicate the 10 most significant, ranking them in order of priority. To evaluate the importance of the priorities 10 points were assigned to the first one, 9 to the second, until the tenth, which received 1 point. All ratings of the 1316 questionnaires which were filled in, were then calculated together to produce the average score (from 0 to 10) for each issue.

ANSWER: Given that so many Kosovars imagine *only* full independence, they will opt for low-scale violence (terrorist-type activities, some of which have already begun), though it is hard to foresee that it will range outside of Kosovo's borders.

QUESTION: What is your sense of the *length* of external support (financial and administrative) that will be required following a "solution?"

ANSWER: First and foremost, this is conditioned by the notion that Kosovars will be dramatically unhappy ("unaccepting") of the solution of the international community. Then, it will be necessary to "compensate" Kosovars for the injustice. "Tremendous" support will need to be forthcoming: economic aid, infrastructure money, resources for education, a role in EU development projects, and special military guarantees. Today, Kosovars feel isolated from the rest of the world. After an unfavorable settlement, the international community will need to aid Kosovo to the point of winning over the destructive and violent parts of Kosovar society. The price will be high and the term indefinite.

QUESTION: Should Albania have any role in the negotiations?

ANSWER: Albania will have to be involved because its politics is extremely influential in Kosovo, and a wide range of outcomes (of the negotiations) will cause violence to spill over into Albania.

QUESTION: What is your sense of the most crucial single change that needs to take place to attract foreign direct investment?

ANSWER: Two answers surfaced. First, the Kosovar Assembly and the UNMIK need to produce a commercial code that provides solid guarantees to foreign investors. Second, international players should guarantee the investments in Kosovo. One scholar added that this should have been done long ago ("too much time has already been lost") and can happen without a "final status" agreement.

These opinions draw attention to the pivotal problems that surround a search for a solution. One could see in them the emotion, inflexibility, and absence of perspective that abound in Kosovo. To be very fair, these are scholars who are functioning in a charged and pressurized environment. However, if this is the texture of opinion from the small scholarly community (a tiny sample from a tiny population), it may be prudent to assume that one will find *more poignant* views in the general population. It is also possible to find in the responses a sense that the responsibility for all things (especially negative things) lies outside Kosovo, which could bode very poorly for any kind of democratic development. Democracy would certainly require a sense of responsibility for events and future direction. The "victim" or dependency mind-set creates an unworkably soft foundation for systemic development.

Dimensions

A recent study by Hartzell and Hoddie (2003) suggests a starting point for the search for a constructive scenario. They studied post–civil war conflict management in the second half of the twentieth century. Though they did not include Kosovo as a case, their data points clearly in a couple of key directions that can be helpful. First, to establish "power-sharing" institutions that address the security concerns of former adversaries, the institutions should be designed to explicitly share power across four dimensions: political, territorial, military, and economic. In the Kosovo environment, this would require multitiered institutions that engaged and provided for both Serbs and Kosovars. The case is coherently made that only by a framework with this breadth can the psychological and tangible security concerns of the parties be addressed. They warn that if only formal issues of the distribution of political power are included, conflict will reemerge. They go on to suggest that "While the ability of power-sharing institutions to balance power among groups is initially likely to be the critical factor for stabilizing the peace, long-term stability seems to depend on groups having learned to transact with one another and perhaps having even developed new rules of conflict management" (320).

The multidimensional strategy has another key asset: insulation against "implementation failure." To ensure that the peace is not jeopardized by any one failure, Hartzell and Hoddie suggest "specifying multiple dimensions of power-sharing in the agreement, [because] the failure of one aspect of power-sharing may not necessarily result in groups becoming permanently marginalized or unable to provide for their own security" (2003, 327).

The second major conclusion of this study is that long-term success requires a "third-party enforcer" (Hartzell and Hoddie 2003, 327). In the Kosovar context, this has been a widely recognized reality. However, the implications for a draw-down or withdrawal from the territory by the international community raise profound questions about commitment to sustained and peaceful outcomes.

The Hartzell-Hoddie study hypotheses, which create a guideline for a solution, are as follows:

1. The more extensive the power-sharing arrangements called for in a negotiated settlement, the more likely it is that peace will endure in the long run.
2. Negotiated settlements constructed by actors with previous experience with democracy are more likely to produce an enduring peace than settlements constructed by actors whose previous regime type was authoritarian.
3. Wars of long duration should increase the likelihood that parties will commit to an enduring peace.

4. Settlements of civil wars characterized by high casualty rates are unlikely to yield a durable peace.

5. Settlements that call for third-party enforcement are more likely to produce a durable peace than those that make no provision for enforcement by third-party actors.

6. Civil war settlements negotiated since the end of the cold war are more likely to foster a durable peace than those negotiated during the cold war.

7. Negotiated settlements are more likely to produce enduring peace when the issue at stake in the conflict is politico-economic rather than identity-based.

8. The risk of war breaking out again following the negotiated settlement should decline with the passage of time. (Hartzell and Hoddie 2003, 330–31)

Briefly, hypothesis 1 tells us that it is crucial to create an agreement that speaks to the four dimensions of interests among the conflicted parties—Serbs and Kosovars. Hypothesis 2 suggests that success is more difficult because both groups have little experience with democracy. Because the Kosovar war was not of long duration and involved relatively light casualties, hypotheses 3 and 4 indicate that an enduring peace may be less likely. Third-party enforcement is possible from either the United States or the EU. Both have become increasingly reticent to commit to a long-term role. The research indicates how crucial that role is. Hypothesis 6 suggests a bit of optimism given that cold war and super-power competition is not a factor in the negotiations. Hypothesis 7 is ominous because most see the conflict in Kosovo as an "identity-based" conflict. Finally, the short three-year interregnum between war and negotiated solution falls in the range that the study would suggest enhances risk. The study, as guidepost to a solution for Kosovo, has mixed messages. Five of the research findings draw one in the direction of deep concern for Kosovo's nonviolent prospects.

Prescriptions for the future of Kosovo include nine preset principles, with other elements to be negotiated, as follows:

+ Negotiations should recognize as key parties Serbia, Montenegro, Kosovo, and the United States.

+ The first three days of the negotiations should be dedicated to an empirical review (briefing) of the assets, liabilities, and prospects for Serbia, Montenegro, and Kosovo in the near and broader-term future and to the implications for viability as independent states.

+ Negotiations should be co-hosted and supervised by the OSCE and the EU. The OSCE will issue annual reports on the implementation of the letter and intent of the agreement.

+ A negotiated plan (in whatever format is determined) should be presented to neighboring states for their comments and refinement before public announcement. These states should include Macedonia, Albania, Bulgaria, Croatia, and Greece. They should be made a party to the negotiated agreement in a second phase. Bosnia should be excluded.

+ The political future of Kosovo shall be negotiated only in a framework where it remains part of a new federation of Serbia, Montenegro, and Kosovo.

+ Security forces for all of the new states (Serbia, Montenegro, Kosovo) will be trained and reorganized by the U.S. military. Forces at all levels will be multiethnic in composition with a negotiated balance among the three groups. Their deployment will be supervised by a special civilian commission (one for each of the three regions) whose makeup will also be multiethnic.

+ Kosovo's economic plight will be addressed through commitment to economic development by external players. Specifically, Kosovo will be induced to accept a World Bank–sponsored economic development plan for the territory built upon the dominant participation of a solicited global agribusiness firm that will remain in Kosovo long-term. Resources should be assigned to this company on a priority basis by the regional authorities.

+ The formal design of the territory's political architecture will provide specific political power and a formal role for the representatives from this mega-enterprise. This amounts to the creation of a neocorporatist political framework. A council of economic advisors dominated by representatives from the designated firm should have to approve all legislation and executive decisions on economic policy.

+ The election system used shall be proportional representation at both the territorial and central system levels. Kosovo elections should be delayed until a significant amount of preparation and public education takes place regarding constituencies, candidate selection, campaign rules, and broad expectations.

The rationale, first and foremost, recognizes the Hartzell-Hoddie requisite that the settlement be multidimensional though with adjustments to the Kosovar situation. It also seeks to put in place new roles for the external players: the United States, EU, and OSCE. Most importantly, it recognizes that the political future of a microstate is so problematic as to make that an unworkable option. Kosovars must accept that "size matters" and that, linked politically with a carefully guided new state, the prospects for EU inclusion, political maturation, and economic development are maximized.

To balance the argument for these provisions, it should be added that the USIP has weighed in negatively on the key notion here that a new union of Serbia, Montenegro, and Kosovo be constructed. "Participants in the Institute meeting agreed that the new governing arrangement for Serbia and Montenegro *offers no serious possibility* of incorporating Kosovo. . . . The majority in Kosovo will not want to join Serbia and Montenegro, even on an equal basis (neither Serbs nor Montenegrins would want it to do so in any event)" (United States Institute of Peace 2003, 2).

On the economic side, the situation is so dire that only a fairly radical framework will have any chance of working. To this end, the "solution" is economic vitality by tying Kosovo's economy to the corporate interests of a successful and sophisticated agribusiness company that will rationalize development in its own business interest. Initial incentive will be created by World Bank development funds, but long-term protection for the corporate interests will be ensured by providing the company's representatives with a measure of real political power. This illiberal element is necessary given the measure of what needs to be done to create productivity in Kosovo. Kosovo cannot realistically imagine itself as a viable economic player in the twenty-first-century world. This plan creates a "company town" atmosphere and reality that will make basic sense to the people and can create jobs, production, and eventually revenue for the system. Realistically, issues of political power and political mechanics will be welcomed and managed *after* the people of Kosovo see some economic opportunity. There is no faster way for Kosovar or Serbian politicians to establish their credibility and legitimacy than to point to the creation of jobs, incomes, and economic stability.

The emphasis on agriculture may require a bit of development. Kosovo has traditionally been a rural region. Village life constructed around basic growing, and husbandry is the norm. People will understand this sort of economic development and may be prone to support it. Perhaps more crucial is the possibility that agribusiness development can stem the tide of young people leaving the villages, given that employment opportunities will be created. Donor support over the past three years has identified the agricultural sector as a focus where tangible progress is possible repairing tractors, restocking herds, supplying fertilizers, and providing veterinary services. Many in NGOs believe that only with stability in the rural villages will Kosovo have a chance to move forward.

Assessing in terms of the three requisites posited earlier—constructing a value consensus, elaborating a functional political architecture, and finding effective leadership—the plan as presented is partial at best. Under the plan, the search for a consensus broadens to all Serbs, Montenegrins, and Kosovars living in the larger system. This is a problem *and* an advantage. To find a premise that can ally all of them is to direct their interests to the economic. Defining the consensus in terms of *quality of life* may be the only consensual premise that resonates at this time. All plans will try to address the political architecture issue. However, most will make the classic mistake of trying to create the appearance of a democratic system where the behaviors and attitudes do not support it—democracy lite. This is a dangerous option. It is far better to concede that the democratic elements of the system will require much longer gestation and that the concentration of power in corporate hands (de facto monopolistic) is more candid and acceptable than the alternative. There is little evidence that this will rankle Kosovars. Finally, political leadership is likely to continue to be a problem. A partial way to address this issue could emerge from the role ascribed to the global firm. Its profit-motivated needs and experience may serve to support interim leadership long enough to nurture evolving political skills. Placing faith in the corporate elite is not so rare even in developed societies and, given Kosovo realities, may be as good as any other oligarchy.

Criticism of this plan can be introduced from many ideological perspectives. Most may be valid. Nonetheless, if the international community wishes to relieve itself from perpetual responsibility in Kosovo and/or from the guilt of walking away from its involvement there, this platform can create a future that can make life in Kosovo livable and significantly more stable than the alternatives.

TEXTURES AND MIND-SET FOR MOVING NEGOTIATIONS AHEAD

The next two sections are broadly prescriptive. They represent the key to creating a successful next step and a subsequent process that can approach results that proximate the goals of the international community. As such, these are absolute requisites, although they are altogether intangible. As posited in an earlier section, the process needs to begin with some nonspecific discussion of values, perceptions, and the future if the current unproductive atmosphere is to be overcome. While there are various challenges facing the "solution," remedies and mechanisms can be created to set in motion processes that have the potential to yield positive results from both indigenous and international perspectives. The concepts that follow are crucial.

State Identity versus National (Ethnonational) Identity

Identity may be the magnifying concept that enables us to see the issues in greater focus and seek strategies for constructive change. All people in modern societies have multiple identities. These are often in conflict but do not manifest themselves in obvious tension, because they are often not juxtaposed as we frame our behavior. We manage these personal strains (who we are) by creating, often semiconsciously, a hierarchy of these identities and by reaching down into the list to accommodate situation-bound decisions. In settings of the sort one finds in Kosovo, the ordered list of identities seems to shorten and to be dominated by those identities that evoke emotional commitment. This has the *seemingly* desired effect of making issues and choices simpler. Politics, then, is a more stark and clear phenomenon than one would find in a more developed society—that is, one with more economic choices, more institutions, and higher levels of personal comfort in the broadest sense. Identities that help define who one is *politically* serve that function in a more essential way in a setting such as Kosovo. The thrust of this idea is simple. Where uncertainty abounds in many aspects of life, the door is open to composite identities that purport to be comprehensive and solution-bearing.

Enter the classic tension between identity with the *state* and identity with the *nation*. In essence, this is a choice between believing in and committing oneself to the politically defined society or the ethnically defined society. The salience of this choice cannot be overestimated. If the construction of the *state* and its political principles is the goal, there is the real prospect that the design of the political society can evolve and can be renegotiated, redefined, and expanded. If the protection of the *nation* is the goal, it has historically defined boundaries (geographic and cultural) and will seek to reify those. Nationalism conceives of itself as a fixed reality bastardized by the injustices of *others*. Its vision of tomorrow is always contextualized in the past. In sharp contrast, those who set out to construct a *state* have the luxury of focusing their attention purposively on the future—not because the past is irrelevant but because the past does *not* bear the seeds of solving the injustices of the past. History, at least in Central and Eastern Europe and more specifically in the Balkans, is not a platform on which a dynamic political future can be built.

This statement certainly seems to be so sweeping that many will presume it prima facie to be academically irresponsible. Nonetheless, as people of goodwill search for constructive solutions to the Kosovo situation, its essence will be unavoidable. Building a viable political future for Kosovo will require a forward-facing mentor and forward-facing indigenous leaders who will ask themselves and each other the penetrating questions about the *future* they want to construct. And this will necessarily preclude asking themselves how to ameliorate the injustices and violence of the recent or distant past. The truism is that a scenario does not exist for the future that rectifies the past. Dwelling on how to compensate or hold current people responsible for vile behaviors of the past will certainly predestine negotiations to failure. In the specific case of Kosovo, we see the classic conundrum: Which moment in time is the moment when a claim to a territory is validated? It is the arrogance of the "nationalist" who claims the right to select the epoch that makes righteous a specific claim or to identify *which* historically validated seizure is the injustice to be rectified.

Analysts naturally should not deny historical events. Recognizing them in more comprehensive contexts certainly helps. However, for those with the specific goal of moving the negotiations about Kosovo toward a society with genuine prospects for the future, the past will need to be marginalized and de-emphasized. Man can face forward and march into the future or face backwards and stumble into the future. Constructing a *state* can be embracing and inclusive if designed with that as an explicit institutional goal. In contrast, if the *nation* is to be the foundation of the state, its texture is bound to be insular and exclusive. In real political terms, this portends more ethnic cleansing, dislocation, and incumbent conflict.[28]

Patriotism versus Nationalism

Whatever vision for Kosovo's future is conjured, there will be efforts to enlist the hearts and minds of the people of the territory. The options are clear. Patriotism will create real positive prospects if constructed as the allegiance to and support for the political principles of the state, especially if they (1) guarantee minority rights and (2) build a broad inclusive texture into the political architecture. If nationalism is framed as the central allegiance and focus of support, the uncertainty for all minorities and even those in the majority who have experienced minority status in another political environment will find it impossible to support the system or to feel secure in it. Such tensions will confound early political efforts and sabotage development.

The key consequence of the exclusionary pressures of nationalism as the framing thesis for society would be the significantly diminished *human capital* available to the society. Only nationalists are prepared to say they are sure that minorities will not contribute to society—that the next great inventor or scientist, scholar or teacher, athlete or artist will not be from those sectors of society.

Political science has informed our analysis to the point that we all recognize the centrality of *legitimacy* in the functional life of political systems. By what strategy can one induce legitimacy into a new Kosovar political reality? There will be those who argue that legitimacy can only be built on the already prevalent foundation of nationalism and ethnic identity in Kosovo. Short-term, this would seem to yield the most measurable results. But it is a bankrupt strategy for the real systemic (political) health of the society. Nationalism is a placebo with side-effects that function like intellectual sedatives. The slogans and myths so embedded in nationalism blur or discourage thinking and political rationality. Long-term prospects for Kosovo *require* that legitimacy be built incrementally on the platform of enlightened principles and tested experience, particularly practices stemming from tolerant and liberal principles.

The case can be made whether one is focusing on the internal dynamics of politics in Kosovo or on the evolving foundation for international relations. An open, accommodating, and pragmatic approach to international relationships will stretch the options and crystallize linkages. An ideologically narrow conception of politics will inevitably strain at least those interactions with Western democratic and resource-laden partners. For the liberal and tolerant (or aspiring to be tolerant) political systems, nationalism is singularly threatening and abrasive. President Bush would go well beyond this characterization and even use the term "evil." The simple and inescapable reality is that Kosovo will need external assistance and support for a very long period, and Kosovars should come to recognize that nationalism will politically sabotage that prospect.

The paradox for Kosovar leadership is acute. Creating a posture that can be popularly supported in Kosovo has necessarily brought leaders to make intolerant appeals and policies. The disparity between international and local perceptions about what is needed for Kosovo is so dramatic that conventional approaches to resolving the issue will not suffice. From the international administration's theoretical perspective, the "prize" is institutional longevity premised upon liberal values. For Kosovars generally, politics is a zero-sum game where gains for the Serbs represent defeat for the Albanian ethnics.

As with any academic look at such issues, this analysis seeks to construct a practical, positive approach. The Kosovar environment (like so many in our world today) resists. In Kosovo province, emotion is the primary political platform, and leaders embrace and evoke this emotion as often as they can in their rhetoric. Evidence abounds but, in my mind, the most vivid evidence is anecdotal. Today, so-called heroes from the struggle in 1999 are buried in fresh graves in the public parks in Pristina. The soil is tilled and flowers are placed to create the image that these are "yesterday's" victories and sacrifices—just yesterday's! These graves are purposefully aligned and marked and celebrated to leave the clear impression that the struggle persists.

On a fairly crisp day in November 2002, a visitor to Pristina would have experienced Flag Day. On that occasion, recognizing the public sentiment for Kosovar independence, I took special note that Kosovo does not have a flag. Indeed, the flag that was so proudly displayed with accompanying fanfare was the Albanian flag. I seemed to be the only person in the capital who found this perplexing. All that the Kosovars seem to require is an anti-Serbian symbol. The numbness that follows any effort to raise issues of Albanian politics or political efficacy is characteristic of political dialogue in Pristina.

Ethnic nationalism, so classically manifest in Kosovo, is the politics of ethnic separation. It has reified the Serbian enclaves where today frustration and alienation build to explosive levels. Enclaves invite violence in order to level the playing field in the society. The ghettoization of Serbs in Kosovo has intensified resolve against compromise and cast doubt on any credible claim by Albanian Kosovars that Serbs will be treated in more enlightened ways than Albanian ethnics were treated in the prewar period.

CONCLUSION

Harri Holkeri, the current UN special envoy in Kosovo, indicated in January 2004 that "the task of the UN Mission in Kosovo (UNMIK) is to help locals prepare the province, which has been under UN administration since June 1999, for the resolution of its future status—and then to leave. But he said this would not work unless Kosovo meets many challenges in 2004, including holding fair parliamentary elections, ensuring the rule of law, promoting multi-ethnicity, encouraging dialogue between Pristina and Belgrade, and establishing an effective market economy." [29]

In the final analysis, a search for ultimate status for Kosovo will require ingenuity, intensity, and a big-picture perspective. It is an uphill journey in an ill-designed and partially assembled vehicle whose engine is the international administrative and donor community. The most probable outcome is a tactical withdrawal of international effort and concern coupled with ongoing local strife unreported by the world's major media. Ironically, what the Kosovars and the international community share is an inventory of unwarranted expectations. With the passage of time, the efforts in Kosovo will be chronicled as an example of well-meaning but ineffective international intervention.

NOTES

1. An interesting analysis can be found in Franzinetti and Curis (2003).

2. This report also is interesting for its effort to lace the most positive picture on the Kosovo situation.

3. For greater insight into the current Kosovo leadership, see *Conference on Integration of Ethnic Communities in Kosova/o* (Pristina: Soros Foundation, December 2002).

4. Arrigoni, Broadbent, and Valier (2001, 19).

5. UN Security Council (2003, 11).

6. Arrigoni, Broadbent, and Valier (2001, 40).

7. Ibid, 42.

8. Ibid, 8.

9. Ibid, 13.

10. Ibid, 4, 15.

11. UN Security Council (2003, 13).

12. Harri Holkeri made a public speech in January 2004 in which he said, "This is really unacceptable. These parallel courts pretend to exercise jurisdiction in Kosovo. International arrest warrants which have no validity have been issued through these unauthorized structures against Kosovo residents. This has already caused serious difficulties and cannot be tolerated. Under Resolution 1244, it is UNMIK that has jurisdiction and authority over the territory." UNMIK Press Release 1049, p. 6, www.unmikonline.org/press/2003/pressr/pr1049.pdf.

13. The dilemma is outlined effectively in Rubin (2002).

14. UN Security Council, "Security Council, in Presidential Statement, Reaffirms Commitment to Multi-ethnic, Democratic Kosovo," Press Release SC/7659, February 6, 2003 (SC Meetings 4702nd and 4703rd).

15. UN Security Council, "Kosovo Has 'Some Way to Go' in Establishing Representative, Functioning Institutions," Press Release, SC/7737, April 23, 2003 (SC Meeting 4742nd).

16. UN Security Council, Press Release SC/7659, February 6, 2003. UN Security Council Resolution 1244 provides the rationale for establishing international control over Kosovo and, importantly, provides for an outcome in which Kosovo is reconnected with Serbia (ex-Yugoslavia) albeit with significant autonomy.

17. In 2002, 2,671 returned and 1 million remain displaced.

18. UN Security Council, Press Release SC/7659, February 6, 2003.

19. Ibid., 1.

20. Ibid., 6.

21. Ibid., 5.

22. Ibid., 11.

23. UN Security Council, Press Release SC/7737, April 23, 2003, p. 1.

24. Ibid.

25. Especially useful for a full-blown description of the positions taken and measure of flexibility for each of the participant delegations.

26. The *Constitutional Framework* is a document prepared by UNMIK that designates the areas of limited authority where Kosovar institutions can begin to organize themselves. It is a very measured document that sets out prescribed goals and preordains both policies and pace.

27. Survey conducted by author at the University of Pristina during late 2002 and early 2003.

28. Illustrated poignantly in Elsie (2002).

29. United Nations Spokesman for the Secretary General, "UN Envoy Urges Kosovo to Take the High Road Towards Peace in 2004" (New York: UN News Centre, 25 January 2004). Recounts commentary by Harri Holkeri made on 13 January 2004 in Pristina.

REFERENCES

Arrigoni, Mauro, Julie Broadbent, and Hannelore Valier, eds. 2001. *Kosovo Concerns: Voters' Voices*. Pristina: OSCE Mission in Kosovo.

Elsie, Robert, ed., trans., comp. 2002. *Gathering Clouds: The Roots of Ethnic Cleansing in Kosovo and Macedonia*. Peje: Dukagjini Balkan Books Publishing House.

Franzinetti, Guido, and Robert Curis. 2003 (March). "The Assembly of Kosovo: One Year On." Research paper of the Conflict Studies Research Centre. Surrey: Defence Academy of the United Kingdom.

Hartzell, Caroline, and Matthew Hoddie. 2003. "Institutionalizing Peace: Power-Sharing and Post-Civil War Conflict Management." *American Journal of Political Science* 47(2): 318–32.

OSCE. 2002. "Supporting Democracy in Kosovo." OCSE Mission in Kosovo Press Release, June. www.osce.org/kosovo/documents/factsheet/democratization/democr_factsheet_eng.pdf.

———. 2003. "Programmatic Priorities for 2003." OCSE Mission in Kosovo Press Release, January 6. www.osce.org/kosovo/documents/factsheet/general/omik_priorities_for_2003.pdf.

Ottaway, Marina. 2003. *Democracy Challenged: The Rise of Semi-Authoritarianism*. Washington, D.C.: Carnegie Endowment for International Peace.

Rubin, Barnett. 2002. *Blood on the Doorstep: Politics of Preventive Action*. New York: Century Foundation/Council on Foreign Relations Book.

Shanker, Thom. 2003. "Aftereffects: Rebuilding; Lessons for Iraq Seen in Balkan Aftermath." *New York Times*, May 22, 2003, final late edition, sec. A, p. 15.

UN Security Council. 2003. "Report of the Secretary-General on the United Nations Interim Administration Mission in Kosovo." S/2003/996, 15 October. New York: United Nations.

United States Institute of Peace. 2002a (July). *Special Report: Kosovo Final Status—Options and Cross-Border Requirements*. Washington, D.C.: United States Institute of Peace.

———. 2002b (November). *Special Report: Simulating Kosovo—Lessons for Final Status Negotiations*. Special Report 95. Washington, D.C.: United States Institute of Peace.

———. 2003 (February). *Special Report: Kosovo Decision Time*. Special Report 100. Washington, D.C.: United States Institute of Peace.

PART SIX

Latin and Central America

SUSAN L. MACEK & HOWARD J. WIARDA

22 Democratization and Political Terrorism in Latin America

INTRODUCTION: DEMOCRATIZATION AND TERRORISM

Political terrorism is a dramatic but poorly understood challenge to democratization worldwide. The United States' southern neighbors are not immune, even as they live in the shadow of the once self-proclaimed policeman of the Western hemisphere and as the so-called war on terrorism has focused U.S. policy attention away from Latin America and toward other areas (Wiarda, forthcoming). The Latin American countries have been struggling for many decades to democratize and to develop at the same time that they have been caught in a maelstrom of activism, extremism, and now increasing criminality often concentrated with violent attention on national politics. In some cases, the struggle for democracy and development has been superseded by the struggle with private terrorist and criminal groups for state and resource control, threatening domestic, regional, and international security. Whether the state and civilian, democratic, government authority in this contest is winning is not clear.

Several explanatory variables exist for political terrorism in Latin America. By analyzing political terrorism's causes and current manifestations, its consequences and hence the successes and failures of policy response may be better elucidated. Some useful generalities may also be extrapolated from the particulars of the Latin American situation, perhaps offering insight into political terrorism as it presents itself in other regions of the world.

In surveying here the most visible and troubling forms of political terrorism in Latin America, we assume a greatly simplified view of democratization as a transitional course bringing about participatory processes and elections and embracing egalitarian values (however incompletely), though not necessarily in identical reflection of the United States. Democratization has at once objective features (regular elections) as well as subjective intonations ("illiberal" democracy), especially within the American political system. Placed within the context of its current war on terrorism, mutual and concurrent interests, and its extensive history of deliberate hemispheric involvement, the United States has justification for careful scrutiny and cautious but active response to political terrorism in Latin America.

THEORY AND CAUSES

Terrorism is the deliberate manufacture or manipulation of fear, used as a tool of coercion. It may draw attention to a person, a group, or a cause. It has been used to demand government or legal reform and to free imprisoned comrades. It is infinitely malleable: it can be employed for a great variety of uses by individuals or groups willing to prey upon fear to achieve their goals. For nations afflicted, not only are lives lost and property damaged, but quality of life degrades and national productivity decreases (Prilliman 2003, 4). Governments must also divert valuable and scarce resources from democratization and development efforts to police, military, and juridical actions.

In Latin America, the confluence of political terrorism, fragile democratization efforts, and depressed economies may be contributing to the decreasing faith in democracy as the appropriate and desirable government form (*Economist* 2002).[1] But however unfortunate, history provides evidence that the tactics and methods of terrorism have been etched into the ethos of Latin America's political violence. Terrorism begets more terrorism and in some countries insinuates into the political culture. Old habits die hard. In some cases, persistent and pervasive terrorism has left governments critically weakened and vulnerable as they limp toward a state that is democratic, stable and consolidated — an impossibility under such conditions (U.S. Department of State 2003). State success is jeopardized, to the detriment of the interdependent global community.

The coincidence of several characteristics among nations suffering under political terrorism is striking. For example, political terrorism in the form of kidnappings is occurring most prevalently in transitional societies and in societies where painful class conflict exacerbates the socioeconomic cleavages in society (Auerbach 1998, 21–23). Upon closer examination, the frequency of coincidence of the characteristics discussed below suggests that they encourage an environment of political terrorism.

The causes of political terrorism are not simple. A single act may have many explanations, of which some focus on immediate demands and others on longer-range patterns. While the true cause of political terrorism within democratizing nations is most accurately described through a number of variables, based on circumstance and context, seven causative conditions are immediately identifiable: the transitional nature of these societies; intense class conflict; a distinct political culture often based around machismo; the perception of a zero-sum game regarding scarce resources; state failure to deliver socioeconomic opportunities, mobility, and safety nets; the self-perpetuating trap of habit; and the absence or decline of traditional restraints (e.g., religion).

Transitional Societies

Societies undergoing a transition from agrarian to industrial or industrial to postindustrial are especially at risk for an upsurge in certain violent crimes (Auerbach 1998, 21–23). The same relationship extends to political terrorism. States in transition frequently have societal conditions conducive to extralegal means of demanding or producing political change, including political terrorism. The advancement of the development process provides an economic base and infrastructure conditions that may also foment crime when coupled with ineffective and corrupt police forces.

Transitions in societies are times of political and/or social upheaval. Instability unsettles society's structures even if the transition itself is not characterized by violence. New cleavages may appear, accompanied by increased lawlessness or corruption. Significant segments of society may have incomes insufficient to support themselves through legitimate means as their nation shifts from one economic base to another. State-funded social safety nets are minimal or absent under a traditional development rubric of austerity. Urbanization increases, yet jobs are scarce and cities lack adequate existing infrastructure to support the population shift. People are lost in societal cracks and left disenfranchised and desperate as old ways of life fade without any clear alternatives provided by the state or the market. Desperation may encourage political terrorism where there is little confidence in the intended result of successful transition and where there are only feeble mechanisms to check violence.

Class Conflict

Class conflict is another explanatory element of political terrorism. While many Latin American countries have experienced increased income over the last decade, income inequality remains higher here than in any other region of the world (Ocampo 1998). Few control the preponderance of power and resources within many of these societies. In most cases, paper currency translates to political currency, allowing the wealthy to be politically influential and marginalizing the overwhelming majority who are poor, working class, or lower class. Thus, masses who often subsist on less than a living wage and who lack basic necessities are left with a sense of impotence in a political system that denies them voice, representation, or equal control.

Political terrorism confronts these class iniquities, perceived or real. Through their acts, terrorists may seek to galvanize political support behind legal reforms, elections, parties, or even revolutionary measures that in some manner address the income and power disparities of society. Political terrorists in societies rife with class conflict may be seeking a redistribution of wealth and a reallocation of power, however crude their methods or poorly articulated their logic.

Political Culture and Machismo

Latin American political culture is often characterized as having strong elements of machismo, even today. In an environment traditionally dominated by men and where respect is earned through conspicuous bravery, expressions of heroic conquest, and decisive action, the methods of political terrorism may resonate with those frustrated by their ineffectiveness within state-sanctioned participatory political processes.

Political culture also represents the political norms, understandings, and mores of society. In Latin America, what may have started as an accident of history—the orchestrated use of violence to achieve either limited or total gain— now has had a certain legitimacy conferred upon it by success, repetition, and societal acceptance. Political terrorism in every corner of the world has been justified as the fight for freedom. Nowhere has that iconography been more celebrated than in the countries of such people as Simón Bolívar, Ché Guevara, Fidel Castro, and Hugo Chávez.

Scarce Resources and Overcoming the Zero-Sum Game

The scarcity of resources confronting some countries of Central and South America has rendered development considerably more problematic. A country with negligible natural endowments or comparative advantage in cash crops alone has no obvious economic base that can be cultivated and reaped for development income. Industrialization becomes nearly impossible because raw materials, finished goods, and skilled labor must all be imported. Democratization is complicated by this lack of natural wealth in two obvious ways. First, the expenses of reform cannot be met through the country's economic base, and second, a middle-class is slow to develop under such conditions.

Resource scarcity encourages an atmosphere conducive to political terrorism. In a struggle for survival, basic resources such as a reliable and potable water supply for drinking and irrigation can spur intense conflict, domestic and transnational. Desperate circumstances promote a competition for survival where the impoverished or those who are the object of systematic government discrimination forcefully take control of the few resources available. Politically, in a context of a stagnant or contracting economic pie, there are never enough pieces to hand out to those clamoring for more. The dilemma becomes a zero-sum game.

Failure to Deliver Social or Economic Reforms or Improvements

Reformist governments are elected because of their promises. Whether these promises are for economic or social improvement, or both, governments may find them difficult to deliver once presented with the complicated reality of bureaucracy, limited resources, entrenched corruption, and so on. The population, with naive expectations of the extent and immediacy of social or economic improvement, become disillusioned and disgruntled when reform fails to appear as quickly or as dramatically as promised and hoped.

Political terrorists may prompt a government that has become unfocused and mired in political infighting by adopting violently coercive means to demand delivery of promised reforms.[2] Or, losing complete faith, political terrorists may eliminate politicians or intimidate the population in order to materially affect election results or to pressure for new parties or politicians. There is an immediacy in the acts of terror that may be lacking from democratic reform, which is ponderous, slow, and burdensome.

Habit and Self-Perpetuating Cycles

Related to the argument that political culture may evolve to include a tacit acceptance or expectation of political terrorism in response to some government failure or political injury, political terrorism can become inculcated into political routine. It becomes "habit-forming" or, more aptly put, part of a self-perpetuating cycle where an act of political terrorism is met by violence that is then answered by more violence. It is an escalating spiral of action-reaction, often fed by official government response and policy.

Absence of Traditional Restraints: The Church and Religion

Last, traditional societal restraints are eroding as the historical influence of structuring mechanisms, such as the Roman Catholic Church, fade. The values instilled by pious acceptance of church teachings are no longer as inviolable and sacred as they once were. In fact, participation in the Catholic Church has greatly declined in recent decades as religious life reorients itself to secularism —or even Protestantism (Mott 2002, 56).

Political terrorists are no longer held in check by their own or society's strict adherence to church doctrine. Communities are less self-policing as each person's responsibility reorients to self-reliance rather than collective reliance. Political terrorists are no longer facing overwhelming community sanction for their violation of church and community standards. Or, they no longer care.

INSTANCES AND PATTERNS

Political terrorism's extensive reach and emerging patterns in Latin America have taken on frighteningly unprecedented proportions. Political violence is not limited to governmental, bureaucratic, or military targets. The poor, the disenfranchised, and the burgeoning middle classes have found themselves increasingly in the crosshairs of terrorists pursuing political change through the promotion of fear (Wilson 2002; Weiner 2002). The methodical evolution of the region's political terrorists suggests not only adaptation to modern circumstances but also a fundamental shift in relationship within and to the domestic and international communities.

Political figures are obvious targets for Latin America's terrorists desiring media attention and a changed political or legal order—for example, revolutionary political forces or opposition parties contesting elections. Politicians may be taken prisoner, or they may be eliminated. They are valuable pawns when trying to exact a prisoner exchange through negotiations with government officials, a tactic used by guerrilla fighters. As a show of power, as a means of leverage, or as an end itself through execution, politicians and government personnel have the most valence in a campaign of political terror. Latin America has witnessed each of these possible violations of politicians and government personnel.

Foreign investment and the operation of multinational corporations are adversely affected by the targeting of businesspeople. Political terrorists rely on kidnapping and terror's negative impact on the business environment as they fight anti-Western, antiglobalization, or antigovernment campaigns. While scant corporate or government reports are publicly available to confirm or refute the effectiveness of this strategy, and the anecdotal evidence is somewhat contradictory, it is apparent that in some cases shifting, hostile environments deter business. One report indicates that "in Honduras, a spate of kidnappings of Taiwanese nationals involved in business led to a threatened withdrawal of Taiwanese investment from the country" (Wilson 2002). In Ecuador and Colombia, terrorism of pipelines and kidnappings of business executives have hampered the development of the petroleum industry. However, the threat may be manageable: "Risks such as kidnapping or guerilla violence may grab the attention, but many investors say such risks are manageable. They are often more concerned by [ ] red tape, and by frequent changes to the 'rules of the game'" (Wilson 2001, 9).

Innocent people have long been the victims of political terror, either inadvertently or as punishment for cooperating with the "enemy." But the stigma against deliberately targeting civilians seems to have faded over the last several decades. Painful, ubiquitous examples of this bombard us from the Middle East, as suicide-bombers choose buses, markets, and cafés to earn their promised deliverance to heaven. Yet, political terror targeting average citizens occurs worldwide with sickening frequency. This is no less true in Latin America. As society evolves and modernity consumes nations, previous taboos, stigmas, and inhibitions are lessened. Alternatively, the sacrifice of innocent lives may be symbolically more poignant and meaningful in the minds of some political terrorists, and thus more attractive.

The face of terrorism has also been changing in recent decades. Members of Colombia's Fuerzas Armadas Revolucionaries Nacional (FARC) are now trained by former members of the Irish Republican Army (IRA) for hire; Iranians have been implicated in Argentina's anti-Jewish terrorism; and Brazil's Cosa Nostra-style favela gang lords are the rule of law and de facto police in urban slums, unafraid of using fear to block political efforts to reclaim power (Simpson 2003; Rohter 2003b). Yet, these are less surprising than the rumored but unconfirmed presence of al Qaeda sympathizers in quite a number of Latin American Arab communities (U.S. Department of State 2003, 66–67, 70). Each has changed the threat posed to the democratizing state by political terrorists.

In 2002, three former IRA members faced trial in Colombia, where they had been contracted by FARC to help train its members. An international terrorist network of groups with disparate aims cooperating through market-style transactions in order to hone their skills, methodology, and effectiveness in killing is a chilling concept. Such high levels of transnationalism were not a serious consideration until the extensive collaboration of various Islamic organizations under the direction of al Qaeda was brought to the attention of policymakers and media as part of the war on terror. The first style of cooperation represents a calculating solution for unemployed terrorists no longer receiving funding—they can become consultants, even "businessmen." The latter is more nefarious, presenting a greater threat to security—multiple organizations capable of reconciling differences in order to magnify their strength.

The favela slumlords of Brazil have, in many cases, managed to seize nearly complete control of the shanty towns' activities, including water supplies, electricity, and governance, to say nothing of drugs and crime. While their principle aim is profit through drug trafficking and racketeering, these mobster-style organizations use the tactics of political terror to first wrest control from the weak state and then to maintain it in the face of government or police attempts to retake the streets. The two most troubling aspects of this form of political terrorism are the totality of control, where even police and military forces hesitate to venture into the favelas, and the complete subordination of the favelas' people. Too often the denizens feel unable to report crime because of the ineffective police and judicial system; they are literally outgunned in any direct confrontation; and their political voice is squelched by thugs who manipulate votes through bribery and violence.

These criminals are generally better trained and equipped than the police forces that are meant to stop them. More than likely, they are also better paid. Their material advantages are coupled with an inhumane disregard for life, much like violent crime's ghettoization in U.S. urban centers. In Latin America and particularly Brazil, state infrastructure is so critically underdeveloped that gang lords have also learned to disdain the state's authority. Thus, political terrorism is used as a method to preserve little more than rule over an impoverished fiefdom.

Just about every country in Latin America has a sizable Arab community. These are diverse nations with multiethnic populations; all the countries of the area are involved in international trade, cultural, and other activities. Rumors (so far unconfirmed) of al Qaeda's presence in South America surfaced in 2002 and should not be unexpected. The State Department included this in its annual report on global terrorism released in 2003, but the report specifically states that no evidence supporting the rumor has been discovered to date (U.S. Department of State 2003, 66–67, 70). It would not be surprising to learn that cells or sympathizers are operating in Latin America, especially in Mexico, the Caribbean, and the so-called Tri-Border Area (TBA), where the borders of Brazil, Argentina, and Paraguay come together in a wild, lawless, contraband-oriented frontier. The al Qaeda network is better connected and more dispersed than first believed in late 2001. The organization has a confirmed presence in nearly every region of the world, except (so far) Latin America. Weak police forces and sizable black market economies would provide an environment where illicit activities could pass relatively unnoticed.

The presence of al Qaeda or its sympathizers would challenge democratization efforts both directly or indirectly. Al Qaeda may choose to target South or Central American governments that have substantial ties to the United States. However, the indirect threat to democratization comes from possible intervention by the United States. If Latin American countries were unable to divert sufficient resources to detecting and arresting al Qaeda elements, the United States would surely pursue the matter with its own forces. The diversion of critical resources and the likely decline of civil liberties as security powers increased, coupled with a desire to protect state sovereignty, would stymie and potentially reverse some democratization efforts in the region. These actions would have particularly devastating effects on democracy in transitional and weakly institutionalized countries.

TERRORISM IN LATIN AMERICA

Colombia confronts the greatest enemy force as it attempts to democratize. It struggles against political and narcoterrorists (often the same groups) that defy the state at all costs in order to protect their dominion, as political goals become lost in profit seeking. Brazil's beautiful beaches and pristine stretches of rainforest cannot erase its infamy for kidnappings, both the political and the purely criminal. Nor can the government's inability to police urban slums be overlooked as a pressing test of government sovereignty and viability. The TBA is particularly lawless. It is known as a fund-raising center for Hezbollah and Hamas as well as a safe haven for fugitives fleeing prosecution in the Middle East for terrorist acts. The TBA must be purged of its foreign terrorists before it becomes a staging ground for domestic and international acts of terror.

Colombia

Colombia's fight against terrorism is forcing criminals to move their operations to neighboring countries, creating transnational crime rings as well as diplomatic tensions among nations and, in effect, spreading the reach of terrorism. They easily cross borders to prey on Venezuelan cattle ranchers and Ecuadorian oil workers. And no location is sacrosanct; the country's guerrillas attack anywhere, including restaurants and churches (Wilson 2002). From powerful cartels to an alphabet soup of purportedly revolutionary groups, Colombia's terrorists illustrate the spectrum of motivational forces and causal factors listed earlier: ineffective government, zero-sum politics, etc. FARC is one of the most visible antigovernment forces in a country where the three largest terrorist organizations were responsible for thirty-five hundred murders in 2002 (U.S. Department of State 2003, 68).

FARC was born from La Violencia, Colombia's bloody civil war that started in 1948 and lasted into the 1960s. The Marxist-Leninist guerrilla group was organized under a mandate officially endorsing violence to foment revolution, seeking to change Colombia's political and social order through any means possible. Disenfranchisement and a failure by the government to deliver social and economic goods initially spurred the group to action during a particularly tough span of time in the state's transition to democracy. The intervening decades have made FARC something of a state institution, negotiating or competing with the government and certainly illustrating the force of habit and self-perpetuating cycles.

Like many other terrorist organizations, FARC lost funding with the collapse of the cold war, creating an income crisis (Odell 2001; Dao 2002). Members turned to kidnapping and drug trafficking to meet this income deficiency. Somewhat counterintuitively and equally intriguingly, many of FARC's kidnappings do not carry a political meaning per se (Sater 1985, 115–16, 120). They are fund-raising activities. Even when not undertaken for monetary gain, FARC's activities have equally pragmatic explanations. For example, the group targeted Rudolph Guiliani during a trip to Mexico, where the former New York City mayor had been contracted to help that country fight crime. The Colombian terrorists possibly feared Guiliani because his efforts, if successful, would have disrupted the drug pipeline running through Mexico to the United States.

In today's world, FARC at times acts as a subcontractor to drug lords, providing protection for their fields and their distribution networks (Celona and Lisi 2002). The common purpose of dislocating the Colombian government has caused a strange and uneasy union between the drug lords and FARC (and other revolutionary groups), though the gulf between their ultimate goals is vast. Other assessments contend that FARC lost any political fervor long ago and now traffics in narcotics from greed (Dao 2002).

In another example, Ingrid Betancourt, a Colombian politician and presidential candidate, was kidnapped. She stood in opposition to the forces of rebel groups such as FARC and institutionalized government corruption. During her campaign for the Colombian presidency, she was fervently delivering her message to the people. On February 24, 2002, FARC forces captured her as she traveled on a campaign trip to San Vincente del Caguan (Galeano 2002). FARC demanded the release of government-imprisoned members in exchange for the release of Betancourt and five other politicians being held by the group.

This illustrates FARC's capacity to successfully hold the government hostage. The senator was warned against traveling to the town by the government, but the government refused her request for armed escort once she was advised of the risk (Galeano 2002). The entwined links of disenfranchisement and underdevelopment motivate FARC, which chooses to couch its opposition rhetoric in Marxist terms even if its zest for revolution has ebbed in favor of profit.

Brazil

As is typical of the region, many political crimes in Brazil go unsolved, despite efforts by police forces, even the uncorrupted. Brazil's staggering poverty and inability to capably harness its resources have resulted in several dramatic changes in government. However, the promises of Brazilian government have often been particularly unrealistic, fueling terrorism and feeding crime. Exaggerated class conflict separates society into racial and economic groups. These cleavages, coupled with the transitional nature of the state, result in an atmosphere ripe for terrorism. Police forces are ill equipped to restrain these forces.

Typifying the most common terrorist threat to the state and among the unsolved political crimes in Brazil is the kidnap and murder of Celso Daniel in January of 2002. Daniel was mayor of Santo Andre, a São Paulo suburb. An innovator, he was engaged in efforts to form an economic system based on social justice rather than on capricious market whims. He was an intellectual and founding member of the Worker's Party (PT). Had he survived, he would have been a member of the presidential administration formed after the election of Luis Inacio "Lula" da Silva. Praise came even from UN Secretary General Kofi Annan, who specifically lauded Daniel for his creative, visionary projects (Rocha 2002).

The death of Daniel was the work of oppositional political forces within Brazil. There had been five other shooting deaths of PT members during the previous two years, and Daniel was the second mayor to die. Other mayors were similarly threatened. Many of the latter threats came from a previously unknown group identifying itself as either the Revolutionary Armed Forces of Brazil or the Brazilian Revolutionary Action Front. This series of crimes sparked fears among Brazilians that more lawless days had returned. Concerned citizens worried that elections might be adversely affected or the outcome altered by violence. This, in fact, was the purpose of the terrorist: they were attacking the socialist PT for having adopted more moderate politics in their fight to reallocate power in Brazil (Downie 2002).

Daniel is only one among many victims. Particularly challenging Brazil's antiterror efforts are the ineffectiveness and corruption of police forces. This is well illustrated through the crusade and ultimate death of investigative reporter Tim Lopes. Lopes died trying to expose crime where state forces fear to go—the favelas.

Lopes was a journalist whose messianic anticrime stance ensured his popularity with the people. He was best known for the extreme lengths he would go to in order to get a story, most often captured on hidden camera and microphone. Lopes's final investigation came after a request for help from residents of the Favela da Grota, a slum of Rio de Janeiro. Having sought police help and receiving none, residents were desperate to reclaim some local authority, especially over the weekend dance parties that had turned into open-air drug markets and where young girls were assaulted with impunity. Residents believed that if their story was seen on television, authorities would be unable to ignore it any longer (Rohter 2002). In fact what they sought was government reclamation of the "parallel state" that had developed in the Favela da Grota, a transformation overtaking many favelas and increasingly middle-class neighborhoods as well (Bellos 2002).

Lopes was captured and beaten by the crime syndicate controlling the neighborhood while residents closed their windows and blinds against his cries (Bellos 2002). Later, Lopes was tortured and killed and his remains burned in order to protect the activities of a local gang leader. Had Lopes not been such a popular figure, his death might have gone unpunished. The gang leader who ordered and participated in Lopes's death had stood trial for murder before, but he was released on a writ of habeas corpus after police officers scheduled to deliver crucial testimony against him failed to appear in court (Rohter 2002). But Lopes's murder provoked demonstrations in Rio. They were answered by the state with the capture of Elias "Maluco" Pereira da Silva (leader of the Red Command crime gang), temporarily dispersing one syndicate.

The Triborder Area

The TBA, encompassing the juncture of Argentina, Brazil, and Paraguay, epitomizes the threat to national and international security posed by political terrorists in weak states. Because of the TBA's weakened infrastructure and underqualified or corrupted police forces, terrorists have been able to seek refuge in the region for years. Fleeing crimes in nations as far away as Israel and Egypt, these terrorists escape prosecution and are able to continue to aid their organizations. Argentina, Brazil, and Paraguay, working with the United States, have adopted formalized efforts to cooperate in the capture of terrorists, shut down Hezbollah and Hamas fund-raising, and eliminate trafficking in forged documents and stolen goods (U.S. Department of State 2003, 70); however, in this semilawless environment, such cooperative measures are hard to implement.

Terrorists in the TBA are not targeting Latin American governments, per se. But they are identifying, cultivating, and fomenting support for their causes, including within Latin America's Arab communities. Some of these terrorists have been linked to crimes against Israeli targets within the region, such as the 1992 bombing of Israel's embassy in Buenos Aires and the 1994 bombing of a Jewish community center in the same city (Associated Press 2002; Rohter 2003a). Criminal acts are being supported directly and indirectly from the presence of these terrorists. That such acts of terror will not remain confined to international targets but could turn domestic is a reasonable worry. From the perspective of the United States, this area could easily become the staging ground for al Qaeda.

U.S. AND LATIN AMERICAN RESPONSES

The preponderance of Latin America's policy response to crime, including political terrorism, has endorsed increased police and military action, often coupled with a zero-tolerance rule—that is, no negotiating with terrorists and no recognition of certain political opposition. There are two main thrusts to the counterterrorism policy debate. The first group observes that increased military and police action has not proven very effective and suggests that new tactics need to be adopted, such as greater social programs, more jobs, economic development, and a better distribution of wealth. The second policy paradigm endorses an increase in military and police action. Proponents believe that military and police action have been less effective than needed and less effective than what they could be due to insufficient troop numbers and a lack of tactical aggressiveness. There is an official recognition that troops and police are most often poorly outfitted, motivated, and trained. As ancillary policy, appropriate remedy of these factors would be necessary (Neto 2003).

Not surprisingly, each camp supports the redress of certain key social and economic indicators within society, although those discrediting increased military and police action emphasize this more emphatically. Almost unanimously, the benefit to the state of economic and social development in eliminating political terrorism is recognized. Both sides of the bifurcated counterterrorism policy debate underscore the importance of prescriptive measures for treating the underlying causes of terrorism—chief among them the seven factors listed earlier. The debate surrounding an increase or status quo of police and military action is interesting and relevant; however, increases in police and military budgets and counterterror activities, in any strength or number, cannot stand alone to eliminate political terrorism or prevent it.

The U.S. response to political terrorism in Latin America has largely hinged on its identification of an economic injury to itself or of a strategic interest, usually related to security or to the overall war on terrorism. Where neither of the aforementioned are clearly identifiable, the United States seems content to deem the matter a domestic affair and not of grave importance. Frankly, the United States has not paid attention to terrorism in Latin America, or to the region in general. When the converse is true, the United States has engaged in different levels of cooperative action mainly with governments. For instance, the United States has sent intelligence and military personnel to the region to aid in the fight against Colombia's narcoterrorsits. The United States has also entered into formal agreements, as in that mentioned above with Argentina, Brazil, and Paraguay, in order to tackle crime in the TBA.

The United States is redefining its approach to cooperation and its policing rights in international politics at the moment, due to both the ideological
inclinations of the current administration and the dramatic illustrations of its
own vulnerability to political terrorism. The outcome of a policy inclination that
favors unilateral action and a Manichaean understanding of the world is not
entirely clear, but some guesses may be hazarded.

The United States is evidencing an inclination for more aggressive direct
intervention. It has more than once sent "observers" or "advisors abroad" who
were in fact actively engaging in conflicts. Considering the evolving needs of security, the current administration, and the political climate in the United States,
low-profile but active engagement will likely continue. This will be especially
true of the TBA and other regions with concentrated Arab communities suspected of militant links. The preference for military operations will remain the
focus of the United States while the underlying causes will not be addressed
unless done so under unrelated and generally uncoordinated aid programs.

U.S. invasion of a country or overthrow of a government is not unprecedented
in Latin America, and any international objections to such an operation do
not appear capable of preventing the United States from embarking on such
a course. However, at the moment, no rift between the United States and any
Latin American government seems vast enough to warrant serious consideration
of regime change or invasion in Latin America. Moreover, the consequences
of U.S. military intervention—such as currently occurring in Afghanistan and
Iraq—in nationalistic and politically volatile and sensitive Latin America are
incalculable.

CONCLUSION

Political terrorism is a grave threat to the democratization as well as the development process in Latin America. While it does not have the power or momentum in most countries to derail the process entirely, fighting terrorism drains
resources and strains government relations within communities as well as
causes war weariness among the people. It adds to the divisions and tensions of
already deeply divided countries. Such tensions tugging at democratization are
contributing to the decline of its appeal to Latin Americans generally. Specifically, dissatisfaction may be slowing progress by manifesting itself in frequent
administration overturn, interrupting policy continuity, diminishing government
effectiveness and ability to deliver social and economic policies, and alienating
people from a political system hinged on enfranchisement and participation,
especially in its earliest stages.

To precisely quantify the damage political terrorism wreaks in countries undergoing political transitions yet facing constant danger is difficult, if not impossible. There are too many losses that are poorly quantifiable. Clearly, however, political terrorism is sufficiently threatening to already fragile societies and governments to more than justify prioritizing it in policy and practice. Current policy has focused, though obliquely at times, on rehabilitating societies and economies by increasing people's levels of social and human development. Policy has also been hampered by debates surrounding the identification of optimal military and police measures to eliminate terrorists and their accomplices. While the answer to this question is important, it could unduly focus governments on counterterrorism measures that are incomplete and thus doomed for failure because they do not holistically remedy the actual causes of political terrorism.

While there are several key variables within these societies that contribute to the rise of political terrorism in Latin America, societies in transition are by definition liminal in some ways. Unfortunately, liminality in Latin America most often equates to weak and unstable transitions to democracy. There is class conflict, creating nearly irreparable cleavages in some cases. These cleavages are based most frequently on the failure of governments to deliver meaningful and substantial economic and social reform, often needed to redress egregious power and income inequalities.

History has played a role by delivering larger-than-life liberators into societies colored by machismo and a political culture that idolizes freedom fighters. Scarce resources for development and their unequal distribution provides a catalyst for the volatile face-off of the impoverished, marginalized, or greedy against the ownership class (government or otherwise), who are the economic as well as the political elite. Traditional society and ways of life, centered so strongly in modern times around faith and devotion within the structure of the Catholic Church, is reorienting to modernity and the secularism it brings to many places. Finally, to a certain degree, political terrorism has become habit or party to a self-perpetuating cycle in many countries. Terrorism is established as the way to effect change or to demand recognition. Its violence is most often met by equal or greater government violence, where tit for tat is inculcated into generations as reasonable policy.

Emerging patterns of terrorism in Latin America now join the already well-documented permutations seen in other areas in recent decades. They include transnational cooperation among disparate groups, entrenched criminality that may eclipse state authority, and diffusion of Middle Eastern terrorism and possibly the al Qaeda network to this far-off region. These patterns represent the never-ending evolution of terrorism and the greatest threat from political terrorism to domestic and international security.

Response has centered around two principle needs in policy: an effective means of capturing terrorists or otherwise physically restraining terrorism, and the mending of societal and economic woes in order to prevent the production of terrorists or an environment conducive to their creation. The former, while critical, will never be able to halt terrorism, so the latter is in that sense more important. To these two factors we would add what seems to be the most critical factor: the need for effective, democratic, pluralist governance, itself difficult in transitional societies.

The United States has chosen to engage itself in aiding Latin America only when there has been a substantial economic interest in doing so or a clear strategic interest, most frequently the latter. In the ever-changing world, the United States will most likely come to engage more actively and aggressively in aiding its southern neighbors. The world is more interdependent than ever, and the United States has its strongest ties to Latin America in history. Moreover, through immigration, culture, trade, tourism, oil, and natural gas, to say nothing of drugs and crime, we are also more interdependent with Latin America than ever before. But there is another consideration that currently preoccupies much of Washington's policy: the global war on terrorism. The war on terror, much like the war on drugs of the 1980s and 1990s, could bring armed intervention from the United States if al Qaeda's presence is proved true and the Latin American states are unable to respond to U.S. satisfaction.

The truest test of transitional Latin American states can be found in the formidable task to democratize in an environment fraught with political terrorism. Proof of Latin America's ability to do so will be found in its ability to identify and adopt effective, responsible, and feasible means of coping with the challenge.

NOTES

1. Observations based on 2002 data compared to 1996 data from table 1 in *Economist* (2002). Article also included on the Latinbarómetro Web site, www.latinobarometro.org While data is available from the site only by subscription, it provides materials that refer to the results of the organization's surveys.

2. Colombia comes clearly to mind. El Salvador, Guatemala, and, in earlier decades, Cuba are other examples.

REFERENCES

Associated Press. 2000. "Pakistani Is Arrested in Argentina Attacks." *New York Times*, August 19, p. A3.

Auerbach, Ann Hagedorn. 1998. *Ransom: The Untold Story of International Kidnapping.* New York: Henry Holt and Company.

Bellos, Alex. 2002. "Brutal Death Sours Cup Joy." *Observer,* July 7, p. 3.

Celona, Larry, and Clemente Lisi. 2002. "Colombia Terrorists Plotted Rudy Kidnap." *New York Post,* December 7, late city final edition, p. 2.

Dao, James. 2002. "The War on Terrorism Takes Aim at Crime." *New York Times,* April 7, sec. 4, p. 5.

Downie, Andrew. 2002. "Brazil Fears Death Squads' Return." *Scotland on Sunday,* January 27, p. 24.

Economist. 2002. "The Latinobarometro Poll: Democracy Clings on in a Cold Economic Climate." Print edition, August 17.

Galeano, Javier. "Guerrillas Kidnap Colombian Candidate." *Toronto Star,* February 25, p. 12.

Neto, Paolo de Mesquita. 2003. "Crime and the Threat to Democratic Governance in Latin America." In *Crime and the Threat to Democratic Governance,* ed. Allison M. Garland, Heather A. Golding, Meg Ruthenurg, and Joseph S. Tulchin, 33–41. Washington, D.C.: Woodrow Wilson International Center for Scholars.

Ocampo, José Antonio. 1998. "Income Distribution, Poverty and Social Expenditure in Latin America." Paper presented at the First Conference of the Americas, held by the Organization of American States in Washington on March 6, 1998. www.eclac.cl/publicaciones/SecretariaEjecutiva/3/lcg2033/ocampo65.htm.

Mott, Margaret MacLeish. 2002. "Democracy in the Catholic South: Iberia and Latin America." In *Comparative Democracy and Democratization,* ed. Howard J. Wiarda, 37–58. Fort Worth: Harcourt College Publishers.

Odell, Mark. 2001. "Colombia, Mexico, Brazil Hot Spots for Kidnappings." *National Post,* April 23, p. E3.

Prilliman, William C. 2003. "Crime, Democracy, and Development in Latin America." Policy Papers on the Americas, Volume 14, Study 6. Washington, D.C.: CSIS Americas Program.

Rocha, Jan. 2002. "Daniel Celso: Key Brazilian Urban Reformer." Obituary. *Guardian,* February 5, p. 20.

Rohter, Larry. 2003a. "Argentine Judge Indicts 4 Iranian Officials in 1994 Bombing of Jewish Center." *New York Times,* March 10, p. A3.

———. 2003b. "Rio Journal: At Your Great Peril, Defy the Lords of the Slums." *New York Times,* June 28, p. A4.

Sater, William F. 1985. "Terrorist Kidnappings in Colombia." In *Terrorism and Personal Protection,* ed. Brian M. Jenkins, 113–28. Boston: Butterworth Publishers.

Simpson, John. 2003. "Why Money Is Potent Weapon in Hunt for CIA Men in Colombia." *Sunday Telegraph,* February 23, p. 33.

U.S. Department of State. 2003. "Western Hemisphere Overview." Pp. 65–75 in *Patterns of Global Terrorism: 2002.* Annual report released April 2003 by the Secretary of State and the Coordinator for Counterterrorism. Department of State Publication 11038.

Weiner, Tim. 2002. "Notorious Kidnapper Arrested in Mexico, but Problem Rages On." *New York Times,* June 7, p. A5.

Wiarda, Howard J. Forthcoming. "Benign Neglect? American Foreign Policy Towards Latin America in the Post Cold War Era." In *Benign Neglect: American Third World Policies in the Post Cold War Era*, ed. Jürgen Rüland. Freiburg, Germany: M. E. Sharp.

Wilson, James. 2001. "Shifting 'Rules of the Game' Add to Colombia's Woes: Fiscal and Regulatory Uncertainty Is Proving as Big a Deterrent to Foreign Investors as Guerilla Activity." *Financial Times*, May 25, p. 9.

———. 2002. "Kidnapping Spreads across Latin America." *Financial Times*, November 29, p. 5.

23 Central America and Political Terrorism

The explosive emergence of revolutionary wars in Nicaragua, El Salvador, and Guatemala at the end of the 1970s surprised their long-standing, rightist military dictatorships, the U.S. government, and the leaders of the leftist revolutionary movements themselves. The United States viewed each war as a Soviet cold war challenge. This engendered a vast increase in U.S. media coverage and intense conflict within Congress and between it and the executive branch. A portion of that conflict involved debate over human rights abuses.

Terror played a large role in each war as well as in the ensuing counterrevolutionary war in Nicaragua, but there were significant differences from one country to the next. In El Salvador and Guatemala, truly massive numbers of noncombatants were killed. The great bulk of them were not killed by long-range artillery and bombing, or even cross fire. Euphemisms such as collateral damage, errant artillery shells, hiding behind civilian shields, or shot while trying to escape do not apply. In the main, civilian victims were shot or otherwise murdered at short range. The overwhelming majority of these deaths were at the hands of government forces, but the rebel groups also killed noncombatants. In Nicaragua, deaths from terror were lower but extensive. In the war against the Somoza family dictatorship, Somoza had his air force bomb urban areas. In the ensuing war against the Sandinista government, guerrilla forces (contras), organized and financed by the United States, regularly ambushed civilians they associated with the Sandinistas and attacked targets that were primarily civilian (such as farms or truckloads of people) where a small proportion of those being attacked did have arms (for protection against contra attacks). The Sandinistas committed violent abuses of human rights during each war, but the evidence does not show systematic abuse suggesting a policy, and at least some abusers were held accountable (America's

473

Watch 1985b; Betancur, Figueredo, and Buergenthal 1993; Historical Clarification Commission 1999).

The immediate effects of terrorism are, almost by definition, devastating. It's impact as a wartime strategy or tactic can be decisive, though it can and did have reverse or "blow-back" effects. Indeed, one could argue that in El Salvador, and to a lesser extent in Somoza's Nicaragua, terror was the last in a chain of causal agents that led opposition groups to wars to overthrow the government.

Despite the naked power of terror, many filters can, and are intended to, obscure the nature and extent of terrorism from those farther from the action. The perpetrators of terror in Central America wanted to eliminate enemies and send a message to potential enemies, but they also attempted to prevent others from seeing this or from identifying the perpetrators. And others farther from the action, even those with an interest in the wars, have their own motivations for not believing, minimizing, or ignoring reports about terror. Wars and battlegrounds and sites of terror are intensely local. By placing these wars within a cold war framework, the United States made them less local so that eventually the issue of human rights abuses became significant in the United States. Despite this, many filters still obscured the extent of terror. Even after the terror subsided in Central America and the wars ended, a contest has remained pitting those who want to reveal the extent of terror and hold protagonists accountable against those who wish to hide it to maintain impunity or wish to forget a painful past.

What were the roots of terror in these wars, and why was the terror so extensive? What role did it play in determining the outcome of the wars? How did terror and the rhetoric of terror affect the debate over Central America in the United States and the outcomes of the wars? What were the extents and consequences, both political and social, of terror? Are there lessons to be learned?

ROOTS OF TERROR AND REVOLUTION IN CENTRAL AMERICA

In each of the three countries, the depression of the 1930s led to deep economic crises and the onset of military rulers supported by the small number of economic elites (with fortunes mostly based on coffee growing and export) who had previously ruled directly, albeit in Nicaragua with fractiousness that had led to wars—wars in which the United States regularly intervened. Each was dominated by one military figure from the early 1930s until the end of World War II. Then their paths diverged.

Anastasio Somoza and, after his assassination in 1956, his sons continued a family dynasty in Nicaragua. In El Salvador, following some upheaval in 1944, an institutional military dictatorship replaced the regime of General Maximiliano Hernández Martínez, who had taken over in 1931. Guatemalans were able to supplant the military in 1944 with a remarkably peaceful revolution that led to two elected governments, both of reformist bent. But a CIA-organized coup in 1954 overthrew the Arbenz government, which had brought about an agrarian reform that affected lands that were not in production of the banana giant, the notorious United Fruit Company, and that had in its governing coalition (and close to President Arbenz) members of Guatemala's tiny Communist Party. The military took over and remained in power until 1985, and most would argue, for several years after that (Paige 1997; Baloyra 1982; Walter 1993; Dunkerley 1988; Gleijeses 1991; Handy 1984).

Each regime was repressive, but there were no human rights groups, such as emerged later, to attempt to measure the extent of repression. But in El Salvador and Guatemala in some periods, repression became so extreme that it could not be covered over.

In 1931, lightly armed peasants in Salvadoran coffee zones revolted. The revolt caused few deaths and, as it had been discovered before it erupted, was put down easily. Then the military, police, and landowners killed all suspects. Estimates range from eight thousand (by a police official in later years) to thirty thousand or, according to another estimate, one in every thirty-eight Salvadorans. The slaughter was limited to a few areas such that in these areas, entire male populations were wiped out (necessitating population shifts to provide a labor force) and the indigenous population of El Salvador was either eliminated or driven underground. Though there were a few short episodes of protest, El Salvador remained repressed for decades (Seligson and McElhinny 1996, 213; Durham 1979; Anderson 1971; Baloyra 1982; Montgomery 1995).

In Guatemala, the 1954 coup that destroyed the ten-year "springtime of democracy" brought repression and the deaths of several hundred political figures as well as a rapid rollback of the agrarian reform. Repression came in a much larger scale in the 1960s as the regime attempted to snuff out three small rural guerrilla groups in eastern regions with counterinsurgency help from the United States. Urban repression was directed at trade union leaders, student groups, teachers, and other leftist opposition figures and extended to political activists who would be considered centrist in most countries but were regarded as subversive in Guatemala. Urban repression included torture, murder, and either a public disposal of corpses or permanent disappearance—each calculated to send frightening messages (Jonas 1991; Handy 1984; Levenson-Estrada 1994). Thus, when protest grew rapidly in the late 1970s, there was ample precedent in El Salvador and Guatemala to respond with large-scale terror.

In the Somozas' Nicaragua, repression had been less dramatic. The family regime thought nothing of eliminating upstart peasants and members of the very small Sandinistas rebel party that had been in existence since the mid-1960s. However, Somoza coopted some potential opponents and even took some Sandinistas prisoner, a concept that remained alien to the Salvadoran and Guatemalan militaries for many years. In Nicaragua, non-Sandinista elite dissidents who did not call for radical social change got no more than short jail terms or a variety of economic sanctions. But in 1978, the regime exceeded this limit by assassinating Pedro Joachim Chamorro, a famous protesting newspaper editor and member of one of Nicaragua's most powerful elite families. Massive protests broke out; repression followed, as did battles and full-scale, though episodic, civil war (Black 1981; Dunkerley 1988).

WHY THREE CONTIGUOUS, SIMULTANEOUS REBELLIONS?

A spate of guerrilla groups around Latin America, inspired by, and to a much lesser extent supported by, the Cuban revolution had pretty well died out by the early 1970s, defeated by increased counterinsurgency capacities in Latin American militaries and by the failure of leftist groups to spark rebellion. Castro had caught the United States by surprise when he successfully confronted a rotten, corrupt military opponent. By the early 1970s, it looked as though there would be no more leftist revolutions in Latin America, particularly after the 1973 overthrow of Salvador Allende in Chile, who followed the "other" road to socialism through the ballot box. The coup there was followed by the torture and disappearance of thousands. In the second half of the decade, the Argentine military conducted its "dirty war" that proved to be devastatingly effective against the two leftist rebel groups.

But then the three wars in Central America broke out. Why? Repression and terror are part of the explanation, but only part. In El Salvador, the slaughter in 1931–32 brought a virtual end to radical protest for decades. The repression following the 1954 coup in Guatemala not only fulfilled then U.S. Secretary of State John Foster Dulles's desire that there be no communists in the government (and none to this day) but prevented any form of rebellion for a decade. Terror worked. On the other hand, it had contrary effects. The killing of the editor Chamorro sparked a civil war. Guatemalan and Salvadoran practitioners of state terrorism might have concluded that Somoza used too little terror. However, the fact is that rebellion had broken out in all three countries by 1979, the year in which Somoza fell, so higher levels of terrorism had not been sufficient to prevent violent rebellion, and, indeed, by eliminating all other forms of protest and even escape, terror could also be said to be a cause of the wars. It added fuel to the fire of rebellion. But it is insufficient as an explanation.

The analysis of the Republican right in the United States was that the revolutionary wars were a cold war product—proxy guerrilla armies encouraged and supported by the USSR and its client Cuba. In the cold war game, three neighboring countries had been selected to maximize the domino effect. When confronted with facts about lack of democracy and deep poverty, the Republicans argued that those conditions existed in dozens of countries where there was no rebellion. This explanation glossed over why the USSR would "target" three poor, small countries with few natural resources.

The three countries each had very long-standing dictatorships, almost no experience in democracy, and histories of repression. They were not "soft" political dictatorships, though some might make that case for Somoza. This meant that significant political change had not been possible. The one exception was in democratic Guatemala during 1944–54, and that exception proved the rule. All three had economies centered in two to four export crops controlled by a small number of large growers. In the 1960s, the new land-hungry export was beef, largely to feed new national burger chains in the United States. Each country had large peasant populations whose already poor life chances rapidly diminished as a result of expansion of lands for export products as well as population growth. Debt, competition with powerful landed elites, and intimidation forced peasants off the land or onto ever-smaller parcels. As a result, more fell into the migrant labor market, in turn creating downward pressure on wages. In virtually all third world countries, urban economies have not expanded rapidly enough to absorb rural labor forces, but in Central America urban economies were particularly small, despite expansion of manufacturing as a percent of GNP in the 1970s. Migration had not become a realistic option. Actually, it had for a time in El Salvador, the country with the highest population density, but a war between Honduras and El Salvador in 1969 had forced tens of thousands of Salvadorans out of Honduras and back into El Salvador. No other countries in Latin America had such extremely combustible mixes of persistent dictatorship, pervasive repression and selective to widespread terror, increasing land shortages and migratory labor, and tiny urban economies (Paige 1975, 1997; Durham 1979; Dunkerley 1985, 55; Dunkerley 1988, 169–218; Williams 1986; Wickham-Crowley 1992).

EARLY WAR YEARS IN CENTRAL AMERICA: LARGE-SCALE TERROR

The Central American wars may be thought of in two stages. First were initial leftist assaults on power. In Nicaragua, this phase led to an overthrow of the Somoza regime in 1969. In El Salvador it led to stalemate by 1984 and in Guatemala to a strategic, though not total, defeat of the left. Second were wars of attrition in each country in which "selective terror" played different, brutal roles aimed at eroding the institutional capacity of the enemy.

Nicaragua

In Nicaragua in the 1970s, the Sandinistas had not been wiped out, but their numbers were small and their military capacity even smaller. They had occasional capacity for a spectacular foray, but those served mainly to gain visibility and to free some of their leaders from prison. However, the Somoza regime was weakening, though this became apparent later. Pervasive corruption had become ever more naked after Somoza's military, the National Guard, openly stole relief goods airlifted into the country after a devastating earthquake hit Managua in 1972 and after firms controlled by Somoza vacuumed up lucrative reconstruction contracts financed by international donors. Unlike the other Central American countries with small economic elites, one family controlled a large, rapidly expanding portion of Nicaragua's economy. Everybody knew that the Somoza family had built its economic empire through its control of the military and the state. Blatant theft enriched, and undermined, the regime.

Thus, opposition to Somoza came also from elites. But elites were divided; some had made alliances with Somoza or a variety of compromises. The assassination of the newspaper editor Chamorro in early 1978 led to broad-scale protests, repression, battles, and war. The Sandinistas alone had been calling for an overthrow for more than a decade. They were the best organized with the most military experience and so took leadership.

As Somoza's military position weakened, he responded with terror. His air force bombed urban civilian areas, and the National Guard took few prisoners. But even though the National Guard was winning some of the battles, adherents flocked to the rebels in many parts of the country—too many for the rather small army (some twelve thousand) to contain. The bombing and the ruthlessness of the National Guard, on balance, seemed to have worked to the advantage of the rebels by creating outrage and further rebellion. So too did Somoza's isolation from large numbers of Nicaragua's most important traditional families with elite roots in the nineteenth century. (The Somoza family origins were modest; the route to power in the 1920s originated with the U.S.-organized National Guard.)

During the Sandinistas' war against Somoza, the U.S. role was decisive in that it did not send in troops to determine the outcome, in sharp contrast to its near-constant military interventions in Nicaragua during the first thirty years of the century. Somoza and his staunch backers in the U.S. Congress felt betrayed by President Carter. Carter had elevated human rights to an important diplomatic element in his foreign policy. U.S. criticism of Somoza had led to substantial reductions in military aid, which had peaked in 1975 at $4.2 million. Under Carter it fell to $400,000 in 1978 and $10,000 in 1979. Once war broke out, the United States attempted to broker solutions that initially attempted to modify Somoza's behavior and preserve the National Guard but eventually called for his removal. At all points, the U.S. positions lagged behind events. The United States attempted to keep the Sandinistas out of any interim government until what turned out to be a few weeks before Somoza's fall, when the United States suggested but one Sandinista to be in an interim junta. For their part, the Sandinistas (and Castro) were careful to have their arms come from non-Cuban anti-Somoza quarters. When Somoza fell in July 1979, he and his allies fled with everything he could steal, leaving but $3 million in the national treasury. The war was enormously destructive—some twenty-five thousand were killed. A UN report predicted that the country, under the best of circumstances, would take ten years to recover to prewar GNP per capita levels. Nicaragua was not to enjoy the "best of circumstances" (Millet 2002; Black 1981; Booth 1985; Christian 1985).

Guatemala

In Guatemala, rebellion grew in the latter half of the 1970s, both in urban and regional trade unions and by reformed and new guerrilla groups. The guerrillas, unlike those of the 1960s, emphasized clandestine political organizing in the Mayan highlands to build a political base and to recruit before attacking the regime. These indigenous groups suffered double and triple discrimination and had been repressed and dominated for nearly five centuries. Most of the rural poor were indigenous, and they made up the bulk of the rapidly increasing migratory workforce that annually descended to lower altitudes to harvest coffee and to the steaming coastal plains to harvest sugar and cotton. This migration was driven by forms of semiforced labor through landlord loan sharking and even vagrancy laws held over from earlier decades. Labor relations on plantations for the permanent workforce were described as semi-feudal (Handy 1984; Black 1984; Paige 1997; Jonas 1991; Dunkerley 1988; Levenson-Estrada 1994).

Unlike Nicaragua, there were no class divisions among Guatemala's economic elite, and unlike El Salvador, there was a military with recent experience in waging brutal counterinsurgency campaigns. Unlike both countries, there was abundant racism against the very large minority (and by some calculations majority) Mayan population that had survived culturally (with twenty-one languages, distinctive weaving, indigenous religion syncretized with Catholicism, and forms of social organization such as the *cofradia*, or village council of elders) despite catastrophic demographic depletion and subjugation. Beginning in the sixteenth century, rebellion from Mayan ranks generated fear among the power elite and repression on a scale that made the 1960s counterinsurgency repression mild by comparison. Guatemalan military figures later referred to this 1980s campaign as the second conquest of the Mayans.

Caught by surprise at the extent to which three different guerrilla groups had organized in the highlands and had commenced attacking, the military launched scorched earth campaigns, burning crops and hundreds of villages, and under two different governments—that of military dictator Romeo Lucas Garcia and his brother Benedicto, and then in 1982 by the government of Efraín Rios Montt, also from the military, who took over after claiming to have been defrauded by another military faction in the March 1982 "elections." Rios Montt saw himself as an anticommunist evangelical reformer who, in his own eyes, mitigated the excesses of Lucas Garcia with programs such as "beans for bullets," building controlled villages, and forming "voluntary" civil action patrols under the thumbs of military commanders. In essence, Rios Montt continued the same scorched earth campaign as his predecessor.

By the end of 1983, the three guerrilla forces, which had united under a coalition of the Guatemalan National Revolutionary Unity (URNG) had suffered a strategic defeat. The military's central weapon was terror—burning villages, massacring inhabitants, and forcing villagers to name (and in some cases kill) supposed guerrilla sympathizers. The military drove remaining guerrillas into very remote areas and hundreds of thousands of refugees into other areas of Guatemala and Mexico. The URNG civilian support base was destroyed. The URNG held on, however. The military never was able to inflict a final defeat, and the war stretched on at much reduced levels until 1996 (Handy 1984; Jonas 1991; Schirmer 1998).

The U.S. role during the Carter administration was roughly parallel to what it had been in Nicaragua. Carter administration criticisms of human rights led to large reductions in military aid. Then the Guatemalan military received supplies and intelligence-gathering techniques from Israel. The Reagan administration was unable to convince Congress to restore aid, even after President Reagan asserted that Rios Montt was getting "a bad rap" on human rights. Guatemala became a minor theme in the Washington debate on Central America, but this was in part due to the reverses suffered by the guerrillas. The Guatemalan military effectively sealed off the worst zones of scorched earth policy from prying eyes for some years.

El Salvador

In the early 1960s, El Salvador began a modest liberalization. Three center and center-left political parties were allowed to compete in local elections and for seats in the rather toothless national legislature. They had some success. By 1972, those parties coalesced to challenge for the presidency. By all accounts, save those of the military, the civilian ticket won, but when the sun came up the next morning the military had construed the ballot count to show that its candidate (a relatively moderate military figure) had won. The military repeated this electoral fraud in 1977, but this time its candidate was a hard-liner, because his predecessor had incurred the wrath of extreme elements among the landed elite by proposing a very small-scale agrarian reform to address the severe land shortages and thereby avoid social explosion.

These fraudulent elections and the growing land crisis led many who had sought reform through elections to abandon electoral politics in favor of participation in new militant grassroots organizations that made demands for better services and higher wages. Protest grew. Three small guerrilla groups also formed and had various ties to the grassroots organizations. Some of the guerrilla groups kidnapped wealthy businesspeople for ransom and in a few cases killed them.

The government responded with increasing repression, and leaders of the grassroots organizations began to disappear. The Carter administration also leveled criticism at the Salvadoran government, but repression did not abate. The military rejected U.S. aid rather than comply with human rights standards, but the Carter administration sent mixed signals when it supported several World Bank and Interamerican Bank loans. Then in mid-October 1979, just three months after the Salvadoran military and elites had witnessed the destruction of the Somoza regime, there was a coup within the military. The new seemingly reformist officers nominated an all-civilian left and center-left cabinet—not counting the minister of defense, who remained a hard-liner. However, the new government failed the litmus test posed by the militant opposition; it made no effort to investigate, much less bring to trial, those responsible for the disappearances and assassinations. They had numbered in the dozens for the first nine months of the year—please pause here to consider the meaning of this number by imagining several dozen political assassinations in an equivalent-sized political jurisdiction such as Massachusetts. But the following October, coup assassinations and disappearances escalated to several hundred in the last ten weeks of the year. The terror campaign was on.

In protest, the civilians resigned from the government. The same military figures appointed a new center-right cabinet at the beginning of 1980. There was another vast increase in assassinations, almost all of them targeting demonstrators, left or center-left figures or persons considered (by someone) to be sympathetic to the left, or persons who lived in neighborhoods or hamlets that were suspect. This new cabinet resigned after two months because well-known figures were being fingered on TV as communists and then assassinated in their homes. In early March, the military appointed a third cabinet, this one with the previously exiled Christian Democrat politician Napoleon Duarte (who had been defrauded in the 1972 election). Within days, the United States declared its support and, over the protests of the most prominent person in El Salvador, Archbishop Oscar Romero, also pledged a renewal of military aid. The new government instantly decreed a substantial agrarian reform (three hundred of the largest farms but not some smaller, more wealthy places in prime coffee territory) and nationalization of banks and of the marketing of coffee, all measures loathed by the far right. So the killing raged on, and before the end of March a death squad assassin murdered the archbishop during a mass. Then, days later, gunmen opened fire on a large crowd gathered to commemorate the archbishop.

By April, open protests virtually disappeared as grassroots organizers went underground, left in exile, moved to rural areas to join the guerrillas, or were killed. In a few months, the ranks of the five guerrilla groups had grown and the guerrillas united, more or less, into a coalition—the Farabundo Martí National Liberation Front (FMLN). El Salvador entered into civil war that continued to have massive levels of human rights abuses for the next three years (Montgomery 1995; Manwaring and Prisk 1988; Stanley 1996; Williams and Walter 1993; Binford 1996; Danner 1993; America's Watch and the American Civil Liberties Union 1982, 1984; Americas Watch 1984).

WHY THREE DIFFERENT OUTCOMES?

Unlike the case of the Sandinistas against Somoza, the left was not able to win in El Salvador. Unlike the case of Guatemala, with its own terror campaign against the left, the Salvadoran government, with a rather different sort of terror campaign, was not able to inflict a strategic defeat on the guerrillas (though it eliminated the largely unarmed urban protestors and organizers). Indeed, in 1983, despite optimistic public pronouncements by U.S. officials about the growing capacity of the Salvadoran military and the prospective demise of the guerrillas, declassified cable traffic indicates that the real view was that the war, from the U.S. perspective, was going very badly and indeed might be lost. Put simply, by 1984 (with the wars not over) one could say that the left had won (Nicaragua against Somoza), lost (Guatemala), and stalemated (El Salvador). Why? If rightist terror had won in Guatemala, why had it failed to win in Nicaragua and El Salvador?

One difference was the role of the United States. It was (more or less) neutral during the war against Somoza. Arguably, that enabled the Sandinistas to win. A mere nine months later, the United States weighed in with military aid in El Salvador—aid that rapidly mounted to extraordinary levels. Arguably, that prevented the FMLN from winning. But that does not explain Guatemala, which had received very little U.S. military aid since 1977 and no real increase once its war intensified.

Another line of argument focuses on the cohesion of the ruling classes. Somoza was like Batista in Cuba—a one-person kleptocracy dominated by a figure not from traditional elite families, who was backed by an equally corrupt, unloved military that had no practice in, or aptitude and aspiration for, fighting a war. In Cuba and Nicaragua, the elite was divided (with a long history of it in Nicaragua). In both, the regimes fell to insurgencies that swelled as victories were gained and as the regime stooped to lower and lower tactics, including terror. In El Salvador and Guatemala, by contrast, the guerrillas were not able to win, and U.S. military aid, or the lack thereof, the argument runs, had very little to do with it. Strong class cohesion of the coffee power elite in both countries meant that they were united in confronting the insurgency and unambiguous about taking what they saw as the necessary steps of "total war" to put it down (Wickham-Crowley 1992).

This explanation encounters three difficulties. It assumes that the elite was in perfect partnership or in control of the military. However, there is evidence of tensions between the coffee elite and the less privileged military (Stanley 1996). Second, if elite solidarity prevented leftist victories in El Salvador and Guatemala, why was it insufficient to produce an elite victory in El Salvador (or was it necessary *and* sufficient for one in Guatemala)? Third, though many (mostly conservatives) have critiqued the efficaciousness of U.S. aid around the world, it beggars the imagination that massive U.S. aid poured into El Salvador was simply irrelevant. Though the Salvadoran elite themselves were not shy about criticizing the United States (for agrarian reform, for restrictions on military practices), none of them ever stood up and said, "Please stop sending the aid; we'd be better off without it."

Differential effects of terror may provide a partial additional explanation. Though Somoza was ruthless, the level of terror in that war was much lower. It was not clear at all for the first year that Somoza was going to lose. Terror clearly was devastating in Guatemala and El Salvador. There is considerable evidence in both countries that some elites were all for the terror and provided financing. In Guatemala, terror wiped out the support base of the guerrillas and forced potential rural recruits to the guerrillas (potential because of their indigenous and poverty-stricken state, but hardly automatic) to flee or to assume increasingly impossible neutrality and eventually join the "volunteer" civil patrols and the terror campaign (Stoll 1993).

Terror seemed to have different effects. In El Salvador, it did not seem to have reduced the ranks of the guerrillas and very likely increased them in two ways. First, as noted, some militant protestors left urban areas to join the guerrillas. Second, some peasants joined the guerrillas because the military had killed large numbers of their families. In interviews during and after the war, FMLN combatants related to me both types of narratives about how they decided to join the FMLN. I have not heard such stories from Guatemala from observers with long experience. Second, the Guatemalan military was perhaps more ruthless and more efficacious. Despite massive amounts of U.S. military aid, the Salvadoran military was less capable of pursuing the war in El Salvador, at least prior to 1985, than was the Guatemalan military. The latter had counterinsurgency military experience. El Salvador's sole military experience had been a two-week war against Honduras in 1969. It was simply completely unprepared for an extended guerrilla war. U.S. military advisors could not get the Salvadoran military to go on small night patrols or to forego large-scale invasions (requiring lots of equipment, food, etc., and therefore opportunities for graft) or prevent officers from driving the short distances to the capital city for weekends of parties. Also, Guatemala's terror was directed at whole villages, not small groups that were semiunderground in urban neighborhoods (Manwaring and Prisk 1988; Schirmer 1998; Williams and Walter 1993; Schwarz 1991; Waghelstein 2002).

On balance, terror worked against all three regimes by contributing to revolt. It did not save Somoza. In Guatemala, a vastly expanded rural terror campaign directed against indigenous villages and backed by a fairly experienced and extremely ruthless military succeeded, in part because of initial lack of international media attention. In El Salvador, a terror campaign, backed by an incompetent military, was sufficient to destroy urban protest but, if anything, aided recruitment to the guerrillas who were advancing more rapidly than their opponents, despite escalating terror, until the United States changed the balance of power in 1980–81 and then changed it again in 1984 with the infusion of troop-bearing helicopters. This led to stalemate.

TERROR IN THE U.S. WAR OF ATTRITION IN NICARAGUA

About half of Somoza's army escaped to Honduras. Soon the Argentine military and the CIA attempted to reorganize them to oppose the new Sandinistas. Argentina's rightist military dictatorship was in the later stages of its "dirty war" against two leftist urban guerrilla groups and began to see itself as the main continental pillar against communist subversion as it witnessed with alarm Carter's human rights doctrine and the victory of the Sandinistas. The Argentines were not purely ideological, however, as they also leapt to sell wheat to the USSR after the United States embargoed wheat sales in protest of the Soviet presence in Afghanistan (Armony 1997).

Reagan's election campaign called for the ouster of the Sandinistas ("another Cuba"), and then the new administration accused the Sandinistas of international terror—that meant shipping arms to the Salvadoran guerrillas, who had attempted a "final offensive" just before Reagan's inauguration. That led to efforts to aid the new "contra" groups fighting the Sandinistas as well as to forays into Nicaragua conducted by CIA paid "assets." And that, in turn, led to a battle with Congress that stretched on to the end of Reagan's second term and beyond. That contest had too many chapters to recount here, but three elements deserve mention (Armony 1997; Arnson 1993; Dillon 1991; Dickey 1985).

First, the contra army grew. Former Somoza National Guardsmen and their officers were joined by peasants, mostly from remote areas. Some were disaffected by Sandinista leftism or were subject to anticommunist propaganda. Others did not like Sandinista efforts to control agrarian markets or were not beneficiaries of the large agrarian reform program. Still others were forced to join or opted to join because in some regions neutrality became virtually impossible. The growth was made possible by increased U.S. funding that, at its peak in 1986, amounted to $100 million (light air craft, shoulder-held missiles, computer-based communication equipment), a sum in excess of the annual military budget of Honduras and twenty-five times the peak amount of aid the United States had given Somoza in any one year (Arnson 1993; Gutman 1988; Kornbluh 1988).

Second, at various times Congress placed restrictions over the amount and types of aid that could be provided, prohibiting until June 1986 lethal forms of military aid. It prohibited military aid and then lethal military aid and, early on, said the aid could only go to an effort to intercept arms going to El Salvador. (The contras never found any. Indeed, at one juncture, Salvadoran guerrillas claimed the contras were selling them arms!) Congress discovered at the end of 1986 that the Reagan administration had cheated on the earlier restrictions. This and the revelation of a secret arms sale to Iran led to the Iran-contra scandal, which, among other things such as indictments and jail terms, led to a vast reduction in aid to the contras, though never to a complete aid cutoff. The contras became passive, retreating to their bases in Honduras, but the economic drain on Nicaragua (combined with various forms of U.S. embargo) continued, as did the threat of never-ending war (Arnson 1993; Gutman 1988).

Third, the contras and the Sandinistas were accused of human rights abuses. In the main, the charges against the Sandinistas were for press censorship, unfair jailing without due process, or harassment of opposition rallies. However, the contras made repeated assaults on civilian targets and assassinations following ambushes. Many of these were documented by international human rights groups and, in interviews, even of the contras themselves, some of whom hardly seemed to realize that they had done something wrong. These abuses were sufficiently widespread to indicate a policy of attacking government workers or agrarian reform farmers. Efforts to police this by the contra command were so isolated and pathetic as to add to the argument that terror was policy. There is evidence that some U.S. personnel involved with the contras ignored abuses to keep scandal from public view. Indeed, the role of the United States in organizing the contras extended to a training manual written and supplied by the CIA that openly called for eliminating local Sandinista leaders (Americas Watch 1985a, 1985b, 1986; Arnson 1993; Dillon 1991; Dickey 1985; Cabestrero 1985; Chomsky 1985; Eich and Rincón 1985; Tayacán 1985; Brody 1985).

The contra abuses fed into the debate by those in Congress opposed to at least some of the forms of U.S. aid to the contras but did so in a relatively minor way. The main arguments Reagan opponents used were fear of getting dragged into another Vietnam or that providing arms to groups to overthrow another government violated international law. (However, Congress and the Reagan administration ignored the process and outcome of the case Nicaragua brought against them in the World Court.) The abuses and the Iran-contra scandal created political conditions that made it possible for Latin American diplomats and President Oscar Arias of Costa Rica to fashion the 1987 Central American peace treaty, the foundation stone of the three peace processes that would culminate in several years (Arnson 1993).

The attacks on unarmed Sandinista personnel made it virtually impossible to carry out government programs in rural areas, and military expenditures, abetted by considerable Sandinista mismanagement, led to near economic collapse, as evidenced by an approximate inflation rate of 30,000 percent in 1987. The threat that the United States would not cut off aid to the contras if the Sandinistas won the 1990 election was the main element in the electoral defeat of the Sandinistas by Violetta Chamorro, though Sandinista arrogance and the fact that the widow of Pedro Joachim Chamorro and mother of a family with partisans on both sides was the perfect candidate were important factors. The United States played a strong role in cobbling together her candidacy and unruly coalition. The devastating war of attrition had worked, and her victory brought the conflict to an end (Nuñez, Cardenal, et al. 1991).

EL SALVADOR'S WAR OF ATTRITION AFTER 1983 AND TERROR

With the election of Napoleon Duarte as president of El Salvador in March 1984, the debate in the U.S. Congress over increasing amounts of military and economic aid to El Salvador stopped (until 1990). That, in turn, led to qualitative increases in military aid and, most importantly, a large increase in helicopters to ferry troops. This then forced the FMLN to forego large, highly visible and damaging operations and to adopt small-unit tactics. Rather than hope that a large operation would spark insurrection, the FMLN shifted to a war of attrition with small-scale attacks on portions of the agro-export economy, transport, and power lines. Some of their units also waged war on small town elected mayors who accepted government sponsorship, in territories in which the FMLN was strong, to establish civilian patrols. The FMLN assassinated several mayors. In contrast to Guatemala, the patrol strategy failed. The FMLN strategy hoped that the enemy would wear down first, but the enemy had what amounted to an infinite supply line from the United States, once debate in Congress quieted.

The rightist terror campaign abated substantially in El Salvador by mid-1984 for several reasons. This should not be taken to mean that violent human rights abuses stopped or even went down to the levels of pre-October 1979. Put cynically, one reason for the reduction in terror was that there were few suspects left to kill. Entire communities fled to refugee camps in San Salvador and Honduras. The terror engendered massive migrations to the United States. Other "targets" had joined the guerrillas.

Second, the campaign against aid in the United States had rested in part on the undemocratic nature of the Salvadoran government (corrected in the eyes of Congress with Duarte's election, even though the runner-up, Roberto D'Aubuisson, was labeled as a death squad organizer and probable intellectual author of the assassination of Archbishop Romero) and in part on the massive scale of human rights abuses. Congress pressured the Reagan administration, and the embassy and the military attachment there, to pressure the Salvadoran military. The effects of that pressure seem to have been minimal for at least three years, which is perhaps another way of saying that the pressure was not all that high. That is not to say that U.S. military advisors were not trying to improve the record by telling their counterparts, for example, that prisoners were more valuable alive than dead. It is to say that it did not have much effect. The Salvadoran military could be quite candid in interviews and told me, even in mid-1985, that they understood they were doing the fighting so that U.S. troops would not have to and that they were not doing anything that had not been done in Vietnam.

In short, the Salvadoran colonels knew that the United States needed them at least as much as they needed the United States. Their ability to stonewall for years even over the human rights cases with the highest profiles in the United States spoke volumes. That only the hit men, after years, were tried and convicted of the late 1980 slaughter of four U.S. nuns and the even more brazen machine gunning in a restaurant in one of San Salvador's two luxury hotels of two Americans assigned as advisors to the hated agrarian reform agency as well as the head of that agency spoke volumes (Bonner 1984; Americas Watch 1984; Chomsky 1985; Arnson 1993; Waghelstein 2002).

However, after Duarte's election, the United States turned up the volume. Ambassador Deane Hinton, who had been telling Congress and reporters for years that El Salvador was making great strides on human rights, read the riot act at a luncheon attended by many of El Salvador's economic elite. He said that as many as thirty thousand people had been murdered in political crimes. This dramatic performance was followed a few months later by a visit from Vice President George Bush, who also delivered a stern message (Arnson 1993).

There is another reason for the decline in political assassinations that is less celebrated in U.S. accounts of the war. To some extent, the increased military and intelligence capabilities of the FMLN enabled it to send messages that it could retaliate against political assassinations. From time to time, it demonstrated that it knew where key people lived, for example. At one point, it kidnapped the daughter of President Duarte in exchange for prisoners.

U.S. POLICY IN CENTRAL AMERICA AND THE MASKS OF TERROR

Raymond Bonner (1984) was a *New York Times* reporter new to El Salvador in early 1980, but as a former Marine was not inexperienced in warlike activities. Early in his book *Weakness and Deceit,* he recounts an emblematic confrontation. Demonstrators from one of the grassroots groups had more or less peacefully occupied the headquarters of the centrist Christian Democratic Party but also held several of its party members hostage. The stated object of this protest was the release of political prisoners and an end to repression. Two weeks later, Bonner and other reporters were covering one of many protest demonstrations when they became aware that the military was headed toward the Christian Democratic building. Though the demonstration had been fired upon by troops (with some return volleys from a few demonstrators carrying pistols), Bonner and others peeled off to follow soldiers and armored personnel carriers toward the party's headquarters. But the military prevented them from seeing its assault on the building. The reporters could only hear grenades and automatic weapons. They were later permitted to advance. They found two dozen terrified teenaged protestors face-down in the driveway. Soldiers then threw them, sobbing, into a flatbed truck piled on top of one another. Inside in the foyer, the reporters found three bodies of somewhat older people who had been shot, some whose body parts had been hacked with machetes.

It wasn't until some time later that Bonner realized that this had not been a firefight. The captured weapons had amounted to two beat-up pistols and a few homemade contact bombs. The bodies had been behind cement walls. Bonner deduced that the glimpse he'd had of one of the protestors being hauled from the others meant that the soldiers had identified the older leaders, dragged them back into the building, and hacked and shot them.

Bonner wrote, "I had coldly recorded it all in my notebook. The significance of what I was reporting did not register. . . . I could not conceive that an army could be so brutal to its own citizens. It just didn't cross my mind that the occupants had been killed in other than a shoot out. . . . What I would not realize until many months later, until I learned more about the history of El Salvador, was that the army that day . . . had behaved as it always had, ignoring civilian pleas for restraint [from the Christian Democratic Party in this instance], using excessive force against all dissent from the left" (3–6).

It took Bonner several months to learn this reality, even though it was obvious to the captured, terrified teenagers that day and to other Salvadorans after the assassination of the archbishop weeks later, and even though Bonner himself was seeing bodies in the street every day that could not be explained either by combat firefight or common crime. This observation is not meant as a criticism of Bonner. Many Salvadorans, particularly from well-to-do families, knew there was violence but had little idea of the scope of the terror campaign and even less idea of the rural conditions that had been one cause of the conflict.

Bonner, however, was the eyes and ears of the leading newspaper in the United States. Traditionally, the U.S. media's international reporting tends to reflect the parameters of debate in Washington, though occasionally its reporting can change the shape of the parameters, such as in the revelations of the Mai Lai slaughter in Vietnam and its cover-up. The Carter administration's policy on human rights was just then in flux as Carter, in an election year, was under rhetorical fire from the right about "losing Nicaragua," the communist threat to El Salvador, the Soviets in Afghanistan, and so on. The *Times* headlines in early 1980 tended to see the Salvadoran left initiating violence or provoking it. But the left in El Salvador saw its protests as a response to the disappearance and assassination of its leaders. In this particular case, it is not clear if Bonner even filed a story on the Christian Democrat headquarters; The *Times* carried a tiny Associated Press notice on page 5.

The newspaper had Bonner there because, in the wake of Nicaragua, it, and the Carter administration sensed another cold war issue. It ran some three dozen stories on El Salvador in January and February, though none made the front page. By contrast, *Times* coverage of the fateful election fraud in 1972 had only amounted to four two-inch stories buried inside the paper—as close to nonnews as a "news" story can get. In early 1980, there was almost no TV coverage of El Salvador. It was a new hot spot. Reporters were not familiar with the history, nor was there one dominant "bad guy" personality such as Somoza. As the assassinations became commonplace, they were less newsworthy. Many were in remote areas. So the terror remained invisible in the United States in early 1980 until a brief spasm of coverage of the assassination of Archbishop Romero in March and then nine months and many thousands of deaths later coverage of the murder of four U.S. nuns (Spence 1983).

Two years later, the landscape had changed. U.S. aid had built to high levels. There was opposition in Congress that began to grow at the end of 1980 when the U.S. nuns were murdered. But the Reagan administration dominated the news frame, and for the next three years it basically fended off the human rights issue. Opponents in Congress could only get weak compromises and slight reductions in the requested aid for El Salvador. (The administration pledged to certify every six months that the government was making progress on the human rights front, a restriction that amounted to little more than an opening for a few days of coverage of the human rights issue in El Salvador.) The dominant news frame was the communist threat and, by 1982, that El Salvador was becoming a fledgling democracy because it was holding elections, even though the party of the probable intellectual author of the assassination of the archbishop emerged in the strongest position in the Constituent Assembly.

Reagan's concept of terrorism arose in that he saw "international terrorism" in a Cuban-Nicaraguan effort to overthrow the Salvadoran government. Though human rights was an issue, the *Times* and the U.S. government did not see, or chose to minimize, the extent of terror, though Reagan, on the other hand, vastly exaggerated Sandinista "terror," accusing it falsely of a genocide campaign against an indigenous group caught up in the contra war.

U.S. reporters had had a more encompassing view of Somoza's terror for several reasons. In 1978 and early 1979, Nicaragua's civil war was not as firmly implanted in the cold war by the Carter administration. Somoza bombed urban neighborhoods, a most public form of mass terror. His troops assassinated a U.S. reporter, and another reporter filmed the act. All this worked against Somoza's interest.

The effect of the news frame being dominated by the cold war was to cast the debate in the United States, and coverage in the U.S. press in a parameter of anticommunism or, for dissenters, the label of being soft on communism. The contrary framework in Congress and therefore in the news had three elements. Once Reagan was in office, Democrats warned that anticommunism would lead to another Vietnam in Central America. A step in that direction would be the U.S. support of repressive, unpopular, and undemocratic governments, as it had been in Vietnam.

Once Bonner realized what was going on, his stories, in subtle ways, went beyond these parameters. He posed critical questions and wrote critical stories. This partial unmasking of the extent of human rights abuses, of corruption, of poverty, and of military brutality through quotes from opponents and affected citizens brought Bonner under attack from various conservative quarters, ranging from the editorial page of the *Wall Street Journal* to the right-wing media outlet *Accuracy in Media*. Eventually, his critics won. The *Times* reassigned him to domestic stories. Bonner then took a leave of absence and wrote the aforementioned book. It was a much harder-hitting critique of U.S. policy than his reportage, but the book's circulation was a mere fraction of that of the *Times*. The successful campaign against Bonner sent a message to other reporters.

The assault by the military on the Christian Democratic Party headquarters was emblematic, then, not only in what it said about the military's habitual use of terror that was then growing exponentially, but also in what it signified about U.S. perceptions of the terror. Bonner didn't understand it for a time, and he was one of a small handful of reporters filing stories. Once he did report a clearer picture, his reporting was criticized. Once human rights became an issue in Congress, terror's full extent was still obscured by claims, for example, that human rights groups in El Salvador were mere fronts for the left, a charge that contributed to the deaths of many staffers of human rights groups. When the killings became more "high profile" and could not be ignored, the initial response of the U.S. and Salvadoran governments was to blame assassinations on the left. This was true in the cases of Romero and of the U.S. nuns and later in the wake of the 1989 murder of six Jesuits.

And even when human rights did become an important issue in Congress, the tendency was to minimize it because it was not comprehensible until someone from the United States was killed. When the nuns were killed, the bloodbath had been going on for a year and was largely ignored in the United States. A congressional staffer noted, "These were Americans, not nameless, faceless campesinos or urban dwellers. It was very hard not to be deeply affected by that, and a lot of Senators were" (Arnson 1993, 62). Of course, some of those anonymous peasants were left quite literally "faceless" as Bonner's account attests, and some senators, as the quote suggests, were not deeply moved even by the assassination of the nuns. There was an effort in El Salvador and from rightist sectors in the United States to portray the nuns as political activists who had perhaps been working with the guerrillas.

A decade and $4 billion in U.S. aid later, this same pattern was to be repeated in 1989 when the six Jesuit priests were slaughtered (that is, made to lie face-down on the ground and machine gunned) by the military on the campus of the Central American University. The government blamed it on the left, with the U.S. embassy echoing the suspicion, and when the right eventually was blamed there was the suggestion that the priests had all been sympathetic to or supportive of the guerrillas. And then the effort was made to claim that this had been the work of a rogue squad in the military rather than what it was—an operation carried out under orders from the high command (Doggett 1994; Whitfield 1995).

Some notion of the terror in El Salvador (though not in Guatemala) did seep through to the U.S. public. Polls consistently showed that a majority opposed U.S. policy toward El Salvador and that there were high levels of opposition to the idea that U.S. troops would be sent there. However, polls also revealed that the Central American issues were not high on the list of concerns of those polled and, in addition, that Americans were substantially confused. A large majority could not accurately answer which side the United States was supporting in both countries. While the majority accepted the idea of many human rights abuses in El Salvador and by the Nicaraguan government, there was no effort in Congress and virtually none in the press to compare them: press censorship and political harassment with some jailing in Nicaragua as contrasted with thirty thousand murders in El Salvador by 1983. By 1982, there was no need to censor the press in El Salvador, as left-of-center presses had been bombed and reporters assassinated (Spence 1987).

THE CONSEQUENCES

We don't know how many people were killed by terror; that's one of its consequences in Central America. In El Salvador, efforts by various human rights groups and by the U.S. embassy could not keep up with terror's victims. That was even truer in Guatemala, though there was a magnificent survey effort there, conducted by the Catholic Church toward the end of the war, to recapture the memory (Archdiocese of Guatemala 1999). In Nicaragua, efforts were rudimentary. Much of the killing was in remote areas. There was no postwar truth-investigating commission.

Seligson and McElhinny (1996) have brought together estimates for El Salvador and Nicaragua of both civilian and combat deaths. They then use their own contemporary surveys to determine who among noncombatants was killed. The estimates they catalogue vary, but using their best estimate, 1 in every 66 Salvadorans died in war-related violence, and in Nicaragua, counting the war against Somoza and the contra war, 1 in every 38 Nicaraguans died. In the United States during World War II, by contrast, 1 in every 387 persons died in war-related deaths. In El Salvador, members of the extreme left were far more likely to die than those in the center or right, but no such ideological pattern is found in Nicaragua (1996, 211–25). In Guatemala, using the estimates of the Commission for Historical Clarification that 200,000 died (42,275 of the deaths were documented) and a 1979 population of 6.8 million, 1 in every 34 Guatemalans died. However, of the documented deaths, 83 percent were Mayans. If we assume that proportion for all deaths and further assume that half of Guatemala's population is Mayan (a high estimate according to government and survey data), then 1 in every 20 Mayans died (Seligson and McElhinny 1996; Historical Clarification Commission 1999; Betancur, Figueredo, and Buergenthal 1993; Nuñez 1991).

In all three countries, the social fabric was shredded. Ten to 20 percent of the population of Nicaragua and El Salvador fled, mostly to the United States, and many more were displaced in their own countries. The Nicaraguan economy, in near collapse at war's end, showed almost no growth for the next five years. Economic damage was severe in El Salvador, but U.S. aid kept the economy afloat. Despite several years of high rates of growth beginning in the last year of the war, poverty levels remained nearly at wartime levels until late in the decade. In Guatemala, the economic damage of the war, measured in national aggregate terms, was not as great, but rural poverty and lack of government services is greater there than in the other two war-torn countries. El Salvador's principle export product in dollars earned, by far, is Salvadorans.

THE LESSONS

It might seem brutal to say, but terror worked to achieve its immediate and medium-term ends. In Guatemala, the military's terror campaign wiped out the support base of the guerrillas and reduced them to a minor fighting force until the end of the war more than a decade later.

In El Salvador, terror wiped out the urban base of leftist organizers, activists, and sympathizers and created similar havoc in the countryside. It is difficult to prove, but one could argue that terror staved off defeat. On the other hand, in Nicaragua, it could be argued that the terror campaign waged by Somoza backfired by sparking revolt. His campaign was smaller than those waged in the other two countries. In the contra war, attrition worked against the Sandinistas, and the assassination campaign was an important part of that.

Another lesson might be that in U.S. politics, a terror campaign against "faceless peasants" was not sufficient to induce the congressional critics of the Reagan administration to reduce significantly the amount of U.S. aid, because they were afraid of being called soft on communism and tarred with the "loss" of El Salvador and because there were filters, some self-created, that obscured a full view of terror. A harsher criticism would be that terror helped stave off defeat for the United States in the region and that the United States, or at least some of its agents, were either well aware of terror's importance or, worse, were providing training manuals on the topic. An unhappy lesson is that terror that does not directly impact U.S. citizens will generally not be sufficient to mobilize a large campaign against it, in part because filters prevent the public from seeing its effects.

However, these "lessons" are complicated by the longer view of the postwar processes. There has been a contest of sorts over memory and lessons that has parallels with the issue of terror during the war. For example, John Waghelstein, U.S. military advisor to the Salvadoran government in the early 1980s, began a recent retrospective analysis by asserting that the U.S. operation in El Salvador was a success because its goal was to prevent a communist takeover. To accomplish that goal, he argued, the U.S. military had to, among other things, convince the Salvadoran military that a live prisoner had value. It took some time to do this, he notes, because by the time of the aforementioned speech of Ambassador Hinton, up to thirty thousand murders might have been committed. But then, by 1984, things got better. Unfortunately, toward the end of the war, a military unit killed the six Jesuits and their housekeeper and her daughter. That Waghelstein, almost twenty years removed from his experience in El Salvador, and speaking, ironically enough, within days of the thirteenth anniversary of the murder of the Jesuits could fail to mention that this reversion to form was at the orders of the Salvadoran high command is but one suggestion that another grim lesson is the staying power of an inclination to veil what happened (Waghelstein 2002; Betancur, Figueredo, and Buergenthal 1993; Dogget 1994; Whitfield 1995).

Terror also expanded the number of enemies of the terrorists, and some of them have fought to keep the memory alive and to bring terrorists to justice. In each of the three countries, human rights groups formed during the wars and made connections with international human rights groups. In El Salvador, the peace treaty called for a civilian commission to investigate the human rights records of all officers and for several high-ranking officers to be removed, an action impossible to imagine a decade earlier. The treaty called for an international truth commission to investigate the more notorious of the human rights cases. Its report named names, though an amnesty law prevented prosecutions. The report was met with a furious but rhetorical response from the military. In Guatemala, the treaty called for a truth commission, though it was not permitted to name names. Its findings, based in part on the records of various human rights groups and on the aforementioned survey conducted by the Catholic Church, were dramatic. The military was responsible for more than 90 percent of the deaths. An amnesty law has not been fully effective in preventing cases against human rights abusers, but in Guatemala, much more than the other two countries, threats and assassinations continue against plaintiffs, witnesses, prosecutors, and judges. The most telling example of the fight over memory has been the assassination of Bishop Gerardi in Guatemala the day after he released the massive study of human rights abuses committed during the war in Guatemala. That case was prosecuted and eventually resulted in the conviction of two military officers—a first in the country's history. However, the process of the case, despite much international attention, included the full array of efforts just mentioned to injure and corrupt the judicial process and maintain impunity, and the convictions may be overturned on appeal.

A major boost to the human rights community was the international case against Chile's former dictator Pinochet and his being held under house arrest in England for months following a writ issued by a Spanish judge. Civil cases have been brought in the United States against Salvadoran and Guatemalan military figures as well as in various international courts. There have been many delays and evasions in all of the cases. Nonetheless, one could conclude that the process to end the war has vastly reduced the scope of human rights abuses and has reduced the power of the military, even in Guatemala. But the campaign against terror, the war of attrition against the impunity enjoyed by the terrorists of Central America, has shown itself to have staying power. It has placed the former perpetrators, for the first time, on the defensive.

REFERENCES

Americas Watch. 1984 (August). *Free Fire: A Report on Human Rights in El Salvador.* New York: Americas Watch.

———. 1985a (July). *Human Rights in Nicaragua: Reagan, Rhetoric and Reality.* New York: Americas Watch.

———. 1985b (March). *Violations of the Laws of War by Both Sides in Nicaragua: 1981– 1985.* New York: Americas Watch.

———. 1986. *Human Rights in Nicaragua: 1985–1986.* New York: Americas Watch.

America's Watch and the American Civil Liberties Union. 1982. *Report on Human Rights in El Salvador.* New York: Vintage Books.

———. 1984 (January). *As Bad as Ever: A Report on Human Rights in El Salvador.* New York: Americas Watch.

Anderson, Thomas P. 1971. *Matanza: El Salvador's Communist Revolt of 1932.* Lincoln: University of Nebraska Press.

Archdiocese of Guatemala. 1999. *Guatemala: Never Again!* Maryknoll, N.Y.: Orbis Books.

Armony, Ariel C. 1997. *Argentina, the United States, and the Anti-Communist Crusade in Central America, 1977–1984.* Athens: Ohio University Press.

Arnson, Cynthia J. 1993. *Crossroads: Congress, the President, and Central America, 1976–1993.* University Park: Pennsylvania State University Press.

Baloyra, Enrique. 1982. *El Salvador in Transition.* Chapel Hill: University of North Carolina Press.

Betancur, Belisario, Reinaldo Figueredo, and Thomas Buergenthal. 1993. *From Madness to Hope: The Twelve-Year War in El Salvador. Report on the Truth Commission for El Salvador.* New York: United Nations.

Binford, Leigh. 1996. *The El Mozote Massacre.* Tucson: University of Arizona Press.

Black, George. 1981. *Triumph of the People: The Sandinista Revolution in Nicaragua.* London: Zed Press.

———. 1984. *Garrison Guatemala.* New York: Monthly Review Press.

Bonner, Raymond. 1984. *Weakness and Deceit: U.S. Policy and El Salvador.* New York: New York Times Books.

Booth, John. 1985. *The End and the Beginning: The Nicaraguan Revolution.* 2d ed. Boulder, Colo.: Westview Press.

Brody, Reed. 1985. *Contra Terror in Nicaragua: Report of a Fact-Finding Mission, September 1984–January 1985.* Boston: South End Press.

Cabestrero, Teófilo. 1985. *Blood of the Innocent: Victims of the Contras' War in Nicaragua.* Maryknoll, N.Y.: Orbis Books.

Chomsky, Noam. 1985. *Turning the Tide: U.S. Intervention in Central America and the Struggle for Peace.* Boston: South End Press.

Christian, Shirley. 1985. *Nicaragua: Revolution in the Family.* New York: Random House.

Danner, Mark. 1993. *The Massacre at El Mozote: A Parable of the Cold War.* New York: Vintage.

Dickey, Christopher. 1985. *With the Contras: A Reporter in the Wilds of Nicaragua.* New York: Simon and Schuster.

Dillon, Sam. 1991. *Comandos: The CIA and Nicaragua's Contra Rebels.* New York: Henry Holt and Company.

Doggett, Martha. 1994. *Chronicle of a Death Foretold.* Washington, D.C.: Georgetown University Press.

Dunkerley, James. 1985. *The Long War: Dictatorship and Revolution in El Salvador.* London: Verso.

———. 1988. *Power in the Isthmus: A Political History of Modern Central America.* London: Verso.

Durham, William H. 1979. *Scarcity and Survival in Central America.* Stanford, Calif.: Stanford University Press.

Eich, Dieter, and Carlos Rincón. 1985. *The Contras: Interviews with Anti-Sandinistas.* San Francisco: Synthesis Publications.

Gleijeses, Piero. 1991. *Shattered Hope: The Guatemalan Revolution and the United States, 1944–1954.* Princeton, N.J.: Princeton University Press.

Gutman, Roy. 1988. *Banana Diplomacy: The Making of American Policy in Nicaragua, 1981–1987.* New York: Simon and Schuster.

Handy, Jim. 1984. *Gift of the Devil: A History of Guatemala.* Toronto: Between the Lines.

Historical Clarification Commission. 1999. *Memory of Silence: Report of the Historical Clarification Commission.* Guatemala City, Guatemala.

Jonas, Susanne. 1991. *The Battle for Guatemala.* Boulder, Colo.: Westview Press.

Kornbluh, Peter. 1988. "Nicaragua: U.S. Proinsurgency Warfare against the Sandinistas." In *Low Intensity Warfare: Counterinsurgency, Proinsurgency, and Antiterrorism in the Eighties,* eds. Michael T. Klare and Peter Kornbluh, 136–57. New York: Pantheon.

Levenson-Estrada, Deborah. 1994. *Trade Unionists against Terror: Guatemala City, 1954–1985.* Chapel Hill: University of North Carolina Press.

Manwaring, Max G., and Court Prisk. 1988. *El Salvador at War: An Oral History of Conflict from the 1979 Insurrection to the Present.* Washington, D.C.: National Defense University Press.

Millett, Richard. 2002. "Short Term Policies, Long Term Consequences: U.S. Relations with Nicaragua's Armed Forces." Paper presented at the Assessing U.S. National Security Cooperation Strategies Conference, Boston University, November 13–14.

Montgomery, Tommie Sue. 1995. *Revolution in El Salvador: From Civil Strife to Civil Peace.* Boulder, Colo.: Westview Press.

Nuñez, Orlando, Gloria Cardenal, et al. 1991. *La Guerra en Nicaragua.* Managua, Nicargua: Centro para la Investigación, la Promoción y el Desarrollo Rural y Social (CIPRES).

Paige, Jeffery M. 1997. *Coffee and Power: Revolution and the Rise of Democracy in Central America.* Cambridge: Harvard University Press.

Schirmer, Jennifer. 1998. *The Guatemalan Military Project: A Violence Called Democracy.* Philadelphia: University of Pennsylvania Press.

Schwarz, Benjamin C. 1991. *American Counterinsurgency Doctrine and El Salvador: The Frustrations of Reform and the Illusions of Nation Building.* Santa Monica, Calif.: RAND Corporation.

Seligson, Mitchell A., and Vincent McElhinny. 1996. "Low-Intensity Warfare, High-Intensity Death: The Demographic Impact of the Wars in El Salvador and Nicaragua." *Canadian Journal of Latin American and Caribbean Studies* 21: 211–41.

Spence, Jack. 1983. "Media Coverage of El Salvador's Election." *Socialist Review* 13: 29–57.

———. 1987. "Covering (Over) Nicaragua." In *Reagan versus the Sandinistas: The Undeclared War on Nicaragua,* ed. Thomas W. Walker, 182–201. Boulder, Colo.: Westview Press.

Stanley, William. 1996. *The Protection Racket State: Elite Politics, Military Extortion and Civil War in El Salvador.* Philadelphia: Temple University Press.

Stoll, David. 1993. *Between Two Armies in the Ixil Towns of Guatemala.* New York: Columbia University Press.

Tayacán. 1985. *Psychological Operations in Guerrilla Warfare*. New York: Vintage.

Waghelstein, John D. 2002. "Military to Military Contacts: Personal Observations—The El Salvador Case." Paper presented at the Assessing U.S. National Security Cooperation Strategeis Conference, Boston University, November 13–14.

Walter, Knut. 1993. *The Regime of Anastaso Somoza, 1936–1956*. Chapel Hill: University of North Carolina Press.

Whitfield, Teresa. 1995. *Paying the Price: Ignacio Ellacuría and the Murdered Jesuits of El Salvador*. Philadelphia: Temple University Press.

Wickham-Crowley, Timothy P. 1992. *Guerrillas and Revolution in Latin America: A Comparative Study of Insurgents and Regimes since 1956*. Princeton, N.J.: Princeton University Press.

Williams, Philip J., and Knut Walter. 1993. *Militarization and Demilitarization in El Salvador's Transition to Democray*. Pittsburgh: University of Pittsburgh Press.

Williams, Robert G. 1986. *Export Agriculture and the Crisis in Central America*. Chapel Hill: University of North Carolina Press.

24 Colombia
DEMOCRACY UNDER DURESS

Not far from here, on that fateful 11th of September, 2,801 citizens of the world died. In Colombia, violence causes as many deaths every month.
—PRESIDENT ALVARO URIBE, Speech to the UN General Assembly, September 13, 2002

Democracy is difficult to achieve. This is especially true when politicians and citizens are constantly haunted by the specter of political violence. Indeed, if political violence can sufficiently disrupt the health of civil society and institutions of democratic governance, can democracy itself survive, led alone thrive? While neither political violence nor terrorism in democracies is a new problem (just consider anti-Israeli terrorism or the Irish Republican Army in the United Kingdom), the events of September 11, 2001, have brought the question of terrorism itself to the fore, and actions such as the U.S. invasions of Afghanistan and Iraq and the subsequent nation-building paths it has embarked upon raises the legitimate question of how to build democracy in the context of ongoing threats of political violence, especially terrorism focused on civilian populations and politicians. To build a body of knowledge to apply to these issues, we need systematic study of cases in which democracy coexists with ongoing violence.

The South American republic of Colombia (unfortunately, for Colombians) is an excellent case for discussing issues of democratization under the persistent threat of endemic, fierce, and prolonged political violence. The enigma that is Colombia is a complex one indeed. On the one hand, Colombia is one of the longest-standing electoral democracies in Latin America, only one of three countries in that region to avoid long decades of military rule in the last century.[1] On the other, Colombia has also had a history of sustained and brutal political violence.

Indeed, classifying Colombia is difficult in terms of both violence and governance. First, what is the Colombian conflict? Is it an ongoing conflict between groups who believe themselves to be disenfranchised by hegemonic oligarchs? Is it the longest-running counterstate Marxist insurgency in Latin America? Is it a law enforcement conflict over the production and trafficking of illicit narcotics (cocaine and heroin)? Is it a mobilization of vigilante groups seeking their own justice? Is it an antiterror fight aimed at multiple actors who wish to cripple the state by attacking civilians and unarmed politicians? It is all of these things: a perfect storm of political violence. Second, there are clear flaws in Colombia's democracy. Some are the result of the violence, while others have helped cause the need in the minds of some to foment violence against the state. Yet Colombia remains a democracy of functioning parties and governing institutions with regular elections that result in legitimate transfers of power.

Both democracy and terrorism are analytically slippery concepts. On the one hand, at first glance they appear to be ideas that we are familiar with and can easily define. Like Justice Potter Stewart in his infamous formulation concerning the definition of pornography, we like to think we know them when we see them; of course, this is not a helpful method of categorizing cases for systematic study. A goal of this analysis is to define those terms as they are relevant to the Colombian case (as well as to a broader discussion of the general topic). Two things are certain: Colombia is not a perfect democracy, nor is it a case where the only relevant political violence is terrorism. As such, it may not be the perfect example of democratization in the context of a terrorist threat. However, there is no doubt that it provides a very dramatic and quite useful look into the possibilities and difficulties associated with democratic governance in the face of substantial counterstate force where there is a substantial element of terrorism. At a minimum, Colombia provides a clear case of a country that endeavors to function democratically while being besieged by political violence over a sustained period of time.

The Colombian case demonstrates that electoral democracy can function under the threat of terror but that clearly the presence of that threat makes the maturation of that democracy difficult. Colombia also demonstrates the importance of elite commitment to democratic rules of the game and of the insidious effects of illicit gains from narcotics production to fuel such violence.

PLACING COLOMBIA IN CONTEXT

Violence absorbs 4% of our Gross Domestic Product.
—PRESIDENT ALVARO URIBE, Speech to the UN General Assembly, September 13, 2002

Colombia is, to put it mildly, a complex place. Like many states, it was born in violence. However, in most cases the violence that precedes and creates independence for a given territory subsides, giving way to political discourse sans regular bloodshed. Colombia, however, took a route that included both. Indeed, political violence has been a hallmark of Colombia's political history. From the fourteen civil wars of the nineteenth century (Bushnell 1992, 13–14) to the major conflicts of the twentieth century, there has been little peace in Colombia's postindependence existence.[2]

However, along with the violence, there has also been a history of civilian government and electoral democracy. Despite the scholarly opinions of some,[3] I would argue that Colombia has been an electoral democracy since 1958, even during the institutional power-sharing arrangement known as the National Front.[4] As such, it is impossible to discuss or understand Colombian politics apart from violence, yet along this trail of carnage there has been a remarkably strong commitment to democratic governance and paradoxical stability over the long haul.

COLOMBIA AND DEMOCRACY

I have nothing to lose, nothing but my life.
—ARCADIO BENÍTEZ, former mayor and current candidate, quoted in the *Miami Herald*, October 6, 2003

There have been uninterrupted national elections and peaceful transfers of power in Colombia from 1958 onward.[5] The caveats are that each election cycle in recent decades has seen some localities having to cancel or postpone elections due to violence and that voter turnout rates have always been low.[6] Also, during the 1958–74 period, elections were held under the National Front power-sharing agreement between the Liberal Party and the Conservative Party.

Indeed, unlike most of their Latin American neighbors, Colombia avoided the cycle of military rule that wracked the region throughout the twentieth century. Instead, there was only a brief military government from 1953 to 1958 under General Gustav Rojas Pinilla.

Aside from regular elections, there are several key examples of democratic governance in recent Colombian history worth noting. Specifically, there was the process to replace the 1886 constitution, which resulted in the current basic law, and the 2003 referendum. Both cases indicate that Colombia has a commitment to democratic governance and also that its government will abide by the outcomes of democratic processes.

The constitutional reform process that began in 1990 was an attempt to foster a deeper and more participatory democracy in Colombia. To that end, a National Constituent Assembly was elected in 1990 to rewrite the country's constitution. Not only was the process to call the Assembly driven by a democratic demand, but the 1990 election to choose that Assembly elected the most politically varied set of officials in the history of Colombia. In that contest, a demilitarized guerrilla group, the Movement of the 19th of April (M-19), won the second largest share of seats and shared in the tripartite presidency of the Assembly with a Liberal and a member of the National Salvation Movement (dissident Conservative group). The document went into effect on July 4, 1991. This was a process clearly run by democratic, not oligarchic, principles, and it demonstrated that the institution of democratic governance in Colombia did indeed function.

A more recent example would be the 2003 referendum on various political reforms under the auspices of the 1991 constitutional order. Like much in Colombia, the results of that process point simultaneously to the presence of democracy and its lack of health. The vote, which consisted of fifteen questions placed to voters on issues of governmental reform, both institutional and fiscal, went forward on October 25, 2003, after the appropriate congressional process. However, the combination of traditional low voter turnout, a boycott by many on the nonviolent left, and the ongoing political violence in the countryside led to extremely low voter turnout. The result was that while each of the reforms won a majority of the vote, they failed to achieve the legally required vote of 25 percent of the electorate to be enacted.[7] Thus, if such a major vote cannot muster sufficient participation to properly function, then clearly there is a problem with democracy. On the other hand, the process did work as constitutionally created—the boycott itself is a method of mass participation, and President Uribe (who had banked on the success of the referendum) will abide by the results. This is democratic governance in the context of substantial difficulty.

Given the flawed, but persistent, nature of Colombian democracy, it is fair to argue that Colombia clearly has what Larry Diamond (1999, 8–13) terms "electoral democracy" and is striving for (with some success) liberal democracy. There can be no doubt that Colombia meets minimal definitions of democracy, which include basic political freedoms (e.g., press, speech, association) and governing institutions populated by officials selected in free and open elections. Diamond himself noted that Colombia qualifies as a democracy in the electoral sense but "fall[s] short" in the liberal sense (10).

Diamond (1999, 11–12) provides the following ten components of liberal democracy:

1. Control of the state lies in the hands of elected officials.
2. Executive power is constrained.
3. Electoral outcomes are uncertain, with a presumption that some alteration of the party in power will take place over time.
4. Minority groups are not prohibited from expressing their interests.
5. Associative groups beyond political parties exist as channels of representation.

6. There is free access to alternative sources of information.
7. Individuals have substantive democratic freedoms such as speech, press, association, assembly, etc.
8. Citizens are politically equal under the law.
9. Liberties are protected by an independent, nondiscriminatory judiciary whose decisions are respected by other institutions within the state.
10. Rule of law is sufficiently strong to prevent "unjustified detention, exile, terror, torture, and undue interference in their personal lives not only by the state but also by organized nonstate or antistate forces" (12).

Clearly, Colombia fails on many of these dimensions and is questionable on others. The most glaring failure on the list is number ten regarding the rule of law, although clearly since the state does not fully control its own territory, number one cannot be claimed in its entirety either. Further, the executive, while more constrained than many examples in Latin American history, is not sufficiently controlled at times, given the historic pliancy of the congress and the available emergency powers that the president has under the constitution, bringing number two into question. The weakness of the Colombia judiciary certainly raises issues with number nine—especially given the death threats (and actual assassinations) of judges involved in drug cases. Indeed, the threats to the judiciary resulted in the infamous *jueces sin rostro* (judges without faces), which clearly brought into question the fairness of the courts and efficacy of justice in Colombia (see, for example, Kline 1999, 173).

Numbers four (protection for minority groups' opinions), five (the existence of associative groups beyond parties), six (alternative sources of information), seven (basic political freedoms), and eight (political equality of all citizens) are present, but weakly in some cases. The only item that can be said to be fully in place is number three (uncertainty of electoral outcomes), as there has been noteworthy alteration of power at the presidential level in the last three electoral cycles, and the election of a leftist to the mayor's office in Bogota in 2003 illustrates that, indeed, elections are open to true contestation.[8]

From that run-down of variables, I would argue that Colombia is an electoral democracy struggling to be a liberal one and that the chief element keeping the country from making the complete move is the unfettered violence fomented by the guerrillas, paramilitaries, and narcotics traffickers in the countryside. The state's inability to control its own territory and maintain the requisite monopoly on the use of violence in its borders makes a full transition to liberal democracy essentially impossible. Furthermore, there are long-standing problems with concentration of power in the hands of oligarchs along with rampant clientelism and corruption, which also hamper attempts to liberalize the democracy. Those problems, however, are difficult to address while the antistate (and anticitizen) violence continues. So yes, the record of democratic success is stained, without question, by the ongoing violence, but there is a record, and it is better than in many countries.

COLOMBIA AND POLITICAL VIOLENCE

Colombia's 102 senators have agreed to wear bulletproof vests as part of their standard business clothing, after being pressured by a local insurance company. The assassination of a prominent senator last month also apparently prompted the decision.
—*CHRISTIAN SCIENCE MONITOR,* September 3, 1997

The promise of democracy is hardly complete in a land that has been accurately called both the murder capital and the kidnapping capital of the world and that is a land of the displaced (at least one million since 1996). Thus, formulating an adequate description of political violence in Colombia is a daunting task. The victims of the conflict are elected officials, judges, candidates, journalists, city dwellers, and peasants—that is, no one has been left untouched. The crimes committed include assassination, intimidation, kidnapping, and displacement. Sometimes the violence is planned and victims are targeted, and at others the victims are simply in the wrong place at the wrong time. Indeed, it is miraculous that society and government function at all in Colombia; yet, somehow, they do.

One fact that needs to be made clear in evaluating political violence in Colombia is that it is not a typical case of either guerrilla violence or organized crime, but I would not argue that is it sui generis and therefore a case that defies comparative analysis. Rather, I would note that there are substantially important variations within the evolution and application of violence in Colombia that require notice before appropriate analysis and comparisons can be made.

A generic case of guerrilla warfare in an archetypical Latin American country back in the 1970s typically had two basic camps of belligerents: the insurgents themselves, almost certainly fighting from a Marxist perspective (sometimes from the Cuban, Guevarist strain, other times from a more Maoist perspective), and the military, usually backed by the United States to some degree. While always complex, the basic rationales of the actors were fairly clear (i.e., social justice versus national security, overthrow of the state versus protecting the constitution, and so forth). The fighting in such a case was normally between combatants, although civilians would regularly get caught in the cross fire. Further, abuse of power by the state (especially in military regimes) would often lead to fomentation of "dirty wars" against civilians thought to be sympathetic to the left. Eventually, this story typically came to an end, with military regimes collapsing and leftist guerrillas running out of ideological steam, or some combination thereof.[9]

The crumbling of the Berlin Wall and the subsequent collapse of the Soviet bloc took away an ideological exemplar for such armed insurgents to emulate. Further, liberalization allowed armed leftists to, in some cases, integrate into civil society. In other cases, the insurgents found themselves defeated (or at least largely so).

When looking at the main example of sustained guerrilla warfare in Latin America with its myriad outcomes, elements of the above tale fit or can be made to fit those cases. However, Colombia is different. Not only is it a case in which political violence has had an endemic place in the development of the country, but the overwhelming influence of the narcotics trade has also transformed the conflict, lending substantial fuel to a fire that has seemingly died in most of the rest of the hemisphere. Indeed, the main problem in clearly assessing the constellations of violence in Colombia is that the presence of the narcotics trade blurs the lines that separate the various actors in this intricate drama.

COLOMBIA AND TERRORISM

In this moment of pain, Colombia cannot surrender. Now, we have to fortify our decision to defeat terrorism.

—PRESIDENT ALVARO URIBE, May 5, 2003, addressing the nation after guerrillas killed
ten hostages, including a sitting governor and a former defense minister

There are two ways in which one can discuss terrorism in the Colombian context. The first is largely rhetorical, the second conceptual. This distinction is useful, and noteworthy, because the way in which the terms "terror" and "terrorism" are used by politicians in Colombia (and Washington) has substantial policy implications in the ongoing conflict, while the conceptual debate helps the analyst get a better handle on the situation. Hence, to classify part of the discussion in terms of rhetoric is not to marginalize that aspect of the terrorism discussion vis-à-vis Colombia but to delineate between two important strands of discussion. The rhetorical usage of the word "terrorism" by both the American and Colombian administrations has escalated markedly since the events of September 11, 2001.

A search of the *New York Times* from 1990 to September 2003 of the terms "Colombia" and "terrorism" in the LexisNexis database reveals the following. From 1990 through September 11, 2001, there was an average of less than 1 such reference a month (.86, in fact). And for the 1990–94 period, such references were almost exclusively leveled at the drug traffickers. However, from September 12, 2001, until September 1, 2003, there was an average of 3.47 such references a month. Further, if one reviews recent works on Colombia, even those focused on violence, one finds that use of the term "terrorism" is limited or nonexistent, with the exception in some cases of the phrase "narcoterrorism." For instance, the last three editions of the literature reviews in the *Handbook of Latin American Studies* on Colombia does not mention terrorism (although they speak quite a bit about violence).[10] Kline, in text specifically on the Colombian state's fight with political violence, makes one reference to "the terrorist escalation of the guerrillas" (1999, 110) as one of a set of problems that besieged the peace process in the 1980s and early 1990s. From there he makes three references to "narcoterrorism" (119, 120, 199). Both the edited volumes by Berquist, Penaranda, and Sanchez (1992, 2001) do not discuss generalized terrorism, but the more recent volume does discuss narcoterrorism in a fairly limited way, referring primarily to the actions of Pablo Escobar's Medellin Cartel.[11]

However, as the LexisNexis numbers demonstrate, a clear semantic shift has taken place. The change is partially due to an overall increase in the usage of the term "terrorism" when political violence is discussed. But more importantly, it is due to an increase in the description by both the Bush and Uribe administrations of the Colombian case as one of terrorism. Furthermore, Colombia's main guerrilla group, the Revolutionary Armed Forces of Colombia (FARC), has shown signs of moving more into the area of urban warfare, which often employs terroristic tactics, and would also account for increased usage of the term.

The main significance here is that in many ways terrorism is becoming the new communism, at least in terms of the national security rationales of both the United States and Colombia. That is to say that in the post-9/11 world, terrorism has become a reason for U.S. intervention (in terms of both actual personnel and aid), and in Colombia the notion of terrorism, whether it be in the guise of guerrillas or narcotraffickers, becomes a driving force in the administration's national security doctrine, where both were fueled by anticommunism during the cold war. In this context, it should be noted that the U.S. Department of State classifies the FARC, the National Liberation Army (ELN), and the United Self-Defense Forces of Colombia (AUC) as terrorist organizations. Furthermore, as the FARC becomes more active in the Colombian frontiers that border Ecuador, Peru, Brazil, and Venezuela—with potential training from Irish Republican Army (IRA) operatives—they start to fall into that rhetorical category of terrorists who have "global reach" and therefore provide potential impetus for further actions by Washington in Colombia.

Hence, the recasting of the guerrilla conflict as a war against terrorism has a threefold effect: it enhances U.S. involvement, intensifies the military's fight against the rebels, and diminishes the chances of a negotiated solution. Furthermore, if the FARC (or others in the fight) turn to terroristic tactics (such as bombing civilians), then this will just reinforce the effects of the rhetoric mentioned above.

Beyond the rhetorical issue, there is also the conceptual issue of studying terrorism as one of classification of political violence. Is there truly "terrorism" to be found in Colombia? The simple answer is yes, but it is not the predominant form of collective political violence.

To admit that defining the term "terrorism" is difficult is obligatory in almost any work that mentions terrorism. This is unhelpful but true, as illustrated by the fact that there is no consensus in international law as to how to define the term (Sofaer 1986). Regardless of the exact definition used, there can be no doubt that the term "terrorism" is a loaded one that evokes emotional responses even among those seeking analytical conclusions.

As is customary, I will offer my own definition for usage in this piece, which builds on Cooper's definition (2001, 883): "Terrorism is the intentional generation of massive fear by human beings for the purpose of securing or maintaining control over other human beings," to which I add that the fear in question is generated by aiming violence at noncombatants. As such, terrorism is irregular warfare directed not at the state but at the citizens of the state for the purpose of generating fear, so that the civilian population will, in turn, pressure the state to act. Groups rely on terroristic tactics because direct confrontation with the state will not yield the desired results—that is, direct military confrontation will not result in the defeat of the state. For the sake of a coherent discussion of political violence, I would argue for at least three categories: conventional war, guerrilla war, and terrorism. This list does not exhaust the universe of collective political violence by any means, but it does provide a basis for the discussion of the Colombian case. Perhaps more specifically, terrorism is a tactic that can be employed in both conventional and nonconventional conflicts. Failure to recognize that fact leads to further confusion in an already complex discussion. Indeed, in this I concur with Merari: "If the definition of terrorism is equally applicable to nuclear war, conventional war and guerrilla, the term loses any useful meaning" (1993, 217). This is not to say that states cannot engage in activities that cause fear in a population (indeed, total war is waged, at least in part, to scare civilian populations enough that they will want their governments to surrender). However, as horrific and violent as such activities can be, I find them to be their own category of action and therefore not terrorism per se.

Given this discussion and definition, clearly Colombia does suffer from a substantial amount of terrorism that compliments the guerrilla war itself and deters the law enforcement fight against drug traffickers. The sources of this terrorism is plentiful.

THE ACTORS

Peace has a lot of enemies, even inside of our country.
—FORMER PRESIDENT ANDRES PASTRANA,
in an interview with the *NewsHour with Jim Lehrer*, October 6, 1998

The actors in this difficult drama are plentiful. Aside from the state itself (in the form of the military and the national police),[12] there are the guerrilla groups, the narcotraffickers, and the paramilitaries. In terms of terrorism as a tactic (as defined above), all of these actors have engaged in such activities over the past two decades. Of the groups utilizing such tactics in a fashion most directly threatening to democratic governance, the guerrillas are the guiltiest.

Guerrillas

We have to grab people from the Senate, from Congress, judges and ministers, from all the three powers (of the Colombian state), and we'll see how they'll squeal.
—JORGE BRICEÑO, a.k.a. "Mono Jonoy," a top FARC commander, in 2002,
as reported by Human Rights Watch

Guerrilla warfare has been an ongoing element of Colombian politics from at least the days of the partisan civil war known as La Violencia[13] to the present. Specifically, the last forty years have seen a number of groups in operation, each seeking the violent overthrow of the Colombian state, with the four most significant being the FARC, the ELN, the People's Liberation Army (EPL), and M-19, as well as a number of smaller groups. The FARC and the ELN emerged in the 1960s in the wake of partisan civil war, while M-19 and the EPL emerged in the 1970s. And while the FARC and the ELN continue to struggle against the state, M-19 demobilized in 1989 to become the Democratic Action/M-19 (AD/M-19) political party.[14] The majority of the EPL also demilitarized and made the transition to the Hope, Peace and Liberty Party (whose Spanish initials conform also to EPL) so as to participate in the 1991 Constituent Assembly process of rewriting the Colombian constitution. Some members of the EPL did not lay down their arms, however, and continue their armed struggle.

The FARC is the oldest active guerrilla group in Colombia (indeed, in all of Latin America). Its origins are in the liberal self-defense groups that fought in La Violencia. The group emerged in the early 1960s as part of the Communist Party of Colombia and was firmly established as an official revolutionary movement by 1964. Currently, the FARC measures somewhere between sixteen thousand and seventeen thousand and operates primarily in rural sectors of the country, with strongholds in the south and east.[15]

The FARC has primarily been a rural guerrilla group during its almost four decades of fighting, with only occasional forays into urban centers. Indeed, the group has established substantial control of areas of the countryside.[16] However, there are indications that the guerrillas are becoming increasingly interested in the cities and may have elicited training in urban terror from members of the IRA and Basque separatists (Wilson 2001). Specifically, the car bombing of the exclusive Club Nogal in Bogota by the FARC in February of 2003, which killed thirty-three people (the worst urban bombing in Colombia for a decade), was linked by authorities directly to the FARC's association with the IRA (McDermott 2003; *Seattle Times* 2003).

The threats aimed at local governing officials by the FARC could be said to be among the most terroristic in terms of specifically threatening democracy. This fact is further illustrated below in the discussion concerning the specific targeting of elections and elected officials by the guerrillas.

Narcotraffickers

> *The only law the narco-terrorists do not break is the law of supply and demand.*
> —FORMER PRESIDENT VIRGILIO BARCO, 1990

There are four distinct eras of organized narcotrafficking in Colombia: the pre–Medellin Cartel era, the Medellin Cartel/Pablo Escobar era, the Cali Cartel era, and the post–major cartel era. Of the four, only the Medellin Cartel/Escobar era is substantially associated with terrorism. It is fair to say Escobar, the leader of the infamous Medellin Cartel, attempted to wage war against the state during much of the 1980s until his death during a firefight with police in 1993. The use of political assassinations is a clear example of this war, as were the car bombs that killed hundreds of civilians in urban centers during January to April of 1993.

By the late 1990s, there was no longer one large narcotrafficking organization to discuss, at least not in the same way that the 1980s and 1990s saw the Medellin and Cali Cartels. Instead of large, fairly visible organizations, we now see a large number of smaller cartels, or "boutique cartels" as Sweig (2002) refers to them. Their influence over the question of terror is now less as a direct player than as a facilitator of the violence due to the very presence of the remarkable profits that illicit narcotics generate.

Paramilitaries

> *The methods the "self-defense" forces used to recover Urabá were no less violent and disgusting than those used by [guerrillas]. . . . This should be absolutely clear! We copied the guerrillas' methods and confronted them with the same tactics.*
>
> —CARLOS CASTANO in his 2001 autobiography, *Mi Confesion*

The concept of private citizens (i.e., neither military nor guerrilla) taking up arms in Colombia is not new,[17] but the 1980s saw the advent a new element to Colombia's political violence: the establishment of formal paramilitary groups operating at the national level and often linked to drug trafficking (and, as noted above, clandestinely with the state). The first such group was Death to Kidnappers (MAS),[18] which was formed primarily by various drug lords (Bagley 1988, 76) but reportedly also included active duty army officers, representatives of a petroleum company, and cattle ranchers (Richani 2000). As the organization's name suggests, its primary raison d'être was to strike back at guerrilla groups engaged in kidnappings (specifically, the abduction by M-19 of the daughter of drug baron Luis Jorge Ochoa).

The current face of paramilitary activity came to fruition in the 1990s with the formation of the national United Self-Defense Forces of Colombia (AUC) in the 1990s under the leadership of Carlos Castano, who, along with his brother Fidel, formed the group after their father was kidnapped by the FARC and died while in its custody (the exact details of his death are unknown) (Dudley 2002).

DEMOCRACY IN THE CROSSHAIRS: TERROR AND ELECTIONS

> *We are offering democracy, so that arms can be replaced by argument. . . . We will not allow the long-standing struggle of the people to elect their next authority to be frustrated by the threat of a bullet.*
>
> —PRESIDENT ALVARO URIBE's inauguration speech, August 8, 2002

Understanding that Colombia's history is one of ongoing violence, it is difficult to pinpoint specific starting points to illustrate different aspects of the evolving conflict. Keeping that caveat in mind, this section provides some key examples of the application of tactics and actions that can properly be defined as terrorism as they specifically apply to the furtherance and general health of democratic governance in Colombia. Clearly, to catalogue all such examples would, unfortunately, require a lengthy tome, so selectivity is necessary. Two key recent presidential campaigns, the 1990 and 2002 cycles, and the example of local elections in recent years demonstrate the effects of terroristic violence on Colombian democracy.

The 1990 Presidential Elections.

All of the presidential candidates have reported death threats. That's normal.

—GENERAL LUIS ENRIQUE, head of Colombia's secret police,
as reported in the *Christian Science Monitor,* June 18, 1998

The 1990 electoral cycle was among the bloodiest in the country's history. During that particular contest, three presidential candidates were assassinated, all by killers linked to the Medellin drug cartel. The most significant of these attacks was that made on Luis Carlos Galan, the Liberal Party candidate, and almost certainly the man who would have been elected to the presidency in 1990. He was cut down by submachine gun fire while at a campaign stop just south of Bogota in August of 1989.

Two candidates of the left were also killed by assassins funded by the cartel. In March of 1990, the Patriotic Union's (UP) candidate, Bernardo Jaramillo, was killed as he awaited a flight in Bogota's airport. The UP, which had its origins in the FARC, was a nonviolent alternative to change. From 1985 to 1990, the UP was essentially wiped out by right-wing violence (linked both to narcotraffickers and to the military).[19] April 1990 saw the death of M-19 candidate Carlos Pizarro Leongomez at the hands of a paid assassin during an airline flight from Bogota to Cartagena. M-19 had recently made the transition from guerrilla group to political party. Further, Cesar Gaviria, who took up the Liberal mantle from the fallen Galan and served as president from 1990 to 1994, received numerous death threats.

The elections themselves were held under threat of violence, as on the eve of the 1990 elections, 230,000 troops patrolled Colombia's majors cities in an effort to both bolster the confidence of voters who feared for their security and thwart political violence, such as the twenty-two hundred pounds of dynamite seized in Bogota, which appeared destined for bombs in shopping malls and near polling booths (Brooke 1990, 17). Overall, this was an especially bloody period of Colombia's history, fueled primarily by the drug cartels. This period, which ran from the mid-1980s until Escobar's death in 1993, was one of the clear utilization of terror by an antistate actor to attempt to alter public policy. The tools of violence, primarily assassinations but also car bombs in public spaces, were used in hopes of getting the state to back off its antinarcotics positions and to specifically halt the extradition of narcotraffickers to the United States.

Key assassinations of the period include the attempted slaying in 1987 of Colombia's ambassador to Hungary (and former justice minister) Enrique Parejo Gonzalez (in the streets of Budapest, no less), and the successful killings of Justice Minister Rodrigo Lara Bonilla in 1984, the antidrug newspaper editor Guillermo Cano Isaza in 1986, Attorney General Carlos Mauro Hoyos in 1988, and Governor Antonio Roldan Betancur of Antioquia in 1989. All of these attempts and deaths were linked to Escobar's cartel and were clearly intended to signal the willingness of that group to use violence to dissuade the Colombian state from interfering with its business activities.

Furthermore, this period was marked by numerous death threats and assassinations of judges engaged in drug-related cases and by a terror campaign aimed at the general populace by the groups of narcotraffickers who had dubbed themselves "The Extraditables" (i.e., those who would be extradited to the United States, if caught, to face drug-trafficking charges). Bagley notes, for example, that from 1981 to 1986 more than fifty judges were killed, and those handling drug-related cases were threatened with death if they did not accept bribes (1988, 83). This number includes the members of the Supreme Court who were held hostage in the Palace of Justice when M-19 seized the building and was subsequently attacked by the military. It is thought that M-19 received $1 million from the Medellin Cartel to fund the attack.[20]

The 2002 Presidential Campaign

I am fighting for the security of 40 million Colombians. If I was only concerned for my security I would be in exile.

—PRESIDENTIAL CANDIDATE ALVARO URIBE as quoted in *The Scotsman*, September 2001

The 2002 electoral cycle marked the national contest most affected by the FARC's interference. While the 1990 cycle was clearly fueled by violence derived from the drug trade, the guerrillas had largely limited their attempts at influencing electoral contests to the local level. The 2002 campaign, however, saw assassination attempts, kidnappings, and general disruption on behalf of the FARC.

The candidate who received the most attention from the guerrillas was Alvaro Uribe Velez, former governor of Anitoquia and eventual winner of the contest. Uribe was considered a hard-liner and was perceived as the candidate preferred by the paramilitaries. As opposed to the promises of Pastrana, who ran on a platform of peace, Uribe ran promising to intensify the conflict. Given the failure of the Pastrana peace initiative, this point of view proved to be quite popular among the Colombian people. Uribe became the first candidate to win an election with an outright majority of the vote since the implementation of the two-round system in 1994. Indeed, his 53 percent to 32 percent trouncing of his nearest competitor (Liberal Horacio Serpa) was among the more lopsided presidential victories in modern Colombian elections.

There were two attempts on Uribe during the campaign. The first, a plot to place a briefcase full of Bibles rigged with explosives outside Uribe's office, was foiled by security forces in September of 2001 (McDermott 2002, 10). The second was a bomb attack in Baranquilla that killed five. The crescendo of attempts on Uribe took place on his inauguration day when rebels launched mortar attacks in the capital city, killing fourteen and wounding at least sixty (Semple 2002). After the elections, a plot to assassinate Uribe was foiled during a presidential visit to the town of Neiva in February of 2003 (Wilson 2003, A25).

In addition to the details concerning attacks aimed specifically at Uribe, there are the numerous high-profile kidnappings that began with the forced landing of a plane containing Senator Jorge Gechem Turbay on February 20, 2002. Three days later, presidential candidate (and former senator) Ingrid Betancourt was kidnapped by the FARC. The organization already held, at the time, a former governor of the department of Meta, a senator, and three members of the Chamber of Representatives. The political kidnappings during the 2002 political season were escalated with the capture of thirteen members of the departmental legislature of Valle (Human Rights Watch 2002).

ATTACKS ON LOCAL DEMOCRACY: THE 1990S

I love my town, but whoever chooses politics is a dead man.
   —MAYOR ORLANDO FLORES of Libano, as quoted in the *Christian Science Monitor*, July 1, 2003

One of the more important aspects, yet less visible to outside observers, of the attacks on democracy in Colombia are to be found at the local level. This can be specifically seen in attacks on the capacity of localities to hold elections (and related activities such as campaign events) as well as on those who seek elective office and democratic governance at the local level. According to a recent public defender's office memo, sixty-three mayors were assassinated in office in the 1998–2003 period, and eighteen were taken hostage in 2002 through mid-2003. Furthermore, eighty-two municipal council members were killed from May 2002 to May 2003, with eighteen hundred being displaced during that same time period. Overall, the Uribe administration concluded that roughly half of all the mayors in Colombia were under direct threat by either the guerrillas or paramilitary groups (*El Tiempo* 2003b).

Guerrillas ordering boycotts of elections, such as they did in the 1997 cycle (departmental and local elections in Colombia run on a three-year cycle), had become commonplace. A clear exemplar of the use of fear as a tool to disrupt democratic governance in Colombia came in mid-May of 2002 when the FARC issued a "resign or die" order to the mayors and other public officials in southern departments where the rebel presence was extensive and then extended the threat to the entirety of the country. As a result, at least 140 mayors (out of 1,097) resigned, as did hundreds of other officials (judges, secretaries, policemen) (Ottis 2002, 26A). One mayor, Luis Carlos Caro Pacheco, of Solita in the department of Caqueta, was murdered during this period, and his death was directly attributed to the FARC's order (Amnesty International 2003, 81). In the 2003 local election cycle, 26 mayoral and council candidates were assassinated (*El Tiempo* 2003a) and 48 candidates decided to end their pursuit of office due to the violence (*El Tiempo* 2003c).

LESSONS AND PROGNOSTICATIONS

These numerous examples from the 1980s to the present clearly demonstrate that Colombia's democracy has existed under a prolonged assault by various actors employing the tools of terror. Given these circumstances, what is the long-term prognostication for Colombia and the health of its democracy? Unfortunately, it is more of the same, especially as long as the cultivation, refinement, and export of cocaine and heroin continue to provide the cash needed to finance various antistate actors.

So, what does this case provide for our inquiry into democracy in the context of endemic terrorism? First, we can say that it is possible for democracy to function even under substantial strain, although with the clear caveat that such a democracy is clearly wounded, and that ongoing intractable violence makes the flourishing of liberal democracy a clear difficulty. Second, we can say that Colombia does provide some clues to help us understand what might make democracy possible even in the context of attacks on the institutions of democracy. Specifically, there has been long-term elite commitment to electoral democracy and strong mass-level association with electoral politics.

One hallmark of Colombian democracy has been the basic commitment of elites to basic partisan politics. On one level, this has often been seen as a flaw in Colombian democracy—the idea that the country has been governed throughout the majority of its history by a traditional oligarchy. Certainly, that is an argument heard from opposition groups, both of the democratic and nonviolence stripe, as well as by the rebels. And, it clearly has been the case that throughout Colombia's history, the leadership of the parties have looked out primarily for themselves. Nevertheless, the utilization of electoral procedures, rather than authoritarian means, to obtain power is preferable and has led to the long-term evolution of democratic institutions in Colombia.

I would argue that Colombian electoral democracy has increasingly become more than simply a "conversation among gentlemen"—as Wilde (1978) put it—although there is no denying that there is still a substantial presence of elite orientation to

Colombia's democracy. However, this record is not exclusively a negative one. An elite-level commitment to electoral democracy is preferable to elites committed to military dictatorship or theocratic rule. A clear example would be that the sole military government of the twentieth century was removed largely because the elites of the two parties were able to cooperate and negotiate a means to return to power.

Another area that has long been identified as a key woe in Colombian democracy, and that has been linked to the elitism noted above, has been the long-standing clientele networks linking rank-and-file voters to specific politicians. No doubt the pervasive clientelism evident in Colombian politics has hampered good governance and sound policymaking by encouraging particularistic political behavior by politicians from the local to the national levels. Furthermore, such a system encourages corrupt practices and the misuse of scarce public funds. However, there is a positive upshot of these types of relationships: they generate a relationship between voters and elected officials, which reinforces democratic rules for the selection of officeholders. A reliance on pork barrel politics as the foundation of a democracy has problems to be sure, but one of the reasons democracy persists in Colombia is that it has been habituated in the population.

Indeed, fierce partisan identification was long a hallmark of Colombian political life, and not always with positive results. Ironically, while this habituation into electoral practices can be seen as a reason for the long-term persistence of democratic rules in Colombia, partisan affiliation also can be seen as a fomenter of violence, as most of the civil conflicts prior to the 1960s were partisan in nature: liberal versus conservative. Indeed, as noted above, La Violencia was a partisan civil war, and the FARC evolved from liberal self-defense groups from that era.

Really, the combination of elite commitment to democratic rules (granted, ones skewed in their favor) and clientelistic practices within the state, which linked policy largesse from the local to the national level with elected politicians, has imbued the democratic habit into a substantial portion of the Colombian populace. It is true that voter turnout is low (a condition that predates concerted attempts by guerrillas to disrupt elections), bringing into question the depth of commitment to democracy in the Colombian public. Still, the juxtaposition of democratic norms and clientelism is ironic given that much of the criticism of Colombian democracy over the years (both by analysts in Colombia and from the outside) have often cited the problems of overconcentration of power in the hands of elite families and the substantial presence of clientele networks.[21] Nonetheless, the basic lesson is clear: the commitment of elites to democratic rule is essential to the habituation of democracy in the mass populace.

A main lesson that Colombia may provide in a broader context is the degree to which a major impediment to political terrorism can take away the sources of power and funding for terrorist groups. In the past, the allure of Marxist revolution fueled a great deal of political violence, some of it terroristic, in Latin America. Its demise led to a commensurate demise of guerrilla war in much of the region. In the case of Colombia, the presence of substantial revenues from narcotrafficking has allowed for a prolongation of armed struggle. This is not unique to Colombia, as the Taliban used opium poppies as a method to generate revenue during the time it controlled Afghanistan, and Kashmiri separatists are reportedly using profits from the opium trade to fund their war as well (Baldauf 2003).

Ultimately, I fear that the stalemate will continue. This means that on the one hand, Colombia will persist, as will its embattled democratic government. However, on the other, it means that the violence will continue as well. There is little doubt that guerrillas and paramilitaries have the resources needed to continue their struggle as long as they wish, given the nearly infinite profits from the illicit trade in cocaine and heroin. However, it is also the case that they lack the military might and, more importantly, the popular support needed to overthrow the state. And the Colombian military lacks the ability to best the guerrillas. As such, Colombia will remain a key example of democratic governance under the constant threat of political violence.

NOTES

1. Colombia, Costa Rica, and Venezuela are considered Latin America's longest-running democracies, each dating back to the late 1950s. Of course, Venezuela's recent experience with Hugo Chávez leads to classification problems with Venezuela.

2. The largest delimited political violence event of the twentieth century was La Violencia, the partisan civil war of the late 1940s and 1950s that took the lives of an estimated 250,000 Colombians. Since then, of course, are the conflicts with various guerilla groups from the 1960s to the current day and the drug wars.

3. For example, Wilde (1978) classified Colombia's democracy as "oligarchical," Martz (1992, 22) considered it "qualified," and Bagley (1984, 25) referred to Colombia as an "inclusionary authoritarian" regime. And, as Diamond (1999, 31) notes, Colombia became less free starting in the early 1990s.

4. Under the National Front, the congress and all local offices were split 50–50 between the Liberals and Conservatives, and the presidency alternated every four years. Competitive elections between members of the parties filled the actual slots. While this system did officially curtail the participation of third parties, it was a fairly porous system with essentially any office seeker having the ability to declare themselves either a Liberal or a Conservative. Indeed, the dissident National Popular Alliance (ANAPO) ran congressional candidates on both Liberal and Conservative lists (and won seats by so doing). For a brief overview, see Bushnell (1993, 228–30).

5. The only national election that was the subject of serious debate vis-à-vis fraud was the 1970 contest, which helped spawn the M-19 guerilla movement.

6. For example, the average rate of participation in Colombian presidential elections from 1970 to 2002 is 45.5 percent (this number excludes the rate for the first round of the 1998 race, which are not available). Source: National Registry of Colombia.

7. Only the first question passed, which was a minor anticorruption measure (Consejo Nacional Electoral 2004).

8. The October 26, 2003, election saw the election of Luis Eduardo Garzon (a.k.a. "Lucho"), a former communist and labor union leader, to the mayoralty of Bogota. Garzon came in third to Uribe in the 2002 presidential elections. His election marks the most significant electoral victory of the left in Colombia's history. Further, he is not the first unorthodox candidate to win election as mayor of Bogota. The 1995 contest saw the election of Antanas Mockus, a math and philosophy professor, to the office. He was reelected to a second, nonconsecutive term (consecutive terms are not allowed under the Colombian constitution) in 2000.

9. For example, see the cases of El Salvador, where a stalemated guerilla conflict led to a negotiated settlement, or Peru, where the guerillas were essentially defeated by the state.

10. The *Handbook*, a publication of the Library of Congress, reviews literature in the United States and in Latin America on the politics and government of the region in each of its odd-numbered issues. The chapters in question here are in volumes 57, 59, and 61 (Chernick 1999; Taylor 2003; Taylor forthcoming).

11. The references are in Bergquist, Penaranda, and Sanchez (2001, 7, 17, 10, 116, 172, 185, 222–23, 234, and 262).

12. The complicity of the military in the actions of paramilitary groups certainly confers to the state the employment of terror by sanctioning (directly or indirectly) political assassinations and peasant massacres — that is, "dirty war" tactics aimed at potential leftist sympathizers. However, since this activity is unofficial and difficult to track, there is no specific discussion of official state action in this section. However, the linkage to the paramilitaries should be noted.

13. At least 250,000 Colombians died in this conflict between liberals and conservatives.

14. The decimation of much of the group during the Palace of Justice confrontation with the military in 1985 helped to encourage this transformation.

15. See Watson (1992, 91–93) for a brief overview of the FARC's history and Serres (2000) and *BBC News* (2002) for an evaluation of its current status.

16. For a fascinating example of the FARC's presence in the rural department of Meta, see Wilson (2003).

17. For example, Law 48 of 1968 allowed for the legal organization of rural self-defense groups. The law was abolished in April of 1989. Decree 356 of 1994 allowed for the creation of Private Cooperatives for Vigilance and Security (CONVIVIR)—which were abolished in 1999. For a discussion of paramilitaries see Cubides (2001), Richani (2000), and Santina (1998).

18. The Spanish acronym MAS stands for Muerte a Secuestradores.

19. Bagley (1988, 84) links at least five hundred deaths of UP members to the narco-funded group MAS between 1985 and 1988. MAS was purported also to have included active duty military officers (Richani 2000).

20. Bagley (1988, 83–84) treats this information as tentative, but Carlso Castano, leader of the paramilitary group AUC, states in his autobiography that this was indeed the case (Hu-

man Rights Watch 2002). Castano's brother, Fidel, who was allegedly killed by the FARC (see Dudley 2002 for that remarkable tale), was an associate of Pablo Escobar's and was involved with MAS before working with his brother to found what would become AUC. The Palace of Justice affair illustrates the complex interaction of players in the Colombian context that has been distorted primarily by drug profits and the need for groups to have adequate funding for their activities. If this net of connection is correct, it demonstrates a most bizarre picture. Allegedly, the cartel wanted the guerrillas to destroy records in the palace related to extradition, while the guerrillas were seeking a huge operation to bolster their flagging fight against the state. So far, so good, except that the Castano brothers were antiguerrilla (although, granted, anti-FARC, due to the kidnapping and murder of their father), while the cartel was anti-M-19, as MAS had been founded because M-19 had kidnapped a drug lord's daughter. For more on the Palace of Justice incident, see Carrigan (1993) and Hudson (1995).

21. See, for example, Archer (1990) and Leal and Davila (1991).

REFERENCES

Amnesty International. 2003. *Amnesty International Report 2003*. New York: Amnesty International. web.amnesty.org/report2003/index-eng.

Archer, Ronald P. 1990. *The Transition from Traditional to Broker Clientelism in Colombia: Political Stability and Social Unrest*. Kellogg Institute Working Paper #140. Notre Dame, Indiana.

Bagley, Bruce M. 1984. "Colombia: National Front and Economic Development." In *Politics and Economic Development in Latin America*, ed. Robert Wesson. Stanford: The Hoover Institute.

———. 1988. "Colombia and the War on Drugs." *Foreign Affairs* 67 (Fall): 70–92.

Baldauf, Scott. 2003. "Heroin Money Could Fund Kashmir's Militants." *Christian Science Monitor*, October 20. www.csmonitor.com/2003/1020/p07s02-wosc.html.

Bergquist, Charles, Ricardo Penaranda, and Gonzalo Sanchez, eds. 1992. *Violence in Colombia: The Contemporary Crisis in Historical Perspective*. Wilmington, Del.: Scholarly Resources.

———, eds. 2001. *Violence in Colombia, 1990–2000: Waging War and Negotiating Peace*. Wilmington, Del.: Scholarly Resources.

BBC News. 2002. "Colombia's Most Powerful Rebels." September 19. http://news.bbc.co.uk/1/hi/world/americas/1746777.stm.

Brooke, James. 1990. "230,000 Troops Patrol Colombia on Election Eve." *New York Times*, May 26, p. 17.

Bushnell, David. 1992. "Politics and Violence in Nineteenth Century Colombia." In *Violence in Colombia: The Contemporary Crisis in Historical Perspective*, ed. Charles Bergquist, Ricardo Penaranda, and Gonzalo Sanchez, 11–30. Wilmington, Del.: Scholarly Resources.

———. 1993. *The Making of Modern Colombia: A Nation in Spite of Itself*. Berkeley: University of California Press.

Carrigan, Ana. 1993. *The Palace of Justice: A Colombian Tragedy*. New York: Four Walls, Eight Windows.

Chernick, Marc. 1999. "Government and Politics: Colombia and Ecuador." In *Handbook of Latin American Studies*, Vol. 57, ed. Dolores Moyano Martin, 456–63. Austin: University of Texas Press.

Consejo Nacional Electoral. 2004. *Resultados Definitivos del Referendo*. Bogota: Republica de Colombia.

Cooper, H. H. A. 2001. "Terrorism: The Problem of Definition Revisited." *American Behavioral Scientist* 44 (February): 881–93.

Cubides, Fernando. 2001. "From Private to Public Violence: The Paramilitaries." In *Violence in Colombia 1990–2000: Waging War and Negotiating Peace*, ed. Charles Bergquist, Ricardo Penaranda, and Gonzalo Sanchez, 127–49. Wilmington, Del.: Scholarly Resources.

Diamond, Larry. 1999. *Developing Democracy: Toward Consolidation*. Baltimore: Johns Hopkins University Press.

Dudley, Steven. 2002. "Dead Man's Bluff." *Washington Post*, November 24, W10.

El Tiempo. 2003a. "Alvaro Uribe asegura que las Farc ordenaron asesinar candidates." October 13.

———. 2003b. "198 alcaldes del pais estan amenazados por la guerrilla o los paramilitares." October 13.

———. 2003c. "Reportan el asesinato de 25 candidatos a las comicios del 26 de octubre." October 7.

Hudson, Rex A. 1995. "Colombia's Palace of Justice Tragedy Revisited: A Critique of the Conspiracy Theory." *Terrorism and Political Violence* 7(2) (Summer): 93–142.

Human Rights Watch. 2002. "Colombia: FARC Kidnappings Documented." *Human Rights News*. April 15. www.hrw.org/press/2002/04/farc0415.htm.

Jenkins, Brian Michael. 2000. "Colombia: Crossing a Dangerous Threshold." *National Interest* (Winter): 47–55.

Kline, Harvey F. 1999. *State Building and Conflict Resolution in Colombia, 1986–1994*. Tuscaloosa: University of Alabama Press.

Leal Buitrago, Francisco, and Andres Davila Ladron. 1991. *Clientelismo: El sistema politico colombiano y su expression regional*. 2d ed. Bogota: Tercer Mundo Editores.

Martz, John. 1992. "Contemporary Colombian Politics: The Struggle over Democratization." In *The Colombian Economy: Issues of Trade and Development*, ed. Alvin Cohen and Frank R. Gunter. Boulder, Colo.: Westview.

McDermott, Jeremy. 2002. "Bogota Bible Bomb Plot Exposed." *Scotsman*, February 10, p. 10.

———. 2003. "Bogota Nightclub Bombing Blamed on Marxist Rebel Group." *Scotsman*, February 10, p. 11.

Merari, Ariel. 1993. "Terrorism as a Strategy of Insurgency." *Terrorism and Political Violence* 5 (Winter): 213–51.

Ottis, John. 2002. "Rebels Tell Colombia's Mayors: Resign Or Die." *Houston Chronicle*, June 26, p. A26.

Richani, Nazih. 2000. "The Parliamentary Connection." *NACLA Report on the Americas*. 34(2) (September/October): 38–43.

Santina, Peter. 1998. "Army of Terror: The Legacy of US Backed Human Rights Abuses in Colombia." *Harvard International Review* 21(2) (Winter 1998–99): 40–43.

Seattle Times. 2003. "Bombing Tied to IRA, Basque Rebels." February 12, p. A12.

Semple, Kirk. 2002. "Undaunted, Colombia's Uribe Presses Security Plan." *Christian Science Monitor,* August 9, p. 7.

Serres, Philippe. 2000. "The FARC and Democracy in Colombia in the 1990's." *Democratization* 7(4) (Winter): 191–218.

Sofaer, Abraham D. 1986. "Terrorism and the Law." *Foreign Affairs* 64 (Summer): 901–92.

Sweig, Julia E. 2002. "What Kind of War for Colombia?" *Foreign Affairs* 81 (September/October): 122.

Taylor, Steven L. Forthcoming. "Government and Politics: Colombia." In *Handbook of Latin American Studies*, Vol. 59, ed. Lawrence Boudon. Austin: University of Texas Press.

———. 2003. "Government and Politics: Colombia." In *Handbook of Latin American Studies*, Vol. 61, ed. Lawrence Boudon, 490–98. Austin: University of Texas Press.

Watson, Cynthia. 1992. "Guerrilla Groups in Colombia: Reconstituting the Political Process." *Terrorism and Political Violence* 4 (Summer): 84–102.

Wilde, Alexander W. 1978. "Conversations among Gentlemen: Oligarchical Democracy in Colombia." In *The Breakdown of Democratic Regimes*, ed. Juan J. Linz and Alfred Stepan, 28–81. Baltimore: Johns Hopkins University Press.

Wilson, Scott. 2001. "Colombia's Peace Bid at Risk; Arrests of IRA Trainers Spark Calls to Close Safe Haven for Rebels." *Washington Post,* August 25, p. A13.

———. 2003. "Colombia's Rebel Zone: World Apart." *Washington Post,* October 18, p. A1.

PART SEVEN

Conclusion

WILLIAM CROTTY

25 International Terrorism
CAUSES AND CONSEQUENCES FOR A
DEMOCRATIC SOCIETY

Terrorism is not going to fade away. If anything, the likelihood is that it will be with us for as far into the future as we choose to project.

Several points seem clear: first, the root causes, as seen in the foregoing chapters, are unlikely to be addressed in any meaningful way. Authoritarian governments, however they choose to label themselves, are likely to persevere; repression will continue; poverty, ignorance, fear of modernity, and religious zealotry will not disappear; and military action over any prolonged period of time is costly, debilitating to the nation relying on it, and potentially destructive of the very democratic values it has been enlisted to serve.

Second, terrorists operate with their own group dynamics. Blind loyalty, authoritarian leaders, eternal rewards (martyrdom), intense social pressures on the individuals recruited to serve the cause, loyalty to the group, and, most surprising for those not caught up in the terrorist mythology, a desire to better the lot of those they identify with and whose cause they perceive themselves as championing serve to reinforce the group's bonds, its objectives, and the subjugation of the individual, whatever the cost, to achieving the goals sought.

Third, terrorism can be highly effective. In a sense, this is its ugly secret. It may well be unethical, immoral, inhumane, and criminal from the perspective of those who are targeted. Nonetheless, terrorist acts can highlight a group's causes, foment terror and fear (as intended) in those seen as enemies, and destroy symbolically or in actuality (through suicide bombings, assassinations, car bombings, plane hijackings, kidnappings, and random killing) those it chooses to attack. The seemingly random nature of such attacks and their legacy of death and horror all serve to promote the ends and political importance of the groups committing the acts. It can be a vicious cycle—a terrorist act, a high casualty rate, condemnation by the country attacked, a rise in concern about and importance for the group carrying out the mission.

Fourth, and ironically, contemporary technology can actually be used to increase the deadliness and effectiveness of terrorist actions; an example is the nuclear threat evident in the world today. The materials for such weapons can be had for a price, and advanced weaponry can be used effectively by small groups against large military or civilian targets.

Fifth, organizations such as al Qaeda have shown a marked ability to adapt and to organize efficiently in order to operate successfully in this modern hi-tech world. In her discussion of al Qaeda, Jessica Stern quotes an American neo-Nazi on strategies to adopt and survive:

> Al Qaeda seems to have learned that in order to evade detection in the West, it must adopt some of the qualities of a "virtual network": a style of organization . . . groups refer to . . . as "leaderless resistance." . . . [H]ierarchical organization is extremely dangerous for insurgents, especially in "technologically advanced societies where electronic surveillance can often penetrate the structure, revealing its chain of command." In leaderless organizations . . . "individuals and groups operate independently of each other, and never report to a central headquarters or single leader for direction or instruction, as would those who belong to a typical pyramid organization." Leaders do not issue orders or pay operatives; instead, they inspire small cells or individuals to take action on their own initiative. (Stern 2003, 33–34)

Adapting to the terrain and taking on the coloration of the society (as al Qaeda did in training and planning the attacks of 9/11) appears to be an attribute of the most successful terrorist networks, and one that works to ensure their survival in the modern world.

Sixth, "transitions to democracy" can be virtually endless; "consolidation" of democracies is hard to achieve. There is no format, or many times not even an identifiable starting point, for a democratic evolution to begin. There also are no specific marking points for when a "transition" may be in its final stages or when a permanent "consolidation" may have taken root. The process is messy, uneven in timing, often facing setbacks in policies or leadership, and extraordinarily difficult to achieve and maintain. Add to this that the international community often loses interest as time passes, and as long as the forms of the democratic process are honored, regardless of the reality of the situation, it is normally satisfied. Perception is the key to politics; unfortunately, it may also be the key to maintaining semiauthoritarian, or even fully authoritarian, states.

Seventh, terrorist organizations can morph themselves, much as do other institutions, into different versions of the same or related species that continue (if with altered objectives and under different pretenses) the life and continuity of the organization. It is a basic principle of group dynamics, not unknown to corporations, governments, and not-for-profit organizations. Unfortunately, the new group dynamic preserves the tactics and violent methodology of its source. Jessica Stern states that

> many terrorists and their supporters have suggested to me that people first join such groups to make the world a better place—at least for the particular populations they aim to serve. Over time . . . terrorism can become a career as much as a passion. Leaders harness humiliation and anomie and turn them into weapons. Jihad becomes addictive . . . and with some individuals or groups—the "professional" terrorists—grievances can evolve into greed: for money, political power, status, or attention. (Stern 2003, 208)

Furthermore,

> In such "professional" terrorist groups, simply perpetuating their cadres becomes a central goal, and what started out as a moral crusade becomes a sophisticated organization. . . . Some groups find a new cause once their first one is achieved. . . . Other groups broaden their goals in order to attract a wider variety of recruits. Still other organizations transform themselves into profit-driven organized criminals, or form alliances with groups that have ideologies different from their own, forcing both to adapt. Some terrorist groups hold fast to their original missions. But only the spry survive. (Stern 2003, 28)

It is a conception familiar to organizational theorists, and it occurs in organizations as dissimilar as the March of Dimes and the U.S. military.

Eighth, exporting democratic values and institutions is not easy. This is seen in much of the world as manifestations of Western culture and as not unrelated to economic expansion and exploitation, an experience most nondemocratic countries are familiar with and one that serves to legitimize much of the terrorist rage against the West. The attack against the World Trade Center, was, in essence, an attack against wealth and the symbol of capitalism. The Pentagon attack focused on the military. Combined, the world's wealthiest and most powerful nation experienced devastating assaults on two of its most proud and representative symbols. None of this, of course, was by accident; rather, it was the outcome of long-term, careful, and technically sophisticated planning.

Ninth, the gap in economic and social resources and in the political cultures of democratic and nondemocratic nations is enormous, a formidable obstacle to democratization efforts of any kind. As Atul Kohli puts it,

> sources of social and political democracy to most developing countries come as imported ideas. As these ideas are translated into institutions of follower democracies and these institutions provide new incentives for political actors to organize and mobilize, the results over the short to medium term are often disquieting. . . . Whatever the mechanisms, cultural conditions in the developing world do not readily mesh with these imported political models. . . . [I]dentities tend to be more local than national; authority in society tends to be dispersed but, within dispersed pockets, quite rigid and hierarchical; and community norms often prevail over narrow individualism. (1997, 72)

There is an issue of modernity and traditionalism involved in this that goes beyond the benefits of democratization. In effect, the effort is to layer one civilization and its values over another. The two can be millennia apart as much as they are products of different historical, religious, and cultural forces.

Tenth, the new "democracy," such as it is, can come from external efforts to institutionalize democratic forms of representation and decision-making. What emerges may look a good deal like the old authoritarianism, with a few fringe elements added (political institutions, regular elections, a written constitution) to satisfy the outside world and justify a long and costly crusade. In Iraq or Afghanistan, as examples, the eventual outcomes and the new governing elites may not be all that different in operation and objectives from the old. "One of the biggest dangers facing postwar Iraq is the prospect of its becoming a classic 'petro-state' (like Nigeria or Venezuela), in which vast revenues from the sale of oil accrue to a shaky national government. Such states are characterized by massive corruption, fiscal profligacy, and vicious zero-sum competition for control of oil revenues. Politicians who gain power in these countries typically invest heavily in repression to retain it" (Lawson 2003, 206). The hope is that places such as Iraq (or Kuwait after the first Gulf War in 1991) emerge overall "better off than they were before" (209)—a modest goal given the effort expended but both programmatic and practical, and incrementally one that other authoritarian states might be pushed into achieving.

All of this can be surmised rather easily in relating democratic development to modern-day terrorism. Terrorism has many causes and takes many forms. It thrives best in societies the least likely to address the causes or conditions that provide its life force. It is not a short-term problem. There are no quick or easy solutions. In its various forms, the likelihood is that it will be with us far into the indefinite future.

This assessment may not be satisfying. The unfortunate fact is that terrorism is what is most likely to occur. If so, the real question may be how to contain its worst features, lessen its impact and global role, and best resolve the conditions and regimes that give it relevance.

APPROACHES TO TERROR

Again, there are no clear, direct, or easy answers in regard to lessening the causes of terrorism and its consequences. There are options, though, that can be pursued. These could include:

1. Diplomatic engagement over the long run, with one objective being to understand terrorism and to attack the conditions that make it attractive to recruits.

2. The use of economic sanctions, claimed to be useful in undermining apartheid in South Africa but embraced cautiously by others who believe the effects are indirect and seldom enforced completely and are, therefore, basically ineffective. Economic sanctions are not a prime option for those seeking significant change in a predetermined framework of time. They have been used against Fidel Castro in Cuba and in Libya. In the latter case, broad international sanctions (which went beyond the economic) could be said to have succeeded, convincing Moammar Khadafi to open his country to international weapons inspectors and in practice removing it from a terrorist designation.

3. Humanitarian aid intended to alleviate the economic and social conditions that breed terrorists. This has been the principal approach taken by the European Union (EU). It also would take a significant amount of time to impact a problem such as terrorism or to advance democratizing efforts in authoritarian cultures. Still, it would seem to be a necessary component of any long-range plan, although on a large if not massive scale. As an example, the European Commission (of the EU) provides approximately one-third (30 percent) of global humanitarian aid, while EU member states acting on their own volition are responsible for an additional 25 percent of the sanctioned humanitarian aid officially distributed worldwide.

   There are two major problems in this strategy. One is convincing governments to reduce domestic spending to supplement international aid. It is, in effect, a zero-sum game and one not likely to be overly popular with the donor countries. The EU has shown that such an approach can work under the proper conditions, as it has in Ireland, Spain, Portugal, and Greece, in upgrading economic conditions and hence the quality of life and in bringing these countries close to the standard of living enjoyed by other European nations. However, an equalization of resources, not a fight against terrorism, was the precipitating motivation. The enlargement of the EU into Eastern Europe may test the validity of this approach and serve to overextend the resources of the core EU nations.

There is also the difficulty of ensuring that humanitarian aid gets to the groups it is intended to help and does not simply refill the treasury of the states and their elites responsible for the repression, exclusion, and underdevelopment that give rise, in extreme situations, to terrorist cultures.

4. Military action, the principal alternative pursued by the United States. What is clear is that military force has its limits. There has to be something more — precise nation-building plans, economic aid, and a long-term commitment to seeing the process through to completion. The American experience in Iraq would indicate also that multinational military efforts are far preferable to unilateral declarations of war and the problems that accompany them.

5. Establishing international sanctions for terrorist states and groups, such as creating multinational peacekeeping forces equipped to move quickly and effectively against terrorism and state and ethnic or religious group terrorism (Kosovo, Rwanda, the Congo, Liberia, Bosnia, the list goes on). Also, the institution of an international court of justice and truth commissions and tribunals would help in bringing a sense of order, reason, and the rule of law to situations as they arose. In many respects, the European community and the United Nations are moving in these directions.

EFFECTS ON THE HOMELAND

The war against terrorism can have significant costs for the nation pursuing it, all of which move beyond democratic bounds: domestic restrictions on transportation; civil rights and liberties; the use of national resources; the operations of institutions designed to be accountable to the citizenry; the abdication of responsibility for policy or outcomes by agencies intended to represent (Congress) or protect (the courts) the public interest; the failure of a coherent opposition to mobilize; the constitutionally questionable awarding of war powers (by Congress) to the president (the "strike first" authorization); the power of the government to gain access to financial records, private communications such as telephone conversations and email messages, health reports, and credit ratings and to spy on those deemed suspect without notification to the individuals involved; and the authority to detain individuals (citizens, aliens, war prisoners) indefinitely without access to the courts, lawyers, constitutional protections, or judicial procedures. The United States is far from being a perfect democracy, as most would recognize. Nonetheless, this is not the direction a democracy would prefer to move in.

Several post-9/11 developments bring into question the fundamental values of American society. U.S. government agencies were restructured to create a cabinet-level superdepartment, the Department of Homeland Security. The CIA was authorized to involve itself in internal domestic affairs (a violation of its charter), and the FBI was authorized to extend powers of investigation and its jurisdiction internationally. The powers of the Defense Department and National Security Agency have also been expanded. Data banks have been created to store personal information, inaccessible and unknown to the individual involved, in federal archives available to security agencies and police. The changes are broad and fundamental. American government is being transformed (Crotty 2004; O'Hanlon 2002; Leone and Anrig 2003). How long-term the changes are—many, it would appear, are beyond being reversed—and what their ultimate consequences are to be is yet to be determined. Modestly put, the America of pre-9/11 is not the America of post-9/11. Indeed, as terrorist attacks occur in one country after another, the world is not the same place. Developing and living in a state of permanent national security is not an attractive option. Recall that during the cold war, in a battle of democracy versus totalitarianism, it was not seen as necessary to institute the restrictions on freedoms or the powers that have been granted the Bush administration in its war against terrorism.

COST AND CONSEQUENCES

There is another major issue involved in all of this. Simply put, what are America's objectives? To end terrorism? Understandable, but unlikely given the policies that are being followed. To place America's (or the West's) stamp on the world? To extend its values, culture, and institutions worldwide? The immediate reaction to terrorism is understandable, but the long-range objectives are questionable. Is the United States to serve as arbitrator of what is good or evil? Which governments should continue to exist and which should not? Which countries should the United States invade and which should it choose to ignore, however egregious their policies of state-based terrorism, nuclear threat (North Korea is a recent example), or aggression against their neighbors? Will the United States assume the role of the world's policeman? Increasingly, there are references to a "Pax America." It is not a comfortable role for a nation with the traditions and history of the United States to undertake or enforce. Yet it may be in progress.

The warning signs are there. Terrorist acts have had an enormous impact on American society and on U.S. relations with other nations. Whether the changes under way will become permanent and the security state expanded or whether there will be a return to the pre-9/11 political order is yet to be seen.

In regard to the terminology by some referring to the United States as "the Reluctant Empire," Paul Kennedy and others strongly reject both the concept of "reluctant" (he and others feel it was planned) and "empire," a role he (and again others) believes would make a casualty of the American democratic system (Kennedy, Perle and Nye 2003; Nye 2002; Carothers 1999). As for "empire," Kennedy states that

> From Okinawa to Kuwait, we wield enormous, disproportionate power. We have military contingents in 40 countries, naval bases in ten, and right now are drawing up plans to turn Iraq into some sort of mandate. [Deputy Secretary of Defense Paul] Wolfowitz [a neoconservative ideologue and the principal author of an influential national security document advocating the position the Bush administration adopted in the exporting of democracy and the targeting of likely countries] has recently set up a panel in Washington to advise him on the rise and fall of empires in the past, and why certain empires lasted so long. . . . [I]f it looks like an empire, and acts like an empire, and increasingly quacks like an empire, well, perhaps you know what it is? (Kennedy, Perle, and Nye 2003, 14)

AS FOR THE UNITED STATES BEING "RELUCTANT,"

> the anti-war demonstrations across the country—the dimensions of which are not fully covered by our too, too-cautious media—suggest a lot of reluctance, dismay, and anger at the White House's decision to go to war in the present circumstances. But among the right-wing think tanks and the hawkish intellectuals, who have been telling each other and telling us for the past years that we need to re-make the Middle East, refashion the Arab world, topple dictators, and force democracy on other societies, among those folks, could one honestly say there was reluctance? When . . . [told] that once we have reached Baghdad we should turn smart right and head for Tehran, is that reluctance? Where do we stop? Ever newer acquisitions bring ever newer frontiers of insecurity. (Kennedy, Perle, and Nye 2003, 15)

Political terrorism is a reality. It is deadly, difficult to deal with, and effective. It has transformed a good deal of America's political infrastructure, and it has also negatively impacted the freedoms of its citizens. The terrorist threat is real. It has worldwide consequences. The issue yet to be effectively resolved is how best to deal with it within a framework that maintains a democratic order and protects the values of a democratic society.

REFERENCES

Carothers, Thomas. 1999. *Aiding Democracy Abroad: The Learning Curve*. Washington, D.C.: Carnegie Endowment for Peace.

Crotty, William. 2004. *The Politics of Terror*. Boston: Northeastern University Press.

Kennedy, Paul, Richard Perle, and Joseph S. Nye Jr. 2003. "The Reluctant Empire: In a Time of Great Consequence." *Brown Journal of World Affairs* 10(1) (Summer/Fall): 11–31.

Kohli, Atul. 1997. "On Sources of Social and Political Conflicts in Follower Democracies." In *Democracy's Victory and Crisis*, ed. Axel Hadenius, 71–80. Cambridge: Cambridge University Press.

Lawson, Stephanie. 2003. *International Relations*. Malden, Mass.: USA Polity.

Leone, Richard C.,and Greg Anrig. 2003. *The War on Our Freedoms: Civil Liberties in an Age of Terrorism*. New York: BBS Public Affairs.

Nye, Joseph S. 2002. *The Paradox of American Power*. New York: Oxford University Press.

O'Hanlon, Michael. 2003. *Protecting the American Homeland: One Year On*. Washington, D.C.: Brookings Institution Press.

Stern, Jessica. 2003. *Terror in the Name of God: Why Religious Militants Kill*. New York: Ecco.

About the Contributors

Abdullah Al-Faqih is Professor of Political Science at Sana'a University in Yemen. He received his PhD from Northeastern University in 2003. His writings and publications are in the area of democratization, the Middle East, Yemen, and regional peace processes.

Chris Barr received his master's in history from Southern Illinois University and has worked with John S. Jackson III at the Public Policy Institute since 2001, focusing primarily on twentieth-century American political history and the history of public policy. He has co-authored or worked on a number of books and articles.

Amílcar Antonio Barreto is an Associate Professor of Political Science at Northeastern University and a member of Northeastern University's executive committee in Latino, Latin American, and Caribbean Studies. A graduate of the State University of New York at Buffalo, where he earned his JD in 1993 and his PhD in political science in 1995, he was the youngest recipient of the Universidad Interamericana's Distinguished Alumnus award (2002). He is the author of three books: *Vieques, the Navy, and Puerto Rican Politics* (University Press of Florida, 2002); *The Politics of Language in Puerto Rico* (University Press of Florida, 2001); and *Language, Elites, and the State: Nationalism in Puerto Rico and Quebec* (1998). His scholarly articles have appeared in the *Canadian Review of Studies in Nationalism, Caribbean Studies, Centro Journal, Homines, Nationalism & Ethnic Politics, Peace Review, Polity,* and *Revista de Ciencias Sociales.* He is currently working on his fourth book—a study of rationality and nationalist movements.

Lenard J. Cohen, Professor of Political Science at Simon Fraser University, British Columbia, Canada, specializes in Russian and East European politics with a particular focus on the Balkans. During the last decade, he has also been working on questions of regional security in Southeastern Europe, international relations, and both Canadian and U.S. foreign policy toward Eastern Europe. Dr. Cohen has published widely in political science journals, edited collections, and written many books concerning Europe. His recent books, both published in 2003, are *NATO and European Security: Alliance Politics from the End of the Cold War to the Age of Terrorism* and *Foreign Policy Realignment in the Age of Terror*. He is currently working on a study of democratization in Southeastern Europe entitled *Embracing Democracy: Political Change in Southeastern Europe.*

Daniel Cox teaches Asian and comparative politics at Missouri Western State College and has long had an interest in researching democratic and economic development in Southeast Asia. He is also interested in U.S. foreign policy as it relates to democracy and capitalism in the region. His most recent publication, a study of U.S. foreign policy titled, "Making Sense of Poll Results: Ambiguity in the Interpretation of Foreign Policy Questions regarding the United Nations," was published in the *International Journal of Public Opinion Research* (Summer 2002).

William Crotty is Thomas P. O'Neill Professor and Director of the O'Neill Center for the Study of Democracy at Northeastern University. Areas of study are democratization and democratic development, political parties, electoral and political behavior, and political representation. Dr. Crotty is the author or editor of a number of publications, including *The Politics of Terror: The U.S. Response to 9/11* (2003); *Political Terrorism and America* (2005); *Ireland and the Politics of Change* (1998); and *Public Policy and Developing Nations* (1996). He is past president of the Policy Studies Organization, the Midwest Political Science Association, and the Political Organization and Parties section of the American Political Science Association, from which he received a Lifetime Achievement award. He teaches courses in democratization, comparative democracies, and American and comparative political parties.

Karla J. Cunningham is Assistant Professor in the Department of Political Science and International Relations at SUNY Geneseo. She joined the faculty in 1999 after leaving the Department of Defense, where she worked as an analyst. With specializations in the Middle East and North Africa, terrorism, and national security, Dr. Cunningham regularly consults for U.S. and Canadian law enforcement. Currently working on a book regarding female political violence, Dr. Cunningham published an article on that topic in *Studies in Conflict and Terrorism* (2003) and has also published on topics related to democratization, the Middle East peace process, and Islamic fundamentalism. She received her PhD from the University of Buffalo in 1997.

Richard Farkas is Professor of Political Science at DePaul University. He is in his thirtieth year teaching about Central and Eastern European politics. He holds an honorary degree from Budapest University of Economic Sciences and Public Administration and has lectured in Russia, Poland, Hungary, Croatia, Montenegro, Greece, and Kosovo. His research compares strategies for political and economic development in postcommunist countries. The future trajectory of these systems is a special focus of his research. Professor Farkas has published articles and books for both academic and public audiences, consulted for some of the largest corporations in the United States and Europe, and has frequently appeared on U.S. and international broadcast media.

Irene Gendzier is currently Professor of Political Science at Boston University. She is affiliated with the University's African Studies Center and is a research associate at Harvard University's Center for Middle East Studies. Her articles and books span the subjects of development, third world studies, and U.S. foreign policy in the Middle East and include works such as *Frantz Fanon: A Biography* (1973, Pantheon/Grove Press; French and Spanish editions published by Seuil and Era/SP); *Development against Democracy* (Tyrone Press, 1995); *Notes from the Minefield: United States Intervention in Lebanon and the Middle East, 1945–1958* (Columbia University Press, 1997, and Westview Press, 1999); "Play It again Sam: The Practice and Apology of Development," in *Universities and Empire*, ed. C. Simpson (1998); and "The Saints Come Marching In: A Response to John Lewis Gaddis," in *After the Fall: 1988 and the Future of Freedom*, ed. G. Katstiaficas (2001). Of particular relevance to the current essay are the following: "Oil, Politics and the Military," in *Masters of War*, ed. C. Boggs (2003); and "Dying to Forget: The U.S. and Iraq's Weapons of Mass Destruction," in the online journal *Logos* (Winter 2003).

Mohammed M. Hafez is Visiting Professor of Political Science at the University of Missouri—Kansas City and the author of *Why Muslims Rebel: Repression and Resistance in the Islamic World* (Lynne Rienner, 2003). He earned a PhD in international relations from the London School of Economics and Political Science and was a Harry Frank Guggenheim Foundation fellow and a United States Information Agency fellow during 1998–99. In 2003, Hafez began a study of Palestinian suicide bombers with a grant from the United States Institute of Peace.

Irm Haleem is Visiting Assistant Professor of Political Science at Northeastern University. She holds a PhD from Boston University (January 2001) in political science with a concentration in South Asian politics. Dr. Haleem is currently working on a book project dealing with the issue of state and legitimacy in Pakistan. She is the author of "Ethnic and Sectarian Violence and the Propensity of Praetorianism in Pakistan" (June 2003) in the journal *Third World Quarterly*. She has also been involved in a number of colloquia at area universities dealing with the impact of 9/11 on Pakistan and its current military regime and was interviewed by Voice of America (May 2002) regarding nuclear tensions between India and Pakistan.

John W. Harbeson is Professor of Political Science in the Graduate Center and at City College in the City University of New York. A comparative politics and international relations specialist, he has written extensively on African politics and development. His *Africa in World Politics* (co-edited with Donald Rothchild), in its third edition, centers on the influences of African domestic and regional politics and global patterns in international relations upon each other. He served as Regional Democracy and Governance Advisor for Eastern and Southern Africa in the Agency for International Development from 1993 to 1995. He has been a Jennings Randolph fellow at the United States Institute of Peace and a Visiting fellow at Princeton University's Center of International Studies.

John S. Jackson III is Professor of Political Science Emeritus at Southern Illinois University Carbondale and Visiting Professor at the university's Public Policy Institute. He is formerly the Interim Chancellor of SIUC, and before that he served as Provost and as Dean of the College of Liberal Arts. His two books, *The Politics of Presidential Selection*, and *Presidential Primaries and Nominations*, were co-authored with William Crotty. He has contributed chapters on national conventions, congressional elections, and presidential elections to numerous volumes, and his research has been published in the *Journal of Politics*, the *American Journal of Political Science*, *Polity*, and *Legislative Studies Quarterly*.

Mehran Kamrava is Associate Professor and Chair of Political Science at California State University, Northridge. He is the author of a number of books on political development and Middle Eastern politics including, most recently, *Democracy in the Balance: Culture and Society in the Middle East*, and the forthcoming *Continuity and Change in the Modern Middle East* (2004).

Susan Macek is a doctoral program graduate student at the University of Massachusetts at Amherst and has worked with Howard Wiarda on several projects.

Suzanne Ogden earned her PhD from Brown University and is Professor of Political Science at Northeastern University. Her research interests focus on Chinese political development, international relations, and comparative politics. Her books include *The Inklings of Democracy in China* (2002) and *China's Unresolved Issues: Politics, Development and Culture* (1995). She currently serves as a Research Associate with the Fairbank Center for East Asian Research at Harvard University.

Lada Parizkova is a native of the Czech Republic and lives in Paris. She has graduate degrees from both Czech and American universities, and has had advanced graduate work at Northeastern University, including research analysis on political terrorism in relation to the European Union and its member countries, at the Center for the Study of Democracy. She specializes in analyses of the European Union, international political terrorism, and democratization in Central and Eastern Europe.

Lawrence C. Reardon received his PhD in political science from Columbia University. His first book, entitled *The Reluctant Dragon: The Impact of Crisis Cycles on Chinese Foreign Economic Policy,* was published by the University of Washington Press in 2001. He has written articles on China's foreign policy for *China Quarterly,* the *Journal of Contemporary China,* the *China Business Review,* and the *Journal of Shenzhen University.* He is Research Associate at Harvard University's Fairbank Center, Luce fellow at the Woodrow Wilson International Center for Scholars, and Special Researcher at Jinan University (Guangzhou, China). Currently, he is Associate Professor of Political Science and Coordinator of Asian Studies at the University of New Hampshire.

James Roberts earned his PhD from the University of North Carolina and is currently Associate Professor of Political Science at the University of Southern Maine. Trained as a Sovietologist, in 1989 he took part in a study tour of Egypt, followed up by visits in the next two years to Egypt, Syria, Bahrain, and Kuwait. These travels led him to a study of the extensive English-language literature on Arab-Islamic intellectual history, with a particular view to understanding how that history relates to the contemporary predicament of the Arab world.

David E. Schmitt earned his PhD from the University of Texas, Austin, and is currently Edward W. Brooke Professor of Political Science at Northeastern University. Research interests include the Republic of Ireland, Northern Ireland, Canada, ethnic conflict, and U.S. and world security policy. His books include *The Irony of Irish Democracy* (1973) and, co-edited with William Crotty, *Ireland*

and the Politics of Change (1998) and *Ireland on the World Stage* (2002). He has written papers, articles, and chapters on the Republic of Ireland and Northern Ireland as well as ethnic conflict theory and Canada.

Jack Spence teaches in the Political Science Department of the University of Massachusetts Boston and is currently the Associate Dean of the College of Arts and Sciences. His research has focused on war, conflict resolution, and democratization in Central America since 1981. As President of Hemisphere Initiatives, he has organized and authored two dozen published analyses of postwar politics.

Rein Taagepera is Professor Emeritus at the University of California, Irvine, where he has taught since 1970, and Tartu University, Estonia, where he has taught since 1992. He earned a PhD in physics, and his main research interest is in electoral systems. He is senior author of *Seats and Votes* (Yale University Press, 1989), received 23 percent of the votes in the Estonian presidential elections of 1992, and was the founding chair (2001–2002) of the new Res Publica Party that was poised to place second or third in the Estonian parliamentary elections of March 2003.

Steven L. Taylor is Assistant Professor of Political Science at Troy State University in Alabama. He is the contributing editor on Colombia for the government and politics section of the *Handbook of Latin American Politics* and is currently working on the issues of drug war politics in the Western hemisphere and elections in Colombia. He has written on democratization in Latin America and elsewhere.

Howard J. Wiarda is Dean Rusk Professor of International Affairs and Department Head at the University of Georgia Department of International Affairs. He was formerly Professor of Political Science and Comparative Labor Relations and Leonard J. Horwitz Professor of Iberian and Latin American Studies at the University of Massachusetts at Amherst. He has written extensively on Latin American politics as well as on foreign policy, comparative politics, and developing nations; has been affiliated with top institutes and research centers; and received many grant awards.

Yahia H. Zoubir is Professor of Global Business and International Studies at Thunderbird, the American Graduate School of International Management, Glendale, Arizona, and currently Director of Thunderbird Europe in France. He is Editor-in-Chief of the refereed *Thunderbird International Business Review* and serves as a member of the editorial boards of various political and business journals. He is the co-author, editor, or main contributor of four books. His scholarly publications have appeared in the *Cambridge Review of International Affairs*, the *Oxford Companion to Politics of the World*, *Democratization*, *Third World Quarterly*, the *Canadian Journal of History (Annales Canadiennes d'Histoire)*, the *Journal of North African Studies*, the *Middle East Affairs Journal*, the *Journal of Third World Studies*, the *Middle East Journal*, *Middle Eastern Studies*, *Africa Today*, the *Journal of Modern African Studies*, the *California Western International Law Journal*, the *Maghreb Review*, the *Middle East Report*, the *Thunderbird International Business Review*, and others. He has published many chapters in numerous edited books. Dr. Zoubir is a well-established scholar on North African and European affairs whose works have been published in the United States, Europe, the Middle East, and North Africa.

Index

attrition, war of: and El Salvador, 487–88; and Nicaragua, 484–87

AUC. *See* United Self-Defense Forces of Colombia

Audiencia Nacional, 357

Aum Shin Rikyo (Aum Supreme Truth), 241

Aum Supreme Truth (Aum Shin Rikyo), 241

Australia, 195, 203, 208, 214, 267

Axis of Evil, 36, 370

Azerbaijan, 99

Azzedine, Baa, 290

Azzem, Abdallah, 289

BA. *See* Barisan Alternatif

Baader-Meinhof, 102, 355

Ba'ashir, Abu Bakar, 196, 202–3, 208, 213, 216

Badawi, Abdullah, 209

Badis, Abdelhamid Bin, 284

Baker Institute for Public Policy, 64

Bali, 202–4, 220, 256, 263–64

Balkans, 93, 362–63, 369, 397, 403, 421, 447

Balochistan, 128, 138

Bangladesh, 93–96, 130

Banna, Hassan al-, 109, 284, 287

Baranquilla, 513

Barcelona Process, 366

Barisan Alternatif (BA), 206, 207

Barisan Nasional (BN), 206

Basque ETA, 20, 356–57, 358

Basque Nationalist Party (Partido Nacionalista Vasco) (PNV), 20

Battle of the Boyne, 374

Battle of Kosovo, 400

Bechtel, 66–67

Beirut, 177

Belgrade: and Kosovo, 436, 437, 450; and organized crime, 398–402, 404, 406, 407, 409, 411, 412; and the UN, 433, 434

Belhaj, Ali, 310–14, 318, 320, 322

Belhajar, Sid Ali, 292

belonging, and identity, 26–27, 172, 231

Ben Bella, Ahmed, 168, 169

Benaissa, Benameur, 291

Bendjedid, Chadli, 286, 308, 310–11, 312, 314–15

Berlin Wall, 505

Betancourt, Ingrid, 464, 513

Betancur, Antonio Roldan, 512

Beureu'h, Teungku M. Daud, 260

Biagi, Marco, 362

Bible, 99

bin Laden, Osama, 10, 35–36, 213, 265; and 9/11 attacks, 59, 177; and Pakistan, 125-29, 137-39; and technology, 109; and Yemen, 147, 157; and USS *Cole*, 153, 156. *See also* Afghanistan; al Qaeda

Birds of Paradise, 74

Black September, 355

Black Tigers, 74

Blair House, attack on, 21

Blair, Tony, 37, 385–86

blasphemy, 113, 289

Bloody Friday, 377

Bloody Sunday, 361, 376

BN. *See* Barisan Nasional

Boeing, 66, 68

Bogota, 503, 509, 511

Bokan, Dragoslav, 402

Bolton, John R., 63

Bonaparte, Napoleon, 108, 117

Bonilla, Rodrigo Lara, 511

Bosnia, 3, 444, 528; and democracy, 93–96, 99, 100, 427-29; and the EU, 369; and Red Berets, 407; and Serbia, 398, 400-403, 410-12; and terrorist groups, 138, 363; undeclared war in, 38, 40, 41, 53

Botswana, 93

Boumediene, Houari, 281, 284

Bouteflika, Abdelaziz, 98, 297

Bouyali, Mustapha, 286, 288–89, 290, 319. *See also* Armed Islamic Movement

Brazil, 15, 461–63, 464–66. *See also* Triborder Area

Brazilian Revolutionary Action Front, 465

Breton Liberation Army (ARB), 358

Brigate Rosse, 230, 231

Britain. *See* United Kingdom

British Government of Ireland Act, 375

Bruguiere, Jean-Louis, 359

Buddhism, 233, 234, 236, 242–43

Buha, Bosko, 408

Club Nogal, 509
cocaine, 15, 410, 500, 514, 516
Code of Associations, 309
collective action, 22–28, 103, 303, 305, 320
Collins, Susan, 54
Colombia, 304, 460, 467; and democracy, 501–4; guerrilla groups in, 508–9; history of violence in, 500–501; and local attacks on democracy, 513–14; and narcotrafficking, 509; and paramilitarism, 510; political violence in, 504–5; prognostications for democracy in, 514–16; terrorism in, 463–64, 505–8. *See also* Armed Forces of Colombia
Colonna, Yvan, 359
combat elasticity, 75
Committee of Constitutional Experts, 341
communism: and Central America, 15; and Europe, 94; fear of, 132, 205–6; and Islamic countries, 94–96; and Kosovo, 425; and Malaysia, 209; and Saudi Arabia, 149; and the United States, 116, 196, 215, 268, 491, 494; and Yemen, 152
Communist Party of Italy, 230–31
Communist Party of Spain, 357
Communist Party of Uzbekistan (CPU), 135
Congo, 13, 276, 528
Conservative Party, 501
Continuity Irish Republican Army (CIRA), 361
Convention on Certain Conventional Weapons, 369
Convention on the Elimination of Discrimination against Women (CEDAW), 332, 334–35; compared to the CRC, 342–43; and Ghana, 341–42; and Uganda, 337–38; and Zambia, 339–40
Convention on the Rights of the Child (CRC), 332, 334–35; compared to the CEDAW, 342–43; and Ghana, 340–41; and Uganda, 336–37; and Zambia, 338–39
Copts, 97, 174
Costa Rica, 486
Counter Proliferation Program (CPP), 364

Counter Terrorism Program (CTP), 364
CPP. *See* Counter Proliferation Program
CPU. *See* Communist Party of Uzbekistan
CRC. *See* Convention on the Rights of the Child
credibility gap, 40, 43
Criminal Code (Amendment) Act, 340
crisis management, and the European Union, 368–71
Croatia, 94–95, 398, 400–403, 411, 412, 444
Crown Prince Abdullah, 151
Crusades, 117, 188
CTP. *See* Counter Terrorism Program
Cuba: and economic sanctions, 527; and the ETA, 357; and Gerry Adams, 386; and missile crisis, 385; and ruling classes, 483; and Puerto Rico, 19; and the USSR, 477. *See also* Castro, Fidel
Cuban Revolutionary Club, 19
Cultural Revolution, 237, 242, 249–50
Curuvija, Slavko, 409

da Silva, Elias "Maluco" Pereira, 466
da Silva, Luis Inacio "Lula," 465
D'Aubuisson, Roberto, 487
Daerah Operasi Militer (DOM), 260
Daniel, Celso, 465
DAP. *See* Democratic Action Party
Dar al Harb (Abode of War), 113, 185
Dar al Islam (Abode of Islam), 112, 113, 117, 185
Dar es Salaam, 177
Darul Islam (Islamic Domain), 201–2
Darwish, Mahmoud, 169
Daschle, Tom, 33, 49
Dayton Accord, 410
Death to Kidnappers (MAS), 510
Defense Department, 48, 50, 66, 67, 69, 529
Defense Policy Board (DPB), 58, 64, 66–69
democracy: defining, 5–6; and linkages with terrorism, 8–11; and minimalism, 431–32; as shield against jihadism, 296–98; and terrorism, 455–56; transition to, 524; values, exporting, 525. *See also individual countries*

Escobar, Pablo, 506, 509, 511–12
ETA. *See* Basque Fatherland and Liberty
ethnic oppression, 229
ethnic violence, 26, 263, 435
ethnic cleansing, 3, 15, 26, 400, 401, 448.
    See also genocide
EU. *See* European Union
Eulmi, Abdenacer El, 290
EUPM. *See* European Union Police Mission
Euro-Mediterranean Partnership, 366
Eurojust, 364–65
European Anti-Fraud Office (OLAF),
    364–65
European Commission Humanitarian Aid
    Office (ECHO), 366–67
European Convention on Extradition, 365
European Convention on the Suppression of
    Terrorism, 365
European Judicial Network, 364
European Union (EU): and Arab-Israeli
    conflict, 368; and Britain, 385; and
    crisis management, 368–71; and
    European arrest warrant, 365; history of,
    353–54; and humanitarian aid, 527–28;
    and Kosovo, 421, 425, 427, 433,
    436–37, 433–44, 439–41; membership
    in, 355, 416; and preventive actions,
    366–67; response to 9/11 attacks, 363;
    and Spain, 357; and Turkey, 96; and
    Yugoslavia, 410, 425, 436
European Union Police Mission (EUPM), 369
Europol, 354, 364
Euzko Alderdi Jeltzalea (EAJ), 20
executive branch, enhancing, 49–53
Extraditables, The, 512
Fahd, King of Saudi Arabia, 151, 173
FALN. *See* Fuerzas Armadas de Liberación
Falun Gong, 236, 240–41, 243–44
Farabundo Martí National Liberation Front
    (FMLN), 482–84, 487–88
FARC. *See* Revolutionary Armed Forces of
    Colombia
Fatah, 82, 98
fatwa, 113, 153, 213, 291–92, 294
Favela da Grota, 465–66
Fazilet, 181
FBI. *See* Federal Bureau of Investigation

Federal Bureau of Investigation (FBI), 55,
    154, 161, 529
Feith, Douglas, 68, 69
Ferghana Valley, 139
FIDA. *See* Islamic Front for Armed Jihad
Fieschi, Pascal, 421
Finland, 94, 110
First October Antifascist Resistance Group
    (GRAPO), 357
FIS. *See* Islamic Salvation Front
Five Principles of State (Pancasila), 199
flag. *See* rally effect
FLN. *See* National Liberation Front
FMLN. *See* Farabundo Martí National
    Liberation Front
Foreign Intelligence Brigade, 357
France: and Algeria, 175, 280, 282, 294,
    324; and counterterrorism, 353, 355,
    358-360, 362; and democracy, 94;
    Muslim population of, 113; and Soviet
    invasion of Afghanistan, 289; and war on
    Iraq, 37
Franks, Tommy, 157
Free Aceh Movement (Gerakan Aceh
    Merdeka) (GAM), 202, 204, 220, 258–
    62, 264–67
free-rider paradox, 22–24, 28
Freedom (Istiglal), 98
freedom fighters, 122–23, 128, 136, 228,
    260, 469
Frenkijevci (a.k.a JSO; Red Berets; Special
    Operation Units), 402, 405, 407, 412–15
Frist, Bill, 54
Front Islamique du Djihad Armé (Islamic
    Front for Armed Jihad) (FIDA), 292, 319
Front de Libération Nationale (National
    Liberation Front) (FLN), 282–83, 301,
    308–12, 314–15, 318
Front for the Liberation of Quebec (Front de
    Libération du Québec), 20
Front de Libération du Québec (Front for
    the Liberation of Quebec), 20
Front Islamique du Salut (Islamic Salvation
    Front) (FIS), 175, 177, 284, 301, 324,
    359; and accommodation and limited
    military, 309–14; and escalating
    militancy, 314–16; and moderation and

retreat from confrontation, 316–18; and RIGs/SJGs, 286-291, 293, 296, 297; and violent insurgency, 318–22

Fuerzas Armadas Revolucionaries Nacional (Revolutionary Armed Forces of Colombia) (FARC), 386, 461, 463–64, 506–7, 508–10, 512–14, 515

Fuerzas Armadas de Liberación (FALN), 20, 21

Fulbright, J. William, 39, 53

fundamentalism, 10, 167-170, 178–79, 183-185, 187, 189, 248

Galan, Luis Carlos, 511

GAM. *See* Free Aceh Movement

Gandhi, Rajiv, 74

GAP. *See* grey area phenomena

Garcia, Benedicto, 480

Garcia, Romeo Lucas, 480

Garzon, Baltasar, 357

Gaviria, Cesar, 511

Gaza, 61, 172, 181

Gendarmerie Nationale, 360

Gender In Development Division (GIDD), 339–40

General People's Congress (GPC), 159

General Union of Algerian Workers (UGTA), 308, 316

General Union of Palestinian Women, 80

genocide, 3, 13, 229, 490. *See also* ethnic cleansing

Gerakan Aceh Merdeka (Free Aceh Movement) (GAM), 202, 204, 220, 258–62, 264–67

Gerardi, Juan, 495

Germany, 37, 51, 94–95, 102, 244, 294, 355–56

Gesta de Jayuya (Jayuya Uprising), 21

Gettaf, Rabah, 290

GFA. *See* Good Friday Agreement

Ghamati, Abdelkarim, 322

Ghana, 342–44; and the CEDAW, 341–42; and the CRC, 340–41

Ghana Plan of Action, 342

Ghana Vision 2020, 341

Ghannouchi, Rachid, 183–84

Ghazali, Mohammed, 284, 287

GIA. *See* Armed Islamic Group

GIDD. *See* Gender In Development Division

Gingrich, Newt, 63

GLDs. See *groupes de légitime défense*

Global Crossing, 67

Golden Circle. *See* U.S. Committee for a Free Lebanon

Golkar, 200

Gonzalez, Enrique Parejo, 511

Good Friday Agreement (GFA), 377–78, 380–81, 383, 385–90, 393

Gore, Al, 33

GPC. *See* General People's Congress

Grand Mosque, 173

GRAPO. *See* First October Antifascist Resistance Group

Great Britain. *See* United Kingdom

Great Proletarian Cultural Revolution, 249–50

Greece, 94, 196, 433, 444, 528

Grenada, 38, 40, 41

grey area phenomena (GAP), 213, 220

Grito de Lares, 19

group belonging, 26–27, 172, 231

Group for the Struggle against the Illicit, 286

Groupe Islamique Armé (Armed Islamic Group) (GIA), 175, 289–93, 319–20, 359–60, 362

groupes de légitime défense (GLDs), 295

GSC. *See* Salafi Combatant Group

GSPC. *See* Salafi Group for Predication and Combat; Salafist Preaching and Combat Group

GSPD. *See* Salafi Group for Predication and Jihad

Guardians of the Salafi Predication (*jamaát humat al Daáwa al salafyia*) (DHDS), 292

Guatemala, 15, 473, 475–78, 482–84; consequences of war in, 492–93; early war years in, 479–80; and lessons of conflict, 493–95

Guatemalan National Revolutionary Unity (URNG), 480

Guiliani, Rudolph, 464

Gülen, Fethullah, 180, 183, 184

Gulf Cooperation Council, 178

Gulf War, 60–64, 157, 173, 311–12, 316, 324, 360. *See also* Bush, George H. W.

Habibie, B. J., 261, 264
Hachani, Abdelkader, 316, 318
Haddam, Anwar, 318
Halliburton, 67
Hama, 174–75
Hamas, 109, 171, 172, 309, 313, 318, 463, 466
Hambali (Riduan Isamuddin), 208
Hamburg, 356
Hamrouche, Mouloud, 312, 314
Hamza, Abu, 293
Han culture, 231–32, 236–41
Hanbal, Ibn, 293
Harakat al-Mujtama al-Islami. See Hamas
Harethi, Qaed Sinan al-, 158
Harkat-ul Mujahidin (HuM), 129, 136–37
Hattab, Hassan, 292, 293
Hawi, Khalil, 169
Haz, Hamzah, 200
headscarf war, 180. *See also* veiling; women
Heritage Institute, 67
heroin, 410, 500, 514, 516
Herzegovina, 369
Hezb. *See* Hezb-ul-Mujahidin
Hezb-ul-Mujahidin (Hezb), 136, 137
Hezbollah (Party of God), 172, 175, 463, 466
Hijab Campaign, 82
hijra wal takfyir, 291
Hinton, Deane, 488, 494
Hizb ut-Tahrir al-Islami (HT), 135–36, 138
Hobbesian state of nature, 274
Holkeri, Harri, 421, 450
Hollinger Digital, Inc., 67
Home Rule bill, 374
Homeland Security, Department of, 4, 48, 55, 529
Homeland Security Act, 48–49, 50, 54
Honduras, 460, 477, 484–85, 487
Hope, Peace and Liberty Party, 508
Hoyos, Carlos Mauro, 511
HT. *See* Hizb ut-Tahrir al-Islami
Hudson Institute, 67
Hui Chinese, 235–36, 243
HuM. *See* Harkat-ul Mujahidin

human rights: and Africa, 275, 279, 334; and Algeria, 295, 297–98; and Central America, 473–75, 491; and Chile, 357; and China, 246; and defining terrorism, 256, 258; and domestic compliance processes, 335–36; and El Salvador, 482, 487, 488, 490, 492; and the EU, 366, 369; and Ghana, 340–42; and Guatemala, 495; and Indonesia, 255, 259–62, 264–66; and international relations theory, 332–33; and Ireland, 389–90, 391; and Islamdom, 110, 113; and Jimmy Carter, 478–79, 480, 481, 485, 489; and Kosovo, 438; and Malaysia, 208–9, 214–15; and Nicaragua, 486; and political Islam, 196; and treaty compliance, 332–33, 335–36; and Uganda, 336–38; and the UN, 334–35; violations following 9/11 attacks, 122–33; and Zambia, 338–40
Hume, John, 378
Hungary, 94, 511
Hussein, Saddam: and defining terrorism, 121; and the Gulf War, 36, 42, 61, 148; and the Iran-Iraq War, 171; and 9/11 attacks, 37, 46, 58, 59, 195; and religion, 173; and the UN, 63; and war on Iraq, 4, 69, 189, 257, 368. *See also* Iraq

IAEA. *See* International Atomic Energy Agency
IASPS. *See* Institute for Advanced Strategic and Political Studies
Ibar Highway case, 411
Ibrahim, Anwar, 183, 184, 206
ICTY. *See* International Criminal Tribunal for the Former Yugoslavia
identity: and collective action, 24–28; and group belonging, 172, 231; state vs. national, 446–48
Idris, Wafa, 82
Ikhwan al-Muslimin (Muslin Brotherhood), 97, 109, 168–69, 174, 181, 259, 325. *See also* Nahrah, Mahfoud; Qutb, Sayyid
IMU. *See* Islamic Movement of Uzbekistan
India, 93–96, 115, 123, 137, 139–143, 232, 235

Indonesia, 93–96, 100, 103; militant Islam and terrorism in, 263–64; and military human rights abuses, 260; and potential consequences of terrorism, 264–65; and political Islam, 199–201; and radical Islam, 201–4; and transition to democracy, 204–5. *See also* Jakarta

Indonesian Democracy Party of Struggle (PDI-P), 200

Indonesian Mujaheddin Council (MMI), 203

Institute for Advanced Strategic and Political Studies (IASPS), 67, 69

Internal Security Act (ISA), 206, 208–9, 214

International Atomic Energy Agency (IAEA), 371

International Code of Conduct, 369

International Criminal Tribunal for the Former Yugoslavia (ICTY), 396, 402, 411, 414–15

International Monetary Fund, 150, 273

International Police Task Force (IPTF), 369

Internet, 45, 116, 235

Inter-Services Intelligence (ISI), 124–25

Interstate Succession Act, 339

intifada, 76–77, 80–84, 86, 172, 174, 181

IPTF. *See* International Police Task Force

Iran: and democracy, 93–96, 100, 148, 150, 151; and Islam, 107, 170, 172, 175, 180, 183-185, 196; and nuclear weapons, 370, 371; and recruiting grounds for terrorism, 126; and think tanks, 68, 69; and U.S. military power, 62, 63. *See also* Iran-contra scandal; Iran-Iraq War; Iranian Revolution

Iran-contra scandal, 63, 485, 486

Iran-Iraq War, 170, 172, 366

Iranian Revolution, 60, 186, 285, 286, 288–90, 324

Iraq: and al Qaeda, 215; and authoritarianism, 174; and democracy, 526; and ECHO, 367; and Gulf War, 150, 157, 285, 311; and military action, 528; and 9/11 attacks, 58-61; and state-building, 423, 429; and U.S.-British relations, 381, 385, 392, 393; and U.S.-EU relations, 368; and U.S.-Malaysian relations, 208; and U.S.-Yemeni

relations, 161; war on, 4, 12, 36–42, 46–49, 52–55, 63–67, 69; and war on terrorism, 189, 195, 196, 257, 530; and WMD, 366. *See also* Hussein, Saddam; Iran-Iraq War; Kurds

Ireland, 80, 122, 361, 373–381, 383, 385–393, 528. *See also* Irish Republican Army

Irian Jaya (Papua), 201, 202, 214, 255–56, 262, 264

Irish Americans, 375, 381–83, 386, 388, 391

Irish Northern Aid (NORAID), 383

Irish Republican Army (IRA): and Britain, 102, 361, 383, 385–88; and defining terrorism, 121–22; and the FARC, 461, 506, 509; and impact of 9/11 attacks, 381-382, 390–92; and loyalist violence, 388–89; and the peace process, 377–81; and religion, 229, 375

IRP. *See* Islamic Renaissance Party

Iryani, Abdul Karim al-, 155, 160

ISA. *See* Internal Security Act

Isamuddin, Riduan (Hambali), 208

Isaza, Guillermo Cano, 511

ISI. *See* Inter-Serices Intelligence

Islah. *See* Yemeni Congregation for Reform

Islam: and Africa, 284–86; and Algeria, 77–79; and anti-Americanism, 176–79; and communism, 94–96; as dominating force, 104–6; and fundamentalism, 168–76, 184–88; and Indonesia, 201–4; and Malaysia, 205–7, 208; and politics, 106–9; and Southeast Asia, 197–99. *See also* Islamdom

Islamdom, 102–4; conditions in, 110–14; and politics, 106–9; and solutions for terrorism, 114–18. *See also* Islam

Islamic Domain (Darul Islam), 201, 202

Islamic Front for Armed Jihad (*Front Islamique du Djihad Armé*) (FIDA), 292, 319

Islamic Groups (Jama'at Islamiyya), 174, 177, 181

Islamic Jihad, 362

Islamic League for Predication and Jihad (LIDD), 292

Islamic Malaysian Youth Movement (ABIM), 206

Islamic Movement for Predication and Jihad (MIPD), 292
Islamic Movement of Uzbekistan (IMU), 135, 136, 138
Islamic Renaissance Movement (*Mouvement de la Nahda Islamique*) (MNI), 309, 313, 318
Islamic Renaissance Party (IRP), 134–35, 136
Islamic Salvation Army (*Armée Islamique du Salut*) (AIS), 290, 291, 293, 319
Islamic Salvation Front (Front Islamique du Salut) (FIS), 175, 177, 284, 301, 324, 359; and accommodation and limited military, 309–14; and escalating militancy, 314–16; and moderation and retreat from confrontation, 316–18; and RIGs/SJGs, 286-291, 293, 296, 297; and violent insurgency, 318–22
Islamic Society Movement. *See* Hamas
Islamic State Movement (*Mouvement pour l'Etat Islamique*) (MEI), 291, 319
Islamic values (El-Qiyam al Islamyya), 283–84
Islamic Youth Association, The, 321
Israel: and anti-U.S. Mulsim sentiment, 11, 110, 129, 248, 297; and Arab conflict, 368; and the EU, 368; and Lebanon, 169, 172; and Palestinian citizenship, 22; and peace process, 60; U.S. relations with, 62–65, 67–69, 178; and women, 75, 76, 80–82, 86; and Yemen, 150–51. *See also* Six-Day War; 1967 War
Israeli-Arab conflict, 107, 114, 115, 366, 368
Istiqlal (Freedom party), 98
Italy, 37, 94, 102, 230–31, 353, 360, 362–63

Jaballah, Abdullah, 309
Jaish-e-Muhammad, 134
Jakarta, 195, 199, 203–4, 205, 214
jamaát humat al Daáwa al salafyia (Guardians of the Salafi Predication) (DHDS), 292
Jama'at Islamiyya (Islamic Groups), 174, 177, 181

Jamaát al Jihad, 288
Jama'at al-Sunna wa al-Shari'a, 309
jamaat al 'ulema (Association of Religious Scholars), 284
Japan, 93, 94, 102, 216, 241, 259
Java, 200–201
Jayash-e-Muhammed (JeM), 128, 136, 137
Jayuya Uprising (Gesta de Jayuya), 21
Jazárists (Algerianists), 291
Jeffords, James, 33
JeM. *See* Jayash-e-Muhammed
Jema'ah Islamiyah (JI), 200, 202–4, 208–11, 213–17, 220, 256, 263–65
Jerusalem, 67, 69, 82
Jewish Institute for National Security Affairs (JINSA), 67, 68
Jews, 68, 106, 111, 195, 207, 461, 466. *See also* Israel; Yemen
JI. *See* Jema'ah Islamiyah
Jihadi Salafi International, 297
jihadism, and democratization, 296–98
JINSA. *See* Jewish Institute for National Security Affairs
job approval ratings, 34, 39, 41, 47
John Paul II, Pope, 210
Johnson and Associates, 66
Johnson, Lyndon, 38–40, 43, 53–54
Johnson, Tom, 49
Jordan, 69, 79, 95–97, 123, 168, 171, 325
Jovanovic, Zvezdan, 396, 413
JSO. *See* Special Operation Units

Kabyl Berber, 98
Kadivar, Mohsen, 183–84
Kalimantan, 201
Karimov, Islam, 135
Kashmir, 122, 126, 136–38, 140–42, 516
Kastari, Mas Selamat, 211
katiba al Ahwal. See Guardians of the Salafi Predication
Kay, David, 60
Kazakhstan, 134, 232
KBR. *See* Kellogg Brown and Root
Kebir, Rabeh, 318
Kedah, 207
Kelantan, 207
Kellogg Brown and Root (KBR), 67

macro impact, 139–42

Madani, Abassi, 284, 286, 310–18, 320, 322

Madrasa Registration Ordinance, 133

madrassahs (seminaries), 130–33, 135, 140, 153, 197, 213

Madrid, 3, 9, 19, 357

mafia, 400, 409

Mahathir, Mohamad, 205, 206–7, 208–9, 219

Mahfouz, Naguib, 111

Maidin, Ibrahim, 211

Makhloufi, Said, 291, 314

Malaysia, 95, 123, 183–84, 197–98; and political Islam, 205–7; and radical Islam, 208; and rational choice models, 219, 220; and transition to democracy, 208–9

Malaysian Chinese Association (MCA), 206

Malaysian Indian Congress (MIC), 206

Maluku, 202

Managua, 478

Manichaean worldview, 196, 215, 221, 468

Mansour, Meliani, 289, 290

Mao Zedong, 237, 249. *See also* Maoism

Maoists, 239

Marín, Luis Muñoz, 21

Markovic, Rade, 402, 411

Marovic, Ivan, 403

marriage, 84, 232, 337, 338, 339, 341–42

Martínez, Maximiliano Hernández, 475

martyrdom, 12, 18, 128–29, 134, 140, 523

Marxist Puerto Rican Socialist Party, 19

MAS. *See* Death to Kidnappers

Masyumi (Modernist Islamic Party), 199, 200

Mat, Nik Aziz Nik, 208

Mauritius, 93

Mawdudi, A. A., 107, 109, 187, 284, 297

MCA. *See* Malaysian Chinese Association

McNeil, Dan, 136–37

McVeigh, Timothy, 9, 103

MEA. *See* Movement of the Islamic State

Mecca, 173, 187, 207, 236

Medellin Cartel, 506, 509, 511, 512

media: Arab, 111; and Central America, 473, 484, 489, 491; and China, 237, 239, 247–48, 250; and embedded journalists, 46, 60; and George W. Bush, 54; and Kosovo, 450; and Malaysia, 206; and policymaking, 39; and post-

9/11 focus, 131, 139; role of, 40–49; and Serbia, 398–400, 403, 414, 415; and terrorists, 230, 460; and war on terrorism, 461, 530; and Yemen, 147, 151, 157, 159

Medina, 184, 187

Megawati, Soekarnopturi, 202, 202, 220, 261, 263–65, 267

MEI. *See* Islamic State Movement

Mekhloufi, Said, 316

Meliani, Mansour, 290

Melos, 423

men: and nationalism, 83; and politically violent women, 74–75

MESA. *See* Middle Eastern Studies Association

Mexico, 462, 464, 480

MIA. *See* Armed Islamic Movement

Miao Chinese, 235

MIC. *See* Malaysian Indian Congress

micro target, 139–42

Middle East Forum, 68

Middle Eastern Studies Association (MESA), 115–16

Mihailovic, Dusan, 408–9

MILF. *See* Moro Islamic Liberation Front

Milosevic, Slobodan, criminal state of, 397–406

Milutinovic, Milan, 411

Mindanao, 209, 210, 214, 265

minimalism, and democracy, 431–32

Ministry of Women in Development, 337

MIPD. *See* Islamic Movement for Predication and Jihad

Misri, Abu Hamza el, 292

Mitchell, George, 377

Mladic, Ratko, 411, 415

MMA. *See* Muttahidda Majlis-I-Amal

MMI. *See* Indonesian Mujaheddin Council

MNFL. *See* Moro National Liberation Front

Modernist Islamic Party (Masyumi), 199, 200

modernity, 78, 108–11, 182, 461, 469, 523

Mohamad, Mahathir, 206

Monahan, 391

Mongolians, 233–34

Montenegro, 398–99, 411, 414, 416, 428–29, 439, 443–45

125; and al Qaeda, 35; and Iraq, 173; and Islam, 107; and madrassahs, 135, 197, 201, 215; and oil, 64; and the Taliban, 126; and war on terror, 69; and Yemen, 148–53
Schengen Agreement, 365
Schultz, George, 66
SCP. *See* Serbian Chetnik Movement
SDLP. *See* Social Democratic and Labor Party
Sedition Act, 209
Sekolah Agama Rakyat, 207
September 11 attacks: Yemen's response to, 156–58; and George W. Bush, 34–35; and media reaction, 44–46; and political impact in Northern Ireland, 381–82. *See also* Afghanistan; al Qaeda; bin Laden, Osama; Taliban
Serbia: and Kosovo, 423, 425, 431-434, 439, 443–45, 449; and Milosevic's criminal state, 396-417
Serbian Chetnik Movement (SCP), 400, 401, 402
Serbian Freethinkers Movement, 400
Serbian Movement of Renewal (SPO), 400
Serbian National Guard (a.k.a. Tigers), 400
Serbian Radical Party (SRS), 400, 411, 416–17
Serbian Volunteer Guard (a.k.a. Tigers), 400, 402, 412
Serpa, Horacio, 512
Seselj, Vojislav, 400–401, 402, 411, 416
SFF. *See* Socialist Forces Front
shari'a, and world values, 99–100
Shariati, Ali, 109
Sharon, Ariel, 68, 368
Sheehan, Jack, 66
Shias, 126, 136
Shi'ites, 113, 170, 172, 184
Shinawatra, Thaksin, 212
Simatovic, Frenki, 402
Singapore, 199, 204, 208–12, 214, 216, 220, 221
Sinn Féin, 377–79, 381–82, 385–91
Sipah-e-Muhammed (SM), 136
Sipah-i-Sahaba Pakistan (SSP), 128, 136
Six-Day War, 80, 168. *See also* 1967 War
SJGs. *See* salafi jihadist groups

SM. *See* Sipah-e-Muhammed
Snowe, Olympia, 54
social change, 76, 78, 79, 181, 304, 476
Social Democratic and Labor Party (SDLP), 376, 378–79, 380, 387
socialism, 168–69, 185, 283–84, 390, 476
Socialist Party of Serbia (SPS), 403, 416
Socialist Forces Front (SFF), 318
Soeharto, 198–202, 207, 217, 260–61, 265
Soekarno, 199, 200, 201, 206, 259–60, 262, 265
Solo, 202
Soltani, Abdellatif, 284, 286
Somalia, 38, 40, 41, 153, 276
Somoza, Anastasio, 474–75, 477–79, 483–85, 490, 493
Soroush, Abdolkarim, 183, 184
South Africa, 10, 13, 22, 123, 295, 527
South Korea, 99, 123, 198
Southeast Asia: and Islam, 197–99; and political Islam's threat to democracy, 195–97; terrorism and secessionist movements in, 265–66
Southeast Asian Regional Centre for Counter Terrorism, 208
Soviet Union, 5, 62, 96, 99, 116, 196, 296, 353. *See also* Afghanistan; Russia
Special Services Group (SSG), 138
Special Operation Units (JSO), 402, 405, 407, 412–15
Special Powers Act, 376
SPO. *See* Serbian Movement of Renewal
SPS. *See* Socialist Party of Serbia
Sri Lanka, 74, 76, 80, 84, 130, 143. *See also* Tamil Tigers
SRS. *See* Serbian Radical Party
SSG. *See* Special Services Group
SSP. *See* Sipah-i-Sahaba Pakistan
Stambolic, Ivan, 404, 409, 413
Stamenkovic, Frenki, 413
Stanisic, Jovica, 402, 413
state-centrism, and Islamic terrorism in Southeast Asia, 216–17
state terrorism, 249, 397, 476
Steiner, Michael, 421, 426, 433–35
Stewart, Potter, 500
Stojicic, Radovan ("Bazda"), 402

Yao Chinese, 235

Yemen: American covert operations in, 160; and democracy, 161–62; background of, 147–49; and expansion of state power, 159–60; response to 9/11 attacks, 156–58; terrorism in, 152–54; and U.S. policy, 147–52

Yemeni Congregation for Reform (Islah), 157, 159

Yemeni Social Party, 153

Yi Chinese, 235

Yugoslavia, 396, 398, 407, 410, 412, 414, 423. *See also* Serbia

Yuldeshev, Tohrir, 135

Zambia, 14, 332, 342–43, 344; and the CEDAW, 339–40; and the CRC, 338–39

Zemun, 409, 412, 413

Zhuang, 233

Zitouni, Jamel, 291–92, 293

Zivkovic, Zoran, 413, 414, 416

Zoellick, Robert, 63

Zouabri, Antar (a.k.a. Abu Talha), 292, 293